W9-CMC-669

# THE FUTURE OF OUR PAST

From Ancient
Greece to
Global Village

## H. J. BLACKHAM

EDITED BY BARBARA SMOKER

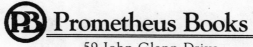 OXFORD-WESTMINSTER CRITICAL STUDIES

**PB Prometheus Books**

59 John Glenn Drive
Amherst, New York 14228-2197
Oxford, England

# The Future of Our Past

From Ancient Greece to Global Village

## H. J. Blackham

### edited by Barbara Smoker

Prometheus Books
Amherst, New York
Oxford, England

Published 1996 by Prometheus Books

*The Future of Our Past: From Ancient Greece to Global Village.* Copyright © 1996 by H. J. Blackham. All rights reserved. No part of this publication may be reproduced, stored in a retrieval system, or transmitted in any form or by any means, electronic, mechanical, photocopying, recording, or otherwise, without prior written permission of the publisher, except in the case of brief quotations embodied in critical articles and reviews. Inquiries should be addressed to Prometheus Books, 59 John Glenn Drive, Amherst, New York 14228–2197, 716–691– 0133. FAX: 716–691–0137.

00 99 98 97 96    5 4 3 2 1

Library of Congress Cataloging-in-Publication Data

Blackham, H. J. (Harold John), 1903–
    The future of our past : from ancient Greece to global village / H.J. Blackham.
        p.    cm.
    Includes bibliographical references and index.
    ISBN 1–57392–042–8
    1. Europe—History. 2. Civilization, Western—Forecasting. I. Title.
D21.3.B58    1996
909—dc20                                                                    95–26135
                                                                                CIP

Printed in the United States of America on acid-free paper

# Contents

## Part Four: The Legacy of the West

# Foreword

A comprehensive thematic essay, *The Future of Our Past,* follows the course of Western history in terms of cultural inheritance and legacy, from Periclean Athens, through the eclipse of the Dark Ages and gradual reemergence at the Renaissance, to the imminent start of the third millennium C.E.

An animal species exists in a habitat to which it is so adapted that there is total dependence. The human species has learned to recognize that survival depends on conservation of necessary planetary conditions. What is less usually considered is that times and places make a more intimate habitat inseparable from the life of every generation. To live at another time in another place, even within the same society, is obviously to live another kind of life, less obviously, to be another person.

Primitive peoples are dominated by their ancestors, a symptom of weak self-confidence. This obsession is generally embodied in ritualistic performances which reproduce, with unfailing exactitude, past behavior that proved successful. This is rehearsing experience by rote instead of learning from it by reflection. For too many history has been learning the past by rote—"1066 and all that"—instead of discerning and grasping the shape things have taken in order to have a firmer hold on the shape of things to come.

There is no possibility that the present in which everyone starts life is not a legacy of the past. To all of which, it may reasonably be answered that all of the past that is relevant is that at hand in the present. It is the past that is not present that is dead and done with. The relevant past that has made the present as a common starting-point for the future is the history of the West. The epigraph on the title-page says it all.

Many, especially if young, are apt to think that because history is about the past, which is dead and done with, it is no concern of theirs. Immersed in the present, they want only to get on with life, perhaps with some thought for the future.

History is in its nature particular, a history of something. There is not enough uniformity for generalization that could be used for prediction. Philosophies of history

7

have been speculative, wholly fallacious, and disastrously influential. The "universals" of history have been of a different kind: the claim of a culture or of a religion or of an *imperium* to be a model for the human race.

Science as the knowledge of nature is organized, systematic, and cumulative. History as the knowledge of human behavior on a macroscopic scale is parallel to natural history, but the phenomena are even more frequently fortuitous. Social continuity is the norm; change occurs by enacted reforms or by violence, deliberate or sporadic. The great social revolutions of lasting effect come about by a fortuitous concatenation of occurrences. There is not enough stability to furnish overall useful laws—predictability. The universals of history are claims to universality for social achievements formed over a period which give a people confidence to speak for the future. With a formed idea of the way things are, they prophesy and institute the future, the way things shall be. Such epochal social achievements may take three or four centuries to get established—that is, to become definitive and proclaimed.

An abstract of history is little more than a mnemonic of rote learning. Understanding requires enough detail to show what makes the shape. The temporal nexus of existence has to be reduced for comprehension, but to go too far is to make a mere inventory and to lose the line.

In the ancient Mediterranean world, Isocrates declared Hellas to be the acknowledged school of the world; Judea declared its tribal god to be the Creator of all that is, and they had his very word for it; Rome adopted the culture of Hellas, declared its destiny to rule the world, destroyed Judea, and adopted its offspring, Christianity.

These three particular projections of a people's achievement as a model for all have indeed been the main formative influences on the history of Europe.

After the collapse of the Western Roman Empire, the Roman Church and the Eastern Roman Empire created Christendom by piecemeal conversion of the settled tribes throughout Europe, including Russia. This was a fourth universal, the Romanized composite of the three which Constantine had created when he established a new capital in Constantinople. After Charlemagne regained by conquest most of what had been lost to Germanic tribes, the Roman Church which inherited the Western Empire combined with him to found "the Holy Roman Empire." For four centuries this venture survived, until the end of the Hohenstaufen dynasty in 1254. Nominally, it lasted until 1806, when it was formally abandoned—though Goebbels thought Hitler was in a position to bring it off at last.

The disintegration that set in with the collapse of the Soviet Union, and the disquieting events that have followed—with the huge social pressures of displaced populations—have induced a prevailing pessimism in the current mood and outlook. But the climate of action is hope, and there are recognized specific tasks for the whole world, such as those in relation to the environment and development.

Central Africa has the natural resources and native talent for achievements which have so far eluded its peoples but remain a natural infrastructure for the long-term future. A string of conditions has hampered performance: neocolonialism in GATT terms of trade; inheritance of arbitrary frontiers; tribal divisions; excessive population; debt and inappropriate aid policies; apartheid; South Africa's systematic destabilization of regimes in neighboring countries; taking over government with little or no administrative experience and a scant supply of adequately educated personnel.

The final universal model of history is now with us, and is concrete; the One World which the West has brought about and organized as a consequence of technological innovation, and has inescapably laid on all humanity. It is the sequel to the Enlightenment. It implies a shared human self-awareness that is a new version and vision of what humanity is.

However, it will not do to leave it at that. For this final universal, so formatively shaped by the three that were the legacy of the ancient Mediterranean world, is a new beginning, in view of the possible future disclosed. There are recognized specific tasks for the whole world (such as the above-mentioned problems of the environment and development). What is not yet recognized is that the outcome of history, which concretely is One World, has an inner implication of shared human self-awareness that is a new version and vision of what humanity is. That is the compelling reason for a reading of history that spells it out.

To see the reach of this long arm, we need samples of the periods in which dominant influences were formed—a finger on the pulse, not an elbow on the table over a chronological chart. Of course, there are multitudinous impulses, many people in many nations. With that in mind, I offer this rereading of Western history from the time of the Greeks to the present day, which shows how the legacies of successive periods accumulated, with the continuity and the transformation that ensued.

Tradition is formative, but every historical society is a collocation of interacting traditions—politico-economic, religious, cultural—conservative or radical, orthodox or nonconformist, classical or romantic. A reader will have sympathies and aversions, and the writer has his own commitments; but the question is the future for all of us, a question of confidence, and a correct aim. Reexamination is called for, second thoughts of the sure-footed.

History has become focused on the future, not a predictable future, the possible future. Will there *be* a future for humanity? If so, its course—the outcome of our history—is already mapped out, and is delineated in the closing stages of this book. Being responsible for the future, we should begin with an informed response to the past. To provoke that is the purpose of this book.

THE
FUTURE
OF OUR
PAST

# Part One
# Three Universal Models

# 1

# *Hellas*

# Antecedents

## Primus Inter Pares

The roots of European civilization are in the fertile soil of classical Greece and Rome and in the arid geography of biblical Israel. Evidence is scattered throughout our schoolbooks, is still visible on our main streets (particularly banks), and is readily apparent in the Bible. The ideals of *Hellas, Romanitas,* and *Zion* crystallized in their classical periods. This crystalline purity is art abstraction, but one that has had the potency of formative ideals.

Ancient Greece matured as one civilization among many: Sumerian, Assyrian, Babylonian, Etruscan, Hittite, Phoenician, Egyptian, Minoan, Mycenian, and Persian; most of them impressive and attractive. These are among extinct species—archaeological sites. Greece alone survives in the continuity of historical influence, beginning with Roman assimilation of Greek culture. It is a fading survival, as the diminished importance of the classics in our schools and universities indicates—as inevitable as the declining importance of English literature in American studies since the time of Emerson. The diminished active influence of these ancient cultures takes nothing from their immeasurable influence on the growth of Europe, their survival in the form and fabric of the contemporary West.

The survival of Greece was not an accident of history, such as might have happened to any one of the civilizations that were lost. From all these ancient civilizations Greece took something of telling importance. What the Greeks assimilated, achieved, and left to posterity, mainly through the genius of Athens, cannot be matched. The Muses were dedicated to the universal plenitude of culture.

In some three and a half centuries until 338 B.C.E., the Greeks turned a rough habitat into a home, for those who spoke their language, woefully deficient in security and stability, but otherwise the most fitting ever occupied for the human imagination, intellect, and body. It was not by any means a paradise or a golden age, but simply a first realization of human capabilities, and a lighting and defining of aspirations.

## Settlement and Unsettlement in Europe

Jericho in 8000 B.C.E. was a thirty-acre walled city with a population of about two thousand cultivating crops and engaging in long-distance trade, importing stone for tools from Anatolia. Some seven hundred years later the town was abandoned and restored some three hundred years after that. This was an exceptional Neolithic anticipation of urban culture based on agriculture that was to spread widely in another four thousand years. It was possible because Jericho was situated near an exceptional desert spring in an area where wild cereals were found. Later development not so favored depended on irrigation. This began as early as the sixth millennium in Anatolian villages, and on a major scale in the valleys of the Nile, the Euphrates, and the Tigris during the middle of the fourth millennium.

Groups from Anatolia crossed the Aegean and moved north along the Vardar-Danube-Rhine, as far as the British Isles perhaps as early as 4000 B.C.E. By this time there were farming villages throughout Europe and the Mediterranean littoral. In Greece, the alluvial plains between the limestone mountains provided ample space and natural conditions for cultivation. The earliest type-site* is Sesklo in Thessaly near the bay of Volos. Here was an unfortified village of brick cabins on stone foundations. Besides cereals, domesticated plants included peas and lentils, olives and vines, and dates and figs, where climatic conditions were favorable. Fishing and maritime trade served the needs of other communities and all these economic variations in ways of life implied cultural difference.

Most distinctively different were the nomads who had domesticated sheep and horses to graze the steppe lands of Eurasia. (By the late second millennium, Indo-European immigrants were coming in.) The plough and wheeled vehicles made the cultivation of heavier soils practical. Sheep and goats were not a monopoly of the nomads, nor were horses. With cattle, pigs, and poultry, they assisted cultivation in the settled lands.

However, the main undertone of "settlement" at this stage was movement, for the rapid expansion of populations that resulted from these economic developments forced out the less successful, or more enterprising, to prey on settlements abroad. For a long, long time to come, predation was a way of life, and often accompanied production and exchange.

As widespread as agriculture was the spread of metal working, mainly from the same source in Anatolia, where there was a good supply of copper. The early copper age, mid-fifth to mid-fourth millennia, extended into the Balkans and northward; during the following millennium the late copper age included, particularly, southern

---

*A *type-site* is an archaeological site that researchers consider typical or representative of a specific culture or time period based on architectural features, types of pottery, and other distinctive features of the site.

Iberia, where there were rich deposits. Greeks and Phoenicians, as seafarers, sought metals in central Italy and Spain. Where there were insufficient local sources, copper was a major import. In the second millennium, tin was mined in Cornwall, Northwest Iberia, and Bohemia. It provided the alloy with copper that made tougher bronze, which gave the founding name to the archaic cultures of the Mediterranean. Iron working brought in a new age with the first millennium.

Four distinct groups are identifiable as occupying areas of the west, the northeast, the south, and the southeast on the Danubian side of the Carpathians: Celts, Slavs, Italics, and Illyrians. These are historic races. Particularly, the Celts were prominent and dominant. By the end of the third century B.C.E., they had moved across Europe to the Atlantic, and had occupied Galatia in Asia Minor. Unlike successful peoples in Mesopotamia, they had not established an empire, but they had developed a culture capable of high-grade art; their fighting capability is evident in exploratory and plundering raids that feature in the history of Rome and of Greece, before the conquest of Gaul by Julius Caesar in 49 B.C.E.

## Features of Prehistory

To try to go back beyond authenticated history, one has in the first place to accommodate mental grasp to millennia instead of centuries, and without any precise date. The prehistory of the Mediterranean basin has been pieced together from collated archaeological evidence in the hundreds of sites excavated. Datings are scientific, not literary, using radiocarbon techniques and readings of tree rings. Peoples and their cultures are identified and named mainly by their pottery remains, and known only by lucky finds. Cooperative study of numerous sites over a long period has established standards of evidence that leave room for disagreement. Whether site evidence of new techniques means learning from contacts or displacement by invaders, or what exactly happened, is not the kind of question that necessarily can be settled conclusively; that kind of margin for error is on every page.

Without ingenious techniques and multiple studies to guide and check him, Thucydides in the fifth century B.C.E. consciously relied on intelligent conjecture when he explained in the first chapter of his history the state of things in mainland Greece before Hellas had a name.

> It is evident that the country now called Hellas had in ancient times no settled population; on the contrary, migrations were of frequent occurrence, the several tribes readily abandoning their homes under the pressure of superior numbers. Without commerce, without freedom of communication either by land or sea, cultivating no more of their territory than the exigencies of life required, destitute of capital, never planting their land (for they could not tell when an invader might come and take it all away, and when he did come they had no walls to stop him), thinking that the necessities of daily sustenance could be supplied at one place as well as another, they cared little for shifting their habitation, and consequently never built large cities nor attained to any other form of greatness.

Prehistory is for Thucydides a blank. He was a critical historian, as much as any modern, and his narrative and reflections are concentrated on the view from Athens of the events of his own time. He continued his speculations confirming his conviction that ancient times were empty of notable achievement, and supplied reasons why this had been so. The idea of power preoccupied him and from the beginning he contrasted the power of Sparta, expressed in superior military capability, which leaves no legacy, with that of Athens, evident to posterity in her monuments.

With evidence we are able to appreciate exactly what Thucydides actually meant by continual movement. The settled were indeed prey to those unsettled. Farming villages were plundered. Impressive cultures were developed, and wiped out—for example, the Hittites. In Asia, loose collections of feudal overlordships were destroyed by tribal invaders from the north and the west. It was with the introduction of iron technology that empires with adequate economic and administrative foundations were in a position to hold their own, and to expand. That time would be roughly 800–500 B.C.E. in the east Mediterranean. In Europe, the final settlement of peoples might reasonably be said to date from the occupation of Britain by the (Viking) Normans in 1066 C.E.

"Colonization" of Europe and European colonization of the New World and of Africa and the Antipodes is the basic theme of modern history.

## Egypt and Mesopotamia

In the alluvial valleys of the Nile, Euphrates, Tigris, and Indus, the need and opportunity for big irrigation schemes brought about the organization from the central governments of the installation and operation of the necessary crops. Population density along the banks of great rivers involved long-distance communications. The enhanced scale of production and distribution required records and accounts, which necessitated the invention of writing. Political unification was earliest in Egypt. Menes of Upper Egypt, armed with copper spearheads, conquered the Delta (c. 2900) to found the first dynasty of thirty that ruled a united Egypt till 342 B.C.E. This longest-lasting, yet stagnant civilization was called by the Greeks, who greatly admired it, "the gift of the Nile."

In Mesopotamia, there was an early development of Sumerian city-states, under a shifting hegemony; and they were the first to use a form of writing. Deficient in stone, metal, and timber, they traded with Iran and Asia Minor. The Akkadians (Babylonians) were in close touch with the Sumerians, and studied to assimilate their superior culture. Sargon, Akkadian minister of the Sumerian king of Kish, the chief city-state at this time, brought the Sumerian cities under central control and founded the first empire, from the Mediterranean to the Persian Gulf. From his expedition into Asia Minor he brought back to Mesopotamia the vine, the fig tree, and the rose, which he domesticated. He became the prototype emperor of legend.

Akkadian became the language of administration, understood from Babylon to Egypt, and the Sumerian language died out, though by this time Sumerian culture had been fully and deliberately assimilated. In this sense, the conquerors were conquered, as the Romans were by the Greeks. Meanwhile, a new power had established itself—

the Hittites, with a capital at Mattushash, on the trading route to the Black Sea. They spread south and sacked Babylon in 1595.

With her productive capacity and rapidly rising population, Egypt became fabulously rich, a prime object of prey, but with exceptional geographic protection. Nevertheless, Asiatic herdsmen, whom the Egyptians called Hyksos (foreigners), did conquer lower Egypt about 1730, and ruled for approximately two centuries. A patriotic uprising then drove them out and reconquered Nubia, through which they had entered Egypt. Thebes was restored as capital of a united kingdom, which then gained further wealth by expansion into Syria through Palestine, almost as far as the Euphrates. This revival under the eighteenth dynasty (1570–1320) was made possible by and associated with a military innovation: use of a chariot drawn by ponies, and of a superior bow, with the requisite skills. This highly effective mobile force, available only to a rich and industrially developed state, was a fulcrum of change, like the use of the stirrup for an armored cavalry in its definitive influence on the social order in the European Middle Ages. Military and industrial inventions or innovations have been hinges of social change down the centuries, and may be used to denominate a particular age, as in our time the internal combustion engine or the nuclear bomb.

The Hittites, of Indo-European stock, had learned from the Sumerian culture of Mesopotamia. Theirs was an empire of vassal kings throughout Anatolia. They had moved south as far as Babylon, and they controlled Cyprus, and had much wider contacts and influence. Their administrative ability facilitated the circulation of goods, ideas, peoples, and language. (The Sumerians had practiced filing, a simple indispensable technique for systematic administration.) Hittites and Egyptians were weakened by mutual inconclusive war for the control of Syria.

By 1200, Ugarit on the Syrian coast was one of the most remarkable cities of the ancient world as a cosmopolitan center, the meeting place of several cultures. The city controlled more than eighty towns and villages, and could equip 150 ships for a trading venture. In the time of the Greeks, Ugarit was to become a Phoenician city, along with Byblos, Tyre, and Sidon, and the Greeks would adopt the Phoenician alphabet.

These impressive empires were vulnerable. Egypt did not succumb totally, but Ramses II, great rival of the Hittites, was the last imperial ruler; her Asian empire was lost. The Hittite empire was destroyed in 1200 by invaders from the northwest. In Mesopotamia, a movement westward of peoples from the edges of the Arabian desert brought in seminomads, who passed from infiltration to the conquest of Palestine, Syria, Assyria, and Babylon. The Israelites were in Palestine before 1220. Domestication of the camel increased the mobility and wealth of these nomads, who eventually conquered Babylon. What happened was piecemeal and fragmentary, disintegrative. Even Assyria, the strongest and most warlike power, could not stabilize her conquests, in spite of ruthless penal sanctions. The petty state was the survivor. When Assyria finally collapsed with the fall of Nineveh to the Medes and Babylonians in 612 B.C.E., a Greek poet found the appropriate epitaph:

> a small, well-ordered city
> When it is built on a rock, is better than senseless Nineveh.

The tribes of invaders from the northeast who overthrew the Hittites and swept down through Syria included the people the Greeks called Palestinians, who gave that name to Palestine where they settled, about 1190. Within less than two centuries of independence they flourished, with wide trading contacts and a well-developed culture for the time. Israelites under David (c. 1006–966) created a kingdom briefly controlling Palestine and Syria, which disintegrated after Solomon. Disparate tribal origins provided no stable basis for these peoples to establish lasting kingdoms. With the fall of the late Bronze Age hierarchic civilizations, it was the growing hegemony of Persia that brought order to the Mesopotamian region, with the rise of Cyrus, whose son Cambyses extended his rule from the Nile to the Oxus. This was the dynasty of the Great Kings, who would threaten to prevent the flowering of Athens, and nearly succeed. This was the power that fascinated Alexander and inspired his dream of a Hellenism that had assimilated Persia and could establish world union.

## Minos and Mycenae

The Bronze Age civilization of the East was adapted and flourished at three independent centers in the Aegean: Crete, the Cycladic Islands, and mainland Greece. This began soon after 3000, and ended about 1100, with the migrations that destroyed Bronze Age sites. For the first thousand years of this period development in these three centers ran an equal course. About 2000, the cultural ascendancy of Crete brought the Cyclades under its influence, and the mainland followed five hundred years later. About 1450, the hegemony passed to the communities of the mainland led by Mycenae. Their power lasted some 250 years, till the Mycenaean world was broken up by a century of wars and disasters, followed by at least three centuries of drastic impoverishment, the so-called Dark Age. There was a gradual recovery, and by the eighth century contacts with the East were renewed. From that renewal developed the Archaic civilization of Greece (c. 700–486) that was more than a foundation of the achievements of classical Greece.

This period of Mycenaean dominance was the legendary Greek Heroic Age celebrated in epic poetry. However, the *Iliad,* composed some four centuries later, drawing on oral tradition, cannot be relied on as a faithful portrayal of the way of life of the Achaean nobles, its heroes. Most likely, their delight was to hunt the lion or the bear, or to feast in the hall and listen to recitals of the glorious deeds of men in war, their own proper business. They exulted in physical strength and prowess in martial arts, admired resourcefulness and guile, but also valued, practiced, and responded to generosity. This focus on exploits was sanctioned by success, the honor and fame of victory, the shame of failure. Its main aristocratic features are recognized in the baronry of the Middle Ages, which the feudal system was intended to form into a social organization. Indeed, on archaeological evidence, Mycenaean society seems to have had more sophisticated organization than the *Iliad* knows about. In any case, as with the barons, the nemesis for their way of life was exhaustion by warfare among themselves. The hero as "sacker of cities" had made the Mediterranean unsafe for trade.

# Incidence of a "Dark Age"

The shape of Greece proper, Archaic Greece, emerged slowly during the early part of the first millennium. The incursions and invasions of what the Egyptians called "Sea Peoples" who wrought these changes cover an obscure series of episodes. What has to be accounted for is not merely the disappearance of Mycenaean rule and the downfall of Hittite power, but also the appearance and established settlements of Dorian Greeks, and of Phrygians, Philistines, and Phoenicians.

Egypt alone survived, though eclipsed as a great power. The historical outcome was the emergence of Persia and of a Greece recolonized and regenerated.

In Greek tradition, the great migrations occurred two generations after the Trojan war, c. 1200. An interesting parallel has been drawn with conditions in Rome's decline, when they were no longer able to police the seas. By about 250 C.E., plundering bands from the Black Sea were coming into the Aegean as far as the coasts of Lykia and Pamphylia, and as far inland as Cappadocia. What was predatory became migratory, in this case part of the movement of peoples associated with the advance of the Goths on the lower Danube. It is a usual pattern, alien to the behavior of the Vikings.

On mainland Greece, Dorian Greeks from the north, led by Mycenaean exiles, it was said, invaded the Peloponnese and pushed south through the islands as far as Crete and Rhodes. The displaced Greeks fled to the hills or as refugees to the Cyclades and the west coast of Asia Minor, particularly the middle region, Ionia. Athens alone held out on the Acropolis, when the rest of Attica was abandoned. She remained the capital of a territory of some 2,500 square kilometers, to be one of the largest of the city-states.

This was no mere shifting around of peoples. It was the impoverishment by destruction and loss that made it a dark age. The art of writing was lost and skilled persons were displaced. Trade and farming lapsed to subsistence level. Civilization begins with overcoming such poverty. Gradual recovery in the first millennium reached the threshold of history with Homer and Hesiod in the eighth century. The ancient Near East had been broken up, and the late Bronze Age civilizations destroyed. There was a legacy.

# 2

# *Hellas*

# Archaic Greece

## The Inheritance

Greece in recovery from the dark age till the defeat of Persia (approximately 750–479 B.C.E.), was in no sense backward, as the traditional epithet "archaic" might suggest. Rather, this was the birth and vigorous early life of the Greek Commonwealth, when all her glorious accomplishments were set in train, and grievous flaws made plainly evident.

There had been a drastic depopulation of Greece at the end of the Bronze Age, with the virtual end of trade and a decline from arable cultivation to pastoral husbandry. A dynamic change came with Greece's marked rise in population during the eighth century. Its communities seem to have more than doubled in size in one generation. Expanding populations and new settlements required an appropriate form of social organization. This was not a restoration of the Mycenaean town. At first, there was an aggregation of villages, politically independent, unified with scattered settlements in a surrounding tract of country. This was successful enough to develop into the characteristic *polis*, probably influenced by the Phoenician cities of the coast. It was also in the eighth century that the Greeks adopted and adapted the Phoenician alphabet, recovering the art of writing with a completely fresh start and a practice that was generally more accessible.

These new beginnings show how complete was the break with the past. Lineages were lost. Every city needed its legendary founder and its patron deity, as each family needed its descendents. In sharing a language and the land, they basically were one people. A place in history was as necessary as in geography. Later, every place in Greece was notoriously steeped in legend, so that Cicero could say: "Walk where we will, we tread upon some story."

At this time, the coming of the Dorians into the Peloponnese was thought of as a return of the Heraclids, descendents of Heracles to their father's country of origin. This was already a legend, with more than one version. As late as the Hellenistic period, royal families would trace their descent from Heracles, the supreme hero. This sounds, and is, primitive; but there are modern versions. *Being There,* a film starring Peter Sellers, is about Chauncey Gardener's virtual nonexistence, because he has no "file."

The vital link of this Greece, reborn in resettlement on its scattered land, with the Mycenaean Age was not historic. Homer's *Iliad* (c.725 B.C.E.) is a portrayal of the legendary Heroic Age, a millennium distant, based on material selected from traditional epics. Like most fiction, it is thematic, not documentary. Homer is "the glorifier of Hero men" (Hesiod). Traditional stories often repeated are a simple people's strongest bond. That is transcended by Homer, who secured an eminent place in the sophisticated diverse cultures of the entire West. How is it that this glorifier of hero men who behave with barbaric savagery can be so profound and have such influence in the nineteenth century on, say, the devout churchman and English Liberal statesman W. E. Gladstone?

A poet claims universality, and in a classic achieves it. In the *Iliad,* the visual world is brought before the eye in images of immediacy; interspersed among the savagery and the supernatural are sights and sounds captured from the natural world in the abounding similes, and elsewhere, from snatches of daily life impregnated with familiar human feeling. The poet glorifies hero men on both sides and introduces the detachment of the historian, the tragic sense of history, and the Greeks' unease at what they do. If Thucydides invented disinterested history, there was the making of it in the work of Homer.

The close link between hero and poet is structural in culture. The deed in itself, however remarkable, is as though it had not been. It inhabits the mind and memory transmitted and transmuted by the poet. To be master equally of speech and action is most desired, but if divided, hero and poet are on the same footing. Pindar thought of himself as equal in performance to the athletic victors he celebrated, and like them in competition.

Finally, Homer is the source of what is characteristically known as Greek. Know and respect the unbridgeable difference between mortals and immortals; study the moderation of human limits (Apollo to Diomedes, *Iliad* V). Strive always to excel, and to surpass all others in honor (Peleus to Achilles, XI). The gods have human shape and passions. Heroes and their legends have a prominent place in the myths. The human image, and with it the human scale, is a Greek norm. The Greek *polis* does not have a priestly caste. Cults of the hearth and of the countryside and of the temple had the Greek diversity that saved their culture from collective bonds. Their mythology, with its judicious part in Homer's human stories, is irreconcilable with what we call ideology.

## The Myths

The *Iliad* and the *Odyssey* are peopled chiefly by gods and heroes, myths and legends. The Greek myths have been a European inheritance that shows how remarkable they were. First of all, in their oceanic volume and copious invention: there were stories for all seasons and for every location. They were raw material for the purpose in hand, not doctrine.

The pantheon had an earthly seat on Mount Olympus. It is appropriate that Zeus, its head, was the son of light and of clear skies. But early cosmic symbolism and personification faded from Greek thought, in spite of ambiguity and ambivalence, giving their stories the human anchorage that makes them distinctively different from Oriental and Gothic tales. Like all the Olympians, Zeus is born and he marries, and fathers the Graces, the Muses, Apollo, and Artemis, with many more, by union with goddesses and innumerable liaisons with mortals.

The mythology includes complicated and varied stories of Athena and Apollo, but they emerge in firmest association with Athens and philosophy in the one, and with Delphi and music and poetry in the other. Athena was the goddess of reason. She sponsored intelligent activity in domestic arts, in martial inventions, in the introduction and use of the olive, and in reflective thought. She was portrayed as tall, majestic, and serene. Apollo was the embodiment of male beauty, the ideal model of sculptors, of great stature, perfectly proportioned, with regular features, and long, curly, black hair. He was said to be in control of the Muses, and was the fountainhead of music, poetry, and eloquence. These two encompass in principle almost all for which the Greeks were outstanding in aspiration and achievement.

Heracles, the exemplary hero, "much the mightiest man on earth," is at one time epic hero, at another folk hero, and in another perspective culture hero in the diverse exploits and episodes of his life. He is supreme in his generosity as well as in his strength and courage, and immensely human in his appetites if superhuman in his deeds. His ultimate attainment of divinity was for conspicuous service to humanity. This supreme Dorian hero of the Peloponnese was paralleled by Theseus as the Attic hero. Of him too there are many themes and connections, but in relation to Attica he was regarded as founder of Athens and of its institutions, including its later democracy. As Heracles reputedly founded the Olympic Games in honor of Zeus, so Theseus was said to have organized the Isthmian Games at Corinth in honor of Poseidon.

This immense Panhellenic repository rooted in Greek habits of thought was integral to their way of life, yet not simply as a golden treasury, rather as a starting point. The myths were there to be put in order, to be put in question, to be interpreted, to be changed, eventually to be allegorized, as well as to be expanded. For the rest of Europe these myths have been a different possession altogether. They offered a spacious realm that the poetic imagination was invited to inhabit. Beginning with the Romans, our poets learned their craft from the Greeks, and thereby "travell'd in the realms of gold." Without any of the complications of a classical dictionary, Western literature is threaded with classical themes and allusions.

> Whence each of the gods sprung, whether they existed always, and of what form they were, was, so to speak, unknown till yesterday. For I am of opinion that Hesiod and Homer lived four hundred years before my time, and not more, and these were they who framed a theogony for the Greeks, and gave names to the gods, and assigned to them honors and arts, and declared their several forms. (Herodotus 2.53)

Herodotus (who should have dated these poets probably not more than three hundred years before his own time) can be assumed to have meant that Homer and Hesiod made all the gods thoroughly familiar to the Greeks through their own poetic works.

Hesiod, perhaps, younger by a generation, is in strong contrast to Homer. Brought up on his father's marginal land in Boeotia, he knows the hardships of peasant conditions, and addresses himself to the realities of daily life. Like William Langland, he is versed in the lot of the poor and the meaning of injustice. He looks up, but not to glorify hero men. In *Works and Days,* he taxes the nobles with injustice, and warns them of the vengeance of Zeus.

With his innovative literary convention of personification, he helped to shift the focus of thought from the hero to the *polis.*

It used to be said that from archaic to classical Greece there was a transition from a "shame culture," to a "guilt culture," from striving for success crowned with honor and avoiding shameful failure to recognition and acceptance that a mature life is not set in black and white. Better to think of it as relinquishing preoccupation with personal supremacy for participation in corporate civic responsibility.

## Festivals

Funeral games for a chieftain or a distinguished warrior were appropriate obsequies in a Heroic Age. After due rites attending cremation of the body of Patroclus, Achilles, to end the obsequies in his honor, engages the princes in races. With the resettlement of Greek lands, periodic competitions became a Panhellenic institution. About 854 B.C.E., Iphitus, king of Elis, contemporary of Lycurgus of Sparta, revived the Olympic Games, which had been interrupted in a time of trouble. This was the beginning of a deliberate initiation of Panhellenic union, in which Iphitus cooperated with Lycurgus and persuaded the people of Elis to found a cult of the Doric hero Heracles, their traditional enemy. Thus Heracles was the legendary founder of the games. Herodotus records how proud the Elians were of the rules laid down for the institution (2.160).

There is a history of some twelve hundred years of continuity in the Panhellenic festivals which followed the success of the Olympiad, at Delphi, Nemea, and the Isthmus. They were for Greeks exclusively, like the language and the land.

The games were keenly competitive for a crown of olives that would remain a badge of honor. However, they did not begin and end with that. The occasion was religious; and as deeply aesthetic and ethical as athletic.

On the practical side, a long list of early Spartan successes at Olympia is evidence of systematic physical training that made her unrivaled in sport and war, until other cities followed her example, and turned the aristocratic amusement in Homer into a main part of the education of the young. The *epheboi,* promising youths who were selected for special education to be trained in athletics and military skills, were also instructed in philosophy and literature by that time. This was especially frequent in Athens, where gymnasia and palaestria became principal places of public resort; their colonnades and shady walks and their rooms and facilities were used for many purposes, including the lectures and discussions of the Sophists.

Physical education remained primary, based on five regular exercises taught progressively, diversified by ball play and dancing, and supplemented by training of teams for torch races, and of choirs for dancing competitions. The five exercises were later integrated in the Pentathlon as a combined competition in running, jumping, discus, javelin, and wrestling. This represented the all-round physical training of the Greeks, superior to specialism, a result of reflection upon practice characteristically Greek.

Wrestling was probably the oldest sport (Theseus is said to have learned the rules from Athena) and the Greeks characteristically saw in it the triumph of knowledge and skill over brute force, of civilization over barbarism. Instruction was strictly progressive: movements, grips, and throws were mastered as separate figures, an advanced pupil paired with a beginner.

The political and social elite were officially and impressively represented at the four Panhellenic festivals, to the great encouragement of the arts in both cases. But the four national festivals were the ones that facilitated intercity political contacts, as well as the mixing of classes—as at the Vauxhall Pleasure Gardens in eighteenth-century England. Philip of Macedon and Alexander identified themselves with them to promote Greek unity. Alexander regarded Olympia as the true capital of Greece, and sent his dispatches from his Asian campaigns to be publicly read there. The new cities he founded on the Greek model included festivals.

Under the patronage of Rome, the festivals survived for four centuries as part of Roman adoption of Greek culture. But Rome could not capture the Greek spirit, virtually extinguished with the loss of independence. Roman health cults (baths/massage) were as remote from Greek athletics as the Coliseum, in which spectacles were put on for popular amusement, with performers drawn from subject races. There was nothing there that could be intellectualized or poeticized in the Greek manner. The Olympics were abolished by Theodosius, to stamp out the relics of paganism. The attempted revival at the Paris Olympics of 1924 was millennia away from the originals, but something of the original spirit was recognized and saluted, before the inevitable commercialism and encroaching professionalism set in.

## The City-State

The roving war leader and his companions, and then the settled kingships great and small of Mycenaean rule, had depended in personal preeminence in valor and strength—the definition of a heroic age, if mystical. With the fall of these warriors and recolonization of their territories, conditions were different. There was still an aristocratic ascendancy, which might share power in oligarchies when increases in numbers and wealth encouraged jockeying for power, with openings for all around capability. If kingship was primordial, it was no longer without alternative. The autocrat or "tyrant" who might emerge from and end an oligarchy was a different phenomenon. The collective rule of an oligarchy induced rotation, election, conventions, spontaneous preliminaries to constitutional government.

The more equal the oligarchs were in wealth, ability, trustworthiness, the more willing they would be to adopt such practices, to institute rules, to regulate power, and safeguard mutual trust. Such regulations might bring satisfaction to the rulers, and oppression to the ruled.

So it was in Athens. The yeoman class of those who lived on and off their land, with little surplus, exposed to the hazards of husbandry, had borrowed on security of their land or person, forfeited on default, and fallen into the hands of the aristocracy, the wealthy landowners. This division of rich and poor threatened civil strife. Solon was elected chief archon to sort it out. He was experienced in high office, had travelled widely, and above all enjoyed a reputation for integrity and wisdom. He accepted the constitution of the state as it was in the main, and introduced only the amendments he saw to be necessary to remedy the situation and prevent its recurrence. That is, he cancelled the contracts of the debtors and prohibited loans on security of the person. He exempted the poorest class from taxation, and gave them the right to attend the Ekklesia and to be members of the Second Council he instituted. *Hubris* was for him not usurpation of the rights of a god, but appropriation of the rights of another human being. "I took my stand like a boundary stone in the debatable land between the two parties." Solon's connection with Athens at so early a stage helped greatly to form the historic reputation of the city. Athena, her patron, was the goddess of reason, and it was Solon who applied reason to affairs of state in an exemplary Greek manner.

Peisistratus as tyrant followed up Solon's reforms with enlightened rule that extended commerce and external relations. By 508, when the rule of Peisistratus and his sons had ended, a return to the old apparatus of aristocratic government was halted by Kleisthenes, whose family had become a focus of resistance to the regime of the tyrants. He won the people over to his side with a popular program, widening the franchise of citizenship. The Spartans did their utmost to stop and reverse this new democratic tendency, but the solidarity of the Athenians and their new political order proved unshakable. These events at the end of the sixth century B.C.E. have been said to be similar to what happened in England after 1642, in France after 1789, or in Russia after 1917; and without a Cromwell, a Napoleon, or a Lenin, for Kleisthenes was no longer in continuous control. Anyhow, it is at least certain that political conditions in Athens by this time were far from those under Mycenaean rule. And it is quite possible that Athens would not have been the household name it is but for these two initiatives in its early history, the reforms of Solon, followed by those of Kleisthenes loyally supported by the people. Herodotus attributed the greatness of Athens to her enjoyment of equal rights, and based a political generalization on the example (V. 78).

With the pressure on food supply because of increasing populations, colonization was the answer, a new movement of peoples that had little in common with the migrations that had repopulated Greece. This was organized emigration planned by "mother cities," sending out armed and equipped parties with an appointed leader to establish permanent independent settlements. Earlier merchants and pirates seeking metals in central Italy and Spain had pioneered the navigational and exploratory information. In the second half of the eighth century the first foundations were established in Sicily, including Syracuse. This first colonizing wave was said to have been completed in 688 with the foundation of Gela by a group from Rhodes and

Crete. Greek colonies were also planted in south and southwest Italy, France, and East Spain, and on the north shore of the Aegean, the Hellespont, the Sea of Marmora, and the Black Sea. To found new societies in new places demanded practical capability and adaptability in the face encountering other peoples and their ways. For metropolitan Greece, the "mother cities," these far-flung newly planted city-states were a New World, as America was to be to Europe in the eighteenth century, but with a closer cohesion. They were united by their language and the myths and associations of a legendary past, and they came together in the regular Panhellenic Festivals. The colonists brought in an infusion of new experience gained from outside contacts and their community building.

By the end of this early period the Greeks were aware of their cultural identity, which had been established institutionally in the festivals, by the solemn procedures, the multiple personal contests of body and mind, and the standards by which they were judged.

Detailed investigation of all that happened in the time between Thermopylai and Plataea reveals a patchy sequence: unexampled bravery of the Spartans at Thermopylai; incidental cooperation and good planning; tactical negligence; reluctant and delayed combination; outright treachery; mean advantage taken of another's jeopardy; in general, the effects of mutual mistrust, enmity, and suspicion. The fact remains that Athens and Sparta, bitter rivals and enemies, did cooperate, to the extent that Athens twice put her combined military and naval forces under a Spartan commander to overcome the conquering Persians, led first by Darius and then by his son Xerxes. Eventually, the invader was driven out.

# 3

# *Hellas*

# Classical Greece

A historical period is separated out as a discernible unit, without a break in continuity. The dates are merely indicative, perhaps symbolic. I would put Classical Greece between 472 B.C.E., when Pericles paid for the production of Aeschylus' *Persians,* and 338, when Philip of Macedon ended Greek independence at the battle of Chaironeia and Isocrates, who had urged him to unite Greece against Persia, is said to have died of shock. Classical Greece is bounded by the menace of Persia, and bound up with the preeminence of Athens. Aeschylus, Pericles, and Isocrates are exemplary patriotic and prophetic Athenians in the time of her greatness, each aware of her unique quality and mission. Each was eminent in a different domain of Greek enlightenment.

Classical Greece is largely identified with the classics. In English scholastic tradition, a classic was a written text studied and annotated generation after generation; the classics collectively were texts that had survived in Greek and Latin. The word today is used less exclusively, but in the context of antiquity it would still bring to mind Homer and Sophocles and the Socratic Dialogues, with Virgil and Horace and Cicero in Latin. Study of a text entailed the discipline of the language. These dead languages, which no one used except in the Church and law and exotic contexts, were brought back to life every day in classrooms, and with virtuosity in school plays. They were extolled above the merits of mere vernaculars as the most resourceful and refined means of developing thought or communicating experience humanly attained; in a word, of philosophy and poetry. Respect for these languages and their literature was an awe that had been made institutional, a holy writ that was not prescriptive but exemplary.

This humanism assumed by Cicero, which Isocrates predicted would make Hellas the school of the world, was the wood, the tree whose branches had grown in poetry, philosophy, and history. Rather, it was the wood that obscured those trees, and removed from view the glades and streams in the depths of the forest. In short, Classical Greece is, and ought not to be, identified with the classics.

After the center of the civilized world had shifted to Alexandria, following the death of Alexander in 323 B.C.E., there were two notable additions to what survives as the corpus of Greek classics: *The Voyage of the Argonauts,* an epic by Apollonius of Rhodes, one-time librarian at Alexandria; and, especially, the *Idylls* of Theocritus. The new epic celebrated the other saga in Greek legend. The distance from Homer is shown most decisively in the psychological attention that reduces his heroes to men, not excluding the superhuman woman, Medea. The poem won respect, registered by borrowers, not the least of them Virgil. Formed and nursed like Wordsworth by the sensations and images of landscape and the simplicities of country life and speech, Theocritus invented a convention for the expression of spontaneous happiness in the presence of the natural scene in a congenial climate.

## Theater

The open-air stadium was constructed to seat a mass audience, perhaps up to thirty thousand. It was a mixed audience, the people of Athens, on a public holiday once a year in spring. The audience on their stone benches were packed close, and participated physically like a modern "rock" audience or a black church congregation. The prototype of what they were attending had been the Dionysiac ritual that involved abandonment to frenzied dances, with shouts and cries, and the sacrifice of animals, torn to pieces alive, their flesh eaten dripping with blood. Hysteria had to be dealt with, and this whole procedure, even as a season of relief, had to be brought under control. Athens was dedicated to Reason. This was introduced first in the dances and songs of the dithyrambic choruses of the Attic tribes, then in the tragedies of the city Dionysia in which they competed.

Aeschylus was choreographer for his productions, himself a dancer and actor. Song, music, movement in dance and procession, inarticulate cries, noises, silence, speech rhythms, gestures, and masks of the actors, the scenes that brought to life terrible episodes of the action, the setting of the auditorium itself: all this and more combined to the total effect, and succession of effects.

## History

If history was invented, as distinct from annals, chronology, propaganda, triumphalism, Thucydides showed the way on his narrow Athenian canvas. He remains a historian of permanent importance, as does Herodotus, the so-called father of history, who worked on a broader canvas. Herodotus was a traveller and a curious observer. He gives his idea of the origins of Greek culture, with the debt to Egypt and the Phoenicians, and is careful to cite his sources (II, 52–53; V, 58). His critical care for evidence and its evaluation is spelled out in many passages. He gives alternative versions, leaving the reader to give credit (III, 122).

Thucydides is equally open about his sources and intentions. His narrative is enlivened with the citation of speeches, and he explains how they were composed in a way to make them generally trustworthy. In narrating events, he says he did not trust sources at hand nor his own impressions, but relied partly on what he saw and partly on what others reported, tested in detail as rigorously as possible. He had been at great pains to reach a probable conclusion when reports differed. His single purpose was to provide a history for inquirers who wanted an exact knowledge of the past as an aid to policymaking for the future, in which there would be parallels and patterns of similarity. In this way, his aim and his hope was to write for all time. This early rational way of addressing the future, when for centuries men had been consumed with anxiety, and were not ready to undertake anything without first resorting to occult predictions, is relatively modern.

Thucydides' history is also political philosophy, more profound than Aristotle's. It was from him, as well as from the English civil war, that Thomas Hobbes, who translated him, learned to formulate in *Leviathan* the ground of political and moral philosophy. Security, stability, and prosperity are the conditions of civilized life.

## Philosophy

Philosophy as we know it was a Greek invention; it is a major item in all we have inherited from them. There was not a Greek philosophy, there is not a modern philosophy. Broadly, there was in this period what has been called the Greek Enlightenment, which, so to speak, fathered the European Enlightenment at the end of the eighteenth century. The development of scientific understanding mainly brought that about in Europe, as philosophy did in Greece; and in both cases it was an application of reasoning.

"Enlightenment" in this context means a rise in the level of human self-awareness. "Know yourself" at Delphi meant simply to know that you are a man, not a god, liable to be struck down by a jealous god if you get above yourself. "Know yourself" for Socrates and for Aristotle meant something entirely different, and not the same in both cases. Aristotle defined man as "a rational animal"; Reason was the god within the mind, akin to the mind within the Cosmos. For Plato and Socrates, a man has to learn that he knows nothing before he can find out how he can know what he should know. There were many other views. What was recognized, however, was the difference between knowledge and opinion, and that a claim to knowledge had to be justified. What would be sufficient justification? In any case, there was the question of knowledge, for knowledge was a question.

Socrates observed that "the unexamined life is not a life for man." Intricacies of thought were disclosed to the man who tried to enlighten himself by examining in reflection the conscious life of which he was aware.

Socrates was a central figure in this classical period. He founded no school, left no writings, taught no explicit doctrine. He made a profound and lasting impression on his disciples, and we have only their barely consistent representations of him. He was a central figure in three respects. He broke with the popular Greek tradition of personal contests for victory in argument, and thus took serious discourse out of a game as old as Akkadian literature—winning a verbal encounter. He turned thought away from speculative interest in the Cosmos, and focused it on ethics, human behavior, and self-discipline, his own version of "Know yourself." He was an influence on several major developments later, particularly on Stoicism. Insofar as he is thought of as a religious figure, he had no teaching about the gods or human destiny, no theology.

Democritus was devoted to the investigation of nature, and had traveled widely to consult the learned amongst other peoples. He had theoretically resolved the problem of knowledge confronted with a panorama of dissolving phenomena by postulating that all things were composed of configurations of atoms moving in a void. Knowledge was obtained by the senses, but these were limited in their reach, so that beyond them "it is impossible to understand how in reality each thing is." A finer investigation is needed, and a tool for distinguishing more finely. Reason and senses are the means of knowledge. Atoms and the void are the unperceived structure of nature. Chance and necessity maintain its continuous process.

Timon, a philosophical skeptic who delighted in making fun of all the dogmatists, regarded Democritus with respect, "among the best I ever read." Like many others, Democritus wrote also on ethics, on logic, on mathematics, and on literature, music, and the arts. There are some three hundred fragments extant.

Diogenes Laertius in *Lives of Eminent Philosophers* (probably in the early third century C.E.) writes:

> Aristoxenus in his *Historical Notes* affirms that Plato wished to burn all the writings of Democritus that he could collect, but that Amyclas and Clinias the Pythagoreans prevented him, saying that there was no advantage in doing so, for already the books were widely circulated. And there is clear evidence for this in the fact that Plato, who mentions almost all the early philosophers, never once alludes to Democritus, not even where it would be necessary to controvert him, obviously because he knew that he would have to match himself against the prince of philosophers.

He quotes Thrasylys, who catalogued the works of Plato and of Democritus: "Democritus was versed in every department of philosophy, for he had trained himself both in physics and in ethics, nay more, in mathematics and the routine subjects of education, and he was quite an expert in the arts." Whatever the truth may have been about Plato's jealousy, with the dawn of experimental science in the seventeenth century Democritus's light was set on a hill where his physics extinguished the dazzle of Aristotle's metaphysics.

Plato's Socratic dialogues remain the best introduction to philosophy, as the Synoptic Gospels are to Christian belief. Plato discovered the "concept" for himself in asking what is bravery in itself, apart from brave acts (*Laches*), a question Achilles could not have asked. Plato went on to apply this principal to "justice," what is it in virtue of which acts are called just? There were three alternatives: one may do an injustice and not have to suffer it; one may do it and have to suffer it; one may neither do it nor suffer it. Why should one not choose the first, if one can get away with it? Why is the third alternative the best, if it is so? The concept "justice" implied for Plato knowledge of its essence. The *Republic* was the answer he worked out, a predetermined structure of society implicit in the natural order; something ordained that can be defied but not escaped. Justice supervenes in the harmony that reigns when the parts act together in fulfillment of their specific roles, as rulers, warriors, workers, corresponding to reason, will, desires in the psyche (its cognitive, affective, and connotative aspects), perfected by practice of the cardinal virtues, Wisdom, Courage, Temperance.

Aristotle was a pupil of Plato, who gradually disengaged himself from the persuasive influence. His omnivorous interests were informed by the methodology he worked out in the logical treatises that had such great influence in the Middle Ages, and maintained a permanent basic place in the curriculum, like Euclid. A thing was to be defined by the class to which it belonged, by its general characteristics, and by what distinguished it as a particular member of its class. Thus a man was an animal distinguished by reason. Nature gave birth to young. Artists made artifacts, and in this way imitated nature. The Idea had to become real in the world as we found it. This kind of analysis was not fully applicable to some subjects, which had to be treated more flexibly and problematically, with an appropriate discipline. Ethics and politics were of this kind. Plato's treatise on ethics was one of the most comprehensive and influential in the history of philosophy. The same is true of his *Metaphysics,* but in this case the influence was extremely unfortunate in perpetuating his supposition that everything is determined finalistically, by the end in view.

For Plato, mathematics was the model; for Aristotle, the organism; for Democritus, mechanics. Epicurus, who owed almost everything to Democritus without saying so, had a short way with Plato and Aristotle: "Justice never is anything in itself, but in the dealings of men with one another in any place at any time it is a kind of compact not to harm or be harmed"; "Nothing is there in order that we may use it, but what is there has its uses." Epicurus did not engage in empirical investigation like Democritus, but he raised the standard: "Nature is its own standard, one thing throws light on another."

## Science

> Whoever makes a close study of the scientific world of Ancient Greece cannot but be filled with veneration and his veneration will but increase, the more he realizes that, beyond all differences and changes, the cosmos of the Greeks is still the rock from which our own cosmos has been hewn.
>
> S. Sambursky, *The Physical World of the Greeks*

A physicist looking back at what the pre-Socratic philosophers were about, Sambursky can say, "We may be called the scientific heirs of Ancient Greece." The Greeks originated the scientific approach, and their thought has a surprisingly close resemblance to our own mental outlook. It has been said with some authority, "Modern science is the continuation and fructification of Greek science and would not exist without it." The second part of that statement may be questionable, the first is not. Aristotle, reviewing the pre-Socratics to find his own starting point in systematic thinking, remarked, "Without being skilled boxers, they sometimes give a good blow." The metaphor applies decisively to the scientific achievement of the Greeks, which was intuitively brilliant, incipiently formative, without a mainspring, and ultimately abortive. Its fate was not natural, but the result of an outside political blow. Modern science may be said to be a "continuation and fructification of Greek science," that had been historically denied that possibility.

The architectonics, dynamics, and collaboration of effective scientific progress, Bacon's Advancement of Learning, were lacking. They were not interested in applying knowledge to "the relief of man's estate," in Bacon's phrase. They had no desire to conquer nature or change the world. They understood deduction and induction, and were fertile in hypotheses, but had not hit on the device of experimental tests. Science as an organized corporate undertaking had a partial beginning in the museum (and library) at Alexandria, inspired by Aristotle, but did not have time to be developed. Science as happy sporadic discoveries and hypotheses is impressively abundant.

The school of medicine founded by Hippocrates in the island of Cos was widely influential and the best example of consistent empirical procedures. An accurate prognosis was sought, so that the patient's confidence could be won and appropriate treatment arranged. Reliance was on diet, good nursing, and the healing powers of nature. (Democritus remarked that men pray for health, not knowing this lies within themselves, and that by lack of control they betray their health to their desires.) They studiously maintained this empirical approach, excluding religious or philosophical presuppositions: "The right-minded aim is either to discover something new or to perfect what has been found out." Within its limitations, it was a foundation of right-minded medical practice.

Anaxagoras in one book on sale in Athens at a bargain price offered a comprehensive philosophy. He had a realistic apprehension of the stellar bodies as material objects held in place by the speed of their revolution, not living bodies moved by voluntary power. He was actively interested in meteorology and atmospheric movement and he used science to discredit divination.

The Greeks were pioneers in the speculative theoretic reach of science, but neglected its practical grasp that seized essential connections by inventive manipulations. They made a disjunction of what is a union. However, this began to be remedied when the momentum of inquiry that had built up in Athens shifted to Alexandria in the Hellenistic Age. This may have been partly the influence of the empirical tradition of the Egyptians they encountered there, evident in their surveying and their mechanical inventions. It was there that Archimedes developed a mathematical theory of the five machines: lever, wedge, pulley, winch, and screw. But the initiative in founding the museum (and library) as a center of learning came from Aristotle and his disciple Theophrastus, who took a hint from the Pythagorean brotherhood devoted to inquiry, organized in association with the museum a research institute for several branches of science, including his own biology or natural history. Aristarchus developed the idea of Heraclides, a pupil of Aristotle, that the earth rotates on its axis and that some of the planets revolve around the sun, into a heliocentric theory of our universe rejected mainly because Aristotle had fixed the earth as the stable center of the universe. Yet Aristotle, the collector and classifier of specimens, was as detailed, absorbed, and painstaking as Darwin himself. The museum established itself as the first university. The library and museum were burned on the orders of the Caliph Omar in 642 C.E.

Aristotle, whose own thinking was flawed by capital mistakes and inconsistencies, so that his *Physics* and his *Metaphysics* perpetuated major errors on his authority, remains a towering intellectual figure and a true representative of the Greek Enlightenment. He launched philosophy and science upon a universal inquiry into the nature of the world and the nature of man. He was one of the founding fathers of the modern world, in that he was aware of the intellectual development of mankind, and of his own position in that progress. He recognized that the advancement of learning was a collaborative endeavor and a cumulative process. Aristotle's axis of thinking was investigation, continuous research, and discovery, whereas Plato's was education and transmission of and control by final and absolute knowledge. If this was the germ of their difference, its end brings into view a mental and moral chasm.

## The Sophists

Some of the philosophers in the last half of the fifth century were sophists, a profession, not a school. They went from city to city throughout Greece to give public instruction for a fee. What they taught varied with demand, which might be for music or mathematics or astronomy. But their specialty was the art of discourse, and their skill and mission had developed from the practice of traveling rhetoricians. When they offered to teach how to speak persuasively, they undertook to help people gain confidence and influence and take a useful part in public affairs, a different matter from teaching philosophy in a school of disciples.

One of the pioneers was Protagoras, a fellow townsman and pupil of Democritus. He said he was trying to promote reflection through discussion to improve the conduct of life in personal and social affairs. He is said to have been the first to introduce the Socratic dialogue. The Sophists were given a bad name by Plato and Aristotle, on the ground that they specialized in disputation, using subtleties of language to make the weaker seem the stronger case, that they prostituted argument for gain, taking money to show people how to win, like a trainer of boxers. Socrates can be thought of as a reforming Sophist.

Protagoras showed that there are two sides to every question, and how to attack and refute any proposition laid down. The justification of that was to alert the reasoner to the duplicity of language, and the need for close attention, and to take account of the strength of the other side. He was the first to call attention to linguistics; he classified types of speech in terms of their work, what they did, and marked the significance of the tenses of verbs. Far from using a license to cheat in the competition of controversy, this was a discipline that unmasked plausibility.

A major controversy in which the Sophists were prominently involved concerned the distinction between laws of nature (necessity) and laws of humanity (convention), *phusis* and *nomos*. This has a partial analogy in modern argument about "fact" and value judgments and "Social Darwinism." Socrates assumes and asserts that ethics is discoverable in what is, a datum of necessity, which is what Plato tried to make good in the *Republic*. Protagoras held that ethics was a work of the will, a human convention, and that this was more useful to men and binding on them than a law of nature. It was the same argument that Epicurus affirmed in his definition of justice. (The force of natural law is expressed amorally in the Melian dialogue above.) Protagoras is generally known for the statement at the beginning of a lost work, "Man is the measure of all things," taking human experience as the subject matter and limit of knowledge and thought. The statement at the beginning of another lost book is the original agnosticism: "As to the gods, I have no means of knowing that they exist or that they do not exist." It has been said by Mario Untersteiner in his *The Sophists:* "Protagoras for the first time proclaims the *regnum hominis*."

In general, the Sophists initiated systematic education, especially of the adolescent. They brought the dawning enlightenment of the age to the people, for they had to make themselves masters of what was currently known and thought. In this they could be compared with the *philosophes* of the European Enlightenment, contributors to Diderot's *Encyclopédie,* who set themselves to modernize the thinking of a generation. In both cases, theirs was a conscious aspiration to a rational human culture, a universal civilization. A lasting feature and consequence of their activity was to involve the public. Propositions proposed and reasons given were submitted to the judgment of the audience.

"Art without practice, and practice without art, are nothing," is another fragment from Protagoras. Demosthenes was a Sophist who most diligently practiced an art to overcome a natural disability; he had an assiduous discipline that became legendary. He repeatedly devoured the history of Thucydides, and he put himself to school with the orations of Isocrates, who was not an effective speaker, but a master and teacher of the art of discourse, and a pupil of Gorgias, its first major exponent, who wrote a handbook on rhetoric, and model orations. Gorgias gave by invitation the Olympian oration at the eighty-fourth Olympiad, on Hellenic unity.

Isocrates provided a rationale for education in opposition to Plato. Human life is highly vulnerable, exposed to unpredictable blows of fortune. The Hero was admired and valued because he had the qualities that enabled him to cope with all occasions and demands, not only strength and bravery, but also resourcefulness. Heracles was the model. What was distinctive in Isocrates was his identification of the art of speech with the art of thought itself. To be able to convince others, one had first to convince oneself. If discourse was practiced on themes drawn from moral philosophy and from history and from poetry, the student was made familiar with all that was greatest in human aspiration and achievement. His was the initiative that formed the content of classical education in the humanities, which was espoused by the Romans, particularly Cicero, himself educated in that way, and was recovered at the Renaissance by the Humanists, so-called because of this educational link. As the staple of higher education, it lasted down to present times, when it has been jockeyed out of dominance by pressing demands for technical and modern subjects.

# 4

# *Hellas*

# Hellenistic Civilization

## Macedonian Hellenism

Macedonia was generally unknown beyond its borders, and was not part of the Greek Commonwealth. A Macedonian prince would not be eligible to compete in, nor even attend, the Panhellenic festivals. Philip II, king of Macedonia, was the first deliberately to make himself an Hellene in the sense meant by Isocrates, one who shared Greek culture, not Greek lineage. As a young prince, Philip had been handed over as a hostage to the Thebans, and he had made himself thoroughly acquainted with the Greek way of life. Back in Macedonia, his leadership and connections led to his being acclaimed king. His ability in arms, shown by notable successes that enlarged his resources and encouraged his aims, including the conquest of Amphipolis, a colony of Athens, brought him to the fore as a force to be reckoned with. He was made head of the Amphictyonic Council, which had charge of Delphi. He had thus insinuated himself into Hellas, and was a Hellene of the Hellenes (even with a victor's crown at Olympia), as well as in a commanding position and with the resources to lead the Greeks in a planned expedition against the "Great King," the Persian enemy. Isocrates had published an address, *Philip,* urging him to unite the Greeks and lead them against Persia.

There was a contradiction at the heart of this situation. Under Philip and his son Alexander, the Macedonians did become identified with Hellas and were more imbued in Greek culture than even the Romans were at the time of Cicero or under the Antonines. Philip obtained the young Aristotle as tutor for Alexander, which helped to form his interests, in science as well as poetry. Alexander claimed descent from Heracles on one side, and Achilles on the other. In imagination, his career was a renaissance of the heroic age of the Achaean aristocracy, with himself as a reincarnation of Achilles. The *Iliad* was his constant reading in his anabasis. This was genuine, if romantic.

35

On the other hand, Isocrates' appeal for a leadership that would unite the Greeks in recourse against their inveterate enemy assumed no interference with the institutions and independence of the *polis*, no tampering with the political foundations of the Greek Commonwealth. A Macedonian conquest of Greece, Greeks as subjects, not allies, of Macedon, Alexander as emperor, that was hardly more tolerable than conquest by Persia. Demosthenes said it all, loudly and clearly. If Philip had not been murdered, which in effect precipitated Alexander's move against Persia, and the need urgently to consolidate his position in Greece, the diplomacy Philip had initiated and was skilled in might well have succeeded in uniting the Greeks voluntarily under his leadership. As it was, in this late fourth century B.C.E., the political and social conditions that had founded the Hellas whose culture Isocrates proclaimed as her gift to the world were in disintegration. The Hellenic world and Hellenistic civilization were due for separation. That was not precisely Alexander's intention. It was the outcome of what he did achieve.

When he had overthrown the dynasty of the Great King and had gone on to establish his rule to the frontiers of India, his dream and his intention was a joint commonwealth of Macedonians and Persians, to the extent that his adoption of Persian dress and customs seriously alienated his Macedonian soldiers, the muscle of his enterprise. Although this was not a Hellenic ideal, it was in accord with a late Hellenic philosophy. Plutarch, referring to Zeno's *Republic,* said its theme was that men ought not to segregate themselves in cities with their own laws, since they shared a common life in a common world order; he said that what Zeno had written as a dream, Alexander had realized. Zeno was given the highest honors by Athens. His master had been the Cynic Crates, a disciple of Diogenes, whose ideal city was one that produced only figs and bread and thyme, for the possession of which men did not take arms against one another. The Cynics did not share the pride of Plato or Isocrates in being Hellenes. They proclaimed themselves citizens of the world, and claimed to follow the laws of virtue rather than those of the city. For this reason, they preferred the Persian empire or the empire of Alexander, just because they thought these political forms were incompatible with, and transcended, the *polis*. The Cynics were committed to the practice of an individual lifestyle offered as a model, not to a doctrine. This practice of virtue was attained by unremitting exercise, like the skill of a flute player or athlete or craftsman. Such ideas may be thought uncharacteristic and eccentric, but they had consonance with new tendencies. The Greeks since Hesiod had never been complacent about war, and their experience of ruinous intercity wars and faction fighting was moving them towards better ways, so that it was said in the third century, "There are many cities, but they are one Hellas." The abridgement and overriding of city independence could not be reversed, and some aspects of the Sophists' teaching had put things in question. Contacts at festivals were helping to develop intercity bodies to settle suits and disputes and establish a common jurisprudence. Private associations and clubs were formed to meet the needs of professional groups, Dionysiac artists, immigrants, philosophical schools, and religious sects. Alexander was to give the *polis*, at this time when it was being put in question and had been subordinated to his dominance, a new trial in a foreign context as an export.

As general of the League of Greek Allies, Alexander was liberator of the Greek cities of Asia Minor from Persia, and avenger of Hellas. As king of Macedonia, he was establishing his own empire, with the security, stability, and prosperity maintained by his own rule. Nevertheless, he conquered the East for the Greeks. He was an Hellene. His policy was to found Greek cities, of which Alexandria became the most distinguished, where some of the most progressive tendencies in Hellenic culture were developed and carried forward; it is one of the three or four sample exemplars of Hellenistic civilization. He celebrated victories with a festival, centered on religious thanksgiving, but with gymnastic exhibitions and contests of singers, musicians, and actors. At the same time, he identified himself with the cults of Egypt and of Babylon, with the normal Hellenic toleration of foreign gods. In his entourage were not only actors and musicians, but also botanists, mining experts, and other scientific staff, who carried out extensively and systematically the kind of investigations initiated by Democritus and sponsored by Aristotle, with whom he continued in touch.

Alexander planned to make Babylon his capital, center of the Asian world, and began excavation of a large harbor, and extension of cultivable land with a series of dikes and canals. In spite of his romantic attachment to Achilles as forebear and model, he was not merely a conqueror in the field at the head of his Macedonian myrmidons, though his reckless dash and personal exposure in the forefront of attack furnished that image and example. He initiated what he did not live to consolidate, an organization of the conquered territories that separated the command, the administration, and the financial system, under central control. This was to establish security, stability, and prosperity, permanent foundations of civilization, sustained by flourishing trade. The king as servant of his people was the Hellenic note. Alexander was still the pupil of Aristotle, and there were philosophers in his entourage, as well as the collectors of specimens and observers of phenomena. The philosophers seem to have included two Cynics, for whom Cyrus was the model king, and Pyrrho, whose ataraxy was probably influenced by contact with ascetic Hindus whom the Greeks called "gymnosophists."

For all his Asian hopes and ambitions, and his espousal of Persia, Alexander was and remained a devout Hellene. He employed the painter Apelles and the sculptor Lysippus, and had a painting of his wedding with the Bactrian Roxane exhibited at Olympia. His love of Greek literature was staunch, preeminently of Homer, but also the tragedians, and he is reported to have taken part in a celebration with his friends by reciting a scene from the *Andromeda* of Euripides. Hellene, but still Macedonian: he had selected beasts from the cattle of Afghanistan sent to improve home breeds in his native land.

Alexander's short career has been one of the marvels of history, and an unattainable model for other conquerors, of whom Napoleon was the last and closest. In effect, he subdued the long-established empires of Egypt and Persia, and if he had made the Euphrates his frontier, which he was advised to do, consolidation would have been possible. But the world was the limit, in defiance of Greek moderation. The conquest of eastern Persia had exacted three years of incredibly tough touch-and-go fighting and marching in the most difficult terrain. The planting of Greek cities strategically sited and held by mercenaries could not be more than a garrison-type occupation, save near the west coast of Asia Minor. It was an imperial sketch to take over and better the model of Persia. In turn, it was the principal influence in bringing about the aim and drive that established the *pax romana,* a model for so long in the West.

The other aspect of his achievement of permanent consequence was the diffusion of Hellenism, which Isocrates prophesied. He and his father were the first Hellenes, and his successors were to prove his followers in this respect. Thus Greek culture, manifest in the exclusive Panhellenic festivals, was brought to the outside world by "barbarians" who became adoptive sons, foreign bodies speaking Greek and Greek in their souls. Of these, none was more an Hellene than Lucian some four hundred years later, a Syrian, a notable influence in European literatures, particularly English. Above all, Roman assimilation of Greek culture was mediated by the Hellenization it encountered. Hellenistic civilization was established under Alexander's successors.

## The Succession: Three Dynasties

On Alexander's death, three of his Macedonian officers seized the initiative: Ptolemy in Egypt, with a strong fleet; Seleucus on the Asian continent, based in Syria; Lysimachos in Greece and Macedonia, the most powerful.

The early Ptolemies ruled Egypt as a conquered country, and it was the least Hellenized of Alexander's conquests.

Alexander founded Alexandria in 331 B.C.E. Ptolemy I planned the museum. In 294, he invited Demetrius of Phalerum, a pupil of Theophrastus and a distinguished scholar who had ruled Athens for ten years, to establish the museum as an academy of learning. Alexandria, having thus the greatest academy of its time, and becoming a trade center of wide importance, was a magnet to foreigners. By the beginning of the second century B.C.E., it was the greatest city of the inhabited world, a city of mixed population, dominated by Greeks, but not a Greek city. Unlike royal libraries that existed in Mesopotamia, the library-museum complex in Alexandria was founded as a public institution for the furtherance of learning and science. An observatory was erected, dissection of human bodies was allowed, a zoological garden was provided, with exotic animals.

Eratosthenes, the second librarian, measured the circumference of the earth. The systematic observations and collections of the specialists in Alexander's entourage were classified and stored, assisting the establishment of exact disciplines. Hipparchus made several important astronomical observations and calculations, and established trigonometry as an independent branch of mathematics. The most advanced school of medicine was developed, founding physiology by using dissection to trace the nervous system, with discrimination of sensory and motor paths. It has been said that the summary of Greek mathematics by Pappos of Alexandria in the time of Theodusius, *Synagoge,* proved the stimulus to the rebirth of mathematics in the mid-seventeenth century. "Thus was modern geometry connected immediately with the ancient one as if nothing had happened between." Astronomy, another science developed in the ancient world, was advanced in accuracy of measurement by the Greeks, and in their use of geometric and mechanical models. In a modern perspective, the lack of scientific instruments was a fundamental handicap. But unfavorable political and cultural conditions proved the fatal detriment. Astronomy was distorted and corrupted by astrology; and magic and astrology gained in favor in the second century.

The production of papyrus and subsequently of parchment, and the employment of educated slaves as copyists, changed the scale of book production. Ships brought rolls from every country. By the first century B.C.E. perhaps some seven hundred thousand rolls were shelved. Philology, already introduced, came into its own. Textual criticism was used to establish definitive texts, which were then produced. Workers from all parts were attracted to this center of organized activity. It was also a model; there were state libraries at Antioch and Pergam and probably at Rhodes. In the Hellenization period, Alexandria displaced Athens as a market center and as the center of learning. After the classics, in the literary field it was an age for classification, compilation, and commentary.

Pergamon was capital of a kingdom from which the western part of Asia Minor was ruled from 228 to 223 and from 188 to 133, supported by Ptolemaic influence, and later by Rome. The Attalids, like the Ptolemies, concentrated on the accumulation of wealth. They were competent. Royal factories produced parchment, textiles, and "Attalid cloth" interwoven with gold thread. Slave labor, mainly female, was employed under state superintendence. The library assembled at Pergamon was second only to that at Alexandria. There were patrons of research at Pergamon as in Egypt; plant and animal breeding was promoted to improve strains and stocks. The famous statue of the "Dying Gaul" memorialized the victory of Attalus I over the Gauls before 230. Later, the gigantic frieze more than 460 feet in length represented the battle of the Titans with the gods in an expression of Hellenism like nothing else in Greek art, the conflict of civilization and barbarism. In spite of this display of Hellenism in science and art, Pergamon, like Egypt, was regarded as unfaithful. Betrayal was sealed in a deed, where Eumenes II instigated Rome to break the Seleucid dynasty, the successors to Alexander who had most consistently striven to continue his Hellenization as a civilizing mission, a service to mankind. Attalus III bequeathed his kingdom to Rome in 133, and made Pergamon a free city.

The Seleucids spent far more of their income on their holdings than the Ptolemies. Their most favored cities would control groups of native villages—which later became a model for Rome. Food supply was the first charge on the administration, then provision of education and welfare, more systematically organized than in classical times.

Asia Minor had been mainly priest-states, on which various conquerors had encroached. Their Hellenization was superficial; their feudal systems were retained. The Seleucids fought feudalism and also the temporal power of the priest-kings, leaving enough land for temple service and bringing the rest into secular use. Their city-states raised the status of the peasantry, releasing them from serfdom. Feudal lands, like temple lands, were transferred to the cities, which enjoyed municipal self-government and corporate institutions. The Greek city seemed to the Seleucids to offer a foundation for security, stability, and prosperity to the diverse multitude of Asiatics. Their accomplishment under adverse conditions must be considered amazing: amorphous native villages were organized, and with selected native towns became Hellenized cities, on a great scale. This was to be taken over and built on by the Romans at a slower tempo.

Seleucid, his son, and his grandson ruled from the Aegean and Mediterranean to Turkestan and Afghanistan. Between 250 and 227 everything east of Media-Susia was lost. In 198 Antiochus III took the rest of Syria from Egypt. In 189 he lost Asia Minor except East Cilicia to the Romans. In 129, the final loss of Babylonia and Judea reduced the Seleucids to a local dynasty in North Syria, one of the centers of their rule. For over a century after Alexander's death, they had been one of the great and enlightened powers of the age. The steady decline in the extent of their rule was temporarily halted by Antiochus III at the end of the third century B.C.E.; but had diminished to unimportance some fifty years later. Their kingdom was weakened by civil war and Parthian encroachment. Inroads from the Central Asian steppes could not be withstood and a Parthian empire was established by Mithridates. The Seleucids were not aggressive, had to rely on mercenaries for defense, and were not willing to spend adequately to do so.

Judea had been a priest-state under Seleucid suzerainty, but won independence by prevailing over Seleucid ineptitude. Simon Maccabeus captured the citadel of Jerusalem in 141, and eradicated Hellenic influence. Antiochus VII invested Jerusalem and starved it into surrender in 134. Simon's son (131–129) pursued the cause of independence, and under his successors the growth of Greater Judea was pushed to the Egyptian frontier in the south and Mt. Carmel in the north. They secured their ascendancy in some parts by forcible conversions. Their introduction of Jewish law into Galilee had unforeseen far-reaching consequences, to rival the conquests of Hellenism. Antiochus VII ended the monarchy, and Pompey finished off Seleucid claims and aims with the annexation of Syria and Cilicia in 65–63 B.C.E.

The Antigonian dynasty in Macedonia was the least successful of the three that had divided the empire Alexander left. Antigonus Gonatas, the wisest and best of them, had to contend with the intrigues of Ptolemy II with the Greeks against him, which spoiled their best chance of stable conditions and security on the mainland under his authority. An Achaean league of cities under Macedonian domination broke free under the daring leadership in commando-type raids of Aratos, a young exile from Sicyon, a city under Macedonian protection. The league was too much for the aging Antigonus. He had inherited Macedonia in a state of exhaustion and anarchy. He succeeded in repairing it, as Alexander's father had. This was his conspicuous service to the Hellenic world, reestablishment of a strong base that was a shield against barbarian invasions from the Balkans. He was a devout Stoic, and a patron of letters.

In Egypt, it was Augustus who "to save what remained of Hellenism, had to return to Ptolemy I, nurse the Greek element, foster the gymnasia, and again break, the reacquired power of the priests."

The outcome was definitive, but mention should be made of counteracting tendencies. There were signs of greater political maturity, and the Greek cities, although deprived of their former independence, were notable for men of outstanding public spirit, ready to spend themselves and their fortunes to help to meet public needs. Hellenic identity and solidarity were reinforced by commercial intercourse and in confrontation with Oriental populations. Forms of intercity liaison, hospitality, consultation, and mutual financial help were developed. Arbitration was increasingly the way disputes were resolved. This tendency in the development of relations between cities was institutionalized in general rules, an *ius gentium,* which, like so many Greek initiatives, found fulfillment through Roman adoption. "There are many cities, but they are one Hellas" was said in the third century.

## Hellenistic Culture

The three dynasties of the Succession were all Macedonian, and Macedonians were not thought of as Greeks until Philip made himself one. At least the upper classes became thoroughly Hellenized in the third century, and their dialect was replaced by Attic Greek.

These adoptive Greeks were well able to do all that could be done to Hellenize the world they conquered. At the same time, they changed the basis of Greek society. They made themselves kings. They founded cities with Greek political forms; but there was not the war-making independence; there was not the local religious tradition that socialized citizens in the attachment of pieties and loyalties to the city and its laws. For the Greek nucleus of these new cities there had to be readjustment to a wider world. The native Olympic gods had also been discredited for educated minds, abandoned to the poets. New forms of philosophical religion here developed and new forms of association, clubs and groups, for particular purposes. In such ways, the Greek world in this period was a new world with old forms. The status of the *polis* became functional instead of foundational, administrative instead of political.

The change was reflected in royal patronage of the arts. In Pergamon, the kings put their private display far second to the public show they made of their city. This new context opened a new chapter in Greek art.

Architecture in the context of town-planning was the most striking and influential development of the period in the visual arts. Landscape architects are thought of as a modern innovation, but their practices and values were dominant in the devices invented to integrate a city with the terrain of its site. This was done in Rhodes, in Alexandria, and in Pergamon with diverse designs for each case. But smaller cities had like treatment; and all were models the Romans studied. A regular feature of these cities was a development of the *Stoa,* a rectangular hall, open on one of the long sides by a colonnade. Sited near the Agora (market-place) this could be used to shape the center of the city.

At this point, it is pertinent to refer to Lessing's *Laocoon* (1766). Lessing was as closely familiar with Hellenic culture and its writers as anyone has been; and in the European Enlightenment he was the Darwin of aesthetic theory. Goethe recalled in *Poetry and Truth*: "One must be a young man to realize the effect which Lessing's

*Laocoon* produced upon us, by transporting us out of the region of meagre perception into the open fields of thought." But that fruitful release into the realm of concepts brought on "an insatiable longing" to look at works of art. What so enlightened and fired the young Goethe was Lessing's comparison of poetry and the visual arts to make nonsense of the current idea that "a poem is like a picture" (*ut pictura poesis*).

A new interest in the portraiture of individuals begins to appear as a characteristic of the Hellenistic age, consonant with the individual's consciousness of himself in a wider world. This was exemplified in biographies and in sculptured portraits. Plutarch's much later famous *Lives* can be taken as the consummation of this new interest. The interest in realism in portraiture, though persistent, was not triumphant in Hellenistic sculpture or painting; it remained blended with or modified by concern for the type or the general. It was the Romans, at first through their contacts in Etruria and south Italy, who seized on this trend, and were to make a booming industry of accurate portraiture, very often employing Greek sculptors for the purpose. Realistic portraiture had a Roman destination and patrons, but the techniques were Greek. They had long known how to execute whatever was wanted.

The successors to Alexander, like modern autocrats, were forward to promote a personality cult and the ubiquitous portrait to bring that about was the head on the coins in circulation, likely to be paid more attention then than now. On these, realism came into its own. Roman eminence in this is famous, as the memorable use of it made by Jesus.

If the structure and dynamism of Hellenism were sustained by the politico-religious discipline of the *polis,* and by the personal discipline of the gymnasium, and the fraternal rivalry of the cities in the festivals, the characteristically Greek spirit they generated could not be exported with the forms of these institutions to alien lands and contacts, even at the cost of the brain drain that brought in Greeks to make them work. Under the royal patronage of the successors, their courts were cosmopolitan, and brilliantly endowed with Greek talent. Asiatic kings were ready to employ Greek experts and to profit by expanding trade opportunities. That did not entail a cultural conversion. Alexander himself had seriously tried to fuse young Persians and Macedonians, giving thirty thousand Persian boys a thorough Greek education. Whether this was a serious Hellenizing mission or a device to establish his authority through union of the two worlds he had impacted, it is impossible to know. In Plutarch's portrait, he is a complex figure, consumed with a desire to excel everyone in everything, exceedingly passionate (Achilles and Hercules), cool and rash in his planning. His successors were deliberate and systematic in their Hellenization. The spirit of the age was unfavorable to Greek rationalism, fostering astrology and magic, cults of the occult. It was to be the conquest of Rome by Hellenism that counted in the history of the world. Augustus was the sole heir of the Hellenistic kings.

Stoicism was the most characteristic philosophy of Hellenistic civilization, readily adopted by Alexander's successors, as later by Romans at the highest level. It can be taken as an index of the paradox at the heart of that civilization. The paradox is that the Hellenization of Alexander's world by Hellenes was not Hellenic. Hellas was an integration of body and mind with a society that strove to cultivate every human activity—a corporate attainment this side of perfection like the incomparable personal achievements of Shakespeare and Mozart. Hellas suffered disintegration with the Macedonian conquest that ended the political independence of the *polis*, and founded the conditions of Hellenization. Stoicism had the provenance of a Greek philosophy. It was deployed in a Greek context, persuasively on offer, not collectively imposed by a state or a church.

The affinity of Stoicism with the cosmopolitan character of Hellenistic civilization was not Hellenic, but that was not what makes Stoicism an index of the paradox of Hellenization. What does so is the dogmatism that turned a philosophical school into indoctrination in a philosophy; for this used philosophy to repudiate the Greek invention of philosophy.

The fourth century had been the great period of Athenian philosophy, but its tradition was established in the Academy and Lyceum. Pyrrho, who had been in Alexander's entourage, had met Hindu gurus, and versed himself in the tradition of *ataraxy,* indifference, based on skepticism and the opinion that all opinions are equal, with a consequent suspension of judgment, imported the case for skepticism into the schools, at least in his person, for he left no writings. He is said to have frequently quoted Homer's likening of the human race to leaves tossed in the wind, as one generation succeeds another (*Iliad* VI, 147). Taken seriously, the outcome of such a position would not be discourse, but an intensive schooling in meditation and nonattachment, on the Hindu model; this seems to have been the mind of Pyrrho. In any case, such absolute skepticism was incompatible not merely with dogmatism, but with any dogma; his followers undermined the foundations of Stoicism.

More central was the development under Arcesilas of the teaching of the Academy, of which he was head from 268 to 241 B.C.E. He initiated the epoch of the New Academy that lasted till the mid-first century B.C.E. He mounted the reaction against the new dogmatisms, and their assumption that a quasiscientific understanding of the cosmos was necessary for the rational conduct of life. Opposing both dogmatism and ataraxy, Arcesilas used dialectic to attack. Diogenes Laertius has given an attractive impression of his lively, generous temperament and of the wit and spontaneity of his lectures. He used dialectic against Zeno in the proper manner, asserting nothing, simply taking the propositions posed by his adversary and drawing the consequences or exposing the inconsistency. He went on to separate the criterion of truth from a rule of conduct, which it was the main point of the dogmatisms to identify as inseparable. You did not have to know First and Last Things before you could decide how to live. Reasonableness and probability were sufficient guides. And the Sophistic tradition of deploying the argument both for and against a thesis was not merely clever and negative, for it could be used to show the need to inquire further. The natural literary form, in itself totally opposed to dogmatism, in this Sophistic tradition was the dialogue, which was revived and continued by Carneades, as later by Cicero and Plutarch.

During the following century, when Rome conquered Macedon (168 B.C.E.), then Greece (146), and Asia Minor (132), after an obscure period at the Academy, Carneades was in charge until his death in 129. He was a profound and subtle thinker who carried the authentic Greek adventure of ideas into the period of Roman rule.

Modern, ever-deepening knowledge of the past diminishes the distance and refocuses the view. We had idealized the Greeks, as they idealized the male nude, without their justification. If a more critical view is based on fuller evidence, that is not only healthier, it is also the path to rediscovery, a path one must tread for oneself, for a prize that is not competitive.

Modern feeling finds the position and treatment of women, and slavery, less than admirable characteristics of ancient Greece. A. R. Burn in the *Pelican History of Greece* writes of hardness as "one of the great defects of classical Greek character" and has in mind particularly their treatment of women and children. He goes on: "The classical world . . . was deficient in *caritas*. For lack of it, those brilliant, hard and gem-like individualists failed to consolidate and make permanent their social achievements" (p. 256). That is a fundamental indictment, and, if one must generalize, would apply to the human race. Hellas is a society occupied and preoccupied with competitive male achievement. Women are out of sight and out of mind, confined to the house where they are part of the property, the part that looks after it, keeps the slaves in order, bears and brings up the children.

In the Hellenistic age women had greater presence and scope. At the top, the Macedonian dynasties produced women who would have their way with the ruthlessness and resolution of Lady Macbeth, without the undoing conscience. Alexander's mother did so. A succession of such women were dominant in the Ptolemy dynasty, beginning with the daughter of Ptolemy I, who married her brother Ptolemy II and turned his halting efforts into the golden age of Egyptian expansion, amply acknowledged in the honors heaped upon her. The famous Cleopatra, Cleopatra VII, whose liaison with Antony, after one with Julius Caesar, brought, with their defeat and suicides, the end of the Hellenistic age. At least three of her predecessors of that name were among the earlier queens whose exploits she was determined to equal; she would revive and dominate the empire.

On the ground, girls in some cities were beginning to get education on a level with boys, and their growing literacy is attested by the production and circulation of novels with a love interest. With education, they had generally more scope outside the home, not only in the arts but also in medicine, and even in civic life as magistrates (recorded in the award of honors). Precedents were being created for a progressive emancipation.

The new interest in women, however, is what most distinguishes the age in this respect from Hellas. They are discovered as interesting in and for themselves, a step in the direction that will develop in more modern circumstances much later, particularly in France. In the visual arts, the female body becomes more realistic on lines that select what is deemed most feminine. The Venus of Milo appeals to the culture of the age. This development broached an inexhaustible modern theme foreign to Hellas.

# 5

# *Zion*

# The Promised Land

## Folk History and World History

There has to be a good reason why the Israelites have a more important place in history than the Edomites, the Moabites, the Ammonites. They were themselves such people. The territory of the Promised Land, "from Dan to Beersheba," was controlled throughout most of antiquity by Egypt or Assyria or Babylon or Persia, or Alexander or his Successors and finally by Rome. It would have been a small part of their dominions, of no importance. David, with an army raised and trained by Saul, did indeed establish a kingdom from Dan to Beersheba, which he consolidated and extended from Damascus to Elath; and he formed a treaty of alliance with Tyre. That was the high point of territorial attainment. After Rome, the remnant of Israelites had no foothold in any territory of their own, till the reformation of Israel in settlements in Palestine that followed Palestine as a British mandate (1918–48), which brought Israel into world history as never before. This could not have happened if there had not been the Israel of folk history, the Israel of the Old Testament.

Folk history is oral tradition and as such contains clues for reappraisal. When history is what is received, perceived, and conceived by a people in respect of its past, it is historical in two senses that may be highly important but are different from eventual history as the record of events. The Bible is historical as an outcome of what happened, not as an account of what happened. The Bible is vastly important as an influence on history; it is not an important history. In this respect, it may resemble other shaping myths. However, as the source of Christianity, it has contributed the second stream to the conflux of European culture, with Greece and Rome. When the Bible's authenticity as the history it professes to be is shown to be untenable in main respects, there is a tendency to write it off altogether as history and take it as literature. In that respect it is acclaimed as a great book, along with Homer's epics, which are also not history.

45

This of course is not how our ancestors took it, until the day before yesterday. In any case, it is not a book like the *Iliad*; it is a complex collection of sixty-six books sealed by selection in a canon. The amplitude and diversity of the material forbids treatment either as history or as literature. If one is to appreciate its historical influence, one must have some understanding of how, why, and when it was put together as it stands. And if the documents are not valid history, their validity and interest nevertheless depend on the historicity of the people whose claims they are making. That historicity has to be pieced together partly from biblical sources critically evaluated, partly from other evidence. Who were the Israelites? What were the actual events behind the account of themselves they give in the biblical record? Answers can only be tentative in respect of the early and most fundamental of the alleged events. David's conquests and hegemony and the outline of subsequent events are hardly in question. Intertwined with the question of events is the question of the sharp conflict between the religious beliefs and practices of the Israelites and those of other settlers in Canaan, in particular the incidence of that conflict. Israel is important solely as the avatar of an historical faith.

## "An Ordinance for Ever"

The ritual celebration of Passover, although enacted only once a year, has at least as great emotional intensity and binding force for the devout Jewish family as the sacrament of the Last Supper has for the regular Christian communicant. It fuses historical and religious beliefs: "By strength of hand the Lord brought us out from Egypt, from the house of bondage" (*Exodus* 13:14).

> Since the night of the Exodus it has become a history feast, and indeed *the* history feast par excellence of the world; not a feast of pious remembrance, but of the ever-recurrent contemporaneousness of that which once befell. Every celebrating generation becomes united with the first generation and with all those that have followed. As in that night the families united into the living people, so in the Passover night the generations of the people unite together, year after year (Martin Buber, 1946).

Continual persecution of the Jews makes for that "ever-recurrent contemporaneousness" that binds the generations together in an historic experience.

In Jewish tradition, the whole story is told in five verses (Deuteronomy 26:5–9): they grew numerous in Egypt, were made slaves and oppressed, complained to the Lord, who brought them out with a mighty hand and great terribleness and gave them a land flowing with milk and honey—salvation and paradise. That it was all the doing of the Lord is of course not reducible to historical terms. That they had been in Egypt some time and had become numerous, and were unendurably exploited, and did find means of escape, and wandered in the Sinai peninsula, hoping to settle in Canaan, is probable. That the Lord would "drive out the Canaanite, the Amorite, and the Hittite, and the Perizzite, the Hivite, and the Jebusite" (Exodus 33:2) in order to give them "a land flowing with milk and honey" is inconceivable.

The story probably begins with the collapse of Sargon's Akkadian empire

(c. 2100 B.C.E.). The movement of peoples involved brought Asiatic nomads into the Egyptian Delta, and these were likely to have included ancestors of the biblical Israelites. Famine is the likely spur to this infiltration. The Hyksos conquered Lower Egypt about 1650. Excavations begun in 1966 by Dr. Manfred Bietak in the neighborhood of Qatir have exposed the site of a city complex on what would have been the eastern mouth of the Nile as described by Herodotus. This has evidence of Canaanite occupation, and seems to have been the capital of the Hyksos dominion (c. l640–1532). The Israelites probably were pasturing their flocks in the fertile environs, living in tents, perhaps since the nineteenth century B.C.E.

It was by superior military technology that the Hyksos dominion had been established. It was by mastery and improvement of that same technology that the Egyptians were enabled to turn them out. In modern technology, what is in production is outdated on the drawing board. At that time, superior resources might outdate the model in production. The composite bow was so called because it used the right kind of wood, tendons from bulls, horn from goats, and animal hair. Increased tension imposed on the bowman a higher requirement of strength and skill. The manufacture of chariots, supply of horses, and training of them for war purposes imposed a further range of demands on resources and selected manpower. Egyptian rulers in Thebes during the Hyksos supremacy seem to have set out to acquire mastery of the resources and technical skills needed to command the military technology of the age, and to have succeeded. Not only did they need this power to reconquer their own land, but also to be equal to the Hittites in competition for the control of Syria. In this way, the Egyptians built up a war machine by which they established the New Kingdom, beginning with the notable Eighteenth Dynasty.

The fifth of the line, Tuthmosis III, consolidated the military organization, building garrison posts and fortifying defense lines. It seems to have been in this work that the Israelites were employed as a labor force, making bricks under the goading supervision of taskmasters who wielded rods and struck heavy blows. The incident described in Exodus 2:11–15, where Moses is said to have killed an Egyptian he saw striking a Hebrew, is a likely enough happening.

## "Conquest"

The "mixed multitude" of the Exodus were akin to the occupants of the oases of the Sinai peninsula in which they sojourned before entry into Canaan, as with the Kenites, the Medianites, and the Edomites who were more permanently settled. All told, whatever their kinship, they shared a common way of life as shepherds originally nomadic. The Exodus party were embroiled in strife with them before their entry into Canaan. The main difference of the Canaanites themselves was that they were settled in cities "and the villages thereof" and were established with a degree of security, stability, and prosperity, enjoying a civilization which the incoming Israelites adopted. Insofar as the cities were under threat from an oppressed peasantry, with relaxed control from Egypt, the infiltration of the Israelites reinforced that threat, and in many cases would help to make good a takeover.

Joshua is described as distributing the "inheritances" in lots, as though indeed they had gone into the Promised Land to be endowed with territories occupied by others.

Embedded in Judges is the Song of Deborah, which is probably a fragment of the form in which much of the oral tradition was passed on. The book contains also the heroic legend of Samson involved in border guerrilla conflict with the Philistines, who first appear in this context. He is the champion hero of a people's Heroic Age:

> With the jawbone of an ass, heaps upon heaps,
> With the jawbone of an ass have I smitten a thousand men.

The Philistines in the story are dominant, the Israelites totally submissive, ready to hand over this champion, their judge, when he has enraged the Philistines, who demand his surrender. It is all legendary and obscure, but it anticipates the decisive struggle for the land of Canaan between the Israelites and the Philistines.

## Union

The Philistines at the beginning of Saul's reign had governors at Gibeah and Geba, near Jerusalem, and at the end of it seem to have commanded the whole plain of Esdraelon (Jezreel). David's raids into Philistine territory during Saul's rule did little to reduce Philistine domination. When David succeeded Saul, the southern tribes he ruled from Hebron were probably held under the authority of the Philistines. After the assassination of Saul's son Ish-bosheth, who had established himself over the northern tribes, David united the two halves and took Jerusalem, a strongly fortified city that that made a wedge between the two Israelite groups. The city of David, as it was thereafter called, was the capital from which he ruled all Israel for thirty-three years. When he was anointed king, the Philistines came up against him, and were defeated (II Samuel 5:17–21 and 22–25); finally he takes their capital (II Samuel 8:1). When at the end of his reign David is in trouble with Absalom's rebellion, the Philistines make no move to take advantage.

"And Solomon sat upon the throne of David his father; and his Kingdom was established greatly." With this consolidation, Solomon, not having to make war, turned his mind to building, and chiefly a temple, which took seven years, and then a palace for himself, which took thirteen years; and another for his wife, the pharaoh's daughter. The building involved lavish expenditure, and, what was more, prodigious labor (I Kings 5:13–18).

## Disintegration

For whatever reason, one Jeroboam, an official of Solomon's court, detached himself from the king and fled to Egypt. Solomon died in 925. When Rehoboam, his son, was to be anointed, Jeroboam reappeared and pledged the allegiance of the Josephites if the heir would provide a milder regime. Rehoboam asked for time to consider what had been said. Having preferred the counsel of his peers to that of the old men, his considered reply made him a high-scorer in the book of notorious follies: "My father chastised you with whips, but I will chastise you with scorpions" (I Kings 12:14). Jeroboam's was the voice of the countryside, speaking the grievances of the tent-dwelling Israelites against the comfortable and oppressive people of the town.

The breach between town and countryside ("cities and the villages thereof") that comes to a head in this incident issues in a mixed division under two kings, Rehoboam ruling from Jerusalem, and Jeroboam from Tirzah. Omri, a later successor to the northern kingdom, is said to have built a new capital on a hill and called it Samaria (I Kings 16:24). He was a strong ruler succeeded by another whose name is better known, Ahab, the husband of Jezebel and the one who killed Naboth and took possession of his vineyard. At this time, he was locked in a life and death struggle with Syria, which continued under his successors. So did the friction between tent and city dwellers.

This undercurrent of the biblical narrative, fragmentation and endemic grievance, was overshadowed, like everything else in the Near East at that time, by the revival of Assyria, whose power had collapsed in 1075. In the ninth century, recovery began with a reorganization of the army and innovations in military technology, especially for the taking of walled cities. With Tiglath-Pileser III in 744, there began nearly a century of conquests, and also of building and works of art, which had not previously been generally recognized. Failure of his predecessors to consolidate conquests, which eventually undermined their power, induced Tiglath-Pileser to devise and carry out a policy of deporting and exchanging subjected populations. The deportation can be thought of as the beginning of the Diaspora.

The recurrence of revolt and repression remains the record until the end under Roman rule early in the second century C.E. From first to last of the Diaspora, the hold on what remained to them in Palestine was ever tenuous, never tentative—perhaps a model of human life on earth.

The small community of Jews in Jerusalem under the Persians was self-segregated, a shrunken remnant with a religious preoccupation that had all but lost a national identity. Under the more open regime of Alexander and his successors, there was emigration within Palestine and beyond. Ptolemaic methods of government allowed them to do better for themselves than had been possible under the Persians. Increased prosperity went along with the attractions of Hellenism, especially to a younger generation. When Antiochus III conquered Palestine (198 B.C.E.) the condition of the people was more prosperous than it had been for centuries, because there was more security and stability. Jewish communities were to be found outside Jerusalem in other parts of Palestine occupied by Ammonites, Moabites, Edomites, and Philistines—neighboring "states." This self-motivated Jewish diaspora was encouraged by the Seleucids in Asia Minor and Syria and by the Ptolemies in Egypt, where Alexandria was the metropolis of Hellenistic Judaism. They were favored as good settlers. There were orthodox in the dispersion as there were Hellenists in Judaea. Jews were in prominent positions at court and in the army. Adoption of Hellenistic ways was socially advantageous, although Greeks were firmly of the opinion than no man's religion was anybody else's business.

However, Antiochus Epiphanes rashly made the suppression of Judaism his business, in his anxiety to unite his motley kingdom in order to be better prepared against the growing menace of Rome. He had been encouraged by reports of the Hellenization of Judaism. In fact the Jews were divided between those who were ready to adopt Hellenism, of whom there was a prominent party in Jerusalem, and those who were loyal to the Law, established by Josiah's reforms and reinforced by the definitive work of Ezra during the captivity in Babylon and after. These loyalists came to be called the Hasidim. Antiochus intrigued with the Hellenizers in Jerusalem, and sent in an army that dismantled the walls. A citadel was built outside to control the town. When the commander of the garrison was assassinated by a village priest and his five sons, who then fled to the hills, the Maccabean revolt was in train. Matthias, a priest, and Judas, his eldest son, initiated a widespread rebellion that went from strength to strength under a succession of leaders drawn from the family, the Hasmonaean dynasty. This began in 165 B.C.E, and by 141 Simon Maccabeus had won autonomy for the Jews. Simon's son John took money from the tomb of David to raise a body of mercenaries, and was able to fight off Antiochus of Syria to defeat massive opposition from his fellow countrymen and annex their territory. Military success enabled him to maintain a stable administration for thirty-one years. When he died in 104, his eldest son, Aristobulus, established the family rule as a monarchy. Annexations of coastal cities, and of Samaria, Galilee, and Idumaea, were made by Simon, John, and Aristobulus. The second king annexed the remaining coastal cities and Greek cities east of Jordan. This was the period of political restoration, 141–76 B.C.E.

Armed struggle between two brothers for the succession brought intervention by the Roman commander in the region, for at this time (66–53 B.C.E.) Pompey was campaigning in the east, and annexed Syria as a Roman province. That intervention led to Pompey's stripping the Hasmonaean dynasty of most of its non-Jewish annexations. Next came the dynasty itself. Pompey had been superseded by Julius Caesar, and the chief person on the Jewish side was Antipater, an Idumaen who had been minister under Hyrcanus II, a briefly legitimate king ousted by his brother. Hyrcanus was restored as ethnarch by the Romans, and Antipater became increasingly powerful, finding favor with Caesar, who made him a Roman citizen. He was also made procurator of Judaea, where he was virtual ruler. He made his second son, Herod, governor of Galilee. Herod made a reputation for himself by suppressing banditry that was afflicting the Syrians. His growing reputation prompted a court faction to have Hyrcanus arraign Herod for exceeding his authority. Hyrcanus was ordered by the Romans to acquit him. Herod was appointed commander-in-chief of part of the province of Syria by the Roman governor, and actually moved to dethrone Hyrcanus, but was dissuaded by his father.

Caesar was assassinated, and civil war followed. Antipater was poisoned, and the Parthians invaded Syria and Palestine, plundered Jerusalem, brought about the death of Herod's brother, and installed Antigonus, son of Hyrcanus's rival brother, as king. Herod, surviving heavy setbacks and infinite difficulties, made his way to Rome, where Octavius, sensible of what Rome owed to Herod and his family, convened the Senate, to whom Herod was introduced. Having heard all that was said, the Senate voted to make Herod king of Judaea. This was 40 B.C.E., two years after Philipii.

Nominated king by the Romans, Herod had to conquer Palestine from Antigonus supported by the Parthians. In this he had the help of the Roman governor of Syria and of Mark Antony; but Antony was corrupted by Cleopatra, who also did her utmost to undermine Herod and to gain control of slices of his territory. It took more than three years to defeat Antigonus, ending with the siege of Jerusalem. The carnage had been fearful, and Herod had to bribe the Romans out of his own resources to prevent their looting Jerusalem. After Antony's defeat at Actium by Octavius, Herod hastened to meet the victor, not to curry favor by excuses for his support of Antony, but simply to say that he owed his throne to Antony and had been undeviatingly loyal on that ground. Augustus recognized the reliable value of this openness, confirmed his position, restored the places detached by Cleopatra, and continued to add to Herod's kingdom. Like most established rulers, Herod engaged in building and rebuilding, and raised many notable monuments. Less usual, he made gifts to foreign cities, especially Greek cities, Athens, Sparta, Pergamon, and particularly Rhodes. Perhaps most notably, he endowed the Olympic games, which were declining for lack of funds. That he was able to maintain this consistent generosity indicates the prosperity of a secure regime. His last years were clouded by murderous family plots and counter plots, parallel to the more notorious horrors of the imperial family in Rome after Augustus. Herod died in 4 B.C.E.

Successive procurators of Judaea aggravated grievances and played into the hands of those in Jerusalem who looked for the opportunity to revolt.

There was a last religious rising, in 132 C.E. under Hadrian, which was suppressed in 135 after a long and bloody struggle. This wiped out Judaism in southern Palestine.

# 6

## *Zion*

## The Chosen People

### The Old Covenant

The political history of the Jews outlined in the previous chapter from the time a mixed multitude left Egypt until Hadrian struck Judaea off the map, a period not far short of a millennium and a half, has to be extracted from the Old Testament (OT), the Apocrypha, Josephus, and other sources. It is not the OT narrative, although generally consistent with it. That narrative is set down by another hand, and is concerned with a different theme. "The Word of God" is not a figure of speech, whatever the claim. The text often reads as dictation of the God of Abraham, Isaac, and Jacob. Jahweh, the tribal god, was "a man of war" (Exodus 15:3). He was the captain of Joshua's host (Judges 7). His favorite servant was the warrior David, a man after his own heart, to whom he gave victory (I Samuel 17), and with whom he was present in the battle (II Samuel 5:23–25).

The Lord of hosts has a driving purpose for his people, and is the *animateur* of the OT narrative. That driving purpose is made explicit in a covenant. Jahweh makes covenants with individuals (as most famously with Noah after the flood [Genesis 9:9–17], or with Phinheas [Numbers 25:12–13]. The definitive covenant that makes for the central theme of the OT narrative is with the children of Israel through their progenitors or their representatives, as it is affirmed and reaffirmed (Genesis 15:18–20; Exodus 2:24; 6:4–8; Deuteronomy 5:2–3; Jeremiah 33:19–26 and 34:13). Anthropological studies show that a covenant is not merely affirmed in words or documents, but mainly is enacted in a memorial meal together of the parties, or a sacrifice, or a sprinkling of blood, some ceremonial act or sign of union, a sacrament. The memorial of the Last Supper does not merely supersede the Feast of the Passover in the Christian calendar, but is mainly the institution of a New Covenant. The Old Covenant was instituted not merely in words, not even in rituals, but materially in cutting the flesh of every male beneficiary, in circumcision (Genesis 17:10–14). Circumcision was a fairly widespread practice, common among Semitic peoples but not peculiar to them. Its specific adoption, however, as an incised badge of a covenanted people, made it a token of separation; if not a test, more than a shibboleth.

A covenant seals a bargain; it is undertaken for mutual benefit, and is two-sided. The covenant with the children of Israel is in the OT text not only initiated by the God of Abraham, Isaac, and Jacob, but almost imposed upon them, although the aid that is promised must have been what they prayed and sacrificed in hope of. This divine monopoly of initiative is fundamental to Judaism, and of historical importance: the will of God is not only paramount, but absolute. However, apart from specific covenants with individuals, there is a distinction in the texts among three types of covenant. There is the one-sided covenant with Abraham, which endows him and his seed with the Promised Land. There is the conditional covenant with Moses on Sinai, which summarily states what is promised, with the attached condition (Exodus 23:20–33). Later, when that condition has been sorely and repeatedly broken, there is Jeremiah's prophecy of a new covenant (Jeremiah 31:31–34) with the house of Israel, written in their inward parts, the new covenant that St. Paul takes as not exclusive to the house of Israel.

## The Prophets

Jahweh is a jealous god who demands exclusive loyalty. The children of Israel are warned not to have anything to do with the inhabitants of the land they will take over; indeed, they must "break down their altars"; they must not inter-marry (Exodus 34:12–16). This is a continual warning (Deuteronomy 4:23–24; 5:9). The consequence of failure to heed the warning is stressed (Deuteronomy 6:15; Joshua 24:19–20): it amounts to extermination. Thus the pattern is set: the Israelites go whoring after strange gods, are visited with Jahweh's displeasure, are sorted out and punished. They do not exterminate Canaanite rituals, and are due for extermination.

The major prophets whose names head books of the OT are not to be confused with the communities of prophets often referred to. They did not belong to such bodies. They spoke and acted independently, and probably had disciples, like the Greek philosophers. They were by no means academics, and did not found schools nor sects. The prophets of the eighth century were from the villages, country born and bred: Elijah, Ahijah, Amos, Micah, Jeremiah. What the prophets did was to shift the center of gravity in Israel's religious history from ritual, even ritual purity, to ethics, from religious observances to social conduct. This is seen conveniently by comparing two versions of the Decalogue that appear in Exodus 20:2–17 and 34:14–28. The earlier one can be summarized as: (1) I am Jahweh your god; you shall not worship another god; (2) You shall keep the feast of unleavened bread; seven days you shall eat unleavened bread; (3) All that open the womb are mine; and all your cattle that are male, the firstlings of ox and sheep; (4) You shall keep my Sabbath; you shall work six days, and on the seventh you shall rest; (5) You shall celebrate the feast of weeks, the first-fruits of wheat harvest; (6) You shall celebrate the feast of in-gathering at the end of the year; (7) You shall not offer the blood of my sacrifice with leavened bread; (8) The sacrifice of the feast of the passover shall not remain all night until the morning; (9) The first of the fruits of your ground you shall bring into the house of Jahweh your god; and (10) You shall not seethe a kid in its mother's milk.

Only the first and fourth of these commandments are in the later revision. All the rest are concerned with arbitrary religious observances and the third requires a barbaric practice that the prophets condemn as an abomination. What they stood for was a root-and-branch transformation of current practices and a reorientation of spirit, with some appeal to an older desert tradition. The ethical content of the revised Decalogue is a measure of their success.

Israel had fallen by her iniquity, but she had not lost the love shown to her from the beginning: "When Israel was a child, then I loved him, and called my son out of Egypt."

There would be a restoration, when as a simple outcome of all her travail, instead of animal sacrifices or trust in alliances and arms or faith in idols, Israel shall say "in thee the fatherless findeth mercy." In the ringing words of Hosea's fatal chapter, the Lord will respond: "I will heal their backsliding, I will love them freely." Jeremiah was steeped in Hosea. He found himself absolutely alone against kings, priests, people, with his immediate communion with Jahweh the abiding reality. "I will put my law in their inward parts." Like the message of the Protestant Reformation, individual fidelity was required, and on that condition no official or institutional mediation or interposition was needed or relevant.

Unless enough of what the prophets had to say had been taken hold of and put into forms of practice before the destruction of the two kingdoms, there would have been no Bible.

## The Law

The prophets did not abolish the priests, as the Reformers would not abolish the Pope. The religious observances were reformed and put in order. This began in little Judah in 621 with the "discovery" by the high priest in the temple in Jerusalem of "the law of Jahweh," the book that was to become the core of Deuteronomy. Ascribed to an ancient source for high prestige, the book was probably the work of a scribe versed in the law and oral tradition, and was devised to anchor the worship of Jahweh in a code of practice. It purposed to be rules for the behavior of the Chosen People in the Promised Land. In effect, it was a program of reforms, which included limiting sacrificial worship to the sanctuary in Jerusalem, thus eliminating Baal-worship. Josiah the king, of noted piety (he was to be a model for Charlemagne), proceeded with the elders of Judah to give effect to the discovered law by rooting out all alien practices "from Geba to Beersheba." That meant the destruction of all existing sanctuaries of Jahweh, since they were tainted by foreign practices. This would hardly have been practicable if the extent of Judah had not been drastically reduced at that time, as mentioned in the previous chapter. A glimpse of the stubborn resistance to the reforms comes through in Jeremiah 44:15–23.

Josiah was killed at Megiddo in 609 B.C.E., and demoralization followed deportation of the ruling classes to Babylonia, leaving others to seek refuge in Egypt or elsewhere. A reforming party among the Babylonian exiles adopted the Deuteronomic code and put it into an "historical" framework that included earlier traditions and records. This was reworked to consolidate and interpret the history of Israel. Others collected and edited and augmented the works of the prophets. The Law and the Prophets were put into books. With Jerusalem destroyed by Nebuchadnezzar in 587, a form of worship had to be devised without temple, priest, and sacrifices. Dispersal had occurred before the Captivity, and continued after. Jews were numerous and prosperous in Babylonia, and were widely dispersed in Persia, in Egypt, in Asia Minor, in the Greek islands. In some of these places there were sizable communities, particularly in Egypt. Prayer and praise (the Psalms), with reading, and exposition of the Law, when established, made a form of service that could be used in exile anywhere. To establish the Law was the purpose and work of groups of priests and lawyers in Babylon, among whom Ezra became prominent. When Nehemiah obtained permission from Artaxerxes to go to Jerusalem to rebuild the walls, he was well received in the city, and the wall was repaired in less than two months. While there he found a wide difference between the Israelites of Jerusalem and those in Babylon who had spent years in reorganizing their religion under a code of rules. Nehemiah wanted to introduce and establish the practice of the new code, and knew that this would not be possible unless a substantial number of those in Babylon could be brought to Jerusalem. He obtained permission from Artaxerxes to do this, and returned with Ezra and a party. The Law, essentially the Pentateuch, though not yet in the final form it has in the Bible, was published. To put it in practice with the population involved separating Jew and non-Jew and putting a stop to mixed marriages. There was scant success in doing this. In 433 Nehemiah got Artaxerxes to appoint him governor of Judaea. In that position he induced the leaders of the people to agree to adoption of the Law, and it was promulgated in an assembly of the people. Nehemiah was narrowly Judaistic, and would not countenance the acceptance of Samaritans under the new regime. They therefore set up their own sanctuary in Shechem. Jew and Samaritan remained apart. The Jews, united on the basis of the Law, became a church rather than a nation; and were represented by their high priest.

A main consequence of Nehemiah's enforcement of the Law was the institution of synagogues, which were served by scribes. The Law was complex, and needed to be taught and interpreted. The will of Jahweh was to be learned not from the inspired teaching of the prophets, but from the custodians of the written Law.

Priestly laws are preoccupied with rites of purification, so that a person is made ready for contact with the divine. "Uncleanness" may have several sources, including disease, infringement of a taboo, a moral offense; distinctions are not made at an early stage. In Jewish law, the comprehensive word is "sin," a breaking of the law, a disobedience, not necessarily a moral term. A sin offering may be for inadvertent transgression of ceremonial prohibitions, or is required after childbirth, sexual intercourse, or from one tainted with leprosy. The physical means prescribed for the removal of uncleanliness of any kind are deemed efficacious against the consequences of wrongdoing, unless the distinction has been made between religious and moral rules.

## The Sects

Pharisees and Sadducees are names made familiar by the Gospels, and they represent the most important sects in Judaism. Before that, the Samaritans had been forced into schism by Nehemiah. They had a version of the Pentateuch, but not the books of the Prophets. What may be regarded as a sect—the Rechabites—appear fugitively. They might be taken as the exemplary Israelites, smaller in number than the "Remnant." They were the nomads who continued to live in tents, and refused to cultivate the soil and adopt the ways of the Canaanites. Not for them the Law.

Similarly, the Essenes were an obscure brotherhood about whom little that is trustworthy is known. What there is comes mainly from Josephus and Philo; there is nothing in the Bible. They seem to have been small groups on the shores of the Dead Sea who lived a monastic life as celibates. Some seem to have travelled to the cities to propagate their doctrines and find recruits. They disappear into the past in the later phases of Judaism. They do not contribute to its development, as do the the two prominent sects.

In the Gospels, the Pharisees are linked with the scribes. The scribes came into existence to teach the people how the Law was to be observed. In status they might be compared with the Greek sophists, both pedagogics, although their jobs were different, the one exclusively religious, the other entirely secular. The Pharisees were an unorganized party of the pious who were special in their total devotion to observance of the Law, and they included many of the scribes. They enjoyed popular support, and even Herod was careful not to offend them. Their influence was immense. This was the time when belief in the immortality of the soul and a last judgment became prevalent. Beliefs of the kind had gained circulation through the influence of the Orphic sects on Plato, and had become general in Hellenic quarters. In Babylon under Persia there had been the influence of Zoroastrianism. The doctrine is given a Jewish setting in the Wisdom of Solomon I and II (Apocrypha); God did not make death; the souls of the righteous are in his hands; righteousness is immortal; death is the portion of the ungodly alone, who have brought it on themselves. The Pharisees were persuaded.

The Sadducees would have none of it, and with the priesthood kept it out of the Law. They were the hierarchical priestly caste, of the old Hasmonaean party, which adhered to the ideal of an independent national monarchy, from which the Pharisees had dissociated themselves in their exclusive devotion to the practice of Judaism according to the Law. The destruction of the Temple by Titus in 70 C.E. extinguished the OT sacrificial cult, and that was the end of the priestly aristocracy.

There was a Hellenizing party, attracted and influenced by Greek ideas and ideals, mainly in the diaspora, and particularly strong in Alexandria. The influence is evident in the Wisdom books of the Apocrypha, Ecclesiasticus and the Wisdom of Solomon, where "wisdom" is thought of as knowledge, secular learning; whereas in the Wisdom books of the OT, Ecclesiastes and Proverbs, "wisdom" begins with "fear of the Lord." It is the different outlook of scribes and sophists. On the whole, Judaism was impervious to Greek thought, but not to Oriental astrology, demonology, and magic, which it could adopt and adapt.

The sect that alone made Judaism a profound influence upon Europe was Christianity. The obsession of Judaism with tradition made it least likely to succeed in a claim to universality: its adherents made themselves a peculiar people. A convert to the new sect, a Hebrew of the Hebrews, brought up a Pharisee, Saul of Tarsus, renamed Paul, set himself to be an apostle to the Gentiles, which required relief from the weight of the Law and the badge of circumcision. Paul had to overcome a stumbling block to the Jews and foolishness to the Greeks in acceptance of the messianic gospel he preached. His position is put succinctly in Galatians 3:23–29, which concludes: "There can be neither Jew nor Greek, there can be neither bond nor free, there can be no male and female: for you all are one man in Christ Jesus. And if you are Christ's, then you are Abraham's seed, heirs according to promise." Stephen had been stoned to death for this new interpretation of Israel's history, a blasphemy against Moses; and Saul had stood by in approval. There were Judaizers among Jewish converts to the sect. They sought to persuade the Galatian Church to observe the Jewish calendar and to require circumcision. Hence Paul's argument. It did not prevail easily with Jewish converts. It did make possible penetration of the Gentile world. Christianity was made a European inheritance because it was eventually adopted by Rome.

## The Kingdom of God

For the mass of the people in the Jewish world after the political destruction of Israel and Judah, the Apocalyptic literature displaced the prophets. It was promise of a new heaven and a new earth in God's good time. The task of the religious leaders of Judaism as they had learned to think of it, freed from the earlier interests of national survival, was to educate the people in the will of God, as the necessary preliminary to the coming of the Kingdom of God. As institutions for this task the school and the synagogue had been developed wherever there were Jewish settlements. The Hebrew Bible was the text in which children learned to read in elementary schools; in the higher schools the Law was methodically studied. This reversed the practice, which had reserved religious learning for the priestly caste, jealously exclusive.

The most striking thing about OT theology is that there is no theology. God forms man in his own image. He speaks to man face to face as a man speaks to his friend (Exodus 33:11). Abraham is the friend of God. The righteous walk with him, albeit humbly. This does not diminish almightiness: Jacob says, "I have seen God face to face, and my life is preserved" (Genesis 32:30). All told, the OT, for all its conglomerate material, and in spite of inconsistencies, is at bottom about a personal God who is accessible, with whom one can walk, who at the same time is maker of heaven and earth. That is unique.

In the Gospels of the New Testament (NT), which are about incarnation, anthropomorphism becomes absolute; man is not merely made in the image of God; God makes himself known in the person of a man. When Jesus of Nazareth preaches the Kingdom of God, what is meant? One might say it is spelled out in a dozen words in the paradigm prayer: "Thy will be done on earth as it is in heaven"—a consensual theocracy, the new covenant. But a prayer is optative, a wish. How is it to be brought about? Sifting the parables and other sayings, there seem to be three phases. "The kingdom of God is within you": it is immediate, enjoyed in fellowship with the Father, and in the fellowship of the disciples with Jesus. It is like a mustard seed that becomes a tree: it is cumulative, a growth, progressive, as in the history of Israel, and in the school, and by social institutions. It will come in the fullness of time with the Day of Judgment, when the wheat will be separated from the tares. That is the Gospel of the NT, in continuity with the OT, without which it would not be.

This was what Paul said was foolishness to the Greeks. It was so because it was sheer anthropomorphism, without question, without theology, a matter of arbitrary assumption and ungrounded faith from beginning to end. The myths of the Greeks were obviously invented and were early brought into question, with the outcome that the whole of existence was put in question: "The unexamined life is not a life for man." The identity of Israel is derived from and bound up with its myths, with the outcome that declares a personal universal God whose will is paramount. Hellenism could give hospitality to Judaism, as an alternative, a choice. Neither Jew nor Christian would have understanding or time for the god of the philosophers.

Both the open humanist culture and the living personal God, with their rival claims to universality, were incorporated into the European inheritance. This would be ambivalence and contradiction at the center, manifested from time to time, and in different ways. The theater of history is not an art form. History throws up themes which work on, and may work out, but not necessarily in a denouement. The earliest of such themes to appear and reappear in the history of the West is this ultimate Either/Or of universal claims.

# 7

# *Romanitas*

# The Imperium

## The Augustan Reconstruction

Rome counts in history as an empire. In extent of territory, the empire was already in existence when Augustus invented and inaugurated the Principate. Indeed, his deliberate purpose was not to extend the frontiers by new conquests. He thought it necessary to consolidate what was held. Security, stability, and prosperity are always and everywhere the material foundations of a durable civilization. To say the least, these conditions did not exist when Augustus took in hand the task he set himself.

If the material foundations were not there, the moral foundations were in the Republic. *Respublica* meant *libertas,* freedom of a people, independence of domination by another power. Dedication to that meant public spirit in the most exacting measure, as searching as a total religious demand. It was forthcoming in Regulus, the Roman consul, taken prisoner by the Carthaginians and sent five years later (256 B.C.E.) with their envoys to sue for peace. Contrary to their intention, he persuaded his countrymen to reject the terms. Since he was on parole, he insisted on returning to torture and death. Another consul, Cincinnatus, some 156 years earlier, had been called to the highest office from his small farm, and, in due course, after notable achievement, returned to the plough. Such legendary heroes were of a different stamp compared with Achilles, who inspired the conqueror Alexander. The hard school of early military service under public authority for survival as an independent people formed the Roman character, and led on to the piecemeal conquests of eventual imperium. Their freedom as a people had to be won and preserved not only against the domination of others, but also and primarily against the tyranny of their early kings. They dated it from the abolition of monarchy and identified it with the constitution of the republic. There was at the same time *libertas populi Romani* and *libertas civis Romani*, freedom of the Roman nation and freedom of the Roman citizen.

Macaulay in his preface to *Lays of Ancient Rome,* an attempt to recreate ballads of early Roman minstrels, attributes to the old Romans great virtues: fortitude, temperance, veracity, spirit to resist oppression, respect for legitimate authority, fidelity in the observing of contracts, disinterestedness, ardent patriotism. That belied history. For if indeed the old Romans had these virtues, there would not have been the successive bids for power and ruthless exercise of it, the civil wars and anarchy that reduced the Republic to the desperate condition in which Octavian addressed himself to picking up the pieces, and became Augustus. At the same time, these were ideals of the Roman character, and were reflected in constitutional principles and institutions they introduced. The Republic that was a shambles embodied ideals in traditions and institutions that were exemplary. The contradiction is not historically unique. Executive authority and power were granted for a limited period, usually one year; and all magistracies were vested in two or more colleagues of equal standing, each empowered to act alone and also to oppose any action taken by his equals or juniors. These conjoined constitutional principles were held to be safeguards of political liberty (libertas). If adhered to, they could have preserved the Republic. That implied consistent loyal cooperation of people, Senate, and magistrates (consuls and tribunes).

Rome's early ascendancy was gained in conflict with neighboring tribes, above all with the Etruscans, and by initiating and leading confederacies within Italy. Carthage was the rival power in that part of the Mediterranean. Greece, with colonies in southern Italy and Sicily, was a declining influence. Carthage had advantage as a sea power, and it was not until Rome built a comparable fleet that she was able to win the first Punic War, which gained her Sicily, Sardinia, and Corsica, her first overseas provinces. This was followed by the famous surprise entry into Italy of Hannibal by crossing the Alps in winter from Spain. The war started in 218 B.C.E. and lasted seventeen years. Hannibal's crushing victory at Trasimeno Lake, which annihilated the Roman army sent to avert his approach to Rome, alarmed the Senate, which appointed as dictator Quintus Fabius to defend Rome. His Fabian tactics are as famous Hannibal's winter crossing of the Alps with some twenty thousand infantry, six thousand cavalry, and a detachment of elephants. The episodes of this part of the war used to be familiar to European schoolboys in the graphic pages of Livy's narrative. In 206, Scipio won a decisive victory in Spain, ending Carthaginian domination there and opening the way for an invasion of North Africa, which he undertook two years later. Scipio's success compelled the Carthaginians to recall Hannibal from Italy. Roman victory in 202 virtually ended the great struggle. Rome was established as the Mediterranean power. The razing of Carthage and of Corinth, her two chief commercial rivals, are among Rome's blackest crimes, even allowing that war is unlimited violence and cunning.

In a position to secure her frontiers in Spain and Africa, and with a sphere of influence in the eastern Mediterranean, Rome was shocked out of complacency in 112 B.C.E. when it was defeated in southern Gaul by migratory tribes who continued to defy attempts at expulsion and inflicted a crushing reverse on another Roman army in 105. This marked a turning point in Roman history, for the Senate elected Marius consul in six consecutive years to tackle the problem; and he instituted a drastic reform of the army that was to make it the tool of conquest. In the new design, 10 cohorts of about 480 men formed the legion, based on a tactical unit of a "century" (80 men) commanded by a centurion, the backbone of the army, promoted from the ranks on merit. This was the more needful since the generals were amateurs, annually elected consuls. With this new model army, Marius was successful in defeating the tribesmen piecemeal, with heavy slaughter. Not only had the army been made a flexible force that could be deployed with great economy to control widespread territory, the loyalty of the legions had been transferred to their generals, when they proved themselves, instead as of old to Rome. Also, the pool of manpower for the army was greatly enlarged when citizenship was granted to the Italians.

Marius was a victim of his own success. Sulla was sent to repel the encroachment of Mithridates in the east. Having completed the mission successfully, he returned to Rome at the head of an army of twenty-three legions, able to quell all opposition, purge opponents, and confiscate land to reward his soldiers. What else he did to impose and reinforce an oligarchic government did not outlast his life, for the army commanders were the executive on whom the Senate depended for implementing their decisions. Both Pompey and Crassus had armies in the field, and were in a position to force the Senate. Pompey was needed to suppress piracy in the Mediterranean, and to deal with a resurgence of Mithridates in Asia Minor. The situation was serious: the seas were practically in the hands of pirates; trade was at a standstill; Rome was threatened with famine. The most capable man was needed, and though the Senate feared Pompey, and resisted his appointment, he was in the end given proconsular power for three years over the whole Mediterranean. He is said to have raised 120,000 men and 4,000 cavalry and had 270 ships in commission. Simultaneous attacks on all the pirates' strong-point anchorages were ordered. They were taken by surprise, and the western area was cleared in forty days. Pompey then turned to the East. He had spared those prepared to be informers, and many surrendered. A hard core of desperadoes, retreating into forts along the Cilician coast with their families and their treasure, prepared to hold out. Pompey gathered siege equipment, and attacked their strongholds. The last fortress surrendered to his mercy, followed by all that remained throughout Cilicia. Pompey recognized that the root cause was poverty, and to prevent recurrence he settled many of the survivors in suitable districts where they could make a fresh start with reasonable prospects. The old Corycian content on a few poor acres, of whom Virgil writes in book IV of his *Georgics,* was a reformed pirate.

After dealing with Mithridates, Pompey in five years defeated the Armenians and annexed Bytynia, Pontus, Syria, Cilicia, and Crete, where he founded cities and installed prudent and humane administrations. Returning triumphant, he was refused by the Senate grants of land for his veterans. There was no financial provision for maintaining and controlling the armies; commanders were left to provide for them by the spoils of war.

Julius Caesar was elected consul in 60 B.C.E., and appointed governor of Cisalpine Gaul, with an army of three legions. Transalpine Gaul was added when its governor suddenly died. Caesar's brilliant eight campaigns in Gaul carried Rome's frontiers to the Rhine and the Ocean and alarmed the Senate. Pompey had allowed himself to support the conservative party. When the Senate decided to recall Caesar and required him to relinquish his command, the issue was forced. Caesar crossed the southern boundary of his original province, the river Rubicon, and marched his army on Rome. Pompey and the senators he supported withdrew from Rome and then from Italy. Caesar defeated Pompey's army in Spain and then returned to Rome, and set out in pursuit of Pompey himself. On the other side of the Adriatic, Caesar's army was defeated; he retreated 200 miles southwest, followed by Pompey. Both sides received reinforcements before their decisive engagement near Pharsalus, in which Pompey's army was put to flight. He escaped by ship to Egypt, where he was treacherously murdered later on the orders of those behind the young king. Although not the end of the civil war, Caesar's triumph was ensured.

Caesar's assassination, intended to save the Republic, was its death blow. There was no army paid and controlled by the state. There was a Senate without an effective executive under its control. Caesar might have been able to reorganize the administration to bring the two together. That task was left to his adopted son and heir, Octavian, when thirteen years later he defeated Mark Antony in a sea battle in the bay of Actium and besieged Alexandria, where Antony and Cleopatra had taken refuge. That concluded, Octavian turned the kingdom of Egypt into a Roman province and set troops to clean out the irrigation canals that had been allowed to silt up. He had in mind grain for the Roman market.

During the vicissitudes that followed Caesar's assassination, Octavian had practiced treachery, murder, and massacre, as they had served his turn. Left with sole power and authority, he practiced due dissimulation, but with the consistent intent to conciliate, disarm, bind, and reintegrate the fragments. In Europe, after the devastation of the First World War, action on all fronts was enlisted under the banner "reconstruction." In Rome during Octavian's time, after years of continuous war, foreign and civil, morale was drained, and there was danger of a lapse into anarchy. Reconstruction was necessary and urgent. Augustus and the Principate were the answer.

The practice of Roman religion had lapsed into obsolescence. Augustus revived it in order to bind the society to the state. Security depended on the army; stability and prosperity (fertility) were associated traditionally with due performance of religious rites. There is classical evidence in Horace's "Secular Ode" or "Centennial Hymn." Augustus commissioned him to compose it when in 17 B.C.E. he revived the Secular Games, a festival that used to be held every 110 years to celebrate the preservation of the state. On the third and last day of the festival an ode was sung by a choir of boys and girls in Apollo's temple. It is in purpose a rededication of the Roman people in their state to their duty and destiny, which the ode sets in an invocation that deftly combines the auspices of their legendary ancestry present in Augustus with the blessing he seeks for the imperium he inaugurates. It is poetic rhetoric, but weighted with indications of actual policies.

Virgil's farm had been confiscated for the settlement of veterans. He went to Rome to appeal to Octavian, and it was restored to him. At the end of book II of his *Georgics* (458–542), he, like Horace, deplores the evil doings of the times, set against the unfailing joys of rural life and the habits of the ancestral past. He too will focus a poem on Augustus. The boldness of the figure of speech foretells the poetic identification of Virgil with Augustus. These are not the courtesies of court flattery. The old Roman *pietas* that Augustus sought to renew by rebuilding temples and resuscitating cults, Virgil embodied in pius Aeneas, whose heir is Augustus—as Jesus was of David.

The setting and imagery of myths exalt a charged imagination. That imagination is shared. Augustus and Virgil and Horace are together and of one mind in their vision; and there is Livy, and probably others, in the background. At this break in their history, a self-conscious moment in which to look back and forth and to sound intent, an historic interpenetration of past, present, and future, the Roman imperium assumes its aim, and is defined. It is to play God, the monumental arrogance. God is supreme power. They see this is theirs. The question for the Caesars is how to use it. Augustus has chosen. His poets couch his choice. Virgil, Horace, and Livy were all on terms of personal friendship with Augustus. All four were necessary to Romanitas. The man of action and the poet were necessary to each other in the ancient world: Alexander and Achilles, to reverse the example.

Ovid was contemporary with Augustus, who was a generous patron, until he banished him for some private reason. Like Pope, Ovid might have said, "I lisped in numbers for the numbers came," and he was the most productive poet. In Europe he was the most readable of Latin poets, and it was the *Metamorphoses* that was most read. Since this relates selected Greek myths in compelling verse, it is literally a Greek book in Latin, though by no means a translation. By implication, it celebrates the adoption by Rome of Greek myths and legends as their own, and that means the Olympian gods. Zeus, Hermes, Poseidon, Athena, and others have Latin names: Jupiter (dove), Mercury, Neptune, Minerva. Some of these were identifications with Latin deities, as particularly Aphrodite with an early Italian Venus. As partly this kind of assimilation, and in greater part outright adoption, this common mythology represents definitively the Hellenization of Rome. Europe generally knows the Greek gods by their Latin names, and by these names they figure in European poetry.

## Assimilation

*Romanitas* is not merely the Roman imperium. It is counterpoint to Hellas, an harmonious vision: the civilization of the inhabited world. Rome was Hellenized, and in turn Romanized the world it conquered, after Augustus. The imperium was Rome's input. Alexander's conquests of unprecedented extent occupied a decade. Rome took more than five and a half centuries to bring Italy under control. Roman supremacy, from the reduction of Macedon to a province to the loss of Alexandria to the Arabs in 640, lasted some 830 years; and a Roman government in Byzantium lasted another 800 years. Beyond that was Rome's immeasurable manifold influence on Europe.

Romanitas as Hellenized Rome was not the Roman imperium plus Hellas. The assimilation produced Roman arts, in particular literature and architecture, to match the Greeks and to crown the arts of government. The Augustan Age transcended its epoch to lend its name to peak cultural achievement. It was Romanitas that in spite of ruin forced the French sixteenth-century Du Bellay, in his twelve-part encomium *Antiquitez de Rome,* to go so far as to say: "Rome fut tout le monde, et tout le monde est Rome" and, "le plan de Rome est la carte du monde," acknowledging the universality the age designed for Romanitas, the evidence left in the stories of the ruined city and in the living words of its dead language.

Horace captured in ten words the historical meaning of Rome's conquest of Greece: "Graecia capta ferum victorem cepit, et artes intulit agresti Latio." (Captive Greece captivated the fierce victor and brought the arts to rustic Latium.) He it is who is most Roman and most Greek, Roman in the fierce pride of his patriotism, Greek in his self-cultivation and in his art. Horace's education, by the care of his father, a freedman, was intensively Greek, in Rome with the distinguished teacher Orbilius, who took him through the *Iliad,* then in Athens, where he became thoroughly acquainted with the poetry and literature and learned something of methodical reflection in philosophy. What he learned from the Greeks, and Pindar especially, was the discipline, the toil, the tireless revision, the polish for perfection, that Pindar found in the competitors at Olympia and commended in the victors he celebrated, and with whom he compared himself, in his training and in the ardors of composition. This reappears in Horace's famous *Ars Poetica,* which was to be so influential. He eloquently articulates his digest of what he learned from the Greeks, reinforced and filled out with reflection on his own experience. Good sense and clear conceptions can be learned from Socrates, to go with observation of things as they are, which of themselves can be trusted to prompt appropriate words. He commends the spirit of Roman poets to go it alone, and says that might have succeeded, as had Roman arms, "Did we not hate the necessary toil of slow correction, and the painful file." The recommendation is to study the Greek models by night and by day.

Roman distinctiveness in literature was in satire. In the tenth satire of book I, Horace says that when in early youth he aspired to emulate Greek poetry, Rome's founder appeared to him in a dream and warned him to forgo a fruitless enterprise, like adding water to the ocean; and he had been driven to think he could succeed only in satire. This is a good example of the truth that to be original is to adopt and adapt. There was early Greek satire in the iambics of Archilochus and later on the stage in the Old Comedy; but they did not make a genre of it as the Romans did. Greeks and Romans shared a promptness to borrow and learn from others, a readiness to adopt and adapt. The Greeks improved on what they took more rapidly and ingeniously; the Romans learned early from the Etruscans military art and their shipbuilding and seamanship, the two departments in which they were to go soonest and furthest. Their first acquaintance with Greek culture was probably through the influence of Greek house slaves, following the conquest of southern Italy. Horace says that it was not until the end of the wars with Carthage that the Romans had the leisure to interest themselves in Greek literature. Since then, their native rudeness in letters had been refined by their Greek studies, and the maturity they had attained was still not without traces of the uncouth. It can be said that the reward of his unremitting polish has been to make Horace the most quotable and quoted author in the language.

Virgil was most simply and wholly dedicated to the new vision of Romanitas.

The *Georgics* is by no means a minor poem. About the labor of body and mind in cultivation of the land, it is rich in deeply worked analogies, of the conditions and experiences of husbandry with the political experience of order and disorder in the world, and with personal experience of joy and suffering: correspondence of people and land, a shared existence, a way of life, continuity; a manner of being, and loss and alienation. Traditional virtues and values, like the goodness of the soil, needed constant regeneration. The tempo and detail of seasonal work was a wordless acquaintance with the "honor" within things, a self-transcendence in entering and inhabiting a world in practicing an art rewarded by the responsiveness of nature, thwarted by its recalcitrance; a life of hazards and demands, in which "everything tends to the worse if left to itself": the bounty and stinginess of nature. Virgil finished his composition of the work as the civil war ended. He read it to Octavian when he had just returned from the final campaign.

The *Iliad* was the model for the *Aeneid,* in the sense that it was an epic and Virgil wanted to compose the epic of Rome. The theme was not in doubt, but the manner seemed an intractable problem, to the extent that when Virgil was dying he is said to have wanted to burn the poem; he had been long in making up his mind, and was hesitant even in the course of composition. How to make a work of contemporary appeal in the manner of the old epic and on the scale he had in mind was impossible. The epic was out of fashion. What he produced had in purpose and substance connections with the conventions of the heroic epic, and profound differences. Virgil insinuates the subtlety of his matured mind and art into the links and differences and into his characters. The influence of the work has been enormous, and wholly different from that of Homer. It has internal "spiritual" dimensions. Dante was inspired by it. T. S. Eliot used it to define a "classic."

A myth gives a people possession of their identity and distinction. This one is identified with a claim to universality. There are of course historical rivals. Marina Warner in her account of the myth and cult of the Virgin Mary, *Alone of All Her Sex,* wrote in the prologue:

> Just as Aeneas provided Roman citizens with historical roots in the noble past of Troy and descent from the goddess Venus, his mother, and at the same time furnished a standard of conduct that they regarded as exemplary—Virgil's "pius Aeneas"—so the Virgin Mary, an ordinary woman who gave birth to Christ, in whom all found new life, becomes the symbolic mother of the Church, gives each of its members a place in God's plan, and also stands as a model of perfect humanity.

Romanitas versus Zion will recur in several contexts.

As Horace said, Latin literature had reached maturity before this period. Catullus died a generation before the publication of the *Georgics.* Cicero was on the proscription list of the triumvirate, and condemned to death by Antony's soldiers. Lucretius belonged to the first half of the first century B.C.E. About 70 B.C.E. a Greek poet, Parthenius of Nicaea, had been brought as a captive to Rome, where he introduced the poetry of Alexandria to educated and gifted young Roman amateur poets.

Callimachus was the most scholarly of the Alexandrians, with a studied taste. The model Parthenius introduced went back to the school of Sappho, neglecting professionals producing works for public competitions in a sophistic tradition of myths for popular edification. In this rediscovered vein, and with the exacting standards of Callimachus, Catullus found the cue for his own genius, and outsoared the fellow poets of his group. With him, and the names that would join his, Latin leapt into the orbit of Greek poetry, bringing all the difference of another language and an alien society.

The theme of Lucretius's great poem is the philosophy of Epicurus, of which it is a full-scale, passionate exposition. It was in this form that the philosophy of Epicurus was made familiar in the West, and the poem was admired and enjoyed for its power by many who rejected the teaching that inspired it. The originality of the poem is in developing into coherent expansion embryonic ideas in the philosophy totally opposed to the dominant thought of the age. Rejecting myths and divine agencies explicitly, he sees the nature of things in terms of process, biological evolution and social development. The evolution applies to plants and animals, and is without design. In the development of society, he traces acquisitions of the arts step by step and stage by stage, and the institution of laws that make society possible. In what he has to say of bringing to perfection all the arts of war, he wonders if men will so fail to see the consequences of what they do that the human enterprise will end in self-destruction. This was prophecy of an altogether different order, and truly universal. The poem did not and could not come into its own until the eighteenth, nineteenth, and twentieth centuries.

The Romans also cultivated the dramatic arts. Many theaters were built in Sicily, and there was a native comic tradition on which were pioneered new forms, which included a type of satirical farce that lent itself to improvisation. Plautus may have emerged from acquaintance with this tradition. The plays he wrote were adaptations of Greek comedies, and are a main source of knowledge about the later Greek theater; but he introduced elements from the native tradition, and as a popular actor brought vitality and familiarity to the play and interplay with the audience. Terence, a generation later, worshiped Menander, on whom most of his few plays are based. This was comedy removed from farce, and was not to popular taste. The language of the dialogue is correct and polished, and it is he who is quoted by a Cicero or a Horace. Popular taste in Rome, however, was not for the theater but for spectacle. By the time theaters were built, the expenditure was put to circus and amphitheater. Terence was eclipsed by the end of his short life. Plautus, with his versatility and universality in comic intentions and resources, although his language was archaic, was in vigorous production for five hundred years and more.

Pollio Asinius, distinguished in public service as a consul and a commander in the field, and in letters as poet, orator, and historian of the civil wars of Pompey and Caesar, and as a generous patron of the arts and founder of the first public library in Rome, wrote tragedies in a Roman tradition that had developed in the third and second centuries B.C.E. but following the Greek theater in themes. He was highly esteemed by Augustus, Virgil, and Horace.

Seneca's poetry is entirely in the form of stage tragedy on Greek themes, and some six of them are the only surviving tragedies in Latin. In treatment they are wholly different from Greek theater; they express their dramatic themes in declamatory verse. Their survival means they are in the classical inheritance, and their considerable influence belongs to European literature.

Seneca was a committed stoic, and has had some philosophical influence down the ages, but not on philosophers. The Romans had little aptitude for philosophy. This was a Greek province they never could possess. Cicero in his late years made it his business and pleasure to introduce his countrymen to the schools of Greek philosophy. As a successful pleader in the courts, his flair had been to state his opponent's case more clearly and effectively than the defendant himself, in order to show the weakness that would justify his dismissal of it. He applied this power of clear statement to the exposition of differing Greek systems, not merely the one he himself espoused but also the one categorically opposed to it. This made him a valuable source for historians of philosophy.

Cicero is the most comprehensive representative of Greek influence on Rome because of the volume, diversity, and quality of his writing, his poetry excluded. He is a direct fulfillment and exponent of Isocrates' philosophy of education, the ground for his declaration that Athens was the school of Hellas and Hellas the school of the world. In a long letter to Lentulus, he says, "I send all my friends who have any zeal for philosophy into Greece; that is to say, I bid them study the Greek writers, in order to draw their precepts from the fountainhead, rather than follow little streams." He himself studied in Athens. His late interest in philosophy was not merely academic, but mainly therapeutic, as a service to himself at a time of stressful misfortune and dire personal grief, mourning the death of a dear daughter. He seeks to show that reason is an efficacious recourse in such circumstances. Since Latin had and was long to have a wider diffusion than Greek, he was of service to more than his countrymen.

His own exemplary eloquence in the service of law and politics had been no small influence on the Roman belief that had inspired it, that *eloquentia* is the glory of the human mind. This belief lasted when there was little scope for the exercise of political oratory. Quintilian's *Institutione Oratoria* gave it a reputation. Voltaire said in a letter to Frederick of Prussia: "Cet grand art des Romains, cette auguste science d'embellir la raison, de forcer les esprits." The extent to which Greek culture, as understood by Isocrates, was assimilated in the training and art of the orator in postclassical Hellas and in Rome goes some way to justify John Stuart Mill in taking Quintilian's book as a compendium of the thoughts of the ancients on education and culture.

Architecture was the art most congenial to the practical genius of the Romans, and monumental buildings most impressively exhibited and recorded preeminence. Their architecture was indissolubly linked with their civil engineering. Together, the massive total achievement of these twin enterprises was superb and supreme. Physical continuance was subject to the ravages of weather and natural disasters and wars, as that of knowledge and ideas and ideals is not, but enough has survived to bring home to successive generations in Europe and beyond, not merely "the grandeur that was Rome," but mainly the example of her achievement.

Basically, it depended on technical innovations. First and most radical was cement, a fine sand mixed with limestone reduced to quicklime in a kiln and poured over a selected aggregate for the purpose in hand. For hardness and cohesion, this was unmatched until the nineteenth-century discovery of Portland cement. The Roman brick was a second new product, and it was extensively used for solidity and for appearance. They were hard-baked, equal in size, of optimum thickness, accurately laid with hard, close joints. As a decorative surface it outfaced marble.

For nothing is the Roman Empire more renowned in the modern world than for its roads. They were a remarkable achievement in two respects. First, in their construction; the standard road was fifteen feet wide and four feet deep, requiring sixty cubic feet of material for each foot of roadway; the foundation of large stones was made solid and lasting, and was covered with rubble and a layer of concrete, surfaced with flagstones or cobble or pounded gravel, and cambered for drainage into ditches or gutters. Since the roads were straight and with minimal gradients, there had to be supplementary cutting, filling, terracing, draining, and bridging and tunneling, according to the terrain. The solidity of the foundations ensured that there would not be expensive upkeep. Our motor roads are shamed by what the Roman engineers achieved two millennia ago.

The second respect in which what the Romans did is remarkable was the network that linked all parts of the empire. This was planned on accurate surveys. These roads were built primarily for rapid deployment of troops in the security of the empire, and the legions were used in their construction. This was the external side of the Pax Romana. They served equally the public business of administration and facilitated a great increase in trade and prosperity—no small contribution to stable government.

This is not the place in which to describe or catalogue the monumental buildings of Rome, comparable in effect no doubt to the Manhattan skyline, incomparable in the design and aesthetic impact of its individual items. Vitruvius Pollio, equally architect and civil engineer, hardly manages such a catalogue, despite dedicating to Augustus a work of ten books on architecture. He was captivated by the Greek models, and their theories of symmetry and proportion. That was what made him the architectural Aristotle of the Renaissance. But his descriptions of Roman buildings do show how the Greek forms they adopted were adapted, mainly by new modes of construction. They used the Greek orders of columns where columns were used, sometimes borrowed from the Etruscans without the Doric purity of the Greek. Both Ionic and Doric deteriorated in adoption, but the Corinthian capital appealed to Roman taste, and where grandeur excelled proportion in their eyes this was the order that could be both adopted and improved, to add splendor rather than grace.

The Romans invented the triumphal arch as a monument of honor; and they used the column for the same purpose, as the Greeks had. Both were made familiar in Europe. Not familiar in Europe in the same way but central to Roman architecture and social life were the baths. In addition to the bathing facilities, with their sophisticated control of temperature and humidity, were large halls to accommodate entertainments, cultural activities, and social intercourse, an enlargement of the Greek gymnasia, a complex housed in great buildings roofed by domes and vaults supported by arches, beyond the reach of Greek architects, who lacked the necessary Roman concrete. The Forum was the open space in the center of a town in which public and private business was carried on. It was of greater importance for political affairs in the Republic than for the Greeks, but with the eclipse of the Republic lapsed the political activities that used to take place in the Forum. When the Pax Romana and the construction of great harbors had encouraged the growth of industry and commerce far beyond simple reliance on agriculture, Trajan's elaborate market complex in Rome behind the Forum added a new feature to town planning. By the end of the Roman imperium, architecture was diverted to building cathedrals in the cities, and in the countryside castles where refugees from the exposed land could seek the protection of their lord. The Pax Romana had passed out of history.

# 8

# *Romanitas*

# The New Rome

## A Second Start

The age of the Antonines was selected by Gibbon as that in which the state of the human race in the West was happier than at any period either before or since. The full weight of barbarian pressure upon the frontiers had not yet made itself felt. The burden of taxation was still light. A large, cultivated middle class enjoyed a rich inheritance of literature in circumstances of great material comfort. Amusements on a lavish scale were provided for the many, the chariot races in the circus, the gladiatorial games and combats of wild beasts in the amphitheater, an easy access to the public baths. A pleasant intercommunion, unvexed by the modern fanaticisms of creed and race, of nationality, language, and color, spread from one end of the empire to the other. In the service of Rome, Syrians and Spaniards, Africans and Britons mingled together without difficulty or wounding discrimination. A wide and indulgent tolerance was the mark of the age. The people of the empire were too close to the Romans in race and too quick to assimilate Roman culture ever to be regarded as natural inferiors. The cities were self-governing and much left to themselves. Of religion as such there was no persecution, for the Roman pantheon was hospitable to every god. Social customs were embodied in the growing fabric of Roman law; local languages—Punic, Lycaonian, Celtic—were permitted to coexist with the *lingua franca* of the empire, which was Latin. Cruelty, indeed, existed then as it exists now, but the humanitarian might reflect that the slave trade had died down, that freedmen could win their way to wealth and authority—even a slave might exercise an influence as an author in a society where careers were open to talent. Of the ultimate fate of the empire there were as yet no apprehensions. It was the universal and comforting belief that Roman rule would endure forever.

The passage echoes Gibbon's periods, and reflects the Augustan vision of

Romanitas, on the eve of the waning of the achievement. Human societies are not organisms like their members, who wax and wane in their fated life cycles. They are associations of generations, and are thus regenerated. But successive generations inherit conditions to which they have to respond, which may be fortunate or unfortunate, unlike other species, which depend on a habitat to which they are adapted. Romans were no longer of Rome; the populations of Italy and of Greece were in decline. In the second half of the second century there had been devastating plagues. The legions became more dependent on noncitizen auxiliaries. Barbarian warriors were brought in to settle on waste land behind the frontiers. Defense and promotion of the traditions of Greek and Roman civilization were passing irrevocably into the hands of aliens. In the third century, there were devastating incursions into the Balkans, into Spain, into Asia Minor, and a king of Persia held Antioch, a strategic center of Roman power in the east. The Roman armies were themselves in rivalry, espousing different claims to the exercise of imperial power. A disabling weakness that would be worse and prove worst was at the base of all, the burden of taxation that drove its victims to desperation.

Nothing short of reorganization could have saved the empire from rapid disintegration (anarchy there was). That was what came at the hands of a Dalmatian peasant, Diocletian, to be modified and powerfully reinforced later by a brilliantly successful commander in the field, Constantine. The reorganization consisted in functional centralization, displaced from Rome, administrative uniformity, a subdivision of powers, including separation of political and military authority, and a subdivision of the provinces. In effect, Diocletian introduced a hierarchical Oriental system, complete with ceremonial.

Defense of the empire on four fronts prompted Diocletian to recognize that army commanders in the several theaters should be brought under the central authority of two emperors in partnership, one for the west, one for the east. Two junior partners, to be known as Caesars, would be appointed as designated successors when the emperors died or retired after not more than twenty years in office. There would be an eastern and a western capital, not Rome. This part of the reorganization did not work out as planned. After the retirement of Diocletian and his partner in 305, army rivalries ensued, and were brought to an end by the very occurrence the plan was designed to avert. Constantine was proclaimed emperor at York by his troops; and by rapid and skillful movements he overthrew his rivals in both west and east.

Two major decisions of Constantine made the final turning point in the history of Rome. The severest external pressure was from the tribes north of the Danube and from Oriental monarchies beyond the Euphrates, including Persia. For the strategic defense of the empire a capital was needed on a site between Asia and Europe. Byzantium offered to satisfy the requirements with its natural aspects. Constantine adopted it for that reason, and adapted it by art to fulfill the destiny of a Roman capital. Within six years Byzantium was endowed with the splendor of which Roman architecture was capable, and crowned with the name of its founder. That was in 330.

Internally, conditions were rapidly deteriorating. Resources had been depleted by deforestation, erosion, exhaustion of mines and quarries, widespread physical destruction in raids and disturbances. Inflation, a debased currency, taxation and its extortion had brought ruin to the peasantry and affected the cities. Municipal councillors were responsible for the collection and payment of taxes. To enforce that, the bureaucracy was increased, and had to be paid for, as well as the army. The peasants in desperation surrendered their holdings for protection, and became serfs. The vicious circle improvised a sort of medieval system, with Roman villas as manorial centers of a subsistence economy supporting local government and defense. With the old municipal (and Greek) conditions of secure, stable, and prosperous social existence thus thoroughly undermined, government of the empire had drifted into an Oriental parallel: a despotism that rested on control by the army, and acted through a royal council arbitrarily appointed by the ruler. It was in this context that Constantine made his other major decision: to adopt Christianity as the religion of Rome.

Thus the Empire, politically one, was divided for civil administration under two parallel hierarchies. Each half was divided into two prefectures, subdivided into dioceses the size of a state. The prefects had vicars of their dioceses, who had governors of the provinces into which a diocese was divided. The military establishment was organized separately. There were permanent garrisons on the frontiers, supplemented by a mobile field army. Cavalry and infantry were separated as independent arms under supreme commanders. Towards the end of the fourth century, the *magister peditum*, infantry commander, was made senior to the *magister equitum*, calvary commander. About a third of the army of a half million or more were in garrisons along the frontiers, with a large concentration on the east frontier, against Persia. A great many of the soldiers were now tribesmen, some talented enough to gain positions of command and distinguish themselves. Roman superiority depended on this. But reorganized power of the army within an empire under the hammer involved growing influence of Germans. Culturally, and to an increasing extent administratively, the reorganized empire was supervised by the Romanized Church, that is, the bishops. A Holy Roman Empire was taking shape.

## The Triumph of the East

In the war between the civilizations of Greece and Persia, and thereafter of Rome and Persia, fortunes were reversed more than once, and Greek values and perspectives did not survive in Roman hands. Alexander infiltrated Asia with Hellenic influence established in Greek colonial cities. The Seleucids and the Ptolemies maintained the Hellenic influence, and its learning, in Syria, Asia Minor, and Egypt. But the East profited by the Roman peace to enlarge its industry and expand its wealth and art, and in one way and another to infiltrate the Mediterranean lands. When Rome became a centralized state under an absolute ruler worshipped as a god, governing through a bureaucratic hierarchy, it was an Oriental monarchy that was the model. Alexander himself had adopted Persian ways. Augustus reorganized Rome on the model of Alexandria, and borrowed fiscal reforms from Egypt. The shift of the eastern capital of the empire was a late move in this direction. The Hellenized Orient imposed itself everywhere through its men and their works, as later it would gain ascendancy over its Arab conquerors in the civilization of Islam. Trajan's principal architect was Apollodorus of Damascus, and the erection of a cupola was learned from the Levant. The taste for luxurious decoration came from the same sources.

Radical politically if compared with the ideal of the Roman Republic and aesthetically if compared with Greek taste, the shift in orientation was most transforming in religion. Here, whatever Hellenic influence there might be was a re-export of an old import, the cults that were sects (Orpheus, Dionysus, Demeter) outside the poetic society of Olympus. The infiltration of Oriental cults in this period, and before, has long been a subject of study (Franz Cumont: *Oriental Religions and Roman Paganism,* 1911). It was the civic focus and function of Greco-Roman religion that was destroyed by this infiltration, devotion to the *polis* or to the state. Egyptian, Semitic, and Persian cults became successively domesticated on Roman soil. They had their sodalities of initiates, and were in the hands of priests who performed a traditional liturgy with scrupulous respect. Their "mysteries" that instilled hopes of future bliss, and the pomp and circumstance of their festivals, were ageless ingredients in the induction of ecstasy. Above this popular appeal, the culture and learning of established civilizations were bound up with these religions and vested in the traditions and training of their priesthoods with unquestioned authority. There was no independent elite, like that of the sophists, who made a business of putting tradition in question and of pursuing methodical inquiry, and who engaged in open-ended discussion. These were systems whose guardians and practitioners exclusively controlled the culture maintained by their state, and not interfered with under Roman rule in the East. These were systems that came to Rome itself, and were domiciled. Mathematics, astronomy, medicine, philology, and history were the province of priests in Egypt and Asia; book-learning, not research, was cultivated in the enclave of Alexandria. Without scientific or philosophic anchorage, cosmic beliefs and ritual practices were afloat, to drift in the movements of psychological currents and speculative winds; astrology and alchemy, magic and demonology were allowed to flourish. The failure of Greco-Roman civic public cults to compete with the claims of these long-established Oriental cults and their appeal to private needs, over the historical period in which the independent *polis* was destroyed by Macedon and then Rome, compelled Rome to come to terms with them. For they not only met private needs more adequately, but also the imperial need for divine sanction that underlay the civic cult. "They supplied the emperors with dogmatic justification for their despotism"—the divine right of kings. The decay of Roman society in the third century increased the opportunity of these imported cults at both levels. The strands of their immediate appeal were gathered to focus aspirations on a life beyond death. This was anticivic in the traditional sense, but it rendered unto Caesar the things that were Caesar's.

The Egyptian, Syrian, and Persian religions, apart from the sporadic influence of Judaism, were the developed cults that impressed successive Roman emperors and were given some form of domestic institution. Egypt was the oldest Mediterranean power, and familiar by reading Herodotus. The early Ptolemies sought to unite Greeks and Egyptians in a common religion, and enlisted Greek sculptors and poets in the celebration of Isis and Serapis. These deities were transformed in idealized figures reflecting Hera and Aphrodite. Bryaxis, a contemporary of Scopas, made a colossal statue of Serapis of which there were many copies. This Greek contribution meant more than merely identification of Osiris with Dionysus or Isis with Demeter. In general, Egyptian worship had been repugnant to the Greeks, and in this way it was selectively modified and made acceptable. Of all Oriental divinities, Isis and Serapis were the only ones to find a place in the Hellenic world. Alexandria was a model for Rome, a city of the highest prestige, and it was this syncretic Hellenized Egyptian religion that came to Rome. In 216 Caracalla built an Isis temple of great magnificence on the Quirinal. The incoherence of Egyptian theology (Plutarch) left it open to eclecticism. Reconciling Egyptian traditions with Chaldean astrology, tinctured with Greek philosophy, Hermes Trismegistus tried to create a theological system universally acceptable, "hermetism." This was to be a system, and still more an enterprise, that would be dominant in Europe for a period within the Renaissance. The syncretic tendency in Egypt was congenial to tendencies in Rome. After worship in the Latin world for five centuries, Egyptian deities disappeared by the time of Justinian.

Emperors were attracted by the idea of monotheism in correspondence with absolute monarchy. Aureliam made *Sol invictus* (the Chaldean Baal) protector of emperor and empire. The Capitoline Jupiter was put in danger by such aberrations. In Asia and in Syria, Babylon even after its political downfall retained cultural ascendancy with a priestly caste that survived. The "Chaldeans" were a learned clergy, and strongly influenced the Jews during and after the Captivity. They were the first to conceive a universe ruled by necessity, instead of gods acting in the world according to their passions, like men in society. They observed that the movements of the celestial bodies were regulated with invariable uniformity, and extended its effects to all social and moral phenomena. Astrology and eventually Manichaeism were influences from this source. Sidereal myths superseded agragian myths. The stars were venerated for their harmonious order, but supreme deity was placed beyond the planets and fixed stars. The image of the Asiatic monarch was projected onto divine omnipotence. Chaldean astrology gave a pictured reality to Semitic traditions that separated the divine from the human. The absolute sovereignty of the supreme God was thus propagated by the religions of Syria and Babylon, as of Judah. Syrian Baal worship on these lines was open and universal, as Judaism was not. The supreme God beyond the stars was made visible in the intermediary of the sun, the known source of all life. The Chaldean-Syrian astrolatry strongly influenced the whole Roman world. "Sol dux et princeps et moderator luminum reliquorum, mens mundi et temperatio" (Cicero's *Scipio's Dream,* widely read, quoted four times by Chaucer, and prompting Dante).

These religious systems which spread in the Roman world and attracted imperial favor were not rival civilizations, as Persia was, the undying enemy of Greece and Rome, repelled yet returning, conquered yet reviving. Mithridates, who claimed descent from Darius, penetrated to the heart of Greece, and was a formidable enemy; and after the mid–third century Persia was sufficiently restored in power and ambition to last until the triumph of Islam. The Jewish diaspora helped to make Persian eschatology and demonology familiar. Alexander's conquest, followed by the Seleucid rule, opened Zoroastrianism to study; and the Library of Alexandria catalogued under that name some two million lines. Roman annexations under the Flavians and Trajan made them neighbors with the Parthians, and there followed an introduction of Mithraic cults, gaining ground as the most important till the end of the fourth century. Persian artistic influence extended into Syria and was a major influence on Byzantium. "Never had Europe a narrower escape from becoming Asiatic than when Diocletian officially recognized Mithra as protector of the reconstructed empire, and the god seemed to be the established authority over the entire civilized world."

Mithraism was not Hellenized, though influenced, as the cult of Isis and Serapis had been in Alexandria. It was completely in the hands of a priestly caste, the Magi. Its beliefs and practices were spread throughout the Latin world by soldiers, merchants, and slaves. A map showing the spread of Mithraism and of Christianity shows them comparable in extent. Ethically, there was a special emphasis on good faith; the lie was a capital source of evil. There was much in this outlook of a feudal, horse-loving aristocracy that appealed to the Romans directly. It was resistant to assimilation. Astrology and magic were persistent influences in all these religions, and they gained quasiscientific standing and philosophical backing for the proper practice of divination, with such as Ptolemy, a genuine astronomer, and Posidonius, a genuine philosopher who had travelled widely. The source of the argument was belief in the continuous mutual influence of all things bound together in interdependence and the observed regularity in the movement of the stars. Carneades, the acutest philosopher in the second century, had no difficulty in mounting a dialectical critique that demonstrated the futility of divination. Rational objections did nothing to affect the survival of astrology and magic throughout the Middle Ages, and an energetic revival with the Renaissance.

These Oriental religions contributed to the failure of the Latin observances that Augustus had hoped to revive as a social foundation for his new political order. They injected a recognition of parallelisms into the syncretism that was going on under imperial patronage. Syncretism could reconcile different traditions with the aid of allegory, needed to make acceptable palpable myth. Cumont felt himself able to summarize his survey of the three hundred years between Augustus and Constantine in a conjectural synthesis as the outcome. This syncretism "pretended to offer to all men a world-conception which gave rise to a rule of conduct and placed the end of existence in the future life." So that, he remarks, this creed and Christianity moved in the same intellectual and moral sphere, adding that it is questionable whether a late Latin writer like Boethius is Christian or pagan. "The religious and mystical spirit of the Orient had slowly invaded the whole social organism and prepared all its nations to unite in the bosom of a universal church."

If this, in general terms, was the historical context, why did Constantine choose Christianity for the protection and unification of the empire, and not Mithraism, chosen by Diocletian? They were equally widespread. There is the legendary explanation, which the Church might adopt as evidence of divine agency. (Eusebius reports that Constantine told him of the vision on the eve of battle.) Constantine had Christian influences in his life, but whatever his private beliefs, Christianity as a talisman of success, favor of the deified fortune, was in uneasy partnership with the Christianity of St. Paul, or of Augustine. However, a ruler who is a professed Christian and who rules as a Christian, a Christian Marcus Aurelius, may be God's agent as well as his servant. The ambiguity was wrestled with later.

What should be made plain in this retrospect is that the syncretism that was made adventitious use of by the imperial power was by no means the stuff of popular religion, such as Augustus had hoped to recover. On the contrary, it was esoteric, arcane, as the Renaissance revival in a strongly Neoplatonist context shows. Christianity was the belief of uneducated fishermen, to the Greeks foolishness, comforting to the poor; it spoke the plainest language of anthropomorphism. Its sodalities offered the firmest foundation of social stability. Whether Constantine recognized anything of this is another matter. He made an historic decision from which major consequences flowed throughout the following centuries. Other aspects of that decision fall under consideration in another universe of discourse.

## The Romanized Church

Constantine let the Christians settle their own disputes, particularly the great Arian divide ("a trifling and foolish dispute about words," to his own thinking); but settle it they had to, since the unity of the Roman Church was paramount. A representative council of bishops was convoked at Nicaea for the purpose. When his son Constantius in turn wanted to modify the Nicene formula, and asserted his imperial authority to do so, he forced an issue with Church leaders for whom Erastianism was not an option, for whom Christian truth could not be compromised. Athanasius with Constantius, Ambrose with Theodosius resisted subjection. The constitutional position of the emperor within the Church was not the same as in the state; in the Church he was in equal subjection with all the faithful to the law of Christ, the will of God. The Church's corporate support was not to be had on other terms. Roman Christendom, the Latin Church of the Middle Ages, was founded in the decisions and conflicts of this fourth century, without a definitive resolution then or later of the troubled relations between these two heads of one physical body.

Constantine might conceivably have embraced Christianity in order to give Romanitas its chance. That was the interpretation of Lactantius, called the Christian Cicero. He revamped classicism by reorienting its ideal on God, the necessary condition on which Romanitas might become humanitas. The *polis* as the center or pius Aeneas as the prototype of human loyalties for the cultivation of civic virtues could not realize justice, the dream of Plato. Loyalty to God alone entailed an equal regard for all human beings, not merely as rational animals, but as animals endowed for self-development through their natural affections oriented on their Creator, enlightened by the Gospel. That other professional sophist, Augustine, on conversion, shifted the humanist program of civilization to a new orbit, *Civitas Dei*. Lactantius was closer to the understanding of Constantine, who appointed him as tutor to his son. The emperor made himself protector of the Church and sponsor of social reforms that alleviated the position of women, children, and slaves in law. But the gravitational pull of Diocletian's corporate state continued to favor the official classes at the expense of the ordinary middle class and peasants.

The Edict of Milan declared the state's religious neutrality. Favors and concessions to the Christian interest were dependent on the emperor's personal inclinations. But successive actions made him not only involved with but also indebted to, dependent on, even manipulated by, ecclesiastics. There was a Christian bandwagon. The Edict of Milan was often observed in the breach. All the same, the strong personal government of Constantine left behind a confusion of ideas and ideals, and therefore of policies and purposes, that brought a drift back to reaction under Julian the Apostate.

How could the culture of the Hellenic Age have been obliterated? After philosophy was emasculated by platform rhetoric in the Second Sophistic; after three main Oriental religions invaded and settled in Rome and the occult was in the ascendancy mixed with whatever science there was; after the empire itself became effectively an Oriental despotism; after the conditions of life in town and country were soured by deprivations and oppressive exactions; when an alternative society was being organized at the grassroots by the Christian Church; when Constantine's favor had increased Church wealth, privilege, prestige, and the opportunity of attractive careers; such changes in the conditions of culture and of politics, to say nothing of the hostile tribes at and within the gates, made the climate in which the apotheosis of the Church did turn upside down the world of a distant Hellenic Age.

However, thus to oppose the eclipse of Hellenistic culture and apotheosis of the Christian Church would be a misleading simplification, since the dominant character of that culture was a cosmopolitanism that was the road that led on to syncretism and Roman hospitality to Oriental cults, and the Roman Church of Constantine was forced to smother its grave and abiding differences.

To get a glimpse of an idea of the situation that had built up, it is necessary to take stock of what was there after Diocletian's reconstruction had ended fifty years of political anarchy. For Romanitas, some four hundred years after Augustus, was replaced by a totally novel model, a Holy Roman Empire.

Varro's sociological classification of the gods is a convenient starting point: there were the gods of the poets, the gods of the philosophers, and the gods of the city. That was a useful formula for Greek religion. Marginally, there should have been added the gods of the people—household gods and those of the countryside, the only proper "paganism," and the gods of the priests, the "mystery" cults. What is specifically Greek, however, is left out of this descriptive coverage of Greek religion; that is the critique of any concept of the divine that implies anthropomorphic notions, broached early by Xenophanes in the sixth century B.C.E., and made fully explicit by Carneades in the second. There were two consequences: either an agnostic humanism that concentrates on the arts and sciences and the advancement of civilization, as with Protagoras or with the reconstructed Stoicism of Panetus and Posidonius; or a refinement of speculative thought about the divine that systematically excludes the anthropomorphic, carried to the highest point of abstract refinement in the so-called Neoplatonism of the system of Plotinus. Judaism lay outside this classification, and was distinctively different in being categorically anthropomorphic, insisting on the one and only God who was the God of Abraham, Isaac, and Jacob, wholly concerned about his people and available to them.

These differences may seem remote and uninteresting, but they had consequences that resounded throughout Europe generation after generation in one context
and another. That came about not through interest in Judaism or in Greek philosophy
but through irreconcilable differences in beliefs about Jesus of Nazareth, who was a
Jew and was seen through the eyes of Jews and through the eyes of Hellenized Jews
and through the eyes of Greeks and eventually in the congealed terms of church
dogma. What was thought about the life and person of this Jew made the turning point
in the history and culture of the West. That thinking was shaped within the syncretism
that had come to prevail in the second period of the Roman Empire, with Diocletian.
It had a history that one could say began with the Assyrian practice of transporting
populations and continued in the Babylonian Captivity and in the general Jewish diaspora. The Hellenistic Age carried it further, and the Roman conquests further still,
mixing East and West. Thus Alexandria, Antioch, and the cities of Asia Minor became
centers for this development. Individuals by eclecticism produced fusions of elements
drawn from different sources. Philo in Alexandria drew on the Pentateuch, on Plato,
on the Stoics, on the Pythagoreans, and on native Egyptian traditions. He reconciled
them simply as abstract and concrete, and resorted to the bottomless resources of allegorical interpretations. He speaks of God as an absolute of whom nothing can be
affirmed but that he is. He is accessible only to a pure spirit detached from the world
and the self. Connection is mediated by the Logos (reason). In this excursion, Philo
was treading the road to Neoplatonism, and was not representative of Hellenistic
Judaism as it appears in Proverbs and Ecclesiastes. Another Egyptian thinker, Trismegistus, drew on Greek philosophy, Chaldean astrology, and Egyptian traditions.
This free-range thinking heralds an explosion of theosophy, known as Gnosticism,
which gave an impulse to the development of nascent Christianity in its mission to
the Gentile world, to which it had to accommodate itself.

"Gnosticism" is a general term that covers a diversity of sects, and is not a given
system. For Gnostics, in general, God is an abstraction, the ground of all existence,
unknowable, not a person. Their basic preoccupation was with evil, identified with
matter, including the human body. The soul was imprisoned in it, corrupted by it, in
need of purification and deliverance from it, and from fate, the mythological demons
who determined the course of human events. This deliverance could be effected only
by enlightenment. The Gnostics worked with mythologies and rituals and magic.
They were not philosophers in the Greek sense. Human destinies were subject to cosmic forces, and could be liberated from them only by initiation into esoteric knowledge, not won by research or disciplined reflection, but communicated directly by
angels or other intermediaries.

This was far removed from the central tradition of Judaism; and indeed Gnostics repudiated the god of the OT as barbaric. This was the mental climate in which
the early Christians had to carry out their mission. Mainly, however, Gnosticism was
Oriental not Hellenic.

Manichaeism was one of its purist products, one that was strongly attractive to
Augustine before his conversion. It was a form of syncretism in Babylon in the
mid–third century C.E., and had regard for Buddha, Zoroaster, and Jesus as sources

of enlightenment in a world in which good and evil, light and darkness, commingled, not as inherent in matter and spirits, body and soul, but rather in tendencies in the soul; earthly life was a sphere of redemption by the separation of the two.

Marcion was a member of the Roman Church who broke away from his own church in the mid–second century based on a personal recension of Jewish and Christian scriptures, influenced by a Syrian Gnostic teacher. Gnostic influence was in a dual concept of God, denial of the Resurrection and of the Incarnation—in the sense that Jesus received the Spirit by supervention at baptism. Marcion practiced asceticism. These doctrines of his church were widespread in the eastern and western empire early in the fourth century, until suppressed by Constantine. They continued to count in eastern Christendom, and were still known in the tenth century.

Valentinus was a gifted and versatile Christian teacher in Alexandria in the mid–second century. He wanted to reconcile prevailing Gnostic thinking with Christian beliefs. He found in Plato's ideal world, reflected in things as they are, a model for bringing the abstract, inaccessible God of Gnosticism into the actual world. This was done in metaphysical terms of emanation, anticipating Plotinus, but full and final authority was given to the teaching of Jesus. It left rather than answered the question of exactly how that authority was guaranteed by the relation of Jesus to his source in God.

His was the Gnostic system that was closest to and had most influence upon Christian thought, not least because it helped to force, though it did not broach, the question of the status and person of Jesus, which was the whole matter of the Christian message. As a Judaistic heresy having to make its way in a non-Jewish world, it was in danger of being swallowed up in the syncretism that was in its Gnostic phase. It gained and maintained its identity by resisting and coming to terms with that danger. Both the resistance and the influence are evident in the language of the first chapter of the Gospel of St. John. There is implicit there the doctrine of the Trinity, which was the outcome of a long and bitter struggle in the third century and beyond, and formulated the specific claim of the Christian faith.

The influence of Gnosticism on Christianity has been summed up under four heads: asceticism, sacraments, mysticism, and theology. The last is the most important, in that it forced Christians to go beyond the NT theology insofar as it was merely claims to the fulfillment of OT prophecies in the life, teaching, and death of Jesus. The first and major step in this Christian theology had to be a Christology, determination of what was meant by the claim that the man Jesus was the son of God, and the presence and revelation of the Father, the creator of the world. This was what was uniquely and totally opposed to the principal assumptions in current Gnostic thinking.

The problem was forced by the existence of the Church formed for the worship of Christ, the man known as Jesus of Nazareth; it was idolatry unless he was in truth divine. To be divine, as the one God, the creator, was, he must have had extra-mundane preexistence from the beginning; in that case, how were there not two Gods? If divine in that sense, how could he also be fully human in all parts as the man Jesus—the how of the Incarnation?

The two opposed arguments in the field were Sabellianism and Arianism, named

from their propounders. The first assumed that God could be known only by manifestation in acts on the world. Thus the Father was creator, the son was Redeemer,
aspects of the one God. The sun is experienced as light or as heat, equally essential
aspects of its existence. The Arians concentrated on the human figure. The Logos was
the dynamic immanent in the creator who becomes the Father in creation of the Son
as partner in the Logos. Thus there was a time when the Son was not, and in that sense
is not, fully divine.

The Church greatly feared both these tendencies as doing away with the reality
of the faith by reducing or eliminating the divinity of Christ. Origen had affirmed the
personality of God in the human terms of intelligence and love. The Son was not in
any sense an emanation, but was the Logos, the self-expression of that personal
spirit, not merely nor mainly an agent. It was this line of thinking that the council convened by Constantine sought to formulate in the Nicene Creed. The trouble was that
it was not possible to state the formula intelligibly. Neither was it possible to refute
Arianism conclusively. Augustine's attempt to unfold and spell out the trinitarian
dogma in book XI, chapter 10, of *The City of God* compounds confusion and elevates
contradiction. A great part of the difficulty was in language, since the central notion
of person had no word in Greek, and in Latin the connotation was in legal usage. This
was nothing new in philosophy. But was the irresolvable difficulty not a committed
insistence on taking metaphorical language literally? At any rate, Nicaea was not the
end. Arianism persisted. New heresies appeared, the Nestorian doctrine particularly.
The Decree of Chalcedon in 451 ruled out all compromise, and sealed the faith in the
perfect humanity and divinity of Christ. The illogical logic of the trinitarian dogma
fixed the premise and made the definition of orthodox Christianity faith. Thus was
institutionalized the consolatory anthropomorphic concreteness distinctive of Christianity, in continuity with Judaism, more than four hundred years after the first Christians naively and devoutly assumed it in practice.

Why so much attention to "a trifling and foolish dispute about words" in this
recapitulation of the Western cultural tradition? Mainly because the ancient Church
when allied with or subject to the power of the Roman emperor turned its conclusions
(dogmas) into instruments of discipline applied by a centralized authority. Parallels
need not be drawn to understand what this totalitarian power might mean. What is
important to understand is that the conclusions that the Church was empowered and
required to enforce were not at all influenced by the state. Even more important to
bear in mind, because of the immense historical influence of Christianity throughout
Europe, is this: what the Church imposed was the set of naive assumptions that had
made Christianity what it was, formulated in a statement that could not be elucidated,
a rigid dogma. True or not, this was the standard of Christian faith.

Arians were good practical Christians, and devoted and successful missionaries.
They converted several of the East German tribes. When the Roman state became
identified with trinitarian orthodoxy, these tribes were enemies whether or not hostile, and although passive in their heresy.

Worth mentioning at this point because of his formative influence in two different connections is Athanasius. He is known of course for his aggressive opposition

to the Arians and the uncompromising anathematical formulation of the creed associated with his name. Probably more important historically was his authorship of the life of the anchorite St. Antony, who founded Egyptian Christian monasticism. This biography was the model for the whole tradition of hagiography, which was a prime means in the Middle Ages and before of spreading Christianity by example. The asceticism that is so pronounced a feature of them could perhaps be more rationally justified by Gnostic doctrines than required by Christian beliefs, and may indeed show a Gnostic influence, but was undoubtedly stamped in by Antony and successive saints, surpassed in influence much later by Francis.

The Roman Church interposed itself between the believer and his Redeemer, and, so to speak, colonized the interim providential order until the consummation. Was the Church in the world for the sake of the world or for the sake of the elect? The new mold had ambiguities, cracks that would widen.

These two human concerns that the period brings to the fore, subjectivity and history, are remarkably documented in Augustine's *Confessions* and *The City of God*. Versed in the abstractions of Manichaeism and Platonism, he expresses in the *Confessions* his astonishment at "the Word was made flesh," and at the Gospel accounts of Christ's human life, and tells how he came to accept this total and actual humanness of Christ as central to the Christian revelation. Convinced, he would convince others. He was a sophist, as Paul was a Pharisee.

*The City of God* is a discursive and diffuse composition, put together over some thirteen years. Augustine was prompted to compose it by Alaric's sack of Rome in 410. The fall of Rome, coinciding with the imperial adoption of Christianity, posed a problem in the interpretation of history. Constantine was a true believer, and he did prosper; but no emperor should turn Christian for hope of attaining Constantine's felicity, because the end of Christianity is life eternal, not prosperity on earth.

History supplied two footnotes to these issues, in terms of names and events: Julian the Apostate and Theodosius I. Julian was born in Constantinople, and was a nephew of Constantine. He was obsessed with a determination to reverse his uncle's policy and its effects. Romanitas had to be restored. Constantine was the Apostate. History had proved the classical lawgivers of Greece and Rome superior to Moses. By repudiating the classical inheritance of philosophy and the arts, to embrace a life of self-abnegation and obedience, Christians chose a servile mentality, incompatible with civilization.

The enlightened part of Julian's reforms was directed to relief of the local officials of the municipalities, lightening the exactions that had demoralized them. Restoration of Romanitas depended critically on recovery of healthy conditions of security, stability, and prosperity in the municipalities and the surrounding countryside. However, like Augustus and many others before and since, Julian thought that the cohesion of society was maintained by the faithful, regular practice of an official, common religion. True religion could not be enforced by blows, only by reason and instruction; but disturbance of the peace by factions and fanatics could not be tolerated. There had to be a state religion, and Hellenism was a religion of good citizenship, as Christianity was not.

In his practical measures for promoting this state religion by instruction, Julian was misguided. The classics were to be taught only by those who believed in what their authors believed, thus turning education into indoctrination. This shocked humanists such as Ammianus, a Greek Roman who truly shared the spirit and imaginative outlook of Isocrates. To promote liberal studies in an illiberal way was subversive of Hellenist culture. For the Christians, their exclusion from the common social culture thus promoted was tantamount to reducing them to an obscure Galilean sect, denied their mission to the human race. The drift towards totalitarianism is evident in these movements within the Roman Empire in the fourth century. It could not be a spurious Hellenism. It had to be a Romanized Church.

Ammianus was closest to Julian, whose portrait he furnished, and whose disastrous Persian campaign he shared as a staff officer. As an historian, he was highly esteemed by Gibbon, who used and relied on him. He aspired to carry on the history of Rome from Tacitus in the disinterested spirit of Thucydides. He was truly a representative of Romanitas.

Ammianus writes of Julian's diligent attention to the administration of justice; he deliberated on how he might give each his due by right decisions, bringing the guilty to order with moderate punishment, and protecting the innocent and the safety of their property. His portrait of the Apostate is of one that should not be remembered merely for an abortive attempt to reinstate the old cult of the city or the state, but mainly as one who near the end, aware of the encompassing disasters, still faithfully represented and exemplified and preached the traditional Roman virtues that justified Romanitas.

It was Theodosius who rescued the empire from another crisis, when Valens was defeated and killed by the Goths in the battle of Adrianople, in which the legions were nearly wiped out, losing two-thirds of their strength. This was a defeat within the imperial frontiers, which succeeded by the enemies' use of cavalry. Theodosius, with a skillful exercise of diplomacy and military resources, was able to stanch the wound.

His troubles were compounded by usurpations, which he eventually dealt with. But the increasing need of funds to cope with multiplying tasks entailed ever harsher methods of conscription and confiscation.

Theodosius was an orthodox Catholic by conviction. He adjusted the state to the requirements and customs of the Church, for example, by allowing the clergy to be tried only in ecclesiastical courts, and by conceding such privileges as tax exemptions; and by state observance of the feasts and fasts of the Christian calendar, including "the Lord's day."

Already, the claim of the medieval Church that the state exists to protect the peace of uniformity established by the Church was anticipated. The prevalent ambiguities of the time were abolished by systematic elimination of the temples and rites and properties and practices of the cults, banning their festivals and calendars and proscribing their priesthoods, all specified in detail. In effect, any form of engagement in a religion other than official Christianity was treated as treason: "this ecclesiastical revolution was conducted with so much discretion and vigour, that the religion of the emperor was established, without tumult, or bloodshed, on all the provinces of the

East" (Gibbon). That anticipates conversion of nations by conversion of their kings in the Roman Church of the Middle Ages.

All churches had to be put under Catholic bishops, and heretics were excommunicated by withdrawing from them rights guaranteed by Roman law—another anticipation. In the Justinian code, heresy is a public crime, injurious to the public interest. By this identification of Church and state, the state was "sacred," to speak in disrespect of it was "blasphemy," disobedience was "sacrilege." This apotheosis of the state in the Church gave it a divine sanction and power, the old-time deification that emperors never achieved. The power of the Church to intervene when acts of the emperor contravened its principles was made good by Ambrose, bishop of Milan, when he excommunicated Theodosius for his responsibility in the "massacre of Thessalonica," and reinstated him only after an act of public penance. A new order was incipient in the commitment and policies of Theodosius; but complete breakdown came first, with loss of the provinces beyond the Alps in 466, and four years later Jerome's epitaph on the sack of Rome: "The city which has captured the whole world is herself taken captive; the bright light of the universe is extinguished; the empire has lost its head; the whole world has perished in a single city." This rhetoric of a Father of the Church who was addicted to Latin shows the ambivalence towards Rome. Rome had suffered ravage before, as Athens did; but this time it was a symptom of the end.

## Dismemberment

Roman rule was decisively at an end in the last half of the sixth century. Three events of different kinds may be said to mark that. The Lombards set up a kingdom in that part of Italy (560–572). Gregory I, the Great, occupied St. Peter's chair in Rome (590). Latin ceased to be the language of Italy. These events, confined to the territory where it all began, follow a millennium after another symbolic event, when the Romans sent to Athens for Solon's laws (454 B.C.E.).

The empire was dismembered mainly by Germanic tribes, beginning, say, with the Alamannic invasion (c. 235 C.E.), about the time of the rise of the new Persian Empire. Settlement brought tribes into closer neighborhood, so that they formed larger units by federation or mixing. The west Germans (Alamanni, Franks, Saxons, Frisians, Thuringians) were thus separated from the east Germans, who remained pastoral and migratory. During the fifth century, the western half of the Roman Empire was occupied from Britain to North Africa mainly by east Germans (Goths, Vandals, Gepids, Burgundians, Lombards).

It was in this context that Rome adopted the policy under Constantine of negotiating treaties by which Germans undertook to keep the frontiers in exchange for subsidies. From the fourth to the sixth centuries, the Germans were nearly all federated to the empire on these terms for a time, before they made themselves the masters.

Nomad hordes known as Huns with pastures near the Caspian and Aral Seas swept over south Russia, displaced by political movements in China. This westward movement of the Huns affected the whole east German world. The Visigoths, drawing south, in 376 sought Roman permission to cross the Danube and cultivate the wastelands of Thrace. The desperate request was granted on onerous and humiliating conditions. Gibbon thought likely an estimate of nearly a million people were thus displaced and seeking refuge. The resident Romans took advantage of the plight of the Goths in effecting a difficult passage of the Danube in flood and settlement of such a large number in Thrace. The Goths were provoked into action; the fighting that ensued brought Valens with imperial forces to the scene, occasioning the disastrous defeat of Adrianople in 378. The terror the Huns had brought to the Goths was now a terror the Goths brought to the Romans.

This was the crisis Theodosius resolved by skillful diplomacy. He eventually established a treaty with the Goths that became the model of Roman policy. They were allowed to colonize available tracts of fertile but uncultivated land, and aided in doing so, subject to conditions that made them allies and defenders of the empire. Theodosius was able to sell this policy, adopted by prudence constrained by necessity, to the tribes on the one hand, and his Roman subjects on the other, employing different considerations. Few emperors had the skill and prudence of Theodosius. Most were too weak or corrupt to meet the needs of a doomed regime.

In Gaul, Euric was the Visigoth king who had the most conspicuous ability and success, extending his frontier to the Loire and the Rhone. He went on to incorporate most of Spain into his kingdom. By 480, his was by far the greatest and most promising kingdom in west Europe. He is said to have seen the tottering state of the Roman Empire, and to have determined to be independent, and to subdue all Gaul. One condition was unfavorable: he and his people were Arians, which involved the antagonism of the clergy and Romanized Gaul.

The first prominence of the Franks is under Childeric, who aided the Romans in frustration of a Saxon attempt in the fifth century to found kingdoms in Gaul as well as in Britain, sailing to the Loire as well as to the Thames. In the destiny of Gaul, however, history has recognized Clovis as the outstanding name between Julius Caesar and Charlemagne. His thirty-year reign began in 481. He reached the Seine in 486, and ten years later conquered the kingdom of the Alamanni, bestriding the Rhine. Clovis's conversion or adhesion to the Catholic faith in 496 made him a client of the Romans in opposition to Visigoths, Ostrogoths, and Burgundians, who were all Arians. His wife, Clothilda of Burgundy, was, exceptionally, a Catholic. He matched his orthodoxy by driving the Goths from Gaul south of the Loire, extending his authority to the Pyrenees, with the wholehearted support of the Romanized Gauls and the Church. Paris was made the center of the new realm. Emperor Anastasius recognized the new Gallic kingdom as within the empire, and made Clovis an honorary consul.

Bohemia was occupied by the Marcomanni for five hundred years. They then migrated, and were succeeded by Slavs. Earliest known settlements of the Lombards were close to the mouth of the Elbe. They migrated south in the second century to the region of Austria and Hungary, and were included in the empire of the Huns. They were admitted by Justinian as federates. They set out to conquer Italy in 568 and established a kingdom in Lombardy independent of Rome, with its own law and administration. In contrast, the Ostrogoth Theodoric, who ruled Italy for thirty-six years with an administration that gave that country security and stability, acted in all respects as an official of the empire, with no attempt to change law, language, or religion, though himself an Arian.

All officials of the civil administration remained Romans; all soldiers and their commanders were Goths. In criminal jurisprudence, the law applied to Goths as to Romans.

In the fifth century, there were three federated German kingdoms in Gaul (Visigoths, Burgundians, Franks); two in Spain (Suevians, Vandals); and at the end the Ostrogoths (Theodoric, grandson of Alaric) in Italy.

A system of federated states within the empire prepared for the system of independent states that was to replace the empire. The Hun empire of Attila (he had a Latin secretary) had retarded Rome's dismemberment by controlling east Germans beyond the Danube and supplying Roman generals with auxiliaries. This retardation gave more time for Roman influence to work on the federates within their borders.

The Vandals, with the Huns the most violent and ruthless of the tribes, like them suffered a permanent decline and fall, and like them had great effect, in their case hastening the Roman decline the Huns had postponed. From Spain they built a fleet with which they established themselves in North Africa, Sicily, and Sardinia. They controlled the corn supply. "The Mediterranean was no longer a Roman lake." Their quietus was the first, most brilliant, successful, and useful exploit of Belisarius.

A brief return to Noricum for a window on the scene during these times. The general crisis of Roman society in the third century was reflected in the ruin of trade and industry in the province following the Alamannic invasion circa 235, with consequent impoverishment of all classes of the population. Diocletian's reforms introduced a stabilization that lasted till the end of the fourth century. He divided the province into two, separated by the chain of the Alps from west to east. Work was restored in mines and forges, new industries started, and building work put in hand to repair the devastation. Socially, the old prosperity could not be restored. The large landowners were the only people able to assume the costly duties of office-holding in the towns. In the fourth century, Christianity gained a hold and spread throughout the province, destroying the Oriental cults, particularly Mithraic, which had been well established. In the fifth century, when the Danubian frontier could no longer be defended, garrisons got no regular pay, leading to dissolution of regular army units. Plundering bands were unopposed. In 451 the Huns and their allies poured through Noricum on their way to Gaul. With the dissolution of Attila's empire in independent movements of Germanic tribes, repeated onslaughts led to the abandonment of northern Noricum in 488. Villas and towns destroyed were never rebuilt. Inhabitants sought refuge where they could. Southern Noricum seems to have enjoyed a certain tranquility under Theodoric, until his death in 526, after which difficult times began again. In 568 the Lombards pushed through Noricum into Italy and gained a strong influence there. At the end of the sixth and beginning of the seventh centuries, incursions of Avars and Slavs from the east and Baiuvari from the northwest brought conflict and confusion in which the last Norican towns went under, about the year 600.

## The Cultural Gap in the West

The cultural gap between the Roman Empire and early Middle Ages, the so-called "Dark Ages," an expression once assumed, more recently deprecated, calls for explanation. In question are the conditions that are needed for and favor the transmission of literary texts, that is, interest in them and the availability of copies. It should not be merely assumed that barbarians overran the empire and their depredations destroyed libraries in which they had no interest. That certainly did happen. On the other hand, there was the solid continuance in the West of the Roman Church as a centrally organized and widely influential legatee of Roman culture, when Roman power had died. The Church was ambivalent towards classical literature, but hardly indifferent. Its clergy owed their education to that source.

Production of the texts was transformed by the shift from the papyrus roll to the codex, a book-form stitching of parchment leaves that came into use in the second century and was usual by the fourth, perhaps stimulated by publication of the Bible in that form by the early Christians. The classics would have to be republished in the new format, and works little read would be destined to disappear. (The cultural clash between Christians and classical humanists was expressed in the debate between Ambrose and Aurelius Symmachus in 384. A picture of the Roman version of classical culture on the eve of extinction is preserved in the *Saturnalia* of Macrobius.)

Surviving monastic productions from sixth-century Italy are evidence of that skill in the hands of the Church. At least in Italy, it was still possible in the year 500 to obtain copies of most of the Latin authors in some of their works. When the Ostrogothic kingdom of Theodoric was destroyed by the Lombards, there was a steep cultural decline in Italy,

After Theodoric's death, Cassiodorus, who had served in the office of state secretary, retired to his estates in Calabria, where he founded a monastery endowed with a library, and encouraged the accurate copying of books connected with an educational program. Classical books were not excluded, but appeared mainly as teaching books and manuals. Very few titles of classical authors are known or believed to have had a place on the shelves. Because Cassiodorus had a Roman education, it has been assumed that he had an interest in the classics; and because he was a prominent official in the administration of Theodoric, that the collection of manuscripts which he transferred to the monastery he founded was largely rescued from the ruins of the libraries of Italy, so that he was "preserving for future ages the intellectual treasure which must otherwise inevitably have perished" (Hodgkin); that he had in mind when he retired from official work what was needed to preserve the continuity of civilization, so that "it is not too much to say that the continuity of the thought and civilization of the ancient world with that of the Middle Ages was due to the life and labours of Cassiodorus." It is too much to say that. Perhaps that is the role he should have played. All the same, the scriptoria of the monasteries were to be the means by which copies of classical texts were made available and interest in the classics promoted, and Cassiodorus seems to have been the first to put the work of the scriptorium firmly and even prominently on the monastic agenda.

The Benedictine Rule for Monte Cassino, which Benedict founded about 529, imposed the monastic discipline that was to prevail for centuries. A period each day was set aside for reading, and although this was laid down as a spiritual exercise, it left open a space that might be filled otherwise, if circumstances and influences favored that. Christian prejudice against the classics in Italy and Gaul at this time, in the sixth century, had the strength of propinquity, fear, and the knowledge of literary inferiority in the eyes of traditional Romans. This would be far different later, in parts removed from Rome, where for the "barbarians" the Church was associated with the Latin language and literature. Meantime, much of that literature was lost because for some two centuries, until the mid–eighth century, the classics were not copied. The accumulation of patristic, biblical, and liturgical material excluded classical texts, which were even washed off originals to make room for works in ecclesiastical demand. The classics could not be objects of care in monasteries at this time. There was no public for them, and parchment was precious.

The net outcome would be chance sporadic survival of copies of the classics in an ecclesiastical climate of general preoccupation with required or useful material. The conjunction of lively interest and available copies, if scarce, was found in what had been on the fringe of the empire, in Ireland first of all. The world of literary imagination is not necessarily born of classical models, though it may feed on them if available. The indigenous literature produced in Europe of the Middle Ages did more to make the Renaissance than the influx of the classics that followed the fall of Byzantium. It was a necessary condition of their excited reception and of what was made of them.

One other factor has to be borne in mind. The education curriculum in the monastic and cathedral schools of the early Middle Ages was the traditional trivium and quadrivium. The educational program was entirely different. The rhetoric that was the central instrument of education in Roman schools (Quintilian) involved and depended on the corpus of classical literature, poetry, history, moral philosophy; the culture of Hellas that Isocrates had declared was the school of the world. The lecture platforms of the Second Sophistic and the schools on which they depended had anyhow been superseded by schools of law. When the sermon superseded the rhetorical performance in due course, the curtain had fallen on cultivation of the original culture. Thus the seven "liberal arts" were entirely different in the ecclesiastical context, and had lost dependence on and reference to classical literature. The education curriculum inherited from Rome continued under the administration of bishops in the First Europe, with a continuity that was basically technical, void of a continued content. This was a main reason for the cultural gap in the "Dark Ages."

## The Legacy of the Roman Empire

The legacy of the Roman Empire to the First Europe is not at all the same as the inheritance of Europe from the Mediterranean world of antiquity, although the empire had adopted Christianity and assimilated Hellenic culture. Successive generations of a population that owns and occupies a particular territory may inherit a culture so long as conditions are stable enough for the necessary degree of continuity. A culture is a complex nexus in place and time, and an inheritance has to be direct and immediate. Elements or parts of that or another culture may be imitated or adopted or adapted. This was evident in the Hellenization and subsequent Romanization of Greek culture, and still further after Diocletian's remodeling of the empire. At the same time, cultural models (rather than model cultures) were formed in and by the exercise of these adaptations: Hellas, Zion, Romanitas. The main elements of an advanced culture can be comprehensively named as sciences, arts, and institutions; and after its conditions have been superseded a residue may remain in language and literature and works of art; its ideas and ideals, and institutions, are then represented or described in the literature, or inferred from that and the surviving works. This differentiation between a culture inherited directly by a population in occupation of an hereditary territory, and transmission of the language and literature and works of art of a cultural model, obvious but liable to confusion, has to be borne in mind when tracing the influence of these models, because succeeding generations perceive them differently and are influenced differently by them, and may not have recognized or may have not cared what the favored culture was to those who possessed and were molded by it.

There are three analogies that may be useful: biological, genealogical, legal. Biologically, a genetic inheritance determines the species. Genealogically, an insulated population inherits a gene pool from which are formed kinship groups transmitting family characteristics, the consequences of mating. Legally, the legacy is personal and willed. Biologically, there is no human motivation; what is, is given, save to the extent that genetic manipulation has become possible. Genealogically, human motive enters in with marriage customs or personal choice. Legally, the testator's will is the whole matter.

The human species has a diverse common habitat on the earth, but not a specific culture. However, there are recognized cultural epochs, from the Paleolithic to the Electrochemical, an ascendancy in the level of human capability as an attribute of the species. In other respects, populations are separated by geography and history, with a territory, language, descent, and institutions as a common inheritance exclusively theirs. Geographically and historically, a group of such peoples may share an inheritance of cultural models, which then differentiates them as a group from other peoples. On the genealogical analogy, this is a heritable difference. On the legal analogy, a dominant ruler or party or tradition may operate like a testator who wills his valued property to selected beneficiaries. This is especially exemplified by a conservative interest; but there are also radical names and traditions. In the history of cultural legacy and inheritance, there are three aspects: universal (the species), general (a group of peoples), particular (a tradition embodying political will). The analogies may help to keep these distinct and appropriately related. It is the principal theme of this work to show how the inheritance of the world from the West has issued in a definitive geocultural legacy to posterity in terms of human capability, an attribute of the race. The exact character of that attribute at the present time and its implications are of a consequence that demands careful statement for the purpose of general understanding of what has happened.

The legacy of the Roman Empire to Europe was complicated. Constantine had purposefully built a new Christian Rome in Constantinople. The empire was divided into east and west for political and administrative convenience and expediency. When the western part of the empire disintegrated, the east was left, not as heir but as the surviving empire itself. That was an assumption never in doubt in Byzantium. Constantine's new Rome was the true Rome. East Rome had supplanted the Rome of Italy as the heart and head of the empire. The Rhomaeans, its citizens, were the Romans. The Roman Empire was an integral part of Europe until 1453. The only heirs were the heirs of the western hemisphere of the empire, Latin Rome. They were principally the Roman Church and such Romanized kings as Clovis and preeminently Charlemagne. Gaul had been the most Romanized province.

Byzantium as a European state belongs to the history of medieval Europe until the mid–fifteenth century. Through the ups and downs of its stormy history of losses and survivals, it maintained the Diocletian tradition of imperial rule and a Christian Church of trinitarian orthodoxy. Culturally, the language and literature were Greek, not Latin. Propinquity made Oriental influences stronger than they had been in the west. Altogether, they were distanced from Augustan Rome and Romanitas, and their legacy to Europe was distinctive. Although in the west their legacy was thought of as what their scholars brought to Italy in 1453, initiating the Renaissance, their particular legacy was to the Russians and Slavs through the Greek Orthodox Church, as that in the west had been to the Germanic tribes through the Roman Catholic Church.

Justinian was the last Roman-minded emperor, a Latin in speech and thought. His concentration of resources on reconquest of the western provinces of the empire in Germanic hands, temporarily successful, drained those resources of the state and alienated by taxation the populations of the territory reconquered. It was a ruinous policy that had to be decisively reversed by exclusive attention to the northern and eastern frontiers of a defensible state. That defense of a European gate that would be precariously held for more than eight hundred years was the most fundamental and precious legacy of Byzantium to Europe.

The final struggle of Rome and Persia was followed by the rise of a new force in the Middle East. Muhammad died in 632. His movement in the following years exploded in parties of mounted raiders, for whom the exhausted empires were easy prey, beginning with Persia, but then Byzantium. Palestine and Syria were conquered; Alexandria fell in 642. Egypt and Syria from early times had provided the timber and skills for shipbuilding, and the Muslims were enabled to make themselves a sea power that captured Cyprus and Rhodes, whence they plundered the Aegean islands and their piracy ruined Mediterranean trade. Constantinople suffered sea attacks. Armenia and the Caucasus regions were lost. Byzantine territory was reduced to Asia Minor and the hinterland of the capital, with the coastland of the northern Mediterranean. Naples, Venice, and Istria were still in her hands, and the complete Lombard conquest in Italy was prevented by her retaining a hold on a corridor between Rome and Ravenna. Slavic tribes established themselves in the Balkan peninsula, severing the highway connecting eastern and western empire. About 680 the Bulgars from Asia crossed the lower Danube, and were to prove a recurrent danger to the capital for the next three centuries. These conditions of medieval Byzantium were addressed by a reorganization of defense. The territory was divided into provinces in which armies were stationed under commanders who were also the governors of the province. In Asia Minor, the main territory, grants of land were made on conditions of military service. This was carried through under Constantine IV (668–685), and was effective in checking Islam's movement towards Constantinople. His successor had to cope with revolutions and anarchy, revolts in Italy, the fall of Carthage to Islam. The Bulgars took advantage of these disasters to establish a position south of the Danube. There were rebellions in Asia Minor. The provinces were ravaged by Islam in an advance on the capital, which was besieged by land and sea throughout 717, the most critical year in the history of Byzantium. In that year Leo III (717–741) succeeded to the throne, the first of a new dynasty; his first and greatest act was to free Constantinople from siege by driving away the investing forces. In that century, he and his dynasty repaired and maintained the military power that enabled Byzantium, the rump of the Roman Empire, to hold a place and play a part in medieval Europe. It was Leo III, on the home front, who initiated the Iconoclast movement, which forced a theological issue that divided Byzantium, and belongs to the history of Europe.

"Byzantine" stands for a distinctive form of the Roman Empire, different not only from that of Augustan Rome, but also from that of Theodosius, the last effective representative of the new Diocletian empire as a whole.

The emperors of Byzantium claimed to be the Roman emperors in line from Augustus. When Charlemagne was crowned by the Pope as the heir of the Roman emperors, Irene, the ruler in Constantinople, assumed the title *Basileus Rhomaion,* "King of the Romans." The imperial rule remained absolute, and this was not questioned constitutionally because the precarious position of the state required it. An Oriental-type court was at the head of government, with an elaborately devised and organized calendar of ceremonies intended to display the majesty of the throne. This was used not only as an instrument of government (more subtle, festive, and impressive in a high degree than modern cults of a totalitarian leader), but also to enhance diplomatic initiatives by a stunning impression on envoys of power and prestige.

The administration that gave effect to imperial decrees and decisions was staffed by highly educated, trained, competent, and well-paid officials, with established career prospects. It had been established long enough for its members to develop a corporate identity and traditions of loyalty—the vested interests of an institution. Its importance, the respect in which it was held, and the power intrinsic to its function and tasks made it the nucleus of the state, promoting its unity, assimilating foreign elements, mediating in practice between emperor and people, both implementing and at times and in ways modifying or even resisting his policies. It held in time of crisis and was conservative, against innovation as imperiling security in a tight situation. It was a main factor in the survival of the state (lacking in the western empire), and reinforced the conservative character of the Byzantine state.

The other main factor in survival was of course the military. It is hardly too much to say that the state had to be on a permanent war footing.

A final, capital point on this remnant of the Roman Empire. Romanitas had proclaimed the ideal of a universal empire and emperor. Rome aspired to rule the world in virtue of Romanitas, the peace and justice it was the mission and destiny of its imperium to establish. This claim to universality had been reinforced by the Christian mission for the salvation of mankind. The Byzantine "Autokrator" claimed in principle the whole world as the goal of his rule.

What survived of Byzantium after 1453 was principally the Greek Orthodox Church; and this church was the principal institution of Byzantium. It used to be thought that Byzantium was Erastian, which is the exact opposite of this. The state upheld the dogmas of the faith and heresy was treason. Emperors were usually anxious to deal leniently or tolerantly with heretics when a body of them were taxpayers, since state business was involved, although the Church remained rigid in persecution. When emperors intervened in religious matters, as supremely when Leo III issued his Iconoclastic decrees, the Church had the last word, literally—since it was the word only that survived. Church and state were frequently in conflict, and in its own concerns the Church prevailed. Ambrose excommunicated the devoutly Christian Theodosius, who had practically identified Church and state. In the last centuries of the state, it was the clergy, not the emperors, who opposed union with Rome.

The "Orthodox" in the title of the Greek church reflects its part in the Christological controversies that established the trinitarian creed. Having adopted Christianity as the religion of the empire, Constantine and his successors were concerned to end theological party and faction within the Church by bringing about a definitive enforceable creed, and convened council after council for that purpose. Resistance to the suppression of "paganism" cropped up with Julian the Apostate, who excluded Christians from the teaching of Greek literature. A compromise was sought, particularly by Gregory of Nazianzus and Basil of Caesarea, who had been brought up on the classics, and were sophists as they were theologians, having been fellow students in Athens. Their writings had the grace, correctness, and persuasion of the sophist rhetoricians. Their theology used the subtlety of Platonic thought to restore the Logos concept to the "one substance" of the trinitarian creed. These Greeks, supported by Latin disciples and allies (Ambrose), on the very eve of the dissolution of the western half of the empire, were the ones who finally united the Church in the orthodoxy of the trinitarian formula of the Christian faith. Rigidity of dogma, orthodoxy, was prized as the conquest of the Greek fathers. The Byzantine church was the preeminent champion and trustee of this orthodoxy. "Greek Orthodox Church" is an integral title.

They are admirable and faithful custodians and transmitters of Greek texts, but there is no continuity with the culture of Hellas, as there is with the language. It is not Greek philosophy they study when they study Plato. The difference of the two cultures can be put in a sentence by saying that "infidel" did not and could not have a meaning in Hellas. In Byzantium, it defined the enemy. The political conditions of an open society did not exist. The universality claimed for its culture by Hellas, and made explicit by Isocrates, was philosophical but not a philosophy: the cultivation of human activities and interests, and the pursuit of knowledge by rational investigation and discourse. Faith in a divine revelation as knowledge could be an option in that culture, but not its ground. The European states would not differ essentially at first in this respect from Byzantium, but differences between and within them would be what made European history, without waiting for the Renaissance.

The Christian art of the East at the beginning of the fourth century drew on Hellenistic traditions still dominant in cities like Antioch and Alexandria, and Oriental traditions that passed from Persia to Egypt, Syria, Mesopotamia, and Armenia. These two influences, opposing one another, combined to give Byzantine art its character. As Christian, the arts that would be influenced from these sources were first and foremost employed in the building and decoration of churches.

St. Sophia's in Constantinople and St. Mark's in Venice have been the two most generally admired and accessible monuments of Byzantine art in Western Europe. St. Mark's is indeed a specimen of Byzantine magnificence in the tenth to twelfth centuries. This was the period in which Byzantine art set the standard for Europe, most evident in Romanesque and Hispano-Moorish art. But to say that anticipates what belongs to the history of medieval Europe. At this point, all that is needed is an indication of the general character of the art developed by the Greek half of the Roman Empire as part of the total legacy. In the thirteenth century a transformation began which in the following century, on the eve of the Italian Renaissance, brought about a return to classical Greek models and ideals.

# Part Two

# The Western Interregnum

# 9

# Foundations of Europe

## The Middle Age

A medieval period in Western history, a Middle Age, intervening between antiquity and the modern world, is recognized retrospectively and was formed in European consciousness at the Renaissance. In the eighteenth century, it might generally have been thought of as the period between Constantine and the fall of Constantinople, but that was more convenient than historically accurate. The division itself is a convenience of thought, and dates for it must be more or less arbitrary, but an addition of a century to the Constantine dates would be nearer the mark.

The first years of this Middle Age used to be thought of and called the "Dark Ages." Jerome's cry on the sack of Rome by Alaric the (Arian) Christian Visigoth in 410, with the words "the bright light of the world is extinguished" anticipates this later description. At the time, the seat of Western imperial government had been removed to Ravenna, and that government did not come formally to an end for another three generations. But the dislocation announced in the full sentence of Jerome's cry was an anticipation of events, by which the axis of civilization shifted from the Mediterranean to that peninsula of Asia that was to be for a millennium and a half historically the most important of the five geographical divisions of the world: Europe. There would not be a European empire. In due course, the peoples of the regions would have defended frontiers and distinctive languages. But it was not until the eleventh and twelfth centuries that this could be discerned and studied, beginning the second part of the Middle Age. Meanwhile, there would be the reign of Charlemagne (742–814); of Alfred (871–901); the Celtic church in Ireland, and the school of Bede in Jarrow (672–735); the administration of Archbishop Dunstan (960–988). These are memorable patches of light in the invisible darkness. Rough and miserable conditions occurred and recurred over a long period into modern times. Indeed, idealized aspects of the Middle Age would be revived in refuge from the modern age.

At first castles and monasteries; at the end universities and chartered boroughs. The curtain falls, but there is unfinished action. Four main agencies are at work in the making of European civilization: the feudal barons, the crown, the towns, the Roman Church. The interests and ideals of each party differed, and were frequently in violent conflict. None established an overall permanent ascendancy; political and social order were attained piecemeal by resolution of the conflicts in one way or another, with shifts in the balance of power within societies and between them. In such circumstances, there are bound to be lapses and setbacks, not steady development. Such language, anyhow, is nonsense unless there is presupposed a commonly defined public interest overriding conflicts. If, politically, civilization is identifiable with a constitutional basis of social order, fundamental law founding the rule of law, with equality and freedom under the law, there is a standard by which history may be judged. In spite of Roman law, that was not one of the classical achievements European nations could recover from the past. Law (Roman law, canon law, the law of nature, and the laws of nations) was prominent in medieval thought, and norms were formulated. In greater part, however, the history of the Middle Age is about Latin Christendom over against and along with Greek Christendom of Byzantium.

Politically, barons, crown, towns, and Church are dominant. Culturally, the sustaining interests are piety, learning, and chivalry, in a remarkable fusion of the indigenous with what was adopted and adapted that emerged and established itself to give the Middle Age an historical identity. This reached a peak in the thirteenth century. This is perhaps the most valid way to think of the Middle Age, as it certainly is the way to enjoy it. As the mid-period between antiquity and modern times, it has been generally seen as a slow climb back to the Roman level of civilization. In that sense, the Renaissance begins early, say with Charlemagne, and ascends gradually to the Augustan age of the eighteenth century, recalling the Roman literary prime, or to the European Enlightenment, which follows the scientific track and registers recognition of the necessary Greek preliminary level of inquiry. No age exists to connect the past with the future. No age exists without doing so. The Middle Age cannot be different. However, it marked rather than marched through time; the interest is in what it was, not in its leading to something else.

## A New Empire

The career of Clovis as a key figure in the making of Europe has been briefly described above in the context of the break-up of the western empire. His dynasty, the Merovingians, lasted from 481 to 716 despite the folly and incompetence of his descendants. Later, the mayors of the palace exercised effective power. An orthodox ruling family who had driven out the Arian Visigoths continued to have the regard and support of the Roman Church and of Byzantium. Thus the Teutonic Franks gave their name to Latin Gaul, leaving the amenable Gallo-Roman population their Roman inheritance. Coherent government was not in royal hands, and the fissiparous tendencies of the over-mighty subject that would plague the feudal system began to be anticipated, with great landowners, predominantly ecclesiastical estates, enjoying "immunities." Even in the domestic disorder, the frontiers were defended.

A Pepin of Heristal was one of the energetic mayors of the palace, virtually a shadow dynasty, under the late Merovingian kings. Bede (V, ix–x) writes of the difficulty and lack of success of missionaries in Frisland at the end of the seventh century. A party of twelve went from England and were well received by Pepin, who had just subdued Hither Frisland and driven out the obdurate king. Thanks largely to Pepin, "the most glorious general of the Franks," they were enabled with Rome to organize the church in Frisland. Later, in 718 the Englishman Winfrid, better known as Boniface, was commissioned by Pope Gregory to preach the gospel to all the tribes in Germany, and did so with great success in Thuringia, Bavaria, Frisland, Hesse, and Saxony. He was appointed archbishop of Mainz in 748. Pepin and his heirs were partners with Gregory and Boniface in this pioneering Christian-Latin thrust into northern territory. Pepin's son, Charles Martel ("the Hammer"), mayor of the palace in 720, was in hard fighting with the Saxons, Alamanni, and Bavarians before his famous battle with the Moors near Tours in 732, a battle said to have lasted between two and seven days, among the most decisive in European history. The Moors withdrew southward, and finally, in 759, across the Pyrenees whence they had come. Charles also hammered the Gallo-Roman church, secularizing the estates of bishops and abbots, an abuse of ecclesiastical power that was to have serious consequences later in connection with the Albigensian heresy.

This was the time of the Iconoclast controversy that followed Leo III's edict ordering the destruction of all images in the churches. There were violent clashes in Ravenna. Gregory III called a council of Italian bishops, which excommunicated the iconoclasts. The authority and status of the Bishop of Rome was at stake. Gregory asked Charles Martel to replace the emperor in Byzantium, and sent him the keys to St. Peter's tomb. Charles was too occupied, and declined. What was abortive then was successful a few years later when Charles, Gregory, and Leo were all dead. The new Pope Stephen came to an understanding with Charles's son Pippin that ended in the recovery of Lombardy. The defeated Lombardy king went back on his undertakings, which required a second invasion by Pippin. Again there was Lombard perfidy, and finally in 774 Pippin's son Charlemagne ended the kingdom of the Lombards, which had lasted two centuries. He handed over territory to the Papal See, and this instituted the Papal States, which would be a main obstacle to Italian unity, and a source of conflict with German emperors trying to make a reality of the "Holy Roman Empire" on Charlemagne's own model. This papal title to the territory was subsequently legitimized by the famous forgery, the "Donation of Constantine." On this disastrous political error for Europe, it is worth reading a few pages of Gibbon that begin:

> The mutual obligations of the popes and the Carlovingian family form the important link of ancient and modern, of civil and ecclesiastical, history. In the conquest of Italy (751, 753, 768), the champion of the Roman church obtained a favorable occasion, a specious title, the wishes of the people, the prayers and intrigues of the clergy. But the most essential gifts of the popes to the Carlovingian race were the dignities of king of France and of patrician of Rome (III, xlix).

The last sentence refers to twenty-six years after Charlemagne's conquest of Lombardy when he was attending a Christmas Mass in St. Peter's, and as he was rising from his knees the pope placed the imperial crown on his head. There was again a western Augustus.

The reality and the ghost of Rome, the mystique of Rome, were such formative influences in the birth of Europe that attention is due to what was meant. Rome was the eternal city, *Roma aeterna,* the source of Romanitas. In Horace and in Virgil, the rock of the Capitol, the symbol of that endurance, is the analogy for the endurance of Horace's lines and of the rule of the heirs of Aeneas (*Odes,* III, xxx, 1:8; *Aeneid* IX, 1:448). This was the core of her reputation as the civilized world, destined to be the whole world.

How impressive that could be to the war leaders of the tribes that eventually brought about the dismemberment of the empire was exemplified in the careers of such as Stilicho, Theodoric, and Clovis. Ataulf, brother-in-law of Alaric, rallied to home on consideration of the inbred lawlessness of his Gothic tribes of men, abandoning his plan to destroy the Roman name ("when experience taught me that Goths would never suffer the restraint of law, and that without law there could be no State, I chose to renew by Gothic strength the fame of Rome, wishing to go down to posterity as the restorer of Roman authority I could not replace"). This was the message that the name and fame of Rome got through to a receptive intelligence on the other side. The invincibly hostile would use the Roman name to express contempt.

When Constantine adopted Christianity as the religion of the empire, and the Church remodeled its organization on the lines of the Diocletian state in order to reach all parts, and formulated an exclusive orthodoxy, not only civilization but also Christendom became coterminous with the Roman Empire. The Pax Romana could be assumed to be fulfillment of a purpose of God. A Christian emperor, autocratic head of the Christian state, was God's regent, recalling David, king of Israel, or Josiah, king of Judah, as prototypes. The head of state was subject to the authority of the Church on matters on which its authority was paramount. This symbiosis was broken in the West when there was no longer an emperor. Rome was represented by the Roman pontiff, whose secular authority rested solely on prestige. Under Gregory I, the Great (590), the authority of Rome was upheld by an exceptionally saintly churchman who was an able administrator and an experienced diplomat. He reconciled the Arian Gothic kingdom of Spain to the Church, and sent missions to England. His successor commissioned Boniface, "the Apostle of Germany." With no emperor in the west, the popes were dependent on conversion of the kings who had established themselves, and on attaching them directly to the Vatican. Insofar as this succeeded, they were forging the strongest bond of union of all peoples and people throughout the "Roman" world, for they would be regularly participating in the same sacraments of one church under the discipline of its clergy. However this was valued as Roman citizenship had been, it was a common cultural foundation for Europe.

The Vatican, like Byzantium and with the greater need, strove to impress its authority on these converted kings, and on all who came to Rome, by pomp and circumstance. Charlemagne was not unsophisticated, but what impressed him enormously and unforgettably on his first visit was the ecclesiastical majesty, complete with relics, discipline, finished ritual, all the splendor of high performance. Here visible and tangible were the credentials of the Christian faith. He was confirmed in his mission to his Frankish world and its extension. When he came back those twenty-six years later, having reestablished a Roman empire in the West, this was of critical historical importance. The tenuous hold of the Roman Church, without the bodily muscle provided by the empire, was decisively reinvigorated. The empire could be restored. A permanent symbiosis, the "Holy Roman Empire," was the new destiny of Rome.

There were two major implications of this New Rome which make the Middle Age what it was. *Roma aeterna* had become *Roma temporalis* in God's hands. The world waited for the Second Coming, and the kingdom of God. The Middle Age would be a model of that regime, not a link between antiquity and modern times. God had consummated antiquity in the Christianized Roman Empire in order to prepare the world for his final intervention and judgment. The other implication concerns the peoples Romanized under this new dispensation. They were to be alienated from the traditions of their folk and to adopt the traditions of their rebirth, like immigrants, a change of identity that would take effect in the schools of Europe. Two notions or conditions were conjoined: the interim city of God on earth and the cultural unity of Europe. History would sort them out.

Charlemagne fought fifty-three campaigns on more than seven fronts in defense and extension of the Christianized West against surrounding enemies; this established the Roman Church in central Europe and founded Germany by admitting Saxons and Bavarians on equal terms with his conquering Franks. His only reverse was more famous in romance than all his successes, the fall of Roland in the pass of Roncevalles against the Gascons. More historical is the Frankish influence by which Latin Christianity penetrated into what became Poland, Bohemian Austria, Hungary. His government was as personal and temporary as that of Alexander, and in its way as historically effective. He brought into parts of Western Europe not touched by Roman rule the presence of a strong civilized government concerned to promote religion and justice and education, and to attend to the needs and appeals of the people. His ubiquitous personal government was not organized administration; the future was being made on the ground by large acquisitions. The Latin empire of the Franks stretched from the Ebro to the Carpathians, over against the Greek Empire of Byzantium and the Saracen empire, governed from Baghdad and Cordova.

Like Alexander's, the empire of Charlemagne broke up after his death; in this case, by the bad old Frankish custom of partition among sons. There was no agreement until after a civil war. Two sons combined against their elder brother and defeated him. Then at Verdun Charles the Bald was allotted Neustria, Aquitaine, and that part of France west of the Rhone and the Saone. Lewis the German got Austrasian Francia east of the Rhine, Bavaria, Swabia, Saxony, and Rhaetia. Lothair, the eldest who had been heavily defeated, got a long intermediate territory from Frisland to the border of Calabria, including the two capitals of Aix-la-Chapelle and Rome. Like Alexander's generals, each of the brothers aspired to imperial rule. The partition of Meersen in 870 eliminated the long neck of Lothair's kingdom between those of his brothers, and something like modern Europe took shape. With the deposition of the incompetent Charles the Fat, son of Lewis the German, the Carolingian dynasty ended. The power of the nobles was growing at the expense of these kings.

## Philosopher Kings

A minor renaissance has been associated with the court of Charlemagne, with some justice. He personally cultivated the liberal arts eagerly, and revered those who taught them. He did his best at astronomy, having learned to calculate, and, as one learns by teaching, would teach this and also rhetoric and dialectic to those around him. He practiced writing diligently in spare moments, but had begun too late, as his biographer says. The Merovingian king Chilperic, grandson of Clovis, had composed Latin verses, but he was the Nero of his age, and Gaul was the most Romanized province. If Charlemagne's accomplishment was inferior, his interest and intention were of a different order. He wanted all his subjects to be instructed in the Christian message, and the first means to that end was a well-trained clergy. Episcopal and monastic schools had existed in the fifth century, but had closed with the turbulence of the eighth. Now the old curriculum was revived (reading, chant, Latin, calculation), and every monastery and bishopric was required to open schools. Enforcement of the requirement meant availability of the clergy who could and would instruct the people and perform the liturgy. In this concern, Charlemagne's model was King Josiah.

He took advantage of a revival that had begun elsewhere, in Spain and Italy, and especially in Ireland and England. Refugee scholars from Arab Spain settled in Gaul. Charlemagne brought scholars back with him from Italy. At least a dozen of these foreigners are known by name and reputation, and where they settled. Foremost in administration of this educational empire was Alcuin of York, whose background brings in Bede of Jarrow, and sources in Ireland. Alcuin had visited Italy, where he met the celebrated grammarian Peter of Pisa, one of the scholars Charlemagne brought over.

Pursuing his intention to form a supply of well-trained clergy, the king had priests examined for their knowledge and understanding. His chief bishops were sent a questionnaire on how baptism was performed and explained in their dioceses. Children baptized were to be instructed by parents and godparents, and to attend religious ceremonies with them. He wanted children to learn to read and write in parish schools. Clerical training was mainly directed to preaching in the vulgar tongue as the most effective method of popular education. There were model homilies to be memorized or to be read.

Charlemagne's sons were as concerned as their father for education. Lothair complained that religious learning had disappeared in Italy by the indifference of those to whom it had been entrusted. He wanted to regroup schools in eight centers. Pope Eugenius II installed masters to teach letters and doctrine in the cathedral schools and in all the parishes in the Papal States. The monastic schools were reserved for novices.

Charles the Bald was the most cultivated of the sons, with the strongest intellectual interests. His palace was said to deserve the name of school, for the time that was spent in scholarly exercises. Outstanding among the scholars in residence there was the Irish monk John Scotus Erigena, who had a knowledge of Greek and made a famous Greek-Latin dictionary, with citations and translations. Far more remarkable was his great philosophical work *De Divisione Naturae*. His Greek had familiarized him with the early Greek fathers and their engagement with Neoplatonist thought. How to relate and reconcile the Christian picture of the world with affinities in this development of Greek idealism was the challenge. He adapted Greek dialogue, between master and pupil, for his exposition. The work astounded his contemporaries, and in due course suffered ecclesiastical condemnation. Charles the Bald was interested and supportive. This was a foretaste of the intellectual activity to come that made universities a main glory of the Middle Age.

St. Patrick is the hero-saint of Ireland, and his character is in the legend. Like Elijah, he was of rugged character, and called by God. The learning for which Ireland gained a European reputation in the sixth and seventh centuries was not his. His Latin was *rusticus,* as he ruefully said; he was a man of one book. If not learned himself, he was the source of the school of learning that developed in Ireland. Never part of the Roman Empire, Ireland had been in contact with Christian communities in Gaul in the second century and in Britain in the third. Conversion was accidental and sporadic, by means of merchants or slaves or returning mercenaries. Circles started in this way had a more personal faith than could be propagated by the evangelizing of a tribe through the conversion of their ruler. But headway could not be made without the good will of rulers. Grants of land were needed for buildings, endowments for a priesthood, royal recognition to safeguard the loyalty of converts: any organized form of Christianity had to begin at the top.

Patrick was able to establish his communities by winning first the toleration of the High King, whose brother he baptized, and then his daughters. There were no cities in Ireland, and a monastery was the institution that served this purpose. He set up a simple scheme for such an establishment. Diplomatic skill, an energetic personality, and (crudely) bribes integrated the new communities piecemeal into the society. Likely lads were recruited for training a native clergy, which at that time could be done by redeeming boy slaves. By the sixth and seventh centuries the churchmen of Ireland were famous in Europe for learning and piety. As Irish bishop, Patrick was illiterate compared with most of the many bishops in Gaul, and he was too well aware of it. Although British born, he was gradually transformed into a typical Irish saint in the Irish imagination, supplied by monks with accounts of his acts in the manner of medieval hagiography that dramatized for edification actual and legendary incidents. Popular taste was formed for such fare.

A prime reason for the reputation for learning acquired by the Irish churchmen was that Patrick did not give them an ecclesiastical literature, including the Bible, in their native language. He and his assistants diffused a knowledge of Latin throughout Ireland, which gave direct access to the Latin fathers, and in time to the Latin classics, a foundation that was built on and is valued to this day. The language was seized on and cultivated as opening a window on the world. Ireland had not been occupied by Roman armies and administrators. Patrick's Christian mission incidentally brought home the majesty of Rome, at the time when dismemberment of the empire was in process. Ireland was a special context for the influence of Roman culture. Since Christianity was not brought to Ireland by Rome, that culture innocently lent its prestige to the faith. Hence Bede's eagerness for all books, all learning.

The school of Armagh was the center of early Irish monastic learning, whence came the scholars who founded Glastonbury. St. Columba landed from Ireland in Iona in 563 and built his monastery, the cradle of Scottish learning for more than a century. Bede in Jarrow is a reliable historian of the conversion of England after Augustine and his party landed in Kent in 597, sent by Gregory I to preach the Gospel to the English. Some sixty years later, there was the question of an archbishop of the English churches. An African abbot called Hadrian was the favored nominee, but he recommended another as more worthy. Eventually, as Bede tells, "a monk, called Theodore, well known to Hadrian, born at Tarsus in Cilicia, a man well instructed in worldly and Divine literature, as also in Greek and Latin," was sent, accompanied by Hadrian. He was consecrated archbishop, the first whom all the English churches obeyed. Theodore and Hadrian toured the country together.

The collection, maintenance, and extension of libraries were central to the sustenance of learning, and Bede's narrative shows this concern. His own abbot, Benedict, had personally founded a library. "The large and noble library, which he had brought from Rome, and which was necessary for the edification of his church, he commanded to be kept entire, and neither by neglect to be injured or dispersed." His successor doubled the stock with visits to Rome.

A manuscript of normal length generally took two to three months to copy. Nearly eight thousand written in the eighth and ninth centuries have been preserved. Certain abbeys became "publishing houses," since they were engaged to make copies for others because the equipment and standard of their scriptoria were famous. The devotion to accurately copied, well edited texts was deep, joyful, and necessary. "Gladly would they learn, and gladly teach."

The young of the aristocracy were given an early grounding in Latin, and if they went to court, studies were encouraged. Intellectual interests were not exclusively clerical. Charlemagne and his sons were bibliophiles in their way and had well-stocked libraries. His own circle read poems they composed, and played literary games, as well as engaging in serious discussions, on questions of astronomy as well as theology, carried on at table or even in the bath.

In England by 800 there had been consolidation in the Heptarchy, first under the overlordship of Northumbria, then of Mercia under King Offa. New invasions shattered this stability in the ninth century, as in Europe: Saracens from Africa, the Magyars from Hungary, the Vikings from Norway and Denmark. The Vikings in persistent and widespread raids damaged beyond recovery the capabilities of the brilliant and distinctive culture established in Ireland, and sacked Iona, by which Irish Christianity had entered Britain. They eventually made settlements. They had destroyed Armagh, but founded Dublin, Waterford, Cork, and Limerick. The Danes established their Danelaw in east England from York to London; and a large territory that would be the nucleus of Normandy was ceded to the Norwegian Rollo in 911. In the first part of the eleventh century England was ruled by Danish kings. Because of kinship, the Northmen in Normandy became French, and those in England became English. That is, in both cases they accepted Christianity and its basic Latin culture. In France, the Capets successfully resisted the Northmen in the defense of Paris, and established a strong dynasty, after the weak government of Charles the Simple. In England, stubborn opposition in Wessex hindered and frustrated complete Danish conquest.

Bede had described the Christian civilizing of the English who had attacked and dispossessed and driven into inhospitable refuge the Celtic British who had been scarcely Christianized by their conquerors. Now, in 787, nearly the same began to happen to Bede's England at the hands of invading Northmen. Nearly, because this time the English were able to maintain and extend a tenuous hold, and eventually to assimilate the invaders. Successive waves of invaders continued for more than two centuries. Mercia had succeeded Northumbria as the seat of preponderant power in Bede's time. Some forty years after the first raid, King Egbert of Wessex conquered Mercia, and was effective ruler south of the Humber. Under its kings, Wessex was the heart of organized resistance to the invaders. Raids gave place to settlements, at first in the isles of Sheppey and Thanet.

Alfred king of Wessex is the hero of this resistance. He belongs to the early days of English exposure to the invasions, for he died almost exactly a century before Canute was born, at the dawn of the tenth century. He became king in 871 at the age of twenty-three. His reign of thirty years may be said to be the most eventful and formative in English history, in terms of personal rule. In driving out the Danes, with temporary cessions, he laid the foundations of a national state. He built a fleet, recovered and restored devastated London, and enabled his son and grandson, Edward and Athelstan, to reestablish English authority, so that by 954 the king of Wessex ruled from the Channel to the Clyde. There was still a Norwegian presence to encourage revival of old aspirations when Ethelred the Unready gave the opportunity. The policy of buying them off with Danegeld invited the invasion under Canute that added England to a Scandinavian empire. *Graecia capta ferum victorem cepit*—the more famous case was to be repeated. Canute became a Christian and went to Rome. He married the widow of Ethelred, and ruled as a native king. England was his center for the conversion of the Scandinavians. The link across the North Sea, however, could not be maintained by Canute's sons. Edward, son of Ethelred (Edward the Confessor), was recalled from Norman exile. The sequel is familiar as "1066 and all that." The Latinized Norman settlement had under a dynasty of vigorous dukes become the most adventurous and militarily effective province in France.

## The New Roman Empire

Germany, the eastern half of Charlemagne's empire, was the first to recover from the ninth century invasions, which gave predominance to the German emperor for three centuries. He claimed the imperial title as heir to Charlemagne in preeminence. Otto, son of Henry I of Saxony (936–973), defeated the Magyars at Lechfeld in 955, lifting the external threat, and bringing the other duchies under his control. In 951 and

961 he intervened effectively in Italy, and was crowned as emperor in 962. This conferred on the German kings the title of emperor of the Holy Roman Empire, which lasted nominally until 1806. It also sealed the historic connection between Germany and Italy. Control of the Alpine passes gave Germany advantage in cultural exchange between the Mediterranean and northern Europe.

In the Carolingian tradition, a Christian drive against the Slavs in the eastern border was started, but halted, and German attention concentrated on the south and southwest, acquiring Burgundy in 1034. Byzantium had begun missionary activity in Russia in the ninth century, and in 989 conversion of the Grand Duke Vladimir and his marriage to the sister of the Emperor Basil II was followed by rapid conversion of the Russian people.

Resistance to this centralization of Germany in the imperial aspiration of the reigning dynasty was favored by a conflict between Henry IV and Pope Gregory VII (Hildebrand). In the course of the quarrel, Henry declared the Pope deposed; Gregory excommunicated the king. Under imperial law, this entailed forfeiture of civil rights and deposition from office. When his subjects appealed to this law against him, Henry was obliged to submit, and in 1077 made his famous journey to Canossa to demonstrate penance and receive absolution. Three years later he resumed hostilities and appointed Clement III as a rival pope. In 1084, after a three-year siege, he took possession of Rome. Intervention by the Norman Duke of Apulia saved Gregory and forced Henry to return to Germany. Gregory died a year later. He had devoted his great ability and unflagging zeal not only to promote paramountcy for the authority of the Vatican, but also to reform the Church itself of grave abuses, and institute a strict discipline. Henry all this time and until his death was embroiled in conflicts with his vassals and the German princes. When Frederick I (Barbarossa) succeeded as emperor in 1152, he too was embroiled in conflicts with his German subjects, with civic republics of Lombardy, and with the papacy. At first he was successful; then his army was reduced by plague and in 1176 he was severely defeated at Legano. This made him change his policy, so that by generous concessions, patronage, and skillful diplomacy he placated the Lombards by recognition of the autonomy of cities in northern Italy, and acknowledged Alexander III as pope. In Germany, he used his patronage to triumphant effect, and established superiority over Poland, Hungary, Denmark and Burgundy. At the height of his power, he joined the third Crusade, and died in Cilicia in 1190. He became a legend that promoted German aspirations.

Innocent III made the greatest claims for the authority of the papacy, temporal and spiritual. He devoted his great abilities to that end and to reforming grave abuses in the Church. In Germany he had encountered a powerful resistant clergy, a rich bourgeoisie not easily to be managed, feudal barons suspicious of his intentions, and Henry VI, the forceful son of Barbarossa, determined to be independent. With Henry's death, and the infancy of Frederick, the pope's ward and grandson of Barbarossa, candidates for the imperial title were Barbarossa's brother Philip and Otto of Brunswick. The German electors chose Philip, and called on the pope to comply. Otto contested the choice, and desolating warfare ensued. Innocent intervened with a judgment that preferred Otto, who had undertaken to restore and recover all estates in the Church domain, and to consent to the formula for his enthronement: "King of the Romans, by the grace of God and the Pope." Philip's party, which included ecclesiastic princes, produced a contrary manifesto, backed by nearly all German clergy and laity. The Pope replied, conceding the right of the electors, by reserving a right of veto. The arbitrament of force would have to prevail. Otto proceeded against Philip, Innocent against the senior clergy.

Ten years of civil war and anarchy followed, ending in Otto's defeat and a temporizing compromise between Philip and Innocent. Philip was assassinated. Innocent engineered support for Otto, which was delivered at the Diet of Frankfort. Otto dissimulated to convince the Pope and secure the imperial title. Temporal rule over Italy was the underlying objective of Innocent, which no German emperor would willingly concede, since Italy was an essential part of the imperial claim. Otto was nephew of Richard I and John of England, and adopted their ideas of strong government. Innocent insisted on five requirements as a condition of Otto's consecration, which Otto accepted, and embodied in solemn declarations, with citations from Scripture.

Underneath, they were locked in mutual intransigence. German opinion would never cede Italy to the Pope. Rupture was inevitable. Otto built up his power in Italy, organizing in the chief towns an imperial administration, so that eventually the high prelates found themselves forced to break their ties with Rome. Innocent's response was the threat of excommunication (which entailed release from a subject's oath of fealty) and an appeal to Philippe-Auguste, king of France, Otto's irreconcilable enemy. Otto was excommunicated, and responded by putting the papacy under interdict, which prevented the pilgrimage to Rome; *la guerre du Sacerdoce et de l'Empire, fleau permanent du moyen age, récommencait* (Luchaire). Innocent worked on the prelates and nobles in Italy; the communes were anticlerical and beyond his reach. Foiled in Italy and Germany, Innocent decided to promote the young Frederick of Sicily as the legitimate and worthy heir to the imperial title. The German magnates, mindful of Otto's uncle John and the English barons, and of Otto's inclination to follow that example, began to assert themselves; the German prelates were ready to enforce the excommunication. A representative diet was held and Frederick elected emperor. Innocent thought he had nothing to fear from his ward, then aged sixteen. The young king of Sicily moved into Germany, where he won over aristocracy and prelates, drawing on the abundant patronage at his disposal when he would be installed as emperor. He came to an understanding with Philippe-Auguste. Otto attacked France with the aid of English and Flemish troops, a superior force that was nevertheless decisively beaten by Philippe-Auguste at Bouvines, near Lille (1214). For Otto, all was lost; and John of England lost standing. Frederick became sole master of Germany and Innocent died triumphant. In 1216, Frederick and the electors, clerical and lay, made documentary renunciation of opposition to papal claims and possessions. To separate an Italian kingship from the German empire, Frederick renounced the kingdom of Sicily to his son.

In Gibbon's words: "As Frederick advanced in age and authority, he repented of the rash engagements of his youth . . . and his ambition was occupied by the restoration of the Italian monarchy from Sicily to the Alps. But the success of this project would have reduced the popes to their primitive simplicity." He had undertaken to Innocent when he was twenty-one to lead a crusade to Palestine, and Innocent's successors insisted on fulfillment. After an abortive start, he was forced to carry out the undertaking. In his absence, Pope Gregory set about recovering the Italian territories with mercenaries and promoting an alternative king in Germany. Frederick's good relations with the Saracens enabled him to return within a year, having obtained Jerusalem, Bethlehem, and Nazareth on a ten-year lease. The Pope's mercenaries were driven out, and Frederick declared his intention of making Rome his capital, soliciting help from France and England. For some time, Frederick maintained his initial success, but the pope, using an alliance with rebellious German princes and Italian cities, gained the upper hand; and in 1248 Frederick's army was destroyed. Two years later, he died.

Frederick was singular, politically a meteor with no lasting influence. In this he resembled the Holy Roman Empire, which fell from the sky with his death. It would and could never have a place in the European firmament, though it continued to be counted by name. Personally, his gifts and interests were such that he has been called the first European. His Sicilian court was a junction of four traditions, Muslim, Jewish, Byzantine, and Latin. All were contributors to European culture, two of them barely acknowledged. He could converse fluently with Saracens in Arabic and was at home in French and Italian as well as Latin and Greek. He founded the university of Naples. "First European" means first Renaissance man. He was anyhow a man of many sides, a love poet in the Sicilian manner and, most remarkably, showing a mastery of empirical observation for a scientific purpose in his treatise on "Hawking," in advance of anything since Aristotle on animals.

Founders of the European States formed after the fall of Rome were haunted by the ghost of Romanitas. The name and fame of Rome evoked the idea and ideal of renewal: there should be universal unity, recalled and instituted in the name of Rome. This was the idea of the Holy Roman Empire. There were three ideas of the way in which it should be brought about. (1) Supreme power should reside in the Church, represented by the Bishop of Rome, vicar of the Almighty on earth. He should be not only chief priest and confessor, but also chief suzerain. (2) Charlemagne had demonstrated the new order in the empire he had achieved; his heirs should rule in the name of Augustus, creating continuity. (3) Opposed claims tend to become intransigent, and to beget conflict and recurrent war. There should be a partnership between the two powers. The pope would crown the emperor, communicating the sanction and blessing of God. The emperor would guarantee protection of the papacy and security of the Roman Church throughout his dominion and would be the secular arm of the Church in the execution of its proper judgments and in upholding its cause against heretics. Together, they carried out divine law, which charged them to see that justice prevailed among men, the wicked were subdued, and the good rewarded.

The coexistence of heaven and earth, of God and Caesar, posed the problem, with the doubts, difficulties, and differences of its due solution. Meanwhile, the duel between the two powers, conducted by some persons on both sides, was the scourge of the Middle Age, this interim period of waiting on God. In effect, the Church became the mirror image of the empire, a different form of the identification that there had been under Theodosius for political reasons. The Pope was emperor of the Church and its lands and possessions. The prelates were also barons with estates. The clergy had a substantial temporal footing and interests, with a lust for expansion, from the top down. The Church was also a corporate profession, with its theory, language, discipline, and functions, a profession generally regarded as fundamental, serving the highest human interests. As a corporate profession, it was a vested interest. All this peaked in the person and conduct of Innocent III, when he supported Otto of Brunswick for the temporal possessions of the Vatican against Philip, the legitimately elected Hohenstaufen emperor. Deviousness and double-dealing on both sides mocked all the exchanges that were not in arms. The Middle Age is also middle in ambiguity and ambivalence. Piety was its binding theme. Was that embodied in a subtle and complex order manipulated by a Christian mafia, itself ambiguous and ambivalent?

With Conrad III, the first of the Hohenstaufen dynasty, in 1138 Germany resumed her expansion to the east. Extension of her territories by two-thirds shifted the center of power from the Rhine to the Elbe, to the advantage of princes on the eastern frontier. Later, the Teutonic knights conquered Prussia. Conflict among the principalities was kept in check by local leagues—as in ancient Greece. The Swiss Confederation of 1291 was the most famous and enduring. The "Golden Bull" of 1356 formally recognized the autonomy of the princes, but the former imperial preponderance in Europe had ended a century earlier. In the thirteenth century national monarchies consolidated rule in Spain, France, and England. Feudal magnates were there to cause civil conflict until Henry VII in England and Louis XI in France, but the general situation was politically in advance of the petty divisions in Germany and Italy that succeeded the disintegration of the German empire and establishment of the Papal States. The Holy Roman Empire had some reality under the Carolingian dynasty, and then for three centuries under the Hohenstaufen dynasty; thereafter, nominal claims. Late in the nineteenth century, when Spain, France, and England had established their empires, Germany and Italy were remodeled to stake their claim. Two world wars were the sequel, if not the consequence, with incalculable suffering and destruction, and a transformation of the problem of international security and stability.

A key to the early medieval history of France is in the division of its composition. The kingdom was organized in and from the northern territory, centered on Paris. Regions south of the Loire were left to local counts and dukes. That was one main reason why English kings, by marriage and otherwise, were able to acquire and for a time hold a French empire. Merovingians and Carolingians hardly established their authority over Aquitaine, a former Roman province, a medieval duchy with a diverse population that had been far less Gothicized than other regions. Where royal authority was weak, papal authority was the stabilizing influence. But the princely ecclesiastics of the region, archbishops and bishops, and especially abbots, had acquired great estates, and were entrenched feudal lords. Even the great Hildebrand was not able to suppress simony and other abuses in these parts, where it was rampant. For the long period of their ascendancy, the counts of Toulouse were virtually kings of the south, and Toulouse was more influential than Paris. That was due not only to its position as capital of the Raymond territory, but also to the affluent bourgeoisie who inhabited it,

supplied its revenues, and controlled its institutions. The counts tried to build an organized state, but their considerable territory was one piece of a random mosaic in which
they were beset by the Plantagenets of England, the kings of Aragon, and the counts
of Provence. Wars-reconciliations-marriages-wars ensued. Nor would Philippe-
Auguste renounce his suzerainty over the south, although engaged in defending the
north from the English. Raymond VI was a popular and able prince, in touch with his
people. His court included one of the great troubadours, Arnaud Daniel, particularly
admired by Dante and Petrarch. This is a hint of the cultural division and rivalry
between the north between the Seine and the Rhine and the south between the
Garonne and the Rhone; between Paris and Toulouse. There were other differences
that would be underlined, and forced into an issue, by the Albigensian crisis.

The Cathars, the heretics associated with Albi, concentrated in Toulouse, Milan,
Florence, and other towns, had a distant origin. A priest named Bogomil, about 950
preached to Bulgarian peasants and artisans a fusion of Christian elements with Oriental dualism. The Oriental source was Manichaeism. The Christian element seems
to have come from Marcion's church in eastern Christendom. The Bulgarian underclass of Bogomil converts accepted their heresy as enlightenment, and identified the
orthodox Church (west or east) as darkness. When the heresy spread to Constantinople it it was given a more sophisticated theology, drawing on Gnostic and Neo-
platonic theosophy. The form in which it came to the West was therefore acceptable
to the educated mind, though still with an appeal to the deprived underclass. However, its strongholds were in the towns. Heretics outnumbered Catholics in south
France. When St. Bernard travelled the whole south in the twelfth century, he found
the churches empty, and at a castle near Toulouse he could not get a hearing for his
sermons. The Cathar missionaries travelled in pairs, on foot, in black habits, carrying St. John's Gospel in a leather wallet. They lived on charity or did odd jobs in the
villages they passed through, ate no meat, practiced chastity, and banned violence and
oaths. What could be more subversive? What could be a starker contrast with ecclesiastical opulence and indulgence? In the squabbles and struggles for the acquisition
of land, the secular lords were given a stick to beat abbots with fat lands, whatever
they may have thought or cared about Cathar beliefs and principles.

Raymond V implored Pope Alexander III to intervene:

> It has penetrated everywhere. It has thrown discord into every house, dividing hus-
> band and wife, father and son, daughter-in-law and mother-in-law. Even the priests
> have succumbed to the disease. The churches are empty and falling into ruins. For
> myself, I am doing everything possible to arrest such a scourge, but I feel my
> strength to be unequal to the task. The most influential people in my country have
> allowed themselves to be corrupted, the masses have followed their example, and I
> neither dare nor am able to suppress the evil.

The papal legates sent in response (1178) were greeted with catcalls in Toulouse.

Those most affected were the middle class and lesser nobility and some of the
artisan corporations, a thoughtful urban element. The Cathars were well enough

organized and disciplined and widespread in the south to have made a bid for independence with a Catharist church feasible under Raymond VI. However, the Cathars eschewed violence and asked only for freedom to preach and to worship in their own way, which they enjoyed in the south. This in itself was a sentence of death, with its threat to a Church that maintained dominion by violence.

For ten years (1198–1208), Innocent tried to redress the situation by sending missions. He recognized that the southern prelates were too corrupted by their temporal interests to sustain and enforce the authority of the Church. His first mission used a group of Cistertian monks with papal authority and the title of legate, many of them natives of the region. They tried to impress and attract by adopting the pomp and display characteristics that played into the hands of the Cathars. In 1206, Dominic Guzman, whose piety and learning had distinguished him at Palencia, where he studied, and who had devoted himself to missionary work among the Muslims of Spain, came with his bishop to redeem the heretics. They were as ascetic and humble as the Cathars, and advised the legates to show the same example. Dominic continued his labors for years and founded the first chapter of his preaching friars at Toulouse from those who had associated themselves with him. Innocent instituted the initiative, like that of Francis, within the Church. This approach of Dominic, parallel with that of the Cathars, did not, could not, make any difference. His immunity, wandering unharmed among them for years, showed the seriousness of their nonviolence. Their widespread obdurate persistence was on a scale that threatened the uniformity of the orthodox Church, the existence of Christendom. When the most high-handed of the legates, Pierre de Castelnau, was murdered, not by the Cathars, things came to a head. Preaching had had little effect. Temporal authorities in the south were no help. Innocent decided on a crusade, and his legate was commissioned to preach it throughout the king of France's territory. Practicing "wise dissimulation," they were to isolate Raymond VI , and not strike him down until he was virtually defenseless. However, in 1209 the "army of the faith" besieged Beziers, whose inhabitants refused to hand over their Cathars. The city fell, and the inhabitants were exterminated. Terror did not end the crusade, which from that point lasted twenty years, with the usual vicissitudes and destruction, not least the burning of Cathars by the hundred. Simon de Monfort, earl of Leicester, was the able and devout commander of the crusade, after some hesitation, until his death in battle in 1218. Under his command, the southerners were consistently defeated, but in his hands toward the end, the religious character of the crusade was encroached on by a resolution of the north to conquer the south, to make de facto the de jure jurisdiction of the kings of France. This phase of the conflict centered on Toulouse. The southerners were roused to expel the French as foreigners and barbarians. They were an occupied country. Raymond VI recovered Toulouse in 1217. But they were alone. Instead of besieging the city, the royal troops ravaged the countryside systematically. Negotiation was forced, and issued in the Treaty of Meaux (1229), which concluded the crusade with virtual capitulation by the count of Toulouse. What the Church had gained under three popes, Innocent III, Honorius III, and Gregory IX, in this twenty-years war tended more to the profit of the French monarchy than to extinction of the Cathars. Depending necessarily on secular arms the Church had strengthened it.

At the very time of the Treaty of Meaux, the Church devised its own instrument of control by establishing and organizing the Inquisition. Everything remained to be done in the suppression of heresy. Gregory IX gave the mendicant orders, especially the Dominicans, the task of a spiritual police. The bishops, since orthodoxy was established, had been charged with rooting out and suppressing heresy. The secular authorities were expected to do the same, since conversion of the northern tribes by the Roman Church. The Inquisition was specially instituted under direct papal control because these regular methods proved insufficient, and because the Cathars continued to offer opposition. A persecution ensued, using secret agents, spreading distrust, which encompassed abettors and sympathizers and included exhumation and public burning of the remains of those posthumously denounced and condemned. Resistance came from burghers and corporations in the towns. Inquisitors were killed, including a massacre of eleven at Avignet, with complicity of Raymond VII. The resistance was inevitably doomed, and with Raymond VII's death the hopes and aspirations of Toulouse were extinguished.

There is a detailed study of Cathars and Catholics in the village of Montaillou, 1294–1324. This village in the Pyrenees was the last to actively support the heresy in southern France, finally wiped out in the last years of this period. The first chapter enumerates the four powers that conjointly directed the lives of the people of the area: the local lord and his bailiff; the Inquisition; the bishop; and, remotely, the king of France. Their unity constituted oppression, whenever the common people challenged religion as heretics or the tithe system as taxpayers.

> People who felt they were being watched used to move about at night; they would be careful what they said; both in towns and villages they were afraid of talking too much, of being caught by the jaw (*capi gula*). Men walked sword in hand and whistled softly to attract the attention of an acquaintance. A man would throw a pebble on the roof or against the shutter of a friend's house so that someone would open the door. The apparatus of power was not a "police" apparatus in the modern sense of the term, but for anyone who did not keep absolutely to the straight and narrow path it was a Kafkaesque world of spies and betrayals.

The study is a portrait of a dominant family, the curé, shepherds, and others, and a sociological description of the conditions of the place and the times.

The uniformity of Christendom as a common civilization throughout Europe implied a rigid orthodoxy (Nicaea and Chalcedon) enforceable if necessary by totalitarian power. There were three forms of that power, without any breach of orthodoxy: the eastern half of the Roman Empire in Byzantium; the Holy Roman Empire of Charlemagne, Otto I, Frederick I, and the Hohenstaufen dynasty; and the "Christian Republic" of Innocent III, with a territorial base in Italy and supreme authority of the pontiff over European states, principalities, and independent cities. In pursuit or defense of its claims, each of these powers was involved almost incessantly in wars that could hardly be won. When that was made manifest, the Middle Age and Christendom had come to an end. Christianity remained the generally professed religion in Europe for at least four centuries, but not with uniformity of doctrine and practice, nor with common assumptions. This opened the door of obedience to the intrusion of questions.

## Nation States

As masters of the sea, the Scandinavian war chiefs pursued profitable careers of violence and destruction wherever they could force access from shores or rivers. However, by the early eleventh century there were Christian rulers in Norway, Denmark, Poland, Bohemia, and Hungary. This did not necessarily mean a renunciation of depredation, as it had not with the Goths and Christianized tribes that settled on Roman territory. Western Christendom was being founded by rulers and peoples who had most threatened it in the tenth century, and helped to bring about the disintegration of Charlemagne's empire. "Having destroyed large parts of Europe in the ninth and tenth centuries, they proceeded in the eleventh and twelfth to play a massive part in the formation of European politics and civilization" (Southern). It was a pattern seen in antiquity.

The making of nations and states was also the making of "nations" and "states"—and "Europe": that is, the use of these terms in recognition of new facts. These developments were not going on everywhere at the same rate. Recognizable features of "modernity" were present in Frederick II's court and kingdom of Sicily; William of Normandy imposed centralized control on his English conquest, which lapsed into feudal anarchy under Stephen. Southern France under the counts of Toulouse was a feudal fief more "advanced" in culture, nationality, and statehood than the suzerain in the north. Forms of unity, and leagues and alliances, appeared and disappeared in a climate of rivalries and aggression. Nationhood and statehood were to be the backbone of that order in Europe, but not everywhere there; this was not a necessary development, nor necessarily a "progressive" one. But in Spain and Portugal, in England and France, and later in Holland, this was their road to to power; and in one sense these were the "history-making" powers.

The foundations of statehood go back to an early period in England. Nationhood means little until the mid-fifteenth century. Clearly, in an "heroic age" when war leaders are mobile, seeking treasure, cattle, slaves, and other such forms of plunder to reward themselves and their followers, they are far from founding a state. The treasure ship discovered at Sutton Hoo (British Museum) is evidence of the kind of goods sought with fame and name by these marauders. Even when converted, they assimilated Christianity to their accustomed lifestyle. Perhaps it is not too much to read into Bede's account of Bishop Wilfrid the style and self-confidence of an aristocrat of the time, an erratic career, and frequent grants of land to found monasteries: one order is being converted by the Church into another.

With settlement, and the demarcation of defensible frontiers, there is a territorial foundation of a state. This territorial thinking is evident in England in the eighth and ninth centuries, conspicuously in Mercia, the first to be organized by division into shires and hundreds, with their courts and sheriffs, and the procedures for *geld* and *fyrd,* taxation and armed service. Land, not treasure, is the wealth sought and granted, for mutual benefit on conditions stipulated in charter records. Coinage is minted to facilitate trade. All this is in place when Wessex under Alfred becomes the nucleus of an English state. Christian as he is, he follows Solomon (I Kings 5:13–14), dividing his magnates into three groups, each of which spends a month at court and two months on their estates. Ecclesiastical unity had been at least foreshadowed when in 669 the newly consecrated archbishop of Canterbury, Theodore, visited all "the tribes of the Angles," and "was the first archbishop whom all the English church obeyed" (Bede). The administrative institutions established are reinforced and extended by Alfred's successors, until England is examined and tallied in Domesday Book.

The Norman conquest of England may be said to be the most pregnant historical event in Western Europe until the Reformation. A remarkable duke of Normandy becomes king of England, not merely, if mainly, by conquest. His enterprise is blessed by the Church; he claims legitimacy, as nominated by the last legitimate ruler, and accepted by the magnates, Norman of course, English though reluctant. He is consecrated at a coronation that endows him with the viceregal authority of Christ in his English dominion, in which he will cooperate fully with Archbishop Lanfranc as protector of the Catholic Church. With the undisputed right and panoply of a medieval king, his authority over his feudatories as duke is exceptionally strengthened, so that to some extent he is able to remodel the feudal polity. Moreover, he is not alone. He is one of those many Normans who in the late eleventh century had crusaded on their own, with the blessing of the Church, conquering Sicily principally, but with interconnections that stretched from Britanny to the Taurus. William's status as king gave him crowning prestige in this far-flung Norman endeavor. His rule, and that of his successors, involves England territorially with the continent, with "Europe."

However, "1066 and all that" was not necessarily "a good thing." For the English, it was "a bad thing": 92 percent of English magnates were dispossessed; the peasants, nine tenths of the population, were exploited by their Norman lords; literature and the arts had scant regard from the uncultivated invaders; women lost the respect they had enjoyed. Moreover, the "Conqueror's" initial success at Senlac took four years of destruction, devastation, and massacre. Historically, all this may rate no more than a footnote. Historically, what was "a good thing" was what William did not do. He did not do what the English had done to the British. The inhabitants of Britain may therefore be called "British," but they are thought of by the French as Anglo-Saxons. That is, William did not drive out the population into inhospitable regions. The language was not superseded by Norman French altogether. Preeminently, English institutions were not abolished, but adopted and adapted. To think of it as a change of succession comparable to the coming of William of Orange would be going too far. Perhaps it was an unnecessary diffusion and transfusion of blood. Norman "blood" was renowned for restless, exploitive energy. The Normans lived on others, with a mastery that turned to their use what they found. They were Vikings, not Vandals. William was an able and intelligent primitive, Henry I was more sophisticated, and when it comes to the Angevins with Henry II in 1154, the sequel to the conquest begins to characterize its political shaping of the state.

With the land in new hands, a new deal was possible. Domesday shows nearly half held directly by the king and the Church, most of the remainder concentrated in the hands of the few greatest Norman families closely associated with William in Normandy and identified with his enterprise. From an initially weak position, he had had to scheme and fight for his ascendancy in Normandy. His conquest gave him the opportunity to forge a tight feudal polity in his kingdom that would also strengthen his hand in the duchy. The grants of land largely coincided with the English fiefs, scattered as they were, with blocks allocated to the most dependable as tenants-in-chief, on whom was imposed military service, with a fixed quota of knights. Disorders arose when there were many armed knights around in the retinue of a magnate; and these were reduced till the quota was supplied mainly by enfeoffment—whereas in Normandy and elsewhere the enfeoffment practiced raised far more than the number due to the suzerain. This enlistment of his magnates in defense of the realm, supplemented as it had to be with English troops and mercenaries, saved William's dominion during almost twenty years of continuous warfare. His administration had to be an aristocracy organized for war. Mainly a defensive war within frontiers, nevertheless it almost renewed the union of a war leader and his companions in their raids and forays.

Under the English kings, sheriffs, landlords who acted in their area as royal agents for the administration of justice and collection of taxes, had been of second rank. William appointed as sheriffs his tenants-in-chief, and when cases of special importance were to be heard, he would send a special representative in his own place to conduct it. Domesday shows that sheriffs who were predatory or corrupt were disciplined and forced to make restitution. There was no independent state; the king's household servants, chaplain, steward, butler, served also in the conduct of public business.

The reorganization of the English church by Lanfranc with William's support was perhaps the most direct and lasting outcome of the conquest. The prelates had been replaced by Normans, and as large landowners this endowment of "religion" made them also feudal barons holding fiefs for military or financial supply. This reinforced a prevalent tendency that fostered the disrepute of the medieval Church. Sees were redistributed, and the authority of the bishops enhanced, subject to the discipline of their metropolitan. The primacy of Canterbury was reaffirmed, on the precedent of Archbishop Theodore, against the objection of York, and without waiting on the consent of the pope. A council at Winchester ordered all bishops to appoint archdeacons (as in Normandy), a key administrative appointment in the hierarchy. Where there had been a collegiate service of parishes, a priest was installed. In such respects, the English church in Norman hands became the Anglican church. This was confirmed for practical purposes in its relations with the papacy, through William's relations with Gregory VII, the Hildebrand who was asserting papal supremacy. William refused his demand for fealty, continued to make ecclesiastical appointments, and suffered no penalty. The Normans were regarded as crusaders for the cause, holy warriors. William's invasion had papal blessing. Above all, Gregory had respect for William's character and conduct, and wrote to his legates: "Although in certain matters the king of the English does not comport himself as devoutly as may be wished, nevertheless he has neither destroyed nor sold the Churches of God; he has taken pains to govern his subjects in peace and justice. . . . In all these respects he has shown himself more worthy of approbation and honor than other kings."

The Norman Conquest consolidated the government of England. Crown and tenants-in-chief were greatly strengthened, and brought into close association and mutual dependence, a fusion of central and local authority. The juridical theory that a whole land is vested in the crown, to be leased on contractual terms, and may be resumed by the crown, has never been more closely justified in practice than in William's legitimate inheritance of England, and his disposal of it.

The Anglo-Saxon Chronicle, which ends with the accession of William's grandson, Henry II, in 1154, records the state of the England that he inherited: after seventeen years of disorder, there were no crops, and "men said openly that Christ and his angels slept." Henry's two main concerns were his French dominions and complete restoration of *avitae consuetudines,* the continuity of rights and privileges comprehended in his grandfather's system of government. He was duke of Normandy, count of Anjou, and (by his wife) duke of Aquitaine, that is, more than half modern France. The attempt to maintain this estate over the next century put off unification of the British Isles until the end of the thirteenth century, at great cost. On the home front, by his personal qualities, with what support he could count on, Henry rapidly restored and consolidated the authority of the crown and systematically reorganized the government, with the purpose of delegating power without losing control, which would facilitate absence abroad in his French dominions. The Conqueror had vested local authority in the sheriff, who was a tenant-in-chief. Henry relied on the cooperation of lesser landlords and ordinary freemen, working to procedures laid down in precisely formulated instructions ("writs"), and administering a "common law" that expanded customary law with cases as they came before and were decided by the justices. In this and other ways, without a bureaucracy and without delegating royal authority to lords and prelates, Henry secured executive action for his authority throughout the land at local level to the satisfaction of the need for practical definition and delivery of justice, as well as, of course, the collection of dues.

Subjection to law of Church and magnates issued in the assassination of Becket as archbishop and the rebellion of 1173. The feudal risings were suppressed, and Henry completed his judicial work in assizes, which in some aspects anticipated statutory law. The Assize of Arms (1181) was an ordinance that revived the old obligation of all English freemen to serve in the fyrd. This gave Henry leverage over the feudal levies; mercenaries were unpopular. The assize required all freemen to provide arms suited to their rank and means. It would be renewed in Edward I's Statute of Winchester. One of Henry's most beneficent reforms was the Grand Assize, his ordinance that substituted inquiry from those well enough informed to give sworn evidence before a jury, instead of trial by battle in disputes on possession of a freehold.

Henry got his positive way in the land, as had his grandfather and great-grandfather, although he reversed the Conqueror's policy in a main respect, reverting to the English precedent, and bidding for English support. An autocrat does not rule by bluff, outside the fairy tale. A medieval king was fairly safe if he complied with general expectations and could count on some respected pillar of physical support. Political stability and security mainly depended on relations between king and barons. Their expectations of the crown were framed by the disposal of patronage, the practice of consultation, and military leadership, with its opportunities of plunder or promotion. These were primitive conditions, to which Edward III and Henry V conspicuously catered. The first two Henrys and Edward I were primarily concerned with a more broadly based order of expectations and grievances, in which there would be popular support for the deliverances of a forceful king. Henry III, Edward II, Richard II, and Henry VI were involved in conflicts and deposition when neither order of considerations prevailed.

The autocratic government of a forceful king was apt to be arbitrary. When King John and his allies lost the decisive battle of Bouvines to Philip Augustus, and with that most of the Angevin empire, an alliance of about one-third of the barons took advantage, renounced allegiance, and captured London. The archbishop negotiated a settlement, that is, a settlement of outstanding grievances. Magna Carta, with its sixty-one clauses, included provisions to remedy all immediate complaints. When it was confirmed the following year by the regent for the boy Henry III, many concessions were omitted and the clauses reduced to forty-two. When confirmed for the fifth time in 1225, there were thirty-seven clauses, and this came to be its accepted legal form. The initial concession and the repeated confirmations implied recognition that the crown was under the constraint of law. Magna Carta, as symbol and in law, anchored the rights and liberties of the subject. Habeas corpus, the writ against arbitrary imprisonment, issued from clause twenty-nine, although its enforcement and reinforcement entailed a long and stormy political history. Magna Carta did not inaugurate the practice of constitutional government. Rather, it initiated the notion of government as a legal contract. The question of the contracting parties, and in that sense the constitution of the state, not the government, was not yet in question.

The makings of that question are discernible under Edward I. Meanwhile, it had been foreshadowed in the Provisions of Oxford (1258) forced on Henry III by the barons. Magna Carta was without sanctions, and depended on the king's good faith. Henry III refused to be accountable, dealing with the realm as his personal estate, although strengthening the structure and promoting the efficiency of centralized government. The Provisions of Oxford imposed a baronial council to meet three times a year, with the appointment of the three chief royal officials in their hands. The Provisions of Westminster followed the next year, when the barons appointed a commissioner to hear complaints in every county against sheriffs and royal officials as a basis for reforms of the common law. They could thus claim to speak not merely in defense of their own interests, but mainly "for the community of the realm." Civil war ensued, ending in 1267 with the Statute of Marlborough, which reaffirmed the Provisions of Westminster and the 1225 version of Magna Carta.

Edward I had helped formulate the Provisions of Westminster. It has been said of this period that the worst king (John) and the best (Edward) were exactly alike: both were out to increase and enforce their authority. The conventional wisdom may be said to be at fault in a kindred main respect: constitutional advance did not march from strength to strength from Magna Carta to the "model" Parliament of 1295 by alliance of the magnates, gentry, and bourgeoisie. Representation in the council was not demanded by gentry and bourgeoisie, but imposed by the king for his own purposes, and resented as an imposition. Edward overrode feudal distinctions, to subject all his subjects to his authority, to monitor local affairs, and to rationalize his revenues—effectively continuing the policy of Henry II. The nucleus of a parliament he instituted as an instrument of control did become the challenge to the royal prerogative, one of the frequent ironies of history, but that lies outside the Middle Age. Within that period, at the end of the fifteenth century, when the wars of the nobility had issued in mutual reduction, the Tudor inheritor was confronted by two centuries of institutional practice it was too late to reverse.

Four knights represented a county when the king's court needed information for inquests into local government or in pursuance of complaints brought against sheriffs; they might present petitions from their constituents to remedy wrongs "that cannot be remedied by the common law." The Parliament of 1265 was the first in which knights of the shires and burgesses of the towns took part at the same time, without any idea of a "house." They were summoned for a particular purpose, and were not in the constitution of the council. In 1294, the king was in desperate need of funds, involved in war with France, a revolt of the Welsh, and a threatened rising in Scotland. The Parliament of 1295 was called "model" as marking the definitive entry of the "communities of the kingdom" into an assembly of the council. The only difference was that here all the elements in the national life previously consulted were brought together at the same time. At a Parliament of 1301, the king sent a "bill" that made the magnates and prelates responsible for enforcement of measures they wanted. Their response was "a bill from the prelates and leaders of the realm delivered to the lord king on behalf of all the community," and presented by a knight in token of this. This was a bill of twelve articles enumerating reforms as a condition of an increase in supply. This early sign of what was to come was deeply resented by the king.

There were five groups in a full parliament of this time, in addition to permanent members of the council: bishops and abbots, earls and barons, inferior clergy, knights, burgesses; members of the first two groups were summoned personally, others through bishops and sheriffs. The business was organized by the judges and officials who were a permanent part of the council. In the Parliament of 1305, about 450 petitions had been received and classified by a commission of four; special commissions were then appointed to examine the several classes over the three weeks of the meeting. The knights and burgesses presented and defended the petitions of their constituencies. In time, the assembly of local representatives would draft collective petitions to be presented by the whole body, the knights of the shires having detached themselves from the magnates to deliberate on a footing of equality with the burgesses of the towns. Royal approval would make such collective petitions law. Royal summons of the first two groups of the five mentioned above constituted the House of Lords, before actual severance; the lower clergy withdrew to Convocation, contrary to royal intention, leaving the Commons composed of knights and burgesses. By such steps and half-steps, the houses of Parliament took shape in the Middle Age; it was an important instrument of government by the time of Henry VIII, when it would begin a short period of momentous change that would put Parliament in the field against the king.

The "public interest" is problematic, and often used to cover the furtherance of sectional interests so that it has sometimes been denied any reality. The "state" as a shared interest, if not equally shared, may be thought of as the institution of a public interest, by which the basic security and stability of a society is organized. Movement from the land as a royal estate administered by servants of the household to organization of estates of the realm to represent sectional interests in a common assembly for public business, as it took place in the Middle Age, not only in England, may be said to have carried the transformation of a kingdom into a state far enough to have been irreversible.

"State" implied the "rule of law," and there was still a very long way to go in terms of accountability, both in the making and in the application of law; but history had endowed the nations that took this course with a political source of both conservative and radical traditions. They must be dubbed the "nations that took this course," for the state was not an international institution like the Church. It was national in the sense that the "community of the realm" was represented in the assembly. But when the king of England was also duke of Normandy, count of Anjou, duke of Aquitaine, or called himself "king of France' (Edward III), or when French was the language in English courts and halls, there was no coincidence of state and nation, and indeed neither state nor nation. But Normandy was lost, and Bouvines ended the Angevin empire. There was a withdrawal from Europe, to unify the British Isles, politically; Oxford University, modeled on Paris, was fully organized by the end of the thirteenth century, and Bracton, who was educated there, had written a systematic and practical manual of English common law; in the following century Froissart was in Britain, and the tourney; English architectural features appeared at Wells and Ely and Canterbury; Chaucer followed Italy and France in a national assimilation of new influences. That is, by the fifteenth century, the common European inheritance from Rome, through the Roman Church in the West, had been reshaped and differentiated in western and northern Europe (England, France, Spain, Norway, Sweden, Denmark) as self-conscious nation states with defined frontiers, a common language, and centralized government. These foundations were not secure, but they proved lasting. Germany and Italy, distracted by the fateful abortive quest for a Holy Roman Empire, were a momentous exception.

## Setbacks

It has been said that, "during the Middle Ages all Europe was a scene of anarchy." This is not true. There was this building of nation states just noticed. There was the literal construction of cities, and of monuments that made an architectural epoch. Nevertheless, foreign wars, civil wars, private wars, episodic revolts were in one form or another almost continuous, and immensely and cumulatively destructive. The Hundred Years War between England and France, followed by the Wars of the Roses, covered a period hardly broken from 1337 to 1485. Some estimate of negative effects is necessary.

At the end of the fifteenth century, it is thought, the population was probably lower than during the Roman occupation. Foundations and remains of Roman villas are commonly found on deserted sites, wastelands and woods, evidence that is indicative, not conclusive. The Black Death (1348–1352) reduced the population of Europe by roughly one-third, and had been preceded by famine.

In the twelfth and thirteenth centuries more land was brought into cultivation than at any time until the world wars of this century. Farming for the market was profitable, so that the greater landowners farmed their demesnes directly, producing grain and wool. With prices trebled and wages static, and with some 60 percent of peasants unfree in the manors of the midlands and southern England, peasants in these regions were on the edge of subsistence; many lesser landowners were in debt to the greater ones. Before the Black Death struck this high-farming community in 1348, there were dramatic climactic changes that brought crop failures and cattle disease in 1315, 1316, and 1322. Recovery was at first rapid after the devastation of the first three years of the plague, but further outbreaks (1361–1362, 1369, 1375) were cumulatively more debilitating, and brought a fall in population to nearly half, with no recovery until the end of the fifteenth century. By 1370 landowners found farming their demesnes for the market no longer profitable. Many hung on by exploitation of their tenants for a couple of decades. By the mid-fifteenth century the manorial system, where it had persisted, had collapsed. The wool trade had fallen to a quarter of its volume, and was replaced by export of cloth. Towns had multiplied. The fall in population did not necessarily mean a fall in the standard of living; and there were great regional variations. What was in common was a relative backwardness compared with north Italy, south Germany, and Flanders. The nation state in the making was not advanced enough to mean economic strength.

This was the variable situation at the time of the so-called Peasants' Revolt (1381), which has been linked with the Black Death. Insofar as the fall in population gave dependent laborers leverage to raise demands, there was a crisis. They were hardly in the position, however, to control the market, like the oil producers of the Persian Gulf in the 1970s. They were under constraint of a government that could and did both compel the able-bodied to work, and at the wage rates of 1346. This was formulated by the first Parliament held after the Black Death in the 1351 Statute of Labourers. This was of special advantage to the smaller county landowners. The statute applied to farm workers, building workers, artisans and all craftsmen, and transport workers. Enforcement failed to maintain the supply of labor at pre-plague level as designed, despite successful prosecutions. A petition submitted by the Parliament of 1376 shows something like a black market in absconding labor, together with banditry and mendicancy, and seeks their general suppression. Evasion of the statute was aggravated by growing discontent with villeinage, and cases of conspiracy to withhold services and collective resistance to distraint by the manor court. They were subject to their lord's court, forbidden access to the royal courts, and otherwise tied to the manor. A 1377 "Commons' Petition Against Rebellious Villeins" refers to the need "to avoid a danger of the sort that recently occurred in the realm of France because of a similar rebellion and confederation of villeins against their lords." This rising in the Ile-de-France of 1358 (the *Jacquerie*) was a consequence of what they had had to endure from an English invasion.

Humiliating defeats in the war with France, helpless endurance in the south and southeast of repeated French raids, ruinous expense of the war, desertions from the army, senility of the aged king Edward III, corruption of those in his entourage and their associates, brought out in the proceedings of the Parliament of 1376, these were the conditions that had brought to a low point royal authority and public morale. What made rebellion of some kind a probability was the imposition of a poll tax in a desperate attempt to meet the expense of the war. The popular hatred concentrated on John of Gaunt, acting as the king's deputy, came from a general belief that he was responsible for its introduction, which in 1377 was an attempt to spread taxation more fairly. Two years later a second poll tax revised the first, assessed now at a graduated rate. Corrupt administration resulted in a totally inadequate collection of the tax, and a third poll tax was granted in the Parliament of 1380. The chancellor (Archbishop Sudbury) had made a speech outlining the straits the country was in and the dire need for money to meet incurred and unavoidable expenses.

The assembly retired to consider what they had heard, and returned to ask for a specific sum to be raised, to be kept to the lowest practicable figure. The amount required was totalled as £160,000 sterling. The commons (knights and burghers) considered this amount intolerable, asked that it be scaled down, and how it was proposed to be raised. After some give and take with suggestions and counter-suggestions, the commons agreed to a general levy of three groats per person, male and female, of fifteen years and older, with means provided by which the better off in each township assessed on this basis should aid the less well off, according to means, so long as no one at all paid less than one groat for himself and his wife. Evasion of the agreed tax led to the appointment of commissioners to enforce collection. The principal persons charged with this enforcement were the sheriff and a royal sergeant-at-arms. The people of Fobbing, a township in Essex, consulted with two neighboring townships, and together refused to pay anything. They numbered a hundred or more, resisted arrest, and threatened to kill the sergeants-at-arms, who fled to London. At first the locals took to the woods in fright. Forced out by hunger, they went from town to town, inciting others to join them. In such a way, it seems, refusal to pay the tax set on foot what was not a "Peasants' Revolt."

Disaffection on several reasonable grounds, not least notorious misconduct of many lords and prelates, makes refusal to pay the tax understandable enough. Less so is the shocking conduct of the crowd in London and on the march there, with many more than a hundred arbitrary beheadings. Crowd theory is some help. Destruction of houses is an annihilation of social distances. "To the crowd in its nakedness everything seems a Bastille." "Of all means of destruction the most impressive is fire." There is a hunting crowd, out to kill, and knowing whom it wants to kill. John of Gaunt was with the army against the Scots, leaving Archbishop Sudbury and Sir Robert Hales as the prime targets. "A special type of crowd is created by a *refusal*: a large number of people together refuse to do what, till then, they had done singly." "Revolutions are times of reversal; those who have been defenseless for so long suddenly find teeth. Their numbers have to make up for the experience in viciousness which they lack" (*Crowds and Power*, Elias Canetti, 1960). The first two types of crowd behavior clearly apply to this revolt; but was it truly revolutionary? It has been marginally claimed for the radical or revolutionary tradition, but is there historical justification for that? It was febrile, fragile, and ephemeral, and totally without gains; this is why it has no more than a mention in general histories.

The rebellion of June 1381 had an obscure background of riots in southeast England, and without a definitive end died out in the autumn, having involved fourteen counties and eleven towns. The outbreak started with two groups, one in Essex, the other in Kent, who eventually converged on Blackheath, on either side of the river, some fifty thousand from Kent, and a like but superior number from Essex. The young king, Richard, aged fourteen, decided to meet them, but was persuaded not to by senior counselors. The rebels then proceeded to London. They had asked the king to grant them the heads of John of Gaunt, their chief target, and fifteen other lords, including Archbishop Simon of Sudbury, the chancellor, and Sir Robert Hales, the treasurer. On their march to London, they had systematically thrown open the prisons, and engaged in a more desultory fashion in breaking into and looting houses and beheading persons. By intimidation, they enlarged their number by forced levies. In London, their principal target was the Savoy, luxurious palace of John of Gaunt, which they broke into and set on fire. Many other houses in and around Fleet Street were also set on fire. They went on to the Temple, which they ransacked for books and records to burn in the street. They proceeded through Westminster to Holborn in the same way. They had broken into groups, of which one went to the Tower where the king was with his entourage, and from where he had watched the raging flames from the Savoy and many other fires. The lords were at a loss to advise him what to do.

After an abortive attempt, with promises, to get them to go home, the king the next day met the congregation of them at Mile End. In the parley, they asked to be allowed to apprehend and deal with all those who had abused their office and behaved illegally. They also asked that all service should be voluntary and regulated by contract. The king made a qualified concession to the demands. Some then immediately proceeded to the Tower, dragged out the archbishop and those with him and on Tower Hill beheaded him, Sir Robert Hales, and one other. Foreigners, especially Flemings, were a special target, and were beheaded as fast as they could be found.

There was a second encounter the following day between the king and the crowd, this time at Smithfield. There the alleged exchange with Wat Tyler took place. The demand was for equal conditions for all, and to that end division of existing possessions, including not least those of the Church, but excluding the Crown. The king returned a temporizing answer. There seems to have followed a scuffle in which Tyler was killed, and both sides scattered. Resolution of the confrontation was effected by prompt action of the mayor of London, who had men from the twenty-four wards arm themselves and come to Smithfield, where "they enveloped the commons like sheep within a pen."

Cade's rebellion sixty-nine years later in 1450 seems closely analogous to the 1381 rising. The men of Kent marched to Blackheath, and with similar grievances. Perhaps attention should be turned to the parallel in the wretched state of the country, brought about by misgovernment at home and failure abroad in the war with France. Kent had been roused to take action by a royal threat of reprisals for alleged responsibility for murder of the duke of Suffolk. The rebels presented Parliament with their complaint under fifteen heads, of which the first is a disclaimer of responsibility for that murder by the commons of Kent; the other items formally specify the malpractices of which they complain. This was not a mob, but rather a delegation raised in due order, and including men of property. Cade, calling himself "Captain of Rent," defeated the king in preliminary skirmishes by superior tactics. Londoners opened their gates, and Cade took possession, and respected persons and properties. However, discipline broke, and excesses ensued that enraged the citizens. After a furious encounter, the rebels were offered a pardon and dispersed. Cade himself recruited a new force by breaking open the jails, but was in the end killed.

Wars were popular, especially in England with the "natural enemy," France, because the spoils of war brought profit, as well as honor and glory. The Hundred Years War began with Edward III's armed assertion of a claim to the French throne at the battle of Crecy (1346), which inflicted a crushing defeat on the French, and ended in 1453 with the ejection of the English from Gascony, their longest-held French territory. The war was not continuous, and ran a checkered course, mainly in two phases. The brilliant successes of Edward III and the Black Prince ended in the loss of their gains by the close of the reign. The war was renewed with vigor by Henry V, dominated by a fanatical determination to prove his kingship by bringing France under the English crown, and ended after his death with the loss of his expensive gains after the siege of Orleans had been raised by the intervention of Joan of Arc.

This protracted English enterprise was wholly misconceived, and politically barren. Henry V was extremely able as a commander and as a politician, but even at his level of blind determination and even if he had lived, there could not have been a possibility that the French would settle down under the rule of the hated English. In Gascony it was different. The duchy had been in English hands some two hundred years earlier, and good government had promoted the arts and social intercourse, commerce, sea transport, and an acceptable fiscal policy, so that there was general prosperity which tied the territory to England. The occupied north, for thirty years, was not governed; it was at the merciless disposal of the army that held it down. The march of war was to kill, loot, and burn. Military occupation was daily indulgence of the power to do what one would; lawless rule.

The English were generally thought of as possessed by an exceptional ferocity. Arbitrary cruelty and destruction continued for a generation at the hands of the English army in the occupied areas of northern France at that time. Apart from massacres and the incidental violations that afflicted any family, and lived in all memories, there was general ruin of the peasantry and the countryside. The only security was in towns and fortresses, the only cultivation what could be snatched under watch and ward immediately around such places, "very small and almost nothing in comparison to the vast extent of all those fields which stayed completely deserted, without a single soul to cultivate them." After eight years of occupation, the population of Normandy was halved by famine and emigration. With more than sixty garrisons stationed throughout, living on the country, there was misery to escape from, if at all feasible.

Henry's operations abroad were bleeding his own countrymen. "The seriousness of the king's financial problems can best be understood by appreciating that when he died the government would have to face a deficit of £30,000, together with debts of £20,000. This was against a total annual revenue of just over £56,000, inadequate for the crown's expenses in peacetime, let alone in wartime."

This was just the interim drain on resources. The war went on, with negative consequences at home as well as abroad. When it did end, the loss of France jeopardized the throne; and the loss of loot fomented the factious spirit that embroiled the country in the Wars of the Roses. England, which had taken opportunistic advantage of the feudal anarchy of France, suffered its own spell of feudal anarchy. The leading families had genealogical ties with the dynasty and rival claims. With the accession of Henry IV and supersession of Richard II, some six families of the large landowners assumed a larger share in the government, and it was their jealousies that precipitated the civil wars.

This was in no sense a civil war for the crown between the house of York and the house of Lancaster. Insofar as this may be a justifiable retrospective view, the conditions which brought it about should be recognized. These were the breakdown of effective central government under Henry VI, the end of a military feudal system for armed service to the state, superseded by pledged service of a greater lord for personal protection and advantage. This disorder, involving private wars, followed on the collapse of the king's order that had provided justice in the king's courts. With contempt for the law and victimization of lawyers and law enforcement officers, landowners with sufficient means deemed private war their prerogative, if they were able to maintain a retinue of retainers and terrorize a county in taking what they wanted, pursuing their claims, or safeguarding their gains. Sir John Fastoff left John Paston in his will Caister Hall, one of his principal properties. The duke of Norfolk wanted it, and contested the will by laying siege to it, and taking it (Paston Letters of September 1469). This was one of the less bloody incidents of the time. The duke of Suffolk and his men were rampant in the area, as Margaret Paston reports; and Sir John Fastoff said that the poor people of Norfolk and Suffolk "have lived in misery and great poverty by many years continued."

Richard, duke of York, was the greatest magnate in the lands he held. Yet he found himself in breach with the court, and appointed to the lieutenancy of Ireland for a period of ten years. He was owed a great deal of money from the king's treasury for his services in France, which the king could not pay, and had been driven to borrow and pawn to meet expenses; he was determined to get into the king's council, from which he was excluded by the influence of his rivals. Richard raised an army in the west Midlands to assert his claims, but the bid was abortive. He had intended to negotiate with the king from strength, but in confrontation was tricked into disbanding his army and arrested. The upshot was that he was isolated, losing even the Irish post.

The situation was suddenly transformed in 1453 when the king was made incapable by mental alienation. York was not invited to attend the meeting of the great council that was called, but the lords would not have him excluded. When the chancellor, Cardinal Kemp, died a few months later, and the king was still incapable, York was appointed protector, which he had been during Henry's minority. The king recovered. York and his allies feared their destruction was being planned, with the backing of the Percies of Northumberland. The council was to meet at Leicester, and the king was proceeding there with some two thousand men, when outside St. Albans they were encountered by superior force under York. Bargaining broke off in a clash of arms, a setting of scores that is counted as the first battle of the Wars of the Roses. The Yorkists were the victors, and Henry was under their control. A Parliament was called, to which the Yorkists invited those peers who were not partisans nor their inveterate enemies. An oath of allegiance to the king was taken by all, as a sign of unity that included an amnesty for the armed assault at St. Albans. The Parliament found time to initiate some reforms.

The most horrific outrage in the chapter of county crimes occurred at this time in the west country, with the deliberate and treacherous murder and plunder of Nicholas Radford, a distinguished lawyer and an old man, by the earl of Devon and his family, who occupied Exeter and continued their extortions. News of the outrages reached London, and the king's intervention was imperative. Parliament assembled, but the king was too indisposed to take part; again York was nominated protector. The clash of arms at St. Albans, of little significance in itself, nursed irreconcilable feuds. Henry, after York's second period as protector, favored him as chief councillor. However, Queen Margaret wore the crown, and she recognized that York in power was the obstacle to all she stood and worried for, the authority of the crown. She therefore sponsored his enemies, and the lines were drawn for civil war. Margaret played her cards by getting her nominees in all the key appointments in the administration. York's principal lieutenant in Wales, where he had substantial estates, Sir William Herbert of Raglan, repossessed by force two castles that had previously been taken in the disturbed state of the principality. This and other high-handed actions of Herbert were deemed a defiance of royal authority.

Relations worsened. At a meeting of the council in London in 1458, one of the servants of the earl of Warwick, York's principal ally, quarreled with a servant of the royal household. The guard set on Warwick and his retinue, and he escaped by fighting his way out. Believing this had been a plot to murder him, he withdrew to Calais. A royal army was sent to meet Warwick and York at Ludlow. York's party broke up without fighting, York escaping to Ireland, Warwick to Calais. York and his chief associates were attainted. Months later, Warwick, with Edward, York's son and heir, crossed from Calais with a force that met the king at Northampton. Betrayal of the king made an easy victory for the Yorkists, leaving Henry in their hands. They meant him no harm, nor disrespect, but were bent on control of the government and recovery of their confiscated estates. Two months later, York returned from Ireland, bent on more than that. He claimed the crown on grounds of legitimacy. To settle the matter, the lords decided that Richard of York should not oust, but should succeed, Henry of Lancaster. This did not suit the queen, who moved against York and ambushed him outside Wakefield. In the fierce fighting, he was killed.

York's allies had not supported him for any claim on the throne. However, the strength of the argument for his legitimacy made them ready to back his son and heir,

Edward, earl of March. After the Wakefield victory, the Lancastrians marched south, to be met at St. Albans by Warwick. He was attacked and overwhelmed. He escaped, but Henry was recovered by the other side. Instead of advancing on London, the Lancastrians retreated northwards. At the Yorkist Parliament in November, Edward was declared legitimate king. This was an act of self-preservation on the part of the supporters of York. Henry had returned, they would be out, according to medieval conventions by which the king was expected to choose his own advisers and officers. Edward sealed his election with a crushing defeat of the Lancastrians at Towton in Yorkshire. He went on to occupy York and Newcastle. Five months later Edward IV was crowned in Westminster Abbey. The Northumberland Percies made two more bids for the Lancastrians, suffering defeat at Hedgeley Moor and at Hexham in 1464.

Edward IV died in 1483. His brother, Richard, duke of Gloucester, was appointed protector of the heir, Edward V. A serious breach in the council between the queen's party and Richard issued in Richard's charging them with a plot against his life. On the alleged ground that Edward and his brothers were bastards, Richard was encouraged to take the crown, and did so. The queen's party then drew close to Henry Tudor of Richmond, who headed the Lancastrians, and who had been kept abroad for his safety because of his possible place in the succession. It was therefore on the field of Bosworth in 1485 that the civil wars ended, when some twenty-one thousand men were engaged in the last of twelve battles.

In the fifteenth century, strict feudalism as a system of government was obsolescent, and "bastard feudalism" mere anarchy. Even more decisively than in the Roman Empire, good government in the nascent medieval state waited on the fortune of a strong ruler. That fortune brought Henry VII in England and Louis XI in France at a time most fortunate for both countries. The development of Europe waited for a shift from exertion of maximum violence to "the tactics of power," a reliance on policy and diplomacy to manage security and stability, the ground of prosperity and easy government, and elimination of the vicious circle of unlimited violence and cunning, which war was in itself. Diplomacy had been a tool in the armory of the Conqueror or the warlord Henry V, used for defense or aggression. Diplomacy in the service of politics was a different art operating in another context. Such a distinction cannot be absolute, but is of great historical importance nonetheless. The shift at this time in the persons of Henry and Louis in England and France is a new orientation that turns toward political control of arms within the state, and a balance of power between states. There will be devastating wars in Europe in following centuries, not least the horrors of the Thirty Years War, one of the most baleful chapters of European history, but the perceptible tendency initiated at this time in the fifteenth century by Henry and Louis helped to ensure that the nation state in these countries would not be merely nor perhaps mainly a war-making machine.

# 10

# Evensong for Christendom

## Chivalry

The "Age of Chivalry" implies the centrality of a concept and a practice. The "Age of Faith" has a similar implication. Each denotes an order dedicated to the provision of a service at the center of the concept. The order denoted by the second is the "religious" who dedicate themselves to the direct service of God in continual prayer and praise, and are segregated to do so. The first denotes an order of "knights," fighting men who dedicate themselves indirectly to the service of God in the redress of wrongs and protection of the weak, and who cultivate proficiency in martial arts in order to do so. The vocation of the religious is realized in a particular religious order governed by an authorized rule; the perfection aimed at by all such orders serves symbolically and vicariously to fulfill what is due from all those men and women who profess the Christian faith. The knight governs himself by a code of conduct in which all knights are versed and by which they are judged. The religious are recruited by "vocation." The knight is destined by birth and connections to belong to his order. The two orders permeate the literatures and arts of the peoples of Europe of this time. Bracketed, they constitute the Middle Age.

Ideals, more often than not, are observed in the breach; they are tangential to the orb of history and belong to poetry rather than to politics. In spite of St. Francis's romantic imagination, and Pope Gregory VII's recruitment of knighthood to deliverance of the holy places, the collective presence of knights-at-arms in the field was about their own business of war and plunder. Edward III and par excellence his son the Black Prince, "the flower of chivalry," were stars in that firmament. Theirs were the exploits that earned the English the undying hatred of the French and their descendents on the ground. A nineteenth-century dictionary of English history soberly notes that the Black Prince "marched from Bordeaux through Languedoc, burning and

125

destroying the towns and villages, and converting the whole country into a desert. . . . On the breaking out of war once more between England and France in 1369, Edward took Limoges by storm, and mercilessly put to death all the inhabitants, without distinction of age or sex. . . . Though full of the spurious knight-errantry of the day, he was mercilessly cruel in his campaigns."

At home at this time of Edward III, errant knights from the swollen retinues of retainers were shattering the security and peace of the countryside, as described in the previous chapter. The towns did not altogether escape. In Suffolk, Sir Simon Pierpoint and his fellow marauders lay in wait for the merchants of Beccles "from day to day, so that scarcely any of them dared to go outside the town to any market." One of them who was set upon died later of his injuries; and the coroner heard no evidence from relatives, who were too intimidated to come forward. Other towns were terrorized in a similar way. In East Anglia, men-at-arms were riding about with banners, seizing persons and holding them to ransom as on a battlefield. Collectors of the king's revenue were killed and robbed. Sheriffs were intimidated by the highest magnates to pervert the course of justice when their retainers were involved in rapine. A petition to Parliament in 1371 sought permission for every man to fortify his dwelling, and for burghers to fortify their towns. Factions within some towns, sometimes maintained from without, practiced extortion. The general picture of callous brutality throughout society at home in the reign of Edward III is in the same tones as that of behavior of the armies in France. The point here is that this reign was the high point of influence of the ideas and ideals of chivalry.

There is no more ardent champion of those ideas and ideals in prose literature than Jean Froissart, who was equally familiar with aristocratic circles in France, England, and Flanders, and whose *Chronicles,* although not history in the broad sense, give us through his own first-hand contacts a closer realization of what chivalry meant for the aristocracy of his time than historians have time for. He writes to celebrate by name and deed the bravest knights.

An historian would briefly and impersonally describe the battle of Poitiers in terms of the posting of the English longbowmen, their striking disorder into the French attack, of which advantage was taken in a counter-attack by the English on foot armed with spears and axes, supported by a flank attack by cavalry. The heavily mailed French cavalry suffered severely, and with the king some two thousand prisoners were taken. At least from the beginning of the twelfth century, knights were generally dismounted on the battlefield, their horses held nearby so that advantage could be taken of enemy disarray or for pursuit. When invention of the stirrup made it possible for a heavily armored mounted warrior to couch a lance so that it was embodied by the pressure of his forearm in his charging horse, a medieval force of shock troops was introduced on the battlefield, tactically superior to infantry, and available only to the ruler of a feudal order. Indeed, that invention and the feudal order may be identified. However, when infantry were not armed with spears, axes, swords, but were longbowmen, able to drive their arrows into horses beginning their charge, and at a hundred yards to let fly a dozen arrows a minute by each man, the charge disintegrated in carnage and wild confusion. Edward I, who conquered Wales, employed

Welsh archers and developed the tactics that gave England supremacy in battle in the French wars. He used large numbers of skilled bowmen trained from boyhood and protected by men-at-arms on foot beside them. When the enemy ranks were thrown into disorder, the bowmen could advance with weapons for hand-to-hand encounters, along with the men-at-arms. When man and horse were armored with plate, the cost escalated and the knight armored cap-à-pie features later in tournaments rather than on the battlefield.

Froissart's description of Poitiers reflects these ground rules. The French king sends out three knights as scouts: "Ride forward, as near the English army as you can, and observe their countenance, taking notice of their numbers, and examine which will be the most advantageous manner for us to combat them, whether on horseback or on foot." They reported their estimate of "about two thousand men-at-arms, four thousand archers, and fifteen hundred footmen"; and they gave a detailed and accurate description of the defenses and formations. They advised attack on foot, with three hundred of the most expert and boldest excellently mounted. The dismounted men-at-arms were ordered to take off their spurs and shorten their lances to five feet. The inevitable happened: the horses struck by arrows wheeled round and threw their riders; the English men-at-arms "rushed among them as they were struck down, and seized and slew them at their pleasure." "To say the truth, the English archers were of infinite service to their army; for they shot so thickly and so well, that the French did not know which way to turn themselves, to avoid their arrows; by this means they kept advancing by little and little, and gained ground." When the English men-at-arms saw this, they mounted their horses, gave a shout "St. George, for Guienne!" and made for the French king.

It is not so much the course of the battle that Froissart is concerned with as the naming and behavior of a multitude of gallant knights. Fifty are named on the French side around the king. "King John, on his part, proved a good knight; and, if the fourth of his people had behaved as well, the day would have been his own. Those, however, who had remained with him acquitted themselves to the best of their power, and were either slain or taken prisoners."

A "career of glory in war" was the whole matter of chivalry. The Black Prince asked after the battle what had become of Lord James Audley, and was told he was very badly wounded. When the lord was brought in a litter, the prince embraced him, saying, "My Lord James, I am bound to honor you very much; for, by your valour this day, you have acquired glory and renown above us all, and your prowess has proved you the bravest knight . . . and to increase your renown, and furnish you withal to pursue your career of glory in war, I retain you henceforward, for ever, as my knight, with five hundred marks of yearly revenue, which I will secure for you from my estates in England."

In the code of chivalry, it was not success that counted most, but conduct in the field. In this respect, it might be deemed superior to the treatment by a *polis* of the failure of their competitor in the Olympics, or by some American high schools of the loss of a game. However, when war is the frame, the context does not make a reasonable comparison.

To end Froissart's account of the battle of Poitiers, "The English . . . were so laden with gold, silver, jewels, and great prisoners, that they did not attack any fortress in their march, but thought they should do great things if they were able to convey the king of France and his son, with all their booty, in safety to the city of Bordeaux."

Since a set battle was avoided as far as possible because of the calamitous loss to chivalry, the encounter of knights was staged in a passage at arms or tilt. This was more commonly on foot than is generally supposed. Froissart gives account of some of these in the wars with France, between English and French knights outside skirmishes and sieges. At Toury, a squire from Beauce came to the barriers, and cried out to the English, "Is there among you any gentlemen who for love of his lady is willing to try with me some feat of arms?" An English squire volunteered, and the match was arranged.

The challenge was, completely armed and mounted, to tilt three courses with the lance, give three blows with the battle axe, and deliver three strokes with the dagger. The earl of Buckingham heard of the combat, and said he would see it, suspending the assault on Toury castle. By the restiveness of their horses, the competitors missed contact in the first onset, and struck each other in the second only "by darting their spears." The earl then had the fight stopped, saying they had done enough, and "we will make them finish it when we have more leisure." They kept the French squire with them, giving assurance by a herald to the governor of the castle that he would be looked after and sent back safely if he survived. Next day the English marched away, and it was sometime later before there was leisure to finish the engagement.

> They met each other roughly with spears, and the French squire tilted much to the satisfaction of the earl; but the Englishman kept his spear too low, and at last struck it into the thigh of the Frenchman. The earl of Buckingham, as well as the other lords, were much enraged at this, and said it was tilting dishonourably; but he excused himself by declaring it was solely owing to the restiveness of his horse. Then were given the three thrusts with the sword; and the earl declared they had done enough, and would not have it longer continued, for he perceived the French squire bled exceedingly: the other lords were of the same opinion.

The French squire was disarmed and his wound dressed. The earl sent him one hundred francs, with leave to return in safety to his garrison and a message that he had acquitted himself much to the earl's satisfaction.

It should be said of Froissart that although he fully shared the class attitudes of a hierarchical society which separated the gentleman as a person of quality, on which chivalry was founded, he did not lack compassion for the helpless victims of a merciless war. He writes of the massacre of Limoges:

> Then was there a scene of great pity, for men and women and children threw themselves on their knees before the prince, and cried, "Mercy, gentle lord!" But he was so incensed that he would not hear; nor was man nor woman listened to, but all were put to the sword, wheresoever found, and though they were in nowise guilty. Nor do I know how they had no pity for the poor folk, who were not in any case to have com-

mitted treason; but these suffered more than the greater people who had been guilty. There is no heart, however hard, that having memory of God, and being in Limoges that day, would not have been filled with tender pity over the great sorrow that there befell, for more than three thousand persons, men, women, and children, were delivered up and beheaded. May God have their souls, for they were in truth martyrs.

Such horrors are not recalled to show the barbarity of the Middle Age, for, indeed, they can be more than matched, and too readily, in our own time. They are the historical context in which chivalry, which was a civilizing ideal and influence, developed. It was the gradual moderation and modification of Viking ferocity, a lineage relevant to history though not to romance.

It can be said that chivalry began with the conversion to Christianity of the kings of the northern tribes by the Roman Church. First and foremost was defense of their frontiers by the warlords after they had settled down. Protection of the Church and where possible extension of the frontiers of Christendom were necessary employments of arms and fighting skills blessed by the Church as pleasing to God. Christian kings fought other Christian monarchs, or their lords were fighting their neighbors, and lawlessness became so extensive that some French bishops tried to ban war and form Leagues of Peace. The Archbishop of Bourges in 1038 ordered every man over fifteen to oppose anyone who took up arms, to the extent of taking up arms against him, which led to armed peasants headed by the clergy attacking nobles in their castles. Irresponsible disorder and destruction and deaths ended in suppression of the Leagues of Peace. Recourse was then made to proscribe warfare at certain times, much as the clergy tried to control sexual intercourse within marriage. The Truce of God prohibited fighting on Sundays and all the major feast days of the Church calendar. The ban was then extended to include Saturdays, the period between Advent and Epiphany, and between Ash Wednesday and the eight days of Easter. In Burgundy, the Church tried to permit fighting only between Monday mornings and Wednesday evenings. There was verbal approval of the Truce of God by many magnates, belied by nonobservance. It was not as practicable as the truce strictly observed by the Greeks for the conduct of their festivals.

If in the West the landed aristocracy was a warrior caste whose fighting propensity could not be curbed, it should be given meritorious scope by being focused on the enemy of the Church, the infidel. Dedication of their military arts and ardor to the service of God in this way would bring them the rewards and blessings of penitents and, if God willed, of martyrs. There was a manifest difference between the magnates and their knights who responded to this religious summons and the tribal leaders who had responded to opportunities of service with authority in the Roman political order; between, say, Louis IX (St. Louis) and Theodoric, even Charlemagne and Stilicho. War leaders who became servants of the Roman state were undertaking a professional job, one simultaneously military, diplomatic, and administrative. Lords who undertook service of the Church in a crusade entered a religious order. Indeed, they served in two orders. By birth, they were bound by the duties of their station, to their superior and to their dependents. By their engagement to serve in a crusade, they took an oath to fulfill an assignment that entailed great sacrifices. As professional fighters, they sought honor and glory for their performance from their peers, with the risk of shame and infamy. Religious military orders were formed by the Church. The Templars, Hospitallars, and Teutonic Knights were warrior monks. Endowed with lands and treasure by the pious, they were enormously wealthy. These were the model religious knights, as the other religious orders were models for the laity. Lords who "took up the cross" for a crusade proved themselves sons of the Church by that undertaking.

The historical account of why Pope Urban II summoned Christendom to the First Crusade tells a story of desperately needed defense. In 1071, the Turks were in Anatolia, and the regent of Byzantium had to act. At the battle of Manzikert his army was annihilated and he was taken prisoner. The mercenaries on whom he depended deserted before the battle, going over to the enemy; cavalry under a Norman leader from the West riding off. After that disaster, the empire was in total disorder for the next ten years until the advent of Alexius Commenus as emperor, an able and statesmanlike young general who in a reign of thirty-seven years restored order and engaged in piecemeal recovery of the imperium. The First Crusade was the joint enterprise of Alexius and Urban.

In 910, Count William of Aquitaine founded the Abbey of Cluny, which was made by a succession of distinguished abbots a pole of the Christian conscience in the West. They organized an extensive system of connections, and were particularly influential in the promotion and administration of pilgrimages as a privilege and a penitence. Jerusalem was the holiest of shrines, the most meritorious of pilgrimages. Pilgrims, who were of all ages and every class, were vulnerable, exposed to the hazards as well as the hardships of their journeys. Their protection was a vocation for the Christian knight.

Urban was a Cluniac, and like Alexius he was a man of outstanding ability who had retrieved his inheritance from weakness and peril. This included annulling the excommunication Rome had imposed on Alexius, and establishing cordial relations. At this time Palestine had become practically inaccessible to pilgrims because of shifts of power on the Turkish side. Urban had heard from Alexius of Turkish inroads that terrorized inhabitants and desecrated their shrines. He called the Council at Clermont, which lasted ten days. On the eve of its closure, he made an announcement. He coupled the plight of the East with that of pilgrims to Jerusalem, and appealed to western Christendom, rich and poor, to march to the East and join in an endeavor to protect the places that were holy to all Christendom. They should leave fighting each other to fight a righteous war, doing the work of God under the leadership of God. Urban was a great orator, and the crowd (it was a public session in the open air) surged in response: *Deus le volt!* In many first-hand accounts of the crusades that cry is almost a refrain. Whatever happens, exultant victory or catastrophic disaster, it is equally God's doing, to be enjoyed or endured with steadfast faith: all events are ordered by God's will.

The First Crusade was launched from its three main European sources in 1096 and reached its climax with the recovery of Jerusalem in 1099, a fortnight before Pope Urban died, without having heard the news. An army under Raymond of Toulouse started from Lyons, one under Robert of Flanders from Vienna, one under Godfrey of Bouillon from Ratisbon, all making their ways to Constantinople. When Alexius heard that whole Frankish armies were on the way, he was alarmed, knowing their propensities, their covetousness and unreliability. He had hoped for small companies of knights. He made preparations to provision and police them. As they arrived in Constantinople, Alexius moved them out of the city and its environment as soon as possible; the first comers had pillaged the suburbs, and even stripped the lead from the roofs of churches. It is estimated that from sixty to a hundred thousand entered the empire from the West between the summer of 1096 and the spring of 1097. Alexius, unable altogether to prevent marauding and attacks on some towns, managed on the whole to effect their smooth passage through the territory he controlled by providing supplies, and by policing their columns with his Petecheneg security force, mercenaries recruited from tribes beyond the Danube who had invaded Byzantium and been defeated; their unfailing obedience made them totally reliable. The Western allies saw the splendors of Constantinople and the elegance of its society with jaundiced eyes. The Greeks of the eastern empire endured the manners of the brigands who had come to their aid as patiently as they could, and without esteem, as they passed through their midst.

After defeating the Turks at Nicaea and Dorylaeum and an eight months siege of the key city of Antioch, the crusaders marched on to besiege Jerusalem. "As they drew near to Beirut the local inhabitants, dreading the destruction of the rich gardens and orchards that surrounded the city, hastened to offer them gifts and a free passage through their lands on condition that the fruit trees, the vines and the crops were unharmed" (Runciman). Jerusalem was heavily fortified. After the failure of their first assault, the crusaders withdrew to equip themselves with more scaling ladders and siege machines. With these preparations, and after fierce fighting, the defenses were breached, and the crusaders poured into the city, to massacre all in sight, or in buildings that were set on fire. "It was this bloodthirsty proof of Christian fanaticism that re-created the fanaticism of Islam" (Runciman).

Recovery of Jerusalem could not be secured until Palestine and Syria were conquered, which was completed in 1124 with the capture of Tyre. Meanwhile, Jerusalem was the capital of this new kingdom, and nomination of a ruler was sought from the crusading prelates and knights, most of whom were anxious to go home. Godfrey of Lorraine accepted. This great success of the First Crusade left Christendom with a kingdom to be protected against an embittered enemy with something to remember and to repay, and left east and west Christendom too well, or too little, acquainted with each other.

A line of castles was built at great expense to hold the kingdom. Under the leadership of Saladin, the Muslims inflicted a signal defeat on the Latin king, which exposed the castles without sufficient defense. This provoked the Third Crusade, in which Richard, Coeur de Lion, inflicted as signal a defeat on the Muslims (1191). However, war between England and France brought him back to Europe, and Jerusalem was left in the hands of Islam. The Fourth Crusade to recover the city was not merely abortive in that regard; it dealt Byzantium a blow from which it never recovered: it became Christendom's civil war.

Geoffroi de Villehardouin, who took a leading part in the crusade, recorded what happened in *The Conquest of Constantinople*. The author was marshall of Champagne, deputy for the province, among the top French nobility, a modest and sincere person, a devout Christian, and a clear-headed, forthright narrator of the events of the campaign. Those who had taken the cross consulted in conference on how to proceed, and agreed to commission six envoys to make all arrangements.

Ships were needed, and the envoys decided that Venice supplied the best facilities. They proceeded there, communicated their zeal to the Grand Council to such effect that the doge himself, although advanced in years, insisted on taking up the cross. The Marquis Boniface de Monferrat accepted leadership of the crusade.

> The Emperor of Byzantium had been blinded and ousted by his brother, another Alexius. The son of the dethroned man, still another Alexius, had escaped; and he was induced to appeal to the crusaders assembled near Venice. Agreement was reached that they would restore him, if he would then aid them in the reconquest of Jerusalem. In the course of the crusaders' assault on the city, the usurper fled, and his blinded brother was restored. A covenant had been entered into by the Prince Alexius that would place the empire under the jurisdiction of Rome, and supply a specified amount of money and men for the recovery of Jerusalem. The restored emperor was asked to ratify the covenant, which he reluctantly did "by oath and by charters with gold seals affixed."
>
> Alexius was now the new Emperor, and he proposed to the crusaders that they should remain with him to secure his hold on the country, where he was not popular, till Easter of the next year when he would be in a position to fulfill his undertaking of a summer campaign against the Saracens. There were many who were happy to make this delay a reason for breaking up the army and going home, but the devoted crusaders prevailed, and their chiefs accompanied Alexius on a tour of his dominion.

Having assured himself of the strength of his position, Alexius reneged on his covenant and a second siege of Constantinople ensued—after the French and Venetians had settled how they would divide the spoils and elect an emperor "if, by God's grace, they effected an entry by force into the city." They did, and they did as they had said. The imperial throne of Constantinople was to go either to the Comte Baudouin de Flandre or to the Marquis de Montferrat, the commander; the electors were divided. To keep both men and their troops with the army, it was agreed that the one of the two not selected should have the lands across the straits and the "Isle of Greece." Baudouin was elected, and the marquis asked for the kingdom of Salonika instead of the proposed lands "because it lay near the territory of the King of Hungary, whose sister he had married." The emperor granted this to the marquis, "who thereupon did him homage for it as his lord . . . no one was more open-handed and generous than he."

The Latins were then in the position of the Normans after Senlac: they had to conquer the land they had divided among themselves; it was war against the Greeks. And it was war on two fronts, because the king of Bulgaria, Johanitza, attacked the Marquis of Montferrat and ravaged the country; he formed an alliance with Theodore Lascaris, who at Nicaea had gathered around him the surviving aristocracy and higher clergy of Byzantium. The Latins made a two-year truce with him in order to concentrate on Johanitza. This respite allowed him, after the defeat of the emperor at Adrianople (1205), to build up in Nicaea a nucleus of Greek renewal, extended by John Vatarzes (1222–1254), who married the daughter of Frederick II ("Stupor Mundi") and secured his alliance. When he died, he left Nicaea in a far stronger position than the Latins who were still in Constantinople. The enforced simplicities of this exile had purged, with good government, the spirit of these Greeks. The Mongol invasion, trouble from Bulgaria, and defections delayed the recapture of Constantinople until 1261, when the last dynasty of the east Roman emperors was installed for the two final centuries of its existence, shrunk to a remnant in extent, but rising to the apogee of its cultivation of the classical tradition, to the subsequent incalculable benefit of Latin Europe.

If the crusades helped to produce a core of paragon knights capable of immense sacrifices for a cause they believed in, and apart from the involvement of the Fourth Crusade in tragic error which doomed the East Roman Empire, the whole enterprise was nonetheless fatally misconceived. What happened in Jerusalem with the triumphal success of the First Crusade inspired in Islam a fanatical hatred only to be appeased in a holy war, which echoes in the memory nearly a millennium later in our own time. The civilized intercourse and diplomatic agreements of Frederick II and the Saracens came to be regarded on both sides as shameful betrayals.

When the great and the good took the cross they deserted the home front where their primary responsibility lay. Neglect on that scale did insidious damage. Agrarian settlements in Europe were exposed at an early date to nomadic invaders from the steppes. The first were the Huns; the last were the Mongols in the mid-thirteenth century. Joinville has a chapter, "The Tartars," in which he relates King Louis's reception of envoys from them offering help in the conquest of Jerusalem. The king sent his own envoys back with gifts for the king of the Tartars, and they returned in due time with Tartar envoys and a letter from that king that celebrated the benefits of peace, but stated, "Since you cannot have peace unless you are at peace with us . . . we therefore advise you to send us a sufficient amount of your money in yearly contributions for us to remain your friends." Joinville had filled five pages about the Tartars with the usual medieval sandwich of thinly spread fact between crusts of wild hearsay. However, the "evil Tartars" really did believe in peace, and did establish a Pax Tartara, as Europe learned from Marco Polo's travels in 1299, since he was for many years the roving secretary of Kubilai Khan the Great, grandson of the redoubtable Chingis, and conqueror of China. He ruled from the Balkans to Indonesia, and brought prosperity with peace to China.

Chingis Khan (c. 1167–1227) created the Mongol empire by uniting warring tribes of Central Asia. When he turned westward, he conquered the Buddhist empire of Kara Khitai and the Islamic Kwarizimian Empire in two campaigns, which included a surprise maneuver that brought him four hundred miles behind the Kwarizimian lines outside Bukhara, by crossing the Kizil Kum desert, thought to be impassable. Chingis Khan and his sons and generals were masters of surprise tactics, and also of strategy, logistics and intelligence; their mounted archers carried a range of arrows for different purposes. They operated with highly mobile units of cavalry, each with its complement of artillery and engineers. They slaughtered, razed, and burned everything in their path, not out of cruelty or rapine, but in order to secure their rear in open country. Chingis had a force of ten thousand fanatically loyal guards. In an assault, he would drive thousands of prisoners or civilians ahead to give cover to his soldiers, whilst an artillery barrage of fire bombs and grenades were catapulted over their heads. In short, he introduced and exploited total war, which Europeans in time learned to improve on. Rommel and Patton were his students and admirers. The advance in twentieth-century armies is in arms, not in the art of war. The fighting over, Chingis Khan was ready to rebuild destroyed cities and reorganize ruined economies, with the help of the conquered civilians to whom he guaranteed security. He did not employ political murder, and rarely torture.

The Mongol conquest and destruction of the two empires around the Caspian Sea had been the triumph of their chief marshal, Subedei, a strategist of genius. After sufficient reconnaissance, he went on to plan the conquest of Europe. When they had conquered the western steppes, they would systematically take kingdom by kingdom to the ocean, as one by one they had conquered the provinces of China. He estimated that it would take eighteen years and require a colossal army. Conscripts from conquered territories (prisoners), rigorously trained, would recruit the strength of the army. They were already being used, and included several corps of Chinese and Persian engineers. The plan was entirely feasible. Kiev, the "mother of cities" to the Russians was stormed on December 5, 1240, and taken street by street, utterly destroyed and plundered. In the following year, leaving the Poles defeated at Cracow, the Mongols encountered near Leignitz a large army of Teutonic knights, German infantry, and remnants of the defeated Polish army. After this confrontation the Mongols crossed the Carpathians and joined their main body in Hungary, where the Hungarian king, Bela IV, with a large army, was routed, with a loss of nearly three-quarters. The Mongols then separated into raiding bands, before returning east to elect a chief khan on the death of Ogedei, son of Chingis. If they had advanced, Christendom would have been wiped out.

Islam was equally threatened in the Middle East. In 1257, Hulegu, the Mongol ruler of Persia, having demolished the "impregnable" mountain fortresses of the "Assassins," advanced on Baghdad, the cultural capital of Islam, and commanded the caliph to dismantle his walls and swear allegiance. The caliph temporized, and agreed to pay tribute. Islam was divided by sectarian disputes. The caliph supported the Sunnites, but his vizier was a Shiite, and sent secret messages to the Mongols, betraying the city's vulnerabilities. The city was taken and sacked and set on fire. Hulegu went on to take Aleppo, inspiring panic in Syria, with the sultan a refugee in his own empire.

In 1259, Mangku, the fourth supreme khan, died. With the news, Hulegu withdrew the bulk of his army to Azerbaijan, and postponed further operations. Islam was saved by the death of Mangku, as Christendom by the death of Ogedei. With fifteen grandsons of Chingis Khan, and a division of Mongol dominion under three khans, there was scope for jealous rivalry among able aspirants within the family.

The threat was lifted, the scars remained. Russia, Poland, and Hungary were severely mauled, as was Persia. Islamic culture was degraded and twelfth-century Arabic learning in the east stamped out with the destruction of libraries. Europe was awakened to the reality of the East. The abortive crusade of Louis IX had been caught up in Egypt in the coup that murdered the sultan, vividly described by Joinville. The Mamluk dynasty that succeeded was drawn from a military elite. They learned from the Mongols, and became the chief power in the eastern Mediterranean, putting an end to the chapter that had begun with the swelling fanaticism and fatal triumph of the First Crusade, a century and a half earlier. The Mamluks expanded into Asia Minor and conquered the Christian kingdom of Armenia. Their power was overtaken by the rise of the Ottoman Turks from a small emirate in northeastern Anatolia, checked by a resurgent Mongol empire under Tamburlane in 1402, but going on, with gunpowder weapons, to end the survival of Constantine's Christian capital in 1453. Their empire reached the height of its ascendancy on land and sea in the next century, and Europe was again threatened and in fear. That was beyond the Middle Age; gunpowder was on the side of newly formed Western armies, and would prove Europe's defense. The "devil's horsemen" of the East and the chivalry of the West had passed into history, and story, books.

## Courtly Love

Froissart was also a poet, at least in youth when he read romances addictively. His youthful heart had been ravished by a beauty, and he had been ready to obey and fear and love her with all that heart. The lady, however, had not been wounded. Froissart came to the English court to attend on Queen Philippa, who was from his own country of Hainault, and who treated him graciously and generously, sending him home with gifts and with instructions to come back. The young poet and rejected lover thus gained the contacts by which he became a chronicler. Frequenting the English court, he learned the conventions of the game of love as well as those of the other related game, the joust. Neither was necessarily Christian. Describing affairs in Africa in a campaign against the Saracens, Froissart remarks of a Saracen "knight" who had shown the most courage: "He was enamoured with the daughter of the king of Tunis, and in compliment to her, was eager to perform brilliant actions." Of course, he was likely to have read into the infidel's behavior the manners he was accustomed to. But in what sense had the sexual behavior of European knights been Christianized?

Whatever the priestly view, and it was slow in forming, they had to reckon with the perceptions and desires and ways of the kings and nobles they had converted. Pope Gregory in correspondence with Augustine in Britain had advised him to bring converts into conformity with the rules and discipline of the Church by compromise with and modifications of their own customs and practices. The concern of the Carolingian kings and their aristocracy in regulating their relations with women was primarily to safeguard the purity of their blood in the descendents who would inherit their property and the family honor. That was to be achieved by negotiated marriages between families of comparable status and achievement. Their belief in the transmission of qualities through blood make them like owners of bloodstock. The random distribution of libido, then and at all times, was another matter, to be accommodated otherwise. Marriage arrangements on such views could be settled by negotiation long before the puberty of the designated pairs. This order of things could only proceed when land-holding settlements had been established; preceding that, a man may have seized a woman of his desire or choice, with or without consent. The generation gap would in part reproduce that difference between the settled and the unsettled: the young, excluded and more hot-blooded, and brought up to hunting, against their elders, in possession and taken up with plans and hopes. In ninth-century texts "abduction" is the relevant crime, upsetting carefully planned arrangements. The cases include widows, nuns, wives, daughters (betrothed or not) as the prey of young men, working havoc in society—or with some "working" the system to get rid of a wife or deprive a sister of her inheritance. By the twelfth century, this propensity had been largely contained by the carefully controlled game of courtly love. Marriage was what had to be protected, from the point of view of the heads of landed families, and equally from the point of view of prelates of the church. Lust might be labeled a sin, and was, but nature had to be dealt with as well as souls.

Roman law recognized *connubium legitimum* between free persons of the same status (the "common-law" wife). Concubinage was recognized in canon 17 of the Council of Toledo in 398. In 829, the Frankish bishops recognized two grades of marriage: with one partner in due strictness and with concubines, as in the OT. A priest could not marry, but might keep a concubine. Pope Leo I: "A man who is married after having put away his concubine is not remarrying . . . not every woman united to a man is his wife." It was wise to leave custom undisturbed. The Church did forbid three things: repudiation of a wife, save for adultery; remarriage; marriage within the extensive prohibition of incest. In Frankish practice, illegitimate children were not concealed. They might, and generally did, live in their father's house. Moreover, this was on the grounds of consanguinity: their mothers were not servant girls, nor prostitutes; they were unmarried daughters of the gentry. Their offspring, bastards, were "noble by birth and by arms," with careers open to their class, not least in the church, if not as heirs, though that too might come their way if legitimacy had not provided otherwise. Plunder had included women; that had to be reduced and contained by the landed nobility for their own ends, as well as by the clergy for theirs. A wife duly introduced into a family was regarded warily because she was a woman; her sexual nature was dangerous, feared by the husband not only because of deception, but also because his virility might not be equal to expectations, which would prompt that deception. Males, old and young, clerical and lay, shared this distrust and contempt of women for their frailty. It was the right and duty of men of the family to discipline their women. That did not mean they were prepared to accept the Church's ban on repudiation, remarriage, and incest. Louis the Pious was willing to listen to the bishops, because he was set on reviving the Christianized Rome of Constantine. His brother, Charles the Bald, resisted with other princes the ban on repudiation and remarriage and thought the ecclesiastical definition of incest was too wide.

The pragmatism of ecclesiastical authority was giving way to asceticism. Jerome:

"To make love voluptuously and immoderately in marriage is adulterous." Peter Lombard reinforces that line of the Latin Father: "The act of procreation is permitted in marriage, but whorish pleasures are condemned." The monks were the "eunuchs" of whom Christ had spoken. Everybody knew that it was the wife who prompted and promoted lust, and that in the natural order it was the husband who had dominion, with the right and duty to keep that in check. Equality was equivalent to disorder in a feudal society, as in the Roman Church. Hierarchy was the foundation of all order, and its faithful observance was harmony in society as in the cosmos. The natural end of marriage was procreation. Hence, the Roman hierarchy laid down rules for the restriction of sexual intercourse.

In the language of the time, *amor* was physical desire, distinguished from *dilectio,* the discretion that in the relations between husband and wife preserved respect for each other and the purpose of their union. This was the ideal condition on which alone marriage could become a sacrament of the Church. From this position the Church was bound to condemn courtly love as scandalous play-acting, affecting to serve a lady with an allegiance a knight owed to his lord alone. The poets were to blame, inventing patterns of behavior that subverted decency and good order. All the same, this perversity did put a light bridle on *amor*; it taught lovers how to behave with elegance and good manners. Even a churchman might see its possibilities in moving from the physical to the spiritual. Most pertinent, it remained outside the strictly separate order of marriage and its proper constraints. Love was outside serious concerns. Libidinous pleasure defiled marriage, which was an order not a game. Courtly love siphoned off excessive ardor in a way that could be found acceptable.

The object of courtly love was most often a married woman, wife of the lover's lord, who was often his uncle. For propinquity counted, and boys were sent early to grow up in a noble household, apprenticed to their class. They served the lord as his son, and the lady, perhaps not much older, was a mother figure who might initiate him in skills other than fighting and hunting. In any case, as lady of the house she was in a position of superiority. If she as his lady was "lord" of her "vassal" lover—and words and gestures of the rites of vassalage were incorporated in the ritual of courtly love—that subverted the true order, as the Church had perceived. But a convention, once established, neutralized that subversion.

The royal court, preeminently, was an educational establishment, bringing up a young man under the prince's eye, and leaving him taught to joust, to hunt, but also understanding music and dancing and etiquette, with daily attendance at divine service.

Magnates offered boys of quality similar schooling in "the art of chivalry." Not only did they have training in appropriate skills by appointed staff, but mainly the example around them of how to dress and conduct oneself, and the opportunity to hear tales and anecdotes that illustrated high society's image of itself. At the end of the twelfth century, princes wanted to domesticate their knights, to attract them to their courts and keep them there, and therefore to provide an environment that would do that. Tournaments were organized not only as a sporting event for high society, but also for the education of young knights.

The approved, regulated form of the tournament was legally instituted in England by Richard I in 1194, and came from France, although the practice was known in England for some fifty years before that. Most young men of quality were obliged to seek their fortune, roaming from tournament to tournament, to display their prowess at serious risk of life, to win fame and favor, and perhaps a wife. "A youth must have seen his blood flow and felt his teeth crack under the blow of his adversary and have been thrown to the ground twenty times": that was the observation of a twelfth-century chronicler on the tournament as a preparation for war. But if war was its justification, it was not war, but a warlike sport, bound by conventions. The knights-errant who wandered from tournament to tournament would be sheltered for the night by country gentlemen, each with a household of "virgins."

> *So did they dally and embrace*
> *That Gawain her deflower'd,*
> *But she gave in with willing grace,*
> *And never said a word*

Courtly love, this interfusion of fantasy and cult, became a staple theme of medieval poetry, and by that door entered with Greek myths into the European imagination.

## A Poetic Landscape

Early in the twelfth century, Notre Dame in Paris was the musical center of Europe for the development of polyphonic music. The music was vocal and choral, words and music were interdependent: hence the lyrics; hence the prosody. This development within the Church, which followed Jewish practice in the synagogue, was parallel to the interdependence of Hero and Poet before the settlement of peoples, and not only in Archaic Greece: "poet" bespeaks the natural need for commemoration and celebration; it is also entertainment. That is, there were musical-poetic traditions within the Roman Church and in the northern tribal societies that developed diversely in religious communities and churches and in courts and halls, with some mutual influence.

Composers and performers of these songs are not necessarily strolling players going from court to court, from hall to hall, from town to town. They might well be academics at the university. Abelard, after his separation from Heloise, at her request composed a *Liber Hymnorum* for the use of her convent, and he composes a short cycle of his own. His sensibility and his subtle and inventive mind were as fruitfully engaged in this exercise as in his dialectic. Nor were such compositions necessarily religious, nor necessarily in Latin. Achilles accompanied himself on the lyre, singing the celebration of the glory of heroes. Many of the rulers in the German courts of the seventeenth and eighteenth centuries were accomplished musicians. There was a long tradition of comparable ability and interest at the highest level of dignity before and after the Middle Age, and it was not broken then.

The earliest known troubadour and one of the best was no less than Guillaume de Aquitaine (1071–1127), grandfather of Eleanor of Aquitaine, a great of the Provencal poetry. Already, the convention of "courtly love" as the theme of the troubadour seems of long standing, for Guillaume deliberately flouts it in a mocking jest that defeats expectations; in another he affects devotion to a lady that does not exist, in order to feel free to turn to one even more desirable, and at hand. In the love songs of Provence and Germany and of Spain and Italy, nature has her way, if not as often as the imposition of convention holds sway. Stylization may conceal, but many times there is frank exultation in and exaltation of the fullness of mutual love, as a human absolute pleasing to God. On the other hand is the ideal restraint of the courtly code, which informs the first part of the *Roman de la Rose,* translated by Chaucer, a code set out by Andreas Capellanus in *De arte honeste amandi* in the early thirteenth century. Outside the conventions of that cult, a gentle knight owed to all ladies the service of good faith, unfailing courtesy and consideration, and protection if needed—which did not banish the frankness of equality. The complexities of the matter occupy a large space in medieval poetic discourse. Courtly love was a game to engage a disengaged knightly retinue. Descants on the theme are generously provided by Chaucer: obviously in the knight and the squire en route to Canterbury, and in their tales, but also in "The Tale of the Wyf of Bath" and "The Frankeleyn's Tale," and even in "Sir Thopas," with "Here the Host stinteth Chaucer of his Tale of Thopas." "The Parlement of Foules" pursues the theme; the moral balade "Gentilesse" delivers a verdict in three stanzas, confirmed in context by Criseyde:

> *For trusteth wel, that your estat royal*
> *Ne veyn delyt, nor only worthinesse*
> *Of yow in werre, or torney marcial,*
> *Ne pompe, array, nobley, or eek richesse,*
> *Ne made me to rewe on your distresse;*
> *But moral vertue, grounded upon trouthe,*
> *That was the cause I first hadde on yow routhe!* (IV 239)

In short, Rome's Christianizing of the northern kings and their warriors spins connecting threads woven into strands that run through characteristic literature of the age, and stretch beyond it.

Poetry is fugitive and rare, even at the best of times, even in the best of poets. If that is too sharp, at least on that assumption one may say that there can be found in a medieval lyric that visitation of power, as well as in the stars of classical repute. Provence in the twelfth century is a source of inspiration for Germany and Spain and Italy, where poets are found fertile in metrical invention, rich in theme, with an authentic personal voice. If four centuries later Ronsard and the Pleiad come along to redeem the verse of their country from ballad-mongering or the mediocrity of Marot, and are able with fresh enthusiasm to adopt and adapt classical models for their inspiration, they can enlarge the vocabulary and enrich the resources of poetry, but they do not eclipse the stars in the medieval firmament. There is continuity, even in musical accompaniments. In England, continuity beyond the age is found in the earl of Surrey, seen by later generations as an anachronism, in reality touching the timelessness of poetry before him and after him, with communication between them.

If the medieval lyric in some examples is capable of this elevation, the narrative poetry and prose of the age has to be seen in a different perspective, because although it does not lack a personal accent it does not have the subjectivity, and in that sense universality, of a lyric. The cycle of King Arthur or the *Roman de Renart* survives as characteristic of the age, though neither is a picture of the age. They are, so to speak, subjective in a collective sense, expressive of an age they indirectly depict.

The production of printed books can be said most decisively to be the watershed that separates the Middle Age from the modern world: a technological advance, like the effective of use of cannon at roughly the same time. What were the books published by the new presses and chosen from the manuscripts that had been circulated through fairs and from hand to hand in various ways? The universities and the monasteries had largely controlled what had been reproduced; lyrical poetry was apart in being performed and heard, and much other material had a popular circulation of that kind. The new enterprise was developed by entrepreneurs with different interests and purposes. Whereas Froben in Basel and Aldus in Venice were interested primarily in scholarly works and the classics, Caxton's list in England represented what had been popular, which had long included a large measure of legend and romance. Gibbon complained of him that he was "reduced to comply with the vicious taste of his readers; to gratify his nobles with treatises on heraldry, hawking, and the game of chess, and to amuse the popular credulity with romances of fabulous knights and legends of fabulous saints." Of the ninety-eight titles published by Caxton, all in English, twenty-two were translated by him from French, Flemish, or Latin. Several were printed in response to a personal request. *The Order of Chivalry* was dedicated to Richard III. *The Faytes of Arms* was translated and printed at the request of Henry VII. In English poetry, Caxton printed *Canterbury Tales,* several other poems of Chaucer, including *Troylus and Criseyde* and *The Parlement of Foules,* Gower's *Confessio Amantis,* and several of John Lydgate's productions. These were the three ranking poets most read at the time.

Another contemporary English classic in his list was *The Noble Histories of King Arthur and of certain of his Knights,* written by Sir Thomas Malory, who appropriated his material from many sources, often French. In his prologue to the edition, Caxton takes Arthur as a national hero, and one of the nine worthies of the world: "In these playsaunt historieyes may be seen noble chyvalrye, curtosye, humanyte, frendlynesse, hardynesse, love, frendship, cowardyse, murdre, hate, vertue and synne. Doo after the good and leve the evyl and it shal brynge you to good fame and renommee." Leave out the moral, which is not in the text, and Caxton's blurb is a fair inventory of the ingredients of Malory's great collection.

Malory's extensive summary of the legends made King Arthur and the Round Table, the court at Camelot, and the enchanted and forested landscape between Tintagel and Joyous Gard on the coast of Northumberland the best known and most influential and representative literary production of the Middle Age. It haunted the poetic imagination.

The other cycle that must be mentioned as characteristic was in strongest and deliberate contrast to the knightly themes: the *Roman de Renart.* This too was not a single work by one author, but twenty-eight "branches" composed between 1174 and 1250 by anonymous French authors, a sequence later taken up and used by others as an available and efficient vehicle of satire and comment. So popular and effective were they in France that the word for fox (*goupil*) was displaced in French dictionaries by the proper name Renard. The Arthurian cycle is a model for parody and for narrative scale and tempo. King Arthur and his knights, Louis VII and his feudal nobility, Noble the lion and the animal seigneurs of his court, Aesop's lion and the beasts he rules and injures, are variations of one pattern. The court of Noble makes the *mise en scène* of *Renart,* where the action starts or to which it returns; behind it is the feudal order of Christendom. In this beast epic, Renart's escapades and escapes were given different turns by different hands, building his reputation for insolent conduct and on mastery of cunning duplicity, so that he cannot be contained and becomes necessary to the establishment. It is this concept of *renardie* that emerges, with a recognition that there is no hope of success in managing the affairs of this world without it. This goes much further than a parody of "curtosye," and anticipates the dilemma of Machiavelli's Prince. The light-hearted gusto and hilarity of the first episodes darkens in the sequels, until the use of Renart becomes in other hands and lands polemical, but with an influence over four centuries. Caxton printed his translation of a Flemish version.

A distinguishing characteristic that separates the Middle Age from all succeeding times is that many-sidedness is still within the compass of a single mind. This is seen incomparably in the literary output of Chaucer. The prologue to the *Canterbury Tales* brings on a parade of medieval types as the cast of a pilgrimage, twenty-nine figures, all memorable persons as well as representatives. Over the four days, they tell their tales, also representative because drawn from the range of actual medieval stories. There is *multum in parvo*; the choice of worthies in the "Monke's Tale," with the misty notion of them and their deeds, samples the eager reach of the medieval mind, without an informed grasp on hearsay lore:

> *The storie of Alisaundre is so commune,*
> *That every wight that hath discrecioun*
> *Hath herd somwhat or al of his fortune.*

Chaucer's representations are his own, and present a humanity that was his own, to join with that presented by others. They enable us to know and feel the humanity of the age.

Chaucer died in 1400. The main literary men who influenced him were the Italians Boccaccio, Dante, and Petrarch, associated with the dawn of the Renaissance. Yet Chaucer belongs wholly and solely to the Middle Age, from first to last. He is detailed above as representative, but his longest poem, *Troilus and Criseyde,* embodies and presents in him the voice of his age.

John Skelton was born more than two generations after Chaucer's death, and was made poet laureate by Henry VII. He died in 1529, and has been said to have some claim to be the first great modern English poet. Since he was alienated by modern trends, a passionate reactionary, politically and culturally, opposed to both Reformation and Renaissance, entrenched in scholasticism and the literalness of monarchy, and at the same time liberal, proclaiming the liberty and duty of a poet to speak his mind, he must count as the last poet of the Middle Age, carrying its voice into the sixteenth century. *Speak, Parrot* delivers his blows in defense of what is about to pass away with a ringing performance of an intelligence nourished on the fare and trained by the disciplines of that epoch. Vigorous, quirky, serious, independent, this display indicates diverse combinations that discount any fixed idea of the Middle Age, save in what it was not.

## The Epoch of Monuments

Above it was stated that the two orders, chivalry and faith, bracketed, constituted the Middle Age. That indulged the nigh irresistible impulse to compound the idea of the Middle Age in a single notion, just repudiated as unrealistic. The many-sidedness just stressed was confined within the span of a contemporary mind, and Chaucer's was used as an example. Even that does not do. For the reality of the Middle Age is not notional even at this remove, but palpably present all over Europe in its most costly legacy. That presence is within reach of the eyes in one's head, soaring vertically or extending axially and transversely within or without. Science and technology, manifest in the Age of Reason (the Enlightenment), in which the Middle Age was notably deficient (the cultural cleavage) was all the time there, reason and technological capability uniquely embodied in these stones of Europe. Over the span of some seven centuries, from Carolingian Romanesque to Gothic, there was a self-contained achievement that enclosed development and the many-sided diversity in unity of Western Europe. Marked off thus from the scientific and industrial revolutions that charged everything, and then changed everything, what was accomplished was fully comparable in terms of human intelligence, invention, and skill. As a whole, it lay within the pattern of the Middle Age as a period of marking time, a waiting on God. It survives as a constant reminder that the human genetic inheritance is a statistical constant within a variable social inheritance.

What happened did start off with a local social inheritance. It should be remembered that the church as a monumental building consecrated to religious worship was a Roman gift to the Christians with political adoption. Their own meeting places had been domestic. Originality is seen in the wild nightly, in dreams that use the material available to them. When established norms return with the light of day, the material is tradition that is adopted and adapted, modified by whatever influences prevail, and by experiment; but also when the material is actual, not metaphorical, constrained by its nature, and renewed by the discernment of innovating possibilities—experiment. In the arts, and particularly in architecture, which is stabilized by utility and available material, this intricate process of continuous adoption and adaptation can be, and has been, traced in detail. This part of the medieval legacy is a fossilized cultural history spread over seven centuries, with fully formed, not vestigial, specimens.

The impetus in architectural thinking was (1) to adapt the Roman inheritance to the needs and habits of the liturgy and of pilgrims, and (2) to find the most appropriate form for the house of God. The arch was the basis of the interior, representing with the vault the grandeur of imperial Rome, a symbol of triumph. The eastern Roman Empire had adopted Oriental models. The northern tribes had their own constructions. Monasteries had priority in Europe, since they could be organized to forward the policy of making a Christian empire; and those on the Benedictine model that had been widely established were well adapted to the purpose. The monks were teachers, farmers, administrators, and their buildings were related to these functions. A plan for St. Gall (c. 820), set out the range of buildings grouped for convenience, of which the largest was the church, a basilica with an apse at each end, designed to serve both the monks and pilgrims. Here was the nuclear arrangement of an ambulatory with radiating chapels developed in the great pilgrimage churches of the eleventh and twelfth centuries. The cathedral complex at Pisa is a much later coherent grouping—a celebration.

This is not the place for any architectural survey or assessment of this vast achievement, with its thematic unities, copious masterpieces, and zonal and regional differences. Enough here to indicate some of the ways in which this does constitute an epoch, something that could not have continued and cannot be rivaled. Like a play, it had its beginning, middle, and end. From a Carolingian beginning, it mounted to the golden age of the Romanesque, and exploded in and with the Gothic. There were contrasting programs. The diverse activities of a monastery reflected in a building complex. The reconquest of Spain, from the ninth to the eleventh centuries, forced the Christians to build castles and churches to secure their foothold piecemeal in reconverted territory; the influence of the mosque engendered a hybrid style. There was a similar process on the eastern frontiers of Europe. In contrast, Charlemagne, immensely impressed by the majesty of Rome, favored grand ritual in a splendid setting. That was reinforced and elevated by the Hohenstaufen dynasty of Holy Roman emperors, echoing Roman triumphalism. Then there was the program that catered to the needs of and staged the ritualistic progress of pilgrims. From the program to the drawing board, a plan gives effect to the idea. From two dimensions to three, structure and composition puts the material in place and relates the parts. Finally, the decoration ornamentation is added or embodied, since the building is both functional and visually harmonious, a center of attraction, making an unmistakable impression of something special.

To accomplish all this there had to be teamwork, the assembly and organization of special talents and skills, geometers and engineers, masons, carpenters, plasterers, painters, enamelists, goldsmiths, silversmiths, and above all, sculptors. As with the Greeks, units of work were finished separately and put together. As with the Greeks, innovations were made by experiment, with reflection on the techniques employed in the light of effects attained. What was not comparable with the Greeks was the problematic course of development the medieval architects set themselves with the huge masses they deployed in oblique components, projections that gave grandeur to their buildings, but required counter-measures to contain outward thrust and to secure stability. The Greeks were content with direct support of the vertical weight, and achieved their variety by the manipulation of proportions. Their architecture was deliberately simple and austere. The many-sidedness of the medieval mind had to express itself; and in this connection it was not scattered and wild, amusing itself with hearsay, but severely disciplined, and with that strength bold and adventurous. The discovery that in the next age would turn in all directions was meanwhile confined to exploration and exploitation within a domain in which which they earned the confidence of increasing mastery.

Carolingian architecture was already remarkably accomplished and diverse, with ingenious and pleasing ornamentation, and spacious in extent. It held to the wood-roofed basilica, and it was the invasion and victory of stonework from top to bottom that largely displaced it with the Romanesque achievement. The arch used in the ribbed vault to sustain the extra weight was developed between 1093, the date of Durham cathedral, and 1144, the date of St. Denis, when Paris was the capital of western Christendom and the Gothic style was introduced. The Romanesque church is a massive structure of compact vaults and thick walls. Pillars combined with rectangular or cruciform piers made a supporting system capable of sustaining an enormous load, a system that was composed of interdependent specialized members. All the technical devices were available resources in the eleventh century, and they prompted invention in facilitating diverse uses. Astonishment and admiration reward even a cursory look at a series of illustrations that samples a geographical spread of churches or selected aspects of them during these centuries.

The Normans at this period showed conspicuous energy and initiative. As well as executing the invasion of England and occupation of southern Italy and Sicily and taking their part in the reconquest of Spain, they were reformers and builders of monasteries and churches. The abbey church at Jumièges with two western towers was a model that Edward the Confessor had in mind for Westminster Abbey. But the catholic taste of the Normans drew on many sources, including Venice and Byzantium. They had supported financially the rebuilding of Monte Cassino; and in the twelfth century they assimilated Greek and Arab traditions with the Romanesque in the Sicilian cathedrals of Montreale and Cefalu. Contact with the Arabs and Byzantium in the Crusades also revolutionized castle-building. Richard I's Chateau Gaillard, 1196–1198, shows what the castle had become. Adapted to the demands of prudent and economic defense, with no regard to appearance, it illustrates medieval church architecture by contrast.

Conditions for the establishment of the Romanesque developed in the eleventh century: there was the parish system, each with its own priest and church; there was the patronage of the laity, who prospered by trade and endowed religious foundations; there was the popularity of pilgrimages. New building thus encouraged new ideas. The liturgy at Cluny was nearly continuous and especially elaborate. The building had to assure undisturbed prayer and at the same time provide for the access of pilgrims to the main shrine behind the high altar. The circular walkway that was the general pattern adopted by the pilgrim churches was the Romanesque ground plan, adopted in the early Gothic cathedrals.

Stonework took over in Romanesque, and this included ornamentation, which was embodied in the stone fabric. The Carolingian churches used ornamentation lavishly, but applied as a veneer, in mosaics or painting or plaster, separate crafts. The Romanesque builders thought in stone and created a stone imperium, its corporate identity neither Carolingian nor Gothic, nor entirely separate from either.

Monasteries had kept alive skills and trades that had survived barbarian invasions and Muslim conquests. They were the patrons who employed or hired laymen for special commissions. The crafts cultivated were metalwork, ivory carving, and manuscript illustration. Brilliant miniature enamels in diptych or triptych forms were placed on altars by devotees, a reminder of the figurines that swelled city treasuries at Greek shrines. Popular taste is evident on corbels and other decorative features on the outside of churches, and in far more finely executed and discriminated detail in the carvings of choir stalls, particularly misericords. Hinged seats had projecting corbels when tipped up, which combined the comfort of sitting down with the dignity of standing for priests during long services. The carved decorations were left to the ideas of the craftsmen employed, with results like the sketchbook of a painter, with scenes of labor, sport, domestic life, or biblical stories. Also common were bestiaries, heraldic animals, domestic and wild animals, unicorns, and dragons and gryphons. This comes to an end with the Renaissance, when craftsmen are organized to execute a given design—a significant change.

Romanesque was from the beginning associated with monasteries, which were planted like farms in favorable rural sites, sheltered and watered. Early Gothic belonged to wealthy cities, manifesting the power of the Church in the hands of the secular clergy. Canon lawyers were in the ascendancy, and with Innocent III in the early thirteenth century Vatican ambition was politically paramount. The cathedral schools were seats of a new learning influenced by the Arab culture of Spain and Sicily, and anticipated the universities that developed out of them.

The emergence of Gothic came with the emergence of France at this time from the anomalous Angevin empire. As a new ally of the papacy, and with the effective end of the Holy Roman Empire after Frederick II's death, France became dominant on the continent, with a cultural as well as political hegemony. Architecturally, she was now at the center of design. The daring engineering experiments that raised the height of roofs and enabled steeples to soar were associated with new ideas about the appropriate form for a Christian church. The inspirational effect of light and color was a primary concern, so there had to be large window space for stained glass, as well as ample circulation space. The pointed arch and ribbed vault had been Romanesque devices that now became central to a style of architecture inspired by the aspiration of the faith and expressing the utmost human effort *ad majorem Dei gloriam,* not a gift from Constantine. Eminently, it was differentiated from domestic and utilitarian buildings, with its towering arched structures. Independent of the walls would be a skeletal framework of vault and piers, buttressed at the corners—a major difference from the massive Romanesque walls. This was achieved by experimentation. Notre Dame in Paris was the first of these great cathedrals, completed by the end of the twelfth century, followed by the rebuilding of Chartres, whose cathedral had been destroyed by fire. The master mason doubled the height of the clerestory. The triumphal power of the Church in its period of political ascendancy was celebrated in these early Gothic cathedrals, a union of physical and spiritual exaltation.

A major influence was the rise of the cult of the Virgin in the twelfth century. Attention was focused on the humanity and suffering of Jesus, picturing his infancy and his crucifixion. A great number of churches were now dedicated to the Virgin, who became the central figure in the art of the period. Attention to her person was associated with her role as intercessor. Henry Adams, writing of Chartres, the most dedicated and celebrated of all her palaces, wrote, "If you want to know what churches are for, come down here to some great festival of the Virgin." An American unbeliever of the nineteenth century, Adams was feeling his way as an explorer into a major period at the end of the twelfth century by dwelling in detail on what was visually present to him in the great cathedral. In doing so, he evokes what the Virgin meant to everyone in thirteenth-century France.

The Middle Age is one of the great periods in the history of sculpture, and what makes it so is its integral use in architecture. In Romanesque use, the sculptures mainly embellish and stand out from capitals or fill the tympanum over a doorway, or are otherwise lodged where the architect wants to attract or rest the eye. It is the architect who directs, the sculptor who performs. The performance is frequently narrative, an illustration, but always a decorative assembly of detail. The architecture is thus richly endowed with a sculpture that is its own.

The Gothic cathedrals use life-size figures to great effect, as in the portal statuary of Rheims and Amiens. Local stone was used in many cases, and where this was soft, it was soon eroded. At Lichfield, one original survives. As the figures became formless the niches were filled from the stone masons' yards, a stone's throw away, with run-of-the-mill substitutes. In the last phase of Gothic architecture, patronage was diffused and Paris no longer magisterial. Cities and merchants were important patrons—for example, the wool trade and the great parish churches of East Anglia—and the buildings they founded were not on the vast scale of the cathedrals. At the end of the period, King Henry VII's chapel at Westminster shows the fusion of sculpture architecture with the invention of artists at the height of their powers.

To think of the Middle Age as Gothic is as ignorant as their own fantasies about antiquity. There was a succession of styles and mobility of style, with immense variety of detail and continual invention and borrowing. The idea of the church was not given and obvious, nor entirely traditional, for it allowed scope for different ideas and ideals, and for the accommodation of whatever practices developed; for example, the barnlike churches of the friars accommodated the people who crowded in to be entertained and edified by their preaching. The gift from Rome was a tradition the clergy transformed into something of their own. If the triumphal arch remained paramount, it was not in the end the same arch that symbolized the triumph of the Roman imperium.

## Tourneys of the Mind

The massive pervasive assumption that made the climate of thought of the Middle Age was faith in the Christian revelation, the anthropomorphism of the Incarnation.

That faith, with its filiation in Jewish thought, had its encounters with Greek philosophy in antiquity. Scraps of that filtered down, mainly through Boethius and Augustine ("the *De Civitate Dei* was the book which, next to the Scriptures, was most surely to be found in every monastery in Europe"); but from Anselm to Ockham there were thinkers in the West who exerted their minds to the limit to reconcile their faith with their reason. It was an honorable endeavor eventually undertaken when what had been inherited from Hellas and from Zion had to be proved reconcilable or incompatible, a main theme in the cultural history of the West. Taken as a whole, what they achieved intellectually in this endeavor transcended the age, as did what they achieved artistically in architecture.

Boethius (480–525), called "the last of the Romans," was the source from which the Middle Age derived the most substantial general inheritance from the philosophy of antiquity. He had translated into Latin the works of Plato and Aristotle, and several of their commentators, but this was not recovered in full until the thirteenth century. Meanwhile, what was available was part of Aristotle's logical works. There was also his own celebrated *Consolation of Philosophy,* written in prison before execution, setting himself to reconcile the injustice and disorderly course of human affairs (of which he was a victim) with the divinely perfect natural order. Platonic and Ciceronian arguments are rehearsed, and espoused with a moving personal testimony to their efficacy. Treatises by Boethius on arithmetic and on music were also available.

At bottom was the traditional education curriculum that had been preserved with Latin, the liberal arts: grammar, rhetoric, geometry, music, to which might be added poetry, medicine, logic, dialectic, and some physics and astronomy. This was a common basis because, in the words of Origen, it "did not contain any view of the divine, nor on the manner in which the world existed, nor on any higher reality, nor on the constitution of a good and happy life"; that is, it excluded the subject matter and themes of philosophy. These propaedeutics were necessary to the education of the clergy, who then applied them in their own pedagogy of edification, instead of ascending by them to a higher branch of learning. For beyond this universally accessible and needful general education was a discernible difference between any higher form of rational learning and "knowledge of the heart" as meant by St. Anthony or St. Francis—or the moral formation at the bottom of stoicism, or the therapeutic function of Epicureanism, or even the intuition of Plotinus. This "knowledge of the heart" concerned a personal relationship with God through Christ, experienced through faith, in the testimony of the Apostles, confirmed and upheld by the Church. This was outside the rationality and rationale of philosophy. But the two languages would in due course force an issue.

St. Vincent of Lerins, one of the founders of monasticism, can be said to have begun the thought of the Middle Age in the West by formulating in his *Commonitorium* the rules to determine the true tradition in matters of faith: "Within the Catholic Church itself the greatest care must be taken that we hold that which has been believed everywhere, always, and by all." Opinions of the Fathers, decisions of ecumenical councils, constituted the mainstream of Catholic orthodoxy; outside these and where there was difference, comparisons should be made to find the common opinion. There could and would be growth, but by inherent development, never by innovation or addition. This set a rule for the maintenance of unity, which excluded any intervention from philosophic thought.

Inherent development expanded by commentaries on the word of God, which themselves repeated and expanded available commentaries by the great teachers of preceding generations, like St. Hilary or St. Augustine. Since there were four recognized levels of meaning, any sentence of the Bible might give scope for expansion. The four levels of interpretation were: literal, allegorical, anagogic (esoteric), and tropological (moral application to life). Not until the end of the eleventh century was there a recovery of genuine intellectual activity. Meanwhile, in monasteries and cathedral schools the same studies were maintained, although libraries were starved by the shortage of parchment after Arab conquests in the East. One of the best off at St. Gall had four hundred volumes in 860. In the twelfth century the library of St. Vincent de Laon contained eleven thousand volumes, following the activity of the religious orders in copying manuscripts.

Associated with the First Crusade at the end of the eleventh century was a reform of the monastic orders, and a movement towards asceticism. Attention turned to stricter regulation of the secular disciplines in learning. Dialectic was declared a servant in the propagation of faith, not an instrument of inquiry. The syllogism was reduced to a rule of statement, without the force of proof. But it had become impossible to ignore the philosophy that had come down from the Greeks. Further recovery, and what was made of that, had consequences for theology by the end of the Middle Age that still obtain.

At this time, Archbishop Anselm, in the Augustinian tradition, tried to institute a stable equilibrium between faith and reason. Scripture and Church imposed on faith certain dogmas (Incarnation) which can only be accepted on authority, since they are not attainable by reason. Once received, however, a man wants to be able to think the dogmas. If you do not believe, you will not understand (Isaiah 7:9). *Fides quaerens intellectum,* faith seeking to understand, is like an intermediary between mere faith and the vision that the elect will have of the divine reality. This formulation of Anselm's was intermediate between outright fideism, which refuses all normal exercise of reason, and a mysticism that strives to introduce into this life the beatific vision.

In meeting the objections of infidels, Anselm was eager to show evidence for the dogmas of faith in "the necessities of reason and the clearness of truth." This exhibition of the reach of reason went outside the thought habits of the age and the slavish commentaries on Scripture: if the idea of God is the ideal of the perfect, it must necessarily include existence. The contemporary attack on this kind of reasoning, which would persist, was that we can have no notion of God other than what is revealed to faith.

From the twelfth until the fifteenth centuries, formulated questions and their systematic discussion dominated first the cathedral schools, then the universities. The practice established in dealing with them was "scholasticism." Peter Abelard at the school of Notre Dame in Paris listed 158 questions about seemingly contradictory opinions of the authorities on matters of importance to Christian faith and conduct.

He does not tell his students authoritative answers. They must examine carefully the statement in question, to establish what exactly it is saying. The pronouncements of Church councils must be respected. Outside what is formally taught by the Church, students must learn to make up their own minds, as recommended by Aristotle, by attention to details. When they had formed their own opinion, insofar as it differed from that of others, they had to defend it in discussion. This was dialectic, in which Abelard's own agile mind delighted. To win the argument, one has to get one's opponent to admit a proposition from which one's conclusion necessarily flows. At any time anywhere, it is reasonable to ask of any serious statement: what does it mean?; on what grounds is it stated?; is it true? This detached critical response to statements was being encouraged at this time in a systematic way that had to sort out an increasingly vast miscellaneous inheritance from antiquity; and their digestion of Aristotle's logical works enabled them to set about it. The four general questions they asked on a work were its subject matter, its aim, its underlying purpose, and the branch of knowledge it belonged to. In those terms it could be lectured upon, discussed, and evaluated.

The textbook in theology that lasted throughout the Middle Age, and that adopted Abelard's critical methods, was compiled by Peter Lombard, bishop of Paris, who died in 1164. His *Sentences,* fruit of his years as a teacher, took the subject matter from the Bible, the Fathers, decisions of the Church councils, and drew on Abelard and Gratian's textbook, the *Decree,* which had reconciled contradictory canon laws for the law school at Bologna. His aim was to alert students to questions and to teach them to reason for themselves. Lombard was to be the foundation of theological studies in the universities, as Gratian of legal studies, in these two works.

This broadening of studies and training of minds in the twelfth century chimed with an increasing need for secretaries and staff in government and administration. The humanists of the Renaissance were to find employment in public affairs on diplomatic missions and in composing letters, and that was anticipated at this time. The main difference was that the rhetoric of this time tended to be animated by biblical imagery and allusion, and later on to be crabbed by scholastic pedantry, whereas, after Petrarch, humanists modeled themselves on the refinements of Cicero, applied with flexibility to the matter in hand.

John of Salisbury (1110–1180) died bishop of Chartres. He had been taught by Abelard, had worked as a clerk in the Curia, had been secretary to the archbishop of Canterbury, and had been sent on diplomatic missions to Rome. He was a personal friend of the new pope, Adrian IV, and well acquainted with Becket, who had been a colleague at Canterbury, and with Henry II. With all the contacts he had made, he was furnished with insight into the machinery of public affairs, great and small, and familiar with the conduct of men in high places. His classical studies, principally of Cicero and Seneca, had helped to form the independence and firmness of his character and the principles of his conduct. He thought that what had so benefited him should benefit others, and the world.

At bottom, John of Salisbury was interested in finding in classical texts maxims and exempla which could be used, like biblical texts, to reinforce with (classical) authority and tradition what he wanted to say to his contemporaries in positions of responsibility. He was hardly aware of the original contexts of the principles he appropriated, the *polis* or the Republic. He did not think of the Curia or the court of Henry II as an institution, nor of political concepts, such as "accountability." Rather, there were acts of officials as agents of the ruler; a matter of personal behavior. Persons had to be convinced of what was wise and right to do, and the wisdom and examples of the ancients could help with that. Conscience was the monitor, not accountability the sanction.

However, there was one supremely important objective regulator: Roman law. The dialectical purging of this inheritance at the hands particularly of Ivo of Chartres and Gratian of Bologna, stimulated by the investiture controversy and contest, produced a synthesis of principles and texts for canon law and civil ("natural") law binding on all, including pope and king. Thus John of Salisbury used the second-hand fragments of Greek philosophy available through Cicero and Seneca to strengthen and stabilize his own character and judgment on natural grounds and in conformity with the rule of reason in natural law.

A century later, there were universities instead of cathedral schools, the whole of Aristotle was available in direct translations from the Greek, the works of the eminent Arab philosopher Averroes had been translated into Latin; and he and Avicenna and Aristotle were being closely studied in Paris by Albert the Great and Thomas Aquinas. The situation was intellectually another world. The focus of interest and attention shifted from Aristotle's logical works to his *Metaphysics,* from what was ancillary to the study of theology to what occupied the space of theology with an investigation of "being," and thus implied a challenge to the existence of theology. The "queen of the sciences" was confronted with a rival claimant to the throne. In the universities of the thirteenth century, philosophy was to mean "metaphysics," and to be given independence as a study in its own right, and a crowning study, in a faculty of arts, separate from the faculty of theology. Moreover, a range of natural sciences (physics, optics, mechanics, astronomy, biology, and above all, medicine) in treatises translated in Greek, Latin, and Arabic had become available. This stock of literature in natural philosophy, for which "metaphysics" provided a plan and first principles, was not only infinitely richer than the meager encyclopedias and compilations eked out with bizarre speculations, which had been the legacy of antiquity to the first Europe, it was a transformation of the context and the agenda of learning: it invented, so to speak, a system of faculties, the university. By 1500, there were some eighty universities in Western Europe, from Uppsala to Cracow to Cantania in Sicily, from Aberdeen to Bordeaux to Lisbon and Seville. Paris, Oxford, Bologna, Rome, Ravenna, and Salerno were among the earliest. About thirty were added in the fifteenth century.

The totalitarian collectivism of the Church might bless or suppress the teaching of outstanding university theologians, but the attempts of theologians in the thirteenth century to produce syntheses, systems of thought that reconciled natural knowledge and the knowledge revealed to faith, could not be prescribed as they might be proscribed when produced.

Different schools of thought were developed, following diverse lines of reflection. Albert the Great, for instance, proceeding from the cosmological argument for

God as first cause, was interested in the study of nature for its own sake, an approach totally different from the bestiaries and symbolism of the early Middle Age. Thomas Aquinas's *Summa* is not a system he invents, but a display of how the arguments are managed, what the views are on topics of importance, how they are justified, and why their contraries and contradictions are rejected. Contrary to attempts in the previous age to reconcile faith and reason (Anselm, Abelard), he definitively separates the two: knowledge founded on sense experience was inapplicable to truths made available by divine revelation. He assumed that truth could not be contrary to truth, and therefore no truth of faith could be inconsistent with rational conclusions. Philosophy remained subservient to faith, not because faith needed philosophy to make it acceptable, but because theology ruled that philosophy was incapable of proving anything that would be contrary to faith. It was exclusively an exterior relationship. This discontinuity between the world known by reason and the world known by revelation would not exist in the world known to God; there was a foothold of common ground, in that the existence of God is rationally demonstrable, as well as revealed. Aristotle's philosophy was truly autonomous and independent of Christian truth, but consistent with it.

Thomas argued that what reason taught could not be contrary to what faith revealed. An Averroist interpretation of Aristotle found conclusions that did contradict faith. Siger of Brabant identified six of major importance to the faith, including the eternity of the world, extinction of the soul with the body, denial of a divine providence. He was of course condemned, and seems to have died in prison. The awkwardness of the discrepancy introduced the notion of "double truth." "Averroism" continued to be studied and expounded, particularly in the university of Padua where Pomponazzi (1452–1524), bred both in Thomism and Averroism, produced a revolutionary critique of both in defense of the proposition that soul and body are mortal. He was forced to revive the doctrine of "double truth," a practical fideism that professed to hold articles of faith on faith, contrary to reason. Pomponazzi was called, not without reason, "the last of the Scholastics and the first man of the Enlightenment."

The familiar ideas of traditional Augustinism and the relation of Aristotle to Christian revelation broached by Thomism were brought into strange company by Duns Scotus (c. 1266–1308), who used the notion of discontinuity with dramatic effect. He deployed all the concepts in discussions of the time, but not to relate or reorganize them in any way. The individual was simply a fact to add to species; "being" in man was the same as in God, not analogous; matter was real, without the necessity of "form"; will was separate from understanding, as matter from form, individual from species, intellect from illumination: will was paramount, and directed understanding. This analysis carried over into his political ideas. Men were at first equal, but of their own will gave up their independence for the protection that an absolute authority alone could provide, to institute and enforce law. This was an explosive that would leave the Aristotelian world in pieces. The dynamic of Aristotle's *Physics* was also attacked: "Everything that moves is moved by another thing." This required a resident mover in the planets. The Parisian nominalists supplied the principle of terrestrial mechanics (ballistics) to replace the mythology of celestial animators, incidentally breaking the ancient link between physics and metaphysics.

The thirteenth-century syntheses oriented to spiritual unity and hierarchical organization were congenial to what was described above as "the totalitarian collectivism of the Church," under the sovereign spiritual power represented by the pope. What seemed possible then was seen to be impossible in the next century, with the evident philosophical contradictions and the nationalistic character of political conflicts in the Hundred Years War. There was not going to be a political union of Christendom that would be universal. The Roman Church would not renounce the ideal, but it could already be recognized as not feasible intellectually nor politically. At the beginning of the fourteenth century, the confrontation of doctrines, the political conflicts, and the situation of the Church itself, following the humiliation of Boniface VIII by Philip IV of France and the removal of the papacy to Avignon in 1305, tended to engender skepticism. Faith might survive if skepticism could systematically be used to show that it was a legitimate option. Faith could not be used to justify the papal claim to political dominion. William of Ockham (1300–1349) took both these positions; if he remains for later thinkers a man of the schools of his time, that is because the times separate different interests, different assumptions, and different starting points. Ockham was certainly not less acute a thinker than the best of later philosophers, and he dealt so comprehensively with all that occupied the medieval schoolmen that he can be allowed the last word on that.

More than half his life was mainly spent in opposing the temporal claims of the papacy based on the fraudulent "Donation of Constantine." What he is best remembered for is a single rule that enabled him to undermine all the constructions of his predecessors: Ockham's razor, *non est major ratio*. This was the argument that one must reject a thesis that is not imposed by a particular compelling reason. Otherwise, one "found no end, in wand'ring mazes lost," though Ockham did not say that.

Neither he nor his fellow schoolmen were confronting skeptics in the modern sense of unbelievers. They were themselves infatuated with Greek philosophy as they knew it, which had come to mean mainly Aristotle. Aquinas had separated natural knowledge, a system derived from sense experience, from theology, truths revealed by the grace of God, and had insisted that they were necessarily separate and complementary. Others had shown that they were contradictory and therefore incompatible. Ockham dealt with Aristotelian logic with which the schools were obsessed by detaching rules of reasoning from the conception of a necessary world with which they were bound up. The only necessity was the logical necessity of the identity of the individual real, that a thing cannot be at the same time what it is and something else. Peter is Peter, not a rational animal. To define him as a man is simply to compare him with others like himself, all different: it does not say what he is. Ockham is making Russell's distinction between knowledge by acquaintance and knowledge by description, and the fundamental logical point that only tautologies are necessary truths, for the purposes of and in terms that come home to the occasions of his own times.

This theory of natural knowledge is compatible with empirical science, but for Ockham it underlay the contingency of the world and the omnipotent liberty of God, save for the logical necessity of identity. Events are predictable that recur regularly in experience without exception, so long as they do so, not because they must. He anticipates Hume, again from reasons that differ with his times. All the five proofs of God's existence are worthless. A natural theology cannot be constructed. Theology cannot be a science. If it is queen of the sciences, that is a paramountcy bound up with its claim to truth not based on evidence, and does not entitle it to judge what is established by evidence. He did not offer the schools a competing system; rather, he drew out implications and demonstrated incompatibilities with a logical rigor that has a modern resonance. He used logic to show the limits of reason, what it could not prove and what not disprove. As an acute thinker himself, on the nature of thought and the problem of knowledge, he was original and relevant. His relevance in later theology is seen in the ground of the thinking of Martin Luther, who read him, and in Karl Barth who in recent times dominated Protestant thought with a reaffirmation of the Lutheran tradition. As a result, in these last centuries of scholasticism, there is the Roman Catholic model in Thomism and the Protestant model in Ockhamism, which both persisted.

Ockham's insistence on the quiddity of individual real was applied by the mystics to God, the supreme individual in whom all would be absorbed. This was a rule of life, not a metaphysical theory, taken from Eckhart and practiced in the religious houses, distinct from the universities, and linked with the masses and popular movements with a millenary outlook, the persistent waiting on God, which may be thought of as another aspect of Ockham's omnipotent liberty of God, a cultivation of the human conditions of union with the divine, not mere fideism.

## The Medieval "Box"

Although this was a time of seething discussion and violent confrontation in the schools, theologians of all persuasions refrained from challenging traditional social and moral doctrines, and kept speculative ideas out of their sermons. Society was still a hierarchy little changed since the twelfth century. The world was as deplorable as ever, but relatively stable in the first half of the fourteenth century. The rules and generalities of preaching, as crafted and drafted by the authorities, needed the spontaneity generated in contact to be effective. That was in the person and mouth of the preacher. The style of the time congenial to the audience was anecdote and narrative or depiction, rather than evangelical histrionics; and here the legendary and mythical past was prepared ground, and the ragbag of compilations provided the pickings. The sermons of the time have been likened to church music: the plainsong in a monastic setting was being superseded by descant in the church choirs under lay masters. A papal bull in 1322 forbade the use of descant in church services, and enlarged on the introduction of ornamentation into the music of the liturgy: the integrity of the chant should not be broken. Oratory had taken over in sermons, tunes in music.

The friars as preachers gave classical poets and philosophers popular currency by using them for exempla and wise sayings. One encyclopedia put together by a team of friars was divided into *naturale, historiale, doctrinale,* and *morale.* The Old Testament merges into universal history in the perspective of divine purpose. Richard de Bury's *Philobiblon* mapped a medieval view of the history of culture: learning had passed from the Orient to Greece, thence to Rome, thence to Paris, and finally to the barbarous peoples far to the West. How wild classical references might be is exemplified in John Lathbury's commentary on Lamentations: the Carthaginians had consulted Delphi on why they had been defeated by the Romans; to decode the oracular reply, they asked "Duke Hannibal" to fetch Virgil from Rome; Virgil came, and interpreted the oracle by a clue supplied in verses written on the main gate at Carthage.

The mythical background that served as universal history began with Genesis and ended in eschatology. In the middle distance of the hearsay past were events associated with prodigious ancestors; Persia, Egypt, Greece, Rome. Such glories made people feel they had come down in the world, and gave zest to the invention of more modern matter, "the matter of Britain" and the like. Chronology, the standard of history, was guesswork. There was no Olympiad to clock their lives.

Classical historians (Herodotus, Thucydides, Tacitus) were aware of their inability to investigate the past with any pretense to authority. They followed a thread of inquiry and sought and tested and amplified relevant information where they could find it; they organized the material they lathered in narrative form, and informed it with their own reflections. Very early in the Middle Age, Bede's *Ecclesiastical History* is nearly of this class; on his selected theme, he sifts and tests the material drawn "from the writings of the ancients, or the traditions of our ancestors, or of my own knowledge." Four of the five books, and more than a third of the first, are based on his own research.

Conscientious historical scholarship on this scale was not achieved again for more than four centuries. William of Malmesbury (born 1195) and Matthew Paris (died 1259) are respected for their superior skill in the chronicling business.

The annals and chronicles that provided material for histories were written by monks. Matthew Paris was a Benedictine monk of St. Albans; he was employed on important diplomatic missions, was accomplished in the learning of his time, and seems to have been intimate with the chief men, including Henry III. He was thus able and inclined to sit close to the events he described. In England after Bede, the main source was the Anglo-Saxon Chronicle(s), supplemented by the lives of saints and some documents. The gradual organization of a centrally ruled state in Britain and France after the Norman Conquest involved written law and documentary instruments, of which Domesday Book is only one early example. Apart from the crown, records were widespread in abbeys and cathedrals and towns, with all corporate bodies, a vast accumulation of meticulously kept archives. In addition were private antiquarians and collectors. The abbey of St. Albans had a strictly annalistic compilation of official records and archives that was the basis of the work of Matthew Paris, and therefore the foundation of his eminence as the greatest master of contemporary history in the Middle Age. This was the climax of chronicle writing. His survey of contemporary international events, with special reference to England, used state documents and official letters. The cartularies of monasteries are still prime sources, for example, in studying the conditions underlying the prolonged failure to suppress the Albigensian heresy. The dissolution of the monasteries and the invention of printing ended these early phases in the history of history, when "history" was not on the agenda of learning, in which it was for edification (lives of saints, ecclesiastical foundation), feats of arms, or utility (titles to property). A more general interest was served by a few biographies (Charlemagne, Alfred) and memoirs (Commines), and by accounts of the Crusades (Villehardouin, Joinville).

## The New Class

With human settlement in occupation of a territory within defined frontiers, there comes the inevitable polarity of town and country, different conditions and ways of life that are mutually dependent. The particular ways in which they differ and are related vary widely historically and geographically, but are always of central social interest. Even the small Greek state had the two elements of *polis*, the city, and *ethnos*, the surrounding countryside. The relation between the two was very different from what might have obtained between a John Gilpin and a Mr. Darcy. For the conditions and ways of life that differentiated town and country became attached to different classes. This was evident already in separation of the knights of the shires from burgesses of the towns in the Parliaments of Edward I. The feudal system was based on landholding.

The Roman Empire was administratively based on municipalities that were virtually self-governing, until they were undermined by ruinous exactions. However, they did survive in Italy and Gaul as major centers of population and organization. In Britain, a Roman outpost, it was otherwise. After the withdrawal of troops at the beginning of the fifth century, there was no continuity of urban life, with no occupying official class to be supplied. The topography of Bede's England in the seventh century is strangely devoid of towns. Preeminently, there is Canterbury as the metropolis of the king of Kent. The city of London is mentioned. Otherwise, important events are sited in rural places. A synod called by Archbishop Theodore was "held in the plain of Heathfield." Searching for large stones for a coffin, monastic brothers come to "a small abandoned city, which, in the language of the English, is called Grantchester." The places named in the narrative were no doubt "towns," but not notable places of business of any kind. As late as the end of the fifteenth century, a Venetian visitor found "scarcely any towns of importance"; a century later, another reported that England "does not possess many large towns, which may be estimated to number twenty-four, a small number for its size, but has very frequent and populous villages and small towns!" In terms of population, less than 10 percent lived in towns by the end of the fifteenth century; and country towns of a thousand or more were rare. York, a sizable provincial capital, had no more than eight thousand. London, with about fifty thousand, was special, the only city comparable with continental cities of importance.

Small in number and in size, the towns were nevertheless the growing points of the nation. As markets, they facilitated and stimulated local trade and production. For their purposes, they needed immunities and freedoms, special conditions, and they acquired them because they were useful allies to the king in securing his needs when opposed by his peers, the landowners. At this stage, their growth was a main means of promoting wealth and constitutional advance.

The concentration of population in towns for business and amenity, however small, required regulation. The merchant guilds, which were associations for trading purposes, were the natural body to take on civic responsibilities. Before the conquest, there were borough courts to order the affairs of the town. Local government shifted from the manors to the boroughs, for their inhabitants gathered there for the purposes of trade. Landed proprietors might found urban settlements for the market convenience of supplies and the disposal of surpluses, and with improved technology agricultural output had risen considerably; but they were not resident. Most of the burgesses would come of trading or artisan stock, and many would aspire to move upwards in their calling. Apprentices chose their trade (or their parents did) and were chosen by their trade, and after their seven years or so were allowed to practice it as journeymen. Sons, perhaps more often than not, followed their fathers in the same trade. At the top end, there was a marked failure of merchant families to perpetuate their dynasties. In the later Middle Age, a three-generation family span had become exceptional in the towns. For one thing, there was the incentive to acquire estates and withdraw from trade when the family was wealthy enough to do so, or to marry into the landed class. For another, there was a high level of infant mortality in the towns. With the appalling dangers of childbirth aggravated by the shortness of life expectancy, epidemics of smallpox, dysentery, tuberculosis, and plague were not among the amenities of town life.

In relative terms, an average merchant's income in a provincial capital could have exceeded the average of the county gentry; and really prosperous burgesses would have assets equal to those of the nobility.

The borough government was in the hands of the merchant guilds, and the craft associations before they became capable of collective action, were clients of the ruling oligarchy. Generally, they were excluded from the franchise of their boroughs, and the guild merchants dictated their wages and conditions of work, and were in a position to try to suppress their attempts to form their own guilds. This naturally engendered class hatred. In some cases, manifest corruption made the oligarchy vulnerable. Even with enlargement of the councils and widening of the franchise, the tendency prevailed for the "wealthier and discreeter sort" to be thought more fit to hold office and conduct the affairs of the borough.

What traders wanted and needed, and what they got, was freedom from dependence on landowners and the obligations and restrictions of the feudal system. With established corporate rights, a borough was able to give political asylum to a villein who got into the town, and qualified by a prolonged stay. With free transferability of land and immunity of their trade from county tolls, prosperous boroughs attained a social and economic self-sufficiency that might enable them to bargain directly with the king. London was a special case, but when Henry I granted the city the right to pay the royal tax direct into the exchequer, instead of having it imposed and collected by the sheriff, it was a precedent set early in the development of self-government in the English boroughs. With borough officials replacing the royal reeve in this matter, a redistribution of responsibilities was general. The guild was paramount in matters of trade as before. In policing the borough and formulating and regulating its customs, initiatives lay with the court. Enlarging and systematizing the jurisdiction of the borough court became the chief objective of reformers of the period after John's charters. Reliable record keeping was fundamental. At this stage, the making of a town was not merely an aggregation of population in one place; it was the making of a new social institution apart from the manorial system, a self-conscious, self-governing community managed by an efficient and accountable bureaucratic administration. At least that was the social and political ideal of an ambitious borough.

A new town founded in the thirteenth century would enjoy three rights as norms: (1) its court would be independent of that of the neighboring manor, and, if it could be achieved, independent of the sheriff; (2) its inhabitants would hold their plots by burgage tenure; (3) their undertakings would be free from tolls. Unless these rights were unequivocally vested in the burgesses, towns were liable to be oppressed by landowners, to the point of extinction. The corporate identity gained in the conduct of their affairs in due course required the protection of legal incorporation, when they looked for sources of revenue other than their tolls, and found it in the acquisition of land. Public services , for public health, for justice, for amenities, with salaried officials, incurred mounting costs, then as now.

English towns, because of the country's insular position, were generally more open than those on the continent. Although more than a hundred did have some defenses, it was less usual to have a completed wall than a firm boundary. There would be occupational zones for convenience. An Italian visitor in the late fifteenth century noted fifty-two goldsmiths' shops in the Strand, outshining all such shops in Milan, Rome, Venice, and Florence put together, he said. Houses were mostly timber-framed, but increasingly with stone cladding from the early thirteenth century. Since the hall remained the main feature of the house even in towns, plots usually ran back from a narrow frontage on the street. Refuge was sought in towns, and there were shanty dwellings on the outskirts, as now in the Third World; self-built hovels on unwanted plots or in occupation of derelict fortifications. Stowe's *Survey of London* (1598) describes the shanty town that had grown up in Whitechapel, aggravated by a rapid increase in migration from the countryside to the towns: Wapping was "a continual street, or filthy straight passage, with alleys of small tenements."

In the town proper, the lowest basin housing, as excavated at Winchester, was in single-cell units, some seventeen feet square, probably partitioned into a living room and a bed cubicle. The "submerged tenth," it is estimated, might number three times that proportion. Over 180 trades were recorded and named in medieval London. By the fourteenth century well-established carting routes radiated out of the city. The interests of trade secured the maintenance of roads, bridges, and waterways, which facilitated the holding and extension of fairs for the sale of goods outside the local market. Boston, Lynn, St. Ives, and Winchester had famous fairs, but all the larger boroughs had their own during the summer months. Edward III established fairs at Bordeaux to promote the economic revival of Gascony. The less common groceries, including spices and wines, dyes and cloth, and other household goods were on display. At that time, wool was almost England's sole export; later it was cloth. The agricultural recession in the mid–fifteenth century affected every borough and market town, and ruined many. Of the forty-five markets of Staffordshire, some twenty-five ceased after the boom years.

The parish system generally came about by the growth of a community, and the building of a church by the landowner. The preconquest church served the needs of an individual estate, and was the personal property of its builder. A town with many landlords had many churches. In the twelfth century, churches were brought under the control of ecclesiastical authorities. Ceasing to be private property, the buildings served a variety of public uses. With a castle and a market, a church made the nucleus of a medieval settlement, and was the focus for the social life of the community. Its size and open-space setting made it the convenient place for meetings on public business, including council meetings, inquests, and audits. Commercial business was also transacted there, with storage of deeds and valuables, even of bulky goods. A market or fair might be held in the churchyard. This multiple use in early times encouraged give and take between the authorities of church and town, for example in the provision of hospitals and almshouses, and in charities generally. Monasteries, which were the province of the friars from the thirteenth century were usually outside the towns. The upkeep of the chancel of a church was a charge on the incumbent, whilst the parishioners were responsible for the fabric. In the later Middle Age, townsmen were more generous than before in the enlargement and embellishment of their churches. Churches were a popular possession, maintained by a strong social habit, apart from religious opinions.

England was largely made up of country parishes, and by the sixteenth century the parish as the smallest subdivision of every county was recognized by the executive of government as an administrative unit throughout the realm. A town like Shrewsbury had fifteen parishes; they were civic institutions, and civic responsibilities devolved on parish officials. Many new tasks in local government were delegated to the churchwardens, particularly care of the poor.

The Italians were pioneers of town planning, having a long tradition of urban life. They gave the town a center, grouping cathedral and administrative buildings with a main square. Most English towns were based on a market, in relation to route junctions. A main street might broaden into the marketplace, with a church or market hall at the end. The burgage plots with narrow frontage on the main street implied a street long enough to provide frontage for all trades and tradesmen. These were towns formed for trade. There were earlier foundations for religious or administrative purposes. Alfred established *burhs,* walled fortresses and perhaps a market, in defense against the Danes. Winchester, his capital, had a palace, cathedral, and mint, and was an administrative center. Alfred was acquainted with the Italian cities and the market towns of Flanders, Ghent, and Bruges; and his idea of a *burh* had the benefit of what he had seen. Although Roman towns in Britain did not survive, elements of their plan, particularly walls and gates, did influence rebuilding on the site. Several towns developed from a market center overshadowed by a castle that had attracted settlement around its gate. Physical features, natural or inherited, were bound to affect planning, but neither these nor architectural design were as important as the social habits, needs, and purposes of the inhabitants who built and rebuilt their towns piecemeal.

There was so great a social transformation in the sixteenth century, with impact on the towns, that to break off formally at 1500, without mention of them, would leave a distorted impression of the place of the towns in English society at the end of the Middle Age. By 1656, the population was double what it had been in 1520. London expanded by seven times at least; provincial towns were magnets as well. Country gentry bought town houses in Norwich or Exeter or Winchester, and made their purchases there. The early towns had been built on overseas trade; now England's home trade brought new business to the provincial capitals with production of many new commodities that had exportable surpluses. The great depression of 1544–1551 had encouraged confiscation of monastic lands after Henry VIII's break with the papacy. Up to 30 percent of the land stock was for public sale, and was available to the towns for investment as well as to the nobility. Great building programs were initiated, mainly for rent. The hall, which alone had been heated, and therefore used for all purposes, was superseded, and became an entrance, with the availability of coal and erection of brick chimney stacks to provide fireplaces to heat bedrooms and living rooms. County towns were places of residence for professional classes as well as traders and artisans. The law had become an attractive profession with plenty of employment, as officials (recorders, town clerks, justices) and in connection with the transfer of lands. Established burgess families were ready to choose the law for their sons instead of apprenticeships. In the first Parliament of Henry VI, many of the burgesses representing towns are lawyers.

Contact in Parliament and social intercourse in the counties between gentry and burgesses became common. In some towns the suburbs were attractive, and elegant houses of gentry and the professional classes were sited in these approaches to country towns. Class was in existence at the end of the Middle Age; divisions carried seeds of different interests that would draw distinct lines of solidarity in the social conflicts that make a nation's domestic history.

"Class" is not an institution. It is a social phenomenon, a self-conscious family grouping into which one is born, associated with income, education, occupation, and common lifestyle—a subculture. Although not an institution, it is a factor of stability, as regular sources of supply for necessary occupations, and with the solidarity of widespread shared interests exerting political pressure. "Class" has been stereotyped on European, and particularly British, lines. Like "elites," it is a concept subject to the discipline of sociological discussion. Enjoyment of social privilege, with which class is identified in the stereotype, is another matter and belongs to politics.

The feudal system, which did not last long in strictness, would be superseded by a class system. This had not happened by the end of the Middle Age, and would not come into its own until the nineteenth century in political terms, but a middle class had emerged and established itself in the towns, already differentiated if not yet graded; and a numerous underclass was encamped on the margins. The social phenomenon was there in a rudimentary form. In time, in England, it would issue in a confrontational or adversarial form of politics, after all the vicissitudes that distanced the nineteenth century from the fifteenth.

*   *   *

I have described the Middle Age as self-enclosed, a time apart, waiting on God. When it ends, however, it is evidently pregnant with what will be born to succeeding generations. It begins with monastery and castle and ends with university and chartered borough. In learning, which it treasured from the first, and in the seven liberal arts inherited from the classical past, it passed from curiosity about curiosities which, as it were, covered the nursery walls with fantasies, to curiosity about nature, which began to inform inquiry. The Middle Age, like the middle class, discloses difference and division on closer inspection. That cannot be surprising over a span of some eight centuries, twice the period between 1500 and 1900.

In sum, these eight centuries between the break-up of the Roman Empire and the establishment of nation states of Europe divide into two. The pageantry and romance for which the whole period is remembered is there on parade at the end with the pilgrims on their way to Canterbury. The seed plot for the next developments is far less evident, but it is there, and is the most interesting and important aspect of the later Middle Age to be discerned. Because it is underground and undeveloped, superficially there is a breach of continuity. Gunpowder, printing, science, voyages of discovery, escape from the Roman Church: there is suddenly a new world. It was the biggest unplanned revolution in human affairs, and like the Industrial Revolution to come was a concatenation of unrelated events. Such revolutions were to prove more far-reaching and long-lasting than political revolutions. Unplanned they are, but so is nature.

# Part Three

# Recovery and Discovery

# 11

# The Rule of Taste

Even the high Middle Age in Europe, almost a set-piece, is not properly to be thought of as a civilization, as one does not generally think of a person's infancy as part of his or her career. This middle period between Greco-Roman civilization and European civilization has continuity with both, but is peer of neither. The name and fame of Rome was legendary, but the discovery of a great pre-Christian civilization, and of the way in which it had been formed over more than a millennium, was not, and could not have been, on the medieval agenda. Discovery of the earth came about in the context of the extension and consolidation of Christendom. The Middle Age was without history and geography, that "other eye of history," and lived in a shadowy world without perspective. There is the Mappa Mundi to show it in Hereford Cathedral.

The natural world was a third area of legend, awaiting piecemeal discovery, even if one does not dwell on the bizarre example of the bestiaries. To attempt to go back in imagination, one would have to deprive oneself of these three areas of awareness in terms of their bearings on all other mental contents.

European history has been marked out in stages in the schoolbooks: Renaissance, Reformation, the scientific revolution, the Enlightenment, the Industrial Revolution, with other labeled divisions that indicate movements and ages. Pedagogically, even conceptually, this is inevitable, for these were all formative social influences that made the history of Europe. However, the period from the Renaissance to the Enlightenment can be embraced in a comprehensive perspective, on the assumption that Gibbon was justified when he considered Europe as "one great republic, whose various inhabitants have attained almost the same level of politeness and cultivation." What, then, were the common features, bespeaking a common inheritance, shared by the civilization of England, France, Italy, Spain, the Netherlands, Germany, even Russia, at the end of the eighteenth century? The educated in each of these societies were to some extent versed in the literature and arts of some of the others; writers and artists in one were subject to the influence of writers and artists in the others. It has been said that by 1700 standards established in music, poetry, drama, painting, sculpture, and architecture were generally approved by what was admired in European capitals. Establishment of a self-conscious European civilization was possible only by discovery of the Greco-Roman civilization as the model: it was in the main an Augustan civilization.

## The Primacy of Music

The surge of creative energy in all the arts associated with the Renaissance, and their dominance in the European concept of civilization, has to be looked at in some detail. Music was the oldest, most constant, and at the same time most esoteric of these arts. Aquinas himself remarked that in musical theory arithmetical observations are applied to sound, which goes back to the Pythagoreans, and is associated with a harmony deemed at the heart of the universe. The Church had been the patron and nurse of choral music for its own needs, and chivalry had bred and developed the chanson in France. Musical performance of some kind was an essential skill of the hero in prehistoric times. Greece established music in the foundation of the educational curriculum. Singing and learning to play an instrument, usually the lute, became a normal part of schooling. Leonardo, among his many accomplishments, was first of all a professional lutanist.

By the early sixteenth century, specialist performers on many different instruments, from different nations, were being mobilized in orchestras, with the majority of executants moving from south to north, and of composers and teachers from France and the Netherlands over the rest of Europe. Music was Europeanized.

Court music was predominantly secular, especially in Italy. Erasmus had protested of church music in England that the monks attended to nothing else. This became a period of stimulus in the formation of musical style, particularly by the cooperation of composers in northern France and the Netherlands with the instrumentalists of Italy under secular patronage.

In general the scope of music was enlarged to express the variety of human experience; the invention and promotion of opera might be seen in this context. The Greeks had insisted on subordination of the music to the meaning of the words, a principle that Monteverdi seized upon when he pioneered the movement that introduced the classical period of European music. But already in the late fifteenth and early sixteenth centuries music had gained a versatility through its natural ramifications in relation to other arts—determinative in forming the concept of "culture" in terms of the several related forms of artistic expression. This was the dawning European consciousness of "civilization."

## The Primacy of Drawing

It has been declared that the rationalization of vision through the invention of perspective was the most significant event of the Renaissance, not the exodus of Greek scholars or the fall of Constantinople. Vasari said that Masaccio (1401–1428) "changed the face of painting," since his paintings of the 1420s introduced a mathematics-based perspective that, as developed in the next generation, permanently affected practice.

Indeed, Vasari, in what he says about Cimabue (1240–1302) and Giotto (1266–1336), indicates how the Italian movement began, and the lacuna that was there before.

Cimabue was born in Florence. At school, he devoted himself to drawing on his books and papers what he saw and what he fancied. The city authorities had invited some Greek painters to Florence for the purpose of restoring the art of painting, which had been lost. Cimabue, who had stood watching them at work, was eventually put to learn from them, and soon surpassed them in both design and coloring.

Painting, sculpture, and architecture were thus reestablished in Italy by outstanding artists, represented with discrimination by Uccello's portrait composition. In the next generation, Leonardo da Vinci (1452–1519), bred in all the arts practiced in the workshop of Verrocchio, a friend of his father, was theorist of "the culture of the workshops," bringing imagination and intellect into interplay with empirical investigation and experiment. Alberti, the model "universal man" of the Renaissance, had formulated and published concepts and guidelines on the arts: *De pictura,* 1436; *De statua,* 1464; *De re aedificatoria,* 1452, published in 1485. Leonardo's orientation was decisively different; he learned the terms of painting directly from observation of nature, the sufficient master. Many-sided as he was, and with said ranging interests multiplying curiosity, and experimental itches, his central and persistent concern was the development and promotion of painting. His statements and example helped to raise the art from its mechanical status as a craft. He placed it not only above sculpture, but also above music and poetry. He was thus not with the humanists (and had not been bred in letters), and was in effect against them. He was not reverent in reference to antiquity. His ample personal library was almost exclusively utilitarian, for information, without literature or philosophy.

Anatomy, like perspective, was taught in the workshops, but Leonardo went much further in associating the exact image of muscular movements with states of mind expressed. In figure and portrait painting, the image was not enough, unless it included representation of what was going on within the mind and mood of the person, which had perceptible physical conditions and consequences. Supremely, this is the human content of his *Last Supper.* The principle eliminates the general or ideal, the Platonic influence.

Most Renaissance architects began as painters or sculptors, or were most famous for their works in those fields, but Andrea Palladio (1518–1580) was more nearly a modern professional when he was appointed by the Venetians to build country houses for prosperous citizens. He adapted what he found by applying the Roman rules and principles the early Renaissance architects had unearthed and reread. His *Quattro Libri dell' Architettura* (1570) gave country villas a distinct section. His villas and the treatise made him a major influence, since the treatise was systematic and exceptionally well illustrated. "It was his comprehensiveness and unrivaled culling of the best models in ancient architecture that made Palladio the most influential architect in the modern period."

The Italian Renaissance transcended in a major respect this revival in terms of piecemeal apprenticeship to rediscovered classical models that would issue in independent achievements of first rank—comparable with Horace's self-apprenticeship to Greek poetry. That major respect is the cultural climate that favored this upsurge of creative energy in all the arts. As in classical Greece, Italy in the fifteenth century was composed of independent city-states, ruled by despots or oligarchies. Venice, Milan, and Florence were the strongest in the north, the kingdom of Naples in the south, with the papal states in the center. But there were many other enterprising cities: Genoa, Bologna, Mantua, Pisa, Perugia, Padua, Siena, Urbino, Verona, Ravenna, and a score more. Here was scope for rivalry and competition. Moreover, when government had been implanted by force and maintained by terrorism, the time came, in the fifteenth century, for more diplomatic methods by which a prince might establish his dynasty and stabilize his regime. Patronage of the arts might be intended to serve the ruler's interest in a personality cult, and at the same time commission artists to express their own vision, in the theater, in buildings, paintings, and sculpture. Documentation and exhibitions have shown this at work in many contexts—the Gonzaga family of Mantua, for instance. A few of these patrons of the arts were themselves enlightened and accomplished, of whom the Medici are the most famous.

The *botega,* the nursery of Leonardo, was like the Hellenic gymnasium in the selection and training of talent and the transmission of example and standards, although different in the activities and skills promoted; and the same could be said of Lorenzo's school in which Michelangelo was bred, founded on the collection of antiques Donatello had been responsible for. Engagement with antiquity and disengagement from it were equal in the independence of both Michelangelo and Leonardo.

The standards set in this way by the High Renaissance in Italy became general on the continent, and the nations manifested their characteristic genius in their achievements in music, poetry, drama, painting, sculpture, and architecture. This diverse display of originality was by common consent rooted in the soil of classical culture, and professed obedience to the same rules.

The insularity of Britain, the strongly marked individualism of the English temperament, at least since the twelfth century, made the place of England in European culture and its adoption of the classical rules especially instructive. The term "Augustan" became as characteristic in Britain as "High Renaissance" in Italy. What justification the term might have had derived from literary associations, but it extended to the settled dominance of classical influences in all the arts. France, which was England's neighbor and rival in everything, was the eldest son of Rome and an early leader in cultural development, so that it seemed to the English that they must always be inferior to Latins in that respect. The assertion of national vigor under the Tudors, in repelling the Spanish Armada, in voyages of discovery and of piracy, in the drama, in Spenser's romantic nationalism, looked more wild and willful than disciplined and classical. So were the great Elizabethan and Jacobean country mansions. The civil war was a rude interruption of what Inigo Jones had begun.

After the Restoration, with Italy and France as the recognized exemplars, the English set themselves to classicize or Latinize their arts. In architecture, the study of Palladio and Vitruvius established a style and a period that had begun with Inigo Jones and ended with Robert Adam, having its own modulations, the most conspicuous known as Queen Anne and Regency.

With the Restoration, too, came in the French formal garden instituted by Le Notre. The laws of Palladio and of Le Notre were complementary. Architecture and formal gardening engaged all who aspired to what was polite. Country house libraries were stocked with great folios of engravings. With the introduction of the Ha-Ha sunken fence, garden and park merged into the cultivated countryside, landscape passed into prospect, art into nature. The generality and solidarity of this collective culture were sustained by a horror of barbarism: uncultivated nature was barbaric; the Middle Age was barbaric; the Orient was barbaric. This was far from the "High Renaissance" response to nature, and these attitudes would be completely reversed in due course.

Meanwhile, the focus on antiquity, when no style was attacked or defended on the ground of its own merits, but only in relation to the rules of taste, led to a closer study of antiquity from which they were derived. Thus came about discovery of the distinction among Greek, Roman, and Greco-Roman, confused for centuries. The Middle Age knew nothing of Republican Rome. A general assumption was that Rome was the mother of all civilization, and that the art of antiquity, like that of the Renaissance, derived primarily from Rome. Ironically, the breach with the authority of the rules began with the discovery of Greece.

Many, particularly in France, wanted a proper revival of antiquity, and association of the arts with politics. With the French Revolution, the idea of republican Rome seemed the model for republican France; and the Greeks and Romans in general had an acknowledged superior status in arts and politics. France, which had been the model in taste and fashion for so many centuries, was still dominant. But England had claims to be considered as civilized as France. The victories of Marlborough and Chatham had restored her self-confidence.

In a rehearsal of Europe's history for its impact on the world, it may seem ill-judged to spend so many pages on the vexed question of aesthetic theory, and to have given space above to the no less vexed question of theological dogma. However, the uniformity imposed by a Rule of Faith under Theodosius was the unity of the first Europe. When that was fragmented by the Reformation, there was still the Rule of Taste, a regime under which nations produced works that were known, enjoyed, and indeed possessed internationally throughout Europe. The Rule of Taste was a European lingua franca.

In literature, the Renaissance came to mean two things, both discoveries. First, the distinctiveness of ancient Greece. Second, the Roman cultural apprenticeship to the Greeks that had enabled them to achieve literary works of comparable standing. This was the model on which the vernacular languages of Europe might learn to mature, and aspire to become classical.

Latin had been the European language of learning and instruction. Latin had been the language in which certain books had come down. Latin had been the language for the study of Greek philosophy. The sixteenth century was the time of the great translations: North's Plutarch, Philemon Holland's Livy, Savile's Tacitus, Chapman's Homer, Surrey's Virgil, many of Ovid. These were not mainly by scholars, some were not even from the original, so that they were not necessarily accurate. What they were warmly appreciated for was that they were vigorously written and immensely readable. They served their generation well. People were given a firmer hold of the classical past, and the *Gesta Romanorum* was made laughable. The grammar schools were being founded in the towns, at first with the idea of cultivating Latin composition in prose and verse as a linguistic discipline; but it was becoming evident that English itself could be made to provide that discipline. Samuel Daniel's *Defence of Ryme* (1602), written in admirable prose, asserted plainly that each language had its own genius and must go its own way.

John Milton (1608–1674) was consciously a paragon humanist poet. That is all that should need to be said for the present purpose, which is simply to indicate the recovery in European literatures of the classical models, and the response to them in original vernacular productions of comparable standard, as the Latins had learned from and responded to the Greeks. Milton has given his own account of his early years: his father's dedication of him to literature; his unremitting addiction to study; the opportunities that came his way at home, at school, at Cambridge; after graduation, his uninterrupted leisure entirely devoted to study of the Greek and Latin classics. After twelve years altogether of solid reading, he made a well-prepared journey to Italy, where he moved among the principal cities, meeting the men of learning he wanted to frequent. After fifteen months, he would have gone on to Sicily and Greece, but for the outbreak of civil war at home, which supervened on his maturely considered plan of education, as had a similar event on that of Horace, who also was fortunately served by an enlightened father.

This diligence and application furnished a mind unexampled, charged, pressed down, running over with stores of knowledge and impressions, remembered legibilities that conserved days and places of the famous past as personal possessions. Steeped in the literature, he had a true insight into the culture of this pre-Christian civilization, communication with the spirit that had informed it. Many of his early poems are in Latin, not merely as exercises in composition, but with the facility and felicity of an alternative language. He is versed also in Italian poetry, and brings back its sonnet for a new spell of example and influence. Milton's prosody combined resources of classical order with the freedom of English verse, like Spenser, who had resisted Gabriel Harvey's attempt to induce him to base his prosody on classical quantity, which he knew was not prescriptive for English.

The Greeks discovered the unending civilizing mission of literature. The Muses were the arts in their singular plural birth manifesting the music at the heart of the universe, particularly that "Blest paire of Sirens . . . Voice and Vers." The discipline and power of the word had been exhibited, and were to be cultivated forevermore. That was the secret that was being rediscovered in humanism. Milton was most conscious of its repossession.

There is a final reason for putting Milton in the historical window. He embodied Hellas, Zion, and Romanitas in cultural integration. He was fully familiar with all three literatures, and constantly consulted them. He had assimilated what they handed down: the culture, the faith, and the need for an imperium.

In the next generation, the Scriblerians, Pope, Gay, Arbuthnot, and Swift, collaborated under Martinus Scriblerus, the Don Quixote of learning, to put his erudition to the gigantic task of reducing to rule the practice in poetry of "Bathos." "The Beggar's Opera," "Gulliver's Travels," and "The Dunciad" proceeded from this initiative against all false tastes in learning, whether "The Art of Sinking in Poetry" or "The Art of Being Silly in Experimental Philosophy." A final act in the Lucianic flouting of rules was an epic in prose, with the hero a common man, the action merely entertaining, and the language familiar and discursive: Fielding's *Tom Jones*. The Augustan age had registered its achievement. The received models, the established genres, the formal rules of taste had done their work and had their day. They had left their permanent mark on the classics under their rule.

# 12

# Discovery of the Earth

## Voyages in Time and Space

The terms "legacy" and "inheritance" although freely used in historical contexts, may
be misleading in that connection. With similar freedom, history itself might be called
an allegory of our own times, insofar as we recognize ourselves under cover of other
times and places; but we would understand that history had no such purpose. In law,
you are a passive recipient of what is bequeathed to you by a personal will. In history, countries havè been bequeathed as dynastic possessions. In general, generations
collectively receive from their predecessors land and language, laws and customs,
works of art and of literature, social institutions. This is the stream of continuity, to
resort to another metaphor. The "legacy" metaphor breaks down when a chief part of
what comes down in the stream is rejected by an active leadership of a new generation that goes back to uncover and appropriate a submerged part of the total inheritance. What is bequeathed cannot be the same as something deliberately chosen and
taken. The historical synthesis stabilized by Theodosius I, the last effective Roman
emperor, which was the model for the Roman Church, had the profoundly important
consequence of molding the first Europe as a united and conscious Christendom. Historically, the synthesis had virtually eliminated Hellas and Romanitas.

Big names and reputations, and established systems (Plato, Aristotle, Plotinus,
Aquinas) perpetuate big mistakes with whatever may be of permanent relevance, and
blot out critical second thought (the New Academy, Arcesilas, Carneades, not Plato;
the reconstructed stoicism of Panetius and Posidonius, not Zeno and Epictetus; Aristotle of the museum, not the peripatetic; Aquinas in the light of Ockham). The Middle Age issued in increasing recognition of the past as an immense unknown, a field
of discovery, an inheritance but not a legacy. Piecemeal recovery of that inheritance
would help to work a transformation, with the mapping of the globe and the explo-

ration of nature. The Theodosian legacy on which the Middle Age subsisted had been an historical synthesis, but it could not endure. The time had come for its dissolution.

The voyage of historical discovery that would ensue would match the geographical voyages that were to inaugurate a new age with discovery of a new world. The transformation of the West that would make an impact on the world reached a way-station in the Enlightenment for reconnoiter of two centuries of the advancement of learning and of the prospects that it encouraged. Discovery of the earth, the habitat, and human self-discovery were gaining impetus, still insufficient for the final decisive impact.

## Caravels of Christ

In the ancient Mediterranean world, seamanship and sea powers piratical or imperial had been formative and often decisive. Minoans, Phoenicians, and Greeks had fleets that enabled them to raid and plunder, but also to establish trading posts and to plant colonies. It was the Athenian fleet that saved Greece from Persian conquest, and tempted or prompted the city's fatal bid for empire. The Vikings found their destiny by boat-building and seamanship, ravaging coasts and penetrating up rivers, touching North America and making an historic settlement in Normandy. This story of rapine, exploration, and settlement is repeated on a global scale by the nascent European nation-states: discovery, expansion, empire. Construction and destruction are yokefellows in this as in almost all human enterprise.

The span of oceanic explorations covers three centuries, from the early fifteenth century to 1780, when all the continents could be accurately mapped, and exploration would be interior. Three main phases are distinguishable: the Portuguese pioneer epic; the Spanish conquests; and rivalry of the British, French, and Dutch for settlements and trade. The first chapter opens with systematic exploration of the west coast of Africa during twenty-six years, promoted by Prince Henry the Navigator. This extended to Sierra Leone in 1460. Portugal was a small and poor country, and it was entirely due to the absolute conviction and resolution of Prince Henry that this enterprise was inspired and sustained. In him, as later in Columbus, there is an avowed and reiterated link between the purpose of the first voyages and the Crusades. Henry's "Plan of the Indies" dreamed of a Portuguese empire that would extend the Christian domain in a way that would exclude and deprive the infidel Muslim, and bring about his collapse. Henry remained single-minded in dedication to the first steps in this task.

To finance the colossal enterprise of his dreams, for which Portugal did not begin to have the means, the prince sought gold dust said to be found on the west coast of Africa. This was accessible, the source of marketable exotic products of value besides gold and slaves, and served as a training ground for acquisition of the skills and experience that would be needed for oceanic ventures. Henry invested in the attraction and employment of the most knowledgeable and skillful persons for his purpose. On the first expeditions he used sturdy vessels of medium tonnage, but soon recognized two desiderata: the capability of negotiating shallow waters and adaptability to the contrary winds that prevailed on the return journey. The caravel was chosen, and he steadily improved them in the light of experience on each expedition. Advantages of ship design were in the hands of seamen, particularly captains and pilots. Prince Henry recognized and insisted on the distinction between the authority of the captain, who had overall command and made and enforced decisions of policy in the conduct and action of the ship, and the navigator, who had the specialized knowledge and skills of a pilot, and in whose hands were the physical progress and survival of the ship. The prince at his base in Sagres schooled this breed of seaman, with the resources then available to the state of the art.

Henry the Navigator did not evangelize India and China, and he was not himself a "navigator." He was a medieval knight, *pur sang,* who devoted himself to his calling with unparalleled enthusiasm. That calling was the Christian military arm of the crusader. On the rim of the Atlantic, and with Portugal's naval interest, he invented the part of his country in oceanic terms. Clever, he mobilized the relevant scientific and technical resources available, organized sources of intelligence, and improved them by experience. Practical, he raised funds for the logistics of his expeditions. Patient, he used the gathering experience of these expeditions for a quarter of a century as the training ground for great adventures. With unwavering confidence, he inspired his mariners with the resolution to overcome their doubts and fears. Not himself one of these mariners, he pioneered for them a role that would eventually translate his medieval vision of a global Christendom into a Western civilization with a global impact. Some four hundred years later, David Livingstone would discover in the African interior that Western civilization was a necessary preliminary to any spread of the Christian faith.

Henry's initiative was sustained in the collective Portuguese endeavor to reach India across the Indian Ocean, after Bartolomeu Dias had rounded the Cape of Good Hope in 1488. Pedro de Covilha traveled through the Mediterranean and down the Adriatic to reach Goa and Calicut. Vasco da Gama crossed the Indian Ocean to the Malabar coast, with the help of an Arab pilot picked up in Mozambique. Successive voyages reached Malacca (1511) and the Moluccas (1512), the "Spice Islands." In 1514 they were at Macao, the mouth of the Canton River. Macao was occupied in 1557; by this time it was one of a system of forts and factories, more than fifty in number, founding a trading empire like that of the Phoenicians but vastly more extensive. This was not what Henry the Navigator had dreamed of for his country, but missionaries played their part. The system of forts and ports controlled the lucrative trade from the Spice Islands, which was a Portuguese monopoly until the Dutch drove them from the Molucca Islands in 1605. The Portuguese controlled the eastern part of Brazil, Angola in West Africa, and a long strip of the eastern coast above and below Mozambique.

## Westward Ho!

The reputedly Genoese seaman Christopher Columbus thought that sailing west would make the shortest and easiest route to the Spice Islands. He had visited Portugal, and in 1477 returned there and married the daughter of a Portuguese mariner who had been settled by Prince Henry on a small island in the neighborhood of Madeira. Columbus seems to have received from his mother-in-law all the charts and papers of her husband, after his death; and this may have been the material that prompted him to think that across the Atlantic he would strike the southeast coast of Asia.

He submitted a plan for an expedition to King John of Portugal, who granted him an interview. He asked for three caravels, with merchandise for barter, and he wanted the king to knight him, make him admiral and viceroy of the lands he might discover, and grant him a tenth of the revenues that might accrue.

The king submitted the plan to his own experts, who could find no sound basis for it; it was therefore rejected in 1484. His actual first voyage was not until 1492, and it was sponsored by Ferdinand and Isabella of Spain.

Columbus kept a day-by-day log of this voyage outward and homeward addressed to his royal patrons. In the month when the Moors were expelled from Granada, he had submitted to them information "about the land of India and about a Prince who is called the Great Khan." "Your Highnesses decided to send me to the regions of India, to see the Princes there and the peoples and the lands, and to learn of their disposition, and of everything, and the measures which could be taken for their conversion to our Holy Faith."

Like Henry the Navigator, Columbus is a medieval figure who links his expeditions with the Crusades. His entry for December 26, 1492 is underlined: "I have already petitioned Your Highnesses to see that all the profits of this, my enterprise, should be spent on the conquest of Jerusalem, and Your Highnesses smiled and said that the idea pleased them, and . . . they had the inclination to do it." Like Henry, he was also a man of the New World, dedicated to a line of close, firsthand investigation and using all available knowledge and skills relevant to his purpose, advancing them by experience. This was how the Greeks had practiced and improved their arts. Unlike Henry, he had lived his life at sea, perfecting the practice of his seamanship. At the time of this first Atlantic voyage, he had been "sailing the seas for 23 years, without laying off for any time long enough to be counted." He was captain of his "fleet," the usual three vessels of different capabilities that formed an expedition, and the other two ships were captained by experienced seamen. Pilots were employed to do the routine navigation: "I worked with my pilot to establish our true position." But this was a voyage into the unknown, and his course, with the availability of favorable winds, was Columbus's constant preoccupation.

On their way, when they were some distance from the Spanish shore, the crew had become terrified that they would never get back, and clamored to return. This fear of the open waters was a characteristic handicap. When Bartolomeu Dias rounded the cape, the crew's resistance forced him to return. Vasco da Gama reached India in spite of the hostility of his crew, by obduracy, cunning, and drastic high-handed action. On land, leaders of the Crusades suffered from the mass desertions of those who found an excuse to go home. At sea, the perils, apart from piracy, were storms and running out of provisions when becalmed or delayed. The unknown increased the risks; established routes that made the best use of calculable winds minimized them. Vasco da Gama discovered the best use of Atlantic winds in getting to the cape. Columbus on his return journey encountered a violent storm off the Azores. His log records the terror-stricken vows they made of pilgrimages if they should survive. As in the records of the Crusades, everything that happens, good or ill, is by the grace or the will of God. "Without God's intervention this country would not have been known as it has come to be known during our time here, and as it will be known by the people I intend to leave here." This was the island of Hispaniola. Cuba he believed was Japan. Columbus tells his royal patrons: "Those lands I have discovered are at the end of the Orient."

Columbus planted great wooden crosses on desirable sites to claim possession for his patrons. Everything and everybody is assumed to be entirely at their disposal. Of the six or seven natives he takes away from the Bahamas, he notes: "After they have learned our language I shall return them, unless Your Highnesses order that the entire population be taken to Castile, or held captive here. With 50 men you could subject everyone and make them do what you wished."

"Beyond doubt there is a very great amount of gold in this country. . . . Also there are precious stones and pearls, and an infinite quantity of spices." Columbus kept insisting that "it was to be the beginning and the end of the enterprise that it should be for the increase and the glory of the Christian religion," to be furthered, of course, by the glory of the Spanish throne in the increase of the realm.

This was the first of the four voyages Columbus made to set foot on China. He returned in 1493 to explore the south coast of Cuba (supposed to be a peninsula of mainland China). In 1498 he discovered Trinidad and the coast of Venezuela; and in 1502–1504 he explored the coasts of Honduras and Nicaragua and Panama, still believing he was on the shores of Asia.

Columbus's signals to Ferdinand and Isabella in the log of his first voyage started the Spanish empire in the New World, first in Hispaniola and Cuba (1511), then in Mexico, finally in Peru (1531–1534). By 1600, Spanish control extended from Mexico to Chile and Paraguay, as well as Cuba, East Florida, Hispaniola, and Puerto Rico. Before noticing the work of the conquistadores, mention must be made of Ferdinand Magellan's epic voyage, because it rounded off the oceanic discoveries of the period, and because he was a Portuguese mariner, although sponsored on this voyage by Spain. He had served with the Portuguese in the East, and submitted a plan to Charles V for reaching the Moluccas by a western route across the Atlantic. In 1519 he set sail from San Lucar with five ships (from 60 to 130 tons). Having coasted Patagonia, he entered the strait named after him, 350 miles long, with dangerous reefs, which he followed for 38 days until he came out into the ocean, which he named the Pacific because it was calm. He turned up the coast of Chile before veering west. More than three months later the Philippines were his landfall. He was killed there in a local conflict. One of his ships got back to Spain in 1552, completing a voyage round the world for the first time. He had shown that it was not the most practicable trade route to the East. More important for the map, he demonstrated practically the scale and unity of the earth, with the interconnection of its oceans.

# Philip II's Holy Roman Empire

It is well enough known that after Spain had conquered and settled in Hispaniola and Cuba, Herman Cortés on his own initiative with an army of some six hundred conquered the Aztec empire of Mexico, setting out from Veracruz, where he had established himself on the mainland a few months previously. The empires of the Aztecs and the Incas conquered by the Spanish contrasted with the Indian tribes of North America. An early civilization is an advanced organization of a numerous population concentrated within the area, supported by a thriving agriculture (surplus), with a margin of energy displayed in monumental buildings. An empire, by definition, is established by conquest and maintained by domination; and that is the usual way in which the central organization of an extensive populated territory was achieved in early times. The conquerors would generally maintain a totalitarian regime, until overthrown.

The civilizations that fluctuated in Mexico, northern Central America, and Peru and Bolivia had origins before 1000 B.C.E., expanding by the domination of successive cities. The largest of these early Mexican empires extended to the highlands of Guatemala, and lasted from about 300 to 600 C.E. There were neighboring civilizations, of which the Mayas are in retrospect the most conspicuous who occupied Guatemala, chiefly in the south. Their agriculture was primitive, and their relatively advanced culture disintegrated when population exceeded the food supply about 900 C.E.

This was before the Incas, moving from the rural south, conquered all the coast and highlands from northern Ecuador to central Chile. They imposed a totalitarian regime by subdividing the population into units of ten, mostly in villages. Urban survivals were of a kind that did not threaten imperial rule.

It may be surmised that the American empires did not have the close contact and mutual borrowing and learning that endowed the Bronze Age empires with fertility passed down culturally, not genealogically, to the European nations.

The Aztec and Inca empires and civilizations were extinguished by the Spaniards. Mexico was conquered by Cortés (1519–1520) and Peru by Francisco Pizarro (1531–1533). These territories were vast in extent, and more than substantial in wealth, especially when silver mines were discovered and exploited. Conquest is seldom dispatched by an initial step, however decisive. After the fall of the Aztec capital, Cortés set about the building of a Spanish replacement and the construction of a fortified harbor, the building of ships, and the manufacture of gunpowder and of artillery. All this, accomplished by ingenuity and energy organized by Cortés on the spot from local resources supplemented by supplies from Spain, is a more astonishing achievement than the taking of the capital. His prospective view of this first endeavor in the New World is indicated in a letter Cortés wrote to Charles V in 1524 about the ships that brought supplies from Spain. "I cannot express how much I value these ships. For I hold it certain that with them, if God will, I shall bring it about that your Caesarean Majesty shall be lord of more kingdoms and lordships than are known in Spain up till now and . . . that your Highness need do no more in order to be monarch of the world." This may have been nonsense and judicious flattery, but the image of Roman imperialism shines through, and in fact the Spanish empire was to exceed Rome's in extent.

Cortés was untiring until his death in further exploration and in expansion and development of the Spanish dominion. He equipped four expeditions to explore the Pacific coasts. One he commanded himself was the first to discover the coast of California, a foothold from which Spain would go on to reach beyond San Francisco and embrace a great part of what is now the southern United States.

The conquest of half the New World, it can be said, was by Spanish privateers operating mainly on land. It was not systematic; it was not consecutive. The Peruvian conquest extended northward to Ecuador and Colombia, and southward to Chile, western Bolivia, and stage by stage into occupation of the region of the River Plate, the most fertile and desirable of all Spain's acquisitions, eventually secured with the foundation of Buenos Aires in 1580. Venezuela was a one-off German enterprise that proved unprofitable, and passed into Spanish hands about 1550. The coast from Cumana to the Gulf of Darien was occupied piecemeal at various points for penetration into the interior.

Thus there was pieced together by the mid-sixteenth century an immense South American Spanish empire of uninterrupted physical continuity. Although acquired piecemeal by individual enterprise, it was organized by the Spanish government in a practical and effective way. The Mexican and Peruvian nucleus was under the two vice-royalties, with governors subordinate to the viceroys responsible for lesser provinces. Municipalities with a territorial jurisdiction were the foundation of administration, as in the Roman Empire. Assemblies, which functioned as administrative councils and judicial tribunals, were seated in the principal capitals. Locally, there were districts under magistrates. Trade with Spain was protected, and under fiscal control. Spain was the first nation to be dominant in Europe. The conquistadores had given history the only realistic version of the Holy Roman Empire.

In 1527 Philip II inherited from his father, Charles V, the rule of substantial European dependencies as well as the Indies: the kingdoms of Sicily and Sardinia and Naples, land in Africa and northern Italy, and the "Spanish Netherlands."

Suleiman the Magnificent ruled an Ottoman Empire equal to that of Charles V. An empire of the Faith was opposed to an equal empire of the Infidel, when the alien faith had recently and painfully been swept from Spain itself after centuries of Moorish occupation. From Tripoli to Spanish Morocco, corsair pirates haunted and hunted the Mediterranean, under the patronage of Suleiman, who garrisoned Algiers, their chief base. He gained a good percentage of their plunder, and had a naval presence he could use to his advantage at will.

France was no friend of Spain, and Venice, with the largest fleet, had favorable trading relations with the sultan. Charles V had allowed the Military Knights of the Order of St. John, unemployed veterans of the Crusades, to settle in Malta, for use against Suleiman's corsair irregulars. They changed their name to the Sovereign and Military Order of the Knights of Malta. Suleiman was persuaded that it was necessary to take Malta. Because of the size of the Turkish fleet, Philip was not willing to go to its aid. Meanwhile, the knights were fighting stubbornly against overwhelming odds, ready to resist to the last man. When at last a fleet did arrive from Spanish Italy, and put ashore 9,600 men, the Turks had abandoned the siege, suffering from fever and afraid of being held there with winter advancing. Nearly half of the knights were dead, and most of the remainder were crippled.

When Suleiman died, there was a new sultan and a new pope, Pius V. The pope was an ascetic wholly dedicated in opposition to the enemies of Rome: the Turk and the Protestant. He wanted to facilitate and make effective the Holy League in the contest with the Ottoman Empire for control of the Mediterranean and the safety of the (mainly) Italians whose shores it washed. Venice and Spain were the principal Catholic powers involved, and they were unwilling partners, not only because of Venetian commercial interests but also because Spain was the totalitarian oppressor of its Italian possessions. Cooperation with Spain, which was the only way in which Turkish designs could be frustrated, was at least as reluctant and unlikely as the alliance of Athens and Sparta against Persia, but it came about when the sultan followed up an ultimatum by capturing Cyprus.

In 1571, Spain, Venice, and the papacy formally proclaimed a treaty of alliance, offensive and defensive, equipped with galleys, transports, infantry, and cavalry, committed to campaign in the open season every year against the Ottoman Turks and their Moorish vassals along the North African coast. The three commanders would make decisions by majority vote. Don John, the bastard half-brother of King Philip, was captain-general of the combined fleets. In August the allied forces assembled at Messina. The Turks had bases in Greece, and advanced to meet the Christians from Lepanto (Naupactos) on the Gulf of Patras.

The battle of Lepanto has been described in detail from accounts of those who took part. The fighting raged from early in the morning to four in the afternoon on Sunday, October 7, 1571. The league lost about seven thousand men and twelve galleys. The Turks lost more than twenty-five thousand men and their battle fleet, 180 galleys captured and many sunk. Twelve thousand Christian galley slaves were freed. Some had filed through their fetters and taken part in the battle. Cervantes, who fought valiantly and was hit twice in the chest and had his left hand permanently maimed, thought that Lepanto was "the greatest occasion that past or present ages have witnessed or that the future can hope to witness." It was not, as reputed, one of the decisive battles of the world, a Salamis, an Actium, a Trafalgar. It did not remove the Turk from the Mediterranean and it was not followed up. It was a tremendous boost to Christian morale because it showed that the Turk was not invincible.

For all its early presence and active role in Europe, Spain was aloof and alien, a foreigner and an enemy. She was hostile to the Reformation, the Renaissance, and the Enlightenment, to the formative principles that transformed Europe. The state was collectivist because of its espousal of Christian orthodoxy. The people were passionate and violent individualists, whose pride preserved their separation, or plunged them to mad excess. Death was ultimate reality, which might encourage a death wish. It is said of those who fought with the conquistadores that eight out of ten perished. Spain made the Middle Age its spiritual empire, and did not join modern Europe until recently, when nations have shown conspicuously how adaptable they can be, since the Second World War.

## The West Rough-Hewn

There are three universal aspects of this European initiative that begin with the voyages of discovery, distinct but connected. There are first the map-making discoveries and the worldwide network of communications. Second, there is European expansion overseas by conquest and settlement. Third are the economic consequences for Europe. The first starts with the rounding of the Cape of Good Hope and the passage to India and ends with Cook's last voyage, a period extending from 1487 to 1780, some forty expeditions that increased geographical knowledge or communication facilities. The pioneer work was done by the Portuguese and Spaniards; the last voyages by Captain Cook were the most scientific in equipment and findings. The explorations were not for the sake of knowledge, but for the hope of gain, for gold, exotic products, slaves, and then for land. The new world of America was conquered and occupied. Empires were acquired by Spain, Portugal, England, France, and Holland, with fluctuations in possession with the rivalry of nations, but expanding the Christendom of medieval Europe, a unity in diversity.

The economic consequences were ultimately decisive for Western ascendancy. The maritime enterprise was consummated in commercial enterprise that became continuous investment in competitive industrial innovation. Wealth invested in industrial expansion rather than in conquest and display was a new theme, a new type of civilization, a European invention. It came about as an outcome of conjunctions of occurrences, not deliberately. At any level, an economic surplus is a necessary condition of a highly organized society. Economic exploitation is more than husbandry and plunder, for it is a system of wealth production consciously managed. It may be disastrous. The bids for world empire, Roman or European or Mongolian or Turkish, were fantasies. Meanwhile, what nobody thought of or strove for came about in stages by the development of ordinary transactions started by voyages into the unknown in the fifteenth century.

European expansion by acquisition of overseas territory discovered by the exploratory voyages was not exactly a "gold rush," but it was intensely competitive. The Portuguese, as the pioneers, were not pleased by Spanish entry into the field. A compromise was arranged in the Treaty of Tordesillas (1494) by which new lands to the east of a meridian 370 leagues west of the Cape Verde islands would belong to Portugal, and those west of the line to Spain. The English, French, and Dutch, not to dispute with Portugal and Spain in the south Atlantic, tried to find a passage to Asia by a northern route. They had no more reason to succeed in that than Columbus, but eleven voyages, from Cabot's rediscovery of Newfoundland (1497) to exploration of the Hudson Bay and the coastline of Baffin Bay (1610–1616) achieved an expansion of European geographical knowledge in leading to the conclusion that there was no practicable northwest passage.

These early voyages of discovery laid the foundations of an expanded commerce in the East and of the New World in the West. Africa was not colonized nor conquered, save for the coastal strips on the east and the west under Portuguese control.

However, it was used as a main source of slaves for the exploitation of land taken into possession across the Atlantic.

Spain, France, England, and Holland were engaged in intense rivalry for possession of islands in the Caribbean, for the production of sugar for Europe. Spain held Cuba, Hispaniola, Puerto Rico, and Trinidad, but the others established possessions, the French in the Windward and the Leeward Islands and the Bahamas, the English in Jamaica, the Dutch in the Lesser Antilles. On the mainland, the English had colonies in the east from Newfoundland to South Carolina; and the French had explored St. Lawrence and the Mississippi to the Gulf of Mexico, establishing fortified posts. In the East, there were Dutch, English, Spanish, French, and Portuguese trade routes, and corresponding places under their control, with Dutch and English preponderance.

Russia under Ivan III (1462–1505) expanded northward to the White Sea, and under his successors across the Urals into Siberia; and with the conquest of Astrakhan Russia gained control of the Volga to the Caspian Sea.

Thus the voyage of Columbus in 1492 initiated a reorientation of Europe, a gradual turning from preoccupation with the past to investment in the future; "investment" because it was actually bound up with economic investment that looked for a return, short-term or long-term, on an international scale. Ocean routes to the East expanded an existing international trade. New lands in the West were exploited by the application of European methods of production. New products, principally sugar, developed new methods of production. New lands increased available natural resources, not least gold and silver. Capital accumulation and the supply of labor were increased. To take advantage of these new opportunities, there had to be political and social changes that would amount to a transformation, innovations or improvements in services, institutions, and organization. Communications required a constantly improving infrastructure, not only in roads and waterways but also in ship-building and navigation, as later in new forms of transport. Public and private confidence in business deals required legally enforceable contracts, security of private property (predictability), insurance, trustworthy accountancy, financial facilities, and legal status for manufacturing and trading companies. The scale of the changes strengthened the influence and enlarged the ranks of "merchants" as agents, agencies, and organizers. Their activities in such functions demanded an area of freedom from restrictions imposed by governments or guilds. Institutions, including states, are constitutionally resistant to change, which normally occurs under external pressure. This pressure is exerted mainly by the mercantile class for the innovations they require and initiate. The underlying condition forcefully making for change was competition, which prevailed massively between states, and inherently between private enterprises.

The transformation worked by these changes together was, as it were, an enlargement to global proportions of the transformation from subsistence to a market economy, when a surplus allows investment for a prospective return. There was thus initiated a process of systematic economic growth: continuous investment in competitive innovative expansion of production and exchange. The process would be, was bound to be, fluctuating, not steady, not a prosperity based on security and stability. All the same, 1492 initiated a process that, in partnership with the advancement of science "for the relief of man's estate" (Bacon), would form a new model in competition with the three inherited from antiquity and the composite idealized in the Middle Age, a new model formulated by Adam Smith in the *Wealth of Nations* that would gain ascendancy in the West, with a claim to universality. Relations between this new model and the inheritance—Christendom, Imperialism, Culture (Hellas)—are generally indirect and indecisive; they are nonetheless competitive, and are with us today, transformed in contemporary issues. From beginning to end, human motivation in terms of material incentives is the determinant. This new social model that supervened on the process initiated by the private enterprise of voyages of discovery is properly named capitalism, but unresolved controversy practically prohibits its use for the purpose. The essence of the matter is "sustained economic growth."

That sustained economic growth is distinctive of the West is illustrated by the case of China, which in the fifteenth century was technologically in advance of Europe, and had a developed administration recruited on merit. With far larger ships than the Portuguese had, China dominated ocean trade with Africa in the early century, and might well have preceded and exceeded Europe in gaining prizes in the wealth of nations. But the motivation was lacking at the top, and her overseas trade came to an end after 1433. At the very top, satisfaction with what may be called ritualistic success ruled, a plateau of economic attainment that was deemed adequate. The bureaucracy had the constitutional resistance to change. There lacked external pressure, the competitive plurality of European nations and governments. Within Europe itself, Spain was all but eliminated from European competition for sustained economic growth. She was "milked" by her competitors, England, Flanders, Holland, France, and Italy, who used her facilities and took her business. Charles V and his dynasty were Hapsburg emperors who employed foreign economic advisers. Longterm, however, was the aloof, profoundly Catholic medieval orientation, an aspect of the Spanish temper. A difference of values, as in China.

## Exploitation of Indigenous Peoples

With the discovery of lands across the Atlantic came the finding of their inhabitants. Something must be said about what the Europeans made of them and what they did with and to them. First, a word or two about the inhabitants as they really were at that time, on the archaeological evidence available and extant Indian traditions. They were named "Indians" because Columbus and subsequent mariners thought they were sailing to the Indies. The lands the mariners discovered had been inhabited for thousands of years, probably not less than twenty-five thousand, and entered from Siberia. The wide range of differences in climate, geology, and topography from Alaska to Cape Horn afforded human habitats of like diversity, with cultures adapted to them. Thousands of distinct technological, artistic, and social traits have been catalogued; and more than two hundred languages have been identified. Local environments were dominant, and for want of advanced tools and techniques, inhabitants were generally highly adapted to specific environments. This is dramatically illustrated by the Eskimos of Alaska, since otherwise physical existence would not be possible in Arctic conditions. Under stress, they are the most innovative among peoples of simple cultures.

European history is spelled out in centuries, prehistory in millennia; although the distinction cannot be applied to what was going on in unknown America, the state of affairs among the inhabitants when Europeans came to settle there was not as it had always been. Glacial ice coverage was a basic condition, with an immense shrinkage between about 9000 and 4000 B.C.E. In the early period big-game hunting was the predominant way of life. With the decline of stocks, the natives had perforce to become hunter-gatherers, foraging for plant foods, fishing, and hunting small game. This would be happening about 4000 B.C.E. Settled farming developed later in some places, and is estimated to have reached its greatest extent about 1000 C.E. This was mainly in the southeast and southwest of North America, leaving out of this account the cultures of Mexico and South America, with their late history mentioned above. Eskimos engaged in sea fishing were by this time inhabiting northern coastal regions. Foraging, supplemented by small game, would have been very different in the western deserts, where resources were sparse, and in eastern woodlands or the well-endowed region of what is northern California and British Columbia, where natural abundance made life easy. In the southwest, influences from Mexico may have encouraged agriculture in an area that required irrigation to make it practicable. Lastly, the thousands of massive mounds, from Florida to eastern Texas and from west of New York to Nebraska, which so mystified European settlers, furnish archaeological evidence of a settled culture built on trading, not agriculture, associated with and only less advanced than the cultures of Mexico and Peru.

The question of what the Europeans made of the Native Americans has to be answered back home. The question of what they did with and to them was answered on the ground. The Europeans most permanently concerned are the Spanish in South America, the English and French in North America, and all three in the West Indies. At the outset, the natives en bloc constituted three distinct European interests; they were souls to be saved; they were subjects to be protected and taxed; they were workers and servants to be used. Christian missionaries of the religious orders, principally Jesuits, were among the explorers of the impenetrable Amazonia. When the Jesuits were expelled from the Spanish dominions in 1767, their property, which was sold, was some measure of their scale of operations. Philip II's laws to protect his new subjects were unenforceable. What was done to them on the ground was the reality for them, and for history.

Before the European conquest of the New World, only about one million people lived in what is now the United States, Canada, and northern Mexico. Probably another million were in the Caribbean. Brazil, the Amazonian region, Chile, and Argentina would have had less than two million all told. This vast numerical disparity between North and South America, with a massive concentration of populations in the area of Mexico and Peru, is the demographic picture to be borne in mind when considering what was done, and the consequences. In general, the Indians, north and south, were not employed by the settlers; there was no partnership. So far as it was tried, the result was not what was expected. That was the main reason for the importation of slave labor, which began toward the end of the sixteenth century and rapidly became a major business extending into the nineteenth century, which introduced a new, non-European population into the Americas, and accelerated the process of capital accumulation. In little more than a century, the Indian population declined by more than 90 percent in Mexico, Peru, and some other highly populated regions. Lacking immunity by their isolations they were prone to European diseases, which could all but eliminate local communities. Moreover, in these areas, the Indians were ousted from their urban cultures and relegated to the countryside, a form of dispossession that permanently alienated them in a way that was different from the alienation suffered by the North American Indians.

The North American Indians have been preserved artificially, so far as they have survived. Their behavior, positive and negative, was persistently misunderstood by the settlers, who judged by their own standards of ownership, hard work, and thrift, what they brought with them from Europe to invest in the new land of opportunity. It was natural to see the Indians as scalping warriors, leaving what little work was done to the women.

The Europeans saw a wilderness of wasteland virtually empty and available, which they could appropriate without injury to anyone; indeed, by making "two blades of grass to grow upon a spot of ground where only one grew before" they and their families could not only prosper but also do well for mankind. Therefore, fields and fences would march over and subjugate the wilderness.

This faceless wilderness was actually a landscape the Indians had made over the years to suit their way of life, by systematically using fire to clear the underbrush and keep an open, park-like forest favorable to the increase of mammals that they hunted for food while the women did most of the gathering and crop-raising. The principle was cohabitation with the animals and plants of their territory, which provided enough for all. Ownership in the way in which tools might be possessed was meaningless to them. On such terms, they were willing to share the land with newcomers, who brought new things of interest to them. The disease germs the newcomers brought with them were lethal as in the south, epidemics claiming a 50 to 90 percent death rate. Later arrivals of immigrants along the coast of New England found Indian settlements wiped out, "the land littered with bleached bones and skulls." For the Puritans it was Divine Providence.

The inexorable demand of settlers for more land as populations expanded and more immigrants arrived required treaties with the Indians, if they were not to be just driven out or exterminated. The Appalachians were made a boundary to contain settlement. It was ruled that Indian land could only be bought. The Indian response was in effect that the land was not theirs to sell, and anyhow was more valuable to them than money: "As a present to you we will give anything we have that you can take with you; but the land, never." Resort was made to the transportation of whole tribes to a designated area, behind a new permanent Indian frontier. But U.S. laws and provisions (like those of the Spanish crown remote from the scene) could not restrain the relentless pressure to move to the West by which the Europeans fulfilled their "manifest destiny." By the 1840s they had reached the Spanish possessions, and the Mexican War of 1846 added an enormous area to what was the United States. When two years later gold was discovered in California, there was the "gold rush." Estimates are that by the beginning of the 1800s there were as many as 260,000 Indians in California, of whom a hundred years later 15,000 to 20,000 remained at most. Vigilante groups had taken it upon themselves to remove a people with whom they had no wish to coexist. The Great Plains remained in Indian hands, where adoption of horse and gun from the Europeans had enabled Indian tribes to find a new way of life by hunting the great herds of bison. The traffic of westward trails across the plains to California and Oregon occasioned conflict that became open war, with massacres and atrocities. The Sioux could not be defeated, and were tackled by destruction of the buffalo herds.

The end was the consignment of all surviving Indian tribes to reservations, amounting in extent to perhaps one-fifteenth of the land they had once occupied; even this was not sacrosanct, if expediency pressed. Deprived of their habitat, as pensioners of the white man, with the image of them entertaining to the new Americans, they did not have even the diminished place in Western society enjoyed by the Indians of South America. They were left with a symbolic culture that recalled their past. The newcomers, having broken their bond with the land, had broken their spirit.

What did the Europeans at home make of these "Indians" who were not in the Bible? The American Red Man and the African Black Man were not just late additions to the human family; they had no necessary connections with the family. Thomas Hobbes defeated the idea of a "noble savage," the idealization of primitive innocence, and added his grounds to the basic Christian notion of the fall of man. This gave a free run to prejudiced selection of whatever was damaging to the reputation of the "Indians," with the formation of stereotypes, the scalping, blood-thirsty warrior, naked cannibals, and the like.

That was the popular view, supposedly based on experience. But the philosophic view was just as prejudiced. If the standard of judgment remains what is contemporary and familiar, there is an insuperable barrier to understanding.

Montaigne's ranging mind could not be representative, but his *Essays* were widely read and influential. Since the new men in the New World were of great interest in Europe, his *Des Cannibales* was particularly discussed. Although he immersed himself in the classics, Montaigne was wary of forming a view shaped by preconceived ideas; he thought he would get closer to reality through the eyes of the seamen and traders who had been to the new lands and had something to do with the inhabitants. He also met in France three natives of Brazil who had been brought there, and questioned them with the aid of an unsatisfactory interpreter. His classical start was to recall that the Greeks called "barbarian" all who did not speak Greek, to make the point that "barbarians" and "savages" were merely different. He describes some of the differences, and parallels, as elicited from his Brazilians. Accepting the negatives, that they are without the civilized arts and sciences, he makes the capital point of their not needing them; they do not have to improve on nature; they enjoy the bounty of a sufficient provision to hand; they can use gold merely for ornamentation. Although his contact is with Portuguese Brazilian captives, he comes near to understanding the orientation of the North American foragers that the Puritans found perverse. He sees the Indians as having a society, as enjoying what is needed, in a state of stability and contentment. He is likely to have been able to make this judgment because of his close familiarity with the ideas of the Stoics and the Epicureans. He possessed a copy of Diogenes Laertius's *Lives of the Philosophers,* in which Epicurus is allowed to speak for himself at length. There he would read:

> Nature's wealth at once has its bounds and is easy to procure; but the wealth of vain fancies recedes to an infinite distance.
>     He who understands the limits of life knows how easy it is to procure enough to remove the pain of want and make the whole of life complete and perfect. Hence he has no longer any need of things which are not to be won save by labour and conflict.

Montaigne would be enabled to see the Indians living the life of that philosophy, as the Puritans were not. He was also interested and amused to hear the views of the Brazilians on what they had noticed about French customs and behavior, opinions that were neither awestruck nor pointless. It broke into the Eurocentric view of the world.

When Hobbes writes of "those qualities of mankind that concern their living together in peace and unity," he is thinking institutionally of a sovereign authority empowered to protect each individual against his neighbor's aggression. That is indeed a condition of civil society, but it is not enough where or when there are ethnic or cultural differences that seriously impair social coexistence.

# 13

# Discovery of Nature

The "Rule of Taste" was established by the discovery of Greco-Roman civilization and of Roman learning from Greek artistic achievements. In the realm of ideas, what was recovered was more unsettling. For it undermined the authority of Aristotelian orthodoxy. New models were looked for, but with basic assumptions in doubt, John Donne could go on to say: "Tis all in pieces, all coherence gone."

The rule of laws, the laws of nature, would reestablish coherence; but that awaited the advancement of learning, a new enterprise. That direction was set more by practice on the ground and a new start in philosophy than by the flotsam of ideas from antiquity, which floated into the prevalent ideological brew.

It is tempting to see Montaigne as the one who "calls all in doubt," steeping himself in the classics and finding nothing assured; and Francis Bacon as fully positive, seeing the advancement of learning "closing up truth to truth, as we find it," in John Milton's phrase. Thus they would stand back to back at this turning point in European history, the one concluding with a negative assessment of the inheritance: "Que scais-je?"; the other opening a new chapter with abundant confidence: "There is all to do, and we now know how to do it." Unfortunately for the graphic, the historical persons do not allow themselves to be represented. Montaigne particularly: nobody's reading of the classics was less barren. He drew on classical poetry and history and moral philosophy, the humanist program Isocrates had commended, and especially on the Romans formed by that experience, not only the Augustans, but also those of the republic and those of the late empire; and he took hold personally of what came home to him, so that he was fertilized and expanded and transported in imagination, with bearings on the human condition; and in reflection he married his reading to his commerce with the world.

Montaigne is feeding on an inheritance that is permanent, not progressive, that expands and charges responsiveness, rather than closes up truth to truth; whilst Bacon is wholly set on a task for which the specific tool that promises to transform the human lot is in hand. These two aspects of the human condition are represented contemporaneously in these two stances at a turning point that can be seen retrospectively to augur a definite human destiny, for which Europe is responsible.

## A Renaissance Philosophy

The nascent movement that in the seventeenth century, "the century of genius," gained strength and recognition for epoch-making successes, the empirical study of nature, then called "natural philosophy," emerged from confusion with the recrudescence of an ancient occult philosophy or theosophic tradition associated with Egypt and Chaldea, and particularly with the name of Hermes Trismegistus. This was an eclectic tradition that picked up elements from Plato, the stoics, Philo, Christianity, Neo-Platonism, Gnosticism, Neo-Pythagoreanism, and the Jewish cabala. Its European revival had two main sources: principally, the Platonic translations and studies initiated by Marsilio Ficino in Florence at the instance of Cosimo de Medici. This was not a straightforward study of Plato's works, for it included what had been attributed in late antiquity to Hermes Trismegistus, Zoroaster, Orpheus, and Pythagoras, as well as the Neo-Platonists. Other influences, Christian and Arabic, contributed their share. The other main source was the Rosicrucian secret religious fraternity that originated in the fifteenth century with Christian Rosencrentz (born 1378) who on his European travels accumulated a store of learning that he collated in his search for the true philosophy that would improve mankind. The fraternity he formed went about relieving the poor and attending to the sick. It was secret to avoid conflict with orthodox, enforceable teaching. After the Protestant Reformation, that was not so necessary in some places; and in the sixteenth century its doctrines and practices became well known and won distinguished adherents, including, in England, Elias Ashmole and Sir Robert Moray, first president of the Royal Society.

It has to be said of this immense revival of theurgy at this time that it was not a minority cult. It was the only traditional body of thought to replace the Aristotelian cosmology, that had been dominant and with which it was irreconcilable. It is thus the Renaissance philosophy that commanded respect from contemporary thinkers. In England, John Dee, one of the most learned Elizabethans, and Edmund Spenser, the patriot poet, dreamed that Elizabeth, scion of a stable monarchy, would make this universal religion prevail imperially throughout Europe and the world—a new version of Romanitas.

However, the fever of ideological revival in Italy included more that was influential, even under Florentine auspices. Fausto Paulo Sozzini (1539–1604) was for twelve years secretary to Cosimo de Medici's son-in-law in Florence. A lawyer educated in the new learning and influenced by an uncle also a lawyer who had Reformation sympathies, whose papers he inherited, Sozzini applied himself as a layman to theological studies; that is, he applied his reason to his own reading of the Bible, as the only authentic source of Christianity. This led to a drastic purge of doctrine. On the death of his Florentine employer, he found his way to Poland, where he organized the radical Minor Reformed Church, later engulfed by the rising tide of the Counter-

Reformation. His successors, Johann Crell (1590–1633) and Jonas Schlichting (1602–1661) established Socinianism in its mature form as a seminal influence. The Socinian purge was a rejection of doctrines that did not square with reason and moral sense, and had no evident foundation in the Bible. England from the mid-seventeenth to the mid-eighteenth century was in a ferment of religious argument, and it was from here that radical religious ideas found their way to France, and to America, many of whose colonists were religious refugees. By the mid-eighteenth century, interest was shifting from theology to political and social issues. The careers of Thomas Paine and Joseph Priestley show the shift and the connection.

Bacon's name has been linked with this occult Renaissance philosophy, but that is superficial. There is an unbridgeable division between his long-term advancement of learning and the immediacy sought in access to all knowledge and power by finding the key to the universe. They are different universes of discourse. John Comenius and others who wanted to combine the "New Philosophy" with alchemical ideas and occult practices failed to understand Bacon's innovation. There was no formula that would unlock nature at one stroke in the laborious Baconian method of closing up truth to truth.

## Natural Philosophy

Empirical science plots in detail the emergence of European thought from obscurity and confusion into the light of understanding by methodical inquiry. This took place over three centuries, from the fifteenth to the end of the eighteenth. In 1600 Giordano Bruno was executed by order of the Inquisition, for which the eminent theologian Cardinal Bellarmine was responsible. Bruno had accepted the Copernican theory of the solar system, but his own cosmology was speculative, and he did not die for the new science, but for freedom of inquiry. The new science emerged from engagement with practical problems, and was not interested in speculative thought about the cosmos. Simon Stevinus (1548–1620) was a military engineer and mathematician, and a designer of ingenious contrivances. As a Dutchman, he was involved in problems of hydraulics in connection with sluices; and he calculated the pressures exerted by water, a non-rigid body, at different depths and directions. This prepared the way for Robert Boyle some decades later to tackle questions of gaseous pressure. Isaac Newton's first law of motion, seen in retrospect as epoch-making, was at close range followed by a constellation of technical questions and further work by himself and innumerable others that in technical detail makes the history of science. In mechanics, ideas of velocity and force, for example, had to be refined in precise conceptions that could describe what actually happened. A constant speed had been thought to require a constant force, the misconception that postulated incorruptible celestial bodies that moved uniformly and in a circle if undisturbed. Galileo, by inference from observations of the behavior of earthly bodies, was led to think of undisturbed motion as uniform. It was acceleration, not speed, that he found constant under constant force. This was the kind of advance that was made at that time, by turning from traditional ideal notions and assumptions to observations secured by mathematics and measurement.

Galileo raised his eyes from observing the behavior of objects on the surface of the planet. Having heard of Dutch experiments that combined lenses for magnification in a telescope, he improved on what had been done, to produce the telescopes with which he made his astronomical investigations. He became convinced that the planets were physical bodies with features like the "corruptible" earth, and that the Copernican theory was correct. Having proved the importance of lenses for astronomy, he recognized the value they would have for microscopy in other fields of science. Craftsmen in Italy and the Netherlands adapted their skill to produce and test lenses for this. Their use required the preservation and preparation of specimens for examination. Observation of the red corpuscles of the blood was one of the first achievements of the microscope. Shortly the Italian pioneer in microscopic anatomy, Marcello Malpighi, saw the blood moving in the capillary vessels of a frog's lung, evidence for William Harvey's proof of the circulation of the blood. Meanwhile, the mechanical aids that had been invented in addition to telescopes and microscopes, such as clocks, thermometers, and barometers, multiplied observations in an accumulation of masses of data. This reinforced the need for cooperation and communication. There were guilds and learned societies; and there was correspondence in letters on subjects of mutual interest. There were informal meetings. Robert Boyle and Christopher Wren, for example, were in the habit of meeting fairly regularly with others in London or Oxford. The Royal Society, the Académie des Sciences, and scientific journals by this informal activity were anticipated before they were established.

The advancement of science is furthered by specialism only when it is organized in a professionally integrated movement, however. The development of chemistry particularly was handicapped by isolation. Few eighteenth-century chemists knew and appreciated the advances made in seventeenth-century physics. A chemist would not necessarily know and use the work of a previous worker in his field.

Classification as a feature of description is scientific if it builds a system that can prompt and guide further research. Carl Linnaeus (1707–1778) is a name as great in botany as Newton's in mechanics; and like Newton he provided a brief, systematic exposition of his innovation, as far as the matter allowed on the model of Euclid. His hierarchical classification was judged complete and fixed, but he himself recognized that it was arbitrary to fix on certain characters to determine the system, and started to take more characters into account. This was the first great biological synthesis before evolution, for it included animals, and by tradition minerals, because of fossils.

Geology was going to be important for evolutionary theory—Charles Lyell preceded Charles Darwin; and supported him. Progress in this earth science particularly was checked by theology, the authority of the biblical account of creation. However, there were mines, there were extinct volcanoes, there were surface rocks and soils, there were fossils. Conjectures at the time of the Renaissance even thought of a possible earlier difference in the distribution of land and sea. No detailed evidence was available; fossils were a puzzle that provoked wild theories. It was the connection of the earth as a planet with the universe of stellar bodies that started a train of thought on the right lines: the solidifying of a molten spheroid.

Georges-Louis Buffon's fairly popular exposition of natural history in its geophysical setting emphasized the immense period of time involved. Sporadic observations and findings were going on all the time. A paper read before the Royal Society of Edinburgh in 1785 by a Scot, James Hutton, "A Theory of the Earth," later expanded in two volumes, was an application of Occam's razor. He deprecated the hypothetical assumption of causes other than those to be seen at work with tested results. The internal heat of the earth extruded molten granite, and igneous rocks were subject to chemical, glacial, atmospheric, hydraulic, and other known and knowable influences, over an immense time scale. This was a comprehensive theory to work with.

Georges Cuvier (1769–1832) followed the work of the microscopists of the seventeenth century who studied and wrote on similarities of construction in different forms of life. His detailed classification of animal species based on innumerable dissections formed a frame of reference for fossil finds, linking paleontology with comparative anatomy, and forcing the conclusion that many fossil remains were of extinct species. The diverse geography of France, England, and Switzerland helped forward, once started, geological mapping and geological theory.

All such findings were leading to conclusions in starkest refutation of biblical chronology and the creation story and its implications.

The scientists of the Royal Society, and, generally, Newton and Boyle and Robert Hooke, were amateur theologians; they were studying the works of God in the book of nature. Insofar as their findings did not square with any text in the Bible, the text could be reinterpreted in the light of the new understanding. Natural philosophy was a revelation open to systematic inquiry that would confirm and fill in the revelation that inspired the Scriptures and was embodied in Christ. Johannes Kepler thought of himself as "thinking the thoughts of God" in his celestial observations and inferences.

Aquinas in the thirteenth century had used Aristotle to provide a rational infrastructure for Christian beliefs, with revelation as the superstructure. Since then, Aristotle's *Physics* and *Metaphysics,* with other relevant treatises, and the many commentaries, Arabic and European, had been welded into an Aristotelian orthodoxy that was practically identified with theology, to the astonishment of Galileo, who did not tire of exposing its absurdity. The model in vogue with the natural philosophers was the atomic theory of Democritus, opposed in principle to Aristotle's physics and metaphysics. Galileo would have nothing to do with any of these philosophies. He wrote in Italian to be accessible to readers uncorrupted by education. Science for him was built on commonsense observations and experiment, guided and developed by mathematics—measurement. That was the Hippocratic detachment from philosophy and from religion, which did not prevent his being a devout practicing Roman Catholic.

Galileo's book *The Assayer,* a manifesto of the new empiricism, was prepared and issued (in Italian) after careful soundings by the author of its likely reception in Rome. The book was a literary sensation, because it rejected submission to authority in philosophy and vindicated the right of research and of free intellectual discussion. Galileo was welcomed and feted in Vatican circles, and by the pope himself. Opposition came from the Jesuits, but they held their fire. In *The Assayer,* Galileo had ridiculed their devotion to the authority of tradition.

The Jesuits were uncompromising partisans of the Tridentine declarations and the

Aristotelian cosmology. They were by far the most united, resolute, forceful, and highly organized of the Catholic communities. They were determined to end the laxity of the Vatican regime, and compel the pope to toe their line. The Holy Office would be their instrument. Their stronghold in Rome was their Collegio Romano, attended by about two thousand students drawn from afar. Father Grassi, the rector, was an accomplished mathematician, at a time when mathematics included astronomy, architecture, and geography. For him Galileo was the enemy, and he anonymously entered a delation in the files of the Holy Office charging the author of *The Assayer* with heresy. The charge alleged incompatibility of Galileo's teaching on the composition of matter with the fundamental decision of the Council of Trent on the dogma of the Eucharist, a reaffirmation of transubstantiation. This had been declared the core doctrine of orthodoxy.

Ever since Constantine, the uniformity of Christendom as a shared civilization had implied a rigid orthodoxy enforceable if necessary by totalitarian power. After the Protestant schism, the Trinity needed replacement by another test doctrine, which would be "transubstantiation." Father Grassi produced a full-length examination of *The Assayer,* to put in the public domain this incompatibility of Galileo's theory of matter with Catholic dogma.

The philosophers of nature were amateur theologians, but the Catholic theologians and colleges were also immersed in scientific studies, researching and publishing boons on all the scientific topics of the day. This was the last redoubt of scholasticism's commitment to Aristotle.

At the end of the eighteenth century, the physical world in the abstract was thought of in terms of substance and attributes; species were regarded as fixed. The concept of substance was not displaced by "process" until the twentieth century. The earth was recognized to have a history, and main features in the making of that history, not least the time span, were appreciated. The notion of conservation, the continuity within change, had become familiar. Thus, when it came, the idea of evolution would not be alien. The confusion and gradual separation in experimental work of the ideas in physics of heat and gases brought out the idea of respiration, which belongs to physiology. The connection is primarily chemical. Use of glass U tubes with liquids in their bends was becoming routine for handling definite volumes of gas at definite temperatures and pressures, following knowledge of Boyle's law, a facility that made possible the later revolution in chemistry of Antoine-Laurent Lavoisier, regarded as the founder of modern chemistry. Early progress in natural philosophy was made in physics (mechanics), chemistry, and physiology. Their connection was made evident in the part of electricity and magnetism in each of them. By the mid-eighteenth century, electricity was popular science.

## Modern Philosophy

In the seventeenth century, a thinker who committed himself to formulation of his thought in unequivocal statements that could be justified conclusively if put in question, in other words a philosopher, had to address the Renaissance amalgam of revived Greco-Oriental theurgic traditions and/or the empirical statements of the natural philosophers, old learning or new. René Descartes (1596–1650) and John Locke (1632–1704) can be thought of in relation to these contemporary situations: Descartes disengaging himself to start anew; Locke abandoning all claims to knowledge to the empirical investigators, to Newton and company.

There is a radical dualism implicit in Descartes's thinking: as something that thinks, he is a mental substance; his body is a physical substance, with material properties. This dualism was to be called by Gilbert Tyle "the dogma of the Ghost in the Machine" (*The Concept of Mind,* 1949), and he dealt with it as a generally held view.

In the "Epistle to the Reader" of his *Essay Concerning Human Understanding,* Locke wrote:

> The commonwealth of learning is not at this time without master-builders, whose mighty designs, in advancing the sciences, will leave lasting monuments to the admiration of posterity; but everyone must not hope to be a Boyle, or a Sydenham; and in an age that produces such masters, as the great Huygenius, and the incomparable Mr. Newton, with some other of that strain, it is ambition enough to be employed as an under-labourer in clearing the ground a little, and removing some of the rubbish that lies in the way to knowledge.

This implies a transition from "natural philosophy" to the "natural sciences," the distinction between philosophy and science, a clear recognition of which is the modern turning point.

In a section in book 4 on "Improvement of our Knowledge," Locke distinguishes between the mathematical-type knowledge that Descartes was exclusively interested in and the knowledge of bodies, which "obliges us to a quite different method"; we are sent "to the things themselves, as they exist. Experience here must teach me what reason cannot." He goes on to discuss grounds of probability and degrees of assent. Philosophy, which is not experimental, cannot extend knowledge. That is the prerogative of science alone. As a freethinking activity, philosophy can debate and assess the claim of science to be true knowledge, or assist science in clearing the ground, particularly in addressing the use and abuse of language; but in forming its own agenda, philosophy cannot undertake to do what science does, and alone can do.

Bacon was the principal herald of the new spirit, to awaken minds to initiate a movement that would transform human life in ensuring human mastery of nature. He had the imagination and application for the undertaking. As a judicial administrator, he knew how to organize, to enlist all concerned (observer, experimenter, theorist) in their special task in a corporate endeavor. The Royal Society was not founded until 1660, but it owed more to the influence and program of Bacon than to anyone. Bacon was not concerned with philosophy in the way of Descartes and Locke; he was of course aware of the Florentine revival of the Greco-Oriental tradition, and found congenial the forward look and the bid for universality that it brought in, with a promise of command over nature by obedience to its laws. In unreservedly approving its ends, he did not underestimate the credulity and imposture in its pseudosciences. They also provided clues and fortunate observations. He was advocate of a method of ascertaining and formulating actual uniformities of nature, instead of the Florentine sympathies and antipathies and analogies and spiritual agencies.

The late scholastic attempt to reconcile reason and religion by accommodation with Aristotle, trusting in faith, was being replaced by an intensity of trust in reason and science that, it was devoutly believed, would profoundly vindicate religion. Religious divisions were separated from the common enterprise of systematic organized inquiry. This was the position of the Royal Society, explicitly stated:

> No difference of *Country, Interest,* or profession of *Religion,* will make them backward from taking, or affording help in this enterprise. And indeed all *Europe* at this time, have two general Wars, which they ought in honour to make: The one a *holy* the other a *Philosophical*: The one against the common enemy of Christendom, the other also against powerful and barbarous Foes, that have not been fully subdu'd almost these six thousand years, *Ignorance,* and *False Opinions.* Against these, it becomes us, to go forth in one common expedition: All civil Nations joyning their *Armies* against the one, and their *Reason* against the other; without any petty contentions, about privileges, or precedence.

This, from Thomas Sprat's *The History of the Royal Society of London, for the Improving of Natural Knowledge* (1667), links the old Christendom of the Crusades with the new Europe launched on voyages of discovery. But the new enterprise had eclipsed the old.

Joseph Glanvill was one of the most energetic supporters of and propagandist for the Royal Society. Knowledge cannot be the work of the mind conversing only with its own ideas; it must take its data from sense observations aggregated and compared. The invention of the compass was worth ten times the number of Aristotles and Aquinases, and did more for the increase of knowledge and advantage to the world than all the subtle disputes throughout the history of all the schools. The Royal Society was instituted not to dispute but to work.

Freedom of inquiry, *libre examen,* was the open-ended program of the Royal Society. It was also the essential spiritual legacy of Hellas.

# 14

# Discovery of History

## The Great Map

The enlargement of European acquaintance with the diversities of mankind took place in a context of commercial expansion, dominant sea power, and missionary enterprise, and thus with an implied assumption of European superiority. The assumption was at the end deemed to have been confirmed: Europe was the light of the world. The acquaintance was informed by prepossessions and prejudice. Nevertheless, it did become better informed, and within measurable distance of a scientifically founded study of the human species.

The Orient figured in the Bible and the classics. Assyria, Babylon, Persia, Egypt, Syria, and Alexander's India were there in the books. They were the conquerors and persecutors of the Jews, and they were idolators. That their civilizations were more advanced was evident, even if it did not count. The general impression brought by this new first-hand contact was of servile populations languishing under despotisms. What civilization there had been was in decline. The cyclical theory of decline and fall after a rise was reinforced.

China seemed the great exception. Early information came from Jesuit missionaries. An impressive picture filtered through. Immense geographical extent was made more astonishing by an assumed central control maintained under an enlightened benevolent despotism by a mandarin elite chosen for their learning by public examination. This ensured a stable unchanging social order at a high level of civilization. Confucius was translated into English from a French version in 1691. Voltaire was impressed. His article on China in his *Dictionnaire philosophique* was on the whole judicious, though as always also a stick to beat fools and fanatics with in the West. He thinks the Chinese constitution the best in the world, and picks out the practices that justify that opinion. He admits they have fallen far behind the West in science, but remembers their achievements when they were far in advance. Indeed, the Ming dynasty from the mid-fourteenth to the mid-seventeenth century was among the very few great periods of sustained social stability at a high level of civilization in human history, and the greatest in geographical extent.

These accounts were to be treated more critically after an expedition, which included a team of specialists, was sent to China in 1793 to negotiate commercial deals. They got nowhere with the official Chinese, impervious to an outside world, who assumed them to have come in homage. The expedition managed to travel by waterways through the country, and to record observations. Blots on the Confucian picture were easy to find on the ground; and at home, satisfaction with the benefits of patriarchal government and unchanging social stability was impermeated with perceptions of the benefits of change that accompanied commercial enterprise.

This restructuring of the subjective approach hardly affected the public appetite for information served by the press. There was John Trusler's three-volume compilation, *The Habitable World Displayed* (1788). An earlier commercial venture had been Thomas Salmon's *Modern History; or, the Present State of all Nations*, a serial publication started in 1724 and continued for fourteen years, with later bound editions and single-volume epitomes. These titles exemplify the ready market. "Mankind" was ceasing to be a commonplace vast and vague concept. The great map was being filled in with defined boundaries across which lived disparate peoples. The tides of travel books and the "geographies" drawn from them was supplemented by an explosion of fiction set off by the immense vogue of the "Arabian Nights" and the collections that followed of Persian, Turkish, Mogul, and Chinese tales, with their European imitators, Voltaire, Joseph Addison, Samuel Johnson, and William Beckford among them. Chinoieserie also became a vogue (reflected in Wedgwood's "willow-pattern"), and the market was exploited by manufacture in bulk for a stay-at-home tourist trade.

The realism of actual contact gradually affected Europe's growing acquaintance with the geography of the world. In his *History of Sumatra* (1783), William Marsden was explicit: "The study of our own species is doubtless the most interesting and important that can claim the attention of mankind; and this science, like all others, it is impossible to improve by abstract speculation, merely. A regular series of authenticated facts is what alone can enable us to rise towards a perfect knowledge of it."

The Royal Society issued memoranda to brief travellers on what to look for and report on when they visited a country—Boyle's "General Heads for the Natural History of a Country." In a very general form, ethnography was thus officially sponsored as a branch of learning.

Some used the new findings to enlarge the context of their own classical or biblical studies. Whatever the scope or focus of interest, detail and accuracy, tested evidence, the standard of science for a science, became increasingly recognized as necessary. Individual travellers made collections, of which the most important formed institutions. Hans Sloane of the Royal Society had collected botanical and geological and ethnographic specimens, which, with his books and manuscripts were bequeathed to the nation. With the Harleian manuscripts, and the Cottonian Library, the collection made the nucleus of the British Museum, formed by an act of 1753. The

Ashmolean had been founded in 1680, the first public museum in the country. At first, the ethnographic scraps were the poor relations in these collections, until it came to be thought that they might be more worthy of study than Roman remains, which merely repeated examples of the familiar greatness of Rome. Indeed, the traditional grand tour that completed the education of an English gentleman could be extended to make the tour of the world in books. He may "make himself master of the geography of the universe in the maps, atlasses, and measurements of our mathematicians. He may travell by land with the historians, by sea with the navigators. He may go round the globe with Dampier and Rogers, and kno' a thousand times more in doing it than all those illiterate sailors" (Defoe).

There was a great modern appendix to the inherited Greek and Roman texts to be taken account of, and parts of this were beginning to be addressed in new academic studies.

Of great prospective importance was the second voyage of Captain Cook, not dominated by Josiah Banks. His journal and those of his highly qualified shipmates pooled a conflux of information and observations, geographical and ethnographic. The accomplished J. R. Forster was especially eager to investigate closely every aspect of the societies they encountered. The questions that were being debated in Europe could be examined on the ground in relation to the circumstances that prevailed. Assuming a common human nature, remarkable differences in behavior could be attributable to remarkable differences in environment, beginning with climate and the natural products and conditions of subsistence, with consequent responses and activities and forms of association.

## Disturbed Foundations

The discovery of America was a cultural shock, since it brought on the scene peoples outside the ken of the Greeks and Romans, and particularly because it put in question the biblical account of the origin and spread of mankind, as the Italian historian Francesco Guicciardini noted. Sir Walter Raleigh in his *History of the World* brought his experience of actual travel and migration to bear on the scale of time required for migrations after the Flood, and the stint of information available in the Mosaic account; his was an essay in reconciliation.

To see in historical perspective what was happening at this time, one should recall the three models formed in antiquity, and how they were insinuated into the European inheritance. The core of the Greek cultural legacy was reason disciplined in discourse. Judea transmitted through Christianity a faith with the discipline of ritual. Rome stamped on the world its imperium disciplined by law. These three elements were fused and confused by Constantine at Nicaea in the Roman state-church, and it was this Roman Church that survived the fall of the western Roman state.

The independent elements of the fusion were identifiable in the Middle Ages. Reason in discourse was studied, and valued in Aristotle's logical treatises, as they became available, and was applied to the faith in scholasticism. The faith made orthodox at Nicaea was maintained and administered through its rituals by the Roman

Church under the papacy. The idea of the Roman imperium was kept alive in the Holy Roman Empire, and by the emerging nation states. Nevertheless, the fusion and confusion remained, engrossed in the Roman Church with its temporal claims.

Restoration of independence began with the schism and the Renaissance: with the schism, because this broke the unity and uniformity imposed by Constantine; with the Renaissance, because this restored for the Italians their continuity with the cultures of Greece and Rome and for the northern Europeans brought into distinction their indigenous cultures and the Romanization imposed upon them by the Church with their conversion. The independence of the Greek legacy was decisively repossessed with the deliberate adoption of a systematic, empirical study of nature in the early seventeenth century. Since its practice was to examine, it could be applied to the two other legacies and to itself, and it was. First, to the faith constructively in scholasticism; later critically to dogmas and to the text of the Bible. It was applied to the Roman republic by Machiavelli in his *Discourses on the First Decade of Titus Livius*, and Guicciardini's *Considerations on the "Discourses" of Machiavelli*, as later by Montesqieu and Edward Gibbon. In general, political theory was formed by learning from history. Thirdly, reason was applied to itself with the detachment of philosophy from science by Locke, in Bacon's philosophy of science, in Descartes finding certainty in the implication of thought.

This gradual repossession of the three legacies in their integrity was, obscurely, what was going on from the time of the schism and the Renaissance to the Enlightenment at the end of the eighteenth century.

There was great confusion and many compromises; and there were also fully conscious undertakings. Among them was the Counter-Reformation, the attempt of the Roman church to restore the status quo. The scientific movement was equally deliberate, and was thought by many and for long to be another road to God.

Alexander Pope's *Essay on Man* is a panegyric on nature's great chain of being, ordained by Nature's God. Natural theology seemed a logical alternative for reason, although David Hume was able reasonably to show that it was not a rational option. When Pope insisted on drawing from his premise his cherished conclusion *whatever is, is right,* Voltaire, who had been in agreement, was forced by experience that culminated in the Lisbon earthquake of 1755, which wrecked the city in a few minutes, to reject the conclusion with his whole being.

There was no safe haven from this tumult of doubt and confusion. The Renaissance had brought a recrudescence of an occult theosophy to replace the discredited Aristotelian metaphysics and to put Christianity into a general context of thought. The relations of that body of thought with the emerging natural philosophy, focused on both sides in Bacon, were curious and spurious. An open-ended natural theology was more congenial to scientists, the other road to God. What was gradually being established was something else entirely. In a couple of phrases, it was the neutrality of science and the neutrality of the state.

Secularization was not hostile to traditional religion, merely an open market: the magistrate had no jurisdiction over conscience (Locke). In the case of research and discovery, why should a worker in this field have to square his findings with received

beliefs? It was up to the believer to defend his beliefs, if those findings were inconsistent with them. There was a shift in the *onus probandi*, so to speak. The advancement of learning as a process was an advance that steadily outflanked those who stood
fast trying to hold the line of tradition.

Myths and fables as fiction that told the truth without being true were familiar.
All the same, the biblical account of man's creation, fall, redemption, and judgment
made first and last things a long-standing possession whose credentials were not to
be compromised. This account of human nature and destiny was unrivaled in authority and completeness. What would be of most influence in diminishing anxiety about
having it put in question was cumulative active interest in the unfolding of the great
map. The phenomena were filling and holding the foreground of attention.

## A Chronological Sketch

A science begins by defining, collecting, arranging, and describing the phenomena to
be distinguished and examined. Theory emerges to complete the description in a way
that makes the phenomena intelligible and consistent with other departments of
knowledge. In this sense, science is a full description of what goes with what and
what follows what, an arrangement in placement and sequence.

The great map showed civilizations at upward or downward stages of their cycle,
and uncivilized peoples living in the state of nature. Transition from nature to society was a current speculative question. Now nature was discovered in the act. "Thus,"
said Locke, "in the beginning all the World was America." Here was a model of the
prehistoric past of the human race. Hobbes looked there for his state of nature without government.

A fatal flaw in the judgments that were made was to import the European way
of life and point of view into what was seen in America, whether by rationalists disillusioned with European institutions or by good citizens who found the Indian way
of life indolent and Indians good for nothing. This began to be recognized and corrected when and where relations on the ground were not disturbed by a struggle for
survival. One of the earliest accounts in English that attempted to be objective was
Robert Beverly's *History and Present State of Virginia* (1705), which gave a systematic description of the Indian way of life, without money or individual property,
but with exceptional physical vigor. Beverly also investigated their religious beliefs
and practices.

Adam Smith in the early part of the *Wealth of Nations* refers to the poverty and
limits of the hunters and fishers of North America, all of whom are active in the same
pursuits that directly procure their subsistence. This is never enough to provide for
all of their dependents, some of whom must be expendable. Only by the division of
labor is productivity increased, and that division is occasioned by the propensity to
exchange, and is developed by the interplay between town and country, and by facilities opened through channels of communication. He draws on history to go into ways
in which this basic mechanics of expansion has been either distorted or forwarded by
policies and institutions.

Buffon's vast *Histoire naturelle* was the first "natural history." Its groundplan was a "Theory of the Earth" and a division of geological periods, "Epoques de la Nature." In this temporal frame man first appeared under primitive conditions. He pictured the American Indian as "no more than an animal of the first order, existing within nature as a creature without significance, a sort of helpless automaton, powerless to change nature or assist her." At the same time, he was not other than human, another species: "Man, white in Europe, black in Africa, yellow in Asia, and red in America, is only the same man tinted with the colour of the climate."

Insight marred by ignorance was limping a way forward to the anthropology that would join natural history with human history in a "science of man."

The historical journey from a state of nature to civil society as represented in Europe presented itself as the course to be mapped. The mode of subsistence was taken as the clue to the changes that had occurred. To move from bare subsistence, where all were engaged in the same pursuits to meet the same primary needs, a division of labor and expansion of exchange made the way forward. Adam Smith was sure that people wanted to improve their condition, and that a man aspired to better himself; but that could only be done by taking advantage of the kind of opportunity the general way of life afforded. Four general stages were identified: hunting and fishing, pastoral, agricultural, and commercial. It was a passage from the rudimentary to the most advanced, from wandering to settlement and from settlement to the amenities of cultivated life enjoyed in Europe.

If the sequence of advance was uniform, diversity amongst advanced societies had to be accounted for. John Millar of the Scottish school of the Enlightenment, a professor of civil law at Glasgow, explained the diversity in his *Origin of the Distinction of Ranks in Society* by stressing the complex interplay of geographical and historical influences, those of the environment and those of the culture. He particularly identified the treatment of women as of paramount importance in the structure and manners of a society.

The course of history envisaged implied an extent of time in which it could be accomplished. Buffon had recognized that nature's great workman was time and that it might extend to half a million years. Georges Cuvier suggested an age of some thousands of centuries for the fossil-bearing strata he studied. Even these modest estimates contradicted the time scale deducible from Genesis, which was at most six thousand years. In the early 1650s, Archbishop Usher of Armagh had furnished a biblical chronology that fixed the Creation at 4004 B.C.E. James Hutton's 1795 *Theory of the Earth* in two volumes argued that, given enough time, geological activity at observable rates could have produced the rocks and the landscape as they are from the massive convulsions that had thrust up igneous rocks and shaped the earth's crust in a distribution of land and water. Two generations later, Charley Lyell made this the orthodox theory in *Principles of Geology*, which was a necessary setting for Darwin's theory of biological evolution of species.

Condorcet's assumption that some achievements in the history of France and of England had been well enough established never to be forgotten and lost might not have been fully justifiable, but was not unreasonable. Two of those achievements had the momentum to carry them forward on the incentives by which they had been promoted: the advancement of learning and of trade and industry, inextricably linked and reciprocally promotional. Others had to be maintained against opposition. Even the necessary independence of the advancement of learning was not necessarily recognized and accepted. Economic expansion by free trade proceeded in cycles of booms and recessions, with severe consequences indefinitely prolonged in each phase, a rough and risky process at the level of trial and error, hardly a science. Accountability of government, and of authority in general, is enforceable only when instituted, and then only when exacted. In other words, the interest has to be strongly felt, and sufficient pressure applied. Secularization (in effect, an open society) comes about when no party is strong enough to impose itself, and when that is generally recognized and accepted; it is not necessarily what everybody wants and will profit by. The fact that they are historical achievements may not imply in itself that they can be lost, but the necessary and sufficient conditions that brought them about and sustain them are always at risk; they have to be understood and actively maintained: the benefits they can deliver have to be sufficiently prized. Dependent on such a complex of conditions, they are not historical gains that perpetuate themselves. Condorcet himself, at the end of his essay, modifies any idea of inevitability by saying that he dares to regard striving for the progress of reason and the defense of liberty "as part of the eternal chain of human destiny . . . which fate can never destroy by a sinister stroke," that is, a reversal. This is a commitment, not merely a faith.

The Enlightenment was a faith that Condorcet shared. His *Sketch* traced stage by stage an enlightenment that had been achieved over the years, which he spelled out in social terms. His faith was that already enough had been learned to inform a "social art" that could be instituted to promote and direct the indefinite perfectibility of the species. Since this was incompatible with faith in a once-for-all revelation by Christ and personal salvation by the grace of God, the Enlightenment was naturally bitterly opposed, and ridiculed, by the establishment and its supporters. Apart from that, it involved a misconception of human nature and of the human task.

The history Condorcet relied on and selected from was the history of particular peoples in a particular period. Humanity in general could not have been the subject or object of history: there was insufficient data for a "science of man." A scientific hypothesis completes the data provisionally, in a way that can be tested, in order to make known facts intelligible. Historical data cannot be completed in any such way. History cannot be spoken for; it has to be waited on to speak for itself. To attribute to it a rationale is gratuitous rather than necessary: contingency is woven into its fabric, because political will counts, within the constraints of political contexts. History's hold on the future is not predictive; it determines the possible, and may suggest odds on the probable. A theory of history is a mistake in principle, whether providence or progress or dialectic. A time would come when there would be sufficient data for a science of man, and when history would speak for itself in terms definitive enough to make humankind a possible subject or object of history. But that time was not yet.

# 15

# British Enterprise

## The First British Empire

In Walpole's day, Britain had scattered stations and settlements abroad. In the Mediterranean, Gibraltar and Minorca; in North America, Prince Rupert's Land (Hudson Bay), Acadaia (Nova Scotia), Newfoundland, the thirteen colonies along the seaboard, the Bahama islands; in the West Indies, Jamaica, the Leeward Isles, Barbados; forts and trading stations of the Royal Africa Company on the Gambia, Guinea, and Gold Coast littoral; St. Helena on the way to Bombay, Fort William (Calcutta), Fort St. George (Madras). These holdings scattered across the seas were acquired piecemeal for and held together by trade, and allegiance to the British crown, on whom they relied for protection. This, and its island position, made the motherland a sea power. This first empire was very different from the British Empire of the nineteenth century that painted the map red and maintained a Pax Britannica, but first and last, the British Empire and sea-power were two sides of the same coin.

William Pitt (Earl of Chatham) measured that sea power as "such a superior naval force that even the united fleets of France and Spain may never be masters of the Channel." These, anyhow, were the main rivals for further acquisition in North America, New France and New Spain, not to mention French rivalry in India. That is, this nucleus of empire obtained by adventurers, footholds here and there, had the huge implication of wars and taxation: it could be held only on those terms, by rivalry and expansion. That was the tragedy of Athenian naval strength that both saved the city and was the means by which it was ruined.

The military acquisition of empire was one thing, its consolidation and administration quite another. There was Canada, inhabited by some eighty thousand French and a sprinkling of British. The composition of the thirteen colonies to the south was entirely different, and alien. The Quebec Act of 1774 established a government that respected the rights and feelings of the French inhabitants, with the effect that an invasion by the southern colonists two years later when at war with the motherland was easily repulsed and a costly failure.

In India, the East India Company had a quasi-independent status. The company's charter empowered it to maintain an armed force, intended to protect its establishments from brigandage, or European rivals. With the decline of the Mogul Empire, which began towards the end of the seventeenth century and rapidly turned into anarchy, the French and then the British were set on a course that plunged them into a twenty-year duel; events turned factory guards into an Indian army. Joseph Dupleix was appointed governor of Pondicherry for the French East India Company in 1742. When France was at war with England in 1744, he thought he had the opportunity to destroy the English settlements. He was eventually frustrated by Robert Clive, and his plans came to nothing after initial successes. Clive's army, the Indian army, was employed by the company. One of its directors noted, "The Sword once surrendered, there was an end to the Company as sovereigns, and, indeed of the British Empire in India." The Indian army was entirely different from units of the British army on service in India, with no love lost between them. The Indian army was officered by adventurers whose social standing excluded them from a career in the British army. Their troops were sepoys, mainly caste Hindus. There were three commands, Bengal, Madras, and Bombay. The number increased tenfold between 1763 and 1805. William Pitt's India Act, 1784, brought Indian affairs under a board of commissioners to supervise the political activities of the East Indian Company, leaving the company the right to appointments in India, subject to royal veto. Opposition to control from London by the Company's servants was led by the Bengal officers. Reference was made to the effect of parliamentary acts obnoxious to the Americans, and "chimerical ideas of independence" were floated. The government gave way, with successive amendments to the act. But the frictions and concern for the defense of British India resolved the government that the Indian army be brought under the control of the crown.

India was held by the sword; empire is a military construction. When the Indian army ceased to be a reliable instrument for the purpose, withdrawal was inevitable, and with it the fall of the defense structure of what had been the British Empire. After 1947, Lord Alanbrooke commented, "The keystone of the arch of our Commonwealth Defense was lost, and our Imperial Defense crashed. Without the central strategic reserve of Indian troops ready to operate either east or west we were left impotent and even the smallest of nations were at liberty to twist the lion's tail."

The dispute between the Parliament of the United Kingdom and the thirteen American colonies should be seen in the context of European international conflict from the time of William III, in which the rival states acquired colonies and control over their production and trade to build their power. In England, centralized control was vested in a board of trade. The network of regulations and relevant authorities was so complicated that the colonies kept resident agents in London. Benjamin Franklin represented Pennsylvania (1757–1762) and also Massachusetts, New Jersey, and Georgia (1764–1765). In 1771, Edmund Burke was acting as agent for New York.

The Declaratory Act was based on resolutions in the House of Lords debated in February 1766. In that debate, the lord chief justice, Lord Mansfield, laid down two propositions that were the groundwork of the resolution debated:

> 1st, That the British legislature, as to the power of making laws, represents the whole British empire, and has authority to bind every part and every subject without the least distinction, whether such subjects have a right to vote or not, or whether the law binds places within the realm or without.

> 2nd, That the colonists, by the condition on which they migrated, settled, and now exist, are more emphatically subjects of Great Britain than those within the realm; and that the British legislature have in every instance exercised their right of legislation over them without dispute or question till the 14th of January last.

The reference to January 14 concerned a speech by William Pitt in the Commons, which began, "I have been charged with giving birth to sedition in America." That was the speech in which he said, "I rejoice that America has resisted." He assented to the general principle of parliamentary supremacy: "Our legislative power over the colonies is supreme . . . Where two countries are connected together like England and her colonies, without being incorporated, the one must necessarily govern; the greater must rule the less; but so rule it as not to contradict the fundamental principles that are common to both."

To tax the colonies for revenue was unconstitutional, and different from duties imposed for the regulation of trade, which during his own administration, he said, had been worth £2 million a year. "This is the fund that carried you triumphantly through the last war . . . You owe this to America. This is the price that America pays you for her protection."

Testimony to Pitt's popularity in the colonies is embodied in public statues in Dedham, Massachusetts; New York; and Charleston; and memorialized in the naming of Pittsburgh. He was a popular idol at home. Charismatic, the Great Commoner, often a lone voice, made his reputation in the Commons. In office as war minister, he inspired and energized those he relied on to carry out his policies. He was no party man, and had no use for intrigue or the political skills of manipulation as practiced at the time for parliamentary control. His absorbing passion was for a British Empire with a shared citizenship based on liberty and affection.

His vision of empire, and his dedication of himself in zeal, energy, and resource to achieve it, was uniquely close to Romanitas. All British citizens throughout the world were to enjoy the equal liberty under the law, shared with English subjects, and commonly enforced. He understood empire to mean the communication of this English benefit worldwide.

"The Unanimous Declaration of the Thirteen United States of America" of July 4, 1776, succinctly asserted the dissolution of all political connection with Great Britain, but in bulk it is an explanation to the world of the reasons for this action, as justification. A short document, eighteen of its paragraphs begin "He," that is,

George III, and detail "repeated injuries and usurpations" amounting to "an absolute Tyranny over these States." "Our repeated Petitions have been answered only by repeated injury." In complicity with the king, "our British brethren . . . too have been deaf to the voice of justice and of consanguinity." The longer paragraph that precedes this catalogue, and begins, "We hold these truths to be self-evident," is grounded in the political thought that was also behind the French Revolution of 1789, and owes not a little to the language and thinking of John Locke, theorist of the English Revolution of 1688. This implicit link between the British version of the ancien regime, the birth of the new nation of the New World, and French attempted destruction of their ancien regime anticipates the confusion of the next century, with the shadow of the past in the Congress of Vienna, and the banner of liberty, equality, and fraternity paraded by several parties and groups, fringed by a radical tendency.

The Declaration of Independence had been the end of the first British Empire. There was a rump: Canada, Newfoundland, and some West Indian islands, a nucleus in India, and some important stations. Pitt's imperial design, the plan of its architect, had not been carried out, and was impracticable. The second model did succeed because it was made practicable by constitutional adaptations to the various dependencies. In the debate with the thirteen colonies over the whole period from the accession of George III to the Declaration of Independence, there was until 1775 a groping movement on the American side towards a constitutional relationship approximating what came to be known in the second British Empire as dominion status. The constitutional principle that "taxation and representation are inseparable" combined with the impracticability of American representation in the Westminster Parliament entailed in logic representative elected legislative assemblies in the colonies. The crown was the executive agent in the British constitution, Parliament made the laws. The crown should execute Westminster laws in the United Kingdom, and decisions of the colonists in America. This was the argument of Thomas Jefferson and of James Wilson (a prominent barrister) in particular. The chartered companies that operated in America provided a pattern of self-governing free association. A chartered colony was analogous, with an elected assembly to deal with law-making and finance, and a governor and council to represent the crown.

It was a last and vain appeal within the terms of the British constitution. Franklin and Thomas Paine had been among those who had hoped for peaceful union and reconciliation on some such conditions, but at and after the second Continental Congress in Philadelphia in 1775 there was a decisive change. Not only were there the Coercive Acts and British intransigence; more momentously, there was a change of heart. The thirteen colonial dependencies, by some years of cooperation in defiance of British coercion, had become conscious of itself as a nascent nation, an independent United States.

## Work and Trade

The center of gravity in the world market had shifted to England, largely by conquest, first at the expense of Holland, then of France. The English fleet was three times its size of a century earlier, and some 42 percent larger than that of France. In manufactures, the new modes of production (machines, coal, steam in place of hands, wood, wind, and water) were limited in extent. They were deployed first and most notably in the cotton industry, not only in factory production, but also in international connections. The calicoes that trading companies had imported from India promoted a demand in Europe, and their re-export made connections that opened a market for European cotton fabrics. The finishing of imported cottons had founded a textile-printing industry, which boosted the industrialization of yarn production. In the next century, there would be scope for vast expansion in the colonial market for cheap cottons. The Indian cotton industry that had started the sequence was thereby destroyed. The raw cotton came from slave plantations. Slaves were themselves a trading commodity. England had gained a monopoly of that trade with Spanish America, wrested from the French after the Spanish War of Succession. With England in first position, France was second, and Holland third, in commercial and industrial expansion by the end of the century. Merchant capitalism was in the process of becoming self-sustained industrial capitalism, with investment in plant and equipment for expanding production of goods as the dynamic of economic development.

The cost of the transformation was borne by the unskilled and semiskilled male, female, and child workers displaced by the changed conditions; a problem for the state that it was tardy in recognizing and tackling. Popular protest and violent agitation were nothing new, but they were aggravated by the changed conditions, until trade unions were able to introduce a measure of discipline with collective bargaining.

Social mobility was a necessary condition of the transformation. Birth had to give way to achievement as the mark of status, not merely in the outstanding case. A numerous and active, and graded, middle class became the driving force of the expansion, although prejudice and snobbery might prevail in social circles.

*The Wealth of Nations* was published in 1776. Although by far the most influential book on economic thinking for its comprehensive character and clear reasoning, it was by no means alone nor the first. Hume had published in 1741–1742 *Moral, Political, and Literary Essays*, of which half the second part, sixteen essays, was devoted to a sequence of economic topics, such as commerce, money, taxes, interest, public credit, and matters of trade. His handling of these themes was deliberately abstract, with historical examples drawn mainly from ancient Greece and Rome. The great difference between the ancient world and the modern was in the margin of difference between the necessaries and the luxuries of life; the ancients spared luxuries to keep men under arms, and most so in their early history: Sparta was the extreme example. "Few artisans were maintained by the labor of the farmers, and therefore more soldiers might live upon it." The modern world could not return to such conditions; the contemporary necessaries of life included general prosperity. Hume is highly critical of contemporary practices: funding a large national debt, the extension of paper credit, national hoarding of gold and silver, national policies to avert an adverse balance of trade. The core of his thinking is that political attention should never be diverted from the basic economic reality, people at work; if everything is done to give incentives to that, reliance can be put on the tendency of other considerations to take care of themselves. There is a market philosophy in the making.

# 16

# The Rule of Law

## Legitimacy

Lawfulness is not in itself a safeguard against injury to one's interests. Hard cases are said to make bad law. That merely points out the generality of law, which is a necessary limitation. "Draconian" as an epithet applicable to law is a reminder that laws may be harsh and cruel, if enacted by a tyrant. Notoriously, the letter of the law may violate its spirit, when a litigant demands his pound of flesh, or a prosecutor makes an example of a trivial case. Law may be a dead letter, lacking the conditions on which it is enforceable. "Enforcement" requires a complete department of law-making, without which a legislature merely debates. The administration that executes the law has necessarily to be allowed discretion in applying the general to the particular; and a bureaucracy, bound to go by the book in order to do what the law requires, is apt to be hidebound.

Law is a deprivation of liberty, under threat of punishment. This can be justified as liberty under the law—equal liberty for all. This justification does not apply equally to all laws, which has given rise to the ideal of minimum law. Governments, on the other hand, are constitutionally inclined to maximize measures in the time available, with deplorable effects on drafting and general consideration. How bills are initiated, and who is entitled to initiate legislation, have been historically basic to law-making.

The independence of the judiciary was early recognized to be a fundamental condition of justice in practice. The tendency of governments to use the judiciary as agents or tools is very strong, for otherwise the government is trammeled by law, as its subjects are. Law as effective justice gets in the way of what many naturally want to do; its restraining influence is in that respect fragile, needing to be bolstered by whatever conventions and devices are found effective. Among these, professional training of those in the judicature and the administration is paramount, including not least provenance and recruitment.

Today, when a very great deal is being said about human rights and when so much moral capital is invested in the talk, it is well to remember what Jeremy Bentham said: it is nonsense to speak of a "right" that has no law to provide redress for its violation; and to say "an imprescriptible right" (that is, an inviolable right) is "nonsense upon stilts."

The phrase "The Rule of Law," like "Human Rights," has the smack of finality— and ought to prompt inquiry. "Law" has no paper validity nor constitutional sufficiency, although both are necessary to its operation, which all the way remains in the hands of human fallibility, corruptibility, and incomplete efficiency. That is to say, the Rule of Law remains an ideal, to be pursued in good faith with improving competence.

Macaulay wrote of the anomaly of English government at this time that the people did not have enough power to make the laws, but did have enough to impede their execution. Both chambers of the legislature were almost entirely aristocratic, the machinery for execution almost entirely popular. The government could obtain from a subservient Parliament laws that the people were unwilling to accept. It was not quite like that. He was thinking of the criminal code and the laws of libel aimed at suppression of disaffection expressed in opinions unfavorable to the government, with juries unwilling to convict. But there were also the Six Acts and other repressive measures, such as the Seditious Meetings and Assemblies Act of 1795, which practically suspended the right of public meetings to discuss political questions unless speakers and their opinions were approved by the government, measures that were opposed by minorities in both houses as unnecessary and destructive of constitutional rights. There was genuine fear of mob rule and of Jacobinism. Inflammatory speculative ideas unleashed by the French Revolution worried even liberal-minded politicians with no aristocratic background.

## Formation of Political Parties (1830–1854)

The outstanding herald of radical new thinking in England was Jeremy Bentham (1747–1832). Bred to the law, though of independent means and not a practicing lawyer, he substituted for the Roman and medieval notion of natural law, *ius naturae*, a practical maxim he borrowed from Claude Helvetius, "the greatest happiness of the greatest number," to institute the principle of "utility," public interest in the good of the community, as a criterion of legislation. As an atheist, he regarded government as a human device for social convenience, to be corrected and reformed in the light of experience. He was particularly interested in the penal system and its reform, but fundamentally in the whole system that applied the rule of law. He found that lawyers formed a corporation more interested in its organization and rewards than in serving the interests of clients for whom it existed, securing for them the remedies the law provided. Therefore the system would never reform itself from within and would resist pressure for reform from without. This, as he learned when he turned his attention to Parliament, was a critique of institutions as such: they were vested interests; their personnel soon became preoccupied with their own rewards, rather than with the purposes of their institution. Institutions tended to be spoils systems, inherently corrupt. This had to be prevented by one means or another.

As heir to the *philosophes*, he thought at first of the enlightened despot as the most hopeful agent of reform uniting information and political will with effective power; however, he became the theoretician of the democrats. In that capacity, he concentrated on securing identity of interests between members of Parliament (MPs) and their constituents, so that the body of Parliament was prevented from forming an independent interest. He thought that annual parliaments would make MPs fully accountable. This was similar to the devices resorted to by the revolutionaries in France in their dread of "faction," banning committees and even the regular seating of members side by side. In both cases, such regulations would make government impossible; and both faction and "vested interest" were controlled as far as possible by competition in the constituencies of organized political parties and the investigations and inquisitions of a free press. These were at last the conditions entirely lacking when Oliver Cromwell was driven to despair of parliamentary government. But neither were such conditions established out of hand with the Reform Act of 1832.

Bentham's preoccupation with the mechanics of "identity of interests" was as myth-making as *ius natura*'s; particular interests and a common or public interest are distinct and cannot be compressed. Particular interests in the country formed associations for their furtherance, as interest groups or pressure groups; and it was similarly on more general lines that political parties were formed. There could be no collective interest of a constituency with which an MP would be identified, as a general rule. Bentham's methodical mind was more apt in seizing on the practical institution of social reforms: investigate; legislate; inspect.

Bentham's associates, principally James Mill, formed a school of thought, Utilitarianism, and a political group, the philosophical radicals. They founded their own quarterly, the *Westminster Review*, to pit against the *Edinburgh Review* of the Whigs and the *Quarterly Review* of the Tories, established as influential organs of opinion, but both equally aristocratic, and tainted with the prejudices and abuses and shortsightedness of the ancien regime. Education was naturally a principal concern of the Benthamite radicals.

As W. E. Forster noted in 1863, "There is a great prize of power and influence to be aimed at on the liberal side of politics." William Gladstone, by his physical presence, his oratorical skill and power, his industrious habits and mastery of business, his robust constitution, his dedication to politics, was the man to seize that prize. At the exchequer in the governments of Aberdeen, Palmserston, and Russell, he had become fully versed in political arithmetic. He made it his first business to phase out revenue from traditional sources in excise and import duties in order to bring in and maintain a free trade system with the help of an income tax. At the same time, he aimed at a budget surplus, with reduction of taxation, pitched at the level of public expenditure the public wanted.

Gladstone included in his cabinet men of discordant opinions from the groups that formed the liberal tendency. The new setting, with Benjamin Disraeli and Gladstone as opposed leaders, was the beginning of a new era in British politics.

Constitutional accountable government was the legacy to Europe of the French Revolution. A reassertion of authoritarianism would not get an easy ride. The issue would be forced when living conditions drove those who suffered to protest. There was a subsistence crisis in 1816–1817, with bad harvests, rising prices, and an increased population. At such times, many left the countryside for the towns, a too familiar phenomenon in our own time in the Third World. In France by 1829 nearly half the population was dependent on poor relief. "By 1830, the whole political order was so unstable that a serious disturbance in any capital of Western Europe would almost certainly lead to outbreaks in a number of other States." The "Three Days" revolution at the end of July 1830 in Paris was followed by outbreaks in ten other states in the next few months. Metternich said the July Days were like the breaching of a dike. In Paris, the restored monarchy was not able to suppress the revolt, and a liberal regime was installed.

This was an interim period, before industrialization was established. After the Napoleonic hiatus, the political legacy of the revolution remained indeterminate. Aristocracy and the ancien regime were back in place, but enfeebled and uncertain. Political ineptitude of the royal rulers was the rule. Metternich's "All or Nothing" was the exception. Concessions short of constitutional government could not appease. Neither concessions nor calling out the troops closed the door to violent protest, when economic depression or political tension occasioned spontaneous unrest. Leadership came from landlords, officials, lawyers, the intelligentsia. Students were more active in politics on the continent than they were in Britain. Artisans had their guild and other forms of organizations and were capable of articulate and forceful representation of their interests. There was no emergence yet of a consolidated middle class exerting its power. Divergence of interests was brought home by the distress suffered, and the consciousness of class divisions intensified. The restructuring of Europe did not take place until later in the century, with the unification of Germany and of Italy; but spontaneous revolts throughout the heartland of Europe at this time, locally occasioned and individual as they were, prompted one another. Europe was a community of peoples politically aware, after 1815, as never before. That was a European community sharply different from the community of Christendom and the Crusades, not yet modern, but already transformed.

By the 1880s, religious questions were losing prominence; development of a mass market and of communications and publicity made it easier to appeal to a national electorate and to organize constituencies in terms of party programs.

## Democracy

As a device of government, democracy at its full extent shares general political responsibility equally among the adult population to be governed. It may be defined loosely as majority rule. Since in the competition for political power the unit is a collective interest (recognized by the stoics), assumptions about political interest have been basic to constitutional arguments. Traditional thinking in terms of "estates" at the time of the 1688 constitutional settlement meant that the majority, those who were not peers of the realm, were deemed to be represented because they were spoken for by a body of them sitting in Parliament, the law-making body. There was no question then of "democracy." The scandal of political manipulation, the repressive measures of wartime government after the French Revolution, and the ideas and ideals of the revolution contributed to an irresistible demand for electoral reform. With that prospect, the notion of "democracy" roused fears of mob law, dispossession of the haves by the have-nots, the majority, with a collective interest in leveling. Democracy was a bad thing, to be resisted. After the Reform Act of 1832, the development and organization of political parties divided on national issues made practicable the election of a party on an advertised program that could command a majority in the House of Commons. The unsuccessful party or parties would be in lawful opposition to the elected majority. The principle of regulated majority rule established in this way in the country, not merely in Parliament, a countrywide choice of alternative legislative proposals. It was found to work. When this happened, political parties had confidence in extending the franchise and democracy was established in principle. This happened historically in England in the second half of the nineteenth century. Democracy was not mob law, but a popular mandate for a specific set of legislative proposals canvassed in an election that set out alternative sets, each already supported by adherents of the sponsoring party.

However, although a device of government, democracy is not merely a set of prescriptive rules that produces a necessary result. Concretely, it works in an historical context, and may as well divide a nation as bring it together. The social dimension is complementary to the structural one. What is to be noticed about the political parties that have filled the offices of state in Britain is that their leaders have deliberately established occupation of the middle ground in politics: Canning, Peel, Disraeli, the Chamberlains, Baldwin, Churchill in the Conservative party; Peel, Aberdeen, Gladstone in formation of the Liberal party; MacDonald, Snowden, Henderson, Atlee on the Labour side, with those others who served in Churchill's wartime cabinet. Peel, Gladstone, Joseph Chamberlain, and Churchill were at different times Tories and Liberals. There have been long spells of coalition government and of consensus politics, as well as shorter spells of confrontation.

Democracy established itself historically in a practical way in Britain when the Corn Laws forced a choice between protection and free trade in terms of a majority for the one or the other, roughly the interests of the landowners versus the rest. This was not a one-off issue. A general way of resolving conflicts of interests was indicated. Those who had the franchise, the electors, had to decide the question by their votes: a question of the majority. Electors were divided by party affiliations or sympathies. There were also extremists, left and right, ideologues with fixed ideas of what they wanted those in power to do, men incapable of compromise or toleration of opponents. They could have no use for democracy save as a means of getting their side into power. That gained, they would throw down the ladder of opportunity for others to replace them. Pragmatists who were not fanatics or doctrinaire had to be a permanent majority as the prime condition of stable democracy, constituting a broad middle ground. Those moderates, while excluding extremists by their permanent majority as a main condition of workable democracy, were also required to tolerate them as spokesmen of radical wings maintaining critical points of view.

On these indications, democracy is not merely a set of rules and principles that a people can be expected or asked to adopt out of hand and put in practice. The required conditions have first to be there to make the system of government workable.

Class divisions have of course existed throughout, with exploitation and oppression. Government was largely in aristocratic hands or under aristocratic influence well into the nineteenth century. From the time of the Conqueror and before, they were involved in local administration and made familiar with problems on the ground. Knights of the shires and burgesses of the towns became merged in the Commons. The contribution of the intelligentsia as political thinkers—Hooker, Hobbes, Locke, Hume, Adam Smith, and as a group, Philosophical Radicals and Fabians—has been pragmatic rather than ideological. On the religious front, Anglicanism is still by law established, but it is noted as a broad church, and not a persecuting one. Nonconformists are sectaries, Congregational, Baptist, Methodist, Quaker. Roman Catholics are virtually among the nonconformists. From no religious quarter is there in this period a threat of fanaticism. Evangelicalism is a form of extremism, and so is Catholicism, but neither figures in Britain in a significant political role.

The main point to be made, looking back over the history, is the establishment of the political middle ground within each of the parties themselves, against their own right and left wings. With that center of gravity supported by the bulk of each party, British politics has been kept in a state of stable equilibrium.

Arguably, democracy can be maintained only on such conditions as a procedure of lawmaking for the rule of law. For Parliament has no legal sanction against enactment of a statute that violates the principle of the rule of law, since its supremacy is the sovereignty of the people. The principle is simply left to the care of the political parties, insofar as they care for the rule of law. A party may care for it only insofar as it gets them into power once for all, to establish what is then called a People's Democracy in which the "people" rule fully and finally because they have destroyed the "enemies of the people." This classes-war version of democracy is of course completely different from and rival to what from that point of view is called "bourgeois democracy," a system of rules and conditions instituting electoral choice, and lawful opposition to the elected majority, in short, alternative government.

Mill says in his *Autobiography* that his motion for an amendment to the Reform Bill "to strike out the words which were understood to limit the electoral franchise to males," was "by far the most important, perhaps the only really important, public service I performed in the capacity as a member of Parliament."

Knowledge that it was a small minority of women who challenged the existing order and fought for votes, and that they were derisively repressed for a long time, and had little support from their own sex, blinds one to recognition that it was glaringly obvious to unprejudiced minds that the exclusion of half the race from rights was monstrous folly, and that this was a prime example of a "due." Condorcet had put it plainly in the final Stage of his *Sketch*:

Among the causes of the progress of the human mind that are of the utmost importance to the general happiness, we must number the complete annihilation of the prejudices that have brought about an inequality of rights between the sexes, an inequality fatal even to the party in whose favour it works . . . This inequality has its origin solely in the abuse of strength, and all the later sophistical attempts that have been made to excuse it are vain.

Particularly, he saw in the equal education of women the ground of individual independence that he believed education to be for men. His statement was more categorical than Mary Wollstonecraft's *Vindication of the Rights of Women* (1792), written out of her own bitter experience, which became the textbook for the next generation of advocates of women's rights.

From 1903, the Pankhursts and the Women's Social and Political Union campaigned for votes for women, with growing militancy as they were rebuffed. By 1910, they found they had roused more opposition than support, and changed their tactics.

The war made all the difference. The nation was together, with marginal exceptions. The enormous sacrifice of manpower on the battlefield required political recognition. Universal suffrage for all men over twenty-one was enacted. Women had demonstrated their public spirit and their personal capabilities. Their frustrated claim to the vote was partially met in 1917 by a vote for women over thirty who were householders or wives of householders. They might also stand as parliamentary candidates. This partway house was abandoned by Stanley Baldwin ten years later when he gave women the same electoral rights as men—the "Flapper Vote."

A committee appointed to advise on employment of women after the war, in the light of that experience, reported in 1919 that women had shown that they worked efficiently in management, supervision, process work of all grades, and laboring. Opportunities for women in industry would cover the whole range of occupations; all clerical posts open to men should be open to women, subject to the same educational tests. Another committee, appointed at that time to advise on relative pay, recommended that, "The principle of Equal Pay for Equal Work should henceforward govern the relation between men's and women's wages." Clerical work became very largely a female occupation, which it had not been before. Women increased in number in the professions, as medical practitioners, barristers, solicitors, architects, even engineers. They remained handicapped by unequal opportunities, in spite of recommendations in official reports of the principle of "a fair field and no favour"; and were almost as rare at the top as outstanding achievement by women in history from the beginning of recorded time: indubitably possible, and as indisputably uncommon.

The most personally fundamental change in women's lot was brought about by the practice of contraception. Of women who married between 1900 and 1909, 33 percent had families of one or two children. In 1930, 51 percent had families of this size. Again, the war was the great divide in attitudes and practice. The propaganda of Marie Stopes was effective; she established the first birth-control clinic for working women. She brought a case for libel against against a Roman Catholic physician who had published a book against her. The confused verdict of a jury directed by a hostile lord chief justice was reversed in her favor by the Court of Appeal, and reversed again in 1924. The Conservative government did not allow information on birth control to be given to women who attended welfare centers.

Political equality and equality before the law were virtually won. Economic equality with men remained sorely to seek in almost every respect. Deliverance from the toil of incessant involuntary child-bearing was at hand. Tremendous as these gains were, there remained grounds for a women's movement to remove handicaps and redress a balance still unfavorable to women. It was a refined legacy of the Enlightenment, and a corollary of democracy—unfinished business.

In democratic theory, which is majority government, majorities must not tyrannize over minorities, and minorities must not obstruct government. But there are no rules on that in legal terms. Democracy carries an assumption of practical tolerance. But absence of repression or oppression is not enough; a minority may be, and commonly is, discriminated against, with an unspoken assumption that the majority has been given the right to do this. It has been said that the American Constitution makes any attempt at majority tyranny abortive; there are too many points at which a sizable minority can defeat discrimination. Nevertheless, discrimination against blacks is practiced even where and when laws and court rulings prohibit it. Passion and prejudice frustrate or pervert the force of law. Minorities are likely to have to organize pressure for the establishment and/or enforcement of legal rights theoretically due in a democracy. The American example shows how protracted, painful, and costly such campaigns can be, and how disillusioning when ultimately successful. The rule of law is always unfinished business.

## Power versus Law

The paradox of democracy is that it is a device for transforming a stark either/or into an accommodating both/and. Political opposition is made legal, on the assumption that the opposition upholds the rule of law as loyally as the ruling party. The abstract walking of different roads to separate destinations becomes concretely following the same road to neighboring destinations. There is nothing esoteric about the theory; there is ever-present risk in the practice. Extremists are in effect outlawed in the game, for they observe the rules with guile: having climbed into power, they throw down the ladder for everyone else. That is why the middle ground is essential to the maintenance of democracy.

Honest and improving practice of democracy, which is the rule of law, is a criterion of judgment in following the course of political events reviewed in this part. Extremists of the right or left can be, and have to be, tolerated in a democracy, so long as they remain minorities. Otherwise, they threaten the survival of democracy, and must be dealt with accordingly by those whose faith is that democracy alone provides the ground rules for human civilization—so long as the conditions obtain on which it can be practiced.

War came in 1914, and victors, having failed with the vanquished to draw the Balkans into a European comity of nations, unwittingly proceeded to Balkanize

Europe itself. Disillusioned by the failure to make political progress, the Allies salvaged the wreck of their hopes in the storms of power politics by staging the war as a "war to end war" and "to make the world safe for democracy." What happened in the circumstances that developed in the aftermath was a deterioration of the polarity of law versus order into one of left versus right, within nations as well as between them. This erosion of the middle ground imperiled democracy everywhere it had been established. The ultimate issue was forced, who shall kill whom.

If this is the scenario for Western history from 1789 to 1939, it remains to point out and point up the events and policies within the outline that justify it, beginning with Versailles, as the previous period began with Vienna.

The war was broken off by an armistice in November 1918. The belligerents were exhausted materially and morally. The Allies, with the late accession of the United States, were in the stronger position, and assumed a German surrender. In the following year, they negotiated among themselves a European settlement, and extracted German assent to a leonine bargain. A hundred years earlier, the Congress of Vienna had given the bruised and doomed ancien regime a blood transfusion that kept Europe safe from democracy, and from war, for at least a couple of generations. The object at Versailles was not to stall history, rather to anticipate it, even less feasible. Germany was left in Central Europe, the largest and potentially the strongest power, with unprecedented possibilities of expansion. This was masked by what the treaty was intended and seemed to provide.

Woodrow Wilson, Georges Clemenceau, and David Lloyd George were the principals in the negotiations. Wilson was the most innovative, idealistic, and free-handed. For him, open covenants openly arrived at was the principle of the new diplomacy, national self-determination the principle on which the political map of Europe should be redrawn, and a covenant of a League of Nations to guarantee collective security should be written into the treaty. Clemenceau was single-minded: Germany had to pay damages, and be made incapable of regaining the military strength to threaten France again, and France must regain Alsace-Lorraine. Lloyd George was most ready to make the rehabilitation of Germany the statesmanlike priority, to avoid planting seeds of another war. He was handicapped by rabid anti-German feeling in Britain, with calls to "hang the Kaiser" and to "squeeze Germany until the pips squeak." He was the man to find tactics that would appease opinion at home, and in practice enable Germany to recover her place and part among European powers. Germany had herself disposed of the Kaiser. She could be given an indemnity bill it would be quite impossible to pay, and enforce a reduction. Keynes's "Economic Consequences of the Peace" in exposing realities was a major contribution to sanity.

Germany herself had been constituted a republic by the Weimar Assembly elected early in 1919 by a great majority. The government, nevertheless, had to suppress serious bids on the left and on the right to displace it, and then had to face France under Raymond Poincaré determined to exact the Versailles pound of flesh by occupying the Ruhr, the industrial heartland. The Germans had anticipated the crushing indemnity by depreciating the mark, a move that triggered runaway inflation. This and passive resistance in the Ruhr frustrated the French maneuver. There was the

Dawes revision of reparations, initiated by the Americans and conducted under an American chairman. For European governments were now debtors to the United States on an immense scale. Poincaré was replaced by Edouard Herriot, who accepted the Dawes plan and evacuated the Ruhr and the Rhineland towns seized as forfeits.

The League of Nations put forward in the "Geneva Protocol" a draft treaty that would bind member states to go to the armed assistance of any member who was attacked: a system of collective security, deploying the strength of all for the defense of each. Logically impeccable, it was politically dubious: for (1) membership of the league was not universal, and (2) it threatened to guarantee a permanently no-change situation. It did not gain assents and instead a particular treaty of guarantee was negotiated in 1925, the Locarno Pact, for the frontier between France and Germany. Gustav Stresemann for Germany pledged not to resort to force of arms to redress her eastern frontiers as determined at Versailles, to which she had strong objections. Briand represented France and Chamberlain Britain in these negotiations. France had at last obtained in a reasonable way the two things Clemenceau had demanded, reparations and a guarantee against German attack, by Britain, Belgium, and Italy. Germany was now admitted as a member of the league, after objection and obstruction of secondary powers to her permanent place on the council. Germany's compulsory disarmament under Versailles made her demand an agreed all-round system of disarmament under the league. Years of delay in moving towards this end did nothing to encourage the German Social Democratic government, which stood for the fulfillment of Versailles as now amended.

France, deeply apprehensive of Germany, formed a Petite Entente with Czechoslovakia, Yugoslavia, Rumania, Poland, and Belgium in a political combination that would be a defensive alliance of the succession states around the central German block. That is, Germany's demand for a radical program of disarmament to follow up the guarantees of Locarno was in practice met by encirclement.

After Adolf Hitler's abortive putsch in Munich in 1923, when he was imprisoned and the paramilitary SA banned, Hitler reshaped it as the party's propaganda unit, turned to politics, and gained a growing membership by making the jobless his constituency and eradication of unemployment his program. When he was made chancellor, on the assumption that he could be used, he resolved to work with the army and with industry, to use them. The army had not accepted military defeat—the politicians had delivered a "stab in the back." Industry would profit by Hitler's initial rearmament; this enabled Hitler to deliver on his employment program. As he settled into government, with the aid of army, industry, and the civil service, the SA served to discipline the workless, keep them under surveillance, and provide them care and vocational training until by 1936 an expanding economy and conscription brought them back into society with a future. It was a unique achievement at that time.

Benito Mussolini formed his Fascist party as a paramilitary political force in 1919 against the Communists. In 1922 his army of black shirts marched on Rome, and, to forestall a seizure of power, the king invited Mussolini to form a government. Mussolini quickly and skillfully consolidated his position as dictator with absolute power. He concentrated public attention on health and fitness, provided employment on public works, and capped police control through the ubiquity of party members with charismatic appearances and displays of dramatic rhetoric. The patriotic theme inevitably recalled the grandeur of Rome—as did the fascist logo. Like Hitler and Joseph Goebbels, Mussolini made Italians think historically, casting further back. When Austrian Chancellor Engelbert Dorfuss was murdered, he moved troops to the Brenner border to forestall Nazi intervention, and denounced Hitler in scathing terms: when the Teutons were illiterate barbarians, Rome was a cultural example to the world, with Augustus and Virgil (tremendous applause). Ethiopia, the last uncolonized African state, seemed an easy target for expansion and a war to gain it Mussolini deemed necessary to brace and prime the spirit of Romans.

The Russians in 1917 found their industrial resources totally inadequate to hold their own against the German armament. The tsar had been induced to abdicate, and a provisional coalition government was formed that proved weak enough to enable the Bolsheviks to seize power. A Council of Peoples' Commissars formed the government, with Leon Trotsky as commissar for foreign affairs. When counterrevolutionary forces were raised, supported by the Allies, he was made war commissar. In that situation Trotsky showed his genius for military planning; he converted a rabble demoralized by shortages and by the humiliating terms of the Treaty of Brest-Litovsk dictated by Germany into a disciplined force that eventually numbered some 5.5 million.

When the White Russians captured a town, they liquidated all its Communists. It was Communist doctrine that they would have to liquidate "the class enemy" to survive and prevail. The political issue truly was reduced to who shall kill whom? Trotsky's raising and handling of the army, moving from place to place within an armored railway car, saved the revolution. In effect, it militarized the administration, imposing a pattern of authoritarian control that had been necessary for survival. Party members had to be summarily posted and moved to replace local Communists murdered by White Guards or their collaborators.

Joseph Stalin, with his close mastery of the administrative machine, worked to isolate the former Menshevik, until he had him physically deported to Turkey, from where Trotsky organized an effective propaganda on an international scale, which included an exposure of Stalin. As a political activist, he was not a welcome guest. He moved to France, to Norway, and finally to Mexico, where at the second attempt he was murdered by one of Stalin's agents. Stalin's paranoia destroyed not only his Bolshevik comrades who had made the revolution, but also a vast number of top people who might be suspected of disaffection with his regime. The army was decapitated, with some 25,600 officers disposed of.

Otto von Bismarck had pushed Austria out of the German leadership as a step on his way to making Prussian Germany the strongest power in Europe. The Austrian Hitler in the 1930s had the lingering rump of Austria to deal with: "In my earliest youth I came to the basic insight, which never left me, but only became more profound, that Germanism could be safeguarded only by the destruction of Austria . . . Even then I had drawn the consequences: ardent love for my German-Austrian homeland, deep hatred for the Austrian State" (*Mein Kampf*). Austria was steeped in anti-Semitism to an extent and in a way that Germany was not; and Hitler confessedly learned his anti-Semitism in Vienna. Germanism required the elimination of such taints. Goebbels's propaganda skillfully and persistently penetrated Vienna and the country with films and written material expounding and extolling the meaning and the virtue of Germanism.

Occupation of the Rhineland by Hitler without a move on the part of France and Britain was a blow to the credibility of French military power and political will. In 1936, when there was a move against the legitimate Republican government in Spain, the newly elected Popular Front government in France under Leon Blum wanted to go to its aid, but Blum recognized that to do so would involve France itself in civil war. When the crisis of Hitler's threat to Czechoslovakia, to whose defense France was pledged, took Edouard Daladier as premier to Munich, he returned after signing the agreement, not like Neville Chamberlain with a message of peace, although that was all that France wanted, but in the profoundest depression that he could do no other than betray the Czechs, because he had been assured by the army chiefs that they could not take on Hitler's rearmed forces, because their preoccupation had been with defense. France then prepared for a war that was all too likely, still with faith in the Maginot line as invulnerable, but now with close military talk and cooperation with Britain. The Soviet-German pact, signed on August 23, 1939, was forced on the Russians by British shilly-shallying: Chamberlain's reluctance and distaste for a Russian alliance and fundamental unwillingness to agree to mutual defense. Instead, and in answer to the Nazi-Soviet pact, under pressure from the House of Commons, a treaty of mutual assistance with Poland was promptly concluded. Chamberlain's diplomatic blindness and blundering had made the worst of both worlds.

Another aspect of power politics which distorted or frustrated the rule of law was conspicuous at this time in the emergence and influence of monopoly capitalism:

> The ruling stratum no longer consists of innumerable subjects who enter into contract but of large power groups controlled by a few persons competing with each other on the world market. They have transformed vast areas of Europe into enormous labour camps under iron discipline. The more competition on the world market develops into a struggle for power, the more rigid their internal and external organization.

In Germany particularly, as this quotation from Max Horkheimer indicates, there were incentives for concentration of industrial power and control. There was again the medieval phenomenon of the over-mighty subject. There was a parallel in the structure and discipline of both monopoly capitalism and Fascist parties that lent them to one another. In using the power of the state to resist or forestall a Communist takeover, Fascist leadership destroyed the enemy of the capitalist system. However, Nazi replacement of the state by the party was not as early and immediate as that of the Bolsheviks in the Soviet Union. Their greatest difficulty was with the *Wehrmacht,* which they regarded as "ultrareactionary and clericalist," and having to be "constantly prodded along." Hitler and Goebbels felt personal affinity with the workers, whom they loved to meet and to address on the shop floor.

However, this coziness was superficial. Workers' organizations were persecuted, their leaders vulnerable to arrest and execution. Groups of them, attached to the Social Democratic party in exile, or Communists, formed an underground resistance throughout the war.

By the mid-thirties, it had been clear to those on the left of politics "that exactly the same forces which hoisted the Nazis to the helm in Germany are at work in all other countries at the present time and that, for better or for worse, there is no possibility of avoiding the issues which these forces present for decision to every man and woman who votes, or thinks, or acts." A "cold war" developed before the war as after 1945, though in a far less rigid form. Anti-Fascist elements formed popular fronts, which in France secured a majority vote under Blum. In Germany, the majority vote seated the Nazis in power under Hitler. A general election is no security against the reign of extremists.

## Sovereignty and State

A state can be defined as a system of institutions for the exercise of political authority and the control and execution of power. Such a definition is applicable generally: "*L'etat, c'est Moi; c'est le Parti; c'est le Peuple.*" Sovereignty is the ultimate political authority and sources of power, beyond which there is no appeal.

Rules may be ritualistic or logical or generative; that is, they may determine exact repetition or necessary consequences or predictable general deliveries. The rule of law requires rules of all three kinds. Procedural law is ritualistic. The "law and order" domain is logical in the sense that it is necessary to the political existence of a society (Hobbes). The rules enacted as public law must deliver public goods: security, justice, services. Defect or deficiency under any of these heads violates the rule of law, although it may be done by law. The "public interest" may be defined generally as the rule of law secured by rules of these three kinds.

Germany was traditionally an organic State. Hitler modified the Weimar Constitution to bring all German institutions into strictest conformity with organic theory, incorporating the *Wehrmacht,* the Labor Front, and the People's Courts. There was no independent judiciary nor bureaucracy; all forms of associations were political instruments of the party. Particularly, the leader-principle was insisted on, a hierarchical system of authority, with responsibility from the bottom up culminating in the leader. A personality-cult of the leader helps to establish the principle in the public mind—as did the ubiquitous salutation, "Heil Hitler!" In an organic state, law-breaking is not infringement of a rule, but is treason; one who is judged as a criminal is condemned as a traitor to the state—as in a theocracy it is blasphemy. Indeed, law functions in an organic state not as rule—the state as power imposes that—but as a kind of rationalization, giving reasons to legitimize what is imposed.

On the Communist side too there was a long tradition, a tradition rather of intense debate than of triumphant power polities, but of debate that was focused on the lessons to be learned from the American and French Revolutions and the Paris Commune. And by contrast this was a debate about democracy, not about nationalism and empire, about equality and liberty. Tocqueville had recognized the danger of democratic centralism that produced a reductive equality. John Mill had taken the cue, and warned that the only safeguard against doctrinaire fanaticism was individual liberty of thought and expression. Condorcet had argued and tried to show that history furnished enough to inform and direct a "social art" that would steadily promote and maintain progress in civilization, in continuation of what had been achieved. A host of others had contributed and would join in: Rousseau, Claude Helvetius, Paul Holbach, Louis Saint-Just, Gracchus Babeuf, Philippe Buonarroti, and Merelly, to name some in the foreground of controversy. The messianic doctrinaire, from Robespierre to Lenin, would prevail, with his fanatical inner certainty and his vision of a new heaven and a new earth in the naturalistic terms of Liberty, Equality, Fraternity—or the Utopian end of government and the need for it, and the state has "withered away."

The war when it came was focused exclusively on Nazi Germany. Winston Churchill and Franklin Roosevelt met for the first time in August 1941 in Newfoundland and composed a declaration of war aims, the Atlantic Charter, a pledge to the world. They looked forward to disarmament, a permanent system of general security, with abandonment of the use of force. The principles of the charter were endorsed by twenty-six governments, including the Soviet Union, with a view to a United Nations.

Thus the war aims of the second war against Germany were the same as in the first war, to end war and to make the world safe for democracy. One partner in the first war was an absolutist tsar, and in the second war a dictator committed to an absolutist democracy. The most prescient participant could not have foreseen that the war would leave both sides to purge their past and recognize and abandon fatal misconceptions. How that happened and what it meant for the rule of law are examined next.

# 17

# Secularization of Europe

Constitutionally, secularization is a legal separation of church and state; or, where that does not apply (as in modern India), legal equality of all religious beliefs and practices within the state. Removal of legal enforceability of a collective ideology, where it happens, has definite dates and is itself simply an enforceable statute with a remedy against the crown for default in the courts. In a general sense, secularization is diffuse, and cannot be given that historical precision. It is a trend, not an event. That moves it into controversy, but not out of history. Taking medieval Christendom as a baseline, there is a chartable movement from that to "civilization," beginning with the schism and made conscious and articulate with the Enlightenment. That was described above as a dissolution of the Constantine merger, and restoration of the independence of the original European models formed in antiquity: specifically, the separation of Hellas and Zion.

In Hellas, religion was one thing among others in its culture—a cultural definition of secularism. Zion was a religious culture, exclusively; and in Christianity, "the one thing needful"; it subordinated all else, and denounced all rival claims as disobedience to the divine will, which was by definition paramount. This was reflected in the dedicated life of the medieval "religious," that is, those who withdrew from the world and vowed lifelong submission to the rules of a religious order. The schism brought in with the reformed churches a different version of the "religious" life; one lived in the world, using ordinary jobs and the duties of one's station, not a life spent in prayer, was service to God, fulfilling his will.

This change, which is not controversial, gave a more central place and greater scope to secular activities, a shift in priorities. The social foreground became crowded with practical activities and demands, increasing in their tendency to dominate thought and interests. Religion had become "one thing among many," subject to a tendency to be pushed into the background—a reversal of the medieval preoccupation with "the next world." Secularization as culturally defined was a condition in most states of constitutional removal of religion from legal establishment. Education in Europe had traditionally been in clerical hands at all levels, at least until late in the nineteenth century. That was vital to their interests; and they would not be persuaded to diminish the scope of their influence on the young in this direct way.

Behind, or underlying, this shift of religion to the background, as one thing among others, is the question of the status of religious faith philosophically. The relations of faith and reason were in active debate in scholasticism, and there were such opposed resolutions of the question as those worked out by Aquinas and Occam. Since the schism, the gradual encroachment of scientific findings on Christian assumptions has filled the chapter with gains and retreats. What will be the upshot of this conflict between the advance of learning and the maintenance of a special tradition?

These are the main matters that have to be looked at in more detail in this chapter.

## By Law Established

There never has been a formal constitutional separation of church and state in England. On the contrary, the Elizabethan settlement still holds: the Church of England is "by law established" in its doctrines, formularies, and practices, as in its hierarchical structure, and is therefore notionally the embodiment of the religion of all citizens. "Notionally" not nationally, for of course England is virtually if not formally a secular state. The Elizabethan settlement was reinstated at the restoration, and redefined in the Revolution of 1688, which provided marginal regulated legal independence for nonconformist sects. The oppressive restrictions were not oppressively enforced; but the Anglican Church used its constitutional position, in Parliament and in the parishes throughout the country, to make its influence politically effective. It was until the nineteenth century an active, not an inert, part of the constitution as formulated in the decisive legislation of the 1688 revolution.

The repeal of the Test and Corporation Acts in 1828 ended legal exclusion of non-Anglicans from public and municipal office. This was followed in 1829 by Catholic emancipation, annulling legislation denying them the vote and election to Parliament and public office. The Jesuits were excluded from England. No Catholic would be allowed to hold the office of lord chancellor, and admission to the universities remained an Anglican prerogative. This far-reaching but not complete removal of civil disabilities is a measure of the meaning of an Anglican Church by law established. The universities were opened to non-Anglicans after Royal Commissions on Oxford and Cambridge recommended broad reforms in 1852–1853, followed by legislation in 1854 and 1856.

The Oaths Act of 1888 relieved non-Christians and those with a conscientious scruple about taking a legally required oath on the Bible. Charles Bradlaugh had forced the issue when elected to Parliament as a member for Northampton. He was well known as a professed atheist and a propagandist for secularism. He claimed to be allowed to affirm instead of taking the oath of allegiance to the crown before taking his seat, or else he would swear on the Bible as a notorious atheist. He was allowed to do neither, nor to take his seat. This happened four times from 1880 to

1886, until the persistence of his electors prevailed. J. S. Mill lost his Westminster seat because he supported Bradlaugh in principle.

Locke, a revered father of liberalism, in his letters on toleration at the end of the seventeenth century, virtually an advocacy of secularism ("the magistrate has no jurisdiction over conscience"), had deliberately excluded atheists, on the ground that the oath was the bond of society. Two centuries later, there was still a widespread feeling that good faith required the guarantee of a divine sanction, provided by an oath on the Bible. Religion was still regarded by many as the bond of political society.

Disestablishment remained, and remains, the unfinished legal business of secularization. In 1869, the Irish Church Act ended establishment of the Anglican Church in Ireland and the seating of Irish bishops in the Lords. Church courts were abolished. The Anglican Church in Wales was not disestablished until 1920. In England, Parliament has exerted its control over the Anglican Church against the will of the clergy in recent times. France was "the eldest daughter" of the Roman Church, as the most Romanized of the provinces of the empire, and the church has had an unparalleled dominance in French domestic history. That dominance has been as a storm center. Louis XIV began with an assertion of Gallicanism, making himself head of the church in France, as Henry VIII had in England, without alteration of doctrine and practice. At the same time, he opened a prospect of ecumenicism, bringing in recognition of the Protestants. Later, this turned to vicious persecution of Protestants in an effort to secure their conversion, followed by revocation of the Edict of Nantes (1685), with massacre and mass emigration. The Jesuits were suppressed in 1763 and their property confiscated, which occasioned a crisis in education, which had been largely and formatively in their hands. The French Revolution had drastically subordinated the church to the state, and from the point of view of the intelligentsia effectively marginalized public profession and practice of religion. Napoleon, recognizing its value to the state in the part it played in the countryside among the peasants and the masses generally, as a still potent, not residual, cohesive social force, negotiated a concordat with the papacy bringing French Catholics back to Roman obedience. The church was by law established, and the clergy were salaried officials of the state. Protestant clergy also were paid by the state. From the point of view of the prelates, compared with the princely regime they had enjoyed, it was an eclipse of the church, its secularization in subjection to the state. In his civil code, Napoleon instituted civil marriage and divorce. This was, and was intended to be, a formula for the secularization of all Europe.

Germany must begin with Prussia, where Christianity came very late. Duty came first, and duty to the state first of all, a substitute religion. Prussia became the classical state of the Enlightenment under Frederick the Great, himself a freethinker, indifferent to religion. In the early nineteenth-century reorganization of the state, 1814–1819, it became officially "devout." Under the "Prussian Union," the king as supreme bishop forced Calvinists and Lutherans into a common organization, with joint authorities and a uniform liturgy. He favored ecumenicism. Politically, Christianity was a state ideology; culturally, there was a romantic invocation of the chivalry and loyalties of medieval Christendom.

## Social Priorities

The business of the other world was unquestionably the paramount priority of Christendom. The business of this world claimed and acquired increasing space and time from the schism onward. The logic of expansion, if it is of some elements and not uniformly of all, is destabilization and disintegration, with the growth of some parts at the expense of others. With enterprise engaged in promoting trade and industry and the advancement of learning as well as national aggrandizements, there was inevitably an increasing demand on time and attention.

The capitalist system posed a problem for a church that condemned usury, which was the principle of commerce—as in a different order of considerations did the findings of science. Self-advancement by self-help was irreconcilable with one's divine lot. The divine order was after all nothing but the conservative status quo, in which there was no inherent social justice.

In England, Bentham's gospel of rationalism could develop untrammeled. His target was thoroughly and comprehensively explicit: the "cold, selfish, priest-ridden, lawyer-ridden, lord-ridden, squire-ridden, soldier-ridden England" in 1828. Naturally, the Evangelicals would have liked to destroy utilitarianism root and branch, but that was out of the question, and the two streams of tendency flowed together in the course of social reforms. The extraordinary mind and personality of Gladstone, high churchman and Tory who remained a high churchman, reconciled a commanding Christian faith with moral trust in the voice of the people, and worked consistently if erratically, in and out of political office, to bring about a political democracy in England. He channeled all the religious influence available into that purpose. This was in starkest contrast with what happened in France and in Germany.

However, the democratic perspective came late in the century. What destroyed the ancien regime was the advance of Dissent, Roman Catholicism, and religious indifference encroaching on the established church. Non-Anglicans numbered about half a million against seven million in 1770, and were slightly over half the churchgoing population in 1851, when over half the total population did not attend church at all.

The Anglican decline prompted the Oxford Movement. From the early nineteenth century, a growing self-conscious "middle class," mainly in nonconformist terms, undermined the ascendancy of the upper class by assertion of its own virtues and values in class terms. Industrialization promoted secularization, so that genuine religious commitment became a subcultural phenomenon under a crust of social convention. Until the end of the nineteenth century there was confidence in a natural order that was providential and supplied a sanction and a corrective. What was Adam Smith's "hidden hand," but just that? Calls for state intervention, a proved need, implied that human wisdom was required to forestall or correct what tended to happen or had happened: an exact reversal of outlook.

The principles of seriousness triumphed because they were the principles of success. Gladstone recognized that Evangelicals did not ally themselves with cultural leaders, but were fully in sympathy with money-getting pursuits. They rationalized and justified worldly success.

G. M. Young has given the best-written and most perceptive and sympathetic portrait of the age. In one of his essays, "The Faith of the Grandfathers," he puts "the decisive secularization of English society and thought" somewhere between 1866 and the end of the century. By then, "The conception of a Church transmitting a tradition and interpreting it by authority had no place in the general English mind or imagination." The "religious catastrophe" of the mid-century is the main theme of the essay "The Victorian Noon-time": "The religious catastrophe" was publication of *The Origin of Species,* which "converted a private, if widely held, doubt into a public issue." "The Darwinian theorem . . . created a new framework of reference for ideas. It breached the cosmology of the old faith, and, with it, the whole metaphysic of redemption; and through the gap surged wave upon wave of criticism gathering for years in the vast receptacle of German learning." All this is set in the full context of Victorian society in his *Portrait of an Age,* to which he appended a chronological table. The survey was published in 1936. A sentence in the final paragraph reads: "To a mature and civilized man no faith is possible except faith in the argument itself, and what leadership therefore can he acknowledge, except the argument whithersover it goes?" These might have been words of Isocrates more than two and a quarter millennia sooner. It has been argued that the plot remains the same age to age when the protagonists in the drama are faith and reason.

The difference (and some similarities) between England, with an empirical tradition of eight centuries, and France or Germany, where philosophical tradition and religious institutions and ethos derive from separate sources to exert and maintain formative influence: this abiding difference is clearly evident in their different course in secularization. The Catholic church has never renounced its intransigence, that is, its intent to restore the seamless unity of Christendom, and has never made concessions inconsistent with that purpose.

With the religious tradition so obstinately true to itself in France, the battle for secularization was fought from entrenched positions. There were liberal Catholics and there were Romantic Catholics, and their names were more prominent and distinguished than those of their ecclesiastical opponents—at least to posterity; but they did not prevail within their church. The Freemasons, a middle-class institution, had a tradition of *libre examen,* free thought and independent inquiry. Before the Vatican Council met, the Freemasons organized an anticouncil, and Protestants sought cooperation of Evangelicals in Catholic countries. Eighteen-seventy was a more critical date for France than the Vatican Council, or anything that might have come from it. With the end of the Second Empire, the church became in the Third Republic a conservative pressure group rather than a national constitutional presence. Battlelines were set, with obsolete assumptions in support of one side and their contraries assumed to justify the cause of the other. Masonry infiltrated the professions and was a skeleton organization of partisans who adopted the outlook of Condorcet and denominated the clergy as the enemy. Thus, by different routes, the point of secularization was reached toward the end of the second half of the nineteenth century in both England and France.

French rationalism, anticlericalism, and the legacy of their heavy borrowing from British empiricism in the Enlightenment establishes traditions and tendencies within a composite culture that had hardly a parallel in Germany, where there was scarcely an alternative to their idealist second nature. Christianity was a historical religion, but the Bible which was its source ceased to be the word of God in the light of history. This was a theme explored by Leibniz, as by Spinoza, and above all by Lessing, in general terms, long before David Strauss or Edward Westermarck applied science to biblical texts and to the history of Israel. It was by this door, half-opened by Vico, that historical thinking captivated the German mind and imagination. As a form of knowledge, this type of thinking was challenged by, or challenged, the natural sciences, as refractory to their discipline. Hence, *geist,* "spirit," became the ruling deity in German metaphysics, not the ascertained laws of nature.

Hegel and Kant made, one or the other, the starting point for succeeding German philosophers, as Plato and Aristotle had been in antiquity—although Kant is the predecessor in Europe. There were neo-Kantian and neo-Hegelian philosophies. Hegelianism was more generally widespread, throughout American colleges and universities as well as in Europe. For at least one generation, it superseded Mill's dominance in British universities.

When Freud introduced the discovery, or rediscovery, of the unconscious, and explored its effects, there was a personal conditioning to affect the mind's operations. These were permanent conditions, not the "conditioning" by an authoritarian society complained of in the Enlightenment. Human capability of being "objective" or "disinterested" was put in question.

The authority and efficacy of "reason" on which the Enlightenment had depended was not only disqualified by upholders of the Christian tradition, but also qualified by Hume on rational grounds. What was in question at the end of the nineteenth century and later had become more than a matter of epistemology or of semantics, for human integrity and human communication were involved. It was recognized that there are different ways of knowing. If science as practiced in the natural sciences is taken as the definition of "knowledge" or the paradigm of knowledge, and is understood to establish general probabilities exposed to qualification or falsification on further evidence, that is the most secure form of knowledge attainable. It is not objective, but has intersubjective warrant; that is, a consensus of workers in each field of expertise, which tends to subdivide into smaller areas of closer acquaintance and competence. Knowledge is the product of a global, organized, progressive tradition of this character, fallible, but, like democracy, the best organization for its purpose humanity can attain. Knowledge secured by this degree of critical rigor is not required for the business of ordinary human commerce in the conduct of daily life, which can be satisfactorily informed by common sense. That middle level of knowledge also derives from experience, and is regularly tested in practice, as though by trial and error.

What, then, is the status of the Christian faith as we approach the end of the twentieth century? So long as it is maintained by its practitioners, it remains available in a culture where it is now one thing among others. The outline review above of what was relevant to secularization in England, France, and Germany suggests that there are two general conditions necessary to establish a secular society: no establishment by law of a privileged system of beliefs and practices organized within the society; social protection and advancement of the sciences, including the social sciences. It could be said that England is not a secular society, with a national church "by law established"; but that would be rather like saying that England is not a democracy, given its monarchy. The Anglican church is privileged, but it is also subject to the control of a freely elected Parliament that may number a majority of non-Anglicans, and nonconformists are no longer legally restricted in its favor. It might be asked what relevance to secularization promotion of the sciences has. Christianity is a metaphysic of a kind and implies, if it does not now profess, a prescientific cosmology and a specific doctrine of human nature. A modern society has institutionalized cognitive standards with an inherent claim to be respected and promulgated, together with the findings they attest: this defines a secular society. The norms of understanding are not Christian: that is the central fact of secularism in European societies.

# Part Four

# The Legacy of the West

# 18

# Confrontation

Whether or not the universe began with a bang, and whether or not our part in it ends with a bang or a whimper, the world of human history began the period after World War II with three explosions. There was of course the bomb launched twice to force the Japanese out of the war, following the defeat of the Nazis. There was the explosion of knowledge associated with nuclear research and the special stimulus to science of the life-and-death competitive struggle of the most advanced nations. And there was, not least but delayed, an explosion of world population trampling the earth. These three explosions effectively displaced the original three models left to Europe. They made a breach with the past by their effect on the future.

The bomb represents nuclear power as a source of energy; as a weapon of war; as a means of space exploration. As a source of energy, it was all promise, blighted by the discovery of complications: the incalculable risks of uncontrolled radiation; obsolescence, with irresolvable uncertainties in dismantling. As a weapon, it transformed the perspectives of war, with the logic of mutual assured destruction (MAD). This affected military thinking and defense procurement and meanwhile carried a constant risk of accidents that might precipitate appalling catastrophe, far exceeding the worst natural disaster imaginable. As a means of space exploration and space occupation, the story is more positively encouraging, in terms of enlarged resources and extended knowledge, rather than in tentatives of the kind exploited for the science fiction market.

The development of nuclear power and these applications of it have altogether involved expenditure of unprecedented magnitude. This priority has disproportionately deprived the funding of other social claims and projects. Its part in the eventual economic collapse of the Soviet Union, if not calculable, was considerable. That does not mean that the economy of the United States was unscathed.

The explosion of knowledge translated into many fronts of spectacular acceleration. This has been evident in information technology, the range of electronics, the

229

generations of computers, the new foundations in microbiology. The infrastructure of science and technology, the research institutes, the laboratories, the research and development departments of all major industries, is international in terms of communication and to an increasing extent in collaboration. This is the reality of the One World platitude that supplements increasing economic interdependence. Like industry, science and technology have developed spectacularly by the division of labor, productivity by specialization. Endless subdivisions have led to broad classification in place of the old distinguishable sciences of the curriculum. There are dictionaries of Physical Sciences, Earth Sciences, Life Sciences, Social Sciences. Secret systems of communications and control are explored in genetics. Anthropology has mapped patterns of culture in their variety. Paleontology is uncovering the remotest organic life on the planet. The figures that characterize all these studies are of an inconceivable magnitude macroscopic and microscopic.

Population does not explode overnight, but the figures are among the more reliably predictable, and on present calculations are alarming. Short of that prospect, present populations are a main cause of most pressing problems. The scale of human need and of human displacement is a growing tax on resources and on caring agencies. When tourists seriously threaten the Alps and very many other target resorts; when industrialized countries and their mass markets are constantly draining exhaustible resources and causing irreparable environmental damage in so many ways that are nigh impossible to bring under permanent control; when the far greater of the total population is living at a level near destitution, and the poor are getting poorer and the rich richer; when China, with the largest national population, in desperation tries to enforce a limit of one child per family: all peoples stare at their increase as the problem of problems.

These scant references to global commonplaces of our time are a reminder that the accelerating enlargement of knowledge and of consequent capability is beyond comparison. As a sequel to the Enlightenment, it is a jump into a new orbit, with an orientation and perspective that transcend the Tenth Stage of Condorcet's *Progress of the Human Mind,* with unforeseeable returns on the investment in knowledge. Unexampled awareness of the earth and its history is accompanied by unexampled awareness of global problems that confront human race. The threat to human survival activates human self-consciousness and is the bond of human union.

The injunction at Delphi, "Know yourself," incorporated in the culture of Hellas, traditional source of European culture, can at last be answered by the human race to whom it was implicitly addressed. The shared capability of the species is the latest addition to what has been learned from all the relevant sciences. This universal knowledge, with the human capability it informs, imposes so decisive a responsibility on the race that it may well be called the upshot of history, although its future course remains unpredictable, with a plenitude of possibilities. To appreciate this outcome, however, it is necessary to look closely enough at the political, economic, social, and cultural development of Europe in the global context since the end of World War II.

# The "Cold War"

The end of the war was by no means an end of the power politics of the powers that had precipitated the conflict. Rather, there was an intensification because of the split in the alliance, and the Soviet menace to Europe; but that heating up was not likely to issue in war or in justice; it was the climate that induced the "cold war."

The Germans themselves were the supreme question. Was there among themselves the kind of division found in the countries the Nazis occupied? Undoubtedly, the Nazis had brought about the war. The nation, forged by war, had learned to think of itself historically and comparatively, and to think of war as an instrument of policy. Defeat in World War I had never been accepted, nor the terms of the treaty that was imposed. The defeat, followed by revolution and runaway inflation, occasioned profound unsettlement and uncertainty, to be reinforced by the Great Depression and six million unemployed.

After Streseman's sudden death, his coalition was superseded by that of the Reichswehr under Paul von Hindenburg and the landowners and industrialists. They needed popular support for the stringent economic policies required, and sought it in the votes of Hitler's popular following, confident of being able to use him. When the boot was on the other foot, the die had been cast. A recognized organized "underground" resistance was less possible in Germany than in the occupied countries. Surveillance was tighter; leaders in great number had left the country when the way things were drifting became evident; the terrain was not favorable to a maquis; the Allies made no attempt to get in touch with and support groups prepared to resist. Apart from the plot to assassinate Hitler that failed; top German scientists did not collaborate to provide Hitler with an atom bomb, as it was in their power to do in a bid to save the Third Reich. In short, Germany was not to be identified with the Nazis; and experience of the Nazis was profound, shocking, and a purge. The German people were in the mind and mood for something entirely different, given a chance, as they could not have been after the Great War, as it used to be called.

Germany, then, was the central problem for the Allies: massively destroyed, what should now be the method and manner of reconstruction and containment? At Yalta, Russian annexation of Lithuania, Latvia, and Estonia had been recognized, new boundaries agreed for Poland, with cessions to Russia compensated by territory transferred form Germany. At Potsdam in 1945, it was decided to hold a foreign ministers' conference to work out a peace treaty. Meanwhile, the four commanders-in-chief should form an Allied Control Commission for four zones occupied separately by their forces. Local government and necessary institutions were to be restored in Germany. The failure of the foreign ministers to agree on conditions of settlement and the de facto consolidation of Russian occupation of Eastern Europe by the end of 1947 enveloped Europe in the East-West division of mutual hostility that was the condition of cold war.

Churchill was aware that Roosevelt intended to get out of Europe as soon as Germany was defeated, and he was anxious to take independent measures against a threat from the East, especially by close alliance with France. His "iron curtain" speech in Fulton, Missouri, in March 1946 upset President Harry Truman, who was conciliatory in his relations with Stalin and felt it was the rhetoric of a warmonger who was out of line. Within a year, came American recognition of the "iron curtain," and the "Truman Doctrine" followed by the "Marshall Plan." Truman's speech to Congress of March 12, 1947, asking for substantial aid for Greece and Turkey, announced that "one of the primary objectives of the foreign policy of the U.S. is the creation of conditions in which we and other nations will be able to work out a way of life free from coercion," and that this entailed a willingness to help free peoples to maintain their free institutions. This projection of a "Free World" of political democracies in opposition to and defense against a totalitarian order of "people's democracies" maintained by a police state was the political division that would be frozen by a preponderant military power poised in a rough match, which the United Nations could not hope to rival, and could do little to influence, since it was composed of the opposing parties.

In June 1947, General Marshall made his Harvard speech, and Truman adopted the plan and put it to Congress, which was strongly influenced in its vote by the coup d'etat in Prague that struck down the democratic regime of Edvard Benes and Jan Masaryk. The Marshall Plan was not only an offer of desperately needed aid in the reconstruction of ravaged and denuded Europe, but also a test of the willingness of Europe, not least the Soviet Union, to cooperate in the reconstruction—a final bid for Roosevelt's warm hopes when the Nazis were seen to be doomed. The Soviet Union was willing to take a lion's share of available aid, as the country that had suffered most, but not to form a partnership in European reconstruction, out of the question anyhow on her intransigent terms.

The tactics by which Stalin had planted and nurtured a Communist spring-growth in Poland and frozen out the government-in-exile in London were a prelude to such moves in other countries freed by the Red Army, Czechoslovakia, Bulgaria, Hungary, Rumania, and East Germany. Whereas, for example, there was a British military delegation in Budapest alongside the Russian one under Marshall Voroshilov (invited to each other's parties), Western policy was to leave politics to the native politicians, whilst the Soviet Union introduced their own agents and worked through Hungarian nationals who were Communists trained in Moscow. The Allies attended at close-hand the course of the Soviet takeover in Eastern Europe, like snooker players in their seats whilst their opponents are in total control at the table.

European nations were no longer dealing with a Russia of familiar mold, a diplomatic partner and rival in the balance of power. The game had changed, and the rules were not known. The Soviet Union was the first state in modern times with the will and the power to apply a clear-cut ideology in all its dealings, in the faith that, since the proletariat alone were interested in the production of plenty for all, they would inevitably gain control of the economic machine and the state apparatus worldwide. When these initial post-war events were seen as a step-by-step achievement of such a program, which counted and built upon a constituency already existing within their own frontiers, Western democratic governments were made understandably anxious. The McCarthy Communist phobia and the Vietnam war were in the making.

The events were open to a different interpretation. The steps the Soviet Union had taken were defensive, not expansionist. The Western capitalist nations were necessarily hostile to Communism. A ring of satellites identified with the Soviet Union was the safest insurance. Such an alternative view, informed and perceptive and detached, was argued with distinction by George Kennan, once U.S. ambassador in Moscow, in the BBC Reith Lectures of 1957, published as *Russia, the Atom, and the West*. The pith of that argument was that to think of defense solely in military terms, and particularly in terms of unusable weapons of unimaginable destructive power, was negative and sterile. NATO was necessary as basic armed defense, but should be secondary to normalized diplomatic relations and the steadfast development of Western traditional liberal institutions into an exemplary way of life. The future of Europe should be staked upon the "European Recovery Program" initiated by Marshall aid, not upon military confrontation. An attempt to build that recovery as an exemplary society based on liberal traditions would be the heart of a positive defense.

This was written after the Berlin blockade and the Western air-lift, the major crisis in the Soviet's probing of limits. Europe did respond positively to the Marshall Plan. Sixteen noncommunist countries set up the Organization for European Economic Cooperation to ensure "a sound European economy through the economic cooperation of its members." The Soviet Union, measuring itself against the "imperialism" of the United States, formed in counteraction the Cominform in October 1947 at a conference of communist leaders from France, Italy, Bulgaria, Czechoslovakia, Hungary, Poland, Romania, and Yugoslavia. The Soviet Union had also mobilized their communist cells in the far East, in Vietnam, India, and Malaya, and in the Middle East, in Syria, and in Egypt. Communist parties in Italy and in France were strong enough to constitute a dangerous political threat. All told, the global position of the U.S.S.R. as it emerged into the clear out of the obscurities of the aftermath of the war was formidable enough to compel recourse to strong measures of containment.

The year 1947 saw Four-Power conferences in March and April and in November and December that concluded the impossibility of agreement over Germany. General Lucius Clay, governor of the American zone, remarked, "The resentment of the Germans against colonial administration is increasing daily. Two and a half years without a government is much too long." The Anglo-American zones were fused, and an economic council established. A council of state was formed with the prime ministers of the Lander and their chief ministers; political parties were reformed. Having taken this initiative, in default of Allied agreement, the three western powers (France joined in) were set on prompting the West Germans into the formation of a new state, which was done by September 21, 1949, by a parliamentary council of sixty-five members from six parties, of which the Christian Democratic Union and the Social Democratic Party numbered twenty-seven each. The new state was expressly provisional, for the new government insisted on a claim to the eventual incorporation of East Germany, in protest against dismemberment.

On that side at about the same time an East German state was brought into existence by three congresses to discuss and determine their future, infiltrated in the usual way by the Soviet Union. Candidates for election to the third of these congresses, which approved the constitution of the German Democratic Republic in October 1949, were from an approved list.

The Russian blockade of Berlin was occasioned by disagreement about the reformed currency for Germany. The Western powers had established a new Deutschmark for the new state. The Russians insisted on their own Soviet issue for the four zones of Berlin, to which the western response was acceptance alongside their own German mark. With refugees deserting the east for the west, and the prospect of a capitalist West Germany supported by the United States as a magnet, Stalin aimed at cutting off Berlin from the West. The unexpected massive airlift with which the blockade was countered, and which was sustained, could not be checked without war, and that was beyond the limit.

Western union had been institutionalized by the Treaty of Brussels signed on March 17, 1948, by Britain, France, Holland, Belgium, and Luxembourg. This had been engineered by Ernest Bevin as British foreign secretary for the defense of democracy in Europe, which he hoped would attract the support of the United States. The communist coup in Prague and the Soviet blockade of Berlin induced recognition of the need for a structured defense to contain the Soviet Union, and the defense clauses of the Brussels Treaty offered the nucleus of such a structure. The North Atlantic Treaty signed on April 4, 1949, was intended as reinforcement of these defense provisions. The five countries of the Brussels Treaty were joined by the United States, Canada, Denmark, Iceland, Italy, Norway, and Portugal. Although a military alliance, it was meant to be integrated with economic collaborations, but in the event the lacing was political not economic.

Marshall aid and currency reform and administrative independence, after more than two years of stalling, enabled the Germans to bring about their own recovery with remarkable speed. Professor Erhard was appointed to direct economic affairs in 1948, and by 1950 production was back to the level of before the war; the country was again a leading manufacturer of steel, chemicals, and electric goods.

Minister of Economic Affairs Erhard in Germany began by dismantling the legacy of Nazi control of industry, encouraging small and medium companies, and the participation of workers in the organization and profit of industry. But government planning was required by Marshall aid; certain central financial institutions remained in place. The banks were used to having representatives on the boards of private companies, with an eye on investment policies and management efficiency. Industries in the forefront of development, like chemicals and electronics, needed promotion. A bank was established for reconstruction and made permanent in 1961 to finance long-term investments neglected by commercial banks. Economic recovery was swift under Erhard's supervision, and during the fifties large surpluses were applied to the provision of social services. Integrated planning was developed and consolidated in Konzertierte Aktion, which brought together government, financiers, employers, workers, and the central bank to formulate policy.

France likewise, having lost nearly half her wealth, had recovered her 1938 industrial level by 1948. The provisional government appointed an economic planning commission under Jean Monnet, whose plan in 1947 set out to modernize

French industry. In 1950, he was associated with Robert Schuman, the foreign minister, in a plan to combine the French and German coal and steel industries, which would block a dangerous German resurgence based on the old military-industrial heartland. This emerged with added members as the European Coal and Steel Community in the Treaty of Paris in 1951, signed by France, West Germany, Italy, and the Benelux countries, which had already formed a customs union. The benefits were exemplary, and in 1955 they appointed a committee "to examine the possibilities of expanding their existing community into an economic association based on free trade, joint social and financial policies, the abolition of restrictive trading practices, and the free movement of capital and labour." The six signed the Treaty of Rome on March 25, 1957, which set up the European Economic Community. The EEC was roughly coterminous with the empire of Charlemagne. Monnet had been awarded the Charlemagne Prize in 1953. These two native citizens of Rome's most Romanized province definitively modernized the legacy with a new form and style of imperium by designing a new Europe to play a central part in global politics, but not to bestride the world.

By the end of 1951, European output was 35 percent above 1939 levels and industrial investment continued rising as firms modernized. By 1958 the gross national product of West Germany, France, Holland, and Britain had at least doubled the 1938 figure. The market was different, with coal increasingly displaced by oil, and steel less important than chemicals. Automobiles were a new main expansionist industry. With a one-third fall in labor employed, agricultural output was one-third greater, aided by machinery, fertilizers, plant breeding, pest control, and government subsidies. Air travel reduced the demand for shipbuilding. There was a drastic scaling-down of traditional industries with the loss of former textile markets on top of these changes. Growth industries were in services, chemicals, pharmaceuticals, and electronics. Young people with money to spend offered a market for exploitation. This growing prosperity, characterized by Harold Macmillan's comment, "You never had it so good," brought an influx of immigrant labor; in England, from the West Indies mainly at first; in Germany, from Turkey; in France, from Africa. The boom would burst in the sixties; but enough has been said at this stage to indicate the radical restructuring of the market that characterized the new Europe that was taking institutional shape.

That institutional structure had permanent foundations by the sixties. The European Community (or European Communities) was a union of the Coal and Steel Community, the Atomic Energy Community (for development of peaceful uses of atomic energy), and the EEC. The EC was administered by a commission constituted by appointed members of the constituent states, who were responsible for carrying out policies decided by a council of ministers of the states. A European Parliament elected in the constituencies of the member states was given consultative functions. A court of justice was instituted by the commission to interpret the treaties that established the EC, and to apply the laws enacted by the council and administrators. NATO was both the de facto organization of Western defense on the ground and the treaty by which that was sanctioned and set up with the cooperation of the United

States. The Organization for European Economic Co-operation set up in response to the Marshall Plan in 1948 became in 1961 the Organization for Economic Cooperation and Development (OECD), a permanent body to monitor economic performance in order to promote growth, expand trade, and coordinate aid to developing countries. Six states outside the EEC in 1960 formed a European Free Trade Association (EFTA): Norway, Sweden, Finland, Iceland, Austria, and Switzerland. Britain would have to sacrifice traditional advantageous trading partnerships, particularly with New Zealand, to join the Common Market, and was both deeply divided on the question and in 1963 blocked by de Gaulle's veto of the British application.

On the other side of the "iron curtain" there were two organizations for the economic association and the defense of the Soviet block: the Warsaw Treaty Organization (Warsaw Pact, 1955), the counterpart to NATO; and the Council for Mutual Economic Assistance (Comecon), formed in 1949 in counterpart to Marshall aid.

Thus, within two decades of the end of the war, in default of a peace settlement, a new Europe had been formed, with a new political map and with institutional forms of economic cooperation and merger frozen in place by the confrontation of two superpowers armed with super-weapons. What had come about piecemeal by shifts and impasses was at the time deemed provisional, as in the long run everything turns out to be, but was regularized by continuance, as things usually are. That regularity made it possible to think and to hope that detente would thaw the climate of cold war. Khrushchev's "peaceful co-existence of different social systems" worked its way slowly into policies and possibilities. Meanwhile, it is worth noticing that even permanent institutions suffer from permanence, and even monolithic totalitarian security suffers from security.

Institutions are social habits formed to prescribe behavior, a performance that is not the property of the institution but of its members, who are affected and motivated by other constraints and interests. When Charles de Gaulle was in power in France, for example, he manipulated, disdained, or rejected the institutions to which France had subscribed, for the majesty and destiny of France that filled his imagination. As time went on, Italy had more governments than years, of the same complexion, but hardly ever able to fulfill all mandates. West Germany was a progressive, pliant, model member, but did not renounce aspirations and former policies that in new circumstances thwarted compliance. Britain went her own way when the shoe pinched too painfully. Not only are the institutions what their members make them, apart from what they are; what they inevitably are, as institutions, has its own fatal logic. What is known as "Parkinson's Law" is the way they work. It is what Bentham found in the corporation of lawyers, and later in other institutions. They are set up to perform a service, and in the second generation are liable to become a vested interest absorbed in or giving priority to self-preservation and self-expansion. They are then not reformable from within, and only by exceptional pressure from outside. Meanwhile, they draw increasing funds expended on increasing floor-space and staff for the production and circulation of massive missives or directives. This semi-automatic manufacture is not wholly and solely under the control of accountable decision-makers. However, these well-known bureaucratic tendencies which are the subject of wry jokes are only incidental, if complementary, to the disparate behavior of the founders of institutions as members of their foundations, capitally exemplified in the UN, and constantly in the European Community. Institutions, in short, *are* their personnel, both as founders and members; and also have a life of their own.

The insecurity of total security in the form of totalitarian government of a police state protected by dependent satellites was evident early on, long before it was demonstrated. Yugoslavia, Romania, and Albania, as Communist as China or Moscow where their leaders were bred, were recalcitrant, not puppet, regimes, maintaining in their own ways their independence. When Hungary and Czechoslovakia went their own way, the tanks were sent in to bring them to heel, for in the latter case there was the pressing danger that East Germany (the linchpin) might be dislodged by Willi Brandt's eastern diplomacy. The Berlin wall had been necessary to stop the hemorrhage. In the year following the imposition on Czechoslovakia there was the insubordination of the Polish workers at Gdansk where they demolished Party headquarters in protest against food price rises. At Gydnia a Soviet ship was set on fire. Moscow knew that if the tanks were sent in, Wladyslaw Gomulka would mobilize the Polish forces against them, a formidable demonstration of political will backed by armed strength. His successor, Gierek, was able undisturbed to introduce far-reaching reforms and open economic relations with the West. In short, in one way and another, the Soviet Union was continuously striving to hold together the imperiled security system sanctioned by force.

The formative motive and inner truth of the new provisional Europe that emerged from global conflict divided by mutual suspicions was the same in both hemispheres: *Never again!*

## The Old Adam

The "dismantlement of colonial empires" is apt to be a summary dismissal of what happened after the war. It was far from that, in the sense that there was nothing voluntary about it. The claim to independence was bitterly resented and fiercely resisted, and to be made good had to be wrenched from the European imperialist power by dedicated leaders of populations or groups with an indomitable will to shake off alien rule. The Dutch, the French, the Portuguese did not renounce their empires. They lost them, for all that they did to retain them. That was an appendix to the chapter that opened a new beginning in Europe. The Western powers were not alone involved. Communism, inspired and aided by the Soviet Union had a dominant part in most contexts.

The war turned things upside down, and the downside, though not in view, is always there. What to the West had been voyages of discovery believed to have been inaugurated by Columbus had been to the Indians invasion and conquest by intruders from the equally unknown. The extension of those voyages to Asia initially introduced access to exotic markets, but commercial contacts, with the expansion of home-based industries, required strengthened hold to secure a reliable supply of raw materials from natural resources. Imperial dominion in these terms was more tenuous than it might appear.

The triumphant Japanese offensive from 1941 can be shown on a map by nearly a hundred arrowheads launched south, west, east, and even north in an enveloping and overwhelming storm that swept out the imperial masters of French Indochina, Dutch East Indies, Britain's Burma, Singapore, Hong Kong, Sarawak, Brunei, and the Philippines, a strategic center of interest and influence for the United States. Although this was won back by 1945 in the Allied counteroffensive at the end of which Japan was knocked out as definitively as Germany, the imperialists had suffered exemplary defeat, and were not to be restored as before in Asia.

The fifties were dominated by Communist bids and threats around the world, as in Malaya, Vietnam, and Cuba. The general unsettlement influenced unrest in British African colonies. The liberal chiaroscuro of indirect rule as demonstrated by Lord Lugard in northern Nigeria was exhibited to all Africans by the South African regime, after leaving the British Commonwealth in 1965, as black and white.

In the Middle East, the ganging-up of France, Britain, and Israel, short-lived and abortive though it was, against Gamal Abdel Nasser of Egypt over control of the Suez Canal in 1956, aggravated as it was by the injection of Israel into Palestine in 1948, demonstrated the end of the old realism of ruling interests, much as Picasso and Francis Bacon did by reinventing nature in painting.

The undisputed new masters of the post-war world were the United States and the Soviet Union, unmatchable in might, military and economic. Both were anti-imperialist in principle. The United States was formed by an alliance of revolting colonies, displacing the authority of birth and privilege with the accountability of elected representatives, as declared by Thomas Paine. The Soviet Union was dedicated by Lenin to bringing about the fated end of the consummation of capitalist economic exploitation in the imperialist phase, for the permanent happy union of mankind.

A treaty of friendship and alliance between the Soviet Union and Communist China in 1950 was the first defeat of American policy in the Far East. China had been rescued from the anarchy of warlords in the 1920s by a national uprising, but then had to be saved from the Japanese aggressor. The leader of the nationalist party, Chiang Kai-shek, was allied to a Communist party, on which he turned in a bloody purge in 1927. During the war the Soviet Union had supported him. It formed an agreement of friendship and alliance with him when the Japanese surrendered. Russian conquest in Manchuria in the last phase had been considerable, and the great quantity of Japanese arms they collected were handed over to the Chinese Communists in 1945, putting them in a strong position to negotiate with Chiang Kai-shek and the Nationalists. General Marshall, who was in China at the time, strongly supported the negotiations, advising close cooperation. Chiang Kai-shek, believing he had the upper hand, refused to compromise, making civil war inevitable, and requiring American military aid on his behalf. The Chinese Communist Party had been formed in 1920 with the support of the Soviet Union. One of the delegates to its first congress had been Mao Tse-tung, an assistant in the library of Beijing University. During more than two years of civil war, the position of Chiang Kai-shek crumbled, and in October 1949 Mao Tse-Tung was able to declare a People's Republic of China. His enemy fled to Taiwan, whence he plotted an invasion of the mainland with military support from the United States, a theatrical coup never enacted. China passed from the American to the Soviet orbit.

Meanwhile, the diplomatic stalemate over Germany at the end of the war had a parallel in the Far East in Korea. The Japanese stationed north of the 38th parallel were to surrender to the Russians, those south of the parallel to the Americans. After evacuation, independent Korea was to have a democratic constitution. Events took over, with a "people's democracy" in the north, and a conservative government in the south. The United States recognized South Korea as an independent state. The Soviet Union and China were committed to unification. In June 1950, the North invaded the South. The United Nations Security Council, boycotted by the Soviet Union, was able to frustrate the General Assembly's condemnation of the act of aggression, which entailed a demand for immediate suspension of hostilities and withdrawal of troops. This unprecedented act commissioned a coalition of forces to enforce it. The Americans furnished the bulk of the troops in support of the South Koreans, with contingents from other nations, including Britain. Under the United Nations, it was a limited use of force, commissioned to enforce the demand for a cessation of hostilities and withdrawal, a legal use of force to suppress an illegal use of force. In practice, the U.N. troops should push the North Koreans back to the 38th parallel, and not go beyond it. In the event, when U.N. troops had succeeded in this, China gave military support that redressed the balance and drove the U.N. forces back. When they regained the initiative and reconquered what they had lost, they pushed on under General MacArthur beyond the 38th parallel, threatening open war. President Truman recalled MacArthur.*

The war dragged on bogged down around the parallel, whilst armistice talks were held, which also dragged on for two years, ending as in Germany with two Koreas sealed in opposition.

The United States, assuming that the Soviet Union was behind Chinese intervention in North Korea, feared that the same would happen in North Vietnam, that the border was not safe. The government therefore gave attention to strengthening the government in South Vietnam, which was in bad shape. A corrupt ruling class that alienated the peasants by denying land reform was fractured by rivalry between Buddhists and Roman Catholics. The regime collapsed in 1963, followed by military coups in the next two years. The Communist Viet Cong, which supported the nationalist party installed in North Vietnam, was steadily gaining influence and territory in the South. In 1962, President Kennedy sent in some four thousand so-called advis-

---

*I was in the United States at that time and happened, in a taxi in New York, to hear President Truman broadcast his announcement that he had recalled General MacArthur. After giving his reason, he said the general would be free to make his own case in the next few days. MacArthur duly did so in a forceful appeal he broadcast to American homes. He said he was not allowed to go on to win and finish the war, so that America's sons would not go on being killed and maimed. He was expected to fight with one arm tied behind his back. When MacArthur came to New York, the city turned out to greet him; the streets were deep in ticker-tape raining down on his motorcade. However, when MacArthur's backers organized public meetings to follow up, they were too scantily attended to be pursued. This first attempt to enforce a U.N. resolution by limited armed intervention was bungled by MacArthur's intransigence. A manifest halt at the parallel would probably have sufficed for the Chinese.

ers to help the Diem regime deal with its own subversive elements. This involvement inevitably escalated. Training South Vietnamese forces was complemented by reconnaissance flights over North Vietnam. Tit-for-tat encounters intensified in 1965; and when North Vietnamese regular troops were sent across the border into the South, two hundred thousand soldiers from the United States were committed in early 1966 to oppose them. This was the beginning of an untoward engagement that sucked in more than half a million young Americans, branded the United States as an imperialist power, spattered atrocities, alienated a large element of the country's student youth, ending in a humiliating scuttle, honored as the best bargain that could be negotiated. In an ugly appendix, backs were turned on unwelcome traumatized victims when they were brought back. The scar was another "Never again."

The generic name of the game of all the players is "power politics," and it operates in internal as well as external relations. The Germans and the Japanese learned to play it the imperial way from the French and the British. The nauseating hypocrisy is unnecessary, and is generally seen through, to the detriment of even minimum respect and trust. International relations would not only have been sweeter but also sounder, at all times, if there had been manifest candor and good faith, as in trading relations, on which an international market depends.

These commonplaces are properly retrospective, relative to the simpler conditions that obtained before the war. The global context of more intimate international relations brought about by the network of rapid communications provided by several expanding fronts of technology introduced two modifying conditions into the unregenerate pursuit of power politics: the new experience of international coexistence and interdependence, with easy and regular contacts with heads of state, a new era of first-hand diplomacy; and many forms of national behavior which necessarily become of legitimate international concern, from acts of pollution that invade neighbors' territories to abuse of human rights from which refugees en masse try to flee to other lands, or the acquisition of weapons of mass destruction by powers regarded not without reason as irresponsible when war with the use of such weapons can no longer be thought of as an instrument of policy. Also, with the increasing mobility of labor, the old habit of exploiting it for large-scale work (Chinese coolies on trans-American railways; Irish navvies on the English canals) has been, as it were, domesticated, bringing in immigrants to do the less attractive work in a society. Thought of as temporary, perhaps on both sides, if and when a majority stay and settle, they tend to establish themselves with their cultural identity that can be assimilated only on its own terms, as a domesticated alien ethnic group. This is happening not least in the United States, which has ceased to be a "melting-pot" in the original sense.

The fight against colonial powers and the fight against apartheid in South Africa and in the United States were the same cause, and even the same movements inasmuch as there was a Communist input in much of it. Of the colonial powers, the Portuguese were the last to give way, undermined from within by a left-wing coup in 1974. Otherwise, in Asia the decisive blows had been struck by the mid-fifties, and in Africa by the mid-sixties, with the bloody eight years of slaughter in Algeria ending in 1962.

The international market economy that was built up at least partially with the benefit of that exploitation is sustained by the terms of trade settled by the market, modified by agreements at the periodic meetings of the industrialized nations in rounds of the General Agreement on Tariffs and Trade (GATT). The underlying market principle is to profit by buying cheap and selling dear. The GATT agreements have invariably set terms of trade detrimental to Third World countries mainly dependent on export of a single primary product, such as coffee or copper. When the developed countries also insist on retaining a monopoly of processing the product, the door is banged shut. When the EEC subsidizes the production of millions of tons of beet sugar to help its farmers, it prices millions of cane sugar workers in the Third World out of the market. This has to be set against the desire and will of the developed nations (the North) to set on their feet the peoples at first called "undeveloped," then "underdeveloped," and finally "developing." The changing nomenclature reflects changing policy, from initial grievous mistakes to recent recognition of what has to be addressed.

It was assumed that undeveloped countries could be helped to catch up by being given the basics of what the developed countries had—massive technical and financial aid to build major industrial plant, particularly hydroelectric dams. The Marshall Plan was a model. In spite of massive grants, the number of destitute in the Third World increased, and was estimated as almost a third of the world's total population. These were people without land or with not enough for subsistence, or who had drifted to the towns in search of work and survived in a hand-to-mouth existence in shanties on the outskirts as "marginal people in marginal places" with no constructive basis on which to improve their lot by their efforts. Aid had failed to reach them for two main reasons. It was received by governments and passed through administrative hands; abundant uses would be found for it before the needs of the absolute poor could be considered. Nothing "trickled down," as donors had assumed. The second reason has to do with the economic plight of most of these governments. Colonial peoples had been generally compelled to sell their exports and buy imports at dictated prices advantageous to the mother country. After independence, to gain a footing in international trade, and to qualify for loans, they had to exploit their export possibilities. This usually forced them to commercialize agriculture, bringing land into cultivation on a scale that displaced subsistence husbandry, which was the livelihood of rural families, driving them into the towns as marginal people in marginal places or into forest land to "slash and burn" and cause long-term environmental damage. When the oil-producing countries of the Middle East, Arab states, formed a cartel, the Organization of Petroleum Exporting Countries (OPEC) and challenged the industrial rich powers by cutting the supply and raising the price to demonstrate their economic muscle, the inflow of foreign currency they received brought about the problem of disposal. Developing countries that had developed an export line to qualify for loans were deemed credit-worthy, and the low interest rates were attractive. But the general unsettlement induced runaway inflation, a sharp rise in interest rates, and the debtor countries could never count on a remunerative price for commodities on which they were dependent for export. The world has heard of their plight: they have been put in the position of having to make a net contribution to the wealth of the developed world, and deprived of conditions for their own growth.

For a general glance at the debt and development problems, Latin America is a useful example. Since the late eighties, there has been a transfer of resources of approximately $20 billion a year to the international funds controlled by the developed world; and still there was no effective plan of the World Bank and International Monetary Fund (IMF) for new lending and debt servicing and repayment targets that would leave enough capital in each developing country for appropriate investment and growth. Without some feasible export growth and the budgetary reform imposed by the IMF as a condition of this facilitation, there was a prospect of bringing these countries (treated case by case) by the mid-nineties to the position of being able to manage their debt responsibly and notch a rate of growth. Without some feasible scheme of burden-sharing, there could be no prospect for developing countries within an international economic system.

Brazil is the largest of these countries in territory and in population, and at the same time it contains the major part of Amazonia, by far the largest remaining tropical forest. Because the rate at which these forests are being destroyed and the irreparable consequences for the planet have been so long and so widely publicized, Brazil brings into focus the conjoined problem of development and environment that have been recognized as a growing threat, one that must be seriously addressed.

In Amazonia this is not simply to check and limit the exploitation of timber. Discoveries of bauxite, copper, gold, tin, lead, iron, manganese, nickel, and silver add mining to logging, the extension of ranch farming, and industrial enterprises for the development of oil, gas, and hydroelectric plant. Brazil is the most diverse and advanced industrializing country in the Third World, which prompts her to jump into a new orbit. At the same time, she is seething with intractable problems. Interests affected are those of the indigenous Indian forest communities displaced, rubber tappers who eke out a living from a resource that once made rubber barons; above all, peasants without any land, forced to work for minimal subsistence wages insufficient to raise a family. The Indians of the forest number some half million; in the sixteenth century when Europeans penetrated into Amazonia they were estimated at about seven million. Overriding interests are those of ranchers extending their monopoly of the land, and those of the companies engaged in exploitative enterprises, together with right-wing political parties and the bureaucracies of the administration.

During the three decades beginning in the sixties, government planned development from afar in the time-honored way with a blank sheet and the book. Amazonia was taken as an empty space for a planned economy on the United States model, without consulting any of the parties.

During the war, Brazil had cooperated closely with the United States. As a junior partner, she hoped to emulate the rapid post-war growth of the states and be catapulted into the major league of industrial states by the end of the century. A measure of that was indeed achieved over the first two decades that began with the sixties, for the Brazilian economy became the eighth largest in the capitalist world after the economic Group of Seven, despite hyperinflation. The downside of this was the concentration of wealth in a few hands. Brazil was near the bottom in terms of the social indicators—life expectancy, infantile mortality, nutrition, literacy, standards that depend on the provision of social services if economic conditions are seriously inequitable. In the third decade, increasing poverty of the majority plunged the country into economic and political crisis. The country might be said to reproduce or to mirror the North/South global divide. By the end of the eighties, there was a political turnabout, with for the first time a mass vote for an independent presidential candidate, Fernando Collor de Mellor, whose campaign focused on government inefficiency and corruption, and promised, in effect, a Thatcherite era of reform by reducing the dominance of the state. In Amazonia, centralized planning would end; civil liberties would allow voluntary associations to champion and further their interests without hindrance.

Against this was the de facto political weight of the ranchers, mining companies, and manufacturers, with their massive vested interest in holding on to what they had, supported by importers abroad, beneficiaries in the developed States, particularly, the United States, the United Kingdom, and Japan. Political rhetoric and campaign promises did not blow this away, even when swelled into a gale by the response of the popular vote. In consequence, the better possibility of a new era did not dawn. There was not a national partnership in policymaking. Room was not made for acceptance of Indian symbiosis with their forest habitat. Modernity was not equated with sustainable, equitable forms of development. Those with a vested interest in environmental degradation continued to ride roughshod over the masses in human degradation. On the eve of the Earth Summit convened by the United Nations in Brazil in June 1992, the government was too unsure of itself to be in control. The consequences of inflation, debt, and unemployment had driven the poor to desperation. Children whose parents did not get wages to support a family, nor state entitlement to social security, lived on the streets, helping themselves by petty crime. To suppress the nuisance, they were systematically shot and killed by hired gunmen glad to earn keep for their own families, even by those of the police who were convinced that this was the best solution in the circumstances.

The extremity of the situation at this time in this place simply highlights a general trend. Urban riots in U.S. inner cities in the sixties prompted Lyndon Johnson to announce his vision of the "Great Society" that made provision for its citizens in need. Nixon reversed this provision of state funds for dependency, with reaffirmation of an imposition of law and order. With the flare-up of racial violence in Los Angeles in May 1992, provoked by an acquittal by a white jury of three policemen charged with the vicious beating of a black man they had arrested, of which there was recorded visual evidence, the unresolved tensions that had surfaced in the Watts riots there and scored a place in the calendar were forced onto the political agenda. Faltering in his presidential campaign for reelection, President George Bush had to deal effectively with the inadequacy of Social Security and the reality of racial inequality, as well as a seriously indebted budget, in the state that had proclaimed itself leader of the Free World.

When Robert Mugabe as leader of the ZANU party became prime minister of Zimbabwe in 1980 his mind was set on establishing a one-party state on the Soviet model. That was an abstract idea like centralized planning, and if he never entirely succeeded, what he did achieve within a decade by the remote lone decision-making entailed was alienation of the mass of the people by reneging on the promise of land, by jobs and privileges for his own tribe, by official corruption, and by failing to associate the people as a whole with policy-making.

When in 1979 Mohammed Reza Pahlavi, Shah of Iran, was forced out and took refuge in the United States, to which he had looked for encouragement and backing in his aspirations to modernize his patrimony, the native population that had been or felt exploited focused resentment and hatred on America. In short, colonialism is not eliminated by doing the right thing at the end of the day in granting independence, nor its bastard apartheid by enacting civil liberties. Developing peoples find themselves still wholly dependent on the political will of those whose development they aided; and citizens can be second class. The developed world is liable to become the settled enemy of the mass of the race.

Whereas the Soviet Union was isolated in its aloofness, and many of the satellite governments likewise, the populations were disoriented and suffering serious privations. Uprooted from their past, they neither wanted to return to a condition that had been semifeudal, nor did they want to stay subject to a "dictatorship of the proletariat" in which they had no say. In large numbers, these populations listened to radio broadcasts from the West: Voice of America, Radio de l'Europe libre, BBC. These broadcasts were from stations mainly staffed by refugee nationals from the countries addressed and aimed at instilling a hope of deliverance, thought of in the West as (an unreal) restoration of liberty. In any case, the listeners were seduced to dally with hopes of deliverance by those who could not deliver. The dilemma in the West forced the issue between those who stood by a policy of containment and some who thought that nothing short of a resumption of war while the West had the edge in military might could resolve the antagonism of contrary social systems. On the latter assumption, the Soviet Union would be delivered an ultimatum that would throw it back to 1945 and redraw the political map of Europe. Capitulation could hardly be counted on, and such counsel did not prevail. It was an echo of the dilemma posed by contradictory hopes and fears that beset the thinking and talking of the three allied heads towards the end of the war: dividing the world into zones of influence by agreement, or collaboration in establishing and policing a global system of international security, prolonging into a new era the common interest that had sustained the defeat of the Nazi bid for the hegemony of Europe. Both sides had lived to recognize that what they had allowed to happen, the balkanization of Europe frozen by a cold war, was a tragic mistake.

What was the society of the United States actually like after the war, when the ambition was to lead the world into a new international economic order? It was unlike any other society in the world, not in having displaced an indigenous population, but in the population that accrued through the open door to uprooted peoples from the Old World, particularly from Europe. These were still a minority, but a substantial minority of tens of millions, to be added to another minority of former slaves. The land of opportunity (from log cabin to White House) was irrefutably true and deceptively false. From the two pools of immigrants and slaves descended to the bottom of the pond a numerous underclass of those who could not make it by the American standard of success in money-making. American society was mobile and lacked the cultural stability and social security of the tribal societies and peasant communities of the late-comers, forced and voluntary. For both groups, the one being dragged into hell, the other buoyantly embarking on a hopeful adventure, but both surviving the ordeal of passage, there was for most a deep and bitter experience of alienation, the malaise of estrangement. For the second generation of immigrants, accommodation was more possible, but often at the expense of alienation from the family. Emancipated slaves had to begin the long journey to civic recognition. That is, there was in American society in the twentieth century a measure of built-in alienation to add to the ad hoc alienation of workers exploited by employers with unfettered power to hire and fire. In sum, there was eminent discrimination, unconscious as well as deliberate, with a harvest of the discarded and the drop-outs. This happens to some extent in any society, and to some extent is compensated by the rule of law. But in the United States of America it was a burdensome part of the social inheritance, evident in their squalid quarters of large cities, in glaring contradiction of the nation's self-image and declarations to the world. Moreover, outside the focus of public awareness, by neglect, this in-built alienation was destined to accumulate and overflow in characteristic symptoms of distress and protest, swelling the statistics of crime, violence, and drug abuse.

The most distinctive feature of the American lifestyle, to the rest of the world, was conspicuous consumption. This was a shop-window for the consumer society that would become a popular dream where it was not already a booming reality. Lavish display and expenditure on a great scale, that included a large measure of unstinted generosity, was at the expense of reckless wastefulness. Little was long-lasting: "built-in obsolescence" was the phrase for it, to keep things moving. In the large cities, large buildings, a prosperous hotel for instance not long erected, would be torn down and replaced, as though on impulse.

At this period, the U.S.A., on behalf of the West, exported to the populations of the East an image of liberation from totalitarian rule and enjoyment of the abundance of a consumer society, which could not be delivered. The Soviet Union responded through the propaganda of the Communist parties in their enclaves in the West with their version of historical destiny based on scientific analysis: American triumphalism was an expiring flare; the alienated classes would grow and would prevail (the meek shall inherit the earth). Let history judge.

The world was comprehensively awakened to the magnitude and seriousness of the threat to the planet by the 1980 Brandt Report, *North-South: A Program for Survival*. Nevertheless, this did not come out of the blue; it came about from a suggestion by Robert McNamara in 1977, when he was president of the World Bank. He himself had been U.S. secretary of state, when a personal conversion to the environmental peril changed the course of his life. The Brandt Commission on International Development Issues had itself been preceded by the U.N. Conference on the Human Environment at Stockholm in June 1972, which instituted the U.N. Environment Program (UNEP) as its main outcome. Among the initiatives of UNEP were a Coordinating Committee on the Ozone Layer, a Global Environmental Monitoring System (GEMS), an International Register of Potentially Toxic Chemicals, a computerized network for the transfer of environmental information, and funds to voluntary associations around the world engaged in pioneering analytical work on the relations between environment and development.

In his Introduction to the Report, Willy Brandt set the perspective for thought and action: "Global questions require global answers; since there is now a risk of mankind destroying itself, this risk must be met by new methods." That required contract and consensus in place of status and compulsion. The peoples of former colonies were striving to be their own masters, and a second phase of decolonization would have to put in question industrialized countries as the model. One condition of this was enlargement of the participation of developing countries in the staffing, management, and decision-making of the IMF. National interests could now be effectively pursued only if sight were not lost of mutual long-term interests. The overriding need for global agreement requited preparation for a Summit of World Leaders.

In 1983 the General Assembly of the UN voted to form a World Commission on Environment and Development, to formulate "a global agenda for change" in order to achieve sustainable development by 2000. "From One Earth to One World" was the title given to the Overview that introduced the report of the Commission, published in 1987.

The essential point in tackling the global problems that the age has learned it has to face—i.e., that there are no "solutions" to be sought because conditions vary and constantly change—was made by the Commission in connection with the "sustainable development" and integration of environment/development problems which were the objectives with which it had been charged: attainment was by "a process of change in which the exploitation of resources, the direction of investments, the orientation of technological development, and institutional change are made consistent with future as well as present needs. . . . Thus, in the final analysis, sustainable development must rest on political will." Lyndon Johnson's "thousand battlegrounds" was not merely political rhetoric, whether he knew it or not. The members of the commission drawn from twenty-one diverse nations, were at least unanimous in their recognition that all nations would be required to take their part "in changing trends, and in righting an international economic system that increases rather than decreases inequality, that increases rather than decreases numbers of poor and hungry." The focus had to be switched from attention to the damage to changing the policies that did the damage. That would make the agenda for the Earth Summit of World Leaders, which the United Nations convened in Brazil in June 1992, at which the perspective on colonialism faded into the perspective on the planet as the habitat of organic life.

What is at stake should not be thought of as "Human Survival," which is a slogan, and originated with the risk of a nuclear holocaust in a World War III. What is truly at stake is the will to learn, and what to learn, about the conditions of organic life—the last phase in Bacon's "advancement of learning," and "for the relief of man's estate." What is happening in an alarming scale is a degradation of the environment, broken down into elements with different effects (acid rain, soil erosion, air and water pollution, destruction of habitats, extinction of stocks and resources by reckless consumption, uncontrollable toxic waste, etc.), locally or globally on life-expectancy and health (brain damage, cancers, bronchial and other organ damage, viral diseases, genetic damage, etc.). A learned respect for nature has become an integral part of self-respect—which is not the same as self-esteem, but is simply due regard for the conditions of one's existence, as respect for a motor vehicle would be regard for its proper maintenance.

Since the human adjustment to habitat is now not automatic, achieved by survival, it cannot be left to nature (as the market cannot be left to "market forces"), and has to be learned. Humans have to manage the environment for their own purposes, which involves a new, sophisticated, responsible relationship. That is what gives a "green" dimension to every human activity, to every government policy and department, to the policies and operations of public corporations and private companies, to all professions, and to consumers' choice and the lifestyle of every person. There is no exemption; everyone counts. One thing that has been learned from the miracles of biological time is the inestimable value in the sum of increments insignificantly small in themselves. Another thing is the infinite value of diversity as a source of life, which shows the monumental folly of the idea of cloning a desired variety of wheat in a monoculture that would eliminate other strains—an idea that has been mooted. Genetic engineering is a central sphere in which intervention demands responsible caution. Interventions there should and must be, since nature has to be used but not abused.

As there are no "solutions," so there cannot be a scale of priorities, although what affects climate and other measures for which time is running out have highest claims. Where particular interests are affected, decisions are properly local. Jamaica, for example, is bankrupt, and after conceding the stringent restrictions imposed by the International Monetary Fund, decided its highest priority should and must be the health and well-being of its people that had suffered, not the payments due on debt. The Indians of New Mexico have been organized to fight colonialism in the form of "environmental racism," the dumping of hazardous toxic waste for incineration in their backyard neighborhood. Environment and development belong together.

Thus countries managed the mixed economy according to national circumstances and the politics of the day. If there was not a uniform model, the objective was the same: annual growth, promoted by investment to increase productivity and gain the edge in competition by innovation. Innovation might bring out a new product or reduce costs and price or improve quality or out-smart rivals in marketing. This might be done by new technology or by more efficient organization. "Growth" and "innovation" were the quickening ideas behind the thrust of the new program. Measures to make them work were taken with the Bretton Woods agreement in 1944 on monetary management, setting up the International Monetary Fund and the International Bank for Reconstruction and Development (the World Bank). The Organization for European Economic Cooperation was set up to facilitate response to the Marshall Plan, and was permanently established later as OECD. In 1947, twenty-three countries signed the General Agreement on Tariffs and Trade (GATT) on the initiative of the UN Economic and Social Council. This increased to some hundred, with regular meetings for the purpose of removing or reducing barriers to trade. This was the institutional framework for a new international economic order initiated after the war principally by the United States, and based on a mixed economy.

In the first decades, there was plenty to be done in Europe that could be put in hand speedily and efficiently in this way; there were shortages and the physical destruction, particularly in Germany where the industrial plant had been removed to Russia from the Soviet zone. Everywhere, there was the hope and intention of catching up with the United States, far in the lead. The Soviet Union had its satellite states under its hegemony, and a Council for Mutual Economic Aid (Comecon) set up in 1949. In the West a Europe of new-born states needed each other as never before and forged the first link with Monnet's Coal and Steel Community. In the political field, there was a significant friendship pact between France and Germany, signed in 1963. The new western states were the basis of the defense strategy the United States developed, its forward position, after the Soviet Union had moved troops into the satellite zone. NATO was under an American commander-in-chief, but it was mutual benefit: the strength of all for the defense of each, the original principle of Wilson's League of Nations, rejected by a then isolationist United States. In political leadership, the United States was at first diffident and faltering in an unaccustomed role. In matters of wealth it was entirely different; there was an ease of manner as natural as gracious patronage was to the aristocrats of the ancien regime: the dollar was almighty in the market.

Control of the trade cycle was a major concern in a managed economy. "Never again" applied to the Depression as well as to world war. Growth was not interrupted in the 1950s and 1960s. Rather, there were consecutive periods of faster and slower growth, an exertion of control by deliberate expansionist and restrictive measures. Instability was controlled, not eliminated, in these two decades. Expansion of international trade was the major contribution to stability, just as national autarky had aggravated recession in the Depression. In the 1950s, Japan doubled its share of world trade and showed a spectacular increase in productivity.

A hiccup occurred in the late 1960s with a spontaneous disaffection among the young in Europe and the United States. It was the time of "hippies" and "flower power." More formally, there was introduced a "counterculture" that made "dropping out" respectable, the approved thing with the public that supported it. In 1968 came the Paris students' revolt, in which universities were taken over, there and in Italy. An alliance with workers of the Renault automobile plant was threatened rather than forged. There were young hero-leaders of the day. No political revolution was actually feasible, but de Gaulle, who quelled the demonstration, resigned in the following year when his proposed constitutional reforms were rejected by the electorate. The forgotten "counterculture" of the period, remembered rather as "the swinging sixties," a generation later was loosely regarded and blamed in conservative circles as the source of a breakdown of morality and family discipline which put a return to the status quo on their educational agenda.

The mixed economy operating in an international context, the program of the post-war order, suffered a setback in the seventies that enforced rethinking and virtually a new start; it brought an end to the first phase. Two particular events marked the change. President Nixon ended dollar convertibility in August 1971 and the Organization of Petroleum Exporting Countries (OPEC) in 1973 deliberately increased the price of oil more than tenfold by restricting supply. This followed the Yom Kippur war of Egypt and Syria against Israel, a sequel to the Six Day War of 1967 and Israel's annexations. This second defeat by the Middle East client of the U.S. angered the Arab world, and provoked the retaliation to embarrass the industrialized West.

In the second half of the seventies there came a world recession, the most serious and prolonged since the prewar slump. The years of boom had produced inflation, and deflationary policies to meet it. The result was "stagflation" and "stop-go" policies to curb and to boost, with high-interest rates, massive unemployment, fluctuations in exchange rates: economic disorientation supervening on the new international economic order. In 1950, the economy of the United States was stronger in terms of output than the rest of the world together, and by the end of the seventies that dominance had dwindled to hardly a fifth of world output. The almighty dollar, devalued in 1971, declined against the Japanese yen and the German mark.

In this decade, the United States increased its oil consumption, with more than half imported at the forced massive price increase from the Gulf states. The consumption of energy per head was twice and three times as much as in Germany and Japan—and more than twenty times that of India. Countries of the outside world were indeed catching up with America. By the end of the decade, Japan had toppled the giant, surpassing the top supplier of the world's most prized manufacture, the automobile.

The world monetary system initiated with the Bretton Woods Agreement ended with the abandonment of dollar convertability. A new ground of reliability and certainty had to be found. The mixed economy had departed far from orthodox economics, a balanced budget, a general balance of imports and exports, a gold standard, debt redemption. A growth ideology had taken the Keynesian cue of expansion and full employment by deficit financing. Inflation was the baffling problem. The unions would not accept an incomes policy; deflationary policies incited a wages explosion. The era of consensus and tripartite cooperation was interrupted, if not ended. An aggravating feature was overcapacity generated in basic industries competing in the market, particularly heavy manufacturing industries, and overmanning in these industries with introduction of technological advances. Drastic measures of reduction entailed large-scale unemployment and had to be pushed through against strongly organized opposition. The new international economic order was caught up in a crisis of confidence that put its assumptions in question, and prompted a strong if confused movement for a return to orthodoxy.

The Japanese had turned the world upside down in Asia in the early stages of the war, and that could not be righted by later Allied reconquest. Japan had taken over French Indochina at the beginning of March 1945. When Japan was defeated, Ho Chi Minh, a Communist who organized and led a nationalist party, occupied the palace in Hanoi and proclaimed the independence of Vietnam, forcing the abdication of the reigning Bao Dai. In August 1945 the French sent a large expeditionary force to reclaim their authority. They recognized the independence of Vietnam within the French Union. Attempts to negotiate a compromise with Ho Chi Minh were upset by violent clashes on the ground, ending in a massacre of French residents in Hanoi. French troops entered, and Ho Chi Minh fled. France then came to an agreement with Bao Dai in 1949 which gave Vietnam independence within a French Union. Cambodia and Laos would be "associated states." This arrangement was recognized by America and Britain. Ho Chi Minh's regime was recognized by Russia and China. Military aid supplied by the United States failed to maintain Bao Dai, who lost credit and was superseded by the return of Ho Chi Minh. After the Korean war, he was supplied with arms by China. The French gave up Cambodia and Laos in 1953, and sent in an airborne force that captured Dien Bien Phu, a base within North Vietnam on the Laos border that constituted the French stake in the area. When it was recaptured in the spring of the following year in a brilliant tactical maneuver by the North Vietnamese, the French military presence was fatally doomed. A conference in Geneva decided that Vietnam should be partitioned between the forces of the Viet Minh (the nationalist party) and the French. In the background, moving into the foreground, in the conduct of the cold war, superseding the colonial powers, was the United States, the main source of military and economic aid. She elaborated a series of encircling alliances to contain Communism by treaty law: NATO in Europe, SEATO in southeast Asia, and CENTO in the Middle East. Linked with these by the same underlying purpose was the Organization of American States (OAS), signed by twenty-one American nations to signify solidarity against aggression, but it was essentially the American Big Brother insisting on a common face against Communism in his own backyard. Encirclement was reinforced by more than fourteen hundred foreign bases in thirty-one countries, including accommodation for nuclear bombers. This ring passed from Europe to Iceland, Greenland, the Pacific islands northeast of Alaska, Japan, South Korea, Formosa, the Philippines, Thailand, Pakistan, Iran, Turkey, Saudia Arabia, Libya, Morocco, the Azores, and Puerto Rico. U.S. fleets were strategically placed in home waters south and north of the American continent, in the Mediterranean, and in the Pacific between the Philippines and Japan.

Counter to this overwhelming military might, the Soviet Union, strategically in the center, had a territory extensive enough to concentrate retaliatory positions within its own frontiers, with China as a buffer in the east. Retaliatory fire power was gained with the acquisition of nuclear weapons: the A-bomb in 1949 and the H-bomb in 1953. The advance of its space program gave the Soviet Union the capability of intercontinental ballistic missiles. The full circus brought both sides to eventual stalemate.

In 1955, a treaty was concluded among Turkey, Iraq, Iran, Pakistan, and the United Kingdom, the Baghdad Pact, designed for military and economic cooperation in the Middle East. It was opposed by Egypt, Syria, Jordan, and Saudi Arabia. When Iraq withdrew in 1959 and the pact's headquarters was moved to Ankara, the organization was renamed CENTO. The United States was an associate member, interested in it as an anti-Soviet military alliance, for Soviet arms and money were being supplied to Syria and Egypt, and to Iraq after the revolution that took it out of the

Baghdad Pact. After the Eisenhower intervention that aborted Franco-British-Israeli action in the Suez crisis, John Foster Dulles was convinced that the action had exposed the Middle East to Communist subversion, and promulgated the "Eisenhower Doctrine," which promised military and economic aid to countries threatened by Communism. To back this up, an American fleet was sent to the eastern Mediterranean in April 1957 to be at hand in support of the Jordanian government. Union of Egypt and Syria in a United Arab Republic and a revolution in Iraq enjoyed cordial welcome in Communist quarters, and the situation prompted division in Lebanon, where there was a pro-Western government that sought support from the United States. American troops were landed in 1958 and stayed until October.

In that year, Fidel Castro began his revolt in Cuba. In the following year he entered Havana and concentrated in himself all political power. At first, the U.S. government was well-disposed to the development; but when it became clear that Castro was a Marxist and opposed to America's way of life and its values, he was recognized as a dangerous threat, an example liable to infect Latin America with the virus of Communism. Indeed, when Castro evoked the delighted welcome and support of the Soviet Union, Cuba was made a focus of U.S. hostility; the cold war was introduced into the Western hemisphere. The United States broke off diplomatic relations in January 1961. Exiled Cubans in the states were given encouragement and arms to venture an attempt to nip the new regime in the bud. Less than two thousand landed at the Bay of Pigs and were promptly captured. This fiasco delighted subversive elements throughout the OAS and elevated Castro as the symbol of resistance to American pretensions. Cuban troops were to become a surrogate force for the Soviet Union in Africa and elsewhere, providing a long arm of military intervention.

Latin American states liberated from Spain in the nineteenth century passed into the hands of military dictators. In the 1970s democratically elected governments in Chile and Argentina collapsed. Salvador Allende was elected president of Chile in 1970, the first Marxist to attain ruling office in the world outside Soviet control. He strove to preserve a parliamentary regime, and to institute socialist measures of nationalization. The policy was frustrated by inflation that could not be brought under control. Even more deadly was a conspiracy of the U.S. Central Intelligence Agency to destabilize the regime. In 1973, a lock-out and a strike by middle-class workers provided the opportunity for a military coup. Allende was killed. General Pinochet, army chief of staff, seized power to "extirpate Marxism." In the same year in Argentina the military government held "free elections" which brought in a candidate who brought back from eighteen years of exile the former dictator Juan Peron, to whom power was transferred. He died in the following year, and was succeeded by his wife. Inflation at an even higher rate than in Chile, factional strife in the Peronist ranks, and guerrilla terrorism on the left precipitated another situation ripe for a military takeover. Improved economic conditions did not prevent an increase in subversive terrorism that invoked countermeasures of terrorism and repressions with the usual "disappearances," torture, and imprisonment without trial. This was typical of other states in the subcontinent where the terrain offered a base from which an opposition could wage a guerrilla war on the government, as in El Salvador.

There were Cuban-inspired guerrilla movements in Guatemala, Colombia, Venezuela, Peru, and Bolivia. There was direct American intervention in Guatemala, Nicaragua, Cuba, Haiti, and the Dominican Republic. Where there was deemed to be a serious Communist threat, American indirect intervention was ubiquitous, undercover through the CIA or in open support of repressive military regimes, as in El Salvador. America had an obsessive social antipathy to anything that smacked of socialism, as threatening to undermine its foundations: in the extreme form of Bolshevik communism, it forced the ultimate political question, Who shall kill whom? Therefore whatever was available that was of use for defense or offense was to be taken advantage of without scruple. This was what had made possible the psychotic Joseph McCarthy witch-hunt that searched out and identified communist sympathizers with lunatic comprehension at a time when the threat within was indeed serious. Japan was promptly rehabilitated and built up after the war for use against the Soviet Union. Fear of the communist element in the government of North Vietnam organized as guerrilla fighters in the Viet Cong made John F. Kennedy, a notable liberal in domestic politics (the "New Frontier"), send his thousands of "advisers" into South Vietnam to ensure that the corrupt and inefficient Diem regime in Saigon dealt effectively with "subversive" elements in the country, a peasantry with good reason to be disaffected. He had induced the OAS to expel Cuba from its ranks. The compromising behavior and forcefully exerted dominance of the self-declared leader of the "Free World" did not earn respect, and tended to alienate members of the OAS, a product of that very policy. He used the CIA as a president's long arm that could be disowned but did nothing without authority. There were twenty-six attempts to assassinate Castro.

In the Middle East and in Africa, the Soviet Union and the United States were opposed in bids for influence that could be decisive and had to be practical. They were dealing with peoples who had come out of the war with resentful determination to gain independence of their colonial rulers. This favored the Soviet Union, the classical enemy of imperialism. Also, there was a general association of nationalism with socialism, which promised a better deal for the numerous lower middle class and rural laborers. The United States, as the pioneer of liberation from colonial rule, had anti-imperial credentials, but was ambivalent about supporting socialist nationalism oriented to the Soviet model. When civil war broke out in Yemen, Egypt backed the republicans with arms and supplies from the Soviet Union. The royalists were supported by Saudi Arabia. The United States used all its means to contain the fighting within Yemen. This, in 1962, helped to form the confrontation in which the United States staked its influence on all-out support of Israel, with the Soviet Union supporting certain Arab states. Gulf oil was of particular interest to the United States, and also the lever of Arab independence.

The colonial powers in Africa did not expect to lose their grip, but it happened with accelerating speed. All French central and West African colonies had full autonomy by 1960. Algeria gained independence in a war, 1954–1962. The Sudan gained independence in 1956, the Gold Coast in 1957. Cyprus was a republic in 1959, Egypt in 1956. The Soviet Union financed construction of the important Aswan High Dam, after the Americans pulled out. When Macmillan made his "wind of change" speech to the South African parliament in 1960, he was announcing the inevitability of a consummation of what could be seen to be happening, with fourteen French former colonies, the Belgian Congo, Somalia, and Nigeria all independent members of the United Nations. An Afro-Asian bloc was forming at the United Nations, which became a forum for aspirants in the decolonizing movement. Just as the "scramble for Africa" in the nineteenth century had been a "not one but all" involvement of European states, the unscrambling of possession inevitably involved all, leaving only frontiers unscrambled.

The nationalist movement in Nigeria was split, and independence delayed until 1960. White settlers in British east and central Africa were dominant influences that complicated and delayed independence involving a transference of power. The whites reinforced the British government in imposing federal solutions that coalesced black and white neighboring territories in an attempt to save white ascendancy. The policy was resisted and frustrated in Uganda and by the Mau Mau insurrection in Kenya. A federation that was composed of Northern Rhodesia and Nyasaland was dissolved in 1963 with the success of the nationalist movement in Nyasaland, headed by Banda in London; Malawi was the successor state. Southern Rhodesia to avert this fate declared independence unilaterally in 1965.

If the end of the sixties was the high point in the initial upsurge of African nationalism it was also a turning point, which occurred with a crisis in the Congo on the precipitate withdrawal of the colonial power at the insistence of the king of the Belgians. Within days, Katanga province, bordering on northern Rhodesia and Tanganyika in the southwest, seceded. This was a region rich in tin, manganese, coal, zinc, copper, iron ore, and (not least) uranium. The Belgians intervened, and the fledgling Zaire government appealed to the United Nations, which supplied troops from many countries, including contingents from African states. However, the governing alliance split into two rival groups and Katanga remained under its secessionist regime; and it was not until 1965 that a settlement was made. In two main ways the Congo crisis and its prolongation affected the issues. The split into two rival groups (apart from Katanga) forced the independent African states to back one or the other. The impasse encouraged South Africa, southern Rhodesia, and Portugal (Angola and Mozambique) to improvise an alliance of resistance. Above all, it drew the United States into African affairs in a more active way.

The split within Zaire which forced the issue amongst the independent African states was virtually between interests which favored good relations and cooperation with the ex-colonial powers and the developed industrialized states, and those who regarded this as a betrayal that played into the hands of the rich and powerful, enabling them to reestablish themselves in neocolonialism. The settlement in Zaire was blatantly favorable to Western mining interests. The difference between radicals and pragmatists (or satisfied neorulers) ran within the new nations as well as between them. This also affected their support for resistance and rebellion in African states still under colonial rule, whether political and military aid or moral support. With the movement of South Africa from severance from the Commonwealth to a policy of apartheid, and then into a vicious phase of enforcement, and a strategy of systematic

covert destablization of neighboring African countries, a new political test of growing significance was instituted. The underlying situation in each of the independent
African states, with all the fluctuations, was the same, and the same as it had been in
decolonized South America, the deficiency of personnel skilled and experienced in
administration, and therewith of working habits and institutions on the ground. This
left them open to tribal rivalries within and political pressures from outside.

These two phases in African liberation coincide with what were virtually two
phases in the cold war. In the first, the Soviet Union was the inspiration, the model,
and the strength, with the one-party state as the political instrument of transformation.
Zimbabwe was the last to achieve independence, in 1979, with Mugabwe determined to establish his one-party state as quickly as possible. Obsessed with this
abstraction, the sequel was alienation from the people; and with Zambia and Tanganyika passing over to political democracy, this marked displacement of the Soviet
model and influence.

By this time both the Soviet Union and the United States had worked themselves
into virtual isolation from their constituents. At the same time, they were drawing
closer together, a move precipitated by two acts of brinkmanship by Khrushchev. The
exodus of 3.5 million East Germans to the West by August 1961 had to be stopped.
Khrushchev announced that West Berlin would be handed over to East Germany.
When the Western powers made it clear that they would not allow this to happen, the
threat was not maintained: the Berlin Wall was the answer. More serious and sustained was the exposure of all parts of the United States to the threat of Soviet missiles installed in Cuba, of which photographic evidence was available in Washington.
An ultimatum backed by American readiness for a nuclear strike, after a short spell
of acute suspense, prevailed. There was an exchange of letters between Kennedy and
Khrushchev; the missiles were removed and the Americans undertook not to invade
Cuba.

In 1960 the U-2 incident in which an American reconnaissance aircraft was shot
down over Soviet territory, and the two occupants baled out and were captured, compromised the United States in neutral eyes, and seemed to justify the stance of the
nonaligned states. That justification came with the actual initiation of detente by the
two parties themselves. The colossal unsustainable expenditure of an arms race, with
all the collateral provisions for gaining and maintaining the edge of superiority, was
a major factor. Not less so was disillusionment with the alienation of their constituents, needlessly denied funds applied to their own needs. It was the clownish
Khrushchev who turned his back on Stalinism, and formulated the positively neutral
"peaceful co-existence of different social systems." It was the pragmatic Nixon who
withdrew from Vietnam and went to Peking at China's invitation; and to Moscow to
agree with Soviet leaders on arms limitation.

Relief of the tension was symbolic of a more general relaxation of the confrontation, an era of detente. In 1963, there was the Test Ban Treaty by which the
Soviet Union, the United States, and the United Kingdom agreed to ban tests of
nuclear weapons above ground. As a measure against the proliferation of nuclear
weapons, it attracted signatures from more than a hundred states, but neither France

nor China signed. At this time too, a "hot line" between Moscow and Washington for the first time assured the world that the superpowers, armed with annihilating military might, intended that no accident should be allowed to occur, and in effect that they would not be used by either party, save as a standing deterrent.

Ostensibly, the two social systems were not only in full opposition, but also in total contradiction. Bolshevik communism under Stalin in the exertion of central control moved inevitably to a rigid if changeable definition of the party line, with ubiquitous attention to arresting the least deviation from it. This stranglehold imposed a deadly uniformity on the official society, with all the consequences. The contrary model was offered by the United States: an open society, with individual freedom to live one's own life in one's own way, within the law. Two contradictory interpretations of the rule of law.

Actually, the United States in defense and offense against the Soviet Union was forced or drawn into repression of evident or suspected leanings to the left (deviations from the Western party line), and into upholding and aiding military regimes that reproduced Franco's Falangist one-party state after the civil war. In the eyes of the nonaligned, they could be seen to mirror one another and to betray their declared ideals. Both sought the uniformity that stifled life instead of the Marxist utopia or the vision of Thomas Paine of a New Age in the New World.

Two superpowers demonstrated the absolute evil of absolute domination. It is worse than simplistic to see this phase as the United States defending the "Free World" from the totalitarian aims of the Soviet Union.

# 19

# Self-Preservation

As rivals in space exploration the two superpowers were in peaceful coexistence, aside from seeking military advantage in space. There were differences in their projects that were of benefit to the general enterprise, which in some measure was inevitably a joint enterprise, if not formally so. The lack of a concerted venture was needlessly wasteful, and when the immense cost began to tell, cooperation was strongly indicated.

Biodiversity, the biggest number and widest spread of variations within species, is the source of the genetic complement of the organisms of the species, the genotype; and it is this mechanism in the natural order that produced the human species, with all others, over an unimaginable period. Human history, from the emergence of Homo sapiens, has no comparable time span. Social development and biological evolution used to be distinguished in principle as different orders not to be confused. There is now a tendency to say that "in principle" there is the same mechanism of natural selection of cultural variations and variations within cultures in history as in nature; and its results are evident in infinitely less time. What is produced is different societies, not different species. With the speeding mechanism, human history surpasses natural history, an incalculable benefit. Confirmation of a parallel might be taken from two historical findings or declarations. "Self-preservation" was declared to be the first law of nature in the medieval doctrine of natural law. Bentham's investigation of the organization and application of law in society showed him that self-preservation by lawyers of that organization and its procedures, by which they prospered, was their principal interest and concern. His later findings in relation to other institutions brought him to the same conclusion: that preservation of the institution becomes the first concern of successive generations of its personnel. It appears that "in principle" self-preservation as the first law of nature (with the best adapted organisms selected to survive) is akin to self-preservation as the general practice within established institutions in societies, with those best adapted to this practice in the society in which they function surviving best. There is equivalence between a principle of biology and of sociology. That would not rule out distinctions that might have importance. For instance, the working of the principle in nature guarantees and safeguards success, whereas in society the equivalent principle guarantees an element of corruption in the human nature of institutions. That is hardly a superficial difference of no account.*

There is one vital identity in the two orders that is indisputable: in any society, individual diversity is necessary as a source of social vitality, which would become enfeebled by unvarying uniformity. Mill's argument in his essay "On Liberty" was not merely for the sake of individual satisfaction and fulfillment, but mainly for preservation of this source of social vitality from extinction by the dominance of a democratic majority that imposed uniformity.

Among the abounding forms of adaptation in the natural world are the insect societies in which individuals are specialized as functional parts of a whole. This is not a model for human society, but some societies may approximate to it in tendency; and it might be suggested that Japanese society conspicuously has that bias. Insect societies of this kind generate a power no individual can match. They act as one in the highest attainable degree. This is a form of uniformity that is expressive, not repressive; it forges in union a popular political will that is sustained and instrumental, not passing in some flash of popular excitement. As an expressive form of uniformity, it is a social variation along with individualism. Jung has argued that collective conformity is the recourse of the very many who cannot bear the isolation of autonomy and are only themselves when merged in identification with a collective unit.

> Collective organization is still so essential today that many consider it, with some justification, to be the final goal; whereas to call for further steps along the road to autonomy appears like arrogance or hubris, fantasticality, or simply folly. (*Late Thoughts*)

Such units would include ethnic minorities with a cultural identity that resist assimilation within a social mold that is not a mother country.

The point of this is that the cold war had none of these options; both sides were flirting with impositions of uniformity they were striving to make absolute. That smothering of life could not have lasted, but it was irresponsible, blatantly ugly and wrong, grossly wasteful, and immensely damaging. Two superpowers demonstrated the absolute evil of absolute domination. That is missed if one is taken in by the claim of the U.S.A. to be defending the "Free World" from the totalitarian aims of the U.S.S.R. That was what the American statesmen of the day genuinely thought; it was the mast to which their colors were nailed. But the requirements of absolute opposition forced them into the likeness to what they opposed.

## Rivals

Peaceful coexistence does not imply social contact. As rivals in space-exploration, the superpowers were intensely aware of and responsive to each other's advances and pro-

---

*Richard Dawkins, who has made most of the identity of the two processes in the natural order and in human cultures, called his best-selling book *The Selfish Gene*.

jects, but not cooperating. Their interdependence in the cold war was malign, but in space science and exploration it was comparatively benign, on the way to a cooperation indicated by the colossal expenditure involved, and the need for shared technology.

The rivalry was launched, so to speak, by the Soviet *Sputnik* on October 4, 1957. The event sent shock waves through the United States, bringing home a realization of the Soviet Union's advanced science program. That mobilized resolve, personnel, and money put into the National Aeronautics and Space Administration (NASA), formed urgently in 1958. The space age had begun. The second Soviet satellite, launched a month after the first, was manned by Laika, a dog. Yuri Gagarin made the first manned flight, orbiting the earth on April 12, 1961, becoming the most famous man in the world and registering another first for the Russians. They were first too in sending unmanned spacecraft to the moon with four flights, *Lunik* I–IV, beginning in 1959. *Lunik II* landed an object on the moon. In 1960, a satellite carrying dogs was safely brought back to earth.

American fixation on the moon was announced by President Kennedy in 1961, with the intention of a landing by 1970. Meanwhile, manned spacecraft *Mercury* (1961–1963) and *Gemini* (1965–1966) were sent on reconnaissance missions. The moon landing was made in July 1969, in a capsule from the *Apollo* spacecraft; two men landed and were watched by the world on television as they clumsily moved around in their spacesuits; they were heard speaking of what they saw and felt to President Nixon and he conveyed to them the admiration, delight, and gratitude of the American people. The Americans had made up their minds to be the first to plant a man on the moon. The Russians had chosen not to adopt this option, for their own good reasons. People in general around the world, immersed in their local concerns, saw on that night a frolic of two of their kind on the surface of the distant planetary satellite. These two were not lone adventurers like stout Cortez and his men. Rather, they were like processed robots, and down there the most intent and intensely engaged of all watchers on the ground were the experts in the NASA team of which the astronauts were a specialized extension. The highest moment of ecstasy was theirs on terra firma when they embraced one another in triumph for their mates on terra incognita. Thus it was that the lady of the skies who had haunted the pages of poets down the ages and attended lovers on their nightly walks was reduced to a sterile arctic waste.

The Soviet Union was the first to launch a space station, *Salyut* 1 in 1971. The U.S. *Skylab* followed two years later. As the American name indicates, these were orbiting spacecrafts large enough to accommodate teams to carry out experimental work in weightless conditions. The Russians launched *Mir* in 1987, a supercraft of this kind. The following year, the Americans announced plans for an international space station to be launched in the 1990s, with the inclusion of Europeans, Japanese, and Canadians in the selected crew. This was anticipated by the Russians, who included an English woman astronaut in their team.

The space shuttle was an American enterprise to provide a reusable craft for space transport. NASA's development of this project was brought into operational use in 1982. It is a complicated and ingenious production, with a large cargo bay from which craft can be launched equipped for long-term scientific probes, or craft manned for laboratory work, and into which spacecraft can be brought for repairs or redeployment or return to earth. They are used also for carrying men and materials to or from a space station. They are designed to be usable up to a hundred times. Test flights ended with that of *Columbia* in 1981; operational flights temporarily ended with the explosion of *Challenger* in 1986 two minutes after blast-off. The shock of this instant loss of the crew of seven who had blasted off with confident hopes after strenuous preliminary training was profound and lasting; the suspension of the program lasted two years. In the year when the program was resumed, 1988, the Soviet Union launched its first space shuttle, *Buran*.

This rivalry in civilian space programs was technological, but several different purposes were being served. There was space exploration, with a first focus on the moon. There were the probes, long-term missions of unmanned craft on a designed route through our universe, equipped to register phenomena and transmit the findings to earth. These have proved successful, and of immense promise. Most prolific have been communication satellites, including weather stations; the sky is littered with some two thousand or more. Laboratory stations served a variety of experimental purposes, including prolonged experience of living in such conditions. Servicing all the purposes was the workhorse, the space shuttle.

This civilian rivalry might be said to have ended with a military clash when President Ronald Reagan insisted on his Strategic Defense Initiative, the venturesome "star wars" research project, at the 1987 summit on arms limitation. Even on the Western side, the project was controversial from the first, for differing reasons. For Soviet leader Mikhail Gorbachev it was doubly repugnant—as a military invasion of space, but above all as incurring heavy additional expenditure in the context of an all-out endeavor to make a drastic cut; the Soviet Union would be forced into a comparable program for its own defense. The United States was better able to afford the cost, or Reagan would have thought so, whereas the inability of the Soviet Union to supply the needs of its population because of arms and space expenditure was the driving force behind the urgent need for reduction.

One vaguer purpose of the space programs needs mention: possible colonization. Stations might be launched or built in space large enough to accommodate a population that maintains contact and traffic with the earth. Or another planet might in some way be made habitable. Such ideas will probably continue to inspire scenarios for fiction or film, and never be realistically attractive enough to engage talent in a real project. At present, anyhow, it is the shadow of a purpose.

## Doing Business

Business of any kind is essentially a transaction between persons, even if the deal negotiated is between parties and has to be ratified collectively to be effective, as in the case of treaties between states. The wartime collaboration of Stalin, Roosevelt, and Churchill was punctuated by agreed decisions of this kind; short-term ones under the exigencies of the war, supported by the political protocol adhered to by each of the three, however nominal that may have been on the part of Stalin. Agreements reached at formally convened conferences, as at Teheran and Yalta, were tentative in preparation for what would be concluded after the war in setting up a United Nations and negotiating a comprehensive peace treaty. The constraint of an urgent and stressful common purpose brought the three together after Hitler launched his invasion of Soviet territory.

In different circumstances, a common purpose re-emerged in crises after the war, first when in 1948 the Russians cut off East Berlin from West Berlin and West Berlin from West Germany, in an apparent endeavor to force the West to abandon the city. The second was the Cuban crisis of 1961. These exercises in brinkmanship brought uppermost the common purpose to prevent a war, which prevailed. Similarly, the common need to reduce exorbitant and escalating expenditure on arms brought the two sides together to convert an arms race into a system of parity controlled by treaty. Forced contacts of these kinds are furthered or retarded by the personal relations that ensue, as well as by the forcefulness, resolution, and skill of one or another of those engaged, for that is what engenders the climate in which confidence can or cannot be built, and mutual trust waxes or wanes. Khrushchev was an odd and boorish customer, and it did not work so well between him and Kennedy as it was to prove so swiftly between Gorbachev and Reagan. Mikhail Gorbachev and Eduard Shevardnadze were both pleasing personalities who complemented and reinforced one another in making a reassuring impact not only on Western leaders but also on their advisers and staffs, in more continuous contact than had been sustained before. Soviet Premier Aleksey Kosygin and Leonid Brezhnev had gone out of their way to assure the West that Khrushchev's policy of peaceful coexistence would be maintained despite his removal from power. When Gorbachev came onto the international scene and made his first round of contacts, British Prime Minister Margaret Thatcher made her famous remark that he was a man "with whom one could do business."

Representation was concentrated in the hands of the president of the United States and the general secretary of the Communist party in the Soviet Union in final negotiations, but there was an imbalance, in that ratification by Congress could not be taken for granted and leaders of the states in NATO did not count for nothing. Treaties, like all laws, are no more than paper and ink unless they are sufficiently supported on the ground by those who have to make them work.

One persistent interest of the West that chafed agreement because it was never left out and never gained Soviet accord was human rights. The common interest that knotted all strands and would hold the parties together to the last as at the first was their determination to prevent the hegemony of Germany in Europe: no further editions of World Wars I and II: *Never again.*

Two particular aspects of the human rights issue affected relations. The United States, as strategically identified with unwavering support of Israel in the Middle East, backed Israel's demand for removal of restrictions on the emigration of Soviet Jews. The Soviet government's realistic fear of decline by hemorrhage to the West imposed the immigration controls that violated human rights. For them it was not a simple matter of right and wrong; rather, of national survival.

Two particular persons were central to the relations: Andrei Sakharov and Aleksander Solzhenitsyn. Both were storm centers within Russia; both were identified in the West with the defense of liberal values; both are complicated and dramatic cases. Sakharov's is the more straightforward and uncontroversial, with parallels in the West. He worked on the thermonuclear bomb exploded in 1954, but protested in 1963 against atmospheric tests of nuclear weapons and initiated work that issued in the atmospheric test-ban treaty of 1963. This preoccupation with nuclear weapons and disarmament carried over into a radical criticism of Soviet society expressed in *Progress, Coexistence, and Intellectual Freedom* (1968) which had to be published abroad, and made him for his government an enemy of the people and for the West a hero.

From Soviet science to Soviet literature, the context is far more complicated and fascinating, with a documentary record that enables an outsider to glimpse the evidence of vitality centered on the conduct of the preeminent literary journal *Novy Mir*. In all this Solzhenitsyn is a novelist among his fellow writers, not a government hack. Abroad, he is that novelist with the powers of expression of a talented writer, but beyond that and specially he is the Russian writer who meticulously and systematically indicts the Soviet Union on the evidence of the labor camps, so that the Soviet historian Roy Medvedev could write of *The Gulag Archipelago*: "I think that few people, having read the book, would be the same as when they opened its first page. In this respect, it seems to me that nothing in Russian or world literature can compare with Solzhenitsyn's book."

*One Day in the Life of Ivan Denisovich* is a vintage sample in the same territory. Khrushchev approved it. This was the period of de-Stalinization and the controversies that movement aroused. Years later Sakharov headed an appeal signed by nine others demanding publication of *The Gulag Archipelago* in the Soviet Union, publication of official material that would give a complete picture of the activities of the state institutions of surveillance and oppression, appointment of an international tribunal to investigate the crimes committed, and protection of Solzhenitsyn from persecution, allowing him to work in his homeland. This was supported by international writers' groups. There were those who, like Sakharov and Solzhenitsyn, were convinced that only pressure from outside, the mobilization of world opinion, could bring about change in the Soviet Union, and there were those who believed that reforms in the Soviet Union could be brought about only from within and from the top; Roy Medvedev was among the latter. For this opinion he was ridiculed by Solzhenitsyn.

Germany was a problem to the Soviet Union, to Europe, and therewith to the United States, and to itself. The kind of political resolution its statesmen and people would look to adopt was the central question for all. Konrad Adenauer, Brandt, and more recently the foreign minister, Dietrich Genscher, have laid down firm lines designed to assure the world, and particularly its neighbors, that Germany's political future is as a reliable partner within the framework of a Europe with established common institutions; that no other option is maintained within the federal republic by any politically viable grouping.

Healing the wound left in default of a peace treaty was the core of the problem. West Germany did not renounce unification, and Willy Brandt's *Ostpolitik* said so. Genscher made this line his own, and as a symptom of nationalism, and as German nationalism had been the scourge of Europe, the uneasiness roused was in all three quarters, the Soviet Union, Europe and the United States, and in Germany itself. To complicate matters for him, Genscher had to work with a succession of six American secretaries of state, with shifts of policy on medium-range missiles stationed on or removed from German territory.

When unification was effected, the new Germany faced two ways in a new context, with a dissolution of the Warsaw Pact alignment and NATO's loss of its instituted role. Moreover, the Soviet Union was a disintegrating disunion, and the United States was no longer a virtual dictator in Europe on grounds of defense as a first priority. Germany might be tempted to see itself in a position to reassert independence, and detach itself from its European commitments. Franco-German relations became the prime indicator. Since Bismarck, France had suffered most from German aggression on the Western side. Mitterand and Kohl were determined to exhibit a close and special relationship to demonstrate that the alliance was definitive. Genscher deployed his skill and used his contacts and spent his influence to strengthen Germany's political prominence with its new bargaining position, showing and hinting ways of its advantage to Europe as a whole. Henry Kissinger, who worked closely with Genscher over three years and kept in touch with him for more than a decade after, rated him "as one of the most important statesmen his country has produced."

Kissinger was tempted from the Arcadia of learning to apply his studies and his talents in the role under President Richard Nixon that made him world famous as America's roving diplomatic wizard. His deepest historical sympathies had been with Europe's diplomatic practice after the Congress of Vienna (1814–1815), which established a new order in Europe. That was the model for his assessment of Genscher's performance in the frozen political order of postwar Europe. It was of course the standard he set for his own operations as well.

The course of detente followed the military path of negotiated disarmament in terms of calculated parities that were verifiably maintained. The immense difficulty in working this out in detail, trying to eliminate all arbitrariness, aggravated by having to use these negotiations dependent upon trust to dispel habitual mistrust, understandably bogged down in protracted talk in Geneva that threatened to be interminable. It was to break the deadlock that the Gorbachev-Reagan summit stepped in, since what both sides needed and desired remained frustrated without a specific mandate at the highest level, targets, and a timetable. Reagan had to dispel his own obscurantist rhetoric about the "Evil Empire," although it expressed his own gut feeling. A man with whom he too felt that he could do business, and whom the world acknowledged to have the ruling voice in that Empire, enabled him to do that. The Gordian knot was cut, neither by force nor evasion, but by compromise and agreed procedures, the way of dealing with real problems that defy "solutions."

The significance of this change at the top is to be seen not merely in resolving deadlock in Geneva over the operational formula Mutual and Balanced Force Reductions (MBFR), but mainly in the change at the top itself, by comparison with the Nixon-Kissinger checkered dealings with Brezhnev in pursuit of detente. Negotiations in Helsinki and Vienna (1969–1972) were strictly between the Soviet Union and the U.S.A. In the course of these negotiations, both sides found that interests other than defense were involved in detente. A poor harvest obliged Russia to buy a huge quantity of grain from Canada and the U.S.A. A growing trade deficit in America made Nixon think of the huge Soviet Union as a market. The two parties issued a declaration of twelve Basic Principles to define their international responsibilities, which included protection of the environment and the conduct of space research. A commercial commission they set up organized a trade agreement in 1972.

Kissinger's diplomatic policy was to create a "web of interests" through which the climate of understanding and trust needed for fruitful negotiations would be brought about. On the other hand, skeptics were able to point to the evidence that Brezhnev was pushing on every front and taking advantage of every opportunity in pursuit of the overthrow of capitalism by communism, not of detente. There were the Cuban troops in Angola, no let-up in the suppression of dissidents, last not least, the invasion of Afghanistan. Even on disarmament, SALT 1 was closely followed by Russian moves that so disillusioned many American experts that they wanted to abandon the pursuit of detente after 1975. The Russians had wanted a European Security Conference. This was not initially welcome to the West. Nevertheless, a Conference on Security and Cooperation in Europe did open in Helsinki in July 1973 and continued in stages until a final document was signed by thirty-five heads of government in Helsinki on August 1, 1975. This was a comprehensively represented assembly covering both sides, with the singular exception of Albania. The accord had been worked out by multinational teams over a period of all but two years. The signatories did not bind themselves legally, but did undertake to adopt the terms negotiated. No machinery was set up to enforce adoption undertaken, and no institution to monitor the signatories' conduct.

Nevertheless, like the Universal Declaration of Human Rights by the United Nations in 1948, the Helsinki "Final Act" was a benchmark for reference, a gospel that actually inspired the democratic evangelists of Czechoslovakia, who formulated "Charter 77" in 1977 in protest against the government's violations of human rights, thereby exposing themselves to drastic sanctions. This prompt use of the document to embarrass a government in default was not effective with an unaccountable regime, but it went into the record for which the regime might one day be brought to account. Insofar as trade agreements were expected to improve the standard of living of the Soviet people, it was argued that this improved the likelihood of their demand for democratic reform— as it had proved a necessary condition in the control of population growth.

The Helsinki accord would hardly have been possible if Brandt's *Ostpolitik* had not developed positively from the Soviet point of view, for Germany was the underlying question, first and last. If *Ostpolitik* was meant to isolate East Germany or bring it into the Western orbit, detente threatened Russia's security. The cold war had ensued in default of a peace treaty, and a thaw without independent assurances would simply plunge the Russians back into their postwar dilemma. Brandt had provided reasonable assurances to the East German government and to the Soviet Union by convincing the West Germans that they should respect the status quo and base their foreign policy on a realistic relationship with East Germany as a separate state. In

1970 Brandt had signed a nonaggression treaty with the Soviet Union that acknowledged existing frontiers, including that between East and West Germany. These were complicated negotiations that involved Poland, because of the Oder-Neisse line and the division of Berlin. In effect, Brandt's treaty was an improvised, ad hoc remedy for the lack of a peace treaty, to meet Soviet needs and fears.

The "Final Act" of Helsinki was in the category of a "facility" that disappoints optimists, is written off by pessimists, and derided by cynics, but is a necessary construct, like habits in personal life or institutions (social habits) in society. Once in place, they are available if and when circumstances become favorable. As important, they select elements in the population whom they attract to form centers of social expectation. They are not short-term casts, but measures to increase the stock. Advances generally have to be inched forward, and clinched.

Brezhnev condemned critics for their condemnation of Russia's record on human rights as interfering in her internal affairs, which they had no right to do. The sequel to that line was confrontation and mutual blame when the signatories met as planned in Belgrade in 1977 to review progress made in giving effect to the "Final Act." From the futility of disputes about human rights, after Belgrade attention returned to disarmament; and in January 1984 representatives of the thirty-five nations in Stockholm made their theme a Conference on Confidence and Security-building. The shooting down of the Korean aircraft that had strayed over Soviet territory on September 1, 1983, was more than "unacceptable" and strengthened the hand of hard-liners, of whom President Reagan was one. However, Brezhnev's word was not the last word and not a word destined to last long.

## Comrades

The words that were soon to become world famous were *glasnost* and *perestroika*. They were structurally connected: the first, "openness," gradually prepared minds for the second, the "new order," that was to follow. Mikhail Gorbachev's name, if he is rated as the most remarkable statesman of the post-war period, and the greatest in achievement, should be hyphenated with that of Eduard Shevardnadze, for it was a close partnership from the outset. It was the general secretary of the Communist party who made his name echo around the world and evoked gales of popular enthusiasm ("Gorby! Gorby!") as he mingled with the crowd in walk-abouts. It was his foreign minister Shevardnadze—later to become president of Georgia—who promptly showed more penetrating insight into how things stood and where they were going at home, and had the last word.

In two years there unfolded the climax of the most dramatic story in the history of the West. Gorbachev, who frequently took holidays at a resort on the Black Sea coast of Georgia, of which republic Shevardnadze was party boss, would consort with him at those times and reinforce their acquaintance as colleagues on the Politburo. The ominous rapid decline of the economy, combined with the Party's obsession with secrecy, alarmed them both: "Everything has turned rotten." They found themselves of one mind about the urgent need for *glasnost* and *perestroika*.

The obsession of the Bolsheviks from the beginning had been that they were carrying out the program of Marx's "scientific socialism," historically grounded and guaranteed. Science was invoked as the rational way forward on every front; the Bolsheviks would prove themselves the legitimate heirs of the Enlightenment. That applied particularly to planning industrialization. In this, they were heirs of some two thousand Russian engineers of the middle class who had pioneered the early phase, and were still engaged and indispensable. The time came, after Lenin, when Stalin thought he could liquidate them, and replace them with Party members and others under orders and surveillance. He organized a "show trial" of bourgeois specialists for "wrecking activities" in 1930–1931 to cover up his own mistakes in collectivization and industrialization. After the war, in 1940, the Gosplan leadership, responsible for the five-year plans, was broken up. Stalin removed Voznesensky, who had been in charge for eleven years, and put other senior officials on trial. Voznesensky was hounded by Beria, and in 1950 arrested and shot. Any centralized system of government is liable and likely to be ludicrously and woefully out of touch with conditions on the ground for which it legislates, aggravated by bureaucrats who interest and justify themselves by inventing and imposing ideas of their own. It happens in the best regulated societies. In the Soviet Union, the mismatch between economic commands and what would be the demands of a market was unexampled and immensely costly. There were not only Stalin's own cherished grandiose projects to change the climate, monumental building programs to celebrate his epoch, reducing new housing to a standstill, and draining scarce resources; but also production of goods in vast quantities that nobody wanted or would or could buy and the building of factories when existing ones were half-used or stood vacant. Moreover, the orders and rules were unquestionable and inviolable. Workers lived and worked under compulsion. No wonder the time came when everything had turned rotten, and an urgent transformation was indicated to avoid total collapse and humiliation before the world of the pioneer regime that would demonstrate the ability of "scientific socialism" to prove history right.

A disaster for *glasnost* as well as for the Soviet Union and the world was the accident at Chernobyl in April 1986. A bungled cover-up attempted "to avoid panic and the spreading of provocative rumours." When Gorbachev finally addressed the nation on television, he had visibly lost credibility, it was said. A regime that for a generation had depended for self-preservation on obsessive secrecy could not be expected to change its ways at a bidding, if not overthrown. Gorbachev himself had been bred under the regime; he was a young man of twenty-five when Khrushchev exposed and denounced Stalin. He believed that Soviet communism could be retrieved, purged of Stalinism. There was no official inquiry into Chernobyl, but questions were raised at meetings with editors about the obscurantist reporting of it; and many editors were replaced. The new men made a breakthrough on that front. Official self-criticism was brought into vogue.

Cultural affairs, penned in social realism, still exposed any writer or performer out of line to imprisonment or exile. Liberation came at a bound in the most public arts of stage and film, boosted if not broached at a congress of the Film-Makers'

Union in 1987, when a spontaneous upsurge of *glasnost* choked off the official voice. That was irreversible when Gorbachev told the bureaucratic overseers to stop "ordering the intelligentsia about, since this was harmful and inadmissible." Otherwise, they were driven to cultivate indifference and cynicism.

Soviet diplomats were assembled in a conference and encouraged to behave in their own way and think for themselves. The heart of the transformation was this: after Chernobyl, Gorbachev was increasingly motivated by concern for the human future as well as the future of the Soviet Union: preservation of the human race superseded class war and the historical triumph of Communism. The "peaceful coexistence of different social systems" was maturing as global initiatives in confronting the problems and tackling the tasks which the human race faces in One World is increasingly of its own making.

Gorbachev took the bold risk of forcing the issue in his prime objective, superpower discussions of disarmament. He resolved to break the deadlock in the endless arms negotiations in Geneva by an offer Reagan could not refuse, and proposed Reykjavik as a midway point for their meeting. What Gorbachev wanted was the elimination of nuclear weapons on both sides, achieved in credible stages and guaranteed by any form of verification that satisfied the other side. That was the program he initiated with the sweeping cuts he proposed at the summit, to which Reagan agreed. The stumbling block was Reagan's pet scheme, the Strategic Defense Initiative—"star wars"—the dream of a defense absolute. He was intransigent in his refusal to abandon it. For Gorbachev, it was virtual sabotage of the arms cut negotiated, for it was tantamount to an invasion of space for the purpose of military superiority, a quest they had agreed to abandon. It threatened to reopen the arms race in a new dimension with escalating costs. Frustrated in his moment of triumph, Gorbachev turned the tables on his partner-turned-opponent by spontaneously telling the media, and the world, at a news conference immediately afterwards what it was that had brought him to Reykjavik, what was so nearly accomplished, and what at the last had thrown it into jeopardy. This impromptu performance of an obviously disappointed man gave him a head start over Reagan in world opinion. The breakthrough he had planned by his bold disarmament bid came through a back door in terms of international credibility. As persona grata his diplomatic and political career abroad was launched.

At home, *glasnost* and *perestroika* spelled political democracy in a society that worked only with institutions made for control. A breakthrough here had to be signaled by a dramatic reversal. One that would mean most to the intelligentsia and his new audience in the West was the unconditional recall and rehabilitation of Sakharov, exiled in Gorky. This unilateral action of Gorbachev, without consultation or warning, outraged the majority of the Politburo, to the loud applause of their opponents within and outside the country. Other liberalizing measures followed piecemeal; institutional transformation could be attained only in step-by-step compromise, on the shop floor, in election procedures, with short lists for selection and larger constituencies with more names on the ballot paper; above all, "broadening inner-party democracy," whatever that might be made to mean. Free comment in the press helped to form and encourage a public opinion active enough to reinforce the influence of Gorbachev and his intimate colleagues, who formed a nucleus within the system.

"The evil that men do lives after them." Khrushchev's exposure of Stalin had focused attention on his crimes. That was the past that was done with, and could be allowed to die. Brezhnev's regime illustrated the point: the system Stalin had established lived on, with its justification of the present by continuous fabrication of the past. "Who controls the past controls the future: who controls the present controls the past" (Orwell). Disinformation and concealment were necessary to totalitarian control. *Glasnost* signaled openness, an about-face; but unless and until the past was allowed to be discovered and shown as it really was, neither the rationale nor the revolutionary character of the political and social change that was in the making could be justified and recognized and accepted. Gorbachev, who had heard Khrushchev and lived under Brezhnev, came to see that the system had to be seen and shown in the light of its making in order to be fully and finally discredited: "History must be seen for what it is." Control from the top down and vested exclusively in the party was identical with fascism, its declared enemy. Property and the economy dependent upon it had been taken over by the state, in the name of the people but in the possession and control of the hierarchy. The frontiers were closed, and the legal system masked with the forms of justice the arbitrary decisions and penalties without appeal imposed by the agencies and agents of a police state. Justification was in terms of the reading of history by Marx, interpreted and applied by Lenin, but trimmed to circumstances in the party line continually determined by the Politburo. The postwar territory of the Soviet Union embraced political unities of diverse ethnic character, some made up by transfers of population, all held under tight central control. The Soviet system cemented a conglomerate that was not a peace-treaty settlement. This was the system Stalin put together in a fortress state, which only officials and escorted parties were allowed to leave. Gorbachev was raised in this system and he set out to dismantle it because he had discerned the nemesis that would ensue. Those who adhered to it and were its beneficiaries, the honest and the dishonest, gradually discerned his moves as a betrayal of its principles.

The corruption of a regime is eventually and inevitably the corruption of a people, save for an exceptional few who are prepared to pay the price in privations and penalties for peace with themselves. Without the West as a model, flawed as it was, there would have been no context in which to see the Soviet Union as it was. Discovery of their history and acquaintance with the West were learning tools of Gorbachev and his close colleagues in promoting reform. Of these, Alexander Yakovlev was the best informed, and served with Shevardnadze as resolute coadjutant. Yakovlev discerned that the moves toward genuine democracy were being recognized as deviations from socialism, a betrayal of principles, and that sporadic opposition would be consolidated. The intelligentsia were unsure of what was happening. This entrenchment of opposition became centered in Yegor Ligachev, Gorbachev's deputy in the Party hierarchy, who believed wholeheartedly in the achievements of the Stalin-Brezhnev period, in the existing culture and economy, in military parity with the United States. Ligachev's line provoked Boris Yeltsin, head of the Moscow Party, to throw in his hand in protest, and request Gorbachev to release him from his duties without more ado, an unprecedented step.

Boris Yeltsin was "awkward" from boyhood, and uncompromisingly direct in denouncing corrupt officials and replacing them where he had the authority to do so. He mixed freely with the people, and his record won him great popularity in Moscow. His innovations there involved him in wrangling with Ligachev on the Politburo, as well as on other matters on which they disagreed, such as the privileges enjoyed by officials and Party members. When Ligachev set up a commission to investigate Yeltsin's rule of Moscow, Yeltsin wrote his letter to Gorbachev requesting permission to resign out of hand. Gorbachev delayed his response: he could not alienate Ligachev, and he was himself irritated by Yeltsin's behavior as a troublemaker on the Politburo. At the Party plenum in October 1987, Yeltsin in a confused speech, not prepared, complained that there had been no progress in *perestroika* in terms of actual change, despite enthusiastic talk, documents, and decrees. People's expectations had been disappointed. Referring to the past, he said that factions had put power into the hands of one man, and that was in danger of happening again: a "cult of personality" must not be allowed to develop. With this warning of the way things were drifting, he brought up his request of resignation, which Gorbachev had not answered. Members of the plenum, unfamiliar with the proceedings of the Politburo, were outraged by Yeltsin's disregard of all the rules, and he was denounced and insulted by speaker after speaker. Rumors of the meeting got out and abroad in spite of endeavors to suppress all news of it. *Glasnost* was compromised. Gorbachev and Yakovlev now were hampered by opponents on the left as well as the right.

Yeltsin was forcing the issue. The strain on him sent him to the hospital with severe chest and head pains. The sequel was abominable. He was dragged out of his hospital bed on Gorbachev's orders to attend a Politburo meeting, followed by a session of the Moscow Party committee, where the speakers, briefed by Gorbachev and Ligachev, insulted and humiliated him, while he listened with his head in his hands. He stumbled to his feet, supporting himself on the backs of chairs to make an incoherent reply that was an admission of most of the charges. His resignation was not accepted: he was demoted from headship of the Moscow Party "for gross shortcomings" and carried by ambulance back to the hospital in a state of collapse. There was agitation in Moscow, with petitions and demands for an explanation, but the conservatives were in the ascendancy, which meant a general clamp-down on dissidents.

Ligachev, who had triumphed over Yeltsin in this round, was as honest and incorruptible, and emotional, as Yeltsin. He was puritanical, unimaginative, totally devoted to the Party and the ideals of socialism, which he believed the Party existed to serve. He was in early sympathy with Gorbachev because he thought they were both concerned to eliminate corruption and wrong-doing. He was put off only when he recognized that Gorbachev was interfering with Party interference, for it was the raison d'être and bounden duty of the Party to interfere in order to ensure that the goals of socialism would be attained. Ligachev was a Slavophile, and found Western ways and thought alien. To pattern reform of the Soviet Union on the West was totally repugnant. Insofar as that became apparent in what Gorbachev and his coadjutants were up to, he would oppose it and frustrate it with all his political skill and will.

The structure of the Soviet Union as a Stalinist artifact, insensitive to geopolitical conditions, put together by ruthlessly Procrustean methods for the sake of absolute central control by the Party, was the Stalinist inheritance Gorbachev was least aware of and therefore least understood and was least effective in dealing with when centralized pressures were relaxed and suppressed racial and cultural manifestations were no longer blotted out under the superior culture of the imperial Soviet Union. He blundered in the first crisis of the kind at the end of 1986, when the corrupt Party leadership of the vast eastern republic of Kazakhstan opposed his democratic tentatives, and he replaced a native Kazakh Communist with a Russian. This was a slight misjudgment compared with what happened early in 1988 in the Caucasus, when an elected council of Nagorny Karabakh in Azerbaijan was encouraged to feel free to withdraw itself from control by the republic of Azerbaijan in order to join Armenia, since the great majority of its population was Armenian—a situation parallel to developments in Yugoslavia later when Serbian domination had lost its hold. Gorbachev promised that a just solution would be brought about. Ligachev was opposed to any change, and the conservatives were in the ascendancy. This was a can of worms, for *perestroika* was threatened by a possible dissolution of the union. But it was immediately threatened directly by a conspiracy engineered by Ligachev in the absence of Gorbachev and Yakovlev abroad. The instrument was an article submitted to the newspaper *Sovetskaya Rossiiya* by a chemistry lecturer in Leningrad who proclaimed Stalin's achievements in what was couched as an anti-*perestroika* manifesto. Encouraged by Ligachev, the editor had the article printed in full and prominently advertised on the front page. Since the newspaper was owned jointly by the government and the Party, the article could not be taken otherwise than as official. The issue was forced on all editors to nail their colors to the mast of *perestroika*, or follow the new Party line. Both Gorbachev and Yakovlev had seen the article while away, and recognized that unless decisive action was taken without delay, editors would not know where they stood, and few if any would have the nerve to take a stand against the sudden turn of events. Ligachev denied complicity when the Politburo met. The conclusion of protracted discussion over two days was to put Yakovlev in charge of the press and ask him to oversee a full rebuttal of the original article, which would be published in *Pravda*. The editor of *Sovetskaya Rossiiya*, who was about to publish readers' letters in support of the article, had a telephone call from Gorbachev, and abruptly dropped them. The day was saved for *glasnost*, by modified employment of the old Party-line diktat—an indication of transition.

This crisis convinced Gorbachev that unless and until he gained mass support he could not prevail against the past and its institutions in establishing political democracy in place of the euphemistic "peoples' democracy," a dictatorship exercised in their name. He had simultaneously to plan stages in the introduction to multiparty democracy, and parry and outsmart the opposition in the Politburo all the way. This occupied the next two years. Early in 1990 the Party's constitutional monopoly of power was abolished. Revolution initiated and incited from above had to be engaged and secured from below.

The first stage was to separate Party and state, so that lawmaking would be enforceable and exclusively in the hands of Parliament and government, reducing the Party from a supervisory to an advisory role. This reform instituted a Congress of People's Deputies of 2,250 members who met twice a year, composed in equal numbers of candidates elected from territorial constituencies, national constituencies, and public organizations. A standing parliament of 542 members formed the Supreme Soviet under a chairman. The prime minister governed with a council of ministers and fifty-seven government departments. The Communist party remained with its general secretary, Politburo, and central committee and departments, effectively an independent organization, not shadowing the government and drastically reduced in numbers. This was more a reversion to Lenin's parliament than to any western model. The chairman of the Supreme Soviet had vested in him the powers of the old Party leader, and he nominated the prime minister and virtually exercised a presidential authority, effecting a transfer of power from the Party to elected and accountable officials. It was the framework of a transformation from arbitrary oligarchic rule, after Stalin, to constitutional government. The Party was represented in the third of the Congress of People's Deputies standing for "public organizations." Local government was also vested in elected councils, leaving the local Party boss to be elected chairman if he had the confidence of the people. The nineteenth party conference at which these changes were debated over four days was marked by lively opposition between Ligachev and Yeltsin, backed by their supporters. Gorbachev contrived a positive conclusion by introducing a resolution of his own at the end of his winding-up speech, which he alleged was an instruction from the presidium, proposing that the changes should be enacted at the next session of Parliament and made effective in the following months. He put it to the vote, and the delegates, taken by surprise, raised their hands in approval. He had gained the upper hand in bringing about their downfall, with their formal approval.

At the grassroots level, voluntary associations were being formed for various purposes, and this formation of groups independent of party control opened the way for the pressure groups needed in democratic politics, which in coalition could develop into an opposition party. In the republics outside Russia, these associations tended to coalesce in concern for recovery of their cultural independence. This move was pioneered by the Baltic republics, the last acquisition of the Soviet Union. Like the colonial possessions of the European nations, they would agitate for independence; and like the European imperial government, the Soviet Union would resist the claims. These movements, in the Baltic and the Caucasus, brought out the high-handed authoritarian side of Gorbachev, the hasty impulsive reactions that marred his political skill; a surprising failure of *nous*. This trait, when it betrayed itself, tended to alienate the intelligentsia, on whom he mainly depended for interpreting and promoting *perestroika* among the people. Yakovlev within the Party leadership was the one they had more confidence in, for his track record of independence in refusing to lend himself to totalitarian practices of which he disapproved was a consistent recommendation. It was he indeed who coined the original practice and promotion of *glasnost*. He had been an exchange student at Columbia University, and he was informed and perceptive about the emergence of a new concerted Europe and a resurgent Japan.

Gorbachev on a five-day visit to Siberia encountered a population articulate about their discontent with the privations and conditions they suffered, while the Party officials enjoyed a privileged life of their own making and taking. When he countered that they should tackle their leaders about this, they convinced him that it would be useless; it was he that was shaken. He then determined to undermine the position of Ligachev who, as his deputy ("second secretary"), had under his direct control the whole administrative apparatus of the central committee, the bureaucracy of twenty departments and several thousand employees. At meetings of the central committee plenum and the Supreme Soviet called at short notice, he proposed and pushed through a replacement of Ligachev's secretariat by six commissions served by one department each and headed by a member of the Politburo. The post of "second secretary" was abolished, and Ligachev was made head of the agricultural commission. All the commissions would be directly responsible to the Politburo and the general secretary. Ligachev was bewildered and disconcerted; he could not think why and how it had happened: it was a great mistake.

Having accomplished a constitutional revolution at the nineteenth party conference, followed by its enactment by the Congress of People's Deputies, and a restructuring of the Party with a diminished role, Gorbachev's position and influence on the international stage in the West was immensely enhanced. Addressing the U.N. General Assembly, his arms proposals were subordinated to impressing on his audience that his domestic policies as well as his foreign policy were inspired by definitive abandonment of class-war thinking in favor of "common human values, consensus, and co-development." One World demanded a common orientation of aims and endeavors, with full toleration of diversities in the way people chose to govern themselves. Gorbachev declared that his reforms guaranteed his intention to establish in the Soviet Union the rule of law, and to bring its practices into conformity with the U.N. Universal Declaration of Human Rights. He then announced his intention to make specific reductions in the armed forces, to withdraw from East Germany, Hungary, and Czechoslovakia, half the tanks, eight hundred combat aircraft, and 8,500 batteries of artillery.

This indication of a willingness to redress the imbalance with NATO forces and retreat to a posture of justifiable defense confirmed the sincerity of the Soviet leader's mental and moral revolution. The change of mind and heart looked like a spiritual conversion, but it was what had been learned the hard way from experience, freely acknowledged in a reappraisal of past mistakes and their consequences. The cold war stood in the way of doing business in the postwar world and threatened calamitous risks to the human race. The speech was not political rhetoric, but, for all its calculation, a thoughtful and honest expression of global statesmanship, to rank in substance if not in form with the most telling and memorable political oratory.

Gorbachev was immediately recalled by an earthquake in Armenia. Ironically, the general human concern that had informed his speech and came home to him in distress on the spot at this particular disaster blinded him to the dominant Armenian concern about Karabakh that was flung in his face when he moved about among the people searching for their relatives. Shocked and disgusted, he treated the core of

Armenian people, frustrated in their representations and demonstrations, as "extremists" to be ruthlessly suppressed when violence broke out. The press was admonished in their reporting of the earthquake to bring out the inhumanity of the "extremists." Party orders were again the order of the day. The exponent of world issues in New York was betrayed by his failure to understand vexed issues on the ground at home.

At the end of 1988 a contested general election was held for the first time under the rules proposed by the nineteenth party conference and subsequently ratified formally by the rubber stamp of the Congress of People's Deputies. The procedures were protracted and chaotic, for it was an unfamiliar and immense organizational task; in spite of corruption and manipulation, an element of genuine choice was operative for the first time. Evidence of it was the election of Sakharov and a landslide victory for Yeltsin, strenuously opposed by a concerted effort of his enemies in the Party. Other radicals were also elected. Unopposed officials had their names scratched out by voters. The rulers of Leningrad were dethroned. They were not prepared to go. Gorbachev, Yakovlev, and Shevardnadze left the country for Cuba and Britain. During their absence, there were peaceful demonstrations in Georgia to demand independence. Ligachev brought colleagues together to respond to the Georgian Party boss who had asked for help, and they arranged for troops to be available to reinforce those at hand. When Gorbachev returned and was informed of this, he insisted that there should be no violence, but negotiations. When the authorities in the Georgian capital ordered the crowds to disperse, reinforced by a plea from the patriarch of the Georgian church, they would not go away. The upshot was an intervention of soldiers in a vicious mood exercising unrestrained violence and leaving twenty dead and hundreds injured. The event was treated in a *Pravda* editorial as a conspiracy that used the mob to "subvert the foundations of society"; deaths in the square were blamed on its leaders, who should be punished. The highly complicated background to this event and its aftermath was a bid of the conservatives headed by the chief of the ousted Leningrad leaders to stem the tide of *perestroika* by claiming that the election had bypassed the "workers" who in the old Supreme Soviet had been guaranteed a 35 percent quota. Gorbachev outmaneuvered them.

Under the new rules, the main purpose of the newly elected Congress of People's Deputies, which met on May 26, 1989, was to elect the 542 members of the Supreme Soviet from its own number. However, the lid was off and it immediately became a forum of open debate broadcast live on television, beginning with a demand from one deputy, "on the instructions of my electorate," for "a report, now and for all to hear . . . about who gave the order for the slaughter of peaceful demonstrators in Tbilisi." The radicals, beginning with Sakharov, challenged everything and had a field day. But there were enough representatives of the old Party among the 2,250 members to ensure the election of a "Stalinist-Brezhnevite" Supreme Soviet. The exclusion of Yeltsin with his popular mandate from Moscow provoked special protest. Yuri Afanasyev, the author of that description above of the Supreme Soviet just elected, was encouraged by Gorbachev to continue his speech, half-smothered by jeers and slow handclapping, which concluded, "We can be obedient. . . . But let us not forget for a moment about those who sent us to this Congress. They sent us here not to behave meekly but to change the state of affairs in this country in the most decisive manner." Yeltsin wrote in his memoirs of the effects of the debates: "On the day the Congress opened, the Soviet people were one sort of people, on the day that it closed they were different people . . . Almost the entire population was awakened from its state of lethargy." All the tabooed topics had been brought up, and were henceforth open to discussion and comment in the press. Most important, the radical speakers who had made their mark in the debates formed the core of a legitimate parliamentary opposition.

On the economic front, there was parallel emergence of a new radical force. This was not in the form of cooperatives, which party officials could frustrate as out of their control, nor in an attempt to transform state enterprises by subordinating them to the market, when the state was the market. It came with a sit-in by coal miners in western Siberia who had no soap. Within two weeks half a million miners were on strike. They wanted more than soap: better working and living conditions, a share in control over the pits and in mining profits, together with political demands for independent trade unions and an end to the privileges and authority enjoyed by the party and its officials. The widespread strike and mass meetings were well organized and responsibly controlled, evidence of political and administrative capability. Regional committees were formed to negotiate with the government. With government concessions to most of the specific demands, the strike was settled. The committees remained as alternatives counter to the official trade unions, and Yeltsin referred to them as "embryos of real people's power." Control of *perestroika* was slipping out of Gorbachev's hands. If he could not continue to manage it at his pace and in his way, the risk of resistance and reversal by consolidation of an alarmed Party greatly increased. Also, he was to be embarrassed by colonial revolt, which he was inept at handling.

The Soviet *Union* was now under test, the forcing together of territories and peoples on Stalin's Procrustean bed. Minorities suffering discrimination provoked virtual civil war. Popular fronts in most republics made changes that alienated and drove out people of a different culture or language. The example of the three Baltic republics kept the unrest at fever pitch. What was to happen some three years later with the breakup of Yugoslavia was anticipated in the ethnic hatred engendered by Stalin's arbitrary mixture of peoples of different races, aggravated by his purpose in extracting their designated output, allowing the retention of little for themselves, and leaving them without adequate means to meet their own needs by imports. It was classical colonial exploitation, a pattern of victimization perpetuated for disadvantaged countries of the Third World in postcolonial times by the terms of trade agreed to by the industrialized countries that dominate GATT.

Meanwhile, *perestroika* was stealing into the Soviet Union's southwestern European satellites. "Solidarity" in Poland, under a workers' leadership supported by the strongest Catholic church in the Communist empire, was able to subvert the official trade unions and undermine the authority of nationals who were virtually agents of a traditional enemy. In strong contrast, the Hungarian Communist government opened its borders with Austria, which enabled East Germans by going on holiday to Hungary to pass over into West Germany, where they were assured of a prompt welcome.

This escape route renewed the hemorrhage the Berlin wall was built to stop. It was too late to check the renewal. The regular popular clamor in demonstrations on the streets was irresistible. Gorbachev himself, attending East Germany's fortieth anniversary celebrations in early October, strongly urged Erich Honecker to recognize that the world situation required a radical change in Communist thinking; if they went on blindly as before, they would be "punished by life itself." That advice was not taken, and events took their course, in East Germany, in Bulgaria, in Czechoslovakia, in Romania. The web Stalin had woven was broken.

This retreat from socialism, with Gorbachev's complacency and encouragement, in the countries the Red Army had liberated from the Nazis, shocked the generals; Ligachev felt vindicated: peaceful cooperation of states with different social systems should never mean submission of socialism to a takeover by capitalism; changes in international relations did not require change in political and economic thinking. Shevardnadze defended what was being allowed to happen in the satellites by insisting that a totalitarian regime had been imposed on each of them, overriding all opposition; that it could not be maintained against the wishes of the people without contradiction of the new thinking initiated in the Soviet Union.

When these events were seen on Soviet television and reported in the press, there were questions about communism and the Party in the Soviet Union. Gorbachev did not want to have the issue forced, which would rally and consolidate the opposition; his timetable gave him scope to stage and maneuver his way to multiparty democracy. But impatience of the radicals and the growing belligerence of the Party opposition were an embarrassment, aggravated by the impetuous demands and actions of the Baltic states, ahead of more than a hundred nationalities and regions in a like state of restlessness within the Soviet borders. There was not the time for his pace of circumspect and constitutional negotiations. Those who jumped the gun could be restrained only by sending in the tanks.

*Glasnost* itself had now become a forcing-bed for *perestroika*. The population as a whole were being made aware of the truth that Gorbachev and his coadjutants had recognized, that the capitalist West had far outstripped the socialist Soviet Union in technological achievements and standard of living, and that they, the Soviet people, had been made by secrecy, deception, and propaganda to believe the opposite of this, and to suffer unnecessary privation. There was engendered a mood of popular revolt. Gorbachev felt that the reforms already in place after the nineteenth party conference had lacked the executive authority to put them swiftly into effect and to enforce the legislation enacted by the new Supreme Soviet. He was persuaded by Yakovlev to institute an executive presidency, and he managed to get this approved, with some difficulty, by the central committee of the Party. A council of the parliamentary leaders of the fifteen republics, together with senior government ministers and his own nominees, formed an advisory body; and he was thus made practically independent of the Party leadership.

Meanwhile, in Leningrad and Moscow the Party had been reduced to opposition, and radicals were in control of the councils. In the Russian Federation, the spine of the Soviet Union, covering three quarters of the territory and more than half the population, Yeltsin was president; in a position to decisively oppose or uphold Gorbachev, who had tried to frustrate his election. Yeltsin immediately declared for the autonomy of the republics, Russia and the others, so that Soviet laws would apply to them only if ratified. Under him, the Russian Federation became a model of government by an elected parliament, not by the Party, a definitive achievement of what was intended in the constitutional reforms proposed by the nineteenth party conference. Yeltsin's radicalism had preempted Gorbachev's tentative moves.

A revolution in management of the economy was involved in far more intractable problems, and would remain so. Gorbachev planned to make the twenty-eighth party congress the forum in which both political and economic issues would be definitively settled, with an unequivocal confirmation of all the reforms in place by a renunciation of the Party of its monopoly of powers. The congress lasted twelve days, and numbered five thousand delegates. Gorbachev put everything he had in mind in the clearest possible terms in his opening speech, and got a frosty reception. These were Party secretaries from all the districts of the union. Over the days, against this blank wall of opposition, Gorbachev demonstrated his virtuosity in persuading delegates to change their minds in spite of themselves, and he ended by getting his way and separating the Party from the government. Yeltsin and the mayors of Leningrad and Moscow formally resigned from the Party, which stimulated mass resignations throughout the union. Gorbachev used his advantage to remove by presidential decree Party controls and to rehabilitate all political prisoners and exiled dissidents, including Solzhenitsyn. He met with Yeltsin for hours of talks, which effected reconciliation and understanding.

The vested interests of the Stalinist establishment were being abolished, and when this came home to them they rallied in self-preservation, still powerful enough to mount a comeback. How formidable they could still be is evident in listing the interests concerned: the hard core of the Politburo; the bureaucrats still staffing the administration; the managers of state industries and collectives; the KGB; the Red army; and the military-industrial complex, which had been favored with the highest endowment of resources. These united to exert their influence in the Congress of People's Deputies. Dismantling the old order had not been matched with a takeover by a new authority, and the country was sliding into anarchy with the disintegration of the union. Gorbachev felt himself bound to resort to old methods of authoritarian rule to exercise presidential power, in a succession of arbitrary actions that mocked *glasnost* and *perestroika*.

His violent behavior, reverting to measures of the repudiated past, spelled desperation. Shevardnadze expressed despair in a passionate speech that warned of a direful impending dictatorship, and announced his resignation as foreign minister. The heroic and Herculean attempt to move the Soviet Union out of the swamp of inertia and stagnation into which it was sinking fast had brought about restless disillusionment, wild hopes, anarchy and chaos, and a concerted backlash. There could be no going back, and there was no certain way forward.

"The Second Russian Revolution" of 1985–1990 was far from an anti-Bolshevik coup. Rather, it had been a five-year plan to abolish economic planning by a centralized authority able to enforce decisions indifferent to economic indicators, unaccountable to those affected. The fatality of that course had become apparent by comparison with the relative success of capitalism and political democracy in the West. Communists would have to apply "new thinking" to the dogmas of the "scientific socialism" they had inherited. They were not heirs to a future guaranteed by history. Meanwhile, a market economy and multiparty democracy were the clues to follow. That might be seen pretty clearly by a Gorbachev, a Shevardnadze, a Yakovlev, but it was more easily seen than accomplished.

What seemed like victory for reaction at this point in 1990, in terms of Gorbachev's loss of direction and control and Shevardnadze's withdrawal, was exposed for the faltering that would inevitably confound it when in the following year their attempted coup to take Gorbachev into their power was decisively foiled, and arguably petered out in humiliating indecision. That outcome perfectly reflected the achievement and the failure of the Second Russian Revolution engineered and conducted by Gorbachev, Shevardnadze, and Yakovlev.

The external side of this internal unresolved upheaval, equally irreversible, was gravitational in its effect, for it reconstituted postwar international relations. The global confrontation of superpowers that had determined policies and events worldwide, domestic and foreign, in Africa, Asia, Latin America, and the Middle East, as well as in Europe, east and west, was lifted, leaving the United States with undisputed powers, but without hegemony, in a world precipitated into unsettlement, a sea of troubles not to be ended by opposing them, and with islands of opportunity. If ever there was a turning-point of history, it had come.

The new postwar world of science and technology which Gorbachev, like Harold Wilson, had hoped would solve the economic problems of politicians had not proved a manageable instrument for that purpose. What it did for politics was in another realm. Nightly evidence around the world on television screens of what was happening in trouble-spots, or wherever the cameras happened to be, made the inhabitants of the world in their masses visually aware of conditions on their planet. This was unparalleled and revolutionary. When the streets of Leipzig were seen night after night crowded with organized demonstrators, and the KGB headquarters was looted and the files torn out, Czechoslovakian dissidents were encouraged to believe that the day had come. Things could never be the same. The civil rights movement in the United States could not have succeeded so well and so quickly if the people in the North had not seen for themselves what was actually going on in the South.

# 20

# New Patterns of Warfare

The military thinking of Karl von Clausewitz (1780–1831) remained relevant until this postwar period and was abundantly exemplified and vindicated in both world wars. The concentration of force and use of speed to achieve victory through a decisive battle was exactly what the Germans did to knock France out in the first active stage of World War II. Morale was a weapon on which Churchill relied when Britain was isolated. If the Russians were not consciously practicing strategic defense by falling back on their lines of communication while the attacker extended his, with diminishing strength, until a culminating point when the defender took the initiative and counterattacked, that is how their victory was achieved. Above all, it was the common political purpose of the Allies, which emerged in the partnership of Stalin, Churchill, and Roosevelt, that was "the supreme consideration in conducting the war." All four points happen to be pure Clausewitz.

The shift in military thinking from how to win the next war to how to prevent war was forced when the effects of the atomic bomb on Hiroshima on August 6, 1945, and on Nagasaki three days later, opened the prospect of a resort to weapons of world destruction. The context of war had been changed, and could never be the same, even if engaged in with conventional weapons. This change of context still involves uncertainties, with changes of policies and prospects, as events continue to change the context itself. There is a chronology to be followed, if not steady development to a new, settled order of international security.

In this chapter, three aspects of the situation will be examined: ascendancy of the superpowers in nuclear capability; continuation of limited wars with conventional weapons in this context; and protracted conflict maintained by guerrilla operations, underground wars, and terrorist tactics. Finally, thinking about war itself will be reviewed and considered. As in general, solutions are not to be looked for, but problems can be broken down and made more tractable, constructive procedures can be identified, criteria can be established for judgments and decisions. Two generations of postwar experience ought to advance learning in this life and death business.

## Nuclear Stalemate

International control of atomic energy would have been a logical continuation of the political partnership that won the war, and like the peace treaty it was frustrated by disagreement between Stalin and the West. An Atomic Energy Commission for the purpose was established in 1946, but without participation of the Soviet Union. The United States and the Soviet Union established their superpower capability in independently pursued programs; it was not until exactly four years after Hiroshima that the Soviet Union was able to test its first atomic bomb. Parity was not reached for another two decades. During the 1950s, the explosive power was increased by fusion instead of fission to produce the hydrogen bomb, equivalent to a million tons of TNT, compared to twenty thousand tons of TNT that was the equivalent power of the atom bomb used on Hiroshima. As great, or greater, improvement was in the means of delivery. By 1956, the Americans had developed the first intercontinental ballistic missile (ICBM), capable of reaching specific targets in the Soviet Union from pits in the United States. By the following year, the Russians were capable of similar retaliation. Both sides were developing ballistic missiles launched from submarines. With special aircraft also designed for delivery, both sides were furnished with a nuclear arsenal of missiles of great complexity, developed in variety over the years to serve particular purposes, some with multiple warheads of at least one megaton each (that is, equivalent to one million tons of TNT). With thousands of these strategically placed and in train for instant use on a coded signal from the one responsible, reliably informed by duty personnel constantly on alert, the day-and-night confrontation of these two systems was the postwar nightmare of international security by mutually assured destruction (MAD), every word of which was guaranteed, but the possible outcome, whether of use or of consequence if used, was incalculable but not unimaginable. Hence the nightmare, and the unprecedented security of this new form of the balance of power, which had converted military thinking to concentration on the prevention of war, that is, the prevention of nuclear war.

First came the wishful thinking formulated as mutually assured complete disarmament, but that was what original disagreements had made impracticable. While the U.S.A. had a long lead in the development of nuclear power, and the Soviet Union was seen as a formidable enemy, a preemptive strike had advocates, and was a tempting possibility, but it was desperate counsel, precipitating what was to be prevented. A sufficient defensive capability was what Reagan dreamed of later on, but it had been early recognized as not technically feasible.

If prevention meant MAD, it is necessary to indicate what that formula entailed in terms of actuality that could and would deter, for it took more than thirty years of research and development to put that in place step by step. A system had to be found and established that would be known to be capable of unacceptable retaliation *after* an unprovoked strategic nuclear attack. There was the inherent momentum of research and development, with innovations out of date on the drawing-board before they are in production: Minuteman I, operational in 1962; Minuteman III in 1970. The first version had a single warhead of one megaton; the third was a multiple, independently targeted reentry ICBM with three separate warheads, of 170 kilotons; in 1980, the three warheads were increased to 335 kilotons. It was mounted in an underground silo, and kept in readiness for instant firing. When such fixed mountings became too vulnerable to missile destruction, ICBMs were mounted for launching from mobile vehicles. This was ideally feasible with the use of submarines. Polaris, with a range of 2,800 miles, could deliver ten separately guided fifteen kiloton warheads in the Poseidon version. Trident, designed to replace Poseidon, and deployed in the early 1980s, had two thousand miles further range and a sophisticated guidance system of great accuracy. Cruise missiles were introduced to confuse defense by changes of direction determined by a computer program. A strategic missile, the MX, with a range of six thousand miles was developed in 1979 for versatile launching possibilities, from ships or submarines, aircraft, land vehicles, or specially reinforced silos. It carries ten warheads. In sum, the United States set out to provide against any nuclear defense contingency that could be thought of, and remain capable of unacceptable retaliation in case a nuclear strike did succeed. The complexity of the arrangements was inherent in the defensive use of nuclear weapons, short of retaliation, by the development of antiballistic missiles relying on their own guidance systems to destroy missiles by radiation from their warheads. These operated against strategic missiles in space.

The credibility necessary to MAD was thus built steadily into the hardware and its disposal and deployment over a human generation that covered successive generations of specific weapons. Even a bomber was enabled to penetrate Soviet air defenses by radar evasion. There was no foreseeable end to this escalation of nuclear capability, in terms of diversity of weapons, increasing sophistication of devices, and growth in number, fire power, and destructive reach and threat. Credibility required not only availability of the means of effective deterrence, but also recognition of a readiness to resort to their use if attacked. That could not be a separate ingredient: it was built into acquirement of the means, a stupefying accomplishment of technical virtuosity, and a prodigious investment of money and resources. There never was so unmistakable a manifestation of political will. These were all strategic or global nuclear weapons, aimed at the Soviet Union and vice versa, aloof from the conventional forces of NATO and the Warsaw Pact facing one another across the East-West divide of Europe, where the danger of a Soviet offensive was most feared. For the Russians were superior in conventional forces. Moreover, they were known to have intermediate range missiles (IRBMs) of lower firepower available for tactical use on the ground. Response was inevitable. The Americans constituted the pillar of NATO. Tactical nuclear deterrence in the European theater was a necessary supplement to strategic deterrence. Thus intermediate nuclear forces (INF) were introduced with thousands of tactical nuclear weapons, including some deployed from submarines and a diversity of missiles and launchers, from specialized guns, aircraft, and mobile mounts, contributed by France and Britain as well as the United States. The Soviet

Union had comparable INF with the same diversity of specialized launchers, and submarines based in the Baltic. Both sides had counter systems of antinuclear weapons with reduced range and power for deployment in the European theater. NATO had superiority in tactical nuclear weapons that balanced Soviet superiority in conventional weapons. It was made clear that first use would be made of them to save the day if an engagement of conventional forces threatened NATO with defeat. Conventional forces were increased to reduce this risk.

The availability of tactical nuclear weapons stockpiled in Europe made a flexible response practicable, adapted to risk. Used to check an aggression likely to succeed, a pause would be offered for second thoughts. Nuclear weapons in the theater of operations would thus be under political control for the purpose of limitation and negotiated settlement (Clausewitz made relevant again). Integration of strategic and tactical systems, with the European confrontation identified as highest risk seemed to complete interlocking systems of credible deterrence and defense formulated and postulated according to the doctrine of mutually assured destruction. The superpowers provided *pax occidentalis*. Unfortunately, it seemed to the European allies that the United States would be in a position to detach strategic nuclear weapons systems for the defense of the North and South American continents, leaving tactical nuclear weapons to assure the defense of Europe, thus reducing instead of reinforcing the credibility of deterrence in Europe. Britain and France had developed nuclear weapons in the late 1940s for national prestige, and later relied on them as insurance against this contingency of American reservation. In 1966, NATO formed a nuclear planning group for consultation and planning. The United States wanted her allies to devote their expenditure to improving and increasing their conventional armament, and claimed the sole right to decide on a resort to nuclear weapons. But her allies were partners, not subjects.

The escalation of nuclear weaponry over the years was of course an arms race, but an arms race with a difference, in that it was all the time planning the invention and production and deployment of weapons in order to deter their use, an indirect way of bringing them under control, in default of cooperation to do so by agreement, which had not been practicable. Did the public see it in this way? The Soviet population was told in the press and otherwise only what their government wanted it to know, whether it was true or not. In the West there was not a homogeneous public even within each nation. Broadly, there was a cadre of informed persons on defense, and there were sections of public opinion catered for by the so-called tabloids and broadsheets and by radio and television, who saw, heard, and read news, information, and opinion on defense matters. There were pressure groups formed to espouse and propagate particular views and policies.

Instituted in response to the new thinking on defense required by the advent of nuclear weapons were the Institutes for Strategic Studies (ISS). Alistair Buchan, son of John Buchan the novelist, who had been called to help set up a Department of Information in 1917–1918, was the first director of the English Institute for Strategic Studies set up early in the seventies. His single-minded drive, wide contacts, and knowledge of the field gave the new venture a resounding start, with the push of his earnest and infectious enthusiasm. People one most wanted to hear on nuclear and defense matters were brought to an informal rostrum, caught on a visit or otherwise induced, to give their views and answer questions from members, equipped to pursue a salient point, to call attention to an aspect omitted, to amplify or emphasize what was felt to be of special or main importance, or otherwise to advance relevant debate. The speaker might be a Russian general, the defense minister, a spokesman for CND, Prince Philip, a defense specialist (like Liddell Hart), an author, an academic in a relevant field, a service chief in retirement or in office, in or out of step (there was a confidentiality rule, announced at the start of every meeting), a war office official, someone in the defense counsels of the United States: the roll drew on names representing the relevant expertise, influences, and policy making. Sometimes a distinguished guest was present. The members included civil servants (ministry of defense, foreign office), members of parliament, relevant specialists, and most importantly defense correspondents of the media. Thus the Institutes for Strategic Studies within the NATO alliance kept in train an articulation of defense opinion and discussion at a general level in touch with public opinion at large, throughout the long period of "new thinking" and planning for international security in the nuclear age. This monitoring function would hardly have been possible for such an existing institution as the Royal United Service Institute. The ISS did for defense what Chatham House did for international relations. Tally was kept on the buildup and deployment of weapons on both sides. The Institutes were a source of information as well as a forum.

The bilateral indirect endeavor to attain international security from nuclear war was seen in a different light by those who were obsessed by the horror of mass destruction brought by the first atomic bomb, and the appalling risks of the escalation of capability that was going on. The dilemma of peace by mutual deterrence mounted by massive arsenals that threatened human survival if used seemed clearly morally indefensible. Fictional scenarios of what might happen were best-sellers. Since the original ideal of mutually assured complete disarmament had not been feasible, the only way to stop the escalation was unilateral repudiation of nuclear weapons.

In Britain, the Campaign for Nuclear Disarmament instituted its ritual annual demonstration, the Aldermaston march to rally public opinion and focus it on research and development, the power-house of escalation. This was steadily maintained, and intensified, throughout the period. At the end, when there was the stalemate of parity, the introduction of American INF weapons, the Cruise and Pershing missiles, since they threatened use in a first-strike, were especially controversial and provoked the women's encampment on Greenham Common on the fringe of the American base where the new mobile weapons were parked and from which they were moved on exercise. The protest was stubborn, courageous, costly to both sides, a real harassment, and well publicized, which kept the issue in the news. It was a political party divide: the Left in most European NATO countries stood for unilateral nuclear disarmament.

## Limited Conventional Wars

The superpowers had decisively put war between themselves with nuclear weapons outside their thinking, but they remained prepared to engage in wars with conventional weapons, so long as they would be limited by their political purpose, and exclude any use of nuclear weapons, including the limited tactical ones. These included the Korean War (1950–1953), the Suez affair in 1956, the Vietnam War (1964–1973), Soviet intervention in Afghanistan in 1979, England's defense of the Falklands in 1982, and the Gulf War in 1991. Wars in which the principal powers were not involved included the Israeli-Arab wars of 1967 and 1973 and the Iraq-Iran war started in 1980.

When the Japanese surrendered in 1945, the Soviet and U.S. governments agreed that the Japanese troops north of the 38th parallel in Korea should surrender to the Russians and those to the south should surrender to the Americans. On evacuation by Russian and American forces, there would be a democratically elected government for the whole of Korea. What actually happened, much as in Germany, turned out to be a "People's Party" in power in the north and in the south a conservative government, under the elderly Syngman Rhee. The U.S. government recognized South Korea as an independent state. The Soviet Union insisted on unification, supported by China, the northern neighbor of the disputed territory. On June 25, 1950, the North invaded the South, which was unable to put up effective resistance. The UN Security Council demanded cessation of hostilities and withdrawal of the invading troops. A United Nations force was assembled to enforce the decision. President Truman ordered an American contingent under General MacArthur to support the South Koreans without proceeding beyond the 38th parallel in driving the Northern troops back.

America's NATO allies were reluctant to grudge their leader support, but there was uneasiness about the legitimacy of the South Korean government. It was recognized that the United States had manipulated the immature Western-dominated United Nations to secure its recognition, as well as the Security Council's resolution condemning North Korea for violation of the charter by an act of aggression. Also, it was known that President Truman was prepared to act alone if necessary, with bipartisan support at home. Fourteen member nations of the United Nations did commit forces to enforce the resolution ordering a withdrawal of the North Korean invading army, and it formally appeared to the world that for the first time the United Nations was able to send in troops to halt an aggression.

The North Koreans had overwhelmed the smaller army of South Korea and captured their capital Seoul before the intervention of the UN forces under the command of General MacArthur. He carried out a brilliant amphibious flank attack, driving the North Koreans back well beyond the 38th parallel to the Chinese border, not heeding serious warnings from the Chinese before the parallel was crossed. MacArthur had his own ideas about the United States' mission in Asia, and he was setting about a forcible reunification of Korea under a government in the Western, anti-Communist camp. His action involved the UN troops in an ambush prepared by a Chinese deployment of masses of "people's volunteers." They were overwhelmed and driven south in disorderly retreat. A war had been precipitated between the United States and China, in what had been started and intended as a police faction by the United Nations, a limited military action, not even a limited war. President Truman recalled MacArthur and relieved him of his command for disobedience. He also lost support of the Republican party for the war. Worse, he jeopardized relations with the allies by revealing in a press conference that the extremity of the situation after the Chinese intervention had prompted serious consideration of the use of tactical nuclear weapons. British Prime Minister Attlee made an urgent visit to Washington to insist on close consultation on major strategic policy decisions if NATO cooperation was to be maintained. The political purpose of halting the aggression was reinstated, albeit not now on a 38th parallel frontier. The forces were bogged down in a war of attrition. Truman was ousted by the Republican Dwight Eisenhower in the 1952 presidential election. Eisenhower's undertaking to bring the war to an end was not easy to fulfill without humiliating concessions of the kind the United States had to submit to later in Vietnam. Eisenhower was even driven to consider the possibility of using tactical nuclear weapons to convince China of the futility of continuation of the war. Negotiations eventually prevailed in a detailed settlement over three months, leading to a cease fire on July 27, 1953.

One main outcome of the war as it affected the United States was a protracted public debate about the conduct of their returned prisoners of war (POWs). There was a tendency in Republican quarters to use them as scapegoats, evidence of the degeneration brought about by the New Deal and soft policies alien to the American spirit of self-advancement by self-reliance. It was grist to the McCarthy mill separating wheat from chaff by blowing away those contaminated by association. Extreme views were heard, similar to the Japanese condemnation of surrender; the mere status of POW was suspect.

At the Geneva conference on Korea in April 1954 things were left as they were. The cochairmen, Britain's Anthony Eden and the Soviet Union's Vyacheslav Molotov, agreed that the armistice line could be assumed to mark spheres of influence so far as the superpowers were concerned, since the fighting had stopped and the question of unification was not urgent. There were more pressing issues elsewhere, as in Indochina.

In Korea itself there was a heavy buildup of arms and military installations by Communists in the North, and with United States aid in the South, a front line for Japan and a key position for U.S. influence in the Far East. The Japanese were rewarded for their backing with supplies and ships not only by payment that boosted their economy but by political rehabilitation in a treaty that integrated them into America's system of Communist containment in the Far East. Taiwan also benefited in this context, with U.S. commitment to their exclusive representation of China in the United Nations. China, for so long in the past exploited and humiliated by the West, had won its own back against the pre-eminent Western power, secured its hold over the mainland, and established itself as a regional power to be reckoned with by Washington. U.S. commitment to NATO was reinforced, and Germany and Japan were rearmed, which was what the Soviet Union was most anxious to prevent after the world war. The Korean episode therefore involved the Soviet Union in putting more resources into building up her own military strength.

Within NATO, the experience of MacArthur and McCarthy raised fears among U.S. allies that American reactions to Communism might do more than Communists to precipitate world war. Especially was this true in Britain where the United States had air bases. There was a sense that America had to be contained by its allies. Churchill was in favor of a detente with the Soviet Union, which the Korean war had derailed. But the United States alone in the West was a superpower, and that was a decisive constraint on all policies. For the United States, escalation of the cost of containment increased ultimate reliance on nuclear deterrence. Eisenhower was more willing to concede North Vietnam to the Communists than to incur another Korean war; North Vietnam attempted to unify the country by force, but the U.S. attempt to frustrate it had predesigned limits. There would be no invasion of North Vietnam. The pattern of the Korean war might be followed in the North, but not in the South.

What should have been an enforcement of the law by police action on an international scale, something the United Nations accomplished that the League of Nations had failed to do, was in fact nothing of the kind, although it was represented as that and popularly believed to be that at the time. Rather, it was a crime against humanity. In the first place, the United Nations was made a tool of the West manipulated by the United States. Second, the South Korean regime, legitimated by the United Nations, was no better than that of North Korea in terms of humanity and human rights, and possibly worse. Third, the sum total of human misery, death, and destruction brought by the war infinitely exceeded what had been wrought by the North Korean invasion of the South and capture of Seoul. The massive use of American technological superiority in aerial and artillery bombardment of villages and Chinese guerrillas (the "enemy") inflicted carnage of obliteration. On James Cameron, who reported for the British media, it made the deepest impression of his life as an experienced journalist, and roused human feelings he could express only with characteristic professional restraint in faithful detailed description that spoke for itself. General MacArthur, the responsible agent, was the most reliable, eloquent, and telling witness: "The war in Korea has almost destroyed that nation . . . I have never seen such devastation. . . . After I looked at that wreckage and those thousands of women and children and everything, I vomited." Not only was the war not a police action, it was not limited in any appropriate sense at all, a cruel mockery of what it purported to be. It flagrantly violated all the rules of Clausewitz doctrine. It was a product of fanatical hatred and fear of Communism endemic in the United States at the time. It was the irreversible opening of the cold war, which it escalated; and the cold war was essentially American preoccupation with a total endeavor to contain communism at all cost. What most needed to be contained then as later was every manifestation of fanaticism.

The Suez operation was both limited and abortive, and equally misconceived and counterproductive. It was a side affair like a fictional subplot; and its effects on the main characters, France and Britain, were very different. For France, it was a passing incident, an embarrassment in their total immersion in the Algerian war. In England, it had an impact in little like that of the Korean War in America, rousing months of heated controversy and blame-casting. But the lasting effect was to register the end of empire, to bring home in a sensitive area, a pivot of imperial hegemony, recognition of radical impotence. The old role had been played out.

The story is familiar. Nasser as president of Egypt was seen and feared by Anthony Eden, prime minister of England, as leader of nationalist expansion in the area when he was known to be acquiring arms from Czechoslovakia and the Soviet Union and supplying arms to the Algerian national uprising, which was what enraged and engaged the French. Eden, applying the lesson of Munich, was anxious that appeasement might again allow a Hitler to wax unchecked. This time, the snake must at least be scotched. When Nasser, frustrated by the West's failure to continue funding construction of the Aswan High Dam, nationalized the Suez Canal, to have that under control and the West discredited, Britain and France felt they had several good reasons to move against him. Israel was also involved because Egypt banned her shipping from passing through the canal and she was permanently under threat from Arab neighbors, who resented a reintroduction into Palestine of a Jewish state. The passage of the canal under arbitrary control was unacceptable to all its users.

The story is a putting together of the details of the movement of events, the sequence of decisions, overt and covert, and the interplay of opinion that took place within the several theaters of England and France, Israel and Egypt, and the United States, and in movements and communications across those frontiers, all rapidly unfolding in the crowded space of eight months from the nationalization of the canal to its reopening in March 1957. That story is of course far from familiar in all its intricate detail. The outline alone is familiar, as a bare chronology of events: Israel's rapid defeat of Egypt in the Sinai; Nasser's blocking of the canal by sinking forty-seven ships filled with concrete; the joint air strike by England and France on Egyptian airfields, secretly planned in concert with the Israeli invasion; the UN call for a ceasefire; Eisenhower's intervention through the United Nations, and later by a conditional offer to help save the run on the pound if the ceasefire was promptly accepted; the strength of political opposition in England to the use of force. An important aspect of the affair was the scrupulous limitation of the application of force to the purpose in hand, using low-caliber bombs accurately and exclusively directed to the military target. This was the model of a police action, outside a legitimating context.

No such control of limitation was feasible in the Vietnam War, although it had perforce to be conducted by the Americans within that parameter. Here the underlying conditions of the commitment need consideration. There was confusion and tension between president and Congress on how far the commitment went in terms of the expenditure of resources; it was never clear what that limit would be, and therefore what the president could count on in conducting the war, particularly what time span he had to act in. The instability and breakdown of the South Vietnam government and the weakness of its army in effect taxed him with the impossible task of a military operation in a foreign country without a political purpose and objective (Clausewitz again). Operations were exclusively in the hands of the general in command, and the political aim was reduced to keep the operations within strict limits, that is, military targets within South Vietnam, not invading North Vietnam, not risking escalation by involving China or the Soviet Union, who were supplying it. The Viet Cong had experience of the French, another Western military power they had decisively beaten. They knew a thing or two that encouraged them on how to demoralize the enemy. Guerrilla tactics were evasive; there were no pitched battles; aerial bombardment was finally elective only if it was followed up on the ground by hand-to-hand fighting that secured and held the objective. General Westmoreland was MacArthur, carrying out this thankless operation he was not to be allowed to win. The Tet offensive of January 1968 was a military success for him, but the political agitation that ensued exposed Saigon as an American administration. This was not what the United States wanted; President Lyndon Johnson recalled Westmoreland, and announced he would not seek reelection. Nixon, with a hint that he might seek a nuclear solution, recognized that "Vietnamization," that is, aiding a South Vietnam government and army to hold its own to repel the invader, was the only realistic policy; but it was unrealistic in the time required. Their experience in Korea and Vietnam pushed the Americans to work out a strategy that would enable them to use their technological superiority in a way that could be followed up in a "fight to win" that did respect political limits. The outcome was a flexible strategy, a multiple of the particular one worked out in the graduated response tactics to a possible invasion of Western Europe.

A human consideration that is perhaps of minor military consequence at present was experienced in the Vietnam War by participants on the side of the United States. In World War I, the breakdown of soldiers at the front known as "shell shock" was a physiological reaction to prolonged severe stress. In the Vietnam War there was psychological breakdown, when men became overwhelmed by a feeling of the inhumanity of what they were engaged in, a paroxysm of withdrawal, a paralysis of guilt. This was no passing mood, but a lasting and crippling damage. At a less pathological level, there were anticommunist believers in the American cause (some of them Catholics) who came to feel more in sympathy with the Viet Cong, their enemy, by their experience of what forceful opposition entailed.

There was a Middle-East theater of confrontation as elsewhere. The special circumstances of the Israeli state required a nation in arms on constant alert, ensuring instant response, unfailing retaliation, and watchful anticipation. Zionism as a Jewish nationalist movement dates back to a congress at Basel in 1897 that set up a World Zionist Organization to establish a Jewish national home in Palestine, and encouraged Jewish immigration into Palestine. The Balfour Declaration in 1917 committed the British government to support the cause, subject to respect for the interests of non-Jewish communities in Palestine, but this consideration was abandoned in 1939 because of unrelenting Arab objections. Britain administered Palestine under a League of Nations mandate from 1920. There was Arab unrest and rebellion provoked by Jewish immigration, and British concessions to the Arabs incensed the Jews, who engaged in underground terrorism. In 1947 the United Nations ruled that Palestine should be divided into Jewish and Arab states, which was accepted by the Jews but not the Arabs; Britain renounced the mandate. The Jews instituted the state of Israel, which was at once attacked by neighboring Arab countries. The Jews repulsed the attacks, managing to hold the territory assigned by the UN commission and to increase it to some extents. Hundreds of thousands of Arab refugees passed over to the West Bank, held by Jordan, the Gaza Strip, held by Egypt, and into Lebanon, Syria, Jordan, and Iraq. A Palestinian diaspora was formed. The Palestinian Liberation Organization was created in 1964 to further oppose the Israeli state. In 1988 it formed a government in exile (in Tunis) for a Palestinian state.

The four Arab-Israeli wars, that of 1949, that of 1956 (the engagement in concert with France and Britain in the Suez Affair), the Six-Day War of 1967, and the Yom Kippur War of 1973, were outside superpower confrontation in the cold war, but indirectly the superpowers were involved in that they used the region as a testing ground for new weapons and equipment supplied, respectively, by the Soviet Union to the Arabs (Syria principally) and by the United States to Israel.

The Six-Day War was a preemptive strike in anticipation of the buildup of threatening Arab forces. Fighter-bombers attacked Egyptian, Jordanian, Syrian, and Iraqi airfields, destroying machines on the ground, and then mounted an armored blitzkrieg, blocking retreat. The UN cease-fire left them in possession of the West Bank and the Golan Heights. The Arabs responded by raids designed to keep Israel mobilized, until the 1970s when they had obtained from the Soviet Union a defense capability against hostile aircraft by a whole range of missiles and cannon specialized for detection and destruction, with antitank-guided weapons on the ground. The Six-Day War could not be repeated, but by 1973, the Arabs were ready to attack to recover the ground they had lost. It was a hard-fought encounter in which they nearly succeeded. The Israelis, however, improvised countermeasures to frustrate the effectiveness of the Soviet weapons sufficiently to deploy infantry and machine-gun fire on the ground to open a way for tanks. In June 1982, responding to Palestinian artillery and rocket attacks on settlements in northern Galilee, they invaded southern Lebanon, with a mobility that took them to the outskirts of Beirut in less than five days, using sophisticated devices to enhance protection and with even more ingenious deployment of advanced technology to pinpoint the exact position of Mobile SAM systems, so that air strikes in the Bekaa valley knocked out most of the Syrian systems in a single day. In all these exchanges, the superpowers, who enjoyed that status by their superiority in research and development, were able to see the most advanced military technology tested in action.

The Afghanistan War started with something like the movement of tanks into Hungary and Czechoslovakia to reinforce and save a Communist regime. The analogy may be in purpose, but is inappropriate in more than scale. For the Soviet Union had no comparable hold on Afghanistan, and poor understanding of the situation in the country. It was unaware of what it would incur by the intervention, as were the Americans in Vietnam; that is the preferable analogy. In the days of the British Empire, there was rivalry between Britain and Russia for possession or position in Afghanistan, where the monarchy held the country together by managing the divisions of tribes and factions. That depended on an efficient army and air force, which the Germans had helped in building up in the 1930s. In the 1950s, the need for modernization required assistance, and an appeal for military aid to the United States was refused. The Soviet Union was the only alternative, with the consequence that officers were trained in Russia to use equipment supplied and serviced by Russia. The tribes and their chiefs were like the armies and warlords of the Middle Ages: the monarch was only the first among equals. The tensions, assassinations, revolts, and reprisals maintained a state of turbulence and anarchy that amounted to chaos by the time the Russians moved in on December 27, 1979. With more than five thousand advisers in the country, some of them murdered from time to time, the Russians had a similar commitment to the Americans in Vietnam. In a similar way, it became a military operation in a political vacuum against the guerrilla forces of the tribes, who were armed through Pakistan by the Americans, even after detente had reached the Gorbachev-Reagan level of mutual trust. As in Vietnam with the Americans, the intervention ended in frustration and unconditional withdrawal, completed by February 15, 1989.

The Iraqi invasion of Iran in 1980 was miscalculated and gratuitous, initiated by Saddam Hussein in his bid for supremacy in the Arab world of the Middle East. He was a maleficent rising star far more like Eden's second Hitler than Nasser ever was or would have been, and not recognized as such until very late in his day, after the futile and inconclusive war that lasted eight years and was an example of unlimited war, with over a million killed and the (disowned) use of poison gas by Saddam Hussein. It was largely a war of fanatical Iranian youth in greater number against superior Iraqi airpower and firepower. It was generally known as the Gulf War, until that name was superseded in the virtual sequel, when Saddam Hussein miscalculated again and invaded Kuwait. In this case, there was the application of a UN military sanction to halt and reverse a violation of international law, which was mistakenly assumed to have taken place in Korea. The influence of the United States was again paramount, but not truly devious as before. The logistics and the brief fighting engagement exhibited and tested in performance state-of-the-art military technology. That was of more value to research and development than the political success in halting the aggression proved to be in the short run to the hopes invested and many of the interests involved.

The Falklands War was an almost incredible feat of British all-round military professionalism, carried out by a task force operated from a remote home base that had to act against an enemy in prepared positions supplied by home bases close at hand. In military terms, the disadvantage was forbidding, even when men and equipment had been transported and were in position: there was not the superiority assumed to be required to dislodge an enemy in position. If the achievement was an unquestionable triumph in every military sense and the political resolve that initiated and sustained the expedition was remarkable, it remained a post-colonial response, a throwback detached from NATO and the post-war remodeling of European armed forces. Like the Suez Affair it evinced inappropriate adherence to a role without a part. True, the small Falklands population to a man or a woman wanted the British connection and craved British protection, felt as British as Ulster or Barbados, and would have felt betrayed if surrendered to a foreign power; but the response to that in the changed conditions of the world was a negotiated accommodation secured and maintained under international auspices, not unilateral conquest and reconquest. Efforts were certainly made to bring about such an accommodation, and failed; but it is questionable whether they were pursued patiently and wholeheartedly enough to succeed. The great cost of the expedition and the greater cost of improving and securing the restored position for the future was a substantial tax to be paid for stubborn denial of the truth. If it could have happened, it would have been far cheaper and materially better for all concerned if the entire tiny population had been offered the chance of resettlement in, say, New Zealand, each with a very generous endowment. That would not have been betrayal, and would have left the Maldivas to the Argentinians, turning the other cheek after a slap in the face.

These wars were limited in the sense that they did not resort to the use of nuclear weapons, held in reserve by the superpowers for mutual deterrence. They were not necessarily limited in duration or carnage, destruction, devastation, violence, or cunning. Of the eight wars looked at here, three evidence the cold war conducted by fighting grievously bloody conflicts; two were post-colonial operations. The first Gulf War began like the second, which evoked unique international police action; the Israeli wars, occasioned by unprecedented circumstances, displayed the limits of defense by attack. The Clausewitz model of limited war, that is, strict conduct of it as a means to a political end for which it was undertaken may apply to half to them. Most were in effect research and development laboratories for perfecting modern weapons of destruction and defense. A limited war controlled by a political purpose is not necessarily justified by that purpose, a just war; that is an entirely different question. The first Gulf War with Iran had a political purpose, but it was neither controlled by that purpose nor justified by it.

## Guerrilla War

Most of the postwar colonial wars were fought by guerrilla forces or against them, and the only reason for giving them a separate classification is to bring out the distinctive character of guerrilla fighting and its special place in postwar politics. An intransigent government will suppress political opposition as necessarily subversive. Opposition is thereby forced to become so, either driven underground or, especially in a favorable terrain, taking to the hills or the bush to mount an armed rebellion. Political opposition under a Marxist government or a military dictatorship could not be a political party. Thus a running guerrilla rebellion (like Napoleon's "Spanish ulcer") was a general pattern in this period of the alternative to democracy.

It is significant that even within Europe at the end of the war, when the inevitability of defeat was recognized, SS leaders were secretly organizing arms caches and cadres for recruitment and training of a resistance movement to operate against Russian occupation. The British Special Operations Executive, set up in July 1940, organized resistance to the Nazis and Japanese worldwide, and was not disbanded until 1946. The office may have been aware of the activities of the "stay behind" Nazi anti-

Communist zealots, as probably was the CIA. When the Russians had occupied Eastern Europe, and were known to be reinforcing their military capability, the ruling Christian Democratic government of Italy felt vulnerable particularly, for they had the largest and best organized Communist party in the West, led by Palmiro Togliatti, an able, clever, and formidable political opponent. They needed to be prepared, either for a Soviet invasion or for the possibility that Togliatti might stage a coup or win an election. The "stay-behinds" offered a ready-made tool for underground resistance in many contingencies. The Central Intelligence Agency was formed in 1947, strictly to operate outside the U.S.A.; intelligence within the country was in the hands of the FBI. At least one of Italy's innumerable prime ministers in rapid succession knew of the Nazi preparations, and failed to hand the information on. The Red Brigade that kidnapped and murdered Aldo Moro in 1978, after he had gained Communist support for the government, seems to have derived from this Nazi source. The "stay-behinds" were war criminals who saved themselves from arrest because they were useful to the West when the partnership with Russia was broken off, and their names did not have the notoriety of those on trial at Nuremberg. Later, many emigrated to Latin America.

The early outstanding success of the colonial guerrilla "freedom fighters" was the victory of Ho Chi Minh's general at Dien Bien Phu in 1954, which forced France to withdraw from North Vietnam. The Dutch had failed to hold their East Indies territory. Britain was in a more secure position in that the Malay people had received concessions and the prospect of independence. Rebellion was pointless. All the same, a Chinese minority with Communist leadership was in rebellion and had to be dealt with. They had a guerrilla force of some five thousand, and concentrated on gaining the villages and disrupting the economy. The British had been prepared to recognize the Malayan Communist Party (MCP) as a legal political party. This was not enough for the MCP, which had hoped to seize power after the Japanese collapse in 1945. They launched an armed struggle in 1948, and moved into the jungle, whence they could make raids and terrorist attacks. Since four-fifths of the country was jungle and a high mountain rib ran down the center, and with the British authority having to reestablish itself with weak resources after the Japanese occupation, the initial advantage was with the rebellion. The government had to introduce emergency laws, necessarily arbitrary and repressive, while it organized a counterinsurgency campaign. The high commissioner asked for an experienced soldier to be appointed as director of operations, and a retired general, Sir Harold Briggs, was sent in. After a tour of inspection, his plan was first to build up complete security in the populated areas, as a condition of eliminating Communist organizations within them, and cutting off their source of food and supplies. They would then be forced to attack the security forces on their own ground. To demonstrate that this was not merely military rule, he persuaded the high commissioner to integrate civil, police, and military committees, so that control of the emergency was in the hands of the community. From this position in the towns, police and troops could move out and secure bases in the villages, driving the insurgents into the jungle. The food- and supply-denying project proved successful. However, some half million Chinese squatters living on the edges of the jungle were still a source of supply. The government decided to resettle them in groups of about five hundred, where they were under control and protected from intimidation. Insofar as this was forcible removal, it had to be done with tact and compensatory advantages. Nevertheless, attacks continued, and the high commissioner was killed in an ambush on October 6, 1951.

The posts of high commissioner and director of operations were merged, and General Sir Gerald Templer was appointed. He reinforced and revitalized the policy that his predecessors had instituted: the whole community had to be involved in defeating the insurgents and had to succeed before Malaya could get self-government. He promised early elections, with independence to follow. Intelligence was improved and a home guard was formed to free the security forces for offensive action. The insurgents were put on the defensive, and many surrendered. When elections were held in 1955, the victorious party offered an amnesty, which was refused. In the next five years, the security force pushed the insurgents back to the Thai border. It was the control of the military operation by a clearly enunciated, well understood, and generally accepted political aim that ensured ultimate success; and of course the government disposed of resources on a scale with which the insurgents could not compete; but this was not so at the start, and took time to build up, and the insurgents continued to have a secure retreat in the jungle, until good intelligence and superior equipment could deprive them of that advantage.

About the same time in Kenya, similar methods were practiced with success in a very different situation, where the settlers were only 1 percent of the population. An emergency was declared to deal with the emergence of the Mau Mau insurrection of the Kikuyu tribe, not generally supported by other Africans in Kenya. Without effective arms, they resorted to surprise attacks and terrorism. The British government was hampered by fierce criticism from the white settlers to their policy of integrating a civil and military approach—"going soft" on Mau Mau. It was best part of a year before the administration was in a position to deal effectively with the uprising, which meanwhile had perpetrated massacres and successful attacks. Nairobi was first purged of Mau Mau suspects and made secure. The country was divided into areas in which policing was normal, and those that were in effect war zones. Devices were used to simulate Mau Mau gangs and gain intelligence and give security to dissidents within the tribe. Mau Mau was put on the defensive and gave up by 1960. The important point was that stringent repressive measures under emergency suspension of law was complemented by political and economic reforms to meet legitimate grievances, reforms that were far-reaching concessions. In effect, Mau Mau lost and gained. What the administration lost could not have been held for long anyway.

What happened in Malaya in 1948 echoed in 1962, when the prime minister of Malaya wanted to bring Sarawak, Brunei, and North Borneo (remaining British colonies) into a Malaysian federation. This was agreeable to the British and to the majority of the populations concerned, but strongly opposed by the president of Indonesia, Ahmed Sukarno, whose plan for a greater Indonesia included some of these territories. A revolt was brought about in Brunei at the end of 1962, which gained initial success. The British sent in forces from Singapore to restore the rule of the sultan, which was achieved in six days. Sukarno opened a new offensive with a guerrilla attack on western Sarawak. The new confrontation was committed to the commander of the British forces in Borneo, Major General Walker, who with limited resources had to build protection for Malays, Chinese, and indigenous population over a mainly jungle territory of great extent. Within that territory there was also a subversive Communist movement, mainly supported by the Chinese, a clandestine force of some twenty-four thousand. Walker had experience of the counterinsurgency tactics employed in Malaya in the previous decade, and he applied them to his task. He instituted a six-point campaign: unified operation; accurate intelligence; speed, mobility, and flexibility; secure bases; domination of the jungle; winning the hearts and minds of the people. Particular attention was given to the last point, on which all depended in the long run. Army and police personnel were sent into the villages to protect and advise the people, and to offer medical and agricultural help, planting small teams to live and work among the villagers. By the end of 1963 the Communist guerrillas were contained, and the Malaysian federation was given support. Sukarno responded by reinforcing the guerrillas with regular Indonesian troops. Britain, Malaysia, New Zealand, and Australia contributed to Walker's resources massively, and he continued his six-point plan. Sukarno lost support in Indonesia, and his successor sought peace with Malaysia, which was concluded in a treaty on August 11, 1966. Denis Healey, British defense secretary called this "one of the most efficient uses of military forces in the history of the world."

In another part of the world, Latin America, the Argentinian Che Guevara, made a notable contribution to guerrilla thinking with his *Guerrilla Warfare* (1960). He had experience of it in Guatemala in 1954, and he was Fidel Castro's chief aide in the Cuban Revolution in 1956–1959. Guevara's key idea was that a small band, the *foco*, operating in a rural terrain as the nucleus of a guerrilla force, could start a successful Communist revolution. They would be the "seed-corn of revolution." Castro, starting with a force of twenty men that had taken to the hills from the city and were without military training and equipment, attacked the largest military forces in Central America and the Caribbean under the regime of the Cuban dictator Fulgencio Batista, who was supported by the United States. This unlikely handful survived to attract recruits and in less than three years to drive out Batista, dominant in the island since the 1930s. The key to their success was less the doctrine of Guevara's *foco* than the collapse of confidence in Batista and consequently of morale and the political will to resist. Guevara himself set out in 1965 with his *foco* to prove his case, and eventually revolutionize Latin America. In October 1967 he was captured by Bolivian troops and shot himself at the insistance of an agent of the CIA. Guevara and the prompt success of the Cuban Revolution acting on his doctrine became a legend. The exceptional circumstances made it a fatally misleading model, and the many Latin American revolutionary movements it inspired were hopeless failures.

By 1964, all British African colonies had attained independence, with the exception of Southern Rhodesia, where Ian Smith, with the support of the settlers, declared independence unilaterally. The Portuguese were the last to hold African colonies, Angola and Mozambique. With neighboring territories in native hands, there were bases for guerrilla operations within these remaining colonies. The peasants in Angola mounted a war of extermination against the white farmers, which exacted even more bloodthirsty reprisals from the Portuguese, who reduced the revolt to a small band of guerrillas cut off in the woods northeast of Luanda. Bases in Tanzania and Zambia were sources for the supply of recruits and equipment, material supplies drawn mainly from the Soviet Union and its satellites, and also from China. The situation in Angola was complicated by division of the revolutionary forces into three antagonistic groupings of which the FNLA (1961) was strongest in the north and UNITA (1966) in the south. Early in 1975 Cubans began to arrive, and by the time Portugal had pulled out and a republic was declared toward the end of the year there was a strong Cuban nucleus, which eventually numbered more than twelve thousand, equipped with artillery, armor, and air support. They drove back the UNITA forces in the south until confronted by a South African army. Mozambique in the east was a theater in which there was close cooperation between Mozambique guerrillas with a base in the neighborhood of Tanzania, and the two southern Rhodesian guerrilla groups ZAPU and ZANU. ZANU and the Mozambique Frelimo shared training facilities in Tanzania and Zambia and campaigned in harmony. The original government of the new Mozambique, like that of the new Angola, was Marxist, opposed by Western-backed guerrilla rebels. Mozambique adopted a new constitution in 1990, after the assassination of its notable and popular president, which provided for opposition parties and free elections. Aside from these legal formalities, and frivolous by comparison, has been the seventeen years of civil war waged by the Renamo guerrillas in opposition to the Frelimo government. Two attempts by mediators to end the conflict in 1992 failed, but at the beginning of July the guerrilla leader Alfonso Dhlakama, agreed to an unconditional ceasefire. In what must have been the understatement of all time, he said: "Between brothers, we can find a solution because this war is not good for Mozambique or the whole region." He had efficiently mounted and maintained continuous destruction all these seventeen years, frustrating the government in protection of the population and in all policies for their welfare and future. Renamo offered them nothing better, only continual deprivation, fear, and misery, with frequent massacres and mutilations, and prompt intervention to scotch any hopeful development. No greater contrast to "winning hearts and minds" for revolutionary success could be imagined. He systematically ruined the country and blighted Southern Africa. The UN's FAO estimated that three million people were starving because of blocked supplies. Robert Mugabe moved in several thousand Zimbabwe troops in an endeavor to keep open road and rail links targeted by the rebels. Of all the many horrors in the postwar history of Africa, and they are many and grievous (think of Uganda), this was decidedly the most protracted and the worst.

Before the war, education had been in missionary schools, and several leaders of revolt in British colonies were actually ministers of religion with a theological training. In 1960, the Russians founded a Patrick Lumumba University in Moscow, and within the next two decades tens of thousands of students from Africa, Asia, and Latin America were in Russia for their higher education. The pattern of colonial revolt exhibited communist leadership and training as well as money and equipment, and the sources were China and the Soviet satellites as well as the Soviet Union itself. The

British protectorate of Bechuanaland was exceptional in its smooth transition to independence in 1966 as Botswana. The major part in this was played by Seretse Khama, who was married to an English woman and had trained as a barrister in London. He returned to Bechuanaland in 1956, and five years later founded a Democratic party. A large part of the country is the Kalahari Desert, and it is generally afflicted with drought. However, it has proved rich in minerals, and diamonds as the main export has helped to make economic growth probably the most stable in all the former African colonies.

The superpowers, having failed to cooperate in control of the development of the atomic bomb which ended the war with Japan, developed it independently in a way intended to prevent a Third World War by mutual deterrence. Tension and conflict between them would not seek resolution by a resort to arms. This was "cold war," and it excluded limited war and guerrilla war, and civil war outside Europe. This cold war was actually conducted by these military operations, in the attempt, on the one side, to assist the "freedom fighters" against the colonial powers; on the other, to resist and contain the advance of Communism. A third European war was avoided, but all told in the four postwar decades these local wars, most of them a military part of the cold war, killed far more millions than the two world wars together, and maimed more, displaced more refugees, ruined more lives, and devastated more of the human inheritance. In this period, the imbalance of disadvantage was heavily augmented, with the plus of human misery entailed, by rash employment of military means for political ends.

After the collapse of the Soviet Union, with the removal not only of inspiration and aid for communist revolt, but also of totalitarian control, outbreaks of uncontrollable fighting for freedom of a different complexion, where ethnic or religious minorities were unwilling to live under alien rule of a new kind, alarmed Europe and America and Russia by the virulent hatred and reckless inhumanity of the conflicts, as in the former Yugoslavian federation. Saddam Hussein's invasion of Kuwait had been halted by allied action under UN auspices. With NATO released from its former role and not disbanded, with the Western European Union and its connection with defense in Europe without U.S. commitment, and with the continuing Helsinki Conference on Security and Cooperation in Europe, there were ready-made European formations which in partnership with Russia had the makings of a system of European security, which should have been able to take appropriate action to prevent or to check military strife in the region, of the kind that broke out in the Balkans and in the eastern Republics formerly in the Soviet Union. A decision was taken to this end at a meeting of the CSCE in Helsinki in July 1992. In Asia, there had been a deployment of U.S. fleets to contain the Soviet Union. With the withdrawal, the resurgence of Japan, China's military might, and Indonesia, Thailand, and South Korea waxing in wealth and influences, what new security arrangements would be instituted? Economic interdependence was not enough in itself to secure peace. The UN could not be expected to bring this about worldwide, although there had been evidence of new authority, resolution, and effectiveness with a change of the Soviet Union's negative play in the Security Council, and a generally shared political readiness and desire to organize any military international intervention under its auspices and sanction. Regional security systems were as necessary to implement and supplement UN authority and resolutions as local government was to central government within any state—at any time, but most especially in a democracy.

## War Considered

The management of crises and the prevention of violent conflict are matters for local and regional agenda. Agreed procedures, contingency planning, have to be thought out beforehand and put in place with the institutional means in a framework of undertaking and commitment. Intelligence, surveillance, monitoring, graduated response, deterrence: all the ingredients of control are only provided and made available at local levels. In sum, security is a system of systems, and is not to be had by ad hoc improvisation, a mobile international force, or any general formula.

The recrudescence of what may be called ethnic violence has to be pooled with the evidence of the general insecurity of modern life in civilized urban society, the more prosperous it is. There are haves and have-nots in all large urban conglomerates, as well as in the world at large. The prevalence of violence in all its forms on an unprecedented scale is a complex of interrelated problems, inseparable like the environment and development. That is why it does not do to look for "solutions": far too many facts and factors are involved. All that can be done is to devise or put together and put on track vehicles of amelioration and accommodation that can be expected to move in the right direction, and in time bring about a difference that makes all the difference. The Cold War was a crude illustration. When the war-time partnership of the Allies could not be maintained, and embodied in a peace treaty, a holding operation was instituted, which with time and experience did eventuate in a new partnership. Such outcomes can never be final, a "solution." They are forever interim because of continually altering contexts; but what was unattainable may be brought about by measures of reduction or ameliorization.

Consideration of new patterns of defense and of conflict raises the question of war itself in the new world context. Historically, it has been associated with honor and glory and noble causes. There has been the Heroic Age and the Age of Chivalry. Heroes of nations have been victorious fighting men: from Alexander the Great the roll is long and majestic, excites emulation, and teaches virtues and values. The Roman legion was a supreme killing-machine that established Rome as a super-power and united the nations in a Pax Romana. Since it is the stuff of conventional history, it is not necessary to underline the influence, directly and indirectly, of war on human thinking and behavior and standards of conduct. The "supreme sacrifice" for one's country is the last secular commandment. "Virtue" is by definition what becomes a man, and that was thought of in terms of strength and valor and endurance, the qualities first of a warrior, second of an athlete.

New thinking about war was recognized as required by the new context that emerged at the end of World War II: the magnitude of destruction in prospect with the development of new weapons. If duelling was banned in the nineteenth century as no longer tolerable in a modern society, by how many more magnitudes is war intolerable in the twentieth. Even in the ancient world, Cicero had argued that even an unjust peace was of more benefit than the justest war; although he had also argued that wars ought to be undertaken for the sake of living without injustice. The contradiction is a dilemma, the human predicament.

# 21

# The State in Question

## Improvements, Not Progress

The human branch in the biological evolution of species is established by the survival of the genetic pools in populations culturally adapted to their geographical habitats. There is no preformed projected perfection towards which evolution carries the species forward, and therefore no possible historical progress of the kind thought of in the nineteenth century, a conjunction of evolution and enlightenment. Biologically, the habitat of a species in nature is constituted by other species in a neighborhood which furnishes given resources for their organic needs, and where they have to adapt to conditions in great part determined by the behavior and interaction of the diverse species in the community. This is the ecosystem and is constituted by interactions of the organic constituents with one another and with their physical environment. It is a stable system, yet in continuous change, since the members of its community are agents of change. The human species emerged from these universal natural conditions, and is glimpsed in prehistoric times in the early ages classified by primitive tools close to such conditions, or more fugitively in surviving tribes found inhabiting parts of a tropical forest in symbiosis with nonhuman species in the ecosystem.

In historic times, there can be thought a parallel when there are contacts and interaction between populations adapted to different cultures. History in general is the course of these interactions, with the communication of discoveries and inventions, and their applications and development. A civilization may resemble an ecosystem, in that its culture is a complex in which subsidiary cultures of constituent peoples have been assimilated over time. The Bronze Age civilizations, and their contribution to the universality of the culture of Hellas, is a rich example. These happenings occur sporadically, contributing to particular developments of the species that are genetically founded but not specifically determined.

The three Mediterranean models described in Part One were brought about empirically by particular contacts and interactions of cultures, until far enough developed to be apprehended conceptually and used to project and forward an ideal version to mold and promote the genius and the mission of a people. Ideals that have been adopted may in time be abandoned or rejected. It is normal to review and revise an initiative in the light of the experience its pursuit has brought about. In the postwar period now under review, the Roman ideal of imperialism has been abandoned by European imperial states in the light of that experience. Nor can Zionism or the Christian faith maintain the claim to universality that was its justification. If the ideal of Hellenic culture still holds, it is modified by a wealth of subsequent experience and achievement into which it has led.

The idea of progress, for example, as developed by Condorcet, is a review and revision of what may be thought of as Bacon's initiative for the advancement of learning. The Enlightenment was generally attacked for substituting a religion of progress for Christianity. Condorcet's "social art" and Pope's "science of Human Nature" are loose generalities with a misleading unitary implication. Condorcet wrote: "The labours of recent ages have done much for the progress of the human mind, but little for the perfection of the human race." Since his day, more, much more, has been done for the progress of the human mind, and the perfection of the human race has been dropped from the agenda. Sociology, in spite of Comte, did not provide a handbook of social management, but disparate studies available for different purposes. The "science of man" consists of a score of specialisms that do not constitute a single discipline, all of which are relevant and essential to an informed concept of human nature. That concept is unitary in embrace of one integrated body of phenomena, without implying a consummation of something in the making, an end in view, a teleology. The planet earth, time and place, the physiology of the species, are human universals, the infrastructure of human existence, so to speak. Human conduct, as adaptation to those particular conditions for survival, is also universal. What is particular in those conditions is not so, by definition. In that sense, the human condition and human behavior are not uniform. The diversity extends from close comparability of human with other species in a natural ecosystem to the population of a modern industrial society in an international world habitat, the ultimate difference between nature and history, with a tendency and trend in history not of progress towards human perfection but towards forms and manners of convergence by interaction. History is the story of a human partnership with nature that eventually brings this about. This progress is in the multiplication of means which are not means to a specific end, but resources for use or enjoyment; always ad hoc, never ad quod. The core of this history is the history of discoveries and inventions, "Progress of the Human Mind'; but that is not finally separable from other events and contexts, political and cultural. History has its specific ecosystem of interconnections and interactions.

Human nature is in the first instance a natural product, and in the sequel an historical product—and therefore unfinished business, and open-ended. Time and place are variables in the infrastructure; the planet and human physiology, the constants. History, and geography, its other eye, bring in the view of the course of the continuous change that brings about the transformation of human kind from primitives to persons of multiple collective capability. The explosion of knowledge and its consequences have brought the world to the point where that capability requires responsible decisions, virtually of all on behalf of all, including posterity.

With the collapse of communism as practiced in the Soviet Union, general attention was called to the abuse rather than use of the state by the Communist Party to provide a legal mask for arbitrary totalitarian control. This stirred into prominence, particularly in Britain under Margaret Thatcher, criticism of even democratic socialism as an abuse of the state, intolerable to free citizens. On other grounds also, especially in the context of the European Economic Community and political union, the state has been put in question as an institution to serve modern political and economic purposes and needs. The state has been the maker of modern history as the pivot of political decisionmaking, whatever the character of the government.

## Society's Functions

In 1969, a revolutionary coup put General Mohammed Siad Barré in dictatorial control of Somalia, and he established a regime of "divide and rule" that disintegrated the clans and allowed him to oppress and exploit the country until he was driven out in 1991. The general rejoicing was short-lived, for his legacy of division and an abundance of arms rapidly led to total anarchy. Food was obtained by the gun. People looted to live, and freely used arms to obtain what they needed or wanted, increasing their armed power by the ample supply of diverse weapons. The state ceased to exist, and what food there was had soon to be sent in as aid from Saudi Arabia and Kenya. Aid agencies such as CARE and the Red Cross and Save the Children could not effect delivery to the unarmed in a climate of incessant sporadic shooting. Thousands died of starvation or bullets. Not until March 1992 did the UN intervene, sending a diplomat and personnel to arrange ad hoc security for delivery of humanitarian supplies and monitoring of their distribution by aid agencies. The long delay had allowed the vicious circle of shooting for food, and the supply of food from outside to harden into a downward spiral hard to break. At the political heart of the strife was the division between the interim ruler who had been appointed and a rival war-lord who would not acknowledge him. The social philosophy of the Somalis is said to be formulated thus: Somalia against the world; my clan against Somalia; my family against the clan, my brother and myself against the family; myself against my brother. That is, no man trusts his fellow. In the same year, the disintegration of the Yugoslav state exhibited similar phenomena of social self-destruction.

The state is instituted to establish and maintain order, and is provided with the means to do so. This is an act of social cooperation and coordination, and like all such acts has to be regularly reenacted to maintain its effectiveness. The Somali state under Siad Barré was identifiable with the order it enforced, which was also the law and in that sense only was it a rule of law. By contrast, a constitutional democracy, while it is necessarily also an enforceable order, is only the fundamental or ground law, the law regulating lawmaking and law enforcement; in that sense it is the rule of law.

The state as an absolute, equivalent to an imposition or order, and the state as an institution for enacting and enforcing laws by agreed rules are distinct in theory and in practice. The difference between a dictatorship or autocracy and a democracy is of course a commonplace, but it is not as generally recognized that this is a difference in the state; that a government of a democratic state, if it violates the rule of law, reduces the state from an institution for that purpose to a mere imposition of order— not in itself wholly negative, but wholly different. The difference is seen most clearly in the exceptional case, when an aggrieved party, particularly a group interest, having exhausted all means of redress the law provides, in desperation breaks the law to register protest. The state in a democracy is bound to punish the infraction, to enforce the rule of law, but in doing so probably violates what the rule of law is instituted to secure by social cooperation, that is, the reciprocal benefit of interdependent interests. The contradiction is not too subtle nor too rare to count, for it has been a principal way by which the rule of law has been made more inclusive in its justice.

The state functions through its personnel, public servants of whatever grade paid out of the public revenue, its functions are specified, and mainly departmentalized. A particular function may be put in question as not needed or objectionable, and this may lead to its withdrawal and exclusion; or it may remain controversial. An effective exclusion of a function may be seen as creeping subversion, diminution of the state power. Philosophical or theoretical anarchy proposes complete subversion. If it is virtually a sociological law that forms of social cooperation and coordination have regularly to be reinstituted, so institutions have regularly to be reenacted to continue to serve their purpose, and if that rarely happens from within, this restructuring of the public service by changes in personnel articulated by key persons may be one way of doing it. On the other hand, it may threaten to undermine the service, as its critics say. At any rate, this is a changing context in which the traditional functions of society must be reconsidered. There are mainly six: defense and security; administration of justice; relations with other states; trade and industry; health and welfare; culture.

Clausewitz formulated the main point in military theory: war was to be strictly controlled and limited by a political purpose, and only engaged in as a people's war in a national, not a dynastic, interest. This moved defense as a social function into a modern context.

Whether the two world wars were precipitated by Germany's fear of encirclement or a German bid for the hegemony of Europe may remain an unprofitable debate. What is of importance is to recognize that the second war introduced a new factor, the invention and use of weapons of mass destruction; both set a new context for defense and at the same time carried on the pattern of European confrontation formed in the past centuries, maintained by bids and fears of bids for hegemony but now conducted worldwide in wars fought under cover of a cold war maintained by two superpowers who disposed of means of mutual annihilation. The containment of Communism by the West and the undermining of Western hegemony by Communists in this new-old context cost an unprecedented expenditure of blood and treasure, an historic travesty of "the prudent views of modern politics" (Hume) that far exceeded "old, unhappy, far-off things, And battles long ago," including those two world wars. With detente, consummated in the disintegration of the Soviet Union and the general collapse of Communism as a discredited political force, the politico-military context was definitively altered, ceasing to be structured by a specific confrontation, and with spreading capability for the production of weapons of mass destruction. In principle this was a shift from defense as a principal function of the state to international security as a global problem and task for all states, requiring new thinking and new institutions.

Events that focused attention on this shift, and put it on the global agenda along with the environment and development were first the invasion of Kuwait by Iraq, and subsequently the disintegration of Yugoslavia in fighting out of control, with consequences not confined to those immediately engaged: in particular, two and a half million refugees thrown on the outside world, most with their homes destroyed. In these circumstances, the UN was found apt for the role for which it had been instituted, and there was available the cooperation and coordination required to begin to reenact its purpose. At the same time, the forces of the NATO integrated alliance, no longer in confrontation with the Warsaw Pact, had to be reduced and, insofar as not disbanded like those of the Warsaw Pact, reconstructed for different employments and deployments, in the new context of UN crisis management, tension defusion, and the monitoring of peace-keeping agreements. In short, in the long term states are called on to provide the armed means of policing the world under the auspices of the UN, and therewith to find their own protection. Control of the production and availability of weapons and war potential of all descriptions is at the heart of this enterprise and its persistent difficulties. It is an international disarmament offensive that may well be defeated. What is certain is that national defense as the first duty of the national state is outmoded by the general need for international security.

The other part of law and order, a part that cannot be internationalized, is internal security, although that also has an international dimension in terrorism. Violence has escalated in the modern world, and defies old forms of control. It has always existed within families and villages as well as in dangerous parts of cities, and been inflamed by drink. The incidence is more general, drug abuse more potent, example epidemic through mass media. Younger age groups are involved, and the police themselves are liable to become targets of guerrilla war in zones of the cities. With mass unemployment, a sizable proportion of school-leavers have no prospect of a stake in society, and are in limbo.

The situation is complicated further by the need to provide bodyguard protection for citizens exposed for one reason or another to personal threats from fanatical groups at home or abroad. Protection of the public by the state has been made more than a routine charge, since it has not merely to be provided on an augmented scale; it is out of control unless and until means are found and applied and funded for greatly reducing the need. That requires simultaneous application of diverse remedies on several fronts. One of these fronts involves the second principal function of the state, the administration of justice.

Foreign relations mean knowledge and contact. Today, correspondents are more useful and important than diplomats. They keep the public informed, if not in touch, and when prime ministers move around the world as they frequently do, they are accompanied by correspondents. Great foreign ministers of the past, in influence not always for the good, like Metternich or Lord Palmerston or Edward Grey, are not outmoded reputations without any modern parallel. Cordell Hull, who was Roosevelt's secretary of state throughout, was far more than his agent in what he accomplished in international affairs, including his part in foundation of the UN. Henry Kissinger, modeled as he was on nineteenth-century exemplars, figured in more headlines of the world press during his time than any other name. But it is not the noise in the world, the rank in general reputation, that counts historically. Rather, it is particular achievements, the work of patient far-sighted diplomacy. Willy Brandt was chancellor, not foreign minister, but it was his far-sighted *ostpolitik* that served to stabilize with concrete reassurance sensitive relations with the Soviet Union in default of a peace treaty, followed up by Genscher throughout a time of many disconcerting changes in rapid succession. If Gorbachev was outstanding for his achievement in transforming relations between the Soviet Union and the West, his foreign minister, Shevardnadze, was the one who underpinned that by his close personal contacts with other foreign ministers that developed mutual understanding and trust. That is the value of the regular and frequent bringing together of the foreign ministers of the EEC, when they plan an agenda and converse in private. This continual mutual consultation has replaced rapprochement. That is what is new.

Modern governments stand or fall by their management of the economy. Yet that is what some say is no business of government, and should be left to market forces and free enterprise. To do so is, and has always been, impossible, although controversial since early nineteenth century. In France, it had long been deeply established and far-reaching. In England, it began in effect with Chadwick's unacknowledged application of Bentham's formula, investigate-legislate-inspect, and its chief characteristic was the institution of inspection into administration. There had for centuries been central and local forms of government, public and private social activities, with customary procedures for their regulation of their relations. The "new state philosophy" was a growth of that stem and withering of the mercantile predilection for monopoly. As between central and local government, there was a natural division between the collection of information knowledge on which instruction is based, and a diffusion of power to give it effect. Supervision was taken care of by inspection. This might be the practical way in which things were constrained to happen. Theory and controversy, as usual, occupied other ground, roughly the organic or historical and the utilitarian or incremental. Entrenched paternalism did not take kindly to pragmatic realism; but neither did the latter want to do other than adopt and adapt what was on the ground. Traditionalists did not favor new state institutions in response to new social problems, and liberals had no patience with unnecessary government interference with personal liberty. The slogans and war cries, collectivism versus individualism or socialism versus capitalism, of course did stand for actual opposition as well as acrimonious polemics, but total laissez faire was totally impracticable and totalitarian rule as unlikely. Meanwhile, the increase of state intervention was unstoppable, and new departments of state were established in the administration.

When the Wall Street crash of 1929 involved the world in a chronic slump and ruinous international competition for an increasing share of diminishing trade returns, it was Roosevelt's New Deal and Hitler's National Socialism, and marginally the ideas of Maynard Keynes, and eventually World War II, that alone offered the rudiments of an effective response. The war ended with the imposed controls in place, charged with planning and supervising the return to normality, as it was phrased. Yet it is experience that the market's failure to deliver is endemic. Investment in training and research and development tends to be undersupplied by the market because industrial firms have to give short-term considerations great weight.

Unemployment is the gravest economic problem, for at a chronically high level it undermines and imperils the whole fabric of society. It hosts a plague of problems. Moreover, full employment is likely to prove a forlorn hope in the modern world. A safer, always attainable, target is maximum employment, which the market left to itself will never attain. There is no limit in sight to work that needs to be done and can be done to inestimable social advantage. This will most certainly not be done without government initiative, planning, and funding, which encourages and enlists private participation. A dogma of the "mixed economy" is that this is a duty of the state to its people and their posterity. There is the National Audit Office in with the duty to monitor the effectiveness of government spending.

The "mixed economy" is by no means yet a model. The new international economic order is far from what it states. On the contrary, the near half-century of vicissitudes is an unhappy story of many grave blunders. Partly of course this is merely the human lifestyle, but mainly it is inevitable that a radical and global change of this magnitude in traditional ways gets established only by trial and error. Thus: the succession of misconceptions and mistakes in programs of aid to Third World countries; the rash expansion of credit facilities, and escalation of irredeemable debt; the era of takeovers, mergers, and diversification, leading to plundering and unmanageability and overstretching, not competitive efficiency, nor the advantage of size; the restructuring of the stock-market. There was a mixture of genuine trial and error and tendencies inherent in institutions. Predominant was the over-mighty corporation with its hierarchical management structure and trading empire, foreseen by James Burnham in *The Managerial Revolution* (1941) as the doom of capitalism. The blurb on the jacket reads: "The capitalist system will soon disappear. Continuous mass unemployment, colossal unpayable debts, wholesale destruction of food while thousand starve, show that it no longer works. The future governing class will not be the possessors of wealth, but the possessors of technical or administrative skill. Already they alone are satisfied, keen and confident." The final statement of the book: "There is no background against which to judge the human situation as a whole. It is merely what it happens to be." The implication of the statement was that his prediction was not a fate, but a warning. A central point he makes relevant to state intervention, and explicates by an analysis of Roosevelt's New Deal and the entrenched opposition of capitalists to it, is that the state has an inherent tendency to consolidate the managerial revolution by intervening to inhibit autonomous institutions like trade unions and the influence of independent private capitalists who together work to maintain the "limited state." The administration favors the rule of administrators. The analysis is a clue to the folly of government policies aimed at the destruction of socialism and trade unionism. State intervention has liabilities, and rules of appropriate conduct, for like all institutions the state is manned and operated by fallible individuals. Another factor in the vicissitudes of the period, and covered in that final statement, was the Wall Street crash of October 1987. It was not explicable in rational terms. Like the South Sea Bubble of 1720, it was a frenzy of panic selling, a madness, not an error, but periodic evidence against the "efficient market" and the sufficiency of the "unseen hand."

Against these follies, failures, liabilities, and uncertainties, there was taking shape a model of the modern responsible joint-stock company, complementary to the model of a modern limited state. This was mainly a product of business studies and business schools as they worked over the experiences of trial and error and the vagaries of the period. The "mixed economy" has a managed economy, with the managers in government, in business, in trade unions—and ultimately in the public as consumers, the market. Underlying this partnership, as its basis, was the assumption of a shared social responsibility. This had been at least nominally present in the British institution of NEDC, the Council set up in 1962 to advise the government on economic policy, and scornfully repudiated by the Thatcher administrations on the assumption that boards of management managed companies, and governments managed civil servants, and trade unions managed obstruction.

The recognized social responsibility of company managers was not merely, if mainly, to and for their workforce for wages and conditions of work and some provision for their welfare, but also to society at large for the consequences of their operations, such as their consumption of scarce or irreplaceable resources and their disposal of waste, with its effects on land, water, and air. All this was elementary but far-reaching, and reduced from the general to the particular, and made explicit, for the first time in recent years. It is the discovery of a new social dimension of free enterprise. Parts of it might be made compulsory by legislation, but on the whole it was to be left in the first place to self-regulation and the development of prudent and rewarding practices in the business community and the workplace, fruits of good management as studied in business schools and exemplified in behavior of reputable firms. In this way was being formed a model of the socially responsible company in the mixed economy, complementary to the pragmatic limited state in the new international economic order being formed with the new outlook and constraints of postwar industrialized western states.

The principal concept in the new thinking of the business schools was the idea of the workforce as human capital, a primary asset of the company for careful investment by top management in procedures that maximized the use to available human resources by infusing incentives that improved productivity, which was the key to the rise in society of "real wages" (purchasing power). To bring this about required changes in the attitude of management that induced responsive changes in the attitudes of all the operatives, that is, there had to be an openness at the top that took the whole company into its confidence. This would be done most effectively by regular disclosure of board policies and decisions diffused in information available to all personnel—remote from the original free enterprise to hire and fire.

New attitudes and concepts on these lines in business schools and board rooms was complemented by new thinking in trade unions and in the sociology of industrial relations.

Producers have to respond to consumer demands, to secure their market, regulated by pricing. Unionized partners in production secure their jobs regardless, by restrictive practices and demarcation. The ultimate common interest that makes them partners willy nilly is at odds with their immediate separate interests in what they put in and get out. This makes the system that is a necessary social function liable to mutual frustration and to that extent disastrously inefficient. A reform of industrial relations must aim in the national interest to reconcile their common interest and their separate interests, which are irremovable as such, and to do so not ad hoc by arbitration in a particular case, but decisively and permanently in a general reorganization of the relations between board room and workplace and between profit and pay, neither of which is determined by the market.

The "mixed economy" as remodeled management of joint-stock companies for maximum performance with social responsibility in a state that invests in maintaining planned maximum employment and funds maintenance of employability is likely to be capped in the next century in a borderless globalized economy, already in the first stages of development by certain firms exporting specialized branded products of quality. This is the new international economic order built from the ground, rather than the postwar American Dream.

Finally, it should be stated that the concepts "capitalism" and "socialism," and the polemics of capitalism versus socialism (ending with "the end of history"), are outmoded by the regime of the mixed economy. The idea that the postwar political consensus engendered a sloppiness only to be redressed by uncompromising confrontation (which undermines the middle ground on which viable democracy stands) has to be reconsidered in the light of the reconstruction in the making of a mixed economy. Similarly with the idea that "privatization" is a release from government control and a reversal of nationalization. For whether it is the introduction of business management in the public sector or the handing over of a public utility into private hands and competition, government does so on stipulated conditions and subject to legally enforceable regulations, with compliance duly monitored: assuming that this is what really happens, it is merely a revised modernized version of "nationalization." The mischief at issue is "privatization" as an ideology, doctrinally imposed for its own sake in all circumstances, as a ready-made prescription for efficiency. Thus generalized, it is abused; in particular use, it is fully justified, and eminently rational.

There remain for consideration the social functions of "welfare and culture." From being virtually run as a spoils system, the state has over the years come to be principally concerned with social services, of which the relief of poverty dated from the first Elizabeth, and public health and education in the last century and this. The welfare state has been, perhaps generally, recognized as a completion of this trend, and regarded by some as a perversion of society, still resisted and rejected in the U.S.A., against encroachments, but also with a growing demand for its provisions. In Britain at least the question is how its growing requirements can possibly be funded, together with other increasing calls on the public revenues, and rising costs all round. Any government is entangled in the same dilemma: partially dismantling the welfare state and reneging on its social pledge, or raising taxes to meet the obligation or providing welfare at the cost of other urgent claims. There is room here for the advocacy of different policies, but not for mere adversarial opposition. A similar change in democratic politics to that in industrial relations has taken place in different circumstances, but in the context of the same events.

The underlying social philosophy of the welfare state is often mistaken, and is of fundamental importance. Made explicit and insistently stressed in the training of social workers and of counselors is respect for the autonomy of clients: what both services are instituted to do is to enable people to help themselves and to facilitate this, never to do for them what they can do or must be enabled to do, whether it be to make a decision (counseling) or to earn a living and pay bills. The line of least resistance is always to do things for people, which makes a fatal tendency in these services that is self-destructive. The principle of responsible autonomy implies a common social morality that is everyone's guide and constraint. Morality has a public and a private hemisphere: the public is the social morality for living and working together—fellow-feeling, good faith, public spirit, self-respect; the private is the virtues and values one chooses to cultivate and cherish, which may be on religious grounds or generally determined by personal feeling and beliefs. Social morality as the ground of social responsibility can and should be part of the publicly provided school program, both within the curriculum and informing the conduct of the school. In a word, self-help is the focus of the properly structured welfare state, instituted by social cooperation and coordination to bring about a society in which people can be truly independent and truly participate.

Escalating costs have to be reduced, if what is socially needed is not to be skimped on. High unemployment is both a steep reduction in revenue and a steep charge. The proposed investment in planned social enterprises to maximize employment would do what can be done to minimize the lost revenue, and the expenditure to bring that about would be investment, not a giveaway.

There is general concern for the control of activities which threaten the extinction of species by reducing stocks to too low a level, whether for ivory or skins or rhinoceros horn or fish supplies. This is not welfare, but existence. The innumerable species in the animal world have together the inestimable value of biological diversity, to which the human species owes its own existence. The dominion which man was allegedly given by the creator over fish and fowl and beast and every living creature misrepresents his status in the natural world, of which he is a product, not the purpose.

The anthropological understanding of culture is the total traditional way of life of a community, derived from the ancestors. The culture of a simple tribal community can be thought of as a very late development from what started when apes that came down from the trees began to colonize the African plains. This was a radical departure from the habitat they were adapted to, and required as radical a change in their behavior to survive. That change began with innovative behavior reinforced and advanced by social learning in elementary communication among members of the group. This slow, cumulative advance was overtaken cumulatively in prodigious length of evolutionary time by a genetic transformation of the physique of these apes; from one line of these the human type derived. Thereafter, with the development of language, social learning far outpaced genetic evolution.

Anthropological studies have shown that this development issued in widely diverse patterns of culture in simple communities, some not merely different, but seemingly perverse, contrary to the normal functions of a society. With increases in population and in feeding capacity and other skills, civilizations were established, again diverse in character. When John Locke wrote in his *Second Treatise on Civil Government*, "In the beginning of all the world was America," he meant that what was to be seen in America as first discovered was "a pattern of the first ages in Asia and Europe." Indeed, there were the several different civilizations found by the Spaniards, and the several tribal cultures adapted to different regions of North America that the other colonists found: altogether, a panorama to exemplify the early course of social development, encountered on one continent by the more advanced Europeans.

When these Europeans came to use the word "civilized," they did not have in mind a civilization, but characteristics they attributed to what a civilization should be, which might summarily be called "humane," having the properties proper to human beings. The difference was between a particular civilization as established and civilization in general, a concept. That concept as it emerged historically was vague and perhaps arbitrary, attributing "barbarity" unjustifiably to earlier, simpler cultures. However, it was an effort to grasp something that is not merely achievable by cultivated humanity, but essentially what is distinctive of the species, what makes it truly *primus inter pares*. Fundamentally, that is human capabilities, and fundamental to that is a learning capacity (furthered by language) that gains from history, the experience of the race, insights into certain permanent social conditions of stability, security, the primary aspiration of developing societies.

What in these pages has been called "civilizing culture" refers to acquired constituent items of this general civilization, such as secularization, the rule of law, freedom of the arts and sciences, and, more recently, a mixed economy and social responsibility for the welfare of the disadvantaged—all functions of the state. The prevalent assumption that "democracy" and "human rights" are right and their violation wrong is testimony to a loose assertion of this trend, which is being reduced to practice in terms of the models taking shape. That is, there is a general civilization actually in the making that would be a fulfillment of human nature and be a concept in people's heads worldwide. Such a global civilization would not replace cultures and subcultures of nations and communities, and all particular forms of association, but they would not be expected to be inconsistent with the civilization that transcended them.

Prominent in the code of civilized rules and values is "free speech." Equally asserted and stressed must be its limits. Sartre in *What is Literature?* castigated European liberals for a betrayal of civilization in upholding toleration and free speech that allowed the Nazis to have their say and get their way. Speech can and does deceive, break up, undermine, subvert, brainwash, enslave, kill, and a world of other mischief, more than ever now that it can be rapidly spread around the world, as in the case of Salman Rushdie's book *Satanic Verses*. Milton in the famous *Areopagitica* "speech for the liberty of unlicensed printing," declared confidently: "And though all the winds of doctrine were let loose to play upon the earth, so truth be in the field, we do injuriously by licensing and prohibiting to misdoubt her strength. Let her and falsehood grapple; who ever knew truth put to the worse, in a free and open encounter's Her confuting is the best and surest suppressing."

That has been taken as the sacred gospel of "free speech" by liberals, but we have learned the hard way that to privatize speech and leave it to the open market leaves truth to be too often "put to the worse" something we know too well, yet not well enough to be alerted to deal with it effectively, which is not by "licensing," save perhaps as a temporary measure in particular cases. And the core statement of the *Areopagitica* is central to a civilizing code: "Give me the liberty to know, to utter, and to argue freely according to conscience, above all liberties."

The dilemma is a supreme example of the sociological rule that "solutions" are not to be looked for. To do so assumes that it can be a problem detached from the network of circumstances and social conditions in which it is enmeshed, the "blank sheet" fallacy. By dealing in appropriate ways on many fronts with the relevant circumstances and social conditions that underlie the tactics of using words offensively and defensively to prevail against the "truth," and make one's side triumph when it is evil or wrong, there can be the hope in time to reduce and marginalize this aberration—as it is the only way to deal effectively with crime.

## Sovereignty

The political concept that governs the authority and power to promote and constrain the six functions of society reviewed above, the function of the state, is what is meant by "sovereignty." That is an abstraction. In practice, political authority and power are conferred by constitutional rules and procedures, "fundamental law," under the rule of law.

A marked difference between the United States and Europe is in the centuries of differential development in the Old World, with the result that "harmonization" of behavior by prescription to ensure conditions of cooperation and coordination is hardly comparable. The U.S.A. is ready-made for entry into an inescapable international order, indeed claiming to initiate one and to lead the way, despite a chronic underlying isolationism that would wash its hands of all the intractable problems that surge around as a legacy of the past.

In nation states, newspaper editors have frequently had occasion or reason to label the government with the character of a nanny or governess, because it has substituted a particular duty for a general responsibility. The only political remedy is the protest, the demonstration, the pressure group, on the part of those who suffer; and without that armory, democratic elections help the voter only generally and indirectly. Particular decisions and policies have mostly to be targeted specially. Adopted policies are general ("hard cases make bad laws"); their applicability to a particular purpose may be relevant to central government, and less so to the small print of a social service or a local government—not the least reason for central government to want to reduce toward elimination the powers of local councils.

The rule of law is abused if a state exceeds its general function. That is an addendum to any constitution, whether in writing or not.

Collapse of the postwar order with one of the poles of the two counter-super-powers, leaving the U.S.A. predominant in power and bidding to inaugurate a new world order as the most influential national agent on the international scene, has been most unwelcome in the greater part of the Third World. The order the Cold War had frozen was not to be generally thawed throughout overnight. At the same time, as noted above, client states had tended to alienation from their patrons as their interests were found in practice to diverge, and dependence gave no national satisfaction. Also, detente had relaxed the constraints that had forced issues and compelled taking sides. Historically, there are always short-term and long-term pictures of the world, to which accommodation has to be made all round all the time.

All the same, international cooperation and coordinations for the institution of a new world order is unlikely to be facilitated by a United States that is suspected of manipulating the UN—as in the Korean War, although since then the General Assembly is vastly more representative of the postwar world. Apart from that, the new demands and opportunities have demonstrated the inadequacy and incompetence of a UN deficient in the resources and support afforded by its members. Unless and until that undermining deficiency is remedied, the UN is halted with a limping impotence. The remedy is hardly to be expected without restructuring reform. Since 1945 in San Francisco, when and where the United Nations was formally inaugurated, nearly half a century of accelerating change has transformed the world in which it was set up to be the international organizing center. The overriding task may still be international security, but that same task is not seen as nor thought of as it was then, because it is not the same. Collapse of one pole left a fragmented disorder rife with acute conflict. The two superpowers, whether in cooperation or in conflict, exerted the constraints of an order. The Security Council as the virtual sovereign has been overtaken by time and perpetuates privilege rather than maintains due representation. A constituent assembly is needed, not to draft a constitution for world government, but to invent an institution for global cooperation in a rapidly changing world. Otherwise, there is likely to be only increasing need of dependence on a fragile crutch.

## Social Identity

There are two kinds or two aspects of social identity, cultural and political. German identity was cultural, not national, before Bismarck, in the culture that was common to all the courts of the innumerable principalities. Nationality, territorial frontiers, and a state administration go with political identity, which each of the principalities had. Social identity has also objective and subjective aspects. Objectively, political identity is the nation-state, although few if any of the states so-called are not pluralistic, more or less multicultural. Subjectively, in a collective sense, a minority ethnic group within a state is socially conscious of its separate cultural identity. Historically, such groups are often survivors of "indigenous peoples" who had their own politico-cultural institutions. The loss of these when incorporated in an alien state reduced them to "ethnic" groups. The only "ethnic" group in medieval Europe would be a Jewish community, which was ghettoed, if not underground. The Reformation painted Protestant communities as cultural minorities in Christendom. In Protestant England, Catholics, nonconformist sects, and Jews were the cultural minorities, to be suppressed or accommodated in the state. They are simple prototypes of the ethnic jungle into which dissolution of the Soviet empire plunged a world already plagued by tribal, factional, and sectarian strife. The dreamed of new world order can never be organized from above. The way in which states deal with their ethnic and other minorities is of basic importance, and there are radically different options.

A consideration of these begins with the distinction between the objective and subjective sides of national identity. "Nationality" is what goes down on forms or in passports. "Nationalism" is equivalent to "patriotism," a subjective relation of citizens to their nation and its land, which may vary from willingness to die for its independence, fighting to preserve it, to anxiety to attain a position of strength that will assure its preservation, by aggression if necessary. In between would be indifference to such issues, a lack of patriotism, for whatever reason. Shades of variation in this complexion of patriotism collect and disperse in the population, and may be brought by events to a flush that favors aggression. The predominant shade may vary from one generation to another.

The nation-state, considered the European norm, is an unreal abstraction, for where is the particular state that is homogeneous in the composition of its population? Because European states have in general composed or concealed the ethnic and cultural differences that do obtain in the territories they govern, it is hardly noticed they are there. With ethnic anarchy and ethnic tyranny abroad drawn to everyone's notice so regularly on television screens and in the daily media, there is suddenly Scottish nationalism and Welsh nationalism and even regional aspirations, a general disintegration of the exemplary states de jure in the wake of the disintegration of the Soviet superstate de facto.

In short, ethnicity has high priority on the agenda of world politics; and the old order of containing it without acknowledging it has broken down. What therefore is on the agenda is for each state how to address the problem of minorities wherever in its jurisdiction; and for the United Nations to address the problem whenever and wherever it occurs that states that fail unacceptably in world opinion to deal with their minority problems. Simplified: "minority rights" is the founding brick with which to build a world order.

In Third World states taken over by the native population on independence from a colonial government, there was usually a dominant ethnic group from which the governing elite was mainly drawn; and their ethnic identity would become with whatever modification the national identity. However, there was a significant if not radical difference between the new state and the home state of the colonial government. For a colonial government was not in occupation, and generally exercised hegemony over a metropolitan area only, leaving outer regions to tribal jurisdiction.

Further, the territory of the new state had been determined by bargaining give and take among the colonial powers for their convenience, and were artificial in that sense, and might cut across tribal integrities. Also there was seldom an administrative cadre educated and trained by the colonial power to take over, for independence had generally been wrested from resisting hands. Therefore, the government of the new colonial state was engaged in building the state rather than the nation, that is, in establishing its rule and the administrative institutions for that purpose. Treatment of minorities followed from that. A different ethnic group was likely to be regarded as a tribal rival, threatening fragmentation, and therefore to be repressed. On the other hand, it might be thought of as a resource to be used, perhaps in the manner of a colonial power, but with little trust. Barré did this in Somalia by a "divide and rule" policy, detaching himself as dictator from both clans, and playing one off against the other. Thus, the identity of the ethnic group was modified inside the colonial state, either as a dominant party or as a subordinate minority in response to government policies. The state was in question in a different sense from the question in Europe of its sovereignty and of the expediency of its interventions; in the Third World, the question was about the kind of state.

Ethnic groups that are minorities in a state claim different forms of accommodation to rectify what they are denied: autonomy, representation, access to resources or land, cultural recognition. Unless the state is intransigent, separation is unlikely to be what is claimed. Political autonomy is to be in control of conditions that vitally affect the minority. Contented minorities, as self-help groups, are a resource, not for manipulations in "divide and rule," but for development, a difference between fertility and sterility. This is of concern to neighbors and the world, not merely of a particular state, as the volume of refugees has demonstrated. Treatment of minorities is generally recognized as a general interest. In the Third World of poor countries, ethnic minorities are self-help communities the state is in no position to serve.

Political analysts have tended to argue that growth in prosperity will in short time eliminate ethnicity in world politics; in short, material values will replace and modernize traditional ones. Perhaps the singular example of Singapore has been misleading. Disintegration of the Soviet Union has demonstrated that ethnic identities suppressed for more than two generations were not replaced by the imposed alien national identity. They actively reasserted themselves as soon as there was opportunity. The Islamic state as projected by Muslim fundamentalism practices the same intransigent exclusiveness as Stalinist Russia. However, it has to be recognized that Islam is not traditionally fundamentalist. The central tradition is that there are different social identities, but Islam is universal. The Koran states, "We have made you into nations and tribes so that you might know one another." That recognizes the social value of kinship groups, whereas Muslim fundamentalists ignore or deny their existence. Social scientists in the United States, with the nineteenth-century background of German training, and their influence on British sociologists, have proceeded on false assumptions about "modernization" for lack of this understanding.

Ethnicity as a social resource has a more positive social value than the negative "divide and rule." Because it roots people in their own customs and traditions against the winds of uncertainty and the climate of the times that is accelerating social change, it gives them an anchorage of stability of advantage to the society in general. If ethnic groups who do have grounds to complain of deprivation and discrimination have their grievances met, they have no reason for disaffection. What they seek may not be acceptable to the society in which they are living. Ethnicity is politically ambiguous, subversive or socializing. Negotiation and compromise in a context of open public debate can hardly be avoided save to make matters worse. In the Third World, kindred groups in neighboring states are apt to be a source of aid and perhaps arms; and addressing the problem directly is the best hope a government can have to putting an end to that. Throughout the Third World, it is the character of the state that is the clue to the contemporary phenomena of ethnicity.

At the UN earth summit conference in Rio in June 1992, the problem of the world's poor was recognized as inseparably linked with that of degradation of the environment That meeting of more than a hundred nations represented generally by their current heads of state revealed and ended in a confrontation of the haves and the have-nots over the issues. European colonialism had in effect been extrapolated into exploitation by the terms of trade. Relations between wealthy and poor nations had been fixed as historically given, unless and until clear recognition issued in the political will to find and follow the means to bring about an alteration.

What was ignored or played down at the earth summit, although it was brought up, was the condition that underlies and aggravates all the global problems, and generates its own: the accelerating expansion of population. International Planned Parenthood reported in August 1992 that five hundred million pregnant women did not have the information nor access to facilities needed for contraception. With the interval between puberty and a social position to maintain a family (biological and social maturity) stretching now from the age of twelve to, say, twice that age, contraception is essential. Sex education, planned enlightenment broadcast through the mass media, and accessible clinics where advice, counseling, and material help can be sought have to be promoted by worldwide campaigns. They are not hard to promote if those who object can be marginalized. There is no more constructive way of taking abortion off the political agenda. It is generally recognized that a rise in the standard of living induces family planning because parents become better off.

To deal with any of these problems effectively, the world has to tackle them comprehensively by international cooperation and coordination, instituting a program that sets out what has to be done, with the procedures and assigned responsibilities required to carry it out, and the monitoring required to ensure performance. This effort does not have to start from scratch. There are piecemeal initiatives already at work within the jurisdiction of the United Nations emanating from international conferences, including Brandt's *North-South*, and the World Commission on Environment and Development's *Our Common Future*, which was consummated by the UN in the Earth Summit.

Such a comprehensive task on such a scale cannot be taken on without first taking the measure of the sacrifices entailed, and their incidence. Those who enjoy luxury and a wasteful lifestyle would be deprived, and there would be a lower upper limit than the market at present provides. Once more, it is short-term particular interests that frustrate general benefit, but the deferred gratification is on the part of living generations for their posterity. The threat to human survival that has been used to shock us into action has to be reflectively translated into a context of human maturity, if all the relevant factors are to be brought together and assessed. It is in this final sense that the state is in question, put in question by inferences from the lapse of law and order that mock the rule of law worldwide, as the fighting factions in Yugoslavia have mocked the United Nations.

# 22

# Humanity Comes of Age

New thinking has been required by what has happened in the last half-century. In science the accelerating pace of discoveries precipitated an explosion that shattered the fabric of science into specialisms, producing contextual science or interdisciplinary science in its applications. Physical sciences, earth sciences, life sciences, science which is abstract and general in character ("pure science") became particular and concrete in its indications of human intervention to human advantage in what is discerned as going on, most innovative and far-reaching in "genetic engineering." Microbiology found numbers as astronomical as in the macrosphere. Ecology discovered the infinite damage done to ecosystems and to the general balance of natural systems. This was recognized as urgent, since extinction of species threatened premature human extinction and time for remedial action was shrinking. Biological evolution of species was at work over geological ages before it produced the world as we know it. Human intervention works on a scale that reduces millennia to centuries and decades. That intervention has to work with nature, or it repeats purposively the destructive practices that were perpetrated ignorantly. Variety was the condition of evolution. Human intervention that eliminates variety is doomed. The gardener, not the engineer, is the model, a partnership with nature. This chapter is designed to spell out what has been learned about nature and human nature, and what that entails for the human future.

## Science Now

Given the contextual character of modern specialisms and their interdisciplinary applications, the question remains of the validity of their findings, their trustworthiness. It has been said that hell is to see the truth too late. But is truth attainable by sciences and how can we be sure if it is?

What lines of research have scientists chosen in their investigations; what are their interests and preoccupations; have they got their priorities right? Unless they have, science, without being at fault, may be in default, deficient. Here lay judgment is relevant; it is evident in the prominence given to all aspects of medicine. Ignorance, poverty, and disease, the age-old traditional foes, are still with us, but the first is being vanquished as the key to victory over the other two. If contemporary scientists are going wrong, it is likely to be in this connection.

If science is being used on projects of human intervention that adopt and adapt natural processes for human ends, whether to correct natural failures or to effect desirable production, as in the food supply, and this is done regardless of consequences in the natural world, the desired short-term results may have in the long-term evolutionary effects as detrimental to survival as currently recognized habits of wasteful consumption and pollution are known to be.

In sum, science in the long-run is the only trustworthy knowledge we can have. But there always remains the question of what lines of inquiry scientists are concentrating on and what alternative priorities might be.

Biological evolution of species is the unplanned universal development of diverse forms of life that die out or survive. How a particular species lives in its habitat is one line of inquiry. More comprehensive is a study of the relations of the various organisms in a habitat to one another and to the habitat: the ecosystem. An ecosystem is a miniature of the natural order of all life on the planet, within the macrocosms and thus of the human condition.

The "biosphere" is a complex of atmosphere, ocean, energy, and soil, the habitat of organisms and an enfolding ecosystem, in which the elements have their function and behavior. In regard to climate and all uncontrollable phenomena, the most useful recourse is reliable prediction in time for adequate preparation. This has notably improved, and continues to be improvable. However what is most critical is the use and abuse of energy, water, and air. The two latter have been generally poisoned by pollutants, to the grave detriment of health, the extinction or drastic reduction of species, and the confounding of ecosystems. Energy is grossly wasted, and is on tap from exhaustible sources. Water, though renewable, has been unnecessarily used, wasted, mostly by swollen populations concentrated in different places. The draw on the land has lowered the water table until the damage is visible in dried water courses and affected soils. Polluted water is a main source of disease and death worldwide, but especially in the southern hemisphere where the poor are congregated. Aquatic animals suffer likewise. Trees and vegetation die under acid rain and other atmospheric pollutants. Not visible is the estimated damage to the protective ozone layer in the upper atmosphere.

What is happening to the land and the ocean speaks most imperatively to nations, and particularly to the industrialized ones, who cause most of the damage and can do most about it. What is happening to energy and water addresses every human being directly, since everyone wastes and has waste to dispose of, and is able to not do so and to recycle waste.

The new knowledge brought recognition of immense disturbance of the finely balanced natural order that had been brought about and was still going on by the "industrial revolution," the more recent commercial agriculture to boost crop production, and by the internal combustion engine in dense masses of vehicles, that is, by a whole way of life of populations living mainly in the northern hemisphere, the developed industrialized states, and particularly the seven known as the G Seven. The developing countries, at different stages of development, were not polluting water, soil, and air to the same extent and in the same way, but were an additional source of damage to the environment. To meet the cost of debt and of needed imports, they had been driven to rely on a crop or a raw material they were able to export. At the same time, the terms of trade and global competition virtually excluded them from the market. The Earth Summit in Rio in 1992 which brought together over a hundred heads of state was planned as a consummation that would embark the world on a definitive program of action, a commitment of political will, in time to secure protection and sustainable development. Instead, humanity is on course to finding itself alone inhabiting a desert occupied before extinction in mutual slaughter. The creator of Adam was contradicted by an American Indian chief taught by nature, when he remarked that the earth does not belong to man because he belongs to the earth, and all things are connected like the blood of one family. Humanity that has been brought about by millions of years is equipped to bring about further developments within spells of thousands or hundreds or decades, whether for its own good or harm.

The food supply can be maintained and increased as necessary only by intensive cultivation, which involves selective breeding of plants and animals for control of yields, elimination of diseases and poisons; in short, to employ all resources that will increase supply. This is done by genetic engineering and good management. But selective breeding for a preferred strain reduces diversity drastically; and pesticides and fertilizers are a source of pollution. This is all apart from the North/South divide and its consequences. The root problem of population has to be tackled. If nothing is done and the total population multiplies threefold, the future will become rapidly dreadful. The recognition is on the map, and the means of prevention are sufficiently known.

The ocean occupies seven-tenths of the earth's surface. Coastal waters are the most actively productive, the source of diversity. They are for an extensive margin territorial waters, with an exclusive claim by the adjoining state. They should belong in common for general benefit. At present they are the source of deepest conflict. The first international conference on control of the seas, under the League of Nations in 1936, brought up both questions to be settled by convention, the common inheritance and territorial rights. Both remain on the agenda. Two UN conferences before 1973 were inconclusive. In 1982 a treaty was signed on the management of coastal waters, categorized in four zones of twelve, twenty-four, and two hundred or more nautical miles, and the continental shelf. The deep sea beds were designated the common heritage, under control of an International Seabed Authority. The treaty required ratification by sixty states to come into force, and the developing countries refused to ratify it, not having the technology to benefit as the North did. Meanwhile many of the industrialized states, including the G7, enacted their own claims. Here again the North/South division is the stumbling-block to advance.

Extravagant lifestyles have come to be recognized as immoral, and in the long run unsustainable. For long, an American way of life was the envy and desire of those who were raised above the degrading poverty of the destitute masses. For those who could drink Coca-Cola throughout the world, the American Dream was their dream. There never had been so wasteful an economy, where everything was expendable, nothing had to make do or go a long way, planned obsolescence and a policy of pulling down replacement, to keep the market moving. Luxury in the past, for which the opulence of the East was legendary, was for the few at the expense of the many. Never was it so general as in the United States of America, despite the abject poverty to be seen on the streets and the racial discrimination. Those excluded from the society of the successful, from the meaning and the message of the dream, showed that it was a dream that faded away in the daylight of reality that uncovered the future, which in that respect is already here.

These cardinal problems have been clearly recognized in their complex interconnection. There are no "solutions," but there is the competence to deal with them constructively by initiatives and measures taken over the years, sustained by the political will to secure the reduction and mitigation attainable. That is a measure of the reorientation and new thinking that begins to turn educated persons from the past to the future with an emphasis and concern that prepares them in general for radical changes of habits and behavior that they have still to embrace with sufficient conviction and resolution.

A further reach in the new thinking has reconsidered the relationship of society with its constituent members. Traditionally, there has been a principal division between political thinkers who have thought of society as an organism, the parts of which are its members who realize themselves by their participation in the life of the community in which they share and for which they make sacrifices. The part is justified and fulfilled in the whole. Philosophically, these belonged to the idealist camp. The opposing school, the empiricists, thought an organism was a false analogy. Rather, society was simply an aggregation of persons more or less independent, but coming together for common purposes and mutual benefit on a contractual basis. Locke held this view distinctively and Bentham argued it forcefully, backed by the formula of the greatest happiness of the greatest number as the maxim for legislation. Marx was neither an organicist nor merely a collectivist. His concrete dialectical materialism sought to draw thought down from metaphysics and anchor it firmly in the bedrock of economic activity (which was nevertheless a natural process: "scientific socialism"). The initial concept was analyzed and developed by Engels and Lenin in its theoretical bearings, but the historical sequel would be spontaneous community production for community consumption, with no political constraint, an integration of individual interests in the public interest. The new perception of the relations between individuals and the society in which they live is different from all three traditional political philosophies, but like Marxism is an historical outcome.

What has been learned from biological evolution is the long-term vital importance of variety to the whole process, and to survival; unification is destructive unless it conserves and does not annul plurality, nor reduce it. Politics are about "interests," their conflicts and institutional means of reconciliation (abolished in the Marxist utopia), individuals associate to serve short-term interests which are immediate aims. These tend to be destructive of long-term interests of general benefit. Political imposition of short-term sacrifices is justified if necessary to secure general benefit in the long run. This was the dogma of socialism, but the new, partially adopted, "mixed economy" and reformed, socially responsible management structure dissolve the capitalist/socialist confrontation and point the way to a global competitive market as the condition of company survival. The market is thought to maximize satisfaction of a general interest, which synthesizes and does not suppress individual interests, an integration of plurality. This new international economic order (the NIEO of frequent reference) would be accompanied and reinforced by a comparable political integration.

As stated in the previous paragraph, the thinking is abstract and the prospect problematic. However, what is seen to be going on in Europe, with all its dubieties and uncertainties, and talk of the need for a new "Bretton Woods" to regulate the currency mismatch of zones and regions of unequal economic performance in the global situation as it has developed since the war, provides evidence that this is the current ideal of a Human Civilization, which will be examined in more detail later in the chapter. Meanwhile, the new landscape in formation can be recognized as a connected and ordered scene comparable with the ecosystems of the natural order. All pluralities rooted in the person are integrated and conserved institutionally in the UN if reformed. Individual identity is itself plural in levels that ascend from the base of family and neighborhood through race, nationality, sex, and age, to recognized possession of a shared human nature in awareness spread by information technology of what that nature is, which has been learned fully and finally. The interdependence traversed in practice in this development is what brings to all a sufficient share of goods and services, instead of deprivation and superfluity, produced by the managed mixed and socially responsible economy, expanded to embrace all production, distributions, and exchange.

Natural disasters, like the unprecedented floods in Pakistan that have brought long-term devastation and loss of land, or unprecedented droughts in Africa, equally bring setbacks to any prospect of betterment, and appalling personal loss and suffering, but they are not obviously man-made, self-inflicted, although the ecological context of human conditions makes the distinction less precise.

## Human Nature

The 1992 earth summit was convened to institute by cooperation and coordination movement into sustainable development for the whole world, for which there was the necessary knowledge and capability. Targets were pinpointed, and a timetable set: greenhouse gases in the atmosphere, biological diversity, forest destruction, protection of coastal areas, integrating environment into the political agenda, a UN commission with the authority to monitor the fulfillment of undertakings. Unfortunately, not only was there formal confrontation between North and South, but in the time since the summit the industrialized states have already begun to renege on their undertakings—always with good reasons. This is not so much want of resolution as a crowded and overloaded political agenda, with too many calls competing for attention—the educational agenda and many others.

The current central obstacle to the way forward has been recognized as the continued dominant power of the industrialized nations. Their aid to the poorest nations, direct and through the IMF, has been largely stultified by denial of the means of self-help, mainly by the terms of trade established by GATT. The first practical step is to begin systematic removal of the handicaps, poverty at the bottom, with illiteracy, malnutrition, and disease, all in general inherited. As these conditions are mitigated, the low vitality that induced supine acquiescence and resignation to the way things are is likely to be replaced by frustration, protest, disobedience: the door is unlocked to the introduction of effective aid to facilitate and support self-help. The resolution and skills that are there but lost for want of opportunity and training become tools for radical improvement. This has been demonstrated by schemes for health care and subsistence husbandry in India. The most striking case is to be seen on the ground in Bangladesh, one of the very poorest and most afflicted countries in the Third World. What is happening there, and could and should be elsewhere, is the root source of development. That is the lesson learned after repeated failures in the postwar mission of the industrialized nations to aid backward peoples to catch up, chiefly governments who were the rebel leaders who had fought for colonial independence.

The knowledge and capability necessary to recognize and redress the ecological complex were equally available to better the human lot directly. The range of these forward-looking tasks can be indicated categorically as physical, chemical, electronic, and genetic: all the mechanical means by which human labor can be replaced or aided, from vacuum cleaners to robots. This separation is misleading, for the knowledge and capability are applied in combination. Biotechnology is a new industry using genetic engineering to produce new kinds of of living cells, not merely chemicals, in making a wide variety of drugs available to deal with almost any physiological condition. The genetic makeup of species can be altered to make them useful to us. Specific genes can be identified and manipulated, which could not be done by the old skills of crossbreeding. Success has been proved by taking simple organisms like bacteria in which to implant human genes to produce human growth hormones, and a whole range of drugs that enhance performance of bodily functions. Similarly, the yields of farm animals can be increased, and the yield of crops. This ability to alter the basis of life at will by reading and changing its coded instructions, the power to change our internal inheritance as well as our environment, was shown above under the section entitled "Science Now" to be a mistaken assumption, since it is subject to an ordained constraint in the long term. However, that does not cancel the capability which allows us to make this assumption; and the point to be made here is that this capability as a human capability, adds a new dimension to human nature. It has been said, "Man has no nature; what he has is history." The knowledge of our nature has been learned in stages, which included a protracted and painful stage of unlearning, and it has not been fully possible until now. The capability that is incorporated into our nature is also acquired cumulatively. The recent explosion of knowledge and consequent capability has been a jump into a new orbit. The "coming of age" is this attainment of independence, instead of providence or fortune: an ability to design human life collectively, which is a transformation of the human condition, however problematic in practice.

Awareness of this new dimension of human nature is inseparable from recognition of the unprecedented responsibility entailed. Unless responsibility for what is done and not done is fixed and persons are made accountable, a tendency to avoid responsibility by fixing blame is likely to prevail, and there is generally a case at hand to justify it.

A responsibility entailed by a property of human nature is both collective and individual, since all are human, but participation in what is shared is different and unequal. Who is responsible for what, and to whom, is always the relevant question. Since the basis of the capability is technology, it seems justifiable to say that the scientists bear the responsibility. They are as much responsible for their product as other producers if not for its misuse by consumers. They certainly are exclusively responsible for the consistency and reliability of their product. However, it is a product that "holds decisive powers for good and evil. *That* is the situation in which scientists find themselves" (C. P. Snow). Left to themselves, they want to get on with their work, and take their share with all citizens in relevant political decisions.

They produced weapons of mass destruction, chemical and biological weapons as well as nuclear weapons and the missiles to carry them, a prodigious arsenal. They need not have done so. They knew what was feasible before it was available. There is some evidence that Hitler would have been likely to deliver the bomb before the United States if top physicists had been more forthcoming, less inclined to avoid the development for the sake of humanity. Robert Oppenheimer headed the team that developed the atom bomb and supported the decision to drop the first bomb on a Japanese town, rather than demonstrate its destructive power on an uninhabited area. He subsequently regretted his part, and was chairman of the authoritative committee that recommended in 1949 that the U.S. government should not embark on production of a hydrogen bomb. But decisions were made by a political and military commission. This is an extreme case, but indicates that scientists are entrained into and used for obtaining noxious products when they are seen to be feasible and are wanted by governments. They cannot be considered instigators. What is relevant here is what science is currently about.

Specific scientific responsibility has been made familiar in the practice of medicine, and is symbolically represented in the Hippocratic Oath, a medical tradition that binds the practitioner to study and serve the interests of the patient, and in that real sense to accept responsibility for what is done. Patients are routinely informed of what is known about their condition and prognosis, and what is done to them is confined to what they have consented to on the information supplied. Medical staff and laboratory staffs behind them bear direct accountability for life and death as other scientists do not and cannot, for they do not function corporately in relations with the public. The technology which endows the species with extensive capability is as much a part of human nature as reason is, of which it is a fruit. Both are cultural products, possessed by common inheritance and acquired individually in the course of education, as language is from an earlier stage. In the universally shared responsibility imposed by that capability every individual has a part, unless impaired by a relevant physical deficiency.

As users and consumers, all are responsibly involved: in wasting or saving energy and water, disposing of waste, in population control, in consumer discrimination, in contributing to pollution or deliberately avoiding to do so, or minimizing what is not avoidable. There is all told a volume of substantial and tiresome responsibilities that has been incurred. This is evident in the organized help that is available. There is a literature on every theme, from a guide to ethical investment to *The Global Consumer,* for helping the Third World—a new slant to the familiar *Which.* There are battery hens and free-range poultry and eggs, and similar choices. Pressure groups like Friends of the Earth and Greenpeace and World Development Movement, as well as Oxfam and the aid agencies, enlist individuals and supporters to organize influence on decision-makers. The young especially are in general well aware of the spread of the call for responsibility, and heed it to some extent. It is collective and individual responsibility to one another for promoting sustainable development in general, and in particular for helping developing peoples to do this for themselves, all for the sake of humanity in the long run. The rationale of this responsibility is clear, and easy to appreciate. It is enforceable mainly through public opinion and the organized means by which that is formed and mobilized. Interest groups are an essential part of democratic accountability. Anyone's part will be small but incremental, like an atom or a cell; and like them not insignificant but indispensable. Everyone should work out what his or her own part should be, and incorporate that in a self-monitored life-plan or life-style. That is to share in the maturity of our species, to grow up. This is the ethical obligation entailed by our acquired corporate capability.

The significance of Apollo's famous "know yourself" was its implied recognition that knowledge of and respect for one's place in the universe is necessary for realistic management of personal life. This was a tottering infant step on the way to the firmer tread of Aristotle's definition of man as a rational animal, which exhibited the triumph of reason in the logic of definition by identity and difference. Biologist though he was, he could not have entertained the thought that two millennia and more would pass before it was learned how this variety of species acquired the unique power by which it was distinguished. For he would have assumed that the kind of inquiry in which he and his colleagues were interested would be maintained. The knowledge of human status which he initiated in the definition has at last reached the stage when human reason has advanced learning to the point when knowledge of the origin and development of human nature has been established. As politically useful knowledge, the biological facts within the frame of Darwin's theory need to be supplemented by generalizations drawn from experience of how men and women do behave, which is both documented in history and familiar to everyday observation and in news reports.

The first stumbling block to learning is in having to unlearn what has long been, and still is, generally taught. Constantine in making Christianity the exclusive religion of Rome made the Bible a source of information of supreme authority. When attention was switched from focus on the word of God to the works of God, with the foundation of organized empirical science in the seventeenth century, it was hoped that the bloody conflicts that had ensued when Protestants wrested the Bible from papal control would be left behind for concentration on the self-revelation of the author's purpose in clues furnished by investigation of what he had brought about. Human nature as such was not on the agenda, and the particular lines of inquiry that were pursued could not be formulated in questions to which answers would have any direct relevance to the creation of man. Nevertheless, Alexander Pope in the next century called for a "science of man," which he assumed was forthcoming and would clinch the proof of God. His *Essay on Man* trumpeted the underlying misconception of the scientific program of which Bacon had been the public relations champion in *The Advancement of Learning.*

In the personal life cycle, maturation takes place in a definitive sequence in a nurturing social group, so that it is vitally affected by the manner of child-rearing, casual or managed, forming an identity personally unique but acquired in shared contexts. The ultimate shared context is global, not experienced in human history until the present time. Thomas Paine called himself "a citizen of the world" to express his identity with the human race and not merely with fellow nationals. He could not then have been aware, scientifically, of what that human nature really is that is universally shared (and at that time it actually was not what it is now, with its acquired capability, self-dependence, and responsibility for the future) in spite of his self-confidence and clear assurance that he was voicing a change in human relations that introduced a new world order, with its debut in France and the New World. That voice of one man, in print, had a popular reach not exceeded until the age of information technology.

The natural history of human nature traced by the sciences is abstract. What is particular, and a necessary supplement, is our remembered experience of the ways in which human beings actually behave, and awareness of like tendencies within ourselves. This adds up to a substantial body of knowledge. It was science itself that gave us concretely the capabilities and responsibility that has made us independent by nature. This other knowledge is of capabilities that are liabilities, negative capabilities that negate the positive ones that have been acquired. The enemy within threatens the partner with nature who could and should design the future and transform the human condition. To consider this negative behavior in particular forms in some detail is necessary now before going on to consider what would be necessary to organize fulfillment of the positive new possibilities.

Rousseau believed that a bad person was bad because he was brought up in a bad society. Brought up outside society (as it was in his day) in a state of nature, a person's innate nature would ripen and blossom and bear fruit in its own natural perfection. He sketched what he meant in *Emile.* Of course he knew it was impracticable, but he went on to wrestle with the problem of producing the perfect society by institutions that could give effect to agreements easily reached by peasants meeting to discuss their affairs in the shade of an oak. Rousseau was wrong in principle, not only in the inevitable result of growing up in the woods, but also in glossing over the inevitability of conflicts of interest that make politics necessary. Marx too assumed a common interest would prevail, once the class division of interests was permanently eliminated, as it could and would be. Thomas More recognized that "Utopia" ("no place") was out of the question, unless it is assumed that human nature is other than it is. There is a common interest, a public interest, without question, but it exists because of, not instead of, sectional and private interests, and consists in the foundations of a society and the mutual convenience of laws and conventions, and particularly in the shifting compromises that accommodate interests that are in conflict, so that they can be lived with and not precipitate a breakdown of law and order.

To identify the evil of oppressive and exploitive behavior with a conflict of interests, so that such behavior would automatically depart with that conflict (the Soviet New Man) was to confuse two related phenomena whose essential difference should not be obscured, for bad behavior is in itself sufficient to obstruct or hamper social improvement. "Man's inhumanity to man makes countless thousands mourn." Wordsworth recalled when he witnessed the outbreak of the French Revolution, "Bliss was it to be alive; to be young was very heaven," for there dawned the prospect of a transformed future, a new humanity. He soon outlived the euphoria, and his meditations constantly brooded on the paradox of man's inhumanity to man, elaborated in the autobiographical third book of *The Excursion,* "Despondency."

The systematic extermination of Jews and "undesirables" as government policy exceeded the religious persecutions of the past, which anyhow had ended by bringing about religious liberty some two centuries before the Holocaust. "Genocide," a neologism that literally implies racial or ethnic discrimination, is used to cover ideological fanaticism which has been a curse of the times, evident in Pol Pot's killing fields of Cambodia, Mao's "cultural revolution," apartheid, "ethnic cleansing," Iran's purges, the connected reduction of Beirut to rubble and divided streets, but also in year upon year of mutual slaughter and atrocities, with lasting desolation of the land, in Angola, Mozambique, and Ethiopia. The point to be made here is that man's inhumanity to man on this scale and in so many cases is so conspicuous and so outrageous that it has shocked those not directly involved into trying to do something about it. In the Gulf War, the oil interest was involved, but it brought the advantage of unprecedented encouragement for the practicability of the policing function for which the United Nations was formed. Since then, Europe, the United Nations, and finally the United States have been jolted into intervention by what is going on in Yugoslavia, aggravated by the fear of imminent escalation. Humanitarian relief was accompanied early on by formal attempts at political reconciliation, during which formal agreements were arrived at and invariably disregarded on the ground. This led to the Geneva Standing Conference, a first trial of the idea that the UN can identify offenders, and if probation fails, can exile the offenders in isolation, so that it is only a matter of time before deprivation compels the nations to submit to the international rule of law. In that global context, gross social evils are not to be listed among human liabilities, for liabilities though they are and of the most serious kind, they are expunged, not allowed to disturb normal social order.

It remains to assess how detrimental to human advance the "normal" liabilities of human nature are. First to be considered must be those that are so general that it is exceptional to be exempt. Most comprehensive is doing as others do, going along with, conforming to social expectations. That most people do this is evident, because if they don't, they make themselves conspicuous, disliked, and punished verbally and by forfeit and exclusion, which is why they are exceptional, the fate of the "whistle blower," which is the public-spirited calling attention to a defrauding of the public. When bad practices get established, they are liable to be maintained even by those who know better, and they are difficult to break.

A notable general tendency has been analyzed by psychologists, particularly in Eric Berne's best-selling *Games People Play* (1964). The underlying theory is that the stimulus of social exchange is essential to human well-being, and that such intercourse is not spontaneously forthcoming, and has to be structured: the games people play are ploys and pleas for recognition, and not straightforward expressions of what he or she feels and thinks. The patterns can be classified, and people will associate with those who play the same games and feel alien in circles addicted to games of another kind. In general, it is a fear and avoidance of candor and intimacy. Since candor and autonomy imply liberation from and defiance of the culture in which one matures and grows up, acquiring a personal identity, the pressure to take refuge in "games" is almost irresistible. Few people may be strong or fortunate enough to be capable of autonomy and candor and intimacy, and the others flock together in these pretended forms of "togetherness" The last sentence of Berne's book: "This may mean that there is no hope for the human race, but there is hope for individual members of it." Precision of analysis may exaggerate the phenomenon, but such a liability if prevalent enough would dash the dawning hope for the human future indicated in this chapter, and be more than the many difficulties from traits of behavior to which we are prone.

"He doesn't want to know": it is natural that having taken pains to make up one's mind, one should be reluctant to consider what would fault it or put it in question. If it is merely an opinion, that may not matter too much. If it is a policy of someone with the authority and power to implement it, the consequence is serious and common: the frustration of those on the ground who are doing the work, quenching enthusiasm, cutting off a growing-point, reducing operations to clocking in to a daily routine.

One might lump together in one inclusive word, "unreliability," behavior that undermines any project or enterprise, but all who take part have their human failings, and not all failings blight what is undertaken with failure. Unreliability should be thought of not as a failing, rather as indicating the seriousness of a specific failing from a cooperative point of view.

The profoundest general question, perhaps unanswerable, is whether there is innate evil in anyone, malignancy that is more than a stance in a particular case. There are people who are antisocial in disposition, with a history that made them so. There is evidence of sadism as an evil that may be dominant in some persons. Even the high-minded may be surprised and alarmed to find themselves off-guard, shocked into a momentary sadistic reaction that is a glimpse into the basement of human nature. But where is the whole person that is evil? Milton's Lucifer is a fallen angel, as the Prometheus of Aeschylus is a rebel against the tyranny of Zeus. Shakespeare's Iago is the more plausible type of villain.

The most famous general liability is Lord Acton's historian's verdict: Power corrupts, and absolute power corrupts absolutely. But that passes over from the general to the particular liabilities characteristic of situations or contexts. One of the most notorious is "Parkinson's Law': "Work expands so as to fill the time available for its completion."

Reflecting on his outlook and output, in 1979 Parkinson made a final point that fixed attention on the vacuum occasioned by the failures of authorities to do what they should do, leaving opportunity for those to rush in for their wrongful advantage. "If the West is to survive it must achieve a measure of unity which is so far conspicuously lacking, but its failure, if it fails, will be in Brussels and Washington, not on the threatened frontier nor even in the countries which cling most desperately to their sovereign status they can no longer afford to maintain."

Bureaucracy is liable to the evil of inflationary manning that incurs extravagant expense and waste, but also the contrary vice of myopic going by the book, to play safe or a pedantic officialdom. This failure to use the discretion needed in the implementation of laws penalizes the beneficiaries.

In all branches of planning, there are those who go by the book in a rather different sense. There are the current models, blueprints for what architects and town planners have decided is their ideal. Planning officers are then apt to try to produce it on the ground, as though they had a clean slate or the drawing board for an area, and not merely a project: there is not the space and it cannot be done, and the result is a botch. In strongest contrast was the pioneer approach of Patrick Geddes, a biologist who became an ecological sociologist and founded the social art of planning. Town planning would begin with a civic survey of what was on the ground in the setting of a regional survey, and informed by knowledge of other geographical features, such as climate, economic activity, historical inheritance. With this preliminary view, consideration would be given to the least interference that would produce the greatest improvement, without preconceptions. The practicality and productivity of this approach was appreciated in England by Sir Patrick Abercrombie and others who established a school of planning on these lines. Abercrombie was employed as a consultant in India, and by the Ministry of Town and Country Planning set up after the war to promote development. Many planning officers appointed by local authorities and chairmen of their committees, as well as civil servants of the ministry out in the provinces, were imbued with these principles, went abroad to gain experience of what was being done elsewhere, and abounded in enthusiasm for adaptable schemes and open-minded discussion. This did happen, and is mentioned here because the contrary also happened, and has remained a liability in the whole range of development, which produces rotting inner cities, the high-rise vandalized blocks, the run-down estates, living conditions that condemn a generation and their progeny to fear, misery, and despair.

Corruption in the political context, and it was not particularly what Acton had in mind, has been in its crudest form virtually eliminated in Britain, where as elsewhere still it once was the system of government. Wherever it is endemic, as in India, it is more than a liability, for it is impossible to get on or to get things done if one ignores it. (It used to be that a doctorate from the London School of Economics could gain promotion without a bribe.) Brazil has found how difficult it usually is to break the system. It is what makes government a spoils system rather than a public service.

Institutions are not persons, but they exist only as manned, and have been called "social habits." Initially established for a social purpose by public-spirited cooperation and coordination, succeeding generations in its offices are likely to put its preservation, and their jobs, before the job it was designed to do. Bentham found that was what lawyers were doing in devious ways when he studied the purpose and operation of law as a social utility. He subsequently found that Parliament also was a corporation of a similar kind in which MPs had a vested interest, at variance with the interests of the constituency voters who had sent them there. Institutions are unlikely to be corrected from within; outside pressure has to be mounted, strong enough to prevail, reinforced by an alerted public opinion. More systematic prevention is effected by accountability, which is the principle of democracy and of all social control, together with official monitoring by inspectors.

There is the well-known liability of crowds to panic and stampede like a herd, and of mobs to run riot and loot and burn, or take the law into their own hands violently and assert deterrence by aggression, to the point of lynching. Passively, crowds have gloated over the cruelty of burning the heretic, and prolonged the agony to prolong their enjoyment. All these are collective liabilities of individuals together, which they would not be likely to have on their own. If a person known to be good natured, kindly and neighborly, and counted on to be so, is liable to be a member of a crowd or mob who behaves irrationally or with reckless violence and savagery, the inference must be that the context of behavior is all-important, that in the analysis behavior is a situational response, not a purely personal manifestation of the individual. As in planning development there is no clean slate, so in thinking of human behavior there is no void. Moreover, materials in manufacture are tested to destruction to make sure of reliability, but very few persons are tested in the course of their lives, to be able to know how they would be likely to behave in trying circumstances; most probably assume a standard of behavior for which they have no evidence and live in naive innocence to the end, untested.

There is a particular historic situation lived through by a generation whose collective response was formative of future behavior. The Great War was entered upon in a fever of patriotic excitement and enthusiasm, and ended in disenchantment, with an enduring change of mind and heart. The call of King and Country would not evoke the same response again. The mood crystallized in a more independent and critical response to the powers that be, a step in growing up. The experience induced an awakening and reorientation essentially different from the rationalism of the Enlightenment, and those who shared in it were alerted to the common but problematic humanity that was shared below or across all barriers, rather than to the advancement of learning and its applications.

What is the outcome of this summary review of the evil in human nature, man's inhumanity to man? Two principal generalizations emerge. (1) There is no satisfactory evidence of innate evil, "original sin," save in the sense that all carry common

behavioral liabilities, and all behavior is in part response to situations in which people are put or find themselves, their fortunate or unfortunate circumstances, not least
those of their birth and upbringing. A corollary would be: The enemy is never an evil
human being; all are in the same human situation together; the enemy is the bad situation to be addressed, and the classic evils of ignorance, poverty, and disease. A
corollary is not a relief of responsibility because of circumstances, for it is what one
does or fails to do that makes all the difference. (2) Parkinson's addendum: the void.
The failure of those in power to do their job effectively invites evildoers to come in
and do what they want to do, which makes the authorities responsible for the evil they
allow to be done. The corollary to that is that doing all that one should do makes one
responsible. Cicero, in a letter to his son, who was studying philosophy in Athens,
pointed out apropos the propensity to act unjustly that it was not enough to refrain
from such acts; it was also one's duty to do all in one's power to ensure that others
who acted unjustly did not gain by it; one must frustrate them and protect their
intended victims, to join in establishing a just society. Much water has flowed under
the bridge since Cicero wrote that letter, and in the West today the individual is
enabled to do what Cicero recommended institutionally by maintaining democracy,
freedom of information, civil liberties, constitutionally enacted rights, an independent
judiciary, and all the sophisticated extra provisions which the volume of modern legislation with a positive and complex social content requires to safeguard individual
interests. This was elaborated as an indication of what the rule of law means today
in the previous chapter with that title. This is no longer a domestic state of affairs in
an advanced industrialized nation, since advanced communications have imposed one
world, leaving advanced nations to take the lead in organizing it.

Of particular social evils, fanaticism has priority today, if not always. It used to
be religious bigotry at the core, which inflamed campaigns of hatred and persecution.
Today, it is mainly in the doctrinal form of "fundamentalism," but ideology of any
doctrinaire character is more comprehensive, and signals the danger in tendencies that
do not run to what would be unacceptable extremes, but are more like a monkey
wrench than grit in the working of democracy.

A final point in this summary survey of liabilities to evil in human nature is the
coexistence of good and evil; they are seldom if ever present as black and white.
There is ambiguity and ambivalence; the uncertainty and hesitancy are liable to
inhibit positive action even when disinclination does not put it out of the question.

Time, the universal condition of existence, has this ambiguity and consequent
ambivalence. It is the paradigm case, for it sweeps all its sons away, as the hymn says,
and buries in oblivion what we shall never know anything about: classics, the things
that are extant, are not necessarily so in virtue of their merit; the destruction is blind,
as indiscriminate as the weather. If time is from our point of view hostile, we are
wholly dependent on it for our existence, for what we are, for our achievements,
incremental, cumulative, historical: we need it and use it for all our enterprises, aspirations, and hopes. That is the frame story of ourselves, our nature, our history, the
theme of this book. Before bringing it up to date, something needs to be said in regard
to the loss and disillusionment of many who are brought to face the finally indis-

putable evidence that the Christian faith, which Constantine made the way of life for what would be the West, is prescientific, and that to continue to take it seriously as a faith to live by would be willful self-delusion. The task is to wean oneself of this accustomed dependency and appropriate the ground of independence human nature has now acquired, which also is collective and shared. All religion is traditional, handed on, acquired from others, convinced by their evident conviction, sanctioned by the witness of the faithful down the centuries, generation after generation, and perhaps confirmed by the inwardness of personal experience in this context.

A vein of new thinking applied to the Christian tradition is derived from the Existentialist movement in philosophy on the Continent, and particularly from Søren Kierkegaard, who was torn between reason and faith. In general, this was dominated by recognition of the time-bound human condition. Nothing can be thought, said, or done definitively, once for all. Reality is in the enactment, which is momentary; something done by choice gratuitously is one's own responsibility. One cannot be a hero, only have been one. A Christian cannot depend on the witness of the apostles, nor on the cloud of witnesses, not because of the distance in time since their day, but simply because nothing can absolve him from having to stand before the Cross as they did, and decide for himself whether this is indeed the Son of God, one with the Father, as he claimed. If one acquires faith in that way, it has constantly to be renewed in that way—as one exists for oneself in perpetual self-renewal.

Buoyed up by faith, one is enabled to project one's need on one who will reinforce weak confidence in one's own inner resources. Those resources are now collectively expanded as the capability of an independent human nature, with responsibility for one's share. The task, then, is to set out for oneself the commitments and priorities that are within one's scope which one should undertake. To do that initiates a break-out from self-absorption, which religion had secured traditionally either by the formal discipline of a religious order, or by prayerful commitment to obediently doing the will of God, like the Son of God. The maturation of human nature is a cultural dispensation.

What can be said to be ethically distinctive of Christianity is not neighbor-love, in the sense of not doing to another what one would not like done to oneself, but exaltation of the poor and the meek; it is they who shall inherit the earth, while the rich and the mighty are pulled down from their seats. Nietzsche singled this out as the corrupting influence of Christianity, which he deplored and denounced as a false premise that alienated humanity from their civilization, with its Greek roots. A realistic eschatology requires the advance of rich and powerful industrialized nations to enable the poorest people to help themselves to become a link in the chain of interdependence. They are not to be blessed in their humility and resignation.

A Christian in a desperate situation at the end of his tether may feel that his faith is hope against hope. An unbeliever, to live in a world found intolerable, may behave as if somehow there is another world. A Christian of doubtful faith may behave as if he were confident. In the history of Western philosophy, there is an "as if" position to accommodate unsurmountable uncertainties. There is no uncertainty in the conclusion to be drawn from the findings of the relevant sciences. But there may well be uncertainty for individuals in coming to terms with that conclusion.

## Cultures and Civilization

A substantial essay might be written on the complications in usage of "civilization," and "culture." Raymond Williams in *Keywords: A Vocabulary of Culture and Society* (1976) gives a meticulous historical account of the complications. In Part One of this book, the claim of Hellas to be a model culture and of home, which adopted that culture, to be a model civilization was the main theme, whether or not the words were explicitly used. These models were shown to be formative influences in the European inheritance. Part Three dealt with the first British Empire of the Elder Pitt on that model, and with European anthropological discoveries as early as the sixteenth century, and British ambivalence in regard to the North American Indians, lapsing into failure to understand their ecological culture, and eventually their ruthless destruction with the push westward. The British Empire became more extensive than Rome, and established at sea a Pax Britannica. By 1945 it was eclipsed by its former rebellious colony, and the age of imperial civilizations was over.

"Culture" is generally defined anthropologically as the shared outlook and behavior of a society. It has these two components of thought and behavior, and is an institutionalized habit formed by success in trial and error. Although stable and not progressive, it undergoes change as individuals introduce innovations that are found acceptable. All these characteristics can hold only for small, simple, homogeneous societies, and have no direct application to a modern, industrialized nation. However, they would have relevance to small groups within a complex society. Rapid social change in adaptation to new circumstances has made "culture" a vogue word in this looser sense of a group's shared outlook and pattern of behavior in a given context. The group may be small, and the settled outlook and behavior ephemeral, for a particular purpose.

European states in this period have taken in immigrants from other cultures meeting better conditions of life. Insofar as they have settled, they form alien minorities, or an ethnic cultural minority in an alien context. The new context has an influence: it may be resisted or to some extent it may be transforming. With all this mixture and merging worldwide in a general context of technology that has shrunk time and space into insignificance, "culture," the shared outlook and behavior of a group, however small or temporary, is the dynamic of an invincibly pluralistic world.

The remainder of this chapter will sample the most typical and influential new cultures of this kind, the transformation of traditional cultures in new contexts, particularly of the humanistic culture inherited from the Greeks, but also of Islam and Communism. The end in view is a global civilization of a new kind that could conserve this immense diversity, like an ecology of ecosystems, but not purposeless. The shared outlook and pattern of behavior would be dominant but partial, composed of what is essentially universal, like the attained human capability. What is happening on the ground in terms of plans and intentions and initiatives undertaken and in progress can be seen in evidence. Whether performance has the scale and effectiveness to displace the void is a question. All this is the thread of what follows.

# Contemporary "Cultures"

The most complete, innovative, and dynamic transformation of a culture in a new context has been the general restructuring of business management initiated by the Harvard Business School, itself an innovation. With more sources of production coming on stream, competition was more testing, and the waste of "human capital" as the most rewarding investment was perceived in the customary hierarchical command structure of management boards, which used the workforce as an inert tool, when it could and should be itself managerial, responsible, and innovative, to the last man or woman, working in small, specialized teams under leaders charged with keeping the team up to the level of its responsibility, not with instructing it. There could not be a more revolutionary transformation, an invention comparable with the internal-combustion engine—insofar as it worked. Ford took it up and put it in practice. The Japanese took it over from America, and recently brought in as consultant the current head of the Harvard School for his ideas on boosting competitiveness.

The new management culture is a shared outlook and pattern of behavior. There has been developed a group technique for breaking a shared pattern of behavior, a form of assisted self-help. The group is composed of a small number of peers, volunteers who are all victims of the same kind of compulsive behavior. They meet confidentially under a form of contract which requires each of them to expose himself as fully and openly as he knows how to the others, and to receive their comment and criticism. Persons who have found themselves in an unhappy or disadvantaged situation have pioneered self-help groups that bring together others who share their plight. These groups are all manifestations of a shared social approach and general pattern of practice which is a remedial or therapeutic culture that compares favorably, for example, with the notoriously corrupting culture of prisons in our penal system. General courses over a long weekend in human relations promoted recently have been made use of by some modern managements for their team-leaders; they have testified to its benefit, and called it "mind management," which testifies to its dubiety. It is loosely organized, and has not been evaluated.

A culture may be maleficent as well as beneficent: the Mafia has been a notorious example. It exemplifies also the transformation in a new context. An underground brigandage in Sicily, with emigrants to the United States from the controlling families, who flaunted their power openly in Chicago during the reign of Al Capone, in Italy itself it corrupted and penetrated local officialdom and central government, itself corrupted by unbroken office of the Christian Democrats since the war. Recently, the Mafia has been so sure of its hold over the government that it has come into the open, and is in the government. Made impotent by the prompt assassination of judges who threaten to succeed in convicting and imprisoning the Mafia leaders, and embarrassed by their weakness as partners in Europe, the government has drawn back from the brink, and has initiated a new phase by purging itself in depth by the removal of untold numbers in and out of office. It bids for a revolutionary cultural change.

"Nationalism" counts among the malign cultures, hating outsiders, shrinking into self-centered preoccupation. When Dr. Johnson spoke of patriotism as the last refuge of a scoundrel, Boswell was of the opinion that he meant "pretended patriotism as a cloak for self-interest." That is an abstract characterization. Concretely, Nazism was an extreme example. Democratic states in Europe are being edged in that direction by the influx from many quarters of foreigners hopeful of a better way of life. Liberalism as the culture of democracy can be saved only by positive action abroad, not by giving way at home, nor by putting up the barriers.

Israel is partly a transformation of an ancient culture in a modern context, partly a daily and detailed resurrection of what Hadrian disposed of in the year 135 by fanatical Zionists with Bible in hand. When the Ayatollah Khomeini on the overthrow of the modernizing Shah returned to Iran from sixteen years of exile in France, his intransigent fundamentalism was the entrenchment of Islam in total opposition to modernity in the image of an America that had seduced the Shah and intoxicated the world with the dream of enjoying an extravagant American lifestyle. The ideals of Islam were refurbished in this context with an austerity that is not traditional, and can hardly be sustained. But Shiite fundamentalism has spread, and is the dread of many Arab states.

Hindus and Sikhs, and Muslims from Pakistan and India and Bangladesh, with Indian traders expelled from Africa earlier, have settled in Britain and set up businesses. Hindu tolerance enables Hindus to appreciate and enjoy the benefits of both cultures. Muslims are more diverse, and include those who are orthodox and organized enough to press demands for equal treatment, particularly for schools of their own on the same terms as Jews, Roman Catholics, Anglicans, and Nonconformists under the Education Act of 1944, and for the protection of the blasphemy law. Girls born into strict Muslim families in England are not all docile and compliant in the matter of arranged marriages, influenced by the comparative independence of English schoolfellows. The original assumption that immigrants who settled would be assimilated, appropriate enough when the great majority were Caribbean, has been superseded by actual coexistence of diverse ethnic groups and their cultures. Even in the United States, the "melting pot" where refugees were born into the possibility of a new life as Americans, American English is ceasing to be universal in a union of states that is polyglot, with a growing dominance of Hispanics, a context that will work a transformation of American culture, as in England it will influence the culture of British democracy, already affected by the irrepressible claims of Scots and Welsh.

The most glaring and alarming example of transformation in a change of context is of course Yugoslavia, where Croats, Serbs, Bosnians, Muslims, and even Albanians had lived side by side peaceably, as acceptable neighbors ruled from Belgrade, and were plunged into mutual slaughter, "ethnic cleansing," with the dissolution of the sovereign power of the regime.

In Africa, tribal divisions with their traditional cultures moved from the context of subjection to British, French, or Portuguese colonial rule, into a context of independence fought for and won mainly under the leadership of the strongest tribe, whose elite took over the government from the colonial power.

## European Culture

Europe inherited in common the Greco-Roman classical cultures embodied since the Renaissance in the core curriculum of schools, the humanities, and mathematics, proficiency in which remained the training and qualification for the elite recruited into government and the higher echelons of public service, until the encroachments of technology and business management imposed other requirements.

Since the low Latin of the medieval period there has been no common language; and the language barrier seems unlikely to have a side gate of that kind. Esperanto is indeed spreading, but the technology of simultaneous translation and its expert staff supply to international meetings facilities for listening in languages in general use that meet the needs of delegations from far parts, despite the fact that some 140 languages are listed worldwide, with innumerable dialects and derivatives.

The classical inheritance is extant, in the sense that a cultivated European is familiar not only with the literature and arts of his country, but also will know and enjoy works of merit in other languages. He need not be a critic to have a broad cultivated taste, and he is probably more generally found in all walks of life on the continent than in England. But this diffused European culture has been and is being transformed in the technological context of the time. The transformed European culture can be termed under a general head as "modernism."

The old frontiers are disregarded and freely crossed in the arts, as they have been in the sciences by the explosion of knowledge. Both arts and sciences that figured in the culture of Hellas have now become contextual and interdisciplinary, and the tendency was at work even in classical times. Picasso declared "painting" outmoded, and diverted his own barely equalled draftsmanship to introduce an inventive and impulsive miscellaneity into his work in an endless range of experimentation in juxtapositions, distortions, and importations, whether prompted by ideas or by attraction from whatever his eyes lighted on in the everyday world around.

Graphic design exploded in invention on posters, signs, and billboards. A famous theater director said, "We want our backdrop to be an iron pipe or the sea or something built by the New Man." That may sound like "socialist realism" imposed on all artists like a death sentence, but it was in no sense an anticipation of Stalinism, quite the reverse; rather, it was an anticipation of the modernism that infects all behavior with the design, invention, and style of fine art.

Music, now inescapably with us on every hand, of all the arts represents acutely the breaking down of barriers, the river that overflows its banks. It is one of the several explosions that characterize the transformation of culture in the context of the postwar age. The flood is an embarrassment to some, the oxygen of their existence to many. One sees the young with their ears plugged, their eyes buried in a book. What is heard, and what is listened to would be an unanswerable question.

Composition in the classical mode continues, although Debussy introduced a revolution when he released from the keyboard a volume of sound instead of the expected note-after-note in the movements of a composition. In general, sound is taken out of the context of harmony, and not safely delivered to the habits of an ear to which it had been tuned, to be exploited experimentally for itself. New instruments are put together, or borrowed from the kitchen or wherever to introduce new sounds, which can be enhanced or distorted electronically.

Rock was and is the currency of youthful revolt. It has not developed the spontaneity and vitality of its sources. Successive lead singers and bands react against one another. The cool correctness of the Beatles becomes wilder and wilder, adding costumes, choreography, properties, lighting, ever new devices of technology, until with Michael Jackson the stage performance has become a show overloaded with "refinements," which lumbers on the road like a circus on the move, which it is.

Music renews itself in endless recycling, and is matched now by performers who, regardless of genre or instrument, are aware only of "music," the universe which is their universe, their life.

Dance is the primary, perhaps ultimate, art, as the body is the human being and source of human renewal. It is partner to music. Nijinsky's premiere in Paris in 1912 of *L'Après-midi d'un faune* bounded out of the steps, conventions, and intentions of classical ballet into interpretation of a work, a pioneering choreography followed by notable successors toward this end of the century. Martha Graham in New York has been succeeded by several outstanding choreographers, each with an idiosyncratic bent, bringing in close-up detail with head movements and facial expression.

On the dance floor, jiving took over with jazz. The Tango was and is special. It comes from Arab, Spanish, and Indian sources, and is marked by a strong, slow, rhythmic beat, bearing overtones of passion and undertones of melancholy. It was taken from Argentina to Finland and Norway, to become an exclusive national dance, expressive of a people's ways and identity like a national anthem.

Fashion is ephemeral, marketing seasonal novelty. The career of Yves Saint Laurent, the Parisian master of haute couture, blazoned in publicity, transformed this run-of-the-mill display of the seasonal collection into a laboratory of art and an epitome of art. Catering exclusively to the well-off, he would not have gained popular renown. However, when he found the commercial market was thriving on ready-to-wear clothes he developed and produced models for off-the-peg pockets and tastes that vindicated his superiority. His materials were fabrics, color, ornamentation, pattern, perfume—a sensuous base. Music accompanied the cat-walk performance. The annual collection had to be pieced together from the work of teams with assigned jobs. The major contribution was detailed craftwork of the highest standard, exacted without concession, as if for a cognoscente. The bits and pieces were programmed for production, assembly, dressing, to make the news at the expected time. Organization of the whole operation was time-tabled commercial logistics. He lent to this industry with an insubstantial product for frivolous consumers an integrity and pursuit of excellence that paralleled the production of Greek bronzes, one of their chief claims to artistic fame, and also put together from separately produced parts.

Cultures are transformed within a new context. The original concept referred to the complex pattern of behavior of a community living in isolation, as studied by an anthropologist. An ecosystem is the parallel in nature. A fixed boundary is necessary to the concept. It is with the general breakdown of barriers and disregard of established boundaries that the notion of culture has been made tenuous, and its usage too loose for description. A new context implies a new boundary, and hence an adaptation of the culture formed within previous borders, as happens in nature with any change in a habitat, short of destruction. Although there has been conspicuous disregard of established boundaries in the arts and in business management, there are still many stable groupings within which there is a formative pattern of community behavior close enough to the original model to be recognized as a genuine culture. These are the subcultures that abound and are of immense sociological importance, some age-old and familiar, like the *particular* group that nurtures the maturation of an infant, or an ethnic group, a profession, a group that forms and firms an outlook and a pattern of behavior, and in that sense the abstract of one's personal identity. The criminal underworld was and is a culture; the world and life of the homeless on the streets less so. A city ghetto ruled by gangs has the boundary and the behavior and outlook; as does a huddle of drug addicts. Where human life has shrunk to a subhuman routine that is shared, culture in that subculture is a parody of itself; but it is there on the ground, evokes a response and is part of the human mix. However, cancerous cells are a threat, not a norm; and the range and variety of multiplying subcultures in our One World is a source and condition of human vitality—not forgetting the therapeutic cultural artifact.

## Human Civilization

Hitherto, "human culture" as "human nature and destiny" has been mainly understood and promoted diversely on the assumptions of the major religious faiths and dispensations. In the pluralistic global context, secularization is universal. The diverse religious faiths remain, but with no global organs of enforcement. Human consciousness as an informed awareness of "human nature and destiny" is not a faith; as knowledge, its universality is virtual and should belong to the future. This has come about through the culture of human learning, which is what brought about the new dimension of human nature, capability, and responsible independence-the "coming of age."

If "human culture" has been since Greek beginnings and its antecedents the culture of human learning, truly universal, as distinct from the universal claims of Christianity and Roman imperialism, human "civilization" is human consciousness as knowledge, not faith and political union as an inclusive pluralism, not imperial rule, not world government. The probable/possible human destiny in these terms builds on positive and hopeful contemporary events and trends.

Institutions for a world order regulated by a representative assembly, a quasi-democratic world government, are already in place in the UN and its agencies, the nongovernmental organizations (NGOs) with consultative status, the standing conferences, the councils and commissions set up to implement and monitor what international summits resolve to do. However, it may well be argued that the UN has survived only because it was impotent. The earth summit of 1992, the most impressive gathering of world leaders and consummation of the public-spirited private initiative of Brandt and his colleagues, followed by the UN conference "All Our Future," have shown that resolutions are words that the institutions they are the rationale for are not empowered to enforce. There is also the ultimate rule of Parkinson's Law of institutional self-preservation, palpably afflicting the UN and its agencies. These depressing indications would reduce the institutions that are in place to blueprints rather than vehicles of effective action.

Some current happenings on the ground are not susceptible to this write-off, or not yet. They are concerned with remedying the failures to act effectively in tackling the primary global tasks of a responsible independent humanity—the system of international security, which the League of Nations and the UN were set up to establish, and the environment/development world ecology and world poverty, which the earth summit was about. To build on these would indicate a positive scenario to set against the negative extrapolations. On the assumption that democracy implies a middle-ground broad enough to accommodate consensus and compromise, the whole-hoggers will prevail only if those who have well-founded doubts and fears fail to act effectively, and leave them the void.

Failure of the developed nations during more than three postwar decades to find the appropriate ways to fund and assist self-help on the ground in the poorer underdeveloped nations is being remedied in cooperation with NGOs; but debt and the terms of trade established by GATT severely handicap self-help in the underdeveloped world, with the net result that the interests of the industrialized nations continue to prevail and dominate the markets, to the detriment of a majority of underdeveloped nations. The earth summit brought this out in broad terms, and signaled the need for an international planned effort to reduce world poverty progressively, which the summit had been convened to launch. The summit in itself marked remarkable progress in the inherently difficult task of forming and informing the political will to get things done on the requisite sustainable scale to make a difference that is all the difference. That it failed to get all the way was failure, but relative failure, dashing but not destroying hope.

The major part of the failure concerned the ecological responsibilities of developed nations whose industrialized agriculture and manufacture is blamed for what has happened and is still happening to a lesser extent and developing peoples who have been driven to forest destruction and soil erosion as self-destructive ways of self-help. The key to removing that obstruction is in an effective plan to aid their sustainable growth, which was the gist of their counter-demand to the demands on them.

What can be said about current attempts to remedy failure to tackle effectively global tasks is that they are in hand or on the political agenda with pressure groups nagging for priority.

The conservation of pluralism in the development of society is comparable with the preservation of variety in the natural process of biological evolution, in that the one is known to have been the necessary condition of evolution, and the other can be assumed to be the condition of a promising human destiny, not merely survival. Therefore, an examination is appropriate of what the pluralism is that should be conserved, and what secures the conservation.

The pluralism in general is mainly a diversity of identifiable forms of association within a society. Most of these have figured in the previous chapter and in this one, groupings and subcultures in constant interaction, so that routines and conventions and traditions are exposed to collisions and challenge, and not conserved indefinitely in isolation. What is conserved in this diversity of pluralism is the agency of change: it is the dynamism of a society and marks the difference between historical societies and isolated primitive communities with a traditional uniform culture, two opposed models. Reorientation from conservation of what is established, with resistance to change, to initiation and direction of continual change has capital exemplification in the restructuring of management in order to employ the entire staff all the time in routine operations subject to their own gainful innovations. Such a revolution follows the grain of things in the temporality of all existence, instead of imposing an alien rigidity. In that respect it is comparable with the discovery of and conformity with the ecological natural order.

If the ultimate justification of pluralism is the all-importance of variety in the long term, its regulation is in the inescapable context of global interdependence long-term, as the discipline for short-term views, and aims. If that discipline works slowly and doubtfully, as is evident in Mozambique and Angola, and is the present stumbling block obstructing peace-making by the Standing Conference in Geneva, one must ask what the alternative is, and the present groping which is on trial is a reading of experience that has concluded that there is no alternative that offers a way forward. Either no hope or trial of an international community, founded on the interdependence in which it is involved, and organized to act with authority and power by withholding the benefits that accrue to its members from any that may fail to conform to agreed requirements. This is the present state of Condorcet's "social art," a long way down the road in a context he could not have imagined in his final chapter of future progress.

UN Secretary General Boutros-Ghali has outlined an agenda for his term of office in a report on "preventive diplomacy." Interviewed by *Newsweek,* he stated as his priority reinvigoration of the UN as an effective institution by requiring membernations to pay their dues promptly for eligibility, and to increase them as an investment, since prevention costs far less than "crisis-management." He wanted closer collaboration and coordination of the agencies, NGOs, quasiautonomous international organizations, and more active participation of member-states than their vote in the General Assembly; they would have a stake in operations by sharing in the provision of personnel for preventive peace-keeping work on the ground. With these enhanced resources, he would be in a position to take initiatives, exercise the influence, and exert the pressures needed for his preventive diplomacy.

The preventive measures the Secretary General has in mind will not necessarily avoid having to resort to crisis-management. A preventive absolute (like all political "solutions" of problems) is not to be looked for. What Boutros-Ghali has in mind is a fact-finding mission to scout out an area of concern, not only for information but also to alert attention to that concern. Intervention would concentrate on the self-interest of the parties in potential conflict, to wean them from preoccupation with what can be gained while relative strength is favorable, and encourage them to recognize that greater and more secure gain can be attained in good time if conflict is avoided and conditions of mutual benefit brought about, specific conditions for which the UN will provide aid if cooperation is forthcoming. This approach of the UN and its particular applications would be advertised to the world and strongly reinforced by the modern publicity of television, radio, and Reuters, reaching all news-desks with immediacy. For it would constitute a world jury for the agreements being negotiated, agreements to be secured by demilitarized zones policed by a proportionate international force. Regional security systems would have to be worked out to provide the world context for such preventive interventions. That network and preventive intervention were seen by the Secretary General as the logical sequel to the UN-European plan broached at the London Conference to deprive breakers of the peace of the benefits of international community. He is committed to trying to see its establishment within his five-year term of office, to use his political will to mobilize the political will of the UN to found an international security system as the global task with urgent priority. Two devastating world wars, and the advent of annihilating nuclear power, have concentrated minds since the Enlightenment propounded a scheme for perpetual peace (Rousseau-Kant).

Human civilization is the comprehensive concept for this plural international order as the context of a pluralistic culture. This culture has been and will be both the advancement of learning and cultivation of the arts. Disciplined learning is science, technology, and scholarship. Without scholarship, there would be scant knowledge of the arts, and no cultivation of them, whatever arts might be practiced. Scholarship provides the immediate context within which the arts function, as distinct from the international political frame. The arts themselves are *sui generis* and not susceptible of progress. A cave sketch may be rudimentary or crude as craft; it is the business of scholarship to provide information about it; a primitive work of art it is not like a primitive tool, it cannot be bettered nor outmoded. The province of art is the variety of experience, not utility. Communication of experience is a specialized traffic, with particular traditions.

The universality and vitality of the dance keep it at the popular center of art forms, and it is probably the best example of immense diversity and adaptability. Seeing a TV film of the Massai tribe in northern Kenya as it lives today, holding on in the last moments to its ritualistic patterns of behavior, one is struck by the parallel with rock groups since the sixties. The dressing-up for the ritual dances, with decorated bodies and heavy personal ornamentation and gorgeous colors, the drums and rhythms, the leaping exuberant participation in what has to be collective, and also individual: both are tribal manifestations of a shared culture, forgetting the competition for "top of the pops." By contrast, the Japanese court dances, secret before the emperor's tentative entry into public life, are models of slow, subtle, graceful movements of some four figures as an anonymous presence of sunbright regular shapes, expressing the secret life and identity of the monarch. By contrast again, the Sun monarch, Louis XIV, structured his court on cultivation of the dance as a public manifestation of his absolute authority and power in continuous celebration. He founded an Academy of Dance, was the initial choreographer of court dances which regulated the court hierarchy, and sent dancing-masters round the European courts, to proclaim

French culture and propagate its influence. His priority and commitment to the dance was the cultural counterpart to the priority and commitment to war. The one brought his country to ruin. The other survived as a source of classical ballet, before falling into desuetude until revived and transformed in the context of epoch-making events and the advent of the Rite of Spring.

The orgiastic experience, intoxication, a drug-induced high, is associated with ecstasy and inspiration. The Pythian oracle at Delphi was "possessed" and rapt and bodily convulsed before uttering the prophecy communicated through her. This mythical inspiration is from above, actual inspiration from below. The rational and purposeful mind in the art of thought formulates the question to be addressed, sorting out inconsistencies and irrelevance, so that an answer is on target for the purpose in hand. Having done what is necessary to provide this context, the conscious mind waits on promptings from the unconscious and subconscious, to be sorted, formulated, and tested.

Contemporary arts include a characteristic of the age: anti-art or no-art. Fundamentally, it is a repudiation of value, nihilism, which has had a philosophical or political resonance hitherto, save that it bobbed up and down in the Dada movement from its inception in 1915 for some forty years. In that movement, it was "an increasingly hysterical demand for the destruction of art," while serious artists in the movement "continued in the tradition of art while using the watchwords of anti-art to open up new paths." To discredit art, works of art had been put alongside manufactures, a coal shovel, a bicycle wheel, or a utility, a urinal. The ultimate answer to that, you could live with a painting and it would grow on you, for you kept finding more in it, because it had more than you could ever find in a bicycle wheel or the like; and that was an everlasting difference. The shock-value of anti-art like a burst balloon loses its point when it has lost its shock.

Traditional culture, in which the dance is usually prominent, has been a consolation prize for authorities who have lost political power, but cling to patronage and promotion of native arts. When Indonesia declared itself a republic in 1950, the ousted royal court in Java sought to establish a new national identity in this way. The Japanese god-king in the postwar regime modernized himself by opening the rituals of the court cult to the public. In Ghana, the Ashanti tribe lost its dominance to a military dictator, and has boosted its cultural festivals—so that Flight-Lieutenant Rawlings is constrained to visit the celebrations, and pay his respects.

A rough scan of cultural pluralism today shows a decadent "modernism" like the disintegrating political order. The map is patchy, but the strongest tendency is to succumb to the pull of commercial values, in the arts as in sport. Money is success, the supreme prize. Image, publicity, wins the most. If this tendency becomes mainstream, more than a corrupting influence, that would occlude any hopeful vision of a human civilization. Is there anything in the cultural scene to match what is being done in the name of the UN to establish a system of international security and on the ecological front to mobilize the political will to act effectively in time?

Histories of the arts within their cultural contexts, like those of states and populations within their boundaries are now materials for scholars to study in a global context with a human perspective. Extant works exist physically in collections housed appropriately and catalogued, exhibited, and maintained by professional keepers, with regulated public access. The jurisdiction of scholarship is being established internationally like that of science, and steady progress is to be expected in the information and critical judgment available in the world's artistic culture. Experiences are the products and commerce of the arts themselves, not commodities, not utilities. Supply and demand create a market, with investment and profit and loss, but that is not business in which artists themselves are engaged.

Experiences are sensuous or emotional or intellectual or imaginative. They are of the human body, its exercise, how it looks, its sex, its age, its postures, of passions, moods, of the natural world, of colors, shapes, patterns, sounds, harmony, discord, contrast, comparison, analogy. Art is arrangement, order, composition. In general, it is the scale of particular experiences that can enter human consciousness or touch the five senses.

A work of art cannot be experienced in any other time and place as it was where and when it was created. Nevertheless, it survives to be experienced differently by others elsewhere, generation after generation indefinitely. That is because of the difference between a work of art and a consumable commodity, one that is usable and will wear out. Art is a product of experience, and transmits experience. The point of the samples listed above was to indicate the inexhaustible range of human experience. Each is a particular part within the dimensions of possibility, and relatively a very small part. As a part, it is not necessarily inexhaustible as experience in general is, nor necessarily exhaustible. Its input is of a kind that unfolds gradually and is discoverable. It is experienced differently by persons whose maturation and formation are in different native cultures, and whose tastes are cultivated in different societies and ages.

Every work is stamped with finality by the artist as it passes into memory, and that is why there is, properly speaking, no progress in the arts, but indefinite progress in the scholarship that informs their study and therewith experience of them. The cave artist is exercising his skill, formulating his feelings and thought, and communicating with his tribe in sketching the figure on the wall. If the tenant of a council house in the twentieth century happens to see some reproduction, what he sees can hardly be expected to transmit what the cave man had in mind. What it would transmit directly and instantly is recognition of a fellow human being.

In these works of body, hand, eye, ear, finger, voice, heart, human beings enjoy supremely the experience of being human. This is the cultural birthright of a species scattered over the face of the earth, organizing itself in differing regimes and practicing diverse walks of life. What has been said here about works of art has been general, ignoring distinctions of prime importance, for the range of works passes from the capricious or the throwaway to the immemorial. Both are "experienced," of course, but one as a passing fantasy, the other an imaginative creation that reshapes the world in powerful images in which obscure implications of experience are communicated. This power of the imagination is educative, not entertainment. Both are within the province of art.

Many early cultures were maintained by shamans who felt a compulsive responsibility to ensure the daily maintenance of the cosmic conditions on which all life depends by practicing sympathetic rituals that were at the same time invocations, celebrations, and active participation in the balance of things that sustains all life. This is still the belief and practice of, say, Mexican Indians, and it lay behind Plato's thinking, evident in the Socratic dialogues and the *Republic*. By an opposed culture of learning, the scattered populations of the earth have now been brought together in actuality by the technology of rapid communication and transport. And the finely balanced conditions needed to maintain life on the planet, which were the object of confirming rituals, are now understood in enough detail to forbid behavior that disregards them and impose measures to redress harm done. The responsibility is a commitment to precisely defined tasks, shared in particular undertakings that involve all, collectively and individually. This shared commitment is the final and actual bond of union that has been imaged as "the brotherhood of man."

So long as there is effective action in addressing the tasks that demand priority, space for a better future is occupied: there is a level playing field in the making for fulfillment of reasonable expectations.

# 23

# Dignity Self-discovered

## WOMEN

### The Legacy

The three societies in antiquity that formed models for Europe were as distinct in the position of women as in their cultures; but with Constantine's adoption of Christianity as the state religion, the prevailing influence of the Church was alien to all three. After so many generations brought up in Christian traditions, Catholic, Orthodox, or Sectarian, neither qualified faith nor outright and widespread loss of faith can merely eliminate this influence as it has been exerted. Because it was a peculiar influence, alien to Greek and Roman and Jew, the particular impact of that influence has not been generally reckoned with.

Because the arts were so highly valued and cultivated in Greece, women had scope they hardly enjoyed elsewhere at the time. Their greatest lyric poet, Pindar, was taught by a woman poet, celebrated in her own city by a prominent statue. Sappho's lyrics were so highly regarded, she was called the tenth Muse. There is a statue in the Vatican Museum and a bust in Rome. Pallas Athene, springing from the head of Jove, was notionally female, with a unique plenitude of attributes, patron of domestic crafts and handicrafts, as well as the liberal arts, endowing mankind with the olive, symbol of peace; Diana invented the first feminist exclusive movement of self-assertion, forsaking sex for hunting. Within Greece itself, there was the strongest cultural contrast in Athens and Sparta, turning on devotion to and rejection of the arts and sciences; in Sparta, military virtues and values alone counted, for male and female alike. The Greek imagination, with a foothold in social experience, was in this as in other matters a theater for the entertainment of all possibilities, that is, the possibilities which make history, and some which do not. The Roman matron is a Roman institution,

341

propagator of the Roman citizen, no mere mother; the nurturing womb is the home over which she presides and in which her children are bound to the service of Rome. The Jews were told to "be fruitful, and multiply." The family was highly valued, and the wife and mother enjoyed authority and respect, so that the power of the Jewish mother was proverbial. The family was the locus of tradition and ritual practices, the cultural genesis of Jewish identity that kept them in the same ethnic family scattered in the diaspora around the world. In all three societies, women had different ideas and expectations of themselves and were differently regarded, but in all three their role was specifically related to promoting what these peoples came to regard as their destiny. With the Greeks, confinement to the home and its duties was humanized by norms of sexual partnership and sexual faithfulness. Hellenic civilization, transplanting the culture of Hellas geographically, introduced transformations, of which one prominent one was a movement for the emancipation of women, their employment in the professions after an education comparable with that of boys, and, most striking of all, discovery of their femininity, interest in them for themselves. Alongside the full equality of men and women in the Garden of Epicurus, as products of nature and as his disciples, and similar inferences may be drawn from Stoic doctrines, these are anticipations of an emancipation that began to be recovered in the European Enlightenment, so many centuries later, and has made a general leap forward not until this postwar period, and as an organized movement particularly in the 1960s.

Simple straightforward recognition of the human equality of the sexes was hindered and delayed by influences from three sources, natural, political, and cultural: childbirth, war, and religion. As child-bearers, women had evident inherent human superiority in simple societies, for which men compensated by instituting male initiation rites for boys, a graduation in the acquisition of manhood. In more complex societies, where rapine and war settle what shall be, the model is the hero whose fame is sung by the poet. "War is both *king* of all and *father* of all," said Heraclitus. That is what made a man's world. Even Cicero, the supreme orator, put the soldier's role above his own, and superior to all. Virtue was preeminently martial virtue (not justice), the proper attribute of *vir,* a man. "Amazonians" are not found in nature, nor in human societies. The influence of religion is more complex, and varies within a religion as well as between them. In the Bible, the "children of Israel" are descendants of the Patriarchs, ancestors of the human race, and particularly of Abraham, chosen by God. When Constantine forces the Church to adopt an enforceable dogmatic theology, it is the dogma of the Trinity that is elected, a divine nuclear family of Father and "only begotten" Son, incarnated through a woman merely to carry out the mission of the Father's will: the "Three-in-One" has no female aspect. The patricians, hereditary aristocracy of ancient Rome, were the sole holders of political and religious offices. Things belonged either to Caesar or to God. In sum, things conspired to vest power and possession in a masculine grip.

Levi Strauss has argued that the monogamous family and mode of upbringing tends to prevail in all circumstances under the constraint of the act of reproduction itself: "You will leave your father and mother" is a necessary rule for a society as such, beyond culture. Variations are relative to this norm.

Christianity is rooted in Judaism, and would not have come into history otherwise. The Old Testament is the foundation of the New, and New Testament theology is the fulfillment of Old Testament prophecies. Beyond this first theology is discourse with Greek philosophy and Gnosticism. If this engendered the first Christian heresies, it is important to remember that whatever else Christianity was, as a sect it was a Jewish heresy. The women who followed Jesus around, ministering unto him as Mark records and were with him to the end included choice spirits like Mary who could enter into communication with him, and one may think of the Epicurean fellowship. Also, he refers to the unity within the marriage bond as divinely ordained, with perhaps Malachi 2:14–15 in mind. But such evidence is essentially irrelevant; the purpose of his mission was to announce the coming of the Kingdom, and to call on those whom he had chosen and convinced to go out into the world and proclaim the good news. John Wyclif was the first modern to discern that this was the essential gospel and mission of the Church, to which she had been unfaithful, an anticipation of Protestant Reformation. Women did not come within the scope of this calling and commission to evangelize. The expectation had been that the Kingdom of God to which the world was to be called was indeed at hand. When it became evident that it was not, the event became the Second Coming in the indefinite future, probably the year 1,000. Meanwhile, those called should live the religious life. The original example of that was the life of St. Anthony, the hermit in the desert, as recounted by Athanasius in his biography. That was the backdoor through which asceticism seeped into Christian tradition, probably from Gnostic sources, since it is not in the New Testament. However, it was stamped in by the sexual neurosis of three very influential Fathers, Tertullian, Jerome, and above all Augustine. These instilled a terror of women as the embodiment of insatiable lust, the standing temptation of Eve to disobedience: an obvious projection. Institutionally, the religious life was practiced by withdrawal from the world into all male or all female communities, usually with a vow to poverty, chastity, and obedience to the superior, in dedication wholly to the service of God. What is in the New Testament is the (apostolic) injunction to wives to obey their husbands; they are deemed in subjection to him in the home as an ordained order of things, imposed on Eve and her sex with the pains of childbirth as the punitive consequences of the primal disobedience (Genesis 3:16). In her thorough examination of the myth of the Virgin Mary, Marina Warner concluded: "Whether we regard the Virgin Mary as the most sublime and beautiful image in man's struggle toward the good and the pure, or the most pitiable production of ignorance and superstition, she represents a central theme in the history of western attitudes to women." That theme is the tendency to idealize woman, counter to the liability to degrade woman by the projection upon her of masculine lust. Both tendencies were within the bosom of the Catholic Church, perhaps equally unhealthy as equally false.

When the Church introduced celibacy as a condition of priesthood, it was apt to be a stranglehold on sex. Penitentiaries show that even within marriage abstinence was made as enforceable as possible in the confessional. Take out periods of pregnancy, menstruation, breast-feeding, when child follows child; add holy days that crowd the calendar, including Sundays; make it a rule in preparation for communion;

precious little opportunity is left for indulgence. Official Roman Catholic prohibitions may be unenforceable and little heeded, but they influenced the climate of opinion in which women in the West grew up before the Reformation. Pathological fear and lust combined to make men hate women enough to make the witch-hunt craze possible. On the other hand, to idolize women as sexless, childlike, and pure was as nonsensical if not as evil.

Courtly love in the Age of Chivalry was a secular rule to which the Church had to make its own adjustment. Otherwise, any role for a woman outside the home in a man's world had to be played as a quasi-male. Within the Church, this might be as a saint or as head of a convent or reformer of an Order (Carmelites). In each case the woman is a permanent virgin. Joan of Arc, *La Pucelle,* wears male attire and lives with the army, and is untouchable. Florence Nightingale compared herself with Joan, alienated from her sisterhood by having thrown in her lot with men. The examination of Joan by the Church showed that what it feared was disobedience, independence of its authority. She is repeatedly asked if she will submit to the Church. Like the Communist Party, the Roman Church had to maintain its bureaucratic control, an exclusively masculine control. Joan's service to France had to be brought within that jurisdiction.

The Reformation, with the priesthood of all believers, should have emancipated men and women from religious authority. Not so. The woman remained imprisoned in the home as wife and mother. The head of the home, the father, was high priest who led the daily prayers for family and servants. This was a root of patriarchal tyranny that became characteristic. This was different in principle from the status of the matron in the Roman household or of a Jewish mother.

The Enlightenment was an interim of detachment from religious prejudice and clerical dominance, with the promise of better things to come. There is not a murmur of the matter in Condorcet's *Sketch,* until suddenly toward the end of the Tenth Stage, "The future progress of the human mind," there are two short paragraphs which are radical in principle, if confined to the family in scope:

> Among the many causes of the progress of the human mind that are of the utmost importance to the general happiness, we must number the complete annihilation of the prejudices that have brought about an inequality of rights between the sexes, an inequality fatal even to the party in whose favor it works. . . . This inequality has its origin solely in an abuse of strength, and all the later sophistical attempts that have been made to excuse it are vain.
>
> We shall show how the abolition of customs authorized laws dictated by this prejudice, would add to the happiness of family life, would encourage the practice of the domestic virtues on which all other virtues are based, how it would favor the progress of education, and how, above all, it would bring about its wider diffusion; for not only would education be extended to women as well as to men, but it can only really be taken proper advantage of when it has the support and encouragement of mothers of the family. Would not this belated tribute to equity and good sense put an end to a principle only too fecund of injustice, cruelty and crime, by removing the dangerous conflict between the strongest and most irrepressible of all natural inclinations and man's duty or the interests of society? Would it not produce what until

now has been no more than a dream, national manners of a mildness and purity, formed not by proud asceticism, not by hypocrisy, not by fear of shame or religious terrors but by freely contracted habits that are inspired by nature and acknowledged by reason?

William Law's *A Serious Call to a Devout and Holy Life* (1728) was a seminal work that influenced Dr. Johnson and William Wilberforce, and through Wilberforce the influential Evangelical party at the beginning of the nineteenth century. Like La Buyere, he uses fictional characters to exemplify the precepts he wants to inculcate, despising the body and the things of this world, wholly devoted to God and good works, living in this world in anticipation of the next. *Miranda* is the model of what a woman should be. *Eusebia* shows how daughters should be brought up. If fathers or husbands should require them to conform to the ways of the world and adopt its vanities, they should in obedience do so, bearing it as a cross, knowing that it is contrary to their true interest and to what is right. At the same time, they should try to persuade husband or father of the truth and of their error, and to bring about their conversion. This manifesto of a radical and literal Christian life in the world in modern times was the main source of the evangelical movement which together with Bentham's Utilitarian movement, with its background in the rationalism of French *philosophes,* was a dominant political influence in the early part of the century.

Mary Wollstonecraft's *Thoughts on the Education of Daughters* (1787) and the more famous *Vindication of the Rights of Women* (1792) are the voice of a woman intellectually standing on the independent ground of reason, to say that women have the universal attributes of humanity as rational and moral agents: sexual characteristics are secondary. If they are treated simply and solely in regard to their sexual characteristics, they will be neither rational nor moral. If they do not have the full attributes of humanity, they have no duties whatever, and should not be allowed what little freedom and share in humanity they do have. She was targeting Rousseau's Sophie. It would do just as well later for *The Angel in the House.** The thrust of Mill's *Subjection of Women* was in the context of representative government: they ought to be represented and speak for themselves, and not have it assumed that their interests were the same or could be adequately spoken for by men—on which he had objected to a paragraph in his father's "Essay on Government." He honored the Saint-Simonians for proclaiming the perfect equality of men and women and an entirely new order of things in their relations with one another. This was deep-seated and original in him, but he notes in his autobiography that he owed to his wife an appreciation of the vast practical bearings of women's disabilities which he had pointed out in the *Subjection of Women*: how the inferior position of women was bound up with all the evils of existing society and with all the difficulties of human improvement. The Saint-Simonians had been most cried down for their championship of women, for this was something the nineteenth century in general did not want to hear about. The subjection, like slavery, was an immense convenience to the owners. Indeed, a whole order was bound up with it. Who otherwise would bear children, look after them,

---

*Sequence of poems by Coventry Patmore.

bring them up, make a home? If not a wife and mother, it would have to be hired females, a domestic staff. And what could they do outside the home, in business, in the professions, in affairs of church or state? How absurd it all was. This was not an order to tamper with.

G. M. Young was close enough and detached enough and versed enough in Victorian England to make his *Portrait of an Age* a perceptive and skillful likeness. He takes representative institutions and the family as unquestionable and unassailable to that age. On the family, he is cautious, for it was a touchy subject, even with increasing secularism. "Sexual ethic had attracted to itself so great a body of romantic sentiment: it was so closely associated, and even identified, with virtue in general, with the elevated, the praiseworthy, the respectable life, that the faintest note of dissidence might attract a disproportionate volume of suspicion and censure." He did not feel at a safe enough distance for a fair judgment on that. He goes on to speak with appreciation of the abounding liveliness and vivacious contact of the large (middle class) families not in need, in spite of the hypocrisy, injustice, suffering, cruelty often found in family life of the time—as in schools, the peer-group subculture was a refuge and resort in defense against tyranny. The upshot of his examination was that the political issue of the vote could not have been raised until a forceful woman's lobby had been made possible by the social transformation by "the rapid improvement of and extension of women's education, and their increasing activity in the professions and Universities, in local administration, in philanthropic work, in the Inspectorates." Over the whole range of criticism and intelligence, he concluded, women had become "an effective element in the articulation of the social mind." Also, in the last quarter of the century the birth-rate of the educated classes began to fall, and with that the old patriarchal cohesion declined, and a new world was dawning.

A Victorian who had a great deal to say about women was John Ruskin: *Sesame and Lilies* is full of it. Men and women were different and complementary; their natures and vocations had equally to be developed. In idealizing both, Ruskin is pure fantasy. *The Angel in the House* was more to contemporary taste. She is a child, an angel, compelling in her total submissiveness. This idealization is far from fantasy, for realism runs between the lines, revealing the enemy in the object in whom affection is totally invested. From this overheated domestic intimacy, it is simple relief to recall earlier ideas of married love in a religious setting. Aquinas: "The greatest friendship is that between man and wife; they are coupled not only by physical intercourse, which even among animals conduces to a certain sweet friendship, but also for the sharing of domestic life." Jeremy Taylor said that marriage was the best of friendships, "a union of all things excellent." These two, Catholic and Protestant, link well with the Sophist Isocrates and Ischomacus in Xenophon's book.

As Levi Strauss saw a link between society itself and monogamy, Young saw a primal link of sex with social union and domestic authority, and could see no end to the consequences of their severance. This was virtually on the eve of the war, and independent of it. The vision of the Enlightenment was the definitive and indefinite progress of mankind, because it was thought that at last reason and morality had been established as acknowledged standards and guides, social norms independent of institutions and traditions. Mary Wollstonecraft had relegated sexual difference to secondary importance, since men and women shared in the same humanity as rational and moral agents. G. M. Young on the eve of the war had felt confident that the future of culture, and with it the universality of the "distinguished intelligence" was safer in the hands of women and was slipping out of the resolution of men.

## Feminism

Young had argued that the Suffragettes, the first forceful women's political lobby, specifically for the vote, could not have mounted their claim unless there had already been a social transformation effected by the penetration of women into educational institutions, which qualified them in the same way as their husbands and brothers for gainful employment, and independence—escape from the universal plight of Daniel Defoe's Moll Flanders. Together with the dissemination of information about the use of contraceptives, which had been a long and bitter moral and legal battle in itself, "a monstrous crime" denounced by the medical establishment with Marie Stopes as the controversial women's champion after Annie Besant, and which facilitated "regulated child-bearing" adjusted to career intentions, conditions were laid that enabled women to organize themselves to raise their voice and exert their pressure to obtain the necessary practical measures to give them political and economic equality with men, unquestionably. Their part in the war reinforced all this dramatically. They had served in the forces and replaced men on the home front, and had been replaced when the men returned. They were not a minority, and the cards were in their hands, but nothing would be done to redress their grievances unless they organized themselves as a pressure group with political clout.

In America, the National Organization for Women (NOW) was founded in 1966 by a group of well-known and influential women, with Betty Friedan as first president. Their intention was to force recognition of "women's civil rights." The Women's Liberation Movement, dubbed (often contemptuously) "Women's Lib," in widespread use since the end of the 1960s, covers more feminist issues than legislation for equal rights; but in America it was in early association with the civil rights movement of the blacks and the agitation of student bodies: what was called the New Left. A strong tendency to squeeze them out, because of the ascendancy and dominant importance of the race issue in the South, forced them on to their own. They gained media publicity, and notoriety, for demonstrations against "sexism"—"bra-burners." By 1970, the Women's Liberation Movement consisted of thousands of small groups and was growing and changing daily. The first National Women's Liberation Conference in Britain was held at Ruskin College, Oxford, in 1970. It has remained a comprehensive movement with local diversity in what it goes about.

To focus the general aims of this organization, it is useful to take the declaration of the WLM Conference in Birmingham in 1978:

> The women's liberation movement asserts a woman's right to define her own sexuality and demands:

1. equal pay for equal work; 2. equal education and job opportunities; 3. free contraception and abortion on demand; 4. free 24-hour community controlled child care; 5. legal and financial independence for women; 6. an end to discrimination against lesbianism; 7. freedom for all women from intimidation by the threat or use of male violence; 8. an end to the laws, assumptions and institutions that perpetuate male dominance and men's aggression toward women.

These private grievances have all been brought into the public domain, and in some degree they have been attended to, some by legislation, as equal pay and nondiscrimination. Full enforcement is not practicable, and the effect on the lives of women belies the promise. All the same, the pressure is maintained and public policy continues to bite and nibble at the problems that have been defined and which the whole population has been required to face, men and women alike.

## The Nuclear Family

Two themes persist, sex equality and sexual difference. Gender equality has been paramount because it is indisputable. "Equal, but different" is regarded with suspicion as a trap. "Separate, but equal" was the formula for apartheid. There is an obvious anatomical difference, but sex has to be distinguished from gender, the one natural, the other cultural—aside from the technology that can make what is natural subject to culturally induced physiological and social modification and adaptation. However, it may be an impoverishment of humanity to treat women not merely as equal to men, but essentially the same. There are passionate arguments in the literature, focused on the interests of women, or on the upbringing of children and the future of the race. To complicate the matter, there is also "feminism" asserting itself as a presumption of feminine superiority and self-sufficiency. Like any extreme, it is not sustainable, and like political and religious extremes it finds expressions and exerts influence. A practical aspect of it is a call on women to devote themselves to what women stand for in the political world as in the prewar Women's International League for Peace and Freedom, aiming at a transformation of society.

Women's access to public life and employment takes the wife and mother out of the home and disrupts the traditional bringing up of the children by the mother in families not affluent enough to employ a nanny and send the boys to boarding school, an epoch of the upper middle class which social changes had eroded out of consideration. Two new considerations prevail: Freud's exposure of the unconscious and of sexuality from birth; the environmental disparity between the home and the industrialized world outside. Did not the old model of upbringing produce misfits in these circumstances? There is a mismatch between the intimacies of a small family and a society of groups whose majorities furnish the examples and form the judgments that are followed.

Dorothy Dinnerstein in *The Mermaid and the Minotaur: Sexual Arrangements and Human Malaise* (1976) argued that the child's tie to the mother is the prototype of the tie to life when all the intimacy of upbringing is left to the mother; the formative life experience is in terms of this bond. A girl grows up to repeat the patterns. A boy is made liable to adult infantilism; and in weaning himself on the male model, breaking the bond, he becomes alienated from and antagonistic towards women. Female domination of early childhood is a root of male domination of public life. The child's perception of the world in being brought up by a mother exclusively is a clue to how it is that women have been held in subjection. The pathology of this type of mothering involves a detailed and controversial etiology, but it is not to be lightly dismissed. The outcome is to say there is evidence for an abiding need of coparenting. The father should have an equal part with the mother in the nurturing care required in early childhood. This is not merely doing a hand's turn in helping with the daily household chores; it is on an entirely different level. Anthropological evidence shows that if deprivation of tactile comfort and security provided by nursing and fondling is prolonged, the infant drifts into a stupor. The same occurs in our own society. A child thus deprived becomes unresponsive and uneducable. The primary classroom has to be turned into a nursery, and women brought in to handle the children, so that they are cuddled and stroked and comforted, and given the experience they need in order to respond. It is at this level that fathers have to play their part along with mothers. With this start in life, it is argued, both men and women would be helped to live with ambivalence and ambiguities, and cope with the tensions of human existence. They would be less apt to exploit and not to conserve, more natural, more ecologically minded: in partnership with one another, men and women would be in partnership with nature.

The call for coparenting has been supported by women who have had great influence in the women's movement, such as the Americans Nancy Chodorow and Alice Rossi, both sociologists who have written on the psychodynamics of mothering. Their findings have particular relevance to boys brought up in increasingly prevalent single-parent families, mainly after male desertion.

## The Man-made World

There are other agencies at work in the socializing of the young outside the family: the school, the peer-group, the diversity of associations. Male dominance entailed the dominance of male values: it was a man's world to which women were seeking access, to join in playing their parts. In the nineteenth century, these were still inherited from the ancient world. Dominant and exemplary figures were Carlyle's heroes: sophists and philosophers (Matthew Arnold, J. S. Mill, Coleridge); priests and prophets (Newman, Spurgeon, Carlyle, Ruskin); poets and artists (Tennyson, Watts, Browning); engineers (Stephenson, Telford); pro-consuls and soldiers (Durham, Curzon, Wellington, Kitchener). Today, they are executives, professionals, technicians, managers, news and publicity agents, teachers, specialists of all kinds, types characteristic of developed industrialized societies driven by competition for consumer choice in an open market, with accelerating social change flowing from investment in research and development. That is to say, women at this late stage are not entering a man-made world they would have either to man or to change, for it is in rapid transition to a common world by impersonal forces not under control, but amenable to control, which could give a footing to women's mission. For meanwhile, there is ubiquitous stress and widespread distress and maladjustment, with drop-outs, unemployment, drug-addiction, vandalism, escalating violence, all the symptoms of frustration, childhood indiscipline, low-achievement, no stake in society, at the heart of a world in unprecedented political disintegration. In sum, an equivocal world.

At the outset in the 1950s, the women's movement was associated with the civil rights movement of the blacks, but also with the student rebellions of the same period which put in question the constraints of authority and the bureaucratic organization of American society. Male power was identified no longer with physical strength and martial prowess, the hero, but with the intellectual ability and technical skills required by industry and technology. Boys developed "a self defined through separation and measured against an abstract ideal of perfection" (achievement); while for girls there was a "self delineated through connection and assessed through particular activities of care." The history of ethics had been a theoretic search for the absolute of moral obligation, a summum bonum, a concept of justice, a definition of virtue, or whatever, in any case an abstraction. This exemplified, not the essential nature of morality but the male habit of thought. In contrast, women prefer a morality that considers the consequences of actions on particular individuals, and they choose to cultivate virtues they are naturally inclined to practice, like nurturing, healing, helping. If they are said to be "deficient in moral development" and without standards, they are simply being judged on a scale devised by male standards of abstract thought. When not browbeaten in this way "by the men on whose support and protection they depend and by whose names they are known," they speak from the convictions of their experience, and what they enunciate is not a new morality, but "a morality disentangled from the constraints that formerly confused its perception and impeded its articulation."

The contention goes beyond a critique of traditional ethics, for it claims that women in virtue of their social position and perhaps of their distinctive nature are able to bring to modern society insights, tacts, and resources serviceable in coping with its specific problems. What people see and understand is a consequence of the material conditions of their social existence—a Marxist analogue. Those who have power are in a position to impose their views on others. Through the struggle, the oppressed have experienced the obverse of the position of those in power and have learned to conceptualize their own position sufficiently for the practical purpose of concerted action, whereas those in power are oblivious to another point of view.

If something like this is true of women as moral agents, something similar is also true of them as rational agents, the two aspects of a common human nature assumed by the Enlightenment. Modernity is a regime of specialization and mechanization that subordinates and frustrates individuals. Women can see this as following from the masculine mental habit of abstraction. Natural laws are discovered, formulated as provisional universals, and used to "master" nature, so that man does what he is enabled to do—Hiroshima, maximum agricultural production, and the like. Mastery of things is inevitably linked with bureaucratic organization of people. The old imperium is consummated in technological capability. Women see this as Bacon's call for a vir-ile science that would conquer and control Mother Nature by learning her secrets, a call that inspired the Enlightenment. This reading of science cuts it off from human needs and interests which it should serve. Science has the authority of consecutive evidence, but that is not an authority for its use. That perception is the pivot of the feminist critique of science. There is no question of a new kind of science, nor of an obscurantist dismissal of science. The argument was directed to the separation "between the production and uses of knowledge, between thought and feeling, between subject and object, or between expert and non-expert"; against the extrusion of science from its social context; against science as an independent self-sufficient endeavor, instead of a socially endowed and accountable productive industry in an historical situation.

Of course, women were not alone among these voices. Current thinking was influenced by environmentalists, interdisciplinary team-work in the social field, educational theory and practice, the sociology of knowledge; and the example has already been given above of a transformation in the structure and management of industry. Indeed, the developed mixed economy, with its long agenda, weaves most of the strands in a responsible use of technological capability and ecological conservation. However, the critique of Chodorow and others of the effect on boys of the traditional mother's monopoly of the fundamentals of child-rearing, forcing them into separation, opposition, and abstract, impersonal, objective ways of thinking, is only one shaft in the aim within feminist theory that has tended to shift from Mary Wollstonecraft's insistence on no difference to founding themselves empirically on the difference, on feminine propensities and values, not necessarily bound up with physiological differences. It has been suggested that mothers should encourage their girls to be "Antigone's Daughters," ready to act against the establishment, the powers that be, if necessary.

The upshot is that for various reasons, of which the women's movement is one, the modern technocratic version of a male-dominated world is losing credibility. The mastery and exploitation of nature, competitive innovative striving for maximum market production for minimum cost, such aims, implicit or explicit, are recognizably on a crash course, to be avoided and paid for. That women should come into their own by their own efforts was due to them, and necessary to human maturity, apart from their reinforcement of what is needed for worthwhile human survival. "Women had found themselves in a culture not their own. They have been tempted to found their own culture, and "women's studies" have been, and are, controversial in this respect. Insofar as the inherited culture, traced in this study from the ancient Mediterranean world, can be perceived and revealed through women's eyes, women's studies will have contributed to a purpose not intended.

## The Self-Assertion in Perspective

The aspect of technology to do with dominance of the machine, automation and cybernetics, is a general social concern. Horkheimer: "The machine has dropped the driver: it is racing blindly into space." That recalls the old saying, "Things are in the saddle and ride mankind." There are old and new technologies that affect human reproduction directly or indirectly: contraception, abortion, artificial insemination, embryo transfers, genetic screening, prenatal screening for abnormalities or for sex, in vitro fertilization, sterilization. Such devices have brought reproduction into the public domain of discussion, at a time when marriage is moving into the private domain of individual arrangements. Shulamith Firestone, one of the most radical and influential of the early feminists, argued that women must use the available technology "to end the tyranny of the biological family," now that artificial reproduction was technically practicable on a "brave new world" scale. That most probably is fantasy, but it brings home even more realistically than Huxley's fiction how technology changes the world. Human nature can be defined and redefined in terms of technological advances that affect the body. What is essentially involved is the expansion of individual choice and the possibilities of social control. The bitterly contested arguments about abortion, although only marginally affected by technology, make a case in point. On one side is the case for women's rights. In 1973 the U.S. Supreme Court ruled in the case of *Roe* v. *Wade*:

> We recognize the right of the individual, married or single, to be free from unwarranted governmental intrusion into matters so fundamentally affecting a person as the decision whether to bear or beget a child. That right necessarily includes the right of a woman to decide whether or not to terminate a pregnancy.

That ruling has been revised and contested ever since, in the name of the "right" of the child to life, at conception or at some stage in the development of the embryo. In Britain, the Abortion Law Reform Association, formed in 1936, worked to get Parliamentary adoption of the 1957 Abortion Bill, and succeeded, the work of a brilliantly led and effective women's pressure-group. That legislation has been contested ever since by a "prolife" movement, mainly of women, to limit as far as possible the time of the pregnancy within which termination is legitimized. This is politics as the art of the possible, for those who are "prolife" are absolutists who do not countenance abortion, unless on medical grounds to save the life of the mother. ALRA changed its name to AWRC, A Woman's Right to Choose. That is the general formulation of the issue also in the United States or Ireland or elsewhere. Ironically, insofar as the feminist element in this advocacy is concerned, and it is the strongest, the "sanctity of human life" is an abstract moral principle, and its indiscriminate application flouts the criticism women made of the type of ethical judgments established by moral philosophy.

The emancipation of women is perhaps the most revolutionary cultural change in the West, and the most formative, one which still has to deliver its radical effects. More has been achieved in legislation than in practice, which indicates a need to influence public opinion, in which the media have the main say.

When, if ever, there is no thought of discrimination against women, will there also be no interest in sex differences? This speculative question may be a reminder of the new interest in women for themselves that occurred in the Hellenistic Age when girls were being educated to the standard of boys and given employment in public life. Is that an indication that liberation which gives women scope to apply and display their genius, unperceived by eyes not informed by expectations will again make them attractive for themselves in a new way? Again, a speculative question; but it brings forward evidence. Preoccupation of feminists with purging the language of "sexism" in the sense of "man" including "woman," a mere convention, overlooks "emasculation," "effeminacy," "femininity" and the like, which are pejorative and offensive in being used to degrade a man by attributing to him the weakness of a woman. In contrast, "manly" and "womanly" are simply different ways of being human, equally attractive. Equally positive was the masculine recognition and appreciation of femininity as a distinctive quality which one must suppose the Hellenistic discovery to have been, and which one must suspect has been a spontaneous finding at all times in the West.

# YOUTH

## Dependency

Animal young in the wild are looked after in ways that generally ensure the survival of most progeny in their habitat. That is a law of nature. Young of the higher mammals are comparatively advanced in development at birth although maturation may extend over a long period. In the young of many species there are innate mechanisms of self-protection, apart from parental care. The point of contrast to be made is that the human young are a resource, a source of innovation, not merely a reproduction of their species.

The persistence in an animal of juvenile features, or of the entire juvenile form, beyond the normal juvenile stage of development, is called "neoteny." Man is thought to be a neotenous form of ape; if the rate of development of the reproductive system is delayed by comparison with the rest of the body, in the period before puberty the young are longer under restraint and instruction, which is necessary for the development of cooperative activities. An anthropological definition of socialization specifies the influences of a culture on the making of a human being: "all those factors, influences, and processes, formalized or implicit, which the culture of the group acting through parents, elders, or other children brings to bear upon the neonate and continues through maturation to adolescence in order gradually to mould the raw stuff of human nature into conformity with group patterns of thought, feeling, and behavior." Different patterns of culture studied by anthropologists on the ground illustrate what this means in practice. It is easier to introduce items of behavior that are imitated and get established in the repertory and routine, but the principle is not different.

Anthropological studies show an immense diversity in patterns of culture sampled in simple societies. These small populations segregated in isolation by their habitat have a deep-seated fear of and respect for ancestors, whose ways they inherit and transmit in ritual performances, repeated exactly to ensure the success being handed on. This is what used to be called "the cake of custom," and where it prevails, innovation is marginal. The large populations organized in empires in commerce with one another as in the Middle East and Mediterranean developed two main types of culture, the open culture of the Greeks with intensive cultivation of arts and sciences, and the closed religious cultures strictly controlled by a hierarchy of priests. The Romans adopted the culture of Greece.

> In India, Greece, and Rome every house is a temple, with the father as priest. The inner family, however, is far from being autonomous; the father has absolute authority over his sons even when they are grown up and have children of their own. It is the death of the father that sets free the sons and so splits up the family. . . .
> It is significant that the three Aryan societies had slaves, serfs, and hired laborers. Without them this individualism is impossible; it is only when retainers are available that a man can become independent of his brothers and live his own life with his own cult. (Hocart: *Social Origins,* 1954)

The Roman Empire under Constantine adopted Christianity as the state religion, and Theodosius enforced it as the law of the land. This was the culture in which the converted tribes of Europe were brought up by the Roman Church after the collapse of the Western Empire.

In Bede and in Alcuin, and at Charlemagne's court, one sees how the young are brought up in that culture. Between the Conquest and the Reformation, children of the nobility after their early years at home went for further training into other noble households, or to universities or to religious houses. This was induction and instruction that trained boys for court and camp or the many offices and tasks of the Church in administration and education. In the towns there were the guilds and liveries in which craftsmen and traders were trained as apprentices and qualified as masters. Supervision and discipline were exerted over the young in one form or another by their elders until they were not merely of an age but also tested and qualified to take their place in society.

A notable comment on the induction of youth into society is Montaigne's essay in the sixteenth century "Of the Institution and Education of Children." The gist of this extensive essay is a denunciation of the ordination of schoolmasters who, under the Church and the universities, have enslaved children to book-learning during the freshest and most active years of their youth; they are made to acquire dead languages which they will never know how to use, unless they become grammarians or logicians. Not only did the system not breed gentlemen, it did not allow free minds; for obedience to the master was imposed, but also unquestioning deference to all established authorities. Against all this he brings the example of his father and his own upbringing. He instances also the example of Sparta in raising the young in action not on books. Thomas Arnold of Rugby will take a similar line in some respects: intellectual attainments come fourth to health, hardihood, and character; model for the public school,* an education for gentlemen and leaders for imperial duties.

---

*In the British sense, "public school" means one of the exclusive, traditional, upper-class boarding schools.

John Locke, a major influence on the French Enlightenment, and on Rousseau, put down *Some Thoughts Concerning Education* (1693) that accord with Montaigne in deprecation of book-learning and the sacrifice of youthful energies to acquisition of dead languages for no good purpose. He is also at one with Montaigne in stout objection to harsh treatment and in encouraging the young to have their own say and take their own part in their education. Having dealt at large with the foundations of health and physical development in terms of habits, exercise, and diet, he goes on: "The younger they are, the less, I think, are their unruly and disorderly appetites to be complied with; and the less reason they have of their own, the more are they to be under the absolute power and restraint of those in whose hands they are." He insists (because he says it is not generally recognized):

> A compliance and suppleness of their wills, being by a steady hand introduced by parents, before children have memories to retain the beginnings of it, will seem natural to them, and work afterwards in them, as if it were so; preventing all occasions of struggling or repining. The only care is that it be begun early. . . . Liberty and indulgence can do no good to children: their want of judgment makes them stand in need of restraint and discipline.

With this absolute foundation of the unquestioned authority of parents and elders implanted in earliest infancy and established in the child as self-restraint, at a later stage, the child's inclinations should be the indication for tasks prescribed. "Children have as much a mind to show that they are free, that their own good actions come from themselves, that they are absolute, and independent, as any of the proudest of you grown men, think of them as you please." In consequence: "they should seldom be put about doing even those things you have got an inclination in them to, but when they have a mind and disposition to it."

This clear and confident perception of the absolute cultural conditions of maturation and upbringing, and it abounds in these pages, the need and the means to enable the child to acquire self-restraint and the cultivation of learning by grafting required tasks on a child's stock disposition and native vigor, anticipates at the end of the seventeenth century the exact pedagogical studies promoted by such as John Dewey and Jean Piaget, who influenced profoundly educational policy and practice world-wide, particularly in primary schools. However, this should be seen in the context of these same years when propaganda by best-sellers persuaded American parents that "liberty and indulgence" was good for their children, that the exertion of authority, restraint, and discipline maimed them for life, so that children were allowed to do what they liked and ruled the house, and parents submitted for the sake of their offspring. This gospel was taken up in England by "progressives" and Neil's school at Summerhill organized a model. The guru who converted a generation, Dr. Benjamin Spock late in the day recognized his disastrous mistakes and printed a recantation.

For Rousseau, the young are corrupted by the culture in which they grow up, the institutions of contemporary society. Society is overdue for reform; meanwhile, for his model of education he takes Emile out of society, and has him brought up in rural retreat in touch with nature and with the unperverted promptings of his own nature. Sophie is trained to be submissive to the service of men. This physical detachment from the culture into which one is born would of course be a return to the wild boy of the woods becoming incapable of becoming human. However, a critical detachment from, for reflection upon, the influences in response to which one has formed one's identity and become what one is is feasible and is a necessary step in gaining personal autonomy. There is a page in the Tenth Stage of Condorcet's *Sketch* which begins: "The degree of equality in education that we can reasonably hope to attain, but that should be adequate, is that which excludes all dependence, either forced or voluntary." The citizen can be taught everything he needs to know in order to manage his life, knowing his rights and his duties, not deceived or fooled, guided by his own reason, not by others. Education is valued for this endowment of independence.

The point here is that the breach with the establishment made by the Enlightenment was not in any way a revolt of youth, a war of the generations. Rather, it was a projection of the revolt of the American colonies, documented in the argument between Burke and Paine, outmoding the ancien regime because reason with the advance of science had emancipated humanity and made populations adult in their independence, as Condorcet made out.

The ancien regime was virtually restored at the Congress of Vienna, but fundamental changes could not be extirpated. The way the young were brought up to conform or adjust to the political and social order and aspirations of their national state was conspicuously different in England, Germany, France, and other European countries. In England, Thomas Arnold's Rugby became the model for some three hundred private public schools that were part of the establishment. Boys were segregated from their families, hardened physically, and bred for public service in the forces and administration throughout the Empire. It was also the education of a gentleman. Napoleon reorganized the system of secondary and higher education in France. At first the lycees were run on semi-military lines and were established only in the larger towns. In Paris, lycees named after famous men became themselves famous: Lycee Condorcet, Lycee Henri Quatre, and later Lycee Napoleon, Lycee Louis-le-Grand, Lycee Saint-Louis. There were several state institutions of specialized higher learning, for professional training. The secondary education developed by the Jesuits since the sixteenth century had been suppressed during the Revolution, but alongside the state schools during the nineteenth century were *ecoles libres* run by the French Catholic Church. The rivalry was intense: a "battle for the mind of the child." Religious and civic education were opposed.

The bid of Prussia in mid-nineteenth century to organize a modern state and displace the premier position of the Habsburg dynasty, together with the independence and eminence of several universities, which attracted the elite of students for their higher education from the Western world, and developed a German culture independent of the political and social order and aspirations of a national state, made Germany a special case. Burkhardt remarked in a letter: "Men cannot simply be left to themselves, they need a universal mould so that at least everyone can fit into the turbulence called modern life." Because there was not a settled social order to grow up in, a mold would have to be devised and adopted for the purpose. The disinterested promotion of humanistic and scientific studies in the universities implied a liberal idea of the state as merely an association of the population for cooperation of individuals for the mutual satisfaction of individual wants. For Hegel, however, the individual was both the creature and the servant of the historical state, and his education must fit him for that: "The basis for all higher study is and must remain the literature of the Greeks primarily, and next, that of the Romans." The excellence of their achievement in the pursuit of excellence was inspired by these studies. It was the business of education to incorporate the individual in the historical world, and the example of the ancients was not followed in Germany unless his education committed him to participation in the public life of the Prussian state in which he was incorporated in an organism as a function, not a mere beneficiary. The young Hegelians, Ruge, Stirner, Bauer, took different lines. The freedom of the arts and science was all right with the Greeks who were "political" through and through as active citizens of a *polis*. How the specialization of higher education in the universities could be joined to incorporating German students in the nascent German state was the German problem. The argument raged and raged.

Nietzsche was loud in his denunciation of German education as civilized barbarism, whether as producing the politically trained man with the prescribed world view, or as fragmented in specialization. His ideal was the old humanist formation of the complete man. Youth movements had a special place in Germany for the young, as a peer group with leadership they were a refuge, a place for belonging and counting; for the state, they were a principal socializing agency outside formal education, weaning the young on meat from the state butchery. Rommel's son, mayor of Strasburg, has testified that the Hitler Youth were treated as adults, brain-washed and trained.

In general, it can be said that during the successive phases of Western history and in the different European states and societies, before the war, the young were regarded and dealt with as the adults in each generation saw fit, whether as patriarchs or as patriots, or indulged as pets, or as pests. John Locke's discernment of the nature and needs of the young, the late child-studies, the vogue of the perverse theory of Dr. Spock were significant but exceptional. What was without exception is the adult point of view and absolute authority, albeit qualified in the exceptional cases. That was what would change after the war.

## Revolt

In the 1950s, a vogue spread among adolescent males in Britain for wearing Edwardian style suits with tails, the "teddy-boy cult." In a TV program that recalled that phase, one man interviewed said that when he failed to find his suit to go out for the evening, his father told him to look outside in the dustbin, where he found it ripped to pieces. He promptly went back into the house and up into his parents' bedroom, took out his father's best suit, to go into the dustbin torn up with his own. His suit was not touched a second time. The incident prefigures both the "generation gap" and the action that will annul it. Self-assertion of the adolescent as a class, flaunted in dress, is epitomized in an essay by Edgar Morin, "The Case of James Dean."

James Dean has also defined what one might call the panoply of adolescence, a wardrobe in which is expressed a whole attitude toward society: blue jeans, heavy sweater, leather jacket, no tie, an unbuttoned shirt, deliberate sloppiness are so many ostensible signs (having the value of political badges) of a resistance against the social conventions of a world of adults. Clothes are a quest for the signs of virility (the costume of manual laborers) and of artistic caprice. James Dean has invented nothing; he has canonized and codified an ensemble of sumptuary laws which allows an age-class to assert itself, and this age-class will assert itself even further in imitation of its hero.

James Dean in his double life, both on and off the screen, is a pure hero of adolescence: he expresses his needs and his revolt in a single impulse . . . "A Rage to Live" and "Rebel without a Cause" are two aspects of the same virulent demand, in which a rebellious fury confronts a life without a cause.

This artless protest of youth which began with the poetic gesture of vesture won the day. Casual wear has marginalized the business suit. Since the 1950s, there is nearly half a century in which this social phenomenon of the self-assertion of a dependent age-class worked itself out, and transformed the world, socially and culturally, and through unemployment politically.

Disaffection swells to revolt against all restraints. The world is my oyster, the exultant cry of the romantic. But there is conflict all the way: the hero is up against it. James Dean is again exemplar, in his life and death, and in his films. As a movie star he is the lonely hero. His mother died when he was nine, and he was brought up by an uncle. He ran away from the university and worked as an ice-breaker, a stevedore, a ship's boy, before he attained the stage and Hollywood. The mythological hero, like Hercules, undertakes many labors to prove his powers, further his ambition to be master, and experience everything. Dean became obsessed by Speed, metaphor for the absolute. The rage to live is the doom to die. In proving it, the hero is killed. In self-assertion, he kills himself. James Dean dies on his racing Porsche at 160 mph, a self-intoxicated god astride a tiger. Dead, he is immortal, hysterically adored as object of an adolescent cult.

In his films *Rebel without a Cause* and *East of Eden* the uncomprehending failure to relate with the father and the mother is portrayed in opposite circumstances of impotence. In *Giant,* his rage is against all the norms and conventions of society. Adolescent identity is normally achieved by a struggle in which parents are called upon to relax their control and forfeit possession, which they are reluctant to do, and they frequently do not recognize the stage at which they should. When the youngster forces the issue and breaks the link, he has to take on escape from the chains of social life. This is the common scenario for the age, and his contemporaries saw in this hero one who represented them in his life and in his films.

Two other paradigms were representative. The motorcycle gangs of skinheads, with their uniform and shaven heads, the intoxicating velocity of their machines, their weekend stampedes and forays wreaking destruction on civilized amenities, rehearsed and expressed prevailing feelings in young people who were often gentle enough at heart and would become respectable citizens. The African beat, the rhythm, color, and velocity of Negro music was absorbed by the abrasive Elvis Presley, who adapted it to electrify American youth with virtuoso songs. His film *Jailhouse Rock*, with the title song and "Treat Me Nice," helped to establish the legend. The Beatles had heard of him, and must have seen his films, when they emerged in Liverpool in 1963. In 1950, there had been Bill Halley and the Comets, with their theme song, "Rock around the Clock." The Beatles were correctly dressed in their own uniform style. John Lennon even thought that he could not appear in glasses. Relaxation came steadily but with accelerating transformation brought about by body movement, lighting effects, diversity of clothing, electric enhancement of sound, stage-business, and properties of all kinds, until the touring groups resembled a circus in the 1990s. By this time, what had been put on by youth for youth, the innovative phenomenon of Rock 'n' Roll, had become not merely a permanent feature of contemporary life but mainly an industry, big business with managers, agents, investment, employing all the connections needed to build it into commerce; in a word, it was a competitive part of "show-biz." However, that is the packaging, more or less parasitical. The essential business, the invention, the content, the purpose remains firmly and absolutely firsthand. The lyrics are a vehicle for their comment on their own experience. In Poland after the turnaround brought about by "Solidarity," their ally the Catholic hierarchy unmistakably expected to take the place of the ousted Communist Party as the governing influence, resuming the established tradition. Many of the younger generation resented this as an unwarranted intrusion into their private lives. With the freedom that had been won, they had formed their own pop groups, and now to find expression for their frustration in their lyrics they felt a compelling need to find their own voice in a music that was their own, and not taken from the style and idiom of the West. By this time in the West, the pop cult was so established that it was part of the establishment. It was given regular prime time on BBC2 presumably for the enjoyment of the young; but treatment of almost any serious topic on radio or television was routinely introduced by a relevant pop song or perhaps rounded off by one. They had gained the status of linguistic currency, though it can hardly be assumed that the adult ear and eye are delighted by high decibels, raucous yelling, gobbled declamation, frenzied gestures and clowning. Of course, that is not the only fare. They are drawing on many popular traditions, and many of the songs are universally pleasing, and some may be haunting.

For a time in the sixties, drugs were a normal part of the pop culture scene, particularly LSD and cannabis; "normal" because of the volume of household drugs on medical prescription, amounting to a drug subculture engendering dependency on amphetamines, "sleeping" pills, barbiturates for sedation, and the like. With a more critical public attitude to drugs and the legal prescription of some narcotics, and the evident consequences of addiction, drugs came to be identified with the hard-core of addicts, and the criminal trade.

Pop groups are not merely young people: singers, song-writers, drummers, guitarists, pianists, players on the saxophone, the double bass, and several other instruments, are professional musicians. Music of whatever kind is not simply invented by the composer; however "original," it is adopted and adapted from one or more traditional kinds.

In what became Rock 'n' Roll, there was the staple African beat, the drums, the exuberance. A more melodic and leisurely movement came from folk music and the ballad. Dance, above all, is wherever music is. One saw this from the first in the compulsive individual movements of the audience. The less musical the yelling, the less rhythmic the response. At first the lyrics were meant to be distinctly heard, as with the Greeks and the madrigals, but later the rush of sound most of the time drowned them out, so that the message came from the sheet or by repute. As professionals, the composers, often the lead singers, are competent, able to bring off what they set out to do, limited though that may be. The question obtrudes: what happens to these young composers when they get older, and how old does that have to be? It seems they are loath to give up, probably because there is no established sequel to follow. Consider the career of the remarkable Mick Jagger. At fifty he insisted he would not give up, carrying on with the image projected by his publicity managers, and his own wry disillusioned outlook. A strong contrast was Louis Andriessen. A versatile virtuoso, he had steeped himself in different kinds of music; at the same time, he steeped himself in different kinds of worthwhile experience, from which he gathered and formulated themes for his music. Thus the making of a material thing, say shipbuilding, in the sequence of operations, would be announced and followed in the inventions of his composition. With him, this was not a gimmick, for his mind was grounded in certain not unreasonable assumptions: that the spiritual is conditioned by material organization; that one is formed as a person by the culture of the group into which one is born. As an anarchist, he assumed the likes of himself would have to be born into an anarchic utopia. He was an absolutist, like James Dean; and this lust for the absolute drove him as a pop musician to strive to establish a life-style that could be pursued indefinitely for the term of the life-cycle.

The decisive phase of revolt, however, was not in dress and pop music, but explicitly in the counterculture of the sixties for an alternative society with its own virtues and values, and lifestyle; the era of flower-power, and the open use of drugs for the enhancement of experience. Aldous Huxley had pioneered drug enhancement experimentally and philosophically in *The Doors of Perception* (1954) and its sequel, *Heaven and Hell* (1956); in which he claimed that "perception can be the same as Revelation," as a "supreme truth." Adolescent experimentation with an addictive drug like LSD was on a different plane; and as an addiction pushed the user into dishonest means of obtaining the money for his daily fix, and the pusher of supplies into exploitation of the need, and the law into prohibition, and the police into search on suspicion, the consequences have persisted to plague families and societies.

Meanwhile, in the sixties the counterculture had a brief link with Renault and political protest in Paris, that led to de Gaulle's withdrawal from government and politics. In Milan, students took over the university, and dictated their terms to their deans and professors and tutors. In Warwick University in Britain, students organized a six-week sit-in, protesting against the funding of the university by industry. Although more than a damp squib, all this had to fizzle out. In depth and extent, it had not been anything that could have been dealt with as puerile. It was taken, as it had to be, as intolerable damage and a serious threat. On the other side, it could not be sustained, and second thoughts came early.

The episode was forceful enough to compel attention to the generation gap, and the need for both sides to bridge it. There is a parallel between the generation gap and the gap between the colonies and the "mother" country after the war, especially, that is, with those acquired by conquest, not populated by emigration. Socialist politician Herbert Morrison said that to give Africans independence would be like giving a boy of ten a latch-key and a gun. It would take at least a generation before Nigeria, which was probably most ready, could take over. Bevin was at this time at the Foreign Office. These were liberal-minded Labour leaders, not imperialists like Churchill.

The effect of forcing recognition of the generation gap was to bring about comprehension that the young had among them those ready and competent to undertake responsibility. Significantly, it was one of the playboys, the pop singers who had cocked snooks at their elders in their lyrics, and were wholly preoccupied in their lyrics with their own adolescent world of feelings and fantasy who stood up and overruled adult authorities with his own moral authority. Bob Geldof was not content to rally his troops in Band Aid at Wembley Stadium in order to raise funds on an unprecedented scale for the relief of starving millions in Africa, dying in unprecedented conditions of drought and civil war. He managed and supervised the distribution of supplies on the ground in the difficult conditions. His personal presence, his realistic appraisals and perceptive eyes, informed a moral rage that galvanized people on the job. It was comparable with the inspiring leadership of great commanders. And the world recognized it, with the aid of television screens. In more recent days, Michael Jackson, a dazzling eccentric star at the center on stage of the gigantic technological circus of his engineered effects, is off stage solicitous for the welfare of children in need, for whom he continues to multiply ways of providing, so that he has invented and runs his own personal "Save the Children" mission.

Attested capability and responsibility of the young, as a reproach to the laxity of their elders, has brought about more general acceptance of Locke's understanding of the natural relations between young and old, growing up into fellowship at adolescence. The legal age of adulthood has been reduced by three years. This specific adjustment is consolidated in the context of a pop culture that is as general as was the culture of "bourgeois" values, so despised and derided by the "avant-garde." This has been established by what was described as "modernism" in the arts. Pop music is no longer a craze of the crazy young; it is an article in the encyclopedia of "music," and may be enjoyed by anyone. The pop music of the seventies shows this broadening. (Take Alex Harvey's "Delilah.") This cultural plateau, worldwide, is a vast assimilation, eclectic but not elitist. Societies are no longer ruled by privileged minorities, with their own exclusive traditions.

With the despondency engendered by prolonged economic depression, the proportion of juvenile offenders in crime statistics has risen sharply. At the level of law and order, public authority inevitably says that circumstances are no excuse, and acts accordingly: the public has to be protected. At grassroots level, sociology sees the matter more closely. There are extensive industrial deserts, not inner cities, where employment has dried up with the extinction of once prosperous industries, like shipbuilding or coal mining. Communities stranded there know they are doomed to a prospect of permanent unemployment, after a generation grows up without a job. Their children grow up on the streets, maturing in a subculture in the making, of which they will complete the development, a perverse subculture with corrupt ideals. Denied the satisfactions, expectations, aims, and rewards of those who have a stake in society, their careers are framed by goals and ideas engendered by opportunity and invention, under peer-group pressure.

Seen by the public, even in their own community, as vandalism, incendiarism, pillaging, burglary, mugging, crimes against property and persons, aggravated by concerted attacks on police and fire service, they are in their own way engaged in the career open to them, with the demand for appropriate skills, expectations, ambitions, failures, rewards, and risks. The life-cycle is lived through in antisocial terms, but the human is necessarily social, and this social soil is a subculture they have been forced into making for themselves. Local authorities, starved of funds, have closed down youth clubs and all play facilities as expendable. This scenario is not the whole story, but it has substance confirmed by questioning on the ground, and by what happened recently in the South Circle of Los Angeles. It was a repetition of what happened a generation earlier, which was thought at the time to have been put behind by a resurgence of aided self-help; taken as a model for rehabilitation of the black community after the Brixton riots that were the subject of Lord Scarman's perceptive inquiry.

Children brought up to throw stones at any who wear the badge of authority, as in Palestine and elsewhere, are disciplined in a transvaluation of values that is probably irreversible.

The general ethos of assumed human equality that tends to prevail since the fundamental discovery of genetic identity makes the context in which old attitudes can hardly be maintained. In the case of youth, unquestioned authority of elders and superiors has been dethroned. Their bluff has been called. Student leaders have pointed out defaults and deficiencies, and asked for their remedy. Speaking frankly and equally to authority did induce reasonable responses, and amicable exchanges and arrangements formerly unthinkable. Justified authority was then respected: each side was able to control the other, both being accountable. It is part of the general dismantling of adversarial attitudes and procedures as short-term policies that in the long-run are disadvantageous to both, made so evident in industry. In the case of youth in the hands of their elders, it could be believed that this was a natural dispensation.

# RACE

## Racial Stock

"Race" is used loosely. In the dictionary, it is a subdivision of the human species distinguished by common physical characteristics. In usage, there is confusion between physical characteristics, which are exclusively genetic, and social characteristics that are cultural. If a white person calls a black person a "nigger," the biological description is incidental; what he has in mind in using this popular contemptuous corruption of "Negro" is a downgrading.

An interbreeding, human population at a given time draws on its "gene pool" for whatever variation may ensue. A "gene flow" is introduced by interbreeding with another such population, and increases the chance of genetic variation. The dynamics of race formation involve many factors, and the detail is still obscure; genetic change, adaptive selection, and isolation of populations have interacted to bring about the evident differentiation of the human species that obtains. Isolation of populations belongs mainly to the early stages of human development. Massive migrations entailed equivalent gene flow, established with the settlement of peoples.

Thus, there is no original human race, and no "pure" race. Also, there is no evidence, nor likelihood, of innate superiority in any of the distinctive racial types. Racial differences are simply patterns of inherited variations maintained within an interbreeding population. Other differences are acquired from the culture in which one is born and brought up. Racial differences reflect the consequence of local differences in the distribution of genes. In discussing and assessing current knowledge of "The Differential Distribution of Genes," J. Z. Young remarks: "It may be that it is not rationally necessary with modern knowledge for us to remain divided into groups, but it seems unlikely that in practice we shall soon cease to be so" (*Introduction to the Study of Man*, 1971).

An informed understanding of "race" does not wipe out prejudice, which by definition is a prejudgment, and not necessarily hostile; but knowledge undermines prejudice, and taxes it with the onus of justification, which it is unable to bear.

This has not come about by the dawn of enlightenment, without the claims and organized pressure of disadvantaged racial groups prepared to stand up for their rights. The movements for civil rights by the blacks in southern states of the U.S.A. took more than a decade to establish a claim to equal citizenship under the Constitution. Apartheid in South Africa was undertaken on an assumption of equal entitlement to independence, but when in practice it became apparent to the world that it was gross discrimination, with inhuman pass laws and the imposition of restrictions that stifled daily existence, the country passed under a cloud of world disapproval marked by economic sanctions, and was forced to begin a slow but growing redress of the situation and public abandonment of the policy.

There is a background of serfdom, long-standing in Russia; and of Negro slavery in the sugar plantations. There is a longer-standing and wider background in empire, in which racial difference, though present, is not prominent. In any case, it is cultural advantage that prevails, as in the so-called Triumph of the West. Indigenous peoples are overrun, driven out, subjugated, annihilated, generally disposed of by invaders in whatever way suits their purpose or their interest. "Aryan" indicates on linguistic grounds a common ancestry for Indians and English, but the British raj, based on conquest, practiced patronage, and indignities that implied an assumption of "racial" superiority. Apart from the Negro, the historical victim of racialism in European history has been the Jew, in which color does not feature among derided characteristics. Beginning with the Crusade of 1096, Church, state, and mob increasingly drove the Jews to the margins of the medieval European world, and beyond. Anti-Semitism remained endemic in Europe. The case of Alfred Dreyfus made it a public issue. Leonard Woolf, himself a Jew, writes of the impact of the case on himself and his friends as students at Cambridge:

> Over the body and fate of one obscure, Jewish captain in the French army a kind of cosmic conflict went on year after year between the establishment of Church, Army, and State on the one side, and the small band of intellectuals who fought for truth, reason, and justice, on the other. Eventually the whole of Europe, almost the whole world, seemed to be watching breathlessly, ranged upon one side or other in the conflict. . . . I still think . . . that the Dreyfus case might, with a slight shift in the current of events, have been a turning point in European history and civilization. All that can really be said against us was that our hopes were disappointed.

He returns to it a few pages later, scanning the whole affair in graphic detail, and raising the court-martial to the level of the trial and death of Socrates and the trial of Jesus before Pontius Pilate. Zola in his article "J'accuse" had started the controversy. Issues are seldom as clear-cut and black-and-white as idealists are apt to see them, and as Leonard Woolf pitched the Dreyfus case. Georges Sorel who was on the side of Dreyfus was put off by the way the affair was used for party advantage, particularly by Jean Jaures; and he ceased his advocacy of democracy. However, there are issues when not to take sides is a betrayal of civilization, an unintentional betrayal to which the liberal intellectual is made liable by detachment and fair-mindedness.

## Negro Slavery

The plantation slavery established in the southern United States was a disturbing influence throughout the nineteenth century, as Apartheid was after South African independence. Diderot's *Encyclopedie* had a short article, "Traite des Negres," which described the slave trade as "un negoce qui viole la religion, la morale, les lois naturalles et tout les droits de la nature humaine. . . . Si un commerce de ce genre peut etre justifie par un principle de morale, il n'y a point de crime quelque atroce qu'il soit, qu'on ne puisse legitimer." There can be no valid rights of property in human beings, no matter what laws a state may enact to the contrary, the article went on to insist. America was in the writer's mind; and the opinion is expressed that, once adjustments were made, if the slaves were freed, there would be no obstacle to prosperity in a land of liberty and industry. Avarice and greed, however, which dominate the earth, would not want to listen to reasons for humanity. The argument was an old one, that there are laws of nature that are universal which the laws of nations may contravene, but without the moral authority to bind the citizen; it is his duty to denounce and defy them.

Henry Thoreau was in the mid-century the most conspicuous exemplar of this line of conduct. Prompted by his rooted opposition to the war with Mexico, he gave a lecture on "Civil Disobedience." The war ended in a vast acquisition of territory in the Southwest that sharpened the division between North and South on the question of slavery. Thoreau went to live on his own in the woods "to drive life into a corner, and reduce it to its lowest terms"—a Tolstoyan mission of self-discovery. He had set out in his lecture what was entailed by sincere opposition on grounds of conscience to acts or policies of the state of which one is a citizen. He was not politically minded. He believed least government was desirable. He was not in the world to change it, but to live in it. He would not oppose laws he thought inconvenient or unjust, unless like slavery they taxed his conscience as morally wrong. In that case, nothing less than exemplary dissociation sufficed: "I cannot for an instant recognize that political organization as *my* government which is the *slave's* government also." Opposition which means what it says involves identification with the victim of the state's injustice.

> Under a government which imprisons any unjustly, the true place for a just man is also in prison. It is there that the fugitive slave, and the Mexican prisoner on parole, and the Indian come to plead the wrongs of his race, should find them; on that separate but more free and honorable ground, where the State places those who are not *with* her but *against* her—the only house in a slave State in which a free man can abide with honor.

It is politically efficacious: "If the alternative is to keep all just men in prison, or give up war and slavery, the State will not hesitate which to choose." Refuse allegiance; do not pay tax bills: "This is in fact the definition of a peaceful revolution, if any such is possible." The strategem of civil disobedience was introduced to underline the language of protest. Gandhi learned it from Thoreau, to make his resistance to colonial subjugation irrepressible.

The Supreme Court tried to take the North-South controversy out of politics by a decision on the Dred Scott case in 1857 that "Congress has no rightful power to prohibit Slavery in the Territories." Lincoln, elected in 1860, said he would not intervene on slavery where it existed. Civil war was precipitated because limited toleration could not satisfy southern slave states. Ambivalence was intolerable when the issue was right or wrong. When the fighting was over in 1865, slavery was constitutionally abolished, and the Negroes were granted civil rights.

Statutes do not change minds and uproot cultures. Civil rights had to be fought out on the ground in the states concerned; and in terms of color prejudice and segregation in the cities, not the economy of the plantations for which slavery had been instituted supplied by the slave trade. Later in the day, Lyndon Johnson in a memorable speech spoke of "a legacy of bigotry and injustice," and identified himself with its victims, concluding with the phrase: "we are all in this together; we shall overcome." What was to be "overcome" was treatment of the colored race as second-class citizens. Legal equality did not entail human equality. The Negro race might still be, or held to be, constitutionally inferior biologically. That was another terrain on which there was a battle to be fought, with statistical analyses and the like tests. Assumptions and prejudice prevailed here, and threatened to blight prospects for those with ambition to get to the top.

Blacks enlisted or employed during the two world wars showed their capabilities and qualities, an opportunity that boosted their self-confidence. It probably influenced the Supreme Court's decision of 1954 in *Brown* v. *Board of Education,* which outlawed segregation in the public schools. In a position to demand full equality, moderate church leaders initiated and organized a civil rights movement, openly committed to peaceful demonstrations. This alarmed the authorities in the states affected, who used their law officers and enforcement agents to thwart, repress, and outmaneuver the black activists. The federal government was fitful in its interventions, but was increasingly forced to overrule reactionary authorities in southern states.

On their part, during 1954–1965 the blacks fought uphill against the odds, with some gains and many set-backs. They were trained and disciplined, exhorted and encouraged, under the resolute leadership of Protestant pastors, whose congregations were the backbone of the movement, with an ally in an independent nonviolent student movement. Desegregation, antiapartheid, was the social issue on the ground: equal access to public places, transport, and institutions, particularly the public schools. Nonviolent revolution included marches, sit-ins, teach-ins, civil disobedience, boycotts, hunger-strikes, and the like, designed to attract publicity, to keep demands on the agenda of authorities, to embarrass them, to impose expense, make complacency and normality of the status quo quite impossible. They suffered casualties at the hands of authorities who did not respond to nonviolence in kind. They kept up their spirits by singing, a prime resource.*

When the social disability of segregation had been removed, there remained the place and part of the Negro in white America. From the militancy of nonviolence evolved the militancy asserted under the aegis of Islam by Malcolm X, who deleted his surname as a relic of slavery. He broke with the Black Muslim movement in 1964 to form an independent Muslim organization prepared to use violence against intransigent social injustice. His influence culminated in the Black Power movement of the late sixties, and the Black Panther Party for Self-Defense. Eldridge Cleaver was a spokesman for this.

> In this land of dichotomies and disunited opposition, those truly concerned with the resurrection of black Americans have had eternally to deal with black intellectuals who have become their own opposites, taking on all the behavior patterns of their enemy, vices and virtues, in an effort to aspire to alien standards in all respects. (*Notes of a Native Son*)

---

*The exuberant temperament of tribal Africans expressed itself in constant chanting and handclapping and rhythmic movement as they went about their work, interweaving song and dance with whatever they were doing. This cultural habitude they took with them unstinted when abducted in the slave trade and transported to the West Indies or the United States. Song and dance was an abiding consolation to them and as their African patrimony it stood for their lost land and their identity. Of even greater significance, it distinguished them in a way that gave them an edge of superiority over their masters. As they discovered this when they had freedom of movement, they went back into their past and brought stimulus to the development of music, song, and dance that captivated ("enslaved") Americans and the white world. Harlem was at first the hub of the development, with nightly shows that forced innovation and invention, with such as Cab Calloway entertaining with surprising antics, always neatly, skillfully, and gracefully executed leading on to dance that was acrobatic without breaking the rhythm. The free flowing movement was in striking contrast with the jerky up and down movements of American dance initiatives, as in jiving. This side of Negro cultural enterprise is less familiar than the music and song that was rapidly adapted.

In this perspective, blacks in America are second-class citizens in a second sense. Why should they want to be American? Africa was not Europe. There was an ambivalence among educated blacks that easily became self-hatred. Eldridge Cleaver began with unqualified admiration of James Baldwin as a first-class black novelist. Then he became ambivalent: was this success helping to destroy black identity? Would it not draw blacks into collusion with the whites?

> The whites are on top in America and they want to stay there, up there. They are also on top in the world, on the international level, and they want to stay up there, too. Everywhere there are those who want to smash this precious toy clock of a system, they want ever so much to change it, to rearrange things, to pull the whites down off their high horse and make them equal. Everywhere the whites are fighting to prolong their status, to retard the erosion of their positions. (*Domestic Law and International Order*)

Rejection of American mercenary values, and sale of the dream of enjoying an American standard of living, which was becoming a middle-class aspiration abroad, can be seen as an anticipation of the Ayatollah's mission on his return to Iran, after the Americanizing Shah had been ousted. Entrenchment in the traditions of Islam, reinterpreted in the fundamentalism that bred fanatics, staked the future on turning the tide of American materialism. Comprehensively, the general recognition dawned that the dominance of the whites and the benefits of their achievements and their culture were theirs. Nonwhites with other roots and traditions, if they allowed themselves to be beneficiaries, came to feel that they betrayed their own race, and sold their birthright for a mess of pottage. Indeed, talented blacks who on the strength of civil rights made it and rose to the top in prominent positions were alienated from the mass of their fellows who remained disadvantaged, and were unwilling to lift a finger to advance their cause. They were content and pleased to become virtual whites. This put race relations in a different context, not only in the United States. If communications have made the world one, and if the races that inhabit it are genetically different but equal, there is still a cloud of misapprehension to be dispersed, and several inappropriate reactions to be politically corrected, not least white resolve to be politically correct in order to meet black determination to rewrite history.

Gandhi encountered racial discrimination and oppression when as a young man he went to work as a lawyer among the Indian community in South Africa. He had read Thoreau's "Civil Disobedience," and employed nonviolent tactics of resistance in South Africa in 1907–14 in his challenge to the Transvaal government's discrimination against Indian settlers. He suffered imprisonment, and he won concessions for the Indians from the government. On his way back, he stayed in England to qualify as a barrister at the Inns of Court. He believed in British justice and had confidence in the liberal principles of British political thinkers. Later in his career in India when he was first in the Congress Party working for independence he was confident that the logic of their system would constrain the British to concede independence when it was made clear to them that this was what Indians wanted and felt entitled to claim.

Disillusionment came slowly, but conclusively, and turned the black-coated barrister into Churchill's "half-naked fakir."

When he returned to India, the Congress Party looked to recruit him. For his part, he was thinking of a political strategy to rouse and raise a peaceful revolutionary opposition of the Indian people, rather than of negotiations at the top. After making himself acquainted with the extent of their poverty and ignorance, he set about representing them in person by stripping himself to a loin-cloth and squatting at a spinning wheel. Like Thoreau, he was ready "to drive life into a corner, and reduce it to its lowest terms," not in preoccupation with himself; on the contrary, to expose to the world the condition of the Indian masses under the British raj. Publicity was of the essence of his campaign, implicitly if not in modern American image and package-making terms. He had to target the masses themselves, the British and colonial public, and not least the alienated British ex-colony, the U.S.A.

His tactics—spinning and weaving cotton, and boycott of British imported cotton; the march to the sea, and to the government salt-works; the call to a day of fasting and prayer, as a general strike—served his strategy of promoting peaceful revolution and non-cooperation, which he punctuated by personal hunger-strikes on critical issues. This sequence of widely reported public events shrewdly planned and resolutely carried through with the strength of the masses forced the government into acts of repression. Gandhi was still confident that this would sooner rather than later induce the British to see the error of their ways, and justice would be done: "Please leave; you know you should not be here in this way." At the same time, the "half-naked fakir" symbolized, and seemed to stand for, a fundamental rejection of modern civilization and all its values.

His was not the only voice in opposition, even apart from Jinnah and the Muslims. But his strategy was too effective to be ignored. Nehru did not have the religious core of Gandhi, and certainly did not repudiate modern civilization, but was content to stand side by side with him in opposing the British raj. Another leading figure in the Congress Party was M. N. Roy. He had been an activist from the age of twelve, and had left India for California, founded a Socialist party in Mexico, and gone to Russia. Lenin sent him with Bukharin to report on the situation in China. He was a leading figure in the Communist International, until he broke with Lenin and the Communist Party on the ground that personal liberty was the most precious human value, the essence of humanity. He returned to India, and was promptly jailed by the British. When the Congress Party favored the Japanese, taking sides against the British in the war with Nazism, Roy seceded from the party on the ground that Fascism had to be opposed by all means, including British arms. He took out with him a loyal following of exceptional men of character, ability, and standing. He formed with them a Radical Democratic Movement, which eventually turned itself into a non-political Radical Humanist Movement, convinced that politics was first and last a pursuit of power, and a prey to corruption. Roy in his exile and converse with the West had become a man of the Enlightenment, and he felt that what India most needed was not the power politics of party government, but the intellectual and moral awakening the Enlightenment had brought to Europe. India had to be brought out of the age-old superstitious and bigoted ways that crippled rational endeavors, as Europe had been out of the ancien regime.

Imperialism itself has had its day. In the West, it has been European hegemony and white supremacy, in times and at times during six centuries in collision with the Ottoman Empire, whose rule extended into the Balkans. European hegemony was not resigned; in each case power was wrested from European hands by force from below.

Immigration has brought the race question home to Europeans in a quite different way. The first phase, to take jobs available because locally disagreeable, in order to send money back home, has been replaced in England since the end of the sixties by ethnic minorities permanently settled and in business, with children born as British citizens: the multicultural population of an historical state. Fair and equal treatment is the reasonable demand of all. Legislation provides for that, but cannot command minds and hearts. Discrimination is rife, but not easy to prove, and bring to court. Of the many changes of context which have come with global unity but not union, this eclipse of historical states threatens to be the most traumatic. The most pressing first problem is to stem the tide that would overwhelm the industrialized states in an invasion. That can be done if enforced restriction goes hand-in-hand with effective measures to improve conditions and prospects on the ground whence people are leaving en masse to seek a better life. Meanwhile, the basic conditions of coexistence for ethnic minorities that have settled are clearly indicated: the indigenous institutions should serve all alike and constrain all alike (the "fair and equal treatment" demanded). Cultural practices not incompatible with this conformity are not affected.

This coalescent pluralism within historical nation-states is going on simultaneously with a fissiparous tendency within these states. England is under pressure from Scotland and Wales for some form of independence; and the status of Ulster is problematic. Dissolution of the Soviet Union has left independent republics, striving to settle claims to further division. Smaller national identities seem inevitable, if far short of "ethnic cleansing." That points in the direction of regional zones, with negotiable internal relations, and cooperation and coordination to establish mutual facilities and promote and safeguard common interests.

In the prolonged aftermath of imperialism, blacks have been killing blacks in South Africa on a scale that has made it a major problem, although apartheid has been sentenced to death. In the United States, crime, including a high murder rate, is high among blacks. Even in Great Britain, blacks killing blacks has become a concern of blacks themselves on some inner-city estates, like Mosside in Manchester. They are victims of a white society that deals directly with the symptoms, the outcome of hopelessness and the resort to drugs and its traffic, without a planned endeavor to transform the situation of which the offenders are the victims.

The Soviet Union that was the mainstay of the freedom fighters against their colonial masters after the war had itself extended its empire in a bastion of satellites. The alien races were in the eastern range of the widespread regime, and gained their freedom when the breakup came.

In general, failure of the power to maintain repression released the races that had suffered subjugation, and they reacted freely to centuries of white enslavement, extermination ("genocide"), and the assumption of white superiority. Nowhere was this so marked and politically explicit as in the United States, a legacy of the slave states.

Black academics addressed Western history and education, which had been exclusively a Western version of events and a Western curriculum, without a glimmer that this might not be "history" and "education" *tout court*. That had to be corrected, by bringing forward and establishing the point of view of those who had been victims of this one-sided exclusion. Overdue redress would be attained by introducing black studies into the curriculum, with university chairs in that field; and equally, indeed primarily, by rewriting history. Without knowing it, black academics had a powerful ally in revising history, because this was the mission of George Said, a Palestinian who for twenty years on the staff of Columbia University for English studies had been doing the research needed for his life-work *Civilization and History* (1991), in which he systematically indicts "history" as universally spelled out as the Triumph of the West with the assumption of white superiority, and total disregard for other civilizations.

The criticism was reinforced by a demand for quotas of blacks in the staffing of educational institutions. There were similar demands from militant feminists. Presidents of universities, duly humiliated, made concessions. This politicization of American universities induced an academic sensitivity comparable with an ecological conscience, and standardized in the label "politically correct."

One of the most senior professors of philosophy, Sidney Hook, a disciple of John Dewey, and like him a philosopher of education, engaged in polemics against this trend as subversive of educational standards and intellectual integrity. He denounced academic presidents scathingly as pusillanimous in giving way to intimidation. He denounced quotas for replacing selection on individual fitness by merit. His main critique was focused on the course in Western culture at Stanford University, with which he had connections. The course had been denounced as racist, sexist, and imperialistic. One of its critics had said of Western culture: "It is not just racist education, it is the education of racists." The Rev. Jesse Jackson had demanded abolition of the course. Hook points out that the course is a faithful history of the legacy of the past essential to understanding the present, that it demonstrates movements to establish the ideals its critics invoke. He concludes: "It would hardly be an exaggeration to say that of all cultures of which we have knowledge, Western culture has been the most critical of itself." Black studies had their due place in modern curricula, which include their critique of Western history; but to black out the true story of Western culture was obscurantism to the point of willful self-blinding. Revenge is notoriously intemperate.

The scientific establishment of genetic diversity and equality takes away any ground for assumption of Western superiority. The fact remains that humanity has been brought together in one world and made aware of its origin and nature, and the transformation of that nature by the acquisition of an expanded capability and responsibility, by the advancement of learning researched and described in the history of Western culture; an unavoidable legacy in concrete terms, which it is understandable but fruitless to disparage in the rhetoric of resentment justified by a history of unforgivable suffering and outrage inflicted by their conquerors. The context has been provided in which reconciliation can prevail.

The racial scene in India is identifiable with the deep religious divisions, liable at any time to erupt in violence and massacre. The white influence remains in language, administration and law, and the secular state, so that government strives to contain the divisions impartially but racial tensions in religious terms are on a greater scale than anywhere else.

China's longest tradition is of singular aloofness, self-containment, and unquestioning assumption of superiority. Her isolationism was rudely broken in the nineteenth century when she became an open field for plunder and manipulation by outside powers, particularly Britain. This was followed by Japanese conquests, until Japan's elimination by defeat in World War II. Conquest and reunification by Mao, with the vicissitudes that followed, contain racial differences that subsist within the widespread territories. Chinese physical features, more sharply distinctive than the Japanese, are evidence of race in every context, whether or not their skills and wares make them welcome.

The Japanese have been sedulous apes of the West, open in their determination to acquire for themselves comparable power and place in the world. That has been a consistent purpose since the nineteenth century, revived under changed auspices since their reformation by General MacArthur who raised them from the dust of defeat. They went on to reassert their skills and their social discipline to excel the performance of this foster-parent.

Racism has been shown to have no rational grounds. Racial identity, like national identity, is characteristically rampant, but essentially ephemeral, in the sense that it is a sentiment, subjective. As a sentiment, it counts for something, and with some for everything, as once it did for the whites, and now in retort for some blacks. When it can be plainly recognized as tribal barbarism, even in the name of civilization, attitudes will begin to come round to a true valuation. For differentiation within the species is variety variation, an enrichment, a source of vitality and productivity. All-white would make pale the future it has brought about.

# SELF

## Self-concept

A concept is general, so that an informed idea of oneself is simply knowledge of human nature which one exemplifies in person. One's own idea of oneself as a particular person distinguishable from all others is a question of identity, all my distinctive individual characteristics focused in my character. Passport particulars amplified in a curriculum vitae abstract the given content of that. What remains is internal: a question of commitments, choices, priorities, what I make of myself, what I do with my life. It may happen that what I do with myself is not positively my own; rather, a routine falling in line with what I think is expected, what others do, what I find myself doing, for one reason or another. This would be an unformed identity, or no firm identity, a lack of distinctiveness, of fundamental self-will, a liability to be easily pushed or influenced. The difference between strong and weak, positive and negative, in this sense emerges in personal development, in one's history,

One's earliest formation occurs during maturation in a nurturing subculture in which one is brought up; and the key factor in this is one's responses to these pressures and influences and expectations, which may include a peer source in siblings responding in their own way to the same influences and expectations. This matrix is not sealed against outside influences, which rapidly gain in strength and possible rivalry. Adolescence is a stage at which these interacting unfolding developmental processes are apt to be checked and brought under review, or they may continue unquestioned. If examined, their tendency or effective influence may be confirmed, totally rejected, or modified. In any case, but most especially if rejected, one is beginning to take oneself in hand, establishing a footing of independence for an autonomous life-style, the foundation of a positive personal identity.

Rather, I am likely to think of my failings and ambitions, of what I am good at and bad at. There will be a conspectus of those I admire and those I despise peopled from the past as well as by contemporaries. These models will help to form my judgment of myself. Self-judgment is exercised in the fields of performance, and motivation, and with regard to success or failure, and ethical norms. There will be performances in which I am most anxious to do well, to focus self-appraisal, and raise me up or cast me down. In the ethical regard, conscience is self-judgment by acknowledged norms of conduct, which may often be uneasy rather than outright. What one cannot know is how one would behave in testing situations one has not been in and which one's way of life is most likely to preclude.

The level of one's self-esteem is an outcome of such self-judgments, and is realistic insofar as those judgments were honest and well-founded. Self-esteem is quite different from self-respect, and they are often confused. Self-respect has a dictionary definition of proper regard for the worthiness of one's character. It is best thought of as respect for one's human nature, rather as respect for one's car or any other property would be care in its use and maintenance. Self-respect is proper regard for one's health, an appropriate regimen, due regard for the states in the life-cycle and what is appropriate to each, with, for example, forward planning and adequate preparation for retirement in advance, not allowing oneself to be overtaken; in a word self-respect is proper self-management.

Selfhood is personal identity, which is a developing process on the lines indicated, modified throughout by experience of oneself, which may or may not prompt corrective action. The practical outcome, distinct from self-esteem, is one's self-confidence. An autonomous person with well-founded self-confidence is the model human being, but his personal identity is particular, and unique. Incidentally, "the quest for identity" often spoken of, looking for it, going back to find it in one's "roots" in the land and culture of one's inheritance, is mistaken in that it is not anything to find, but something to fashion.

## Relations with Nature

The model is the ecological life-style of the North American Indians, the very people the British colonists who settled misunderstood, despised, and decimated as they moved West, for whom there is a modern spokesman in the Native American chief who said: "The earth does not belong to man because he belongs to the earth, and all things are connected like the blood of one family."

Adam is not the master of all creatures put there to serve him; rather, he is the privileged inheritor of astonishing capabilities who can never be independent of the blood supplied from one family. Of course, the modern human life-style cannot be that of the few surviving peoples found living in the depth of the rain forests that survive. This model is only a pattern of a partnership with nature, which is seen closer to home and up-to-date in the gardner and the farmer, particularly perhaps in organic cultivation, as a redemptive mode of agriculture. This partnership belongs to self-respect as self-management.

The most subtle and fruitful partnership with nature is with the temporal conditions of all existence. This is manifest in management of the personal life-cycle, referred to above in regard to self-respect. Business management is also closely concerned with anticipating the future for survival in the market. Success, which is survival in biological life as in commercial competition, is about sustainable fulfillment of necessary and sufficient conditions, a forward dimension. It has been repeated in previous chapters that "problems" are seldom solved outright, if they are real problems—by definition, they should be insoluble. "Solutions" are brought about in partnership with time by initiating moves calculated to break down what is insurmountable and make it more tractable.

This was exemplified in the UN approach to effectively outlawing war. All achievement is an integration over a period of integers, units of action, and is planned in such terms. "Planning" is plotting a course of action on a time-scale. The blessed word "strategy" loosely prevalent in contemporary talk, is just such a plan on a large time-scale. All the performing arts dance to the music of time; and music itself is an art that is in intimate partnership with time, as is film-making and exhibition, and all work in the theater. Science as such fills out deficient description "by using an hypothesis on trial, anticipating future experience." Everything has a history from which it is inseparable. Human nature has been shown in these pages to be historical, temporal. Human individuals come to terms with that in partnership with the temporal conditions. History gives one's experience an orientation and context.

## Relations with Society

The affiliation of individual and society is inherent, for the human embryo does not become human unless and until socialized. We exist in a society from the outset or not at all. Society is not outside the individuals who come together to compose it by contract, as theorists used to imagine: since there is no individual standpoint independent of society. Personal identity of any individual is formed within society, and under its influence; but this society is a generic term, not limited to the particular society into which an individual happens to be born. As has been indicated above, social influences beyond the matrix into which one is born rapidly gain in strength. If this leads at adolescence and beyond to a break with one's upbringing and an autonomous identity, that does not, cannot, break the social bond. Personal isolation at its peak is Robinson Crusoe living on his social past, a privation, survivable only because he has that social past. Autonomy does not go further than a critical detachment that makes necessary associations deliberate, a choice.

The independent standpoint of autonomy is pertinently evident in a personal moral judgment. The underlying process structure of such a judgment is to set out the relevant alternatives as nearly as possible to a disjunction, in order to consider the notable consequences of acceptance and of rejection; then the bearing of the relevant general principle or principles is brought into the equation; weighing these considerations forms the judgment. Such a procedure is not necessarily formally followed through, but it is implicit in a reasoned judgment characteristic of autonomy in practice. The person with a collective identity goes along with the ready-made opinion of his fellows.

## Human Experience

Experience is individual, but may be shared in what happens to the society of which one is a member, shared experience of a war or an economic depression, or the like. There is inherited experience, as embodied in institutions, territory, traditions, a common history, and culture.

Human self-knowledge as demanded at Delphi is general, and was not fully available until science provided the answer. Particular knowledge of oneself is liable to be flawed, and is limited by uncertainty of how one might behave in trying circumstances; nor can one comprehensively sample all the categories of experience—achievement, contemplation, gratification, communication, service, exploration, discovery, types of work. That is, the program of experience remains open, and virtually inexhaustible.

A comprehensive sampling of experience should dwell on two examples. First, the experience of being human: the appropriation and maintenance of one's part in responsibility for global tasks is a fundamental experience of this kind. More intimately enjoyable and fulfilling is performance of specifically human acts in the context of the arts or the sciences or sports or any of the activities characteristic of and exclusive to the species. Engaged in such activities, one is probably never conscious of human privilege; but an occasional pause to savor just that is not out of the way.

Fundamental is one's disposal of oneself, how one employs the privilege of human existence. The quasi-immortality of fame, prominent in the ancient world and conspicuously revived in the Renaissance, is illusory—"seeking the bubble reputation." No longer "in the cannon's mouth," but even on the screen, in stardom, , with perpetuation made all but everlasting by technology, the parade vanishes on the morrow, banished to the archives: Transcendentalism in terms of personal immortality is less plausible than ever. Self-transcendence, however, is a genuine option, if not a moral obligation. It means using one's station in time and place for purposes beyond oneself, as a tool for accomplishments to fulfill one's existence. The grain of wheat that dies in the earth "beareth much fruit." This teaching of Jesus reports an observable fact, a reminder, outside the context in which he is reported to have preached it. Unselfishness, radical disregard for self-centered preoccupations, is not simply "living for others," which literally is nonsense, or misguided in principle. Rather, it is using oneself as an agent for the production and promotion of what one judges of general or particular benefit. It is the difference between fertility and sterility, and inwardly between discontent and joy.

In the ethical sphere of morality, there are public and private hemispheres: obligation and choice. Duty is in the public domain. Choice is personal and private; in ethics outside obligation there is a choice of values for cultivation, say, candor, courage, simplicity, generosity, in which one feels regretfully deficient. Hume said that public spirit is the better part of virtue. Let it be so for the sake of the world; there remains the other part, in which one cultivates oneself with some ideal in mind. This may not be self-transcendence in the direct sense intended above, but all idealism in as far as it is genuine is transcendence, an unattainable aim that is the nerve of striving.

## Self-Determination

The old form of self-observation, with the saint as model ("Be ye perfect"), was a nightly examination as to progress or backsliding (Defoe). The perspective has changed. Today it is more likely to be a look back at the maladjustments of childhood, what went wrong and why, with a background understanding of the stages of development that are the norm in our society, the critical incidents from birth through weaning to puberty and adolescence, with gains and setbacks.

Only an autonomous person achieves full identity; others, who share identification, are nevertheless individuals, not clones. With the acceleration of social change and an outlook of uncertainty, it becomes increasingly important that the achievement of autonomy should become the norm, while conditions make it less likely.

At the beginning of the century, it was a commonplace of educated conversation that the conveniences of life enjoyed by the middle classes accrued from human capability that was recent and accelerating. They were the passive beneficiaries. Now, at the end of the century, what were the conveniences of life have become the conditions of One World, transformed by information technology, telecommunication, and air transport. The advancement of learning that was accelerating ended in an explosion of knowledge that is a breakthrough in human capability with command over the source of life in genetic engineering, entailing responsibility for the planet and the life it contains. The educated middle-class person can no longer be a passive beneficiary. Human responsibility is borne by individuals, though not shared equally.

Human culture has been brought about not through a convergence of cultures but through the advancement of learning initiated by the Greeks, and thence through an assimilation of diverse sources, a life-blood of communication. Is there in the making a human culture that can provide a globally shared pattern of behavior for human identity?

## Acceleration of Social Change

Information technology has produced instant communication in the One World. Technology in general has enhanced human capability to the pitch of supplanting evolution, and, by manipulating the source of life in genetic engineering, makes humanity responsible for life on the planet. The "hubris" warning of Delphi is consummated in the barely calculable risks entailed, principally the extinction of variety, the supreme natural resource, for short-term gain in a particular genetic product.

Human culture can therefore be defined as a globally shared pattern of behavior with a program of specific tasks. These include ecological conservation, population control, unification of North and South by initiatives of the dominant GATT powers, and international security. Human responsibility has meaning only in terms of individual responsibility, and it is for individuals to work out and undertake their share in accomplishment of the program.

Whatever society an educated person belongs to at the end of the twentieth century is transcended in One World by escalating human capability that commands, and is therefore responsible for, the future of the planet. That responsibility is specified in certain global tasks, such as ecological conservation, population control, and unification of One World by redress of the imbalance of North and South.

In addition to an individually worked-out and undertaken program to discharge a due share of this responsibility, a whistle-blowing vigilance on several vital fronts has to be maintained. The political dimension of ethics, recognized since Aristotle and stressed by Hume ("public spirit is the better part of virtue"), has this contemporary specificity as an upshot of history, in a development of human nature, consummated in self-understanding.

The history of Western culture traced in this essay ends here with its focus in oneself. For all selves have been brought together in an historical transformation of human nature.

# Abstract

Following the break-up of the Bronze Age civilizations of the Mediterranean world, the peoples of Greece, Israel, and Rome, formed and formulated, as an outcome of generations of experience, three claims to universality for their examples and destiny. These examples were destined to exert a formative influence on the development of Europe, from the first Europe after the fall of Rome to the two World Wars which mark the watershed between the history of Europe and its upshot in One World. The three examples for which universality was declared are designated in this study: Hellas, Zion, and Romanitas.

Greece in the classical period in which Hellas was formed was composed of more than two hundred small independent city-states, without political union or social cohesion. They enjoyed, however, social contact and cultural union in the regular festivals at which cities competed for wreaths of honor in all the arts. The Olympic Games pioneered these festivals, and are the best remembered; but all the arts were developed by striving for excellence in these intercity competitions.

Sparta and Athens were the two most famous cities, and were polar opposites in both constitutions and ideals. Sparta was dedicated exclusively to military arts, and was a totalitarian closed society. Athens was an open society, with an educational program that included all disciplines. The oracle of Apollo at Delphi subsumed the ancestral wisdom of Greece for all inquirers in two apophthegms, "Know yourself" and "Nothing too much": i.e., know that you are mortal; don't get above yourself as though you were one of the immortals; beware of hubris.

Aristotle went on to define human nature formally: "Man is a rational animal." Plato's Socrates unwittingly provided an operational definition with the remark "The unexamined life is not a life for man": that is, the business of human beings is inquiry, the advancement of learning; what you are, when bidden to know yourself, is an inquirer. On the eve of Alexander's invasion of Persia, at the end of the classical period in Athens, the sophist Isocrates declared that Hellas was known not as a race but as a culture: "the school of the world."

Israel propagated a precisely opposite idea of human nature, proclaiming that the god of their ancestors—the God of Abraham, Isaac, and Jacob—had created Adam in his own image and likeness for dependence and obedience and had expressly forbidden him to eat of the fruit of the Tree of Knowledge which grew in the Garden of Eden. Adam's nature, flawed by his sin of disobedience, was bequeathed to all begotten of his seed, the human race. Though they might strive for knowledge, they could not find out anything that was not ordained by the will of God, the almighty Creator; they could not escape his providence and their dependence. In the sequel, the children of Israel were chosen to redeem mankind by their faithfulness, bearing witness to the world that God had promised to take back into his benevolence all who turned from their disobedience to faithful dependence.

The Romans, from small scattered beginnings under the neighboring Etruscans, slowly over many years built up their influence and power throughout Italy, and in doing so formed their character and reputation for endurance and public spirit, readiness to defend their independence, to quit the plow for military service when called upon to do so *pro bono publico*. Building a fleet and finally defeating their archrival Carthage, they launched the Republic on a career of imperial conquest in emulation of Alexander. Republican public spirit did not prevent bids for power by rival military leaders. After Julius Caesar's defeat of Pompey, followed by his own assassination and then years of devastating conflict, Octavian Caesar emerged as victor, with the Republic in a state of anarchy. As Augustus, he initiated the Principiate, a reconstruction that, while preserving a nominal Senate, a simulacrum of restoration, recognized in the acquired provinces of non-Romans an empire, on which he imposed autocratic absolute rule in the Principiate, to be maintained by successive emperors.

As Horace put it, Rome had conquered Greece but Greek culture had captivated Rome. He had been sent to Athens for his higher education. He, Virgil, and Augustus, in their consultations, conceived the ideal destiny of the new Rome, articulated in two famous lines of the Aenead, as spelled out to Aeneas by his father Anchises in the Underworld: The destiny of the Romans, the seed of Aeneas, was to impose on the nations the rule of law, with peace, leaving to others cultivation of the arts and sciences.

In these legendary terms, *Romanitas* was dramatically declared in Virgil's epic and Horace's odes. It had political reality in the policy and program of Augustus. Moreover, it had feasibility in the practice of Roman uniformity of government by law, served by Roman genius in civil engineering that provided an infrastructure for administration with a network of phenomenally durable roads. Thus Romans made themselves masters of government, and were destined to rule.

After Marcus Aurelius, the Empire fell into corruption and decline until rescued from anarchy by Diocletian, who embarked on a reconstruction for which he took the oriental hierarchical model, including the court ceremonial and a religious sanction. Augustus had tried elaborately and persistently to revive the old political religion of the Republic, but it was too official and formal to meet personal needs, and he failed. Diocletian favored the Eastern religions of Egypt, Persia, and Syria, which had been hospitably received in Rome. Constantine eventually chose the heretical Jewish sect of Christianity as the religion of the Roman state.

Christianity was by that time as widespread as Mithraism, which was popular in the army. Christianity was not arcane, nor priest-ridden; it was monotheistic (a sanction for autocracy); its apostles were humble fisherfolk, not a hegemony of prelates; and its bishops had organized it efficiently. To make it enforceable, however, required an established orthodoxy.

Most Christians were Arians, whose notion of the divinity of Jesus was that it supervened at his baptism by John, so that he was not inherently divine. At Nicaea, the bishops decided that Jesus had to be fully divine and fully human: the only begotten Son of the Father for partnership in divine rule, incarnated in a woman with an exclusively human ancestry. The contradiction was resolved in the Nicaean (Trinitarian) creed, which was inexplicable but mandatory.

Theodosius, the last effective Roman emperor, was a believer, and he enacted a union of Church and State in an indissoluble identity. Church and Empire were one and indivisible.

Thus, after the loss of the Western provinces, the bishops maintained continuity with Rome, without an emperor, and, converting the rulers of the settled and half-settled tribes in the first Europe, imposed an ecclesiastical administration. When Charlemagne conquered the lost provinces and was crowned by the Pope in 800, the virtual restoration was designated the "Holy Roman Empire." This enterprise was not destined to survive the death of Frederick II (*Stupor Mundi*) in the thirteenth century, save as a disastrous distraction from the building of centralized nation states that would acquire in time their own empires, initiated by another Norman, the Conqueror, and consummated in England by Henry VII, Francis Bacon's model monarch, with the suppression of the feudal anarchy of the warlords.

The legacy of Rome to Europe was twofold, Greek as well as Latin. In the East, there was no break in the continuity of imperial rule. The fall did not come until 1453, to the Ottoman Turks. The particular legacy of Byzantium was handed down to the Russians and Slavs through the Greek Orthodox Church.

Greek was the language and literature of Byzantium. Justinian was the last Roman-minded emperor, Latin in speech and thought. He drained the resources of Byzantium by setting out to reconquer the western provinces, an aberration from which his successors turned decisively to attend to the north and east frontiers of a defensible state. This defensive European gate, precariously held for more than eight hundred years, was the invaluable military achievement. Bellisarius, by destroying the North African kingdom of the Vandals and their sea power, which had cut off the corn supply from Egypt, had made the one positive contribution to European security of Justinian's regime.

The vicissitudes of loss and recovery in the checkered history of Byzantium show how precarious their survival was; however, it lasted long enough for them to develop their distinctive adoption and adaptation of Greek classical texts, which they copied and reproduced with scrupulous accuracy, solely for moralistic ecclesiastical instruction. The Greek Fathers had put the final stamp on Christian orthodoxy at Chalcedon;

the Greek Orthodox Church proclaimed itself in its title to be champion and trustee of that orthodoxy. Their scholars and copyists transmitted reliable codices of classical texts which aided the literary revival of learning in the Italian Renaissance, but they did not share, nor appreciate, Greek culture. When they studied Plato it was not the dialectic of the Socratic dialogues. Their society was incompatible with the open society of Athens. Defining the enemy as "infidel" would have been an unintelligible concept to the Hellenes, for whom religion was but one thing among many in a culture that was the competitive pursuit of excellence in all human activities.

Thus, the legacies of the Roman Empire in the East, as in the West, cut off from the European inheritance the legacy of Hellas, the advancement of learning as the school of the world.

After the waning of the Middle Ages, an underlying theme in the history of Europe is the recovery, by discovery, of the independent claims to universality for Hellas, Zion, and Romanitas. Rediscovery of primitive Christianity and popular repossession of the Bible came with the Protestant Reformation that eventually brought religious liberty and secularization with the neutrality of the state.

Zionism might well be likened to the Holy Roman Empire as a bid to restore the past, much as the American Dream dawned as an anticipation of the future in a New World. Both exemplify the need for adjustment to temporality. It is part of the human condition to have to come to terms with history as well as with nature. By no means all Israelis, and probably not a majority, seek a restoration of all the territories of biblical Israel, but a hard core do, demanding defensible frontiers in a hostile environment. The present is endowed by the past, but also bedeviled by it.

The rule of law was established stage by stage, and affirmed as the foundation of society and guarantee of free association and civil liberties.

Advancement of learning became the screw under the water, propelling modern historical progress, when Newton and Galileo and others made their resounding physical discoveries. That was what induced Locke to recognize that the empirical methodology of scientific investigation held the only key to tested knowledge and that metaphysical philosophy had been definitively superseded. The scientists themselves believed they were turning for revelation from disputes about the Word of God to investigation of the Works of God.

God was said by some to be on trial during the next century and a half. The issues were articulated during the Enlightenment. Condorcet, in the weeks of hiding from his opponents and the guillotine before giving himself up, ended his life with a *Sketch for a Historical Picture of the Progress of the Human Mind,* in which he traced the checkered course of the progress of the human race motored by the advancement of learning to the point when an informed purposive "social art" would ensure directed social progress. Though obscured by the reaction of the Romantic movement, Condorcet's vision necessarily prevailed with the discovery of geological time and the fossil evidence of primitive and developing forms of life. This led Darwin to demonstrate a nonpurposive order of nature that had produced a vast variety of living forms of which some survived as self-propagating species, among them *Homo sapiens sapiens.* A steady accumulation and spread of knowledge followed, but the revolutionary discovery of genetic programming was needed before the origin and development of human nature could be fully spelled out and the Delphi injunction at last be fulfilled. The application of abstract knowledge brought about an incalculable escalation of human capability: the actualization of Bacon's knowledge "for the relief of man's estate."

Not until our own time has it been possible for humanity to possess adequate self-awareness, in the light of science and of history. In addition, applications of the escalating knowledge have endowed human nature with a capability of determining the future of life on the planet in specific ways, including even a reshaping of genetic inheritance.

Information technology and rapid transportation have brought about One World, with the specific global tasks and paramount obligation this entails. Awareness of this One World strikes us in evident disorders: disproportion between the prosperity enjoyed by the few industrialized nations and the penury endured by thousands of millions in the so-called Third World; the aggravation of overpopulation; the ecological damage, entailing serious threats to the survival of many species, and even of life on the planet; the existence and availability without adequate controls of annihilating weapons that make international security a political priority.

Responsibility for consequences, good and ill, is at last recognized as being global and shared. This recognition of specific interconnected tasks brings with it the responsibility of addressing them effectively: a responsibility shared worldwide, collectively and individually. Everyone has the moral obligation to work out and undertake his or her appropriate part in the collective tasks, and there are pressure groups and charities organized and equipped to help us. In fulfilling this obligation, one enacts one's personal human identity. This is the bond of human union and the final historical universal that supersedes the claims of Hellas, Zion, and Romanitas to universality.

There remains, however, a caveat to this conclusion. It is an up-to-date version of More's point that his Utopia depended on human nature being other than it is. Human nature, in Darwinian terms, is a concept; human behavior is the practicality. In its variety it cannot be generalized unless characterized as essentially good or evil, and there is insufficient evidence for this. Empirically, it can only be assessed in terms of liabilities, personal but also institutional, as Bentham and C. Northcote Parkinson have demonstrated. The behavioral element in economics defies and defeats science. (Fear and greed may be mentioned.) Thus, human behavior may well defy and defeat, or betray, the moral obligation that develops one's personal human identity and is the bond of humanity.

The questions asked of history (say, by Hegel and Marx) are answered by questions history asks of us today.

# Bibliography

## General

Barraclough, Geoffery, ed. *Times Concise Atlas of World History.* 1982.
Butler, Audrey. *A Dictionary of Dates.* 1987.
Fisher, H. A. L. *A History of Europe.* 1936.
Fukuyama, Francis. *The End of History and the Last Man.* 1992.
Garraty, John A., and Peter Gay. *The University History of the World.* 1985.
Gombrich, E. H. *The Story of Art,* 14th ed. 1984.
Hawkes, Jacquetta. *The Atlas of Early Man.* 1993.
Holmes, Richard. *The World Atlas of Warfare.* 1988.
Malreauz, Andre. *The Voices of Silence.* 1974.
Sweetman, John. *A Dictionary of European Land Battles.* 1984.
Wedgwood, C. V. *The Spoils of Time.* 1984.

## Part One: Three Universal Models

*Hellas*

Antecedents:

Edey, Maitland A. *Lost World of the Aegean.* 1975.
Hamblin, Dora Jane. *The First Cities.* 1973.
Pritchard, James A., ed. *The Ancient Near East.* 1958.
Roe, Derek A. *The Lower and Middle Paleolithic Periods in Britain.* 1981.
Trump, D. H. *The Prehistory of the Mediterranean.* 1980.

Archaic Greece:

Blundel, Sue. *The Origins of Civilization in Greek and Roman Thought*. 1986.
Brehier, Emile. *Histoire de la philosophie*. 1948.
Burn, A. R. *The Pelican History of Greece*. 1985.
Cicero. *De Officiis*. Tr. Thomas Cockman. 1909.
Corn, F. M. *From Religion to Philosophy*. 1912.
Diogenes, Laertius. *Lives of Eminent Philosophers*. Tr. R. D. Hicks. 1925.
Farrington, Benjamin. *Science and Politics in the Ancient World*. 1939.
———. *Greek Science*. 1944.
Fiehleman, J. K. *Religious Platonism*. 1959.
Finley, Jr., John H. *Four Stages of Greek Thought*. 1966.
Finley, M. I. *Ancient Sicily*, rev. ed. 1979.
Freeman, Kathleen. *Companion to the Pre-socratic Philosphers*. 1946.
———. *The Greek Way*. 1947.
———. *Ancilla to the Pre-Socratic Philosphers*. 1948.
———. *Greek City States*. 1950.
Freeman, Kenneth J. *Schools of Hellas*. 1907.
Griffin, Jasper. *Homer*. 1980.
Grimal, Pierre. *A Dictionary of Classical Muthology*. 1986.
Guhl, E., and W. Koner. *Everyday Life of the Greeks and Romans*. 1989.
Guthrie, W. K. C. *In the Beginning*. 1957.
Halliday, William R. *The Growth of the City State*. 1923.
Hicks, Jim. *The Empire Builders*. 1974.
How, W. W., and J. Wells. *A Commentary on Herodotus*. 1912.
Kirks, G. S. *The Songs of Homer*. 19562.
Laurie, Simon. *Historical Survey of Pre-Christian Education*, 2nd ed. 1900.
Levi, Peter. *Guide to Greece*. 1971.
Murray, Oswyn. *Early Greece*. 1980.
Murray, Gilbert. *Five Stages of Greek Religion*. 1925.
Nilsson, M. P. *Greek Piety*. 1948.
Ormerod, H. A. *Piracy in the Ancient World*. 1924.
Sambursky, S. *The Physical World of the Greeks*. 1956.
Sarton, George. *Ancient Science and Modern Civilization*. 1954.
Snodgrass. Anthony. *Archaic Greece*. 1980.
Zervos, Christiaj. *L'Art en Grece*. 1934.


Classical Greece:

Adkins, A. W. H. *From the Many to the One*. 1970.
Bonnard, Andre. *Greek Civilization*. Tr. R. C. Knight. 1961.
Bowra, C. M. *Landmarks in Greek Literature*. 1966.
Bulgar, R. R. *The Classical Heritage and Its Beneficiaries*. 1954.
Bullfinch, Thomas. *The Age of Fable*. 1910.

Butcher, S. H. *Aristotle's Theory of Poetry and Fine Art,* 4th ed. 1923.

Chadwick, H. M. *The Heroic Age.* 1912.

Cornford, F. M. *Principium Sapientae.* 1952.

Crawford, W. S. *Synesius the Hellene.* 1901.

Dodds, E. R. *The Greeks and the Irrational.* 1951.

Ferguson, John, and Kitty Chisho, eds. *Political and Social Life in the Great age of Athens.* 1978.

Finn, David, and Caroline Houser. *Greek Monumental Bronze Sculpture.* 1983.

Gardiner, E. Norman. *Greek Athletic Sports and Festivals.* 1910.

Guthrie, W. K. C. *Orpheus and Greek Religion.* 1935.

———. *The Greeks and Their Gods.* 1950.

Holland, Virginia. *Kenneth Burke and Aristotle's Theories of Rhetoric.* 1959.

Isocrates. *Antidosis.*

Isocrates. *Panegyricus.*

Jaeger, W. W. *Paideia: The Ideals of Greek Culture.* Tr. Gilbert Highet. 1939–45.

Jarret, James L., ed. *The Educational Theories of the Sophists.* 1969.

Lever, Katherine. *The Art of Greek Comedy.* 1956.

Little, Alan M. G. *Myth and Society in Attic Drama.* 1967.

Lord, Louis E. *Aristophanes: His Plays and His Influence.* 1925.

Marrow, H. I. *History of Education in Antiquity.* 1956.

Mitchell, H. *Sparta.* 1952.

Raeburn, Michael, ed. *The Architecture of the Western World.* 1980.

Rand, Edward Kennard. *Founders of the Middle Ages.* 1929.

Stanford, W. B. *Greek Tragedy and the Emotions.* 1983.

Untersteiner, Mario. *The Sophists.* Tr. Kathleen Freeman. 1954.

Whittaker, Thomas. *Macrobius.* 1923.

Zenophon. *Memorabilia.*

Zimmern, Alfred. *The Greek Commonwealth,* 4th ed. 1924.

## Zion

Josephus. *The Jewish War,* rev. ed. Tr. G. A. Williamson. 1981.

Roshwald, M. *Moses.* 1969.

Wellhausen, Julius. *History of Israel.* 1878, 1905.

## Romanitas

Allison, Francis G. *Lucian: Satirist and Artist.* 1926.

Anderson, Graham. *Studies in Lucian's Comic Fiction.* 1976.

Athanasius. *Life of St. Antony.* Tr. Rovert T. Meyer. 1950.

Baldwin, Barry. *Studies in Lucian.* 1973.

Baynes, Norman H. *Constantine and the Christian Church.* 1930.

Beurlier, G. *Essai sur le culte recdu aux empereurs romainains.* 1891.

Bompaire, J. *Lucian Ecrivain.* 1958.

Causse, A. *Essai sur le conflit de Christianisme primitif et de las civilisation.* 1920.

Charlesworth, M. P. *The Virtues of a Roman Emperor: Propaganda and the Creation of Belief.* 1937.

Cicero. *De Legibus.*

———. *De Natura Deorum.*

———. *De Republica.*

Clarke, M. L. *Rhetoric at Rome.* 1953.

Cochrane, C. N. *Christianity and Classical Culture.* 1940.

Costa, C. D. N., ed. *Seneca.* 1974.

Croiset, Maurice. *La vie et les oeuvres de Lucian.* 1882.

de Witt, Norman Wentworth. *St. Paul and Epicurus.* 1954.

Dill, Samuel. *Roman Society From Nero to Marcus Aurelius.* 1904.

Duff, J. W. *A Literary History of Rome.* 1960.

du Roy, Olivier. *L'Intelligence ded la foi en las Trinite selon et Augustine.* 1966.

Grant, Michael. *Julius Caesar.* 1969.

Gwynn, A. *Roman Education from Cicero to Quintilian.* 1926.

Hodgson, Geraldine. *Primitive Christian Education.* 1906.

Kelly, J. N. D. *Early Christian Doctrine.* 1958.

King, Anthony. *Archaeology of the Roman Empire.* 1982.

Levick, Barbara. *The Government of the Roman Empire.* 1985.

Lot, Ferdinand. *The End of the Ancient World and the Beginning of the Middle Ages.* Tr. P. Leon and M. Leon. 1931.

Lucian. *Nigrinus.*

———. *Timon.*

Hodgart, Matthew. *Satire.* 1969.

Momigliano, Arnaldo, ed. *The Conflict Between Paganism and Christianity in the Fourth Century.* 1963.

Murray, Gilbert. *Stoic, Christian, and Humanist.* 1940.

Nock, A. D. *Conversion.* 1933.

Oaksmith, John. *The Religion of Plutarch.* 1902.

Ovid. *Metamorphoses.*

Plutarch. *Lives.*

Rist, J. M. *Epicurus: An Introduction.* 1972.

Roissier, V. G. *La religion romaine d'Auguste aux Antonins.* 1874.

Schlatter, Adolf. *The Church in the New Testament Period.* Tr. Paul P. Levertoff. 1926, 1955.

Simon, Marcel. *St. Stephen and the Hellenists in the Primitive Church.* 1958.

Stobart, J. C. *The Grandeur That Was Rome,* rev. ed. 1912, 1961.

Wacher, John. *The Roman Empire.* 1987.

Wilkinson, P., ed. *Ovid Survey.* 1962.

Wirszubski. C. *Libertas as a Political Idea at Rome During the Later Republic and Early Principiate.* 1950.

Hellenistic Age:

Ammianus Marcellinus. *The Chronicle of Events.*
Baynes, Norman. *The Hellenistic Civilization of Eastern Rome.* 1946.
Grant, Michael. *From Alexander to Cleopatra.* 1982.
Ingram, John Kells. *A History of Political Economy.* 1888, 1967.
Peters, F. E. *The Harvest of Hellenism.* 1970.
Renault, Mary. *The Mask of Apollo.* 1966.
Tarn, W. W. *Hellenistic Civilization.* 1927.
———. *Alexander the Great.* 1948.
Theophrastus. *Characters.*

## Part Two: The Western Interregnum

Adames, Henry. *Mont-Saint-Michel and Chartres.* 1980.
Almgren, Bertil, et al. *The Viking.* 1975.
Barber, Richard, ed. *The Arthurian Legends.* 1979.
Baynes, Norman, and Eileen Power. *Europe Throughout the Middle Ages.* 1929.
Bede, the Venerable. *The Ecclesiastical History of the English Nation.* 1947.
Birch, Walter de Grey. *Domesday Book.* 1887.
Bray, Barbara, tr. *Montaillou.* 1978.
Campbell, Yeoman. *The English Yeoman.* 1942.
Collins. Marie. *Caxton's Description of Britain.* 1988.
de Breffny, Brian. *In the Steps of St. Patrick.* 1905.
Douglas, David C. *William the Conquerer.* 1966.
Dronke, Ptere. *The Medieval Lyric,* 2d ed. 1981.
Dunlop. Ian. *The Cathedrals' Crusade.* 1982.
Elias, Norbert. *The Court Society.* Tr. Edmund Jephcott. 1983.
Focillon, Henri. *The Art of the West.* 1963.
Freeman, E. A. *The Norman Impact Upon England.* 1888, 1964.
Freemantle, Anne, ed. *The Age of Belief: The Medieval Philosophers.* 1954.
Gardner, Arthur. *Medieval Sculpture.* 1937.
Gilby, Thomas, ed. and tr. *St. Thomas Aquinas Philosophical Texts.* 1951.
———, ed. and tr. *St. Thomas Aquinas Theological Texts.* 1953.
Gilson, Etienne. *The Philosophy of St. Thomas Aquinas,* 3d ed. rev. Tr. Ed Bullough. 1929.
Guelluy, Robert. *Philosophie et Theologie de Guillaume d'Ockham.* 1947.
Guenee, Bernard. *States and Rulers in Later Medieval Europe.* Tr. Juliet Vale. 1985.
Haskins, C. H. *Studies in the History of Medieval Science.* 1927.
Huizinga, J. *The Waning of the Middle Ages.* Tr. F. Hopman. 1924.
John of Salisbury. *Policracticus.*
Joinville, Jean de, and Geoffroi de Villehardouin. *Chronicles of the Crusades.* Tr. M. R. E. Shaw. 1963.
Langland, William. *Piers the Ploughman.* Ed. W. W. Skeat. 1906.

Leff, Gordon A. *Medieval Thought.* 1958, 1980.

Madaule, Jacques. *The Albigenisan Crusade.* Tr. Barbara Wall. 1967.

Maitland, F. W. *Domesday Book and Beyond.* 1897.

Malory, Sir Thomas. *Le morte d'Arthur.* 1868, 1901.

Mandeville, Sir John. *Mandeville's Travels.* Tr. Phamelius. 1916.

Marsh, Henry. *Dark Age Britain.* 1970.

Morris, Richard, ed. *An Old English Miscellany.* 1867–8.

Morris, Richard, ed. *Specimens of Early English.* 1887.

Osgood, Jr., C. G. *The Pearl.* 1906.

Phillpotts, Bertha. *Kindred and Clan.* 1974.

Platt, Colin. *The English Medieval Town.* 1976.

———. *The Atlas of Medieval Man.* 1979.

Plitz, Anders. *The World of Medieval Learning.* Tr. David Jones. 1981.

Riche, Pierre. *Daily Life in the World of Charlemagne.* Tr. Jo Ann McNamara. 1973.

Runciman, Steven. *The First Crusade.* 1980.

Sisam, Kenneth, ed. *The Lay of Havelok the Dane,* 2nd ed. 1915.

———, ed. *Fourteenth Century Verse and Prose.* 1921.

Skeat, W. W., ed. *Minor Poems of Chaucer.* 1888.

———, ed. *Chaucer's Complete Works.* 1919.

Southern, R. W. *The Making of the Middle Ages.* 1953.

Storey, R. L. *The End of the House of Lancaster.* 1986.

Swann, W. *The Gothic Cathedral.* 1984.

Sweet, Hy, ed. *Anglo-Saxon Reader.* 1908.

Warner, Marina. *Alone of All Her Sex.* 1976.

Whitelock, Dorothy, et al. *The Norman Conquest.* 1966.

Wyatt, A. J., ed. *Beowolf,* rev. ed. R. W. Chambers. 1920.

## Part Three: Recovery and Discovery, and Part Four: The Legacy of the West

Adams, W. E. *Memoirs of a Social Atom.* 1900–1902.

Aiken, D., ed. *The Age of Ideology: The Nineteenth Century Philosophers.* 1956.

Andrews, Michael. *The Birth of Europe.* 1991.

Arnold, Matthew. *Culture and Anarchy.* 1867.

———. *Literature and Dogma.* 1873.

Aspinall, A. *The Early English Trade Unions.* 1949.

Aston, Margaret. *The Fifteenth Century: The Prospect of Europe.* 1968.

Aulaard, A. *Histoire politique de la Revolution Francaise.* 1909.

Bacon, Francis. *The Achievement of Learning.* 1605.

———. *History of the Reign of King Henry VII.* 1622.

———. *New Atlantis.* 1627.

Barbu, Zevedei. *Le development de la pensee dialectique.* 1947.

Barker, Ernest, ed. *The Social Contract.* 1947.

Bate, Walter Jackson. *The Achievement of Samuel Johnson.* 1961.

Becker, Carl L. *The Heavenly City of the Eighteenth Century Philosophers.* 1932.

Beeching, Jack. *The Galleys at Lepanto.* 1982.

Beloff, Max. *Thomas Jefferson and American Democracy.* 1948.

———, ed. *The Debate on the American Revolution, 1761–1783.* 1949.

Benesco, Georges, ed. *Oeuvres choisies de Voltaire.* 1887.

Best, Geoffery. *The Permanent Revolution.* 1988.

Besterman, Theodore, ed., tr. *Selected Letters of Voltaire.* 1963.

Blum, Carol. *Diderot: The Virtues of a Philosopher.* 1974.

Briggs, Asa, ed. *They Saw It Happen: An Anthology of Eyewitness Accounts of British History.* 1962.

Brookfield, Charles and Frances. *Mrs. Brookfield and Her Circle.* 1905–6.

Browne, Sir Thomas. *Religion Medici.* 1643.

Burke, Edmund. *Reflections on the Revolutin in France.* 1790.

Calder, Angus. *Revolutionary Empire: The Rise of the English Speaking Empires From the Fifteenth Century to 1780.* 1981.

Cannadine, David, ed. *Patricians, Power, and Politics in Nineteenth Century Towns.* 1982.

Carlyle, Thomas. *Sartor Resartus.* 1833–34.

———. *The French Revolution.* 1837.

Cassara, Ernest. *The Enlightenment in America.* 1988.

Cassirer, Ernst. *The Philosophy of the Enlightenment.* Tr. F. C. A. Koelln and J. R. Pettegrove. 1951.

Chadwick, Owen. *The Secularization of the European Mind in the Nineteenth Century.* 1975.

Chamberlain, Muriel E. *Lord Aberdeen.* 1983.

Church, Clive. *Europe in 1830.* 1981.

Churchill, Winston. *My Early Life, 1874–1908.*

Cobban, Alfred, ed. *The Debate on the French Revolution, 1789–1800.* 1950.

Coleman, Dorothy Gabe. *Montaignes's Essais.* 1987.

Cragg, G. R. *From Puritanism to the Age of Reason.* 1950.

Craig, Albert M., et al. *The Heritage of World Civilizations Since 1500.* 1986.

Crampton, R. J. *The Hollow Detente: Anglo-German Relations in the Balkans: 1911–14.* 1979.

David, Edward, ed. *Inside Asquith's Cabinet: From the Diaries of Charles Hobhouse.* 1977.

Davis, I. M. *The Harlot and the Statesman: Elizabeth Armistead and Charles Jason Fox.* 1986.

Denton, W. *England in the Fifteenth Century.* 1888.

Dickinson, H. T. *Liberty and Property: Political Ideology in Eighteenth Century Britain.* 1977.

Diderot. *Le neveu de Rameau.*

Dixon, Peter. *Canning.* 1976.

Drake, Stillman. *Galileo.* 1980.

Edsall, Nicholas C. *Richard Cobden.* 1881.

Emden, Cecil S. *The People and the Constitution: The People's Influence in British Government*. 1956.

Ereira, Alan. *The People's England*. 1981.

Esquemeling, John. *The Buccaneers of America*. 1987.

Fletcher, F. T. H. *Montesquieu and English Politics*. 1939.

France, Peter, tr. *Diderot's Letters to Sophie Volland: A Selection*. 1972.

Franchini, Raffaello. *Le Origini Dealla Dialecticca*. 1961.

French, Peter J. *John Dee*. 1972.

Furbank, P. M. *Diderot*. 1992.

Fuson, Robert, tr. *The Log of Christopher Columbus*. 1987.

Garaudy, Roger. *Les sources francaises du socialisme scientifique*. 1948.

Gooch, G. P. *Frederick the Great*. 1990.

Gore, John, ed. *Thomas Creevey's Papers, 1793–1838*. 1985.

Greene, John C. *The Death of Adam*. 1959.

Groethuysen, B. *Origines de l'esprit bourgeois en France*. 1927.

Haffner, Sebastian. *The Rise and Fall of Prussia*. 1980.

Hall, Hubert. *Society in the Elizabethan Age*. 1902.

Hampshire, Stuart, ed. *The Age of Reason: The Seventeenth Century Philosophers*. 1956.

Hampson, Norman. *Will and Circumstance: Montesquieu, Rouseau, and the French Revolution*. 1983.

Hazard, Paul. *La crise de la conscience Europeenne, 1680–1715*. 1935.

Held, F. E., tr. *Christianopolis*. 1916.

Hibben, John Grier. *The Philosophy of the Enlightenment*. 1910.

Hill, Brian W. *British Parliamentary Parties, 1742–1832*. 1985.

———. *Sir Robert Walpole*. 1989.

Hobhouse, Christopher. *Fox*. 1934.

Hodgen, Margaret T. *Early Anthropology in the Sixteenth and Seventeenth Centuries*. 1964.

Holton, R. J. *Cities, Capitalism, and Civilization*. 1986.

Hooker, Richard. *The Laws of Ecclesiastical Polity*. 1594–97.

Huggin, Frank E. *The Land Question and European Society*. 1975.

Hughes, Stuart. *Consciousness and Society: The Reorientation of European Social Thought, 1890–1930*. 1958.

Hugo, Victor, and Oliver Goldsmith. *Voltaire: Studies*. 1954.

Hyde, Ed, Earl of Clarendon. *History of the Rebellion in England*. 1702–4.

Kaul, R. K. *The Augustans*. 1981.

Kenyon, John. *The Civil Wars of England*. 1988.

Kriegel, Abraham D., ed. *The Holland House Diaries, 1831–40*. 1977.

Lalande, Andre. *Vocabulaire de la philosophie*, 5th ed. 1947.

Lamartine, Alphonse de. *History of the French Revolution of 1848*. 1849.

Langan, Mary, and Bill Schwarz. *Crises in the British State, 1880–1930*. 1985.

Laprade, William T. *Public Opinion and Politics in Eighteenth Century England*. 1936.

Law, William. *A Serious Call to a Devout and Holy Life.* 1728.

Leavis, F. R., ed. *Mill on Bentham and Coleridge.* 1950.

Lefebvre, Georges. *The Coming of the French Revolution.* Tr. R. R. Palmer. 1947.

Leroy, Maxime. *Les precurseurs francaises du socialisme: Condorcet a Proudon.* 1948.

Levi, Anthony. *French Moralists.* 1964.

Lough, John, ed. *Diderot: Selected Philosophical Writings.* 1953.

———, ed. *The Encyclopedie of Diderot and D'Alembert: Selected Articles.* 1954.

Lowith, Karl. *From Hegel to Nietzsche.* Tr. David E. Green. 1965.

Marshall, P.J., and Glyndwr Williams. *The Great Map of Mankind: British Perceptions of the World in the Age of Enlightenment.* 1982.

Martin, Kingsley. *French Liberal Thought in the Eighteenth Century.* 1954.

Mason, Haydn. *Voltaire.* 1981.

Mason, Philip. *The English Gentleman: Rise and Fall of an Ideal.* 1982.

McCarthy, Justin. *A Short History of Our Own Times.* 1901.

McClellan, Woodford. *Revolutionary Exiles.* The Russians in the First International and the Paris Commune. 1979.

McLachlan, H. John. *Socinianism in Seventeenth Century England.* 1951.

Meissner, Erich. *Confusion of Faces: The Struggle Between Religion and Secularism in Europe: A Commentary on German History, 1517–1939.* 1946.

Merson, John. *Roads of Xanadu: East and Wesst in the Making of the Modern World.* 1989.

Meyer, R. W. *Leibniz and the Seventeenth Century Revolution.* Tr. J. P. Stern. 1952.

Meyers, William. *Restoration and Revolution.* 1986.

Mill, John Stuart. *A System of Logic.* 1843.

———. *Essay on Liberty.* 1859.

———. *Utilitarianism.* 1861.

———. *The Subjection of Women.* 1871.

———. *Autobiography.* 1873.

———. *Three Essays on Religion.* 1874.

Miller, John. *Seeds of Liberty: 1688 and the Shaping of Modern Britain.* 1988.

Montaigne. *Essais.*

Montesquieu. *De l'esprit de Lois.* 1748.

Morley, John. *The Life of Richard Cobden.* 1881.

Morris, Richard B. *The Basic Ideas of Alexander Hamilton.* 1957.

Namier, Sir Lewis. *The Structure of Politics at the Accession of George III.* 1957.

Neumann, Franz. *The Rule of Law.* 1986.

Newman, Gerald. *The Rise of English Nationalism.* 1987.

Nicholl, Charles. *A Cup of News: The Life of Thomas Nashe.* 1984.

Paine, Thomas. *Rights of Man: Being an Answer to Mr. Burke's Attack on the French Revolution.* 1791.

Panovsky, Agrippa E., and R. Klibansky. *De occulta philosophia.* 1964.

Parkin, Charles. *The Moral Basis of Burke's Thought.* 1956.

Pascal. *Les provinciales.* 1656–57.

Perry, Maria. *Elizabeth*. 1990.

Polka, Brayton, and Bernard Zeleechow, eds. *Readings in Western Civilization,* vols.
    1 and 2. 1970.

Powell, J. Enoch. *Joseph Chamberlain*. 1977.

Powys, LLewelyn, ed. *The Life and Times of Antony à Wood*. 1961.

Price, Roger. *A Social History of Nineteenth Century France*. 1987.

Purver, Margery. *The Royal Society*. 1967.

Quinton, Anthony. *Francis Bacon*. 1980.

Raleigh, Walter. *Relation of Cadiz Action*.

Renault, Gilbert. *The Caravels of Christ*. Tr. R. Hill. 1959.

Renouvin, Pierre. *Histoire des relations internationales,* vol 5. 1954.

Reynolds, Robert L. *Europe Emerges*. 1961.

Richardson. R. C., and T. B. James, eds. *The Urban Experience: English, Scottish,
    and Welsh Towns, 1450–1700*. 1983.

Roberts, David. *Paternalism in Early Victorian England*. 1978.

Robertson, Sir Charles Grant. *Chatham and the British Empire*. 1946.

Romein, Jan. *The Watershed of Two Eras: Europe in 1900*. Tr. Arnold Pomerans.
    1978.

Roots, Ivan. *Speeches of Oliver Cromwell*. 1989.

Rosenberg, John D. *The Darkening Glass: A Portrait of Ruskin's Genius*. 1963.

Ruskin, John. *Time and Tide*.

Ruskin, John. *Unto This Last*.

Sagarra, Eda. *A Social History of Germany, 1648–1914*. 1977.

Salgado, Gamini. *The Elizabethan Underground*. 1977.

Sampson, R. V. *Progress in the Age of Reason*. 1956.

Sandor, Paul. *Histoire de la dialectique*. 1947.

Santillana, Giorgio de. *The Age of Adventure: The Renaissance Philosophers*. 1956.

Saran, Mary. *The History of the German Labour Movement*. Tr. Edith Korner. 1985.

Sedgwick, Romney, ed. *Lord Harvey's Memoirs*. 1952.

Seidman, Steven. *Liberalism and the Origins of European Social Theory*. 1983.

Seward, Desmond. *The First Bourbon*. 1971.

———. *Henry V as Warlord*. 1987.

Smith, D. W. *Helvetius: A Study in Persecution*. 1965.

Snyder, Louis L. *Fifty Major Documents of the Nineteenth Century*. 1955.

Sorel, Georges. *Reflexions sur la violence*. 1907.

———. *Les illusions du progres*. 1908.

———. *De l'utilite du pragmatisme*. 1917.

Sorel, Albert. *Montesquieu*. Tr. Gustave Masson. 1857.

Steegman, John. *The Rule of Taste: From George I to George IV*. 1936.

Stromberg, Roland N. *Religious Liberalism in Eighteenth Century England*. 1954.

Tagliacozzo, Giorgio. *Vico and Marx*. 1983.

Thoreau, David. *Walden*.

Thurssfield, J. R. *Peel*. 1901.

Tihany, Leslie C. *A History of Middle Europe*. 1976.

Trvelyan, G. M. *The Life of John Bright*. 1913.

———. *English Social History*. 1942.

Usherwood, Stephen and Elizabeth. *The Counter-Armada 1596*. 1983.

Vico, Giambattista. *La Scienza Nuova*. 1928.

Voltaire. *Dictionaire philosophique*. Ed. Julien Benda.

von Greywerz, Kaspar, ed. *Religion and Society in Early Modern Europe*. 1984.

W. Townson. *Illustrated Atlas of the World in the Age of Discovery*. 1981.

Walker, Eric A. *Colonies*. 1944.

West, Sir Algernon. *Recollections, 1832–1886*. 1899.

White, R. J. *The Conservative Tradition*. 1950.

Whitman, Walt. *Democratic Vistas*.

Wilberforce, William. *A Practical View of Society*. 1797.

Wiley, Margaret L. *The Subtle Knot: Creative Skepticism in Seventeenth Century England*. 1952.

Williams, Raymond. *Culture and Society, 1780–1950*. 1958.

Williams, Norman Lloyd. *Sir Walter Raleigh*. 1962.

Willis, Irene Cooper. *Speeches During the French Revolution by Fox*. 1924.

Wilson, Arthur M. *Diderot*. 1972.

Wright, Esmond. *Washington and the American Revolution*. 1957.

Wrightson, Keith. *English Society: 1580–1680*. 1980, 1982.

Yates, Francis. *Elizabethan Neoplatonism Reconsidered*. 1977.

Young, Alan. *Tudor and Jacobean Tournaments*. 1987.

## Law and Politics

Acheson, Dean. *A Citizen Looks at Congress*. 1956.

Annan, Noel. *The Curious Strength of Positivism in English Political Thought*. 1958.

Baldwin, Robert, and Christopehr McCrudach, eds. *Regulation and Public Law*. 1987.

Barker, Ernest. *The Development of Public Services in Western Europe, 1660–1930*. 1944.

———. *Principles of Social and Political Theory*. 1951.

Bell, Colin R. *Middle Class Families: Social and Geographical Mobility*. 1968.

Blackham, H. J. *Political Discipline in a Free Society*. 1961.

Branson, Noreen. *Britain in the 1920s*. 1975.

Bristow, Peter. *Judge for Yourself*. 1986.

Butler, D. E. *The Study of Political Behaviour*. 1958.

Cairns, Huntington. *Legal Philosophy From Plato to Hegel*. 1949.

Carr, E. H. *Studies in Revolution*. 1950.

Chomsky, Noam. *American Power and the New Mandarins*. 1969.

Cox, Harvey. *The Secular City*. 1965.

Dent, David. *The Language of Ordinary Experience: A Study in the Philosophy of Education*. 1979.

Diamond, A. S. *The Evolution of Law and Order*. 1951.

Donoughue, Bernard. *Prime Minister: The Conduct of Foreign Policy Under Wilson and Callaghan.* 1987.

Duver, Maurice. *Poltical Parties.* Tr. Barbara and Robert North. 1954.

Ellwood, Charles A. *A History of Social Philosophy.* 1938.

Erikson, Eric H. *Children and Society.* 1950.

Fasnacht, G. E. *Acton's Political Philosophy.* 1952.

Ford, P., and G. Ford, eds. *Foundation of the Welfare State: A Breviate of Parliamentary Papers.* 1969.

Freedland, Mark, and Paul Davies. *Labour Law,* 2d ed. 1984.

Ginsberg, Morris. *Reason and Unreason in Society.* 1947.

Greaves, H. R. G. *The Foundations of Political Theory,* 2d ed. 1966.

Hancock, Graham. *Lords of Poverty.* 1989.

Hart, H. L. A. *The Concept of Law.* 1961.

Honigmann, John. *Culture and Personality.* 1954.

Horowitz, I. L., ed. *The New Sociology.* 1965.

Howarth, Stephen. *August '39.* 1989.

Kirk, Russell. *The Conservative Mind.* 1954.

Lane, Peter. *Europe Since 1945.* 1985.

Larrabe, Eric. *Commander in Chief: Franklin Delano Roosevelt, His Lieutenants, and Their War.* 1987.

Lasswell, Harold D. *An Analysis of Political Behaviour.* 1947.

Law, Richard. *Return from Utopia.* 1950.

Lewis, roy, and Angus Maude. *Professional People.* 1952.

Lippmann, Walter. *The Public Philosophy: On the Decline and Revival of the Western Society.* 1955.

Lubenow, William C. *The Politics of Government Growth: Early Victorian Attitudes Toward State Intervention, 1833–1848.* 1971.

Mann, Thomas. *Diaries, 1918–39.* Ed. Herman Kesten. Tr. Richard and Clara Winston. 1984.

Mannheim, Karl. *Ideology and Utopia.* Tr. Louis Wirth and Ed Shils. 1936.

———. *Man and Society.* 1940.

———. *Freedom, Power, and Democratic Planning.* 1951.

Marcuse, Herbert. *Reason and Revolution: Hegel and the Rise of Social Theory.* 1941.

Mason, A. T., ed. *Free Government in the Making.* 1949.

Mayo, Elton. *The Social Problems of an Industrial Civilization.* 1949.

Moore, Jr., Barrington. *Injustice: The Social Bases of Obedience and Revolt.* 1978.

Mumford, Lewis. *The Culture of Cities.* 1938.

———. *Sketches from Life.* 1982.

Nicolson, Harold. *Diplomacy.* 1939.

Nokes, Peter. *The Professional Task in Welfare Practice.* 1967.

Page, Norman. *The Thirties in Britain.* 1990.

Parsons, Talcott. *The Social System.* 1952.

Perham, Margery. *African British Rule.* 1941.

Plamenatz, John. *On Alien Rule and Self-Government*. 1960.

Prothero, I. J. *Artisans and Politics in Early Nineteenth Century London: John Gast and His Times*. 1979.

Robertson, Sir C. Grant, ed. *Select Statutes, Cases, and Documents to Illustrate English Constitutional History, 6th ed*. 1931.

Rosen, Connie and Harold. *The Language of Primary School Children*. 1973.

Schapera, I. *Government and Politics in Tribal Societies*. 1956.

Shapiro, Harry L., ed. *Man, Culture, and Society*. 1960.

Sharp, Cecil J., and A. P. Oppe. *The Dance*. 1924.

Smith, Goldwin. *A Constitutional and Legal History of England*. 1990.

Stillman, Edmund, and William Pfaff. *The New Politics: America and the End of the Postwar World*. 1961.

Symons, Julian. *The Thirties and the Nineties*. 1990.

Taylor, Sir Thomas Murray. *The Discipline of Virtue: Reflections on Law and Liberty*. 1954.

Taylor, A. J. P. *The Trouble Makers: Dissent Over Foreign Policy, 1792–1939*. 1957.

Wade, E. C. S., and G. Godfrey Phillips. *Constitutional Law, 5th ed*. 1955.

Ward, Geoffery C. *Before the Trumpet: Young Franklin Roosevelt, 1882–1905*. 1985.

Weldon, T. D. *States and Morals*. 1946.

Wheare, F. C. *Government by Committee: An Essay on the British Constitution*. 1955.

Wheatcroft, Geoffery. *The Randlords: South Africa's Mining Magnates*. 1986.

White, Morton, ed. *The Age of Analysis: The Twentieth Century Philosophers*. 1955.

Williams, Glanville. *The Reform of the Law*. 1951.

Williams, Raymond. *Keywords: A Vocabulary of Culture and Society*. 1976.

Zander, Michael. *The Law-Making Process*. 1980.

## Science

Bolter, J. David. *Turing's Man*. 1986.

Brand, Stewart. *The Media Lab*. 1987.

Clark, David H. *The Cosmos From Space*. 1987.

Dennett, Daniel C. *Consciousness Explained*. 1981.

Dixon, Bernard. *The Science of Science*. 1989.

Gifford, Don. *The Farther Shore: A Natural History of Perception, 1798–1984*. 1990.

Ginsberg, Morris. *The Idea of Progress: A Reevaluation*. 1953.

Gould, Stephen Jay. *Time's Arrow, Time's Cycle*. 1988.

Judson, Horace Freeland. *The Eighth Day of Creation: The Makers of the Revolution in Biology*. 1979.

Kenney, A. J. P., et al. *The Development of Mind*. 1978.

Kinsman, Francis. *Millennium*. 1990.

Levine, George, ed. *One Culture: Essays in Science and Literature*. 1987.

Morley, David. *The Sensitive Scientist*. 1978.

Newell, Joihn. *The Gene Shifters*. 1989.

Otto, Max. *Science and the Moral Life.* 1949.
Pledge, H. T. *Science Since 1500.* 1939.
Priest, Steven. *Theories of the Mind.* 1991.
Ravetz, J. R. *The Merger of Knowledge With Power.* 1990.
Redondi, Pietro. *Galileo: Heretic.* Tr. Raymond Rosenthal. 1988.
Reichenbach, Hans. *The Rise of Scientific Phiosophy.* 1962.
Ridley, Mark, ed. *The Essential Darwin.* 1987.
Smith, Neil, and Dierdre Wilson. *Modern Linguistics: The Results of Chomsky's Revolution.* 1979.
Snow, C. P. *The Physicists.* 1981.
Stanley, Manfred. *The Technological Conscience.* 1978.
Young, J. Z. *An Introduction to the Study of Man.* 1971.

## Economics

Abrams, Philip, and Richard Brown, eds. *UK Society: Work Urbanism, and Inequality.* 1984.
Anderson, Victor. *Alternative Economic Indicators.* 1991.
Bleaney, Michael. *The Rise and Fall of Keynesian Economics.* 1985.
Brown, Hy Phelps. *The Origins of Trade Union Power.* 1983.
Burnham, James. *The Management Revolution.* 1942.
Crouzet, Francois. *The Victorian Economy.* Tr. A. S. Forster. 1982.
Davis, Ralph. *The Rise of the Atlantic Economies.* 1973.
Foreman-Peck, J. *A History of the World Economy: International Economic Relations Since 1850.* 1983.
Frank, Andre Gunder. *World Accummulation, 1482–1789.* 1978.
Fraser, W. Hamish. *The Coming of the Mass Market, 1850–1914.* 1981.
Galbraith, John Kenneth. *American Capitalism: The Concept of Countervailing Power.* 1952.
———. *The Affluent Society.* 1958.
Greeves, Ivan S. *London Dock. 1800–1980.* 1980.
Hawtrye, R. G. *Economic Destiny.* 1944.
Heller, Robert. *The Naked Manager: Games Executives Play.* 1985.
Himmelfarb, Gertrude. *The Idea of Poverty: England in the Early Industrial Age.* 1984.
Holderness, B. A. *Pre-Industrial England.* 1976.
House, J. W. *The UK Space,* 3d ed. 1982.
Jennings, Humphrey. *Pandemonium!: The Coming of the Machine as Seen by Contemporary Observors, 1660, 1886.* 1985.
Kamenka, Eugene. *Bureaucracy.* 1989.
Keynes, John Maynard. *The End of Laissez-Faire.* 1926.
———. *The General Theory of Employment, Interest, and Money.* 1936.
———. *Two Memoirs.* 1949.
Kitzinger, Uwe. *The European Common Market and Community.* 1967.

Kriedte, Peter. *Peasants, Landlords, and Merchant Capitalists: Europe and the World Economy, 1500–1800*. Tr. V. R. Bergbahn. 1983.

Langton, John, and R. J. Morris, eds. *Atlas of Industrializing Britain, 1780–1914*. 1986.

Longmate, Norman. *The Breadstealers: The Fight Against the Corn Laws, 1838–1846*. 1984.

Macdougall, Donald. *Don and Mandarin: Memoirs of an Economist*. 1987.

Marx, Karl. *Herr Vogt: A Spy in the Worker's Movement*. Tr. R. A. Archer. 1982.

McCarthy, Terry, ed. *The Great Dock Strike, 1889*. 1988.

Myrdal, Gunnar. *Economic Theory and Underdeveloped Regions*. 1957.

Prest, A. R. *Public Finance in Developing Countries*, 3d ed. 1985.

Rimmer, Douglas. *The Economies of West Africa*. 1984.

Robinson, Joan. *Economic Philosophy*. 1962.

Rosenberg, Nathan, and L. E. Birdzell. *How the West Grew Rich*. 1986.

Rubinstein, W. D., ed. *Wealth and the Wealthy in the Modern World*. 1980.

Sampson, Anthony. *The Midas Touch*. 1989.

Shonfield, Andrew. *Modern Capitalism: The Changing Balance of Public and Private Power*. 1965.

Smiles, Samuel. *Life and Labour: Characteristics of Men of Industry, Culture, and Genius*. 1887.

———. *Self-Help*. 1897.

———. *The Locomotive*. 1904.

Stearns, Peter N. *Lives of Labour: Work in a Maturing Industrial Society*. 1975.

Stevenson, John, and Chris Cook. *The Slump: Society and Culture During the Depression*. 1979.

Tribe, Keith. *Land Labor, and Economic Discourse*. 1978.

van der Wee, Herman. *Prosperity and Upheaval: World Economy and Society, 1945–1980*. Tr. Robin Hogg and Max R. Hall. 1986.

Wood, Jonathan. *Wheels of Misfortune: The Rise and Fall of the British Motor Industry*. 1988.

Wright, Thomas. *Some Habits and Customs of the Working Classes*. 1867.

# Index